THE HANDBOOK
OF HUMAN-MACHINE INTERACTION

The Handbook
of Human-Machine Interaction
A Human-Centered Design Approach

Edited by

GUY A. BOY

Florida Institute of Technology, USA,
Florida Institute for Human and Machine Cognition, and
NASA Kennedy Space Center, USA

CRC Press
Taylor & Francis Group
Boca Raton London New York

CRC Press is an imprint of the
Taylor & Francis Group, an **informa** business

CRC Press
Taylor & Francis Group
6000 Broken Sound Parkway NW, Suite 300
Boca Raton, FL 33487-2742

© 2011 by Guy A. Boy
CRC Press is an imprint of Taylor & Francis Group, an Informa business

No claim to original U.S. Government works

Printed on acid-free paper
Version Date: 20160226

International Standard Book Number-13: 978-0-7546-7580-8 (Hardback)

Visit the Taylor & Francis Web site at
http://www.taylorandfrancis.com

and the CRC Press Web site at
http://www.crcpress.com

Contents

List of Figures

List of Tables

Notes on Contributors

Gregory Belenky is Research Professor and Director of the Sleep and Performance Research Center at Washington State University. Dr Belenky received his BA degree in Psychology from Yale University and his MD degree from Stanford University. During medical school, he worked in the laboratory of Dr William Dement, a pioneer in the field of sleep and sleep medicine. Dr Belenky completed an internship in internal medicine at the University of Utah and a residency in psychiatry at Yale University. From 1984 to 2004, Dr Belenky led the US Army's program of research in sleep, sleep loss, fatigue, and human performance. Dr Belenky specializes in the study of human sleep and sleep loss and their role in performance, productivity, safety, health, and well-being. Dr Belenky's laboratory and field studies inform the emerging science of fatigue risk management.

Thierry Bellet has a PhD in Cognitive Psychology and Master in Artificial Intelligence. Since 1999, he has been a researcher at the Ergonomics and Cognitive Sciences Laboratory (LESCOT) of IFSTTAR (French National Research Institute on Transport and Safety). His fields of research are (1) Human Driver Modeling and (2) Cognitive Engineering for driving assistance design. Regarding Human Modeling, his main areas of interest are Mental Representations study and Situational Awareness computational modeling. Research collaborations on this topic take place in the frame of French or European projects. Since September 2008, he is involved in the FP7 European Project ISi-PADAS, dedicated to driver modeling and simulation, for virtual design of vehicle automation devices. He also currently participates in several projects focusing on drivers' risk awareness and motorcyclists' attitudes toward risk and risk taking while driving. Regarding Cognitive Engineering and Driving Assistance, his field of research is more specifically focused on Adaptive Technologies design. Adaptive Technologies means "system being able to adapt the assistance according to (a) the driving context and (b) the current drivers' needs." This Human-centered Design approach is applied to different types of driving aids, like "On-board Information Manager," collision avoidance systems, or lane departure warning.

Guy A. Boy is University Professor at the Florida Institute of Technology, Chief Scientist Human-Centered Design at NASA Kennedy Space Center, and Senior Research Scientist at the Florida Institute for Human and Machine Cognition (IHMC). He was the President and Director of the European Institute of Cognitive Sciences and Engineering (EURISCO) from 1992 to 2008. He is the Chair of the Technical Committee for Aerospace Human Factors and Ergonomics of the International Ergonomics Association. He was the Executive Vice-Chair of ACM-SIGCHI (Association for Computing Machinery—Special Interest Group on Computer Human Interaction) from 1995 to 1999. He holds a University Professor Habilitation in both computer and cognitive science from the University of Paris, a PhD in automation and system design from the University of Toulouse (ISAE-SUPAERO: French Institute for Aerospace Engineering). He is a fellow of the Air and Space Academy.

Jeffrey M. Bradshaw, PhD, is a Senior Research Scientist at the Florida Institute for Human and Machine Cognition (IHMC) in Pensacola, Florida (www.ihmc.us/groups/jbradshaw/). He leads the research group developing the KAoS policy and domain services framework. Formerly, he led research groups at the Boeing Company and the Fred Hutchinson Cancer Research Center. Jeff's research has explored a wide range of topics in human and machine intelligence and their interaction. Among many other publications, he edited the books *Knowledge Acquisition as a Modeling Activity* (with Ken Ford, Wiley, 1993) and *Software Agents* (AAAI Press/The MIT Press, 1997).

Barbara K. Burian is a Research Psychologist in the Human Systems Integration Division of NASA Ames Research Center. She studies the cognitive and operational workload demands of two-crew and single-pilot operations aboard commercial aircraft and in very light jets, and other technically advanced aircraft during normal and emergency conditions. She also conducts research related to the use of automated and electronic procedures, and intelligent agents on the flight deck, as well as research on checklist design and use, and pilot weather training, knowledge, and decision-making.

Joshua D. Cameron graduated from the University of Virginia (BA, Biology) and joined the Florida Institute for Human and Machine Cognition in 2005 as a Research Associate. He has contributed to the development of a number of techniques for evaluation of cognitive state, particularly those associated with cognitive impairment due to disease or traumatic brain injury. Mr Cameron will begin medical school in the fall of 2010.

John M. Carroll is Edward Frymoyer Professor of Information Sciences and Technology at the Pennsylvania State University. Research interests include methods and theory in human–computer interaction, particularly as applied to networking tools for collaborative learning and problem-solving, and design of interactive information systems. Books include *Making Use* (MIT, 2000), *HCI in the New Millennium* (Addison-Wesley, 2001), *Usability Engineering* (Morgan-Kaufmann, 2002, with M.B. Rosson) and *HCI Models, Theories, and Frameworks* (Morgan-Kaufmann, 2003), *Rationale-Based Software Engineering* (Springer, 2008, with J. Burge, R. McCall and I. Mistrik), and *Learning in Communities* (Springer, 2009). Carroll serves on several editorial boards for journals, handbooks, and series. He is editor of the *Synthesis Lectures on Human-Centered Informatics*. He received the Rigo Award and the CHI Lifetime Achievement Award from ACM, the Silver Core Award from IFIP, the Goldsmith Award from IEEE. He is a fellow of ACM, IEEE, and the Human Factors and Ergonomics Society.

Serge Debernard is born in 1963 and received a PhD in Automatic Control in 1993. He is full Professor at the University of Valenciennes since 2007. He conducts research on Human–Machine Systems and more specifically on Human Machine Cooperation in Air Traffic Control Domain since 1988 trough several projects in collaboration with DGAC. His scientific production covers about 90 publications.

Margery J. Doyle earned her Masters Degree in experimental and cognitive psychology from the University of West Florida and joined Lockheed Martin in 2007. Since then, she has completed work towards a PhD in Cognitive Science while developing cognitive engineering and modeling methods for evaluation of cognitive workload, situation awareness, situation understanding, decision-making under uncertainty, automation, adjustable autonomy, trust in automation, cognitive reliability, software systems safety, augmented cognition, and remotely piloted systems. Recently she has focused on multiple autonomous agents and stigmergic processes relating to pervasive computing. In 2009, she founded Cognitive Architects and Engineers, LLC.

Michael Feary is a researcher in the Human–Systems Integration Division at NASA Ames Research Center. He is investigating the development of tools to aid evaluation of Human–Automation Interaction during design of aerospace systems in NASA's Aviation Safety and Human Research programs. Dr Feary's current focus is on the application of formal analysis techniques to analyze complex procedural interactions and the impact of automation design changes.

Paul J. Feltovich is a Research Scientist at the Florida Institute for Human and Machine Cognition (IHMC). He holds a PhD from the University of Minnesota and was a post-doctoral fellow in cognitive psychology at the Learning, Research, and Development Center. He was professor in Medical Education at Southern Illinois University School of Medicine from 1982 to 2001. He has conducted research on expert-novice differences, conceptual understanding for complex knowledge, and novel means of instruction for difficult knowledge domains. Since joining IHMC (2001), he has been investigating coordination, regulation, and teamwork in mixed groups of humans and intelligent software agents. He has authored over one 120 articles and three books. In particular, he is co-author of a designated Science Citation Classic paper on problem-solving in physics and is a co-editor of *Expertise in Context: Human and Machine; Smart Machines in Education;* and the first *Cambridge Handbook on Expertise and Expert Performance.*

Philippa Gander is the founder and Director of the Sleep/Wake Research Centre, Massey University, New Zealand. She gained her PhD in chronobiology at the University of Auckland, and following a Senior Fulbright Fellowship at Harvard Medical School, she joined the Fatigue Countermeasures Program at NASA, working primarily on the physiological and safety impact of shift work and jet lag in aviation. This work received a NASA Group Achievement Award in 1993. In 1998 she was awarded a BP International Chairman's Award for Health, Safety, and Environmental Performance for a program addressing alertness management in heavy vehicle operations. She has served as a scientific advisor to numerous industry groups and government agencies and is currently on the ICAO Fatigue Risk Management Task Force. In 2009, she was elected to the Fellowship of the Royal Society of New Zealand.

Curt Graeber is President of The Graeber Group, Ltd., a human factors consultancy. He was a Senior Technical Fellow at Boeing Commercial Airplanes where he served as Chief Engineer of Human Factors until retiring in 2008. Prior to joining Boeing he led the Flight Crew Fatigue program at NASA's Ames Research Center and served as principal investigator for much of the fundamental research that now forms the basis of fatigue risk management. He holds a PhD in Neuropsychology from the University of Virginia and is a Fellow of the Royal Aeronautical Society and the Aerospace Medical Association. Curt has received numerous international awards for his contributions to improving aviation safety through human factors advancements. He co-chaired the Flight Safety Foundation's Ultra Long-Range Crew Alertness Initiative and currently leads ICAO's Fatigue Risk Management Task Force. He also served as the Human Factors Specialist for the Presidential Commission on the Space Shuttle Challenger Accident.

Gudela Grote is Professor of Work and Organizational Psychology in the Department of Management, Technology, and Economics at the ETH Zürich. She holds a Master's degree in psychology from the Technical University in Berlin and a PhD in Industrial/Organizational Psychology from the Georgia Institute of Technology, Atlanta. She has published widely on the interplay of organization and technology, safety management, and changing employment relationships. Gudela Grote is associate editor of the journal *Safety Science*. Special interests in her research are the increasing flexibility and virtuality of work and their consequences for the individual and organizational management of uncertainty.

Don Harris BSc, PhD, is Managing Director of HFI Solutions Ltd. Prior to founding the company, Don was Professor of Aerospace Human Factors at Cranfield University. He has been involved in the design and certification of flight deck interfaces; worked in the safety assessment of helicopter operations for North Sea oil exploration and exploitation and was an accident investigator on call to the British Army Division of Army Aviation. Don is a Fellow of the Institute of Ergonomics and Human Factors and a Chartered Psychologist. He is a member of the UK Human Factors National Technical Committee for Defence. In 2006 Don received the Royal Aeronautical Society Bronze award for work leading to advances in aerospace and in 2008 was part of the Human Factors Integration Defence Technology Centre team that received the UK Ergonomics Society President's Medal "for significant contributions to original research, the development of methodology and the application of knowledge within the field of ergonomics."

Steven R. Haynes is a Professor of Practice in Information Sciences and Technology at the Pennsylvania State University. His research interests include design rationale, scenario-based methods, design science, and theories of explanation. He has worked at Apple Computer, Adobe Systems, and several start-up software companies in the United States and Europe. He has been involved in the development of commercial and custom software solutions as a software developer, analyst, architect, and development project manager. His PhD is in Information Systems and Social Psychology from the London School of Economics.

Erik Hollnagel is Professor and Industrial Safety Chair at MINES Paris Tech (France) and Visiting Professor at the Norwegian University of Science and Technology (NTNU) in Trondheim (Norway). He has worked at universities, research centers, and industries in several countries and with problems from many domains. His professional interests include industrial safety, resilience engineering, accident investigation, cognitive systems engineering and cognitive ergonomics. He has published widely and is the author/editor of 17 books, including four books on resilience engineering. The latest title from Ashgate is *The ETTO Principle: Why Things That Go Right Sometimes Go Wrong*.

Christopher Johnson is Professor of Computing Science at the University of Glasgow. He heads a small research team investigating ways of improving incident and accident reporting across a range of industries. He was part of the EUROCONTROL teams that developed European guidelines on Contingency Planning, including pandemics and volcanic ash. In the last 12 months, he also helped to author guidance on accident investigation for the European Railway Agency. He has authored approximately 200 peer-reviewed papers and is chair of the SESAR Scientific Advisory Body within European Air Traffic Management.

Matthew Johnson has worked at the Institute for Human and Machine Cognition (IHMC) in Pensacola Florida for seven years. He received his BS in Aerospace Engineering from the University of Notre Dame in 1992 and an MS in Computer Science from Texas A&M—Corpus Christi in 2001. Prior to working for IHMC, he spent 10 years in the Navy flying both fixed and rotary wing aircraft. He has worked on numerous projects including the Oz flight display for reducing the cognitive workload in the cockpit, Augmented Cognition for improving human performance, the DARPA Little Dog project developing walking algorithms for a quadruped robot on rough terrain, and several human–robot coordination projects for both NASA and the Department of Defense. Most recently he has worked on development of the NASA humanoid based on Robonaut. Matthew's research interests focus on improving performance in human–machine systems and include the areas of teamwork, coordination and human–robot interaction.

Josef F. Krems, Professor of Cognitive and Engineering Psychology, graduated at the University of Regensburg in 1980. He then joined the group for Cognitive Psychology as a research assistant and did a PhD in psycholinguistics (1984). For his habilitation (second PhD) he worked on Computer modeling and expert systems (1990). From 1991 to 1993 he was a Visiting Assistant Professor at Ohio State University, Columbus (OH), where he worked on computational models of diagnostic reasoning. Then he became an Assistant Professor at the Centre for Studies on Cognitive Complexity at the University of Potsdam (1994–1995). Since 1995 he is full professor at Chemnitz University of Technology. In 2006 he was invited as Visiting Professor to Chung-Keng University, Taiwan. His current research projects are on Man–Machine Interaction, Safety, In-vehicle Information systems, Adaptive Cruise Control, Enhanced night vision systems and so on. Josef Krems published or co-edited nine books and more than a hundred papers in books, scientific journals or congress proceedings.

Saadi Lahlou is director of the Institute of Social Psychology at the London School of Economics and Political Science. He is the scientific director of the Cognitive Technologies program at Fondation Maison des Sciences de l'Homme (Paris); and associate researcher at Centre Edgar Morin (CNRS-EHESS UMR 8177). Previously he has directed the Consumer Research department at Crédoc; and various research units at EDF R&D, where he founded the Laboratory of Design for Cognition. Professor Lahlou's current research interests are in the application of social sciences to the real world, and especially the design of human-friendly and sustainable socio-technical systems.

Annemarie Lesage is a PhD candidate and a part-time faculty at the School of Industrial Design of the University of Montreal. She is doing her thesis on the autotelic experience, which is a dimension of the user experience. She is currently co-teaching a design studio on experience and technology and has taught graphic design for over 10 years in universities in Canada and United States. In 2000–2001, she was part of XMod, the experience modeling group who did the user-experience research at Sapient, a technology consultant. Her interests revolve around experience design, design research, and design process, as it applies to the design of interactive systems supporting the ideation process, thus catering to active and creative users. As a researcher at the Hybridlab, she has published articles through conferences and design journals.

Wen-Chin Li is the head of Graduate School of Psychology, National Defense University, Republic of China, and Visiting Fellow in the Department of Systems Engineering and Human Factors, Cranfield University, United Kingdom since 2006. He is an Aviation Human Factors Specialist of European Association of Aviation Psychology and a Registered Member of the Ergonomics Society (MErgS). His research areas include Human Factors in Flight Operations, Aeronautical Decision-making, Accident Investigations, Cross-cultural Issues in Flight Deck, and Aviation Stress Management. He won the prize for the best paper of 2007 International Society of Air Safety Investigators (ISASI) Seminar and the Best Paper Award Winner of HFES Aerospace System Group, 8th International Conference on Naturalistic Decision-making 2007.

Lynne Martin is a Senior Research Associate with the San José State University Foundation at NASA Ames Research Center, California. She works on the design and human-in-the-loop testing of far-future flight deck displays and automation.

Célia Martinie is a PhD Candidate on Informatics at the University Paul Sabatier (2009–). Previously she has been at Motorola Mobile Devices for eight years (2001–2009) working as a software engineer in the design and development of embedded services and innovative technologies for mobile applications. She holds a Master's degree in Electronics and Telecommunications from the EDF Engineering School, Sceaux, France (2001) and a Master of Philosophy in Digital Telecommunications Systems from the Telecom ParisTech School, France (2001). Her current research interests focus on model-based approaches to design and evaluate interactive systems. Other topics of interest include software engineering, formal methods and safety critical systems.

Patrick Millot, born in 1953, received a PhD in Automatic Control (1979) and is Docteur d'Etat et Sciences (1987). He has been full Professor at the University of Valenciennes since 1989. He conducts research on Automation Sciences, Artificial Intelligence, Supervisory Control, Human Machine Systems, Human Reliability with applications to production telecommunication and transport systems (Air Traffic Control, Road

Traffic, Trains, Metro.). His scientific production covers about 180 publications, collective books, and conference proceedings. He has been Research Director of 36 PhD students and 9 HDR since 1989, as well as a reviewer of 50 PhD theses and 9 HDR from other universities. He was Head of the research group "Human Machine Systems" in LAMIH since 1987 till 2004 (25 researchers), Vice-Head then head of LAMIH between 1996 and 2005 (222 researchers and engineers) and Vice-Chairman of the University of Valenciennes since October 2005 in charge of research; scientific head or Member of the scientific board or manager of several regional research groups on Supervisory Control (GRAISYHM 1996–2002) on Transport System Safety (GRRT since 1987, pôle ST2 since 2001 with 80 researchers of 10 labs); member of the French Council of the Universities (1996–2003), member of the scientific board of the French national research group in Automation Sciences supported by CNRS (1996–2001); partner of several European projects and networks (HCM networks 1993–1996, two projects since 2002 on Urban Guided Transport Management Systems and the Network of Excellence EURNEX since 2004); IPC member of several International Conferences and Journals; Member since 2000 and Vice-Chairman since 2009 of the IFAC Technical Committee 4.5 Human Machine Systems.

David Navarre is a lecturer in Computer Science at the University Toulouse 1. He has been working since 1998 on notations and tools for the specification, prototyping, validation and implementation of Safety Critical Interactive Systems. He has contributed to the improvement of the formal description technique called Interactive Cooperative Objects (ICO) by making it able to address the modeling of post-WIMP safety critical interactive systems. By working on several large projects (industrial or not) he applied the approach to several application domains including Air Traffic Control, Military and Civil aircraft Cockpits as well as several real-time command and control systems (such as multimodal interfaces for satellite control rooms). Since 2000, he has been involved in the development of tool support for interactive systems modeling using the formal description technique ICO, based on the Petri net tool called PetShop, developed and used in the team since 1995.

Philippe Palanque is a Professor in Computer Science at the University Toulouse 3 and is head (since 1998) of the HCI research group in Toulouse. He has been and is still involved in research projects dealing with the notations and tools for the specification of real-time interactive systems (including Command and Control systems for drones and for multimodal interfaces for military cockpits, new civil interactive cockpits …) as well as air traffic control and satellite ground segments. He edited and co-edited 17 books or conference proceedings. As for conferences, he was general chair of HCI in Aeronautics (HCI Aero 2010) and of IFIP INTERACT 2011. He is a member of the Executive Committee and of the Conference Management Committee of ACM SIGCHI as well as French representative in IFIP TC 13 on HCI. He is the author and co-author of more than a hundred international peer-reviewed publications.

Maria Panou has a notable experience in working in European and national research projects, with participation in over 15 such projects. She is an Electronics and Computer engineer, with an MsC on Advanced Control, a PhD on personalized services, holding a position as a Research Engineer at the Hellenic Institute of

Transport. She is the Technical Project Manager of SAVE ME project (FP7-SST-2008–1-234027), the Coordinator of a 6th FP STREP (TRAIN-ALL) and sub-project leader in 2 IPs (ASK-IT–IST-2003–511298–and OASIS–ICT-215754–of the 6th and 7th FP respectively). Her main fields of expertize are driver behavior modeling, Telematics Applications for Transport and their personalization, Infomobility services and content personalization, development of Multimedia Tools for training purposes, Ambient Intelligence framework services, Transportation of persons with special needs. She has more than 40 publications in conferences, 9 publications in scientific journals, and 5 more in books.

Marta Pereira has a PhD on Ergonomics by the Technical University of Lisbon. She is presently working at the Chemnitz University of Technology–Department of Psychology (Germany). She is carrying out a post-doc as Experienced Researcher in the frame of the ADAPTATION European Project/Marie Currie Initial Training Network. Marta Pereira has performed her PhD thesis as Early Stage Researcher of the HUMANIST Network of Excellence (FP6: 2004–2008) with a PhD grant. From 2008 until January 2010 she was integrated as a researcher at UNIVERSITAS/High Institute for Education and Sciences/Department of Science and Technology. She has been involved in the INTERACTION European Project, which main aim is to better understand the driver interactions with In-Vehicle (mature) Technologies and identify patterns of use of these systems in order to highlight individual and cross-country differences in Europe. Marta Pereira will come back to Portugal in February 2012 after finalizing her post-doc to continue working as a researcher on Human Factors.

Anke Popken was born in Germany in 1980. She received the PhD and the MS degrees in Psychology from Chemnitz University of Technology in 2004 and 2009, respectively. She worked as a research scientist in several European and National research projects with the focus on human-centered design of driver support systems. Her research interests are drivers' cognitive processes and their behavioral adaptation to the increasing automation of the driving task due to advanced driver assistance systems.

Amy Pritchett is the David S. Lewis Professor and Director of the Georgia Tech Cognitive Engineering Center. She is responsible for founding and administering an inter-disciplinary research and education program spanning cognitive engineering, piloted control, flight mechanics, guidance, navigation, automatic control, and aerospace design methods. In 2008–2009 Dr Pritchett also served via an Intergovernmental Personnel Agreement (IPA) as Director of NASA's Aviation Safety Program. In this position she was responsible for planning and execution of the program across multiple NASA research centers. She has also served on several executive committees, including the OSTP Aeronautic Science and Technology Subcommittee, the executive committee of the Commercial Aviation Safety Team, the Aviation Safety Information Analysis and Sharing (ASIAS) executive board, the FAA Research, Engineering and Development Advisory Committee (REDAC), and the National Research Council's Aeronautics and Space Engineering Boards. She received her SB, SM and ScD from MIT's Department of Aeronautics and Astronautics.

Anil K. Raj received his MD from the University of Michigan School of Medicine in 1990 and joined the Florida Institute for Human and Machine Cognition as a Research Scientist in 1996. His research focuses on human physiologic and psychological responses in dynamic environments where veridical sensory information may be interrupted. He has been involved with the development, test, and evaluation phases of the US Navy/NASA's Tactile Situation Awareness System and has developed human centered, multimodal sensory substitution interfaces and automated systems for tracking, analyzing, and changing human responses in complex dynamic environments.

Jean-Marc Robert is full Professor in Industrial Engineering at Polytechnic School of Montreal, and Director and founder of the Research Laboratory on Human–Machine Interaction at Polytechnic. He holds a BA and Master's degree in Psychology from the University of Montreal (Canada), a doctorate in Psychology (Cognitive Ergonomics) from University Paris V (France), and he has completed post-doctoral studies in Human Factors Engineering at NASA-Ames Research Center (California). He teaches Cognitive Ergonomics and Human–computer Interaction at the graduate level to a multidisciplinary student body. His research works are concerned with the themes of Accessibility, Usability, and User Experience in various application domains; they address questions related to cognitive task design, collaborative work, the interaction with mobile systems, and the use of virtual reality. Dr Robert is the author of more 160 scientific publications in books, journals, and conference proceedings.

Anabela dos Santos Simões has a PhD on Ergonomics by the Technical University of Lisbon. She was Full Professor at the Technical University of Lisbon/Faculty of Human Kinetics, Ergonomics Department until December 31, 2005. On February 1, 2006, she moved to UNIVERSITAS/High Institute for Education and Sciences/Department of Science and Technology on February, where she is integrated as a Full Professor. Anabela Simões is involved in several European research projects focusing on Intelligent Transport Systems and Human–Machine Interaction issues since 1991. She is a member of the HUMANIST (Human-Centered Design for Information Society Technologies) Association, which is a European research network acting as a virtual center of excellence. Anabela Simões has been the President of the Portuguese Ergonomics Society (APERGO) from 1997 to 2003 and has been a Council member of the International Ergonomics Association (IEA) since 2000. She is also a Chairperson of the Technical Committee on Transport Ergonomics of the International Ergonomics Association since 2008.

Sandra Steere has been a Ground Segment Engineer in the CNES Generic Ground Systems Department since the end of 2008. She has a Master's degree in Human–Computer Interaction and Ergonomics from University College London and obtained her PhD from Toulouse University in 2006 working on formal specification techniques, human "error," system modeling and task modeling in the domain of safety critical interactive systems. Her current interests lie in improving operations in ground segments.

Alexandre Lucas Stephane is involved in the Cognitive Engineering field and focuses particularly on the integration of Human Centered Design methods with Information Technologies aiming to improve socio-technical systems' information gathering and sharing within organizations. Lucas Stephane has a Master of Science degree in Experimental Psychology and an International Master of Science in Business Intelligence. He started working as an IT Manager/Analyst and Human Factors Engineer during the late 1990s and was involved in the early Java-Corba environment. He continued as a Research Engineer at the European Institute of Cognitive Sciences and Engineering in France, where he was involved in various projects related to aeronautics, automotive, and telecom. Beyond several scientific papers, in 2006 his research in Cognitive Modeling and Eye Tracking was awarded two international patents. Currently he is a Research Assistant at the Florida Institute of Technology being mainly involved in cognitive engineering of nuclear power plant control rooms.

Frédéric Vanderhaegen obtained a PhD in Automatic Control in 1993 and an Habilitation to Manage Research in 2003. He worked until 2004 as researcher at the CNRS in France on human error analysis, cooperation and barrier design, validating his contributions in different domains such as manufacturing systems or transport systems. In 2004 he became the Head of the Human–Machine Systems research group of the LAMIH in Valenciennes, France. In 2005, he became full Professor at the University of Valenciennes. He is now vice-director of the Automatic Control and Human–Machine System research group of the LAMIH. He manages national and international research projects and PhD students with academic and industrial partners (for example, MODSafe-FP7, ITERATE-FP7 of the European Commission; PHC SAKURA with Japan; IFAC TC HMS, and so on). He is the director of the European Research Network HAMASYT (Human–Machine Systems in Transportation and Industry) involving Netherlands, Italy, Denmark, Germany.

Marco A.A. Winckler is a Lecturer in Computer Science at the University Toulouse 3. He came to Toulouse France in 2000 to work for his PhD thesis (completed in 2004) whose main focus is the navigation modeling of complex Web applications. During the Master's thesis he worked on remote usability evaluation methods to support the assessment of Web-based interactive systems. His current research mingles Human–Computer Interaction methods and Software Engineering methods applied to the development of Web-based interactive systems. His goal is to propose models, methods and techniques to support the development of usable, sound and effective Web applications. Most recent projects include methods to design and evaluate e-services applications for e-Government initiatives and formal description techniques to deal with navigation modeling of Web applications. Other topics of interest are automation of guidelines inspection; model-based usability evaluation; navigation and dialogue modeling through formal description techniques; task models.

Introduction

A Human-Centered Design Approach

Guy A. Boy

RATIONALE

Nobody questions the use of the clock today: the main function of a clock is to provide the time to its user. A modern watch uses several resources that include a battery, internal mechanisms and the ability of its user to (re-)adjust time when necessary or change the battery when it is no longer working. You interact with your watch as you would with someone who will tell you "hey, it is time to go to the next meeting!" This automaton can be programmed and consequently act as an agent that supports many time-related facets of your life. More generally, automation brought up and consolidated the concept of human–machine interaction (HMI).

HMI, as a field of investigation, is quite recent even if people have used machines for a long time. HMI attempts to rationalize relevant attributes and categories that emerge from the use of (computerized) machines. Four main principles, that is, safety, performance, comfort and esthetics, drive this rationalization along four human factors lines of investigation: physical (that is, physiological and bio-mechanical), cognitive, social or emotional.

Physically, the sailor interacts with his/her boat by pulling sail ropes for example. Cognitively, I interact with my computer writing the introduction of this book. Of course I type on a keyboard and this is physical, but the main task is cognitive in the sense that I need to control the syntax and the semantics of my writing, as well as spelling feedback provided by my text processing application. Software makes it more cognitive. You may say that the sailor needs to know when and how to pull the ropes, and this is a cognitive activity. Indeed, learning is required to optimize workload among other human factors. Socially, it happens that my colleagues and I wrote this text for a community of people. Any production, which is targeted to a wider audience than its producer could anticipate, becomes a social production that will need to be socially accepted. This is true for an engineering production, but also for a legal act or an artistic production. Emotionally, the artist uses his/her pen or computer to express his/her emotions. But, emotions may come from situations also where adrenalin is required to handle risky decisions and actions. More generally, esthetics involves empathy in the human–machine relation (Boy and Morel, 2004).

For the last three decades, cognition has been central to the study of human–machine interaction. This is because automation and software mediates most tasks. Hollnagel and Woods (2005), talking about the growing complexity of interaction with increasingly computerized systems, introduced this concept of changing balance between doing and thinking. But, what do we mean by "doing" today when we permanently use computers for most of our everyday tasks. Doing is interacting … with software! HMI has become human–computer interaction (HCI). However, in this book, HMI is more than HCI even if it includes it. Driving a car, flying an airplane or controlling a chemical plant is obviously not the same as text processing. In this sense, HMI is not the same as HCI (Hewett et al., 1992; Card et al., 1983; Myers, 1998; Sears and Jacko, 2007).

HMI has become a mandatory field of research and engineering in the design and development of nowadays systems. Why? As already said, this is because what is commonly called a user interface is currently made of software … and this user interface has become deeper and deeper! We now interact with machines through software. The main issue is to develop systems that enable appropriate task execution through them. We often think that we simplify tasks by piling layers of software, but it happens that resulting interaction is sometimes more complicated and complex. Indeed, even if HCI strongly contributes to decrease interaction complexity, the distance between people and the physical world increases so much that situation awareness becomes a crucial issue, that is, we must not lose the sense of reality.

Therefore, what should we do? Should we design simpler systems that people would use without extensive learning and performance support? To what extent should we accept the fact that new systems require adaptation from their users? Where should we draw the line? An important distinction is between evolution and revolution. For example, cars are getting more computerized, for example, in addition to the radio, new systems were introduced such as the global positioning system (GPS) that supports navigation, an autopilot in the form of a speed control system and a line keeping system, an onboard computer that support energy consumption, a collision avoidance system, an hand-free kit that enables the driver to communicate with people located outside of the vehicle, and so on.

Even if the initial goal was to improve safety, performance, comfort and esthetics, the result today is that there are far too many onboard systems that increase driver's workload and induce new types of incidents and accidents. On one side, software technology attempts to help people, and on the other side, it induces new types of life-critical problems that any designer or engineer should take into account in order to develop appropriate solutions. A simple alarm provided by the central software of a modern car may end up in a very complicated situation because neither the driver nor a regular mechanic will be able to understand what is really going on; a specialized test machine is required together with the appropriate specialized person who knows how to use it.

This handbook proposes approaches, methods and tools to handle HMI at design time. For that matter, it proposes a human-centered design (HCD) approach. Of course, it must be considered as a starter toward a deeper search into the growing bulk of HMI and HCD literature and field. It is based on contemporary knowledge and know-how on human–machine interaction and human-centered design. It is targeted at a diverse audience including academia and industry professionals. In particular, it should serve as a useful resource for scholars and students of engineering, design and human factors, whether practitioners or scientists, as well as members of the general public with an interest in cognitive engineering (Norman, 1982, 1986), cognitive system engineering (Hollnagel and Woods, 1983, 2005) and human-centered design (Boy, 1998). Above all, the volume is designed as a research guide that will both inform readers on the basics of human–machine interaction, and provide a look ahead at the means through which cognitive engineers and human factors specialists will attempt to keep developing the field of HMI.

HUMAN-CENTERED AUTOMATION

Current machines heavily rely on the cognitive skills of their users, who acquire and process data, make decisions and act in real-time. In particular, we will focus on the use of automated machines and various kinds of innovative artifacts developed to overcome limitations of humans facing the growing complexity of their overall environment. Automation will never stop.[1] This is currently the case of the evolution of air traffic management (ATM) where controllers have to face the difficult challenge of managing a growth of 4.5 percent per year average for the last 20 years; this growth is very likely to remain the same during the next decades. Machines are becoming more complex even if the goal of the designers is to facilitate their use during normal operations; problems happen in routine as well as abnormal contexts. This is why human reliability needs to be taken carefully from tow points of view: (1) humans have limitations; (2) humans are unique problem-solvers in unanticipated situations.

Cognitive engineering should better benefit from operational experience by proposing appropriate models of cognition that would rationalize this experience. Rasmussen's model has been extensively used over the last two decades to explain the behavior of a human operator controlling a complex dynamic system (Rasmussen, 1986). This model is organized into three levels of behavior: *skill*, *rule*, and *knowledge* (Figure I.1).

Historically, automation of complex dynamic systems, aircraft in particular, have led to the transfer of human operators' skills (for example, performing a tracking task) to the machine. Autopilots have been in charge of simple tracking tasks since the 1930s. This kind of automation was made possible using concepts and tools from electrical engineering, mechanical engineering, and control theories, such as mechanical regulators, *proportional-integral-derivative* controllers (PID), Laplace functions, and stochastic filtering. Autopilots were deeply refined and rationalized during the sixties and the seventies. Human skill models were based on quasi-linear models' functions and optimal control models. Human engineering specialists have developed quantitative models to describe and predict human control performance and workload at Rasmussen's skill level. They have been successfully applied to

---

1 Bernard Ziegler, a former Vice-President of Airbus Industrie, made the following observations and requirements from his experience as a test pilot and distinguished engineer: "the machine that we will be handling will become increasingly automated; we must therefore learn to work as a team with automation; a robot is not a leader, in the strategic sense of the term, but a remarkable operator; humans will never be perfect operators, even if they indisputably have the capabilities to be leaders; strategy is in the pilot's domain, but not necessarily tactics; the pilot must understand why the automaton does something, and the necessary details of how; it must be possible for the pilot to immediately replace the automaton, but only if he has the capability and can do better; whenever humans take control, the robot must be eliminated; the pilot must be able to trust automation; acknowledge that it is not human nature to fly; it follows that a thinking process is required to situate oneself, and in the end, as humiliating as it may be, the only way to insure safety is to use protective barriers" (Ziegler, 1996).

study a wide range of problems in the aviation domain such as handling qualities, display and control system design and analysis, and simulator design and use.

The second automation revolution took place when the rule-based level was transferred to the machine. In aviation, a second layer was put on top of the autopilot to take care of navigation. The *flight management system* (FMS) was designed and implemented during the eighties to provide set points for the autopilot. A database is now available onboard with a large variety of routes that cover most of the flights in a specific geographical sector. Pilots need to program the FMS by recalling routes from the database and eventually customize them for a specific flight. Once they have programmed the FMS, the aircraft is "capable of flying by itself" under certain conditions, that is, the FMS is in charge of the navigation task in pre-programmed situations.

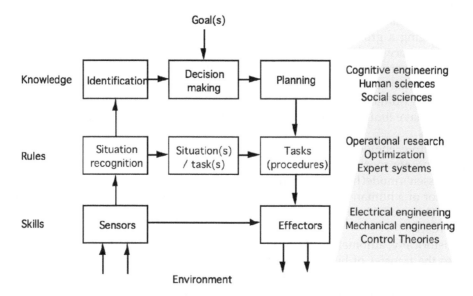

Figure I.1   Rasmussen's model, automation evolution and contributing discipline emergence

Today, human operators mostly work at Rasmussen's knowledge-based level where interpretation has become an important work process. Basic operations are delegated to the machine, and humans progressively become managers of (networked) cognitive systems. Humans need to identify a situation when there is no pattern matching (situation recognition) at the rule-based level, to decide according to specified (or sometimes unspecified) goals, and to plan a series of tasks. These are typical strategic activities. Some people are good at strategic activities, others prefer to execute what they are told to do. In any case, the control of cognitive systems requires strategic training. For example, using the Web has totally transferred the shopping task to Rasmussen's knowledge-based level, that is, the selection of food items is made using virtual objects, and delivery is planned with respect to the customer's schedule and the nature of the food.

Technology has always contributed to shaping the way people interact with the world. Conversely, interacting with the world has direct impact on how technology evolves. Rationalization of experience feedback influences the development of theories that make new artifacts emerge. In a technology-driven society, this goes the other way around, that is, the use of artifacts induces new practices, and new jobs emerge, as film technology induced the art of film making for example. The twentieth century was rich in technology innovation and development. The speed of evolution of technology and resulting practices is very sensitive to economical impacts. In some cases, when economical benefits were not obvious a priori, but the evolution of human kind was at stake, technological advances were decided at the political level, such as designing and developing a technology that enables a man to walk on the moon. Today following these grandiose projects, we realize that human-centered automation, and more generally human-centered design and engineering, is not enough effectively taken into account at the political level yet. A new paradigm needs to be found to better understand the optimal allocation between human and machine cognition together with the evolution of organizations.

The term "human-centered automation" (HCA) was coined by Billings (1991) in the aviation domain, and, among a large variety of research efforts, further developed (Boy et al., 1995). Human-centeredness requires that we focus on some distinctions. When it was conceived, HCA differed from human-centered design (HCD) in the sense that automation is something added to an existing system. Since software technology is dominant in the systems that we develop today, HCA becomes necessarily HCD. But, I think that there is an even more important distinction between HCD and human-centered engineering (HCE). HCD is the mandatory upstream process that enables a design team to incorporate human requirements into the design of a system. Usually, HCD is scenario-based and prototype-based. It consists in gathering human factors issues from an appropriate community of users or, more generally, actors who are anticipated to act on the system being designed. These actors may be direct end-users but also maintainers who will have to repair the system in case of failure for example. In this case, it is not only design for usability, but also design for maintainability. At this stage, we need to investigate possible scenarios that make actors requirements as explicit as possible. In the same way, and as architects do for the design of buildings, mock-ups need to be developed in order to incrementally validate actors' requirements (this is formative evaluation). HCE follows HCD. Human factors engineers are required to check the various steps of the production of the system. If HCD is creativity-driven, HCE is a systematic process that is based on a body of rules that need to be applied. In aeronautics, HCE is now a common practice and is formalized by official national and international regulatory institutions, for example, ISO,[2] ICAO,[3] IATA[4] and EASA.[5] Examples of such rules are provided in EASA CS.25–1302 (2004) and ISO 13407 (1999). In this book, we will mainly focus on HCD, even if some of the chapters treat parts of currently-practiced HCE, and insist on the fact that end-user expertise and experience should be used during the whole life cycle of any artifact.

---

2 International Standard Organization.
3 International Civil Aviation Organization.
4 International Air Transport Association.
5 European Aviation Safety Agency.

THE AUTOS PYRAMID

The AUTOS pyramid is a framework that helps rationalize human-centered design and engineering. It was first introduced in the HCD domain as the AUTO tetrahedron (Boy, 1998) to help relate four entities: Artifact (that is, system), User, Task and Organizational environment. Artifacts may be aircraft or consumer electronics systems, devices, and parts, for example. Users may be novices, experienced personnel or experts, coming from and evolving in various cultures. They may be tired, stressed, making errors, old or young, as well as in very good shape and mood. Tasks vary from handling quality control, flight management, managing a passenger cabin, repairing, designing, supplying or managing a team or an organization. Each task involves one or several cognitive functions that related users must learn and use. The AUT triangle (Figure I.2) enables the explanation of three edges: task and activity analysis (U-T); information requirements and technological limitations (T-A); ergonomics and training (procedures) (T-U).

The organizational environment includes all team players who/that will be called "agents," whether humans or machines, interacting with the user who performs the task using the artifact (Figure I.3). It introduces three additional edges: social issues (U-O); role and job analyses (T-O); emergence and evolution (A-O).

The AUTOS framework (Figure I.4) is an extension of the AUTO tetrahedron that introduces a new dimension, the "Situation," which was implicitly included in the "Organizational environment." The new edges are usability/usefulness (A-S), situation awareness (U-S), situated actions (T-S), and cooperation/coordination (O-S).

HMI could be presented by describing human factors, machine factors and interaction factors. Using AUTOS, human factors are user factors, machine factors are artifact factors, and interaction factors combine task factors, organizational factors and situational factors. Of course, there are many other ways to present this discipline, we choose the five AUTOS dimensions because they have been proved to be very useful to drive human-centered design and categorize HMI complexity into relevant and appropriate issues. Therefore, I use them to structure this introduction of HMI. These aspects include design methods, techniques, and tools.

MACHINE FACTORS (THE A OF AUTOS)

Since this book is devoted to support designers and engineers in the design and development of human–machine systems, technological aspects are important concrete bricks that will enable them to perform their jobs. In this handbook, machine factors will not be developed from an engineering viewpoint, but a usage viewpoint.

Hardware Factors

Today, people at work typically face computer screens of various forms and use a variety of control devices. We usually refer to the user interface, that is, a system in between a user (or human operator) and a process to be controlled or managed.

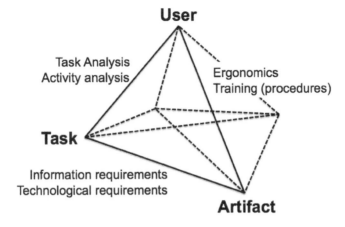

Figure I.2   The AUT triangle

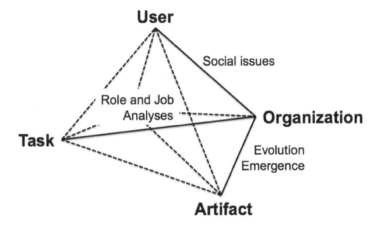

Figure I.3   The AUTO tetrahedron

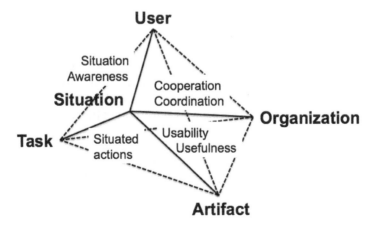

Figure I.4   The AUTOS pyramid

The terms "human operator" and "user" can be equally used. The former comes from process control and the human-system engineering community. The latter comes from the human–computer interaction (HCI) community. In these two communities, automation took various forms and contents. In process control, automation was driven by control theories where feedback is the dominant concept. In HCI (office) automation was driven by the desktop metaphor for a long time to the point that usability often refers to the ability to use a graphical interface that includes menus, buttons, windows, and so on. It is interesting to note that the process control discipline took care of real-time continuous processes such as nuclear, aerospace, or medical systems where time and dynamics are crucial issues together with safety-critical issues. Conversely, HCI developed the interaction comfort side. HCI specialists got interested into learnability, efficiency, easy access to data, direct manipulation of metaphoric software objects, and pleasurable user experience. Human operators are typically experts because industrial processes that they control are complex and safety-critical. Users, in the HCI sense, can be anybody.

For all these reasons, hardware factors are different if we talk about process control or "classical" HCI. The very nature of processes to be controlled needs to be analyzed and understood well enough to determine what kind of hardware would be suitable for the safest, most efficient and comfortable human–machine interaction. However, HCI strongly influenced our lives during the last decade to the point that usability has become a standard even in process control interface design and development. People are now very familiar with menus and windows. This is fine, but this also assumes that these interaction styles cover the various constraints of the process being controlled.

I recently heard the term "interactive cockpit." What does that mean? I always thought that an aircraft cockpit was the ultimate interactive interface with a dynamic safety-critical process, and therefore interactive. But "interactive" means something else today. It does not mean continuous interaction through a steering wheel or a handle physically connected to rudders; it means interacting with a piece of software … typically through a computer screen with a pointing device and a keyboard! This (r)evolution started with the glass cockpits in the mid-eighties; we were talking about "fly-by-wire." Today, the car industry is talking about "drive-by-wire," but the meaning has also changed following this technological evolution where software is the most important component.

There are hardware factors that incrementally emerge from the design of these new machines. Among them, the following are important: force feedback, loudspeakers, screens, signals, buttons, keyboard, joystick, mouse, trackball, microphone, 3-D mouse, data glove, data suit (or interactive seat), metaphor for interaction, visual rendering, 3-D sound rendering, 3-D geometrical model, and so on.

From the time of the first flying machines at the end of the nineteen century to the Concorde, the number of instruments in an aircraft cockpit grew up to 600. At the beginning of the eighties, the introduction of cathode ray tubes (CRT) and digital technology in cockpits contributed to drastically decrease this number. Today, the number of displays in the A380 is considerably reduced. This does not mean that the number of functions and lines of software code is reduced. As a matter of fact, software size keeps increasing tremendously.

Software Factors

Software is very easy to modify; consequently we modify it all the time! Interaction is not only a matter of end product; it is also a matter of development process. End-users are not the only ones to interact with a delivered product; designers and engineers also interact with the product in order to fix it up toward maturity … even after its delivery. One of the reasons is that there are software tests that cannot be done without a real-world exposure. It is very difficult to anticipate what end-users would do in the infinite number of situations where they will be evolving. We will see in this book that scenario-based design is mandatory with respect to various dimensions including understandability (situation awareness), complexity, reliability, maturity and induced organizational constraints (rigidity versus flexibility).

What should we understand when we use a product? How does it work? How should it be used? At what level of depth should we go inside the product to use it appropriately? In the early ages of the car industry, most car drivers were also mechanics because when they had a problem they needed to fix it by themselves; the technology was too new to have specialized people. These drivers were highly skilled engineers both generalists and specialists on cars. Today, things have drastically changed; drivers are no longer knowledgeable and skilled to fix cars; there are specialists that do this job because software is far too complex to understand without appropriate help. Recent evolution transformed the job of mechanics into system engineers who know how to use specialized software that enables to diagnose failures and fix them. They do not have to fully understand what is going on inside the engine; a software program does it for them and explains problems to them — when the overall system is well-designed of course. This would be the ideal case; in practice, most problems come from organizational factors induced by the use of such technology, for example, appropriate people may not be available at the right time to fix problems when they arise.

Software complexity can be split into internal complexity (or system complexity) and interface complexity. Internal complexity is related to the degree of explanation required to the user to understand what is going on when necessary. Concepts related to system complexity are: flexibility (both system flexibility and flexibility of use); system maturity (before getting mature, a system is an accumulation of functions — the "another function syndrome" — and it becomes mature through a series of articulations and integrations); automation (linked to the level of operational assistance, authority delegation and automation culture); and operational documentation. Technical documentation complexity is very interesting to be tested because it is directly linked to the explanation of artifact complexity. The harder a system is to use, the more related technical documentation or performance support are required in order to provide appropriate assistance at the right time in the right format.

In any case, software should be reliable at any time in order to support safe, efficient and comfortable work. There are many ways to test software reliability (Lyu, 1995; Rook, 1990). In this handbook, what we try to promote is not only system reliability, but also human–machine reliability. We know that there is a co-adaptation of people and machines (via designers and engineers). Human operators may accept some unreliable situations where the machine may fail as long as safety, efficiency and comfort costs are not too high. However, when these costs become high enough for them, the machine is just rejected. Again this poses the problem of product maturity (Boy, 2005); the conventional capacity maturity model for software development (Paulk et al., 1995), systematically used in most industries, does not guarantee product maturity, but process maturity. Product maturity requires continuous investment of end-users in design and development processes. At the very beginning, they must be involved with domain specialists to set up high-level requirements right; this is an important role of participatory design. During the design and development phase, formative evaluations should be performed involving appropriate potential end-users in order to "invent" the most appropriate future use of the product.

Interface complexity is characterized by content management, information density and ergonomics rules. Content management is, in particular, linked to information relevance, alarm management, and display content management. Information density is linked to decluttering, information modality, diversity, and information-limited attractors; that is, objects on the instrument or display that are poorly informative for the execution of the task but nevertheless attract user's attention. The "PC screen do-it all syndrome" is a good indicator of information density (elicited improvement-factors were screen size and zooming). Redundancy is always a good rule whether it repeats information for crosschecking, confirmation or comfort, or by explaining the "how," "where," and "when" an action can be performed. Ergonomics rules formalize user friendliness, that is, consistency, customization, human reliability, affordances, feedback, visibility, and appropriateness of the cognitive functions involved. Human reliability involves human error tolerance (therefore the need for recovery means) and human error resistance (therefore the existence of risk to resist to). To summarize, A-factors deal with the level of necessary *interface simplicity, explanation, redundancy*, and *situation awareness* that the artifact is required to offer to users.

HUMAN FACTORS (THE U OF AUTOS)

Human factors have been heavily studied during the last five decades in the HMI context. After the Second World War, human factors specialists were mainly physicians, medical doctors, who were taking care of both physiological and biomechanical aspects of humans at work, that is, ergonomics.[6] Work psychology, and later on cognitive psychology, progressively emerged in the seventies to become the leading discipline in human factors in the eighties. The main reason of this emergence is the introduction of computers and software in work places and, more generally, everyday life. All these approaches were essentially based on the Newell and Simon's information processing model that is typically a single agent model (Newell and Simon, 1972). The development of computerized systems and more specifically networked systems promoted the need for studying social and organizational factors. We have then moved into the field of multi-agent models.

HMI involves automation, that is, machines that were controlled manually are now managed through a piece of software that mediates user intentions and

---

6   Professor Grandjean declared founded the International Ergonomics Association (IEA) on April 6, 1959, at a meeting in Oxford, England. Today, IEA is a hyper-organization that has 42 federated societies, 1 affiliated society, 11 sustaining member organizations, 6 individual sustaining members and 2 networks. It also has 22 Technical Committees (www.iea.cc). IEA includes all forms of human factors at work.

provides appropriate feedback. Automation introduces constraints, and therefore rigidity. Since end-users do not have the final action, they need to plan more than in the past. As already said, work becomes more cognitive and (artificially) social, that is, there are new social activities that need to be performed in order for the other relevant actors to do their jobs appropriately. This even becomes more obvious when cognition is distributed among many human and machine agents. Computer-supported cooperative work, for example, introduced new types of work practices that are mandatory to learn and use, otherwise overall performance may rapidly become a disaster.

Human Body-Related and Physiological Factors

Work performed by people can be strongly constrained by their physiological and biomechanical possibilities and limitations. Understanding these possibilities and limitations tremendously facilitated the evolution of civil and military aviation. Cockpits were incrementally shaped to human anthropometrical requirements in order to ease manipulation of the various instruments. This of course is always strongly related to technology limitations also.

Anthropometry developed its own language and methods. It is now actively used in design to define workspaces according to human factors such as accommodation, compatibility, operability, and maintainability by the user population. Workspaces are generally designed for 90 percent to 95 percent coverage of the user population. Anthropometric databases are constantly maintained to provide appropriate information to designers and engineers. Nevertheless, designers and engineers need to be guided to use these databases in order to make appropriate choices.

Work organization is also a matter of trouble for professionals. Fatigue is a major concern. Therefore, it is important to know about circadian rhythms and the way people adapt to shift work and long work hours for example. Consequences are intimately associated with health and safety risks. Fatigue studies provide more knowledge and know-how on how to proceed with work time schedules, appropriate training, systematic checks, and health indicators following. Of course, this needs to be integrated in regulatory procedures.

Cognitive Factors

Cognitive factors start with workload assessment. This statement may seem to be restrictive and old fashion, but the reader should think twice about workload before starting any work in human factors. On one side, workload is a concept that is very difficult to define. It is both an output of human performance and a necessary input to optimize performance; that is, we produce workload to perform better, up to a point where we need to change our work strategy. But on the other side, we need to figure out a model that would quantify a degree of load produced by a human being while working. Of course, this model should be based on real measurements performed on the human being. Many models of workload have been proposed and used (Bainbridge, 1978; Hart, 1982; Boy and Tessier, 1985). Workload also deals with the complexity of the task being performed. In particular, people can do several things at the same time, in parallel; this involves the use of several different peripheral resources simultaneously (Wickens, 1984). Sperandio (1972) studied the way air traffic controllers handle several aircraft at the same time, and showed that the time spent on radio increased with the number of aircraft being controlled: 18 percent of their time spent in radio communication for one controlled aircraft whereas 87 percent for nine aircraft controlled in parallel. In other words, task complexity tends to increase human operator efficiency.

Human–machine interaction moves into human–machine cooperation when the machine becomes highly automated. In this case, it is more appropriate to talk about agent-agent cooperation. Hoc and Lemoine studied dynamic task allocation (DTA) of conflict resolution between aircraft in air-traffic control on a large-scale simulator. "It included three cognitive agents: the radar controller (RC), in charge of conflict detection and resolution; the planning controller (PC), in charge of entry-exit coordination and workload regulation; and a conflict resolution computer system. Comparisons were made on the basis of a detailed cognitive analysis of verbal protocols. The more the assistance, the more anticipative the mode of operation in controllers and the easier the human-human cooperation (HHC). These positive effects of the computer support are interpreted in terms of decreased workload and increased shared information space. In addition, the more the controllers felt responsible for task allocation, the more they criticized the machine operation" (Hoc and Lemoine, 1998).

Situation awareness (SA) is another concept that is useful to introduce here, especially as a potential indicator for safety in highly automated human–machine systems. During the last decade, lots of efforts have been carried out to assess SA such as the Situation Awareness Global Assessment Technique (SAGAT) (Endsley, 1987, 1996). Several efforts have been developed to assess SA in the aeronautics domain (Mogford, 1997; Stephane and Boy, 2005); the main problem is the characterization of the influence of action on situation awareness. Indeed, human operator's actions are always situated, especially in life-critical environments, and SA does not mean the same when actions are deliberate as when they are reactive. In human–machine interaction, this is a very important issue since actions are always both intentional (deliberative) and reactive because they are mainly performed in a close loop.

Obviously, there are many other concepts and processes that need to be taken into account to investigate cognitive factors. I would like to insist on the fact that cognition must be thought in a multi-agent perspective where human–machine interaction is in fact a dynamic network of interactions among human and machine agents. Consequently, cognition should be taken more broadly than in cognitive psychology and extend it to a social and organizational perspective.

Social Factors

There are two fields of research that grew independently for the last three decades: crew resource management (CRM) in aviation, and computer-supported cooperative (CSCW) work in HCI. The former was motivated by social micro-world of aircraft cockpits where pilots need to cooperate and coordinate to fly safely and efficiently. CRM started during a workshop on *resource management on the flight deck* sponsored by NASA in 1979 (Cooper, White, and Lauber, 1980). At that time, the motivation was the correlation between air crashes and human errors as failures of interpersonal communications, decision-making, and leadership (Helmreich et al., 1999). CRM training developed within airlines in order to change attitudes and behavior of flight crews. CRM deals with personalities of the various human agents involved in work situations, and is mainly focused on teaching, that is, each agent learns to better understand his or her personality in order to improve the overall cooperation and coordination of the working group.

Douglas Engelbart is certainly the most influential contributor to the development of the technology that supports collaborative processes today. He invented the mouse and worked on the ARPANET project in 1960s. He was among the first researchers who developed hypertext technology and computer networks to augment intellectual capacities of people. The term "computer-supported cooperative work" (CSCW) was coined in 1984 by Paul Cashman and Irene Grief to describe a multidisciplinary approach focused on how people work and how technology could support them. CSCW scientific conferences were first organized in the US within the ACM-SIGCHI[7] community. Conferences on the topic immediately followed in Europe and Asia. Related work and serious interest already existed in European Nordic countries. During the late 1970s and even more during the 1980s, office automation was born from the emergence of new practices using minicomputers. Minicomputers and microcomputers were integrated in many places such as travel agencies, administrations, banks and so on, to support groups and organizations. People started to use them interactively, as opposed to using them in a batch mode. Single user applications such as text processors and spreadsheets were developed to support basic office tasks. Several researchers started to investigate the way people were using this new technology. Computer science is originally the science of internal functions of computers (how computers work). With the massive use of computers and their incremental integration in our lives, computer science has also become the science of external functions of computers (how to use computers and what they are for). We, computer and cognitive scientists, needed to investigate and better understand more how people appropriate computers individually and collectively to support collaborative work. Multidisciplinary research developed involving psychologists, sociologists, education and organization specialists, managers and engineers.

In parallel with these two fields of research, two others developed: human reliability (Reason, 1990) and distributed cognition (Hutchins, 1995). The former led to a very interesting distinction between two approaches of human reliability whether the focus is on the person or the system. Each approach induces a quite different philosophy of error management from the other. Reason developed what he called the Swiss cheese model (Reason, 1997). He stated that we cannot change human limitations and capabilities, but the conditions in which humans perform their tasks can be changed. Therefore, these conditions, which can be viewed as technological and organizational constraints, should be clearly identified in order to create defensive barriers against the progression of an unsafe act.

Distributed cognition was first developed to take into account the sharing of meaningful concepts among various agents. Extending the phenomenological school of thought, agents are considered as subjects and not objects. They have

---

7   Association for Computing Machinery—Special Interest Group on Computer Human Interaction.

different subjectivity, and therefore they need to adapt among each other in order to develop a reasonable level of empathy, consensus, and common sense sharing; this is what intersubjectivity is about: "The sharing of subjective states by two or more individuals" (Scheff, 2006). This line of research cannot avoid taking into account intercultural specificities and differences. It is not surprising that most leaders of such a field come from anthropology and ethnology. Obviously, the best way to better understand interactions between cognitive agents is to be integrated in the community of these agents. In the framework of human–machine systems, we extend the concept of distributed cognition to humans and machines. The extension of the intersubjectivity concept to humans and machines requires that we take into account end-users and designers in a participatory way. To summarize, U-factors mainly deal with *user's knowledge, skills*, and *expertise* on the new artifact and its integration.

INTERACTION FACTORS (THE TOS OF AUTOS)

Task Factors

Human–machine interaction is always motivated by the execution of a task. Therefore, the way the task is organized and supported by the machine (prescribed task), and executed by the human user (effective task) is crucial. Obviously the effective task, that is often called "activity," is different from the prescribed task.

Activity analysis could be defined as the

> identification and description of activities in an organization, and evaluation of their impact on its operations. Activity analysis determines; (1) what activities are executed, (2) how many people perform the activities, (3) how much time they spend on them, (4) how much and which resources are consumed, (5) what operational data best reflects the performance of activities, and (6) of what value the activities are to the organization. This analysis is accomplished through direct observation, interviews, questionnaires, and review of the work records. See also job analysis, performance analysis and task analysis. (*Business Dictionary*, 2009)

Task complexity involves procedure adequacy, appropriate multi-agent cooperation (for example, air-ground coupling in the aerospace domain) and rapid prototyping (that is, task complexity cannot be properly understood if the resulting activity of agents involved in it is not observable). Task complexity is linked to the number of sub-tasks, task difficulty, induced risk, consistency (lexical, syntactic, semantic, and pragmatic) and the temporal dimension (perception-action frequency and time pressure in particular). Task complexity is due to operations maturity, delegation, and mode management. Mode management is related to role analysis. To summarize, T-factors mainly deal with *task difficulty* according to a spectrum from best practice to well-identified categories of tasks.

Organizational Factors

Interaction is also influenced by the organizational environment that is itself organized around human(s) and machine(s) in the overall human–machine system (HMS). More explicitly, an HMS could be someone facing his/her laptop writing a paper; it could also be someone driving a car with passengers; it could be an air traffic management system that includes pilots, controllers, and various kinds of aviation systems. People are now able to interact with computerized systems or with other people via computerized systems. We recently put to the front authority as a major concept in human-centered automation. When a system or other parties do the job, or part of the job, for someone, there is delegation. What is delegated? Is it the task? It is the authority in the execution of this task? By authority, we mean accountability (responsibility) and control.

Organization complexity is linked to social cognition, agent-network complexity, and more generally multi-agent management issues. There are four principles for multi-agent management: agent activity (that is, what the other agent is doing now and for how long); agent activity history (that is, what the other agent has done); agent activity rationale (that is, why the other agent is doing what it does); and agent activity intention (that is, what the other agent is going to do next and when). Multi-agent management needs to be understood through a role (and job) analysis. To summarize, O-factors mainly deal with the required level of *coupling* between the various purposeful agents to handle the new artifact.

Situational Factors

Interaction depends on the situation where it takes place. Situations could be normal or abnormal. They could even be emergencies. This is why we will emphasize the scenario-based approach to design and engineering. Resulting methods are based on descriptions of people using technology in order to better understand how this technology is, or could be, used to redefine their activities. Scenarios can be created very early during the design process and incrementally modified to support product construction and refinement.

Scenarios are good to identify functions at design time and operations time. They tend to rationalize the way the various agents interact among each other. They enable the definition of organizational configurations and time-wise chronologies.

Situation complexity is often caused by interruptions and more generally disturbances. It involves safety and high workload situations. It is commonly analyzed by decomposing contexts into sub-contexts. Within each sub-context, the situation is characterized by uncertainty, unpredictability and various kinds of abnormalities. To summarize, situational factors deal with the *predictability* and *appropriate completeness* (scenario representativeness) of the various situations in which the new artifact will be used.

OVERVIEW OF THE HANDBOOK

Of course, hard decisions needed to be made on the main topics that are developed in this handbook. In addition to this introduction and the conclusion, the book is organized into three parts (analysis; design and engineering; and evaluation) and 20 chapters. These chapters include transversal perspectives on human–machine interaction, methods, and tools for human-centered design and engineering, and continuity and change in human–machine systems.

A handbook on human–machine interaction cannot avoid human operator modeling. Thierry Bellet presents an account on analysis, modeling, and simulation of human operator's mental activities. Even if he limits his illustrations to car driving, the various descriptions and methods are applicable to other safety-critical systems. Most readers know what car driving is in practice, therefore examples will be better understood.

Following up on human factors, situation awareness became a major topic over the last two decades mainly because the sophistication of technology tends to increase the distance between human operators and the actual work. Anke Popken and Josef Krems present the relation between automation and situation awareness, and illustrative examples in the automotive domain.

There are several aspects of human factors such as psychophysiology and performance that are certainly very important to take into account at design time. Anil Raj, Margery Doyle and Joshua Cameron present an approach and results that can be used in human-centered design. They focus on the relationships between workload, situation awareness and decision effectiveness.

For the last three decades, human reliability was a hot topic, mainly in aviation, and more generally in life-critical systems. Christopher Johnson presents a very comprehensive approach to human error in the context of human–machine interaction, and more specifically in human-centered design.

Complex systems cannot be operated without operational support. Barbara Burian and Lynne Martin present a very experienced account on operating documents that change in real-time. Software enables the design of interactive documents, electronic flight bags, integrated navigational maps, and electronic checklists for example. New technology enables the integration of information from different sources and ease the manipulation of resulting data in real-time.

Human–machine interaction was thought as a human operator interacting with a machine. Today, the human–machine social environment changes toward multi-agent interactions. Guy A. Boy and Gudela Grote describe this evolution and the mandatory concepts that emerge form this evolution such as authority sharing and organizational automation.

Designing new systems involves the participation of several actors and requires purposeful and socially acceptable scenarios. Scenarios are coming from stories that are incrementally categorized. They are necessary for strategic design thinking. John Carroll and Haynes present the scenario-based design approach that support human-centered design of complex systems.

Design is or must be a socially anchored activity. Complex socio-technical systems have to be developed in a participative way, that is, realistic stakeholders have to be involved at an early stage of design, by developing the new system in actual contexts of use. Saadi Lahlou presents a series of socio-cognitive issues that a design team should take into account to design things for the real world.

Design is certainly a creative activity, but it has to be incrementally rationalized. Following up his 1998 book, Guy A. Boy presents a new version of the cognitive function analysis of human–machine multi-agent systems. He introduces general properties such as emerging cognitive functions, complexity analysis, socio-cognitive stability analysis, and flexibility analysis. He insists on the fact that taking into account experience is a key factor in design, and maturity is a matter of product testing, as well as practice evolution and emergence identification.

Automated processes involve cooperation between humans and machines. Patrick Millot, Frédéric Vanderhaegen, and Serge Debernard present several dimensions of human–machine cooperation such as degree of automation, system complexity, and the richness and complexity of the human component. They insist on the need for a common frame of reference in cooperative activities, and on the importance of the authority concept.

David Navarre, Philippe Palanque, Célia Martinie, Marco Winckler, and Sandra Steere provide an approach to human-centered design in the light of the evolution of human–computer interaction toward safety-critical systems. They emphasize the non-reliability of interactive software and its repercussions on usability engineering. They introduce the "Generic Integrated Modeling Framework" (GIMF) that includes techniques, methods and tools for model-based design of interactive real-word systems while taking into account human and system-related erroneous behavior.

Most of the chapters in this handbook deal with automation. It was important to address the various properties of human–automation interaction that support human-centered design. Amy Pritchett and Michael Feary present several useful concepts, which include authority (a recurrent issue in our modern software intensive world), representations, interface mechanisms, automation behavior, and interface error states.

As already said, software is everywhere in human–machine systems nowadays. Jeffrey Bradshaw, Paul Feltovich, and Matthew Johnson present a variation of human–automation interaction where automation is represented by artificial agents. The concept of artificial agent emerged from the development of semi-autonomous software in artificial intelligence. It is consistent with the concept of cognitive functions already presented.

Evaluation was for a long time the main asset of the human factors and ergonomics discipline. Jean-Marc Robert and Annemarie Lesage propose, in two chapters, a new approach of evaluation going from usability testing to the capture of user experience with interactive systems. Interaction design has become one of the main issue, and consequently activity, in the development of modern technology. Traditional design is typically done locally and integration happens after. Using a user experience approach involves holistic design, that is, the product is taken globally from the start. This is what I call the evolution from the traditional inside-out engineering approach to the new outside-in design approach.

An example of technique and tool for measuring human factors during design is eye tracking (ET). Lucas Stephane presents the core ET research in the field of human–machine interaction, as well as the human visual system to better understand ET techniques. Real-world examples in the aeronautical domain are taken to illustrate these techniques.

Among the many factors useful to assess human–machine interaction, fatigue is certainly mostly hidden because we tend to continue working even when we are tired, and extremely tired. Philippa Gander, Curt Graeber, and Greg Belenky show how the dynamics of fatigue accumulation and recovery need to be integrated into human-centered design, more specifically by introducing appropriate defenses. When operator fatigue can be expected to have an impact on safety, systems being design should be conceived as resilient to human operator fatigue in order to maintain acceptable human–machine interaction.

People performance changes with respect to their age. Anabela Simões, Marta Pereira, and Mary Panou address older people's characteristics and design requests to accommodate their needs in order to ensure efficient, safe, and comfortable human–machine interactions with respect to context. They present the issue of safe mobility for older people and technological solutions with the related advantages and inherent risks.

The various effects of culture and organization influence human–machine interaction. Don Harris and Wen-Chin Lee present the influence of these effects on human errors. People do not use systems in the same way when they come from different cultures. This pragmatic aspect of human–machine interaction needs to be taken into account seriously in life-critical systems in particular.

The Francophone school of ergonomics makes the difference between prescribed task and activity (that is, the effective task). Sometimes we believe that task analysis as a normative approach will guaranty a straight human-centered way of designing systems. This assumes that system boundaries are well-defined. In the real world this is not the case. Systems are loosely coupled in the environment where they are working. They need to absorb change and disturbance and still maintain effective relationships with the environment. Promoting this kind of reflexion, Erik Hollnagel presents the diminishing relevance of human–machine interaction.

The conclusion of this handbook focuses on the shift from automation to interaction design as a new discipline that integrates human and social sciences, human–computer interaction and collaborative system engineering. For that matter, we need to have appropriate models of interaction, context, and function allocation.

REFERENCES

Bainbridge, L. (1978). Forgotten alternatives in skill and workload. *Ergonomics*, 21, 169–185.

Bainbridge, L. (1987). Ironies of automation. In J. Rasmussen, K. Duncan and J. Leplat (Eds.), *New Technology and Human Error*. London: Wiley.

Beaudouin-Lafon, M. (2004). AVI '04, May 25–28, 2004, Gallipoli (LE), Italy.

Billings, C.E. (1991). *Human-centered Aircraft Automation Philosophy*. NASA Technical Memorandum 103885, NASA Ames Research Center, Moffett Field, CA, US.

Boy, G.A. and Tessier, C. (1985). Cockpit Analysis and Assessment by the MESSAGE Methodology. *Proceedings of the 2nd IFAC/IFIP/IFORS/IEA Conf. on Analysis, Design and Evaluation of Man-Machine Systems*. Villa-Ponti, Italy, September 10–12. Oxford: Pergamon Press, pp. 73–79.

Boy, G.A., Hollnagel, E., Sheridan, T.B., Wiener, E.L. and Woods, D.D. (1995). International Summer School on Human-Centered Automation. EURISCO Proceedings. Saint-Lary, Pyrénées, France.

Boy, G.A. (1998). *Cognitive Function Analysis*. Westport, CT, US: Ablex Publishing, distributed by Greenwood Publishing Group.

Boy, G.A. and Morel, M. (2004). Interface affordances and esthetics. (in French) *Revue Alliage*, Edition du Seuil, Paris, France.

Boy, G.A. (2005). Knowledge management for product maturity. Proceedings of the ACM International Conference Knowledge Capture (K-Cap'05). Banff, Canada. October. Also in the ACM Digital Library.

Bradshaw, J. (1997). *Software Agents*. Cambridge, MA, US: MIT/AAAI Press.

Business Dictionary. (2009). www.businessdictionary.com/definition/activity-analysis.html.

Card, S.K., Moran, T.P., and Newell, A. (1983). *The Psychology of Human–Computer Interaction*. Hillsdale: Erlbaum.

Cooper, G.E., White, M.D., and Lauber, J.K. (Eds.). (1980). *Resource Management on the Flightdeck: Proceedings of a NASA/Industry workshop (NASA CP –2120)*. Moffett Field, CA: NASA-Ames Research Center.

Degani, A. and Wiener, E. (1997). Procedures in complex systems: The airline cockpit. *IEEE Transactions on Systems, Man, and Cybernetics*, 27, 3, 302–312.

EASA CS.25 1302 (2004). www.easa.eu.int/doc/Rulemaking/NPA/NPA_15_2004.pdf.

Endsley, M.R. (1987). *SAGAT: A methodology for the measurement of situation awareness* (NOR DOC 87–83), Hawthorne, CA, Northrop Corporation.

Endsley, M.R. (1996). Situation awareness measurement in test and evaluation. In T.G. O'Brien and S.G. Charlton (Eds.), *Handbook of Human Factors Testing and Evaluation*. Mahwah, NJ: Lawrence Erlbaum Associates, pp. 159–178.

Hart, S.G. (1982). *Theoretical Basis for Workload Assessment*. TM ADP001150, NASA-Ames Research Center, Moffett Field, CA, US.

Helmreich, R.L., Merritt, A.C., and Wilhelm, J.A. (1999). The evolution of Crew Resource Management training in commercial aviation. *International Journal of Aviation Psychology*, 9, (1), 19–32.

Heylighen, F. (1996). The Growth of Structural and Functional Complexity during Evolution. In F. Heylighen and D. Aerts (Eds.), *The Evolution of Complexity*. Kluwer Academic Publishers.

Hewett, T.T., Baecker, R., Card, S., Carey, T., Gasen, J., Mantei, M., Perlman, G., Strong, G., and Verplank, W. (1992). *ACM SIGCHI Curricula for Human–computer Interaction*. New York: The Association for Computing Machinery. (ACM Order Number: S 608920), http://sigchi.org/cdg/cdg2.html#2_1.

Hoc, J.M. (1988). *Cognitive Psychology of Planning*. London: Academic Press.

Hoc, J.M. and Lemoine, M.P. (1998). Cognitive Evaluation of Human-Human and Human–Machine Cooperation Modes in Air Traffic Control. *International Journal of Aviation Psychology*, Volume 8, Issue 1 January, 1–32.

Hollnagel, E. and Woods, D.D. (1983). Cognitive systems engineering: New wine in new bottles. *International Journal of Man-Machine Studies*, 18, 583–600.

Hollnagel, E. (1993). *Reliability of Cognition: Foundations of human reliability analysis*. London: Academic Press.

Hollnagel, E. and Woods, D.D. (2005). *Joint Cognitive Systems: Foundations of cognitive systems engineering*. Boca Raton, FL: CRC Press/Taylor and Francis.

Hutchins, E. (1995). How a Cockpit Remembers its Speeds. *Cognitive Science*, 19, 265–288.

ISO 13407 (1999). *Human-centered Design Process for Interactive Systems*, TC 159/SC 4.

Lyu, M.R. (1995). *Handbook of Software Reliability Engineering*. McGraw-Hill publishing.

Mogford, R.H. (1997). Mental models and situation awareness in air traffic control. *The International J. Aviation Psychology*, 7, 4, 331–342.

Myers, BA (1998). A brief history of human–computer interaction technology. *Interactions*, 5, 2, 44–54, ACM Press.

Newell, A., and Simon, H.A. (1972). *Human Problem-solving*. Englewood Cliffs, NJ: Prentice Hall.

Nielsen, J. (1993). *Usability Engineering*. Academic Press. London.

Norman, D.A. (1982). Steps toward a cognitive engineering: Design rules based on analyses of human error. *Proceedings of the Conference on Human Factors in Computing Systems (CHI'82)*, Gaithersburg, Maryland, US, pp. 378–382.

Norman, D. (1986). Cognitive engineering. In Norman, D., and Draper, S. (Eds.), *User-centered System Design*. Hillsdale, NJ: Lawrence Erlbaum Associates, Inc.

Paulk, M.C, Weber, C.V., Curtis, B. and Chrissis, M.B. (1995). *Capability Maturity Model: The guidelines for improving the software process*. The SEI Series in Software Engineering, Addison Wesley Professional.

Rasmussen, J. (1986). Information Processing and Human–Machine Interaction: An Approach to Cognitive Engineering. In A.P. Sage (Ed.), *System Science and Engineering*. North Holland Series.

Reason, J. (1990). *Human Error*. New York: Cambridge University Press.

Reason, J. (1997). *Managing the Risks of Organizational Accidents*. London: Ashgate.

Rook, P. (Ed.) (1990). *Software Reliability Handbook*. London, UK: Centre for Software Reliability, City University.

Scheff, T.J. (2006). *Goffman Unbound!: A New Paradigm for Social Science*. Paradigm Publishers.

Sears, A. and Jacko, J.A. (Eds.). (2007). *Handbook for Human Computer Interaction* (2nd Edition). CRC Press.

Sperandio, J.C. (1972). Charge de travail et régulation des processus opératoires. *Le Travail Humain*, 35, 86 –98. English summary in *Ergonomics*, 1971, 14, 571–577.

Stephane, L. and Boy, G.A. (2005). A Cross-Fertilized Evaluation Method based on Visual Patterns and Cognitive Functions Modeling. *Proceedings of HCI International 2005*, Las Vegas, US.

Suchman, L.A. (1987). *Plans and Situated Actions. The problem of human–machine communication*. Cambridge, England: Cambridge University Press.

Wickens, C.D. (1984). Processing resources in attention. In R. Parasuraman and D.R. Davies (Eds.), *Varieties of attention*. London: Academic Press.

Ziegler, B. (1996). *The Flight Control Loop*. Invited speech. Final RoHMI Network meeting. EURISCO, Toulouse, France, September 28–30.

PART I

Analysis

1

Analysis, Modeling, and Simulation of Human Operator's Mental Activities

Thierry Bellet

1. INTRODUCTION: THE CHALLENGE OF MENTAL ACTIVITIES MODELING FOR COGNITIVE SIMULATION

If the analysis of the human thinking is an objective shared by a set of scientific disciplines, the aim to propose computational simulation models of mental activities is a concomitant project with the development of the cognitive science, considered as a unified approach. It is typically in this cognitive science integrative logic that this chapter is written. The challenge is not only to present alternative theories on human cognition, but rather to propose a general framework for modeling mental activities in a unified way, at the articulation of different theoretical positions, in respect of their specificities, of course, but permitting to identify similarities and complementarities of these approaches beyond their differences.

The main heart of our scientific approach of human cognition is Ergonomics. Ergonomics is essentially an applied science which imports a large part of these theoretical models from other scientific disciplines, but which rebuilt these models into the frame of its own operational aims and scientific objectives: the naturalistic observation and the analysis of the human operators' activity, in all its natural complexity, though also in all its banality of the everyday life. Many scientific research efforts on cognition are essentially based on laboratory experiments, including totally artificial tasks. This is surely a relevant approach according to the Claude Bernard (1856) "experimental method," which was designed for the medical science investigation during the nineteenth century. Applied to cognition, this method aims to propose artificial tasks to the participants (the farthest of the competencies that subjects were able to develop in their daily life), in order to overcome the inter-individual differences that the scientist cannot experimentally control. The benefit of this approach is to "make equivalent" the participants, irrespective of their own personal history, and thus, to discover some invariants—or universals—shared by all the human beings. Nevertheless, the paradox of the experimental method applied to cognition study, is that it partially destroys its own object of analysis, when applied. It is like trying to study life in a completely sterile environment, devoid of oxygen. Soon, the researcher does not observe living organisms, but dead things. It is also the case of the natural cognition in experimental conditions: laboratory artificial tasks partially kill the "living cognition." Certainly, medicine has substantially improved scientific knowledge on life through the dissection of corpses. But not any medical scientist had ever thought to find the life itself into a corpse: s/he knows that life is already away, and s/he precisely seeks what are the reasons for its disappearance. Scientists interested in studying human mental activities must be aware of this methodological risk: the more the experiment is based on artificial tasks, the more the scientist investigates humans "stripped" of their own knowledge, and only a very limited part of their natural cognition can resist to this treatment. This is one of the major contributions of ergonomics — or naturalistic psychology — to cognitive science: to preserve the mental activities studies of the destructive consequences of the experimental paradigm reductionism. Focused on the activities of the human *"Operator"* (that is, a human *able to act*), the ergonomist does not study human cognition *"in vitro,"* as a laboratory specimen, but *"in vivo"*: the *"Living Cognition"* in its dynamic interactions with the surrounding environment, that is, cognition such as it is immersed into situation and implemented through the activity. From there, the new challenge of the cognitive science is to dynamically simulate the human mental activities on computer, opening thus the door to the *"in silico"* study of the living cognition.

In accordance with this general background, this chapter is organized into three main sections. The first one (that is, section 2) will focus on the *Analysis of mental activities* by jointly considering three complementary theoretical fields: (i) Cybernetics and Human Information Processing theory, (ii) the Russian theories of the activity, and (iii) the ecological approach of the human perception. Then we will attempt to propose an integrative approach of these three theoretical fields in a mixed-way, based on a Perception-Cognition-Action regulation loop, and we will illustrate the functioning of this iterative regulation loop in the particular frame of the car-driving activity.

The third section of the chapter will be devoted to the challenge of *Cognitive Modeling*. In contrast with the preceding section, the modeling step aims not only to provide a descriptive analysis of the mental activities based on empirical observations, but tries to propose formal models of human thinking that may be subject to scientific debates. For being comprehensive, a model of the human operator's mental activities should provide an in-depth description of the cognitive system at three levels, which are; (i) its cognitive architecture, (ii) the cognitive processes implemented for the information processing and reasoning, and (iii) the data-structures used for knowledge and mental representations modeling. Then, we will present an integrative model of the human cognitive system, which distinguishes the implicit, the explicit, and the reflexive cognition.

Section 4 will be centered on *Cognitive Simulation* purpose, requiring to develop computational programs able to virtually implement and then dynamically simulate the operator's mental activities on a computer. Cognitive simulation requires us to define models of the human cognitive system jointly based on human sciences theories, artificial intelligence formalisms, and computer science techniques.

Designed in continuity with the Analysis and the Modeling levels, Simulation is the necessary core step for studying the *living cognition*: it is only when the mental activities are simulated on computer that it becomes possible to analyze them in their dynamic interactions, and to apprehend them in their natural complexity.

With the aim to concretely illustrate these different sections, we will borrow some examples of mental activities implemented in the specific context of car-driving activity. This applied field presents the main advantage of being both a familiar task, probably practiced by a large share of the readers of this book, yet still a complex activity involving all levels of the human cognition. Moreover, because of the recent developments of driving assistance in terms of on-board information systems as well as for vehicle automation, some critical issues in ergonomics have emerged during the two last decades. Human-centered design methods based on in-depth understanding of the drivers' cognition are then required, in order to develop future advanced assistance systems—like intelligent copilots—sharing a part of their cognitive abilities with the human driver. In this framework, the mental activities modeling is not only relevant for theoretical research in cognitive science, it also becomes one of central topics of cognitive engineering research.

2. ANALYSIS OF MENTAL ACTIVITIES: "GOD SAVE THE LOOP!"

When engaged in our everyday activities, like reading a book, to move in a familiar place, or to drive a car, a large share of the mental processes that support these activities escape to our own field of consciousness. This reflects the fact that these activities were pre-learnt before and that they are currently based on integrated abilities, a sequence of procedural skills, which trigger themselves successively, without systematically requiring an explicit and conscious monitoring of our thoughts by our cognitive system. They only emerge in our awareness some decision-making steps, like the intention we pursue or the goal we try to reach. However, if the situation suddenly becomes abnormal, or critical, or if one drifts too far from the limits of validity framing the routine regulation process, then the "waterline of the iceberg of awareness" lowers: our attention focuses on the problem to be explicitly solved and our activity becomes then intentionally monitored. To all intents and purposes it is clear that implicit awareness and explicit awareness cannot be seen as two separate entities. These two levels of awareness support themselves and are embedded in each other. In reality, they are two sides of the same coin: one cannot exist without the other. If a coin is placed on the table so that only one side is visible, this does not mean that the other side has disappeared. It is still there, at least in latent state, as a base for the visible side. As a function of the human operators experience and skill, or according to the familiarity of the situation, by contrast with a new or critical situation, their awareness will alternate between the more dominantly explicit, decisional and attentional level of cognition *versus* implicit awareness, mainly based on skills and automatic cognitive processes.

The understanding of the relation between *implicit* versus *explicit* awareness of the situation, as well as between *automatic* versus *attentional* control of the activity is the key issue of the living cognition paradigm, which constitutes the central topic of this chapter as a whole. To investigate these questions it is, however, essential to primarily consider the human's activity as an *iterative loop of regulation* between the human operator and the surrounding environment in which s/he is currently immersed. This approach, considering human activity as an adaptive process of regulation, is mainly based on three classical scientific traditions, unfortunately too often opposed to each other: (i) *Cybernetics* and *Human Information Processing* approaches, (ii) the Russian *theory of activity*, and (iii) the *ecological approach of human perception*.

2.1 From Cybernetics to Human Information Processing Theory

According to Wiener's cybernetics theory (1948), human being can be defined as a self-adaptive system who regulates its interactions with the external environment through a feedback regulation mechanism. Human operators' mental activities are then described in this frame as a "Black Box" owning information processing mechanisms, able to generate outputs (that is, communication or behavioral actions) from environmental perceptual inputs, in order to adapt itself to the situation. As and when this cycle repeats itself recursively, the human cognitive system perceptually assesses the effects of its action on the environment, and then determines which new action is needed to achieve the state of the surrounding world that s/he would like to reach. And this iterative process will continue until the expected state-goal is obtained. Although cybernetics has finally introduced a radical epistemological break with the behaviorist approach in psychology, the initial model proposed by Wiener was fully compatible with the Skinner's "S-R" approach, until the Pandora's *Black Box* was opened. With the development of the Human Information Processing theory, the internal mechanisms implemented into the black box, like mental representations elaboration, reasoning (for example, problem-solving, decision-making, and so on) and behaviors planning, became the central topics of the modern cognitive science. Nevertheless, according to the experimental method used in laboratory for studying cognition in well-controlled conditions, the Cybernetics "loop logic" has been partially lost for two main reasons. First, the experimental paradigm in cognitive science requires to artificially segment the human operators' mental activity into several cognitive functions, that are indeed individually investigated. Moreover, and maybe more critical from the living cognition point of view, laboratory tasks generally correspond to a standardized linear sequence of several steps:

1. Stimulus presentation (that is, input occurrence),
2. Perception (that is, detection of the stimulus and perceptive processing),
3. Interpretation/understanding (that is, mental representation elaboration of the stimulus),
4. Reasoning (that is, from problem-solving to decision-making, in order to identify the appropriate response),
5. Action planning (in accordance with the experimental task goal),
6. Response (that is, performance measured through the experiment),
7. "Game Over!" (that is, new stimulus occurrence, without any link with the previous one).

The last step (that is, "Game Over") is not an explicit phase of the experimental method itself, but it is rather an implicit requirement of this scientific approach. Indeed, repetitive independent measures of similar responses, collected for a similar artificial task, in similar conditions, is the basic fundament of the experimental paradigm in natural sciences, applied or not to cognition study. Therefore, the "story must restart" after each stimulus, as if it was a totally "new story," in order to allow the scientists to rigorously control their experiment. After each "*Stimulus — Response*" sequence, the experimental task is thus completed, without any expected feedback effect (except in the specific frame of the experimental tasks that are explicitly focused on learning or inter-stimulus effects study, like the "priming" effect). Consequently, by using the experimental method, cognitive science ended up losing the notion of "cycle," however so important in the initial cybernetics theory through the feedback process, in favor of a sequential string of information processing functions more or less complex (Figure 1.1).

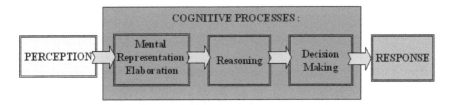

Figure 1.1   The sequential string of cognitive functions in the Human Information Processing classical theory

Even if the circular nature of these cognitive processes seems to still be true, because only requiring to add an arrow between a Response and a new Stimulus, the "Game Over" strategy which is implicitly contained in the experimental method to scientifically control any learning effect risk, definitively breaks the Cybernetics regulation loop and then, the fundament of the living cognition. This is one of the major criticisms that can be addressed to the experimental paradigm applied to cognition, which dominated the Human Information Processing approach during the 1970s and the 1980s. In order to study human operators' mental activities in their natural dynamics, which is the central aim of the living cognition approach as defined in this chapter introduction, it is therefore necessary to consider other theoretical alternatives, like the Russian *theory of activity*, or the Neisser (1976) *ecological theory of human perception*.

2.2 The "Theory of Activity"

Like Cybernetics, the Russian "Theory of Activity" school considers the human operators through their dynamic interactions with the external environment. But in this approach, *Activity* is the starting point and the core topic of the scientific investigation of human cognition, because it is argued that activity directly structures the operator's cognitive functions. The fundamental postulate of the Theory of Activity is well summarized by Smirnov (1966): *human becomes aware of the surrounding world, by acting on it, and by transforming it.* Following the works of Vygotsky (1962), exploring activity as "mediated" by tools (that is, *artifacts*) and concluding that human is constantly enabled or constrained by cultural contexts, Leontiev (1977) described human activity (p. 87) *as a circular structure: initial afferentation → effector processes regulating contacts with the objective environment → correction and enrichment by means of reverse connections of the original afferent image. The circular character of the processes that realize the interaction of the organism with the environment appears to be universally recognized and sufficiently well described in the literature.* However, the most important point for Leontiev (p. 4) is not only *this circular structure as such, but the fact that the mental reflection of the objective world is not directly generated by the external influences themselves, but by the processes through which the subject comes into practical contact with the objective world.* Through activity, continued Leontiev (p. 87), *a double transfer is realized: the transfer object → process of activity, and the transfer activity → its subjective product. But the transfer of the process into the form of the product does not take place only at the pole of the subject (.) it also takes place at the pole of the object transformed by human activity.*

The process of the mental *"introjection"*[1] of the objective world through the activity has been more particularly investigated by Ochanine (1977) within the concept of *Operative Images*, corresponding to functional mental models of the external object properties, as discovered through the practical activity of the operator. From this standpoint, the human operator is not a passive cognitive system who undergoes the stimulus given by the external environment, and who reacts in order to adapt himself under the pressure of events. S/he is an active observer, with inner intentions, able to voluntary act on the world and to modify the current situation by their own activity, in accordance with their own needs. Indeed, behind activity *there is always a need, which directs and regulates concrete activity of the subject in the objective environment* (Leontiev, 1977; p. 88). As a consequence (p. 99), *the concept of activity is necessarily connected with the concept of motive. Activity does not exist without a motive; "non-motivated" activity is not activity without a motive but activity with a subjectively and objectively hidden motive. Basic and "formulating" appear to be the actions that realize separate human activities. We call a process an action if it is subordinated to the representation of the result that must be attained, that is, if it is subordinated to a conscious purpose. Similarly, just as the concept of motive is related to the concept of activity, the concept of purpose is related to the concept of action ... Activity usually is accomplished by a certain complex of actions subordinated to particular goals that may be isolated from the general goal; under these circumstances, what happens that is characteristic for a higher degree of development is that the role of the general purpose is fulfilled by a perceived motive, which is transformed owing to its being perceived as a motive-goal.*

These considerations, so essential in ergonomics and so evident in our every day life as psychological subject with needs, intents, and will, has been nevertheless progressively forgotten by the modern cognitive science, when based on the experimental paradigm. *Under laboratory conditions,* wrote Leontiev (1977, p. 101), *we always place before the subject a "ready" goal. For this reason the process of goal formation itself usually escapes investigation.* However, all human activities in every day life require

---

1 In order for a human being to control a phenomenon, the brain must be able to form a reflection of it. The subjective reflection of phenomena in the form of feelings, perception and thoughts provides the brain with the information essential for acting efficiently on this phenomenon in order to achieve a specific aim (Leontiev, Lerner, Ochanine, 1961).

two conditions for being: *the existence of a need, and the possibility of the surrounding environment to satisfy it* (Ouznadzé, 1966, p. 249). Through laboratory experiments, inner needs and spontaneous motives disappear, as well as the dynamic "life cycle" of the natural cognition.

2.3 The "Ecological Theory of Perception"

The same criticism against the destructive effect of experimental method applied to human cognition study has been formulated by Neisser (1976), through his *ecological approach of human perception*. Neisser's work was initially based on the *direct perception* theory of Gibson (1950, 1979), who postulates that some invariants or *affordances*,[2] corresponding to properties of the objects available in the current environment, are directly perceived by the organism. Then, the organism "resonates" with or is tuned in to the environment, so that the organism's behavior becomes adapted to it. Nevertheless, by contrast with the Gibson "un-cognitive" theory of perception, Neisser admits the existence of mental subjective functions, even if he seriously criticizes the sequential vision of cognitive processes which dominated the Human Information Processing theory during the 1970s (cf. as presented above in Figure 1.1).

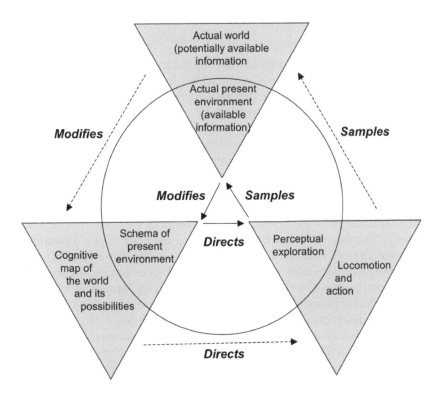

Figure 1.2   Neisser's cyclic model of the human perception (1976)

---

2 In Gibson's Theory, "affordance" means the possibilities for action that are "offered" by an object (for example, a tree affords possibilities for climbing, or hiding behind).

In a synthetic way, Neisser considers perception, including attention, as a skilled and iterative process. Like the Russian theorists of operative activity, he argues that human beings are not passive receivers of perceptual inputs, but that they are active in the world, in accordance with their own motives, their abilities, and their expectations. His model (see Figure 1.2) describes perception as a dynamic cycle focused on the relationships between pre-existing knowledge and the human information-gathering activity. According to this perceptive cycle, the perceiver actively explores the surroundings, and then constructs a dynamic understanding of the current environment. The mental structure that supports such processes of perception, attention, and categorization is described as an *active schema* of the present environment, which is continually modified by the new perceptual information, and which also contains anticipatory expectations. This mental schema includes a *cognitive map* of the world and therefore directs perceptual explorations of the environment, or prepares the mind for perception of anticipated events. It can be consequently considered as a kind of control structure of the perceptive processes (from "bottom up" information integration and processing, to "top down" active exploration of the external environment).

2.4 Illustration: Car-Driving Activity as a "Perception-Cognition-Action" Regulation Loop

To conclude this section, we would like to propose an integrative approach of human operator's mental activities which summarizes, in a very simplified and intuitive way, the main conclusions of the different theories presented above. To be more concrete, we will take the car driving activity as an illustrative example. Although a familiar task of everyday life, car driving is nonetheless a complex activity that potentially involves every level of human cognition. Figure 1.3 provides a synthetic overview of this activity, considered as an iterative "Perception-Cognition-Action" loop of regulation between the human driver and the road environment (see the sub-figure, on the right).

Indeed, as with any dynamic environment, the road environment requires constant adaptation from the driver. From this point of view, car driving has several similarities with other human activities requiring the control of a dynamic process. An important characteristic of a dynamic process is that the situation will change even if the operator does nothing. The driving task does not escape this constraint. Car driving can therefore be defined as an activity of regulating and maintaining the status of the dynamic process as a whole (that is, the driving situation) within the limits of acceptable and safe changes. In terms of mental activities, it requires that drivers; (i) select relevant information into the surrounding environment, in accordance with their current goals and the driving task demands, (ii) understand the immediate situation (that is, mental model elaboration) and anticipate its progression in the more or less long-term, (iii) make decisions in order to interact appropriately—via the vehicle—with the road environment and the other road users, and (iv) manage their own resources (physical, perceptive and cognitive) to satisfy the time constraints of the activity inherent to the dynamic nature of the driving situation. The selective dimension of information collection is especially important as drivers cannot take

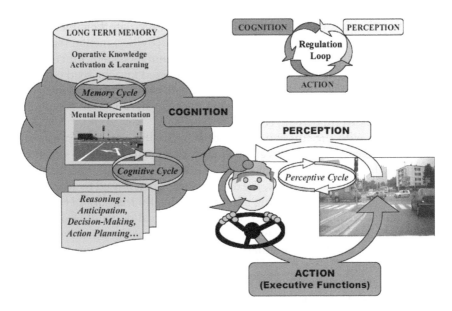

Figure 1.3 Car driving activity as a "Perception-Cognition-Action" dynamic regulation loop

in and process all the information available in the road environment. In accordance with Neisser's theory of perception, this information is not selected haphazardly, but depends on the aims the drivers pursue, their short-term intentions (that is, tactical goals, such as "turn left" at a crossroads), and long-term objectives (that is, strategic goals, such as reaching their final destination within a given time), the knowledge they possess (stemming from their previous driving experience) and their attentional resources available at this instant. Information selection is the result of a *perceptive cycle*, whose keystone is the driver's mental representation of the driving situation. This mental representation, based on operative knowledge stored and then activated (that is, *memory cycle* on Figure 1.3) in Long-Term Memory (LTM), is also the central component of a *cognitive cycle* involving decision-taking and anticipating functions (that is, via mental simulation based on the current state of the world). When an appropriate action to the current driving context has been identified, selected, or cognitively planned, it is implemented by the driver on the vehicle (that is, *executive functions*) for progressing into the dynamic road environment.

In accordance with the *Cybernetics theory*, car driving activity is defined in Figure 1.3 as an continuous dynamic loop of regulation between (i) *inputs*, coming from the road environment, and (ii) *outputs*, corresponding to the driver's behaviors implemented into the real world via the car, which generate (iii) *feedback*, in the form of a new inputs, requiring new adaptation (that is, new outputs) from the driver, and so on. From this general point of view, the first iteration of the Perception-Decision-Action regulation loop corresponds to the moment when the driver starts up the engine, and the last iteration comes when the driver reaches the final trip destination, and then stops the car.

In accordance with the Human Information Processing theory, the human operator is not described here as a closed black box, but as a set of perceptive, cognitive, and behavioral functions allowing the driver to dynamically regulate their interactions with the surrounding environment. In terms of cognitive activities, mental representation of the driving situation plays a key-role in the cognitive system functioning. This mental model, based on perceptive information extracted into the road environment, corresponds to the driver's awareness of the driving situation, and therefore determines directly all their decision-making concerning the relevant adaptive behaviors to be carried out in the current driving context.

In accordance with the Russian theory of activity, this mental representation is also based on pre-existing operative knowledge, practically learnt "*in situation*," and corresponding to a subjective "introjection" of previous activity implementation into similar driving contexts. Moreover, the driving task is performed by using an *artifact* (that is, the vehicle), and the driving situation is directly *transformed* by the human operator's activity (for example, car position on the road depending of the driver's action on the vehicle controls), as well as the situation *modifies* the driver's cognitive states (in terms of mental representation updating, for example, or new operative knowledge learning).

In accordance with the ecological theory of Neisser (1976), driver's perception in Figure 1.3 is based on a dynamic cycle when (i) an active schema directs gathering-information activity (that is, top-down processes) and (ii) focus driver's attention on a sample of pieces of information currently available in the environment. Then (iii), this active schema is continuously modified as a function of the new pieces of information thus collected.

Lastly, but not least, in accordance with the living cognition paradigm as defined in this chapter introduction, this Perception-Cognition-Action loop of regulation integrating three internal underlying cycles (that is, the perceptive, the memory, and the cognitive circles of Figure 1.3) and which is explicitly based on pre-existing experiences, is "per nature" a naturalistic model of everyday cognition. And we can be pleased, because a car driver driving without a living cognition is a generally a near-dead driver.

3. COGNITIVE MODELING: TOWARDS AN INTEGRATIVE MODEL OF THE HUMAN OPERATORS' MENTAL ACTIVITIES

In order to follow up the in-depth analysis of the human operator's mental activities it is, however, necessary to propose a more formal description of them, in the frame of a theoretical model of the Human Cognitive System. For being comprehensive, a model of mental activities should provide a formal description of the human cognitive system at three main levels, which are; (a) its cognitive architecture, (b) the cognitive structures, like mental representations or operative knowledge, encompassed into this cognitive architecture, and (c) the cognitive processes implemented on this mental data-structures for the information processing and the reasoning deployments. The two first components will be discussed in this section, and the cognitive processes modeling topic, being intimately linked with the cognitive simulation purpose, will be more particularly investigated in the section 4.

3.1 Cognitive Architecture

The following Figure (Figure 1.4) provides a synthetic overview of the human cognitive system architecture, distinguishing two main types of functional *memory structures*: the Long-Term Memory (LTM), which hold human's permanent knowledge, and the Working Memory (WM), which contain *mental representations* of the objective world.

Four main dynamic cycles regulate the internal functioning of the human cognitive system. The *perceptive cycle* supports the human perception functions, allowing the operator to actively explore the surrounding environment, according to their current needs and objectives (top down *perceptive exploration* processes) and/or to integrate new information into their mental representations (bottom up *cognitive integration* processes). The memory cycle plays a central role in terms of knowledge activation (supporting *categorization* and *matching* processes permitting to fit pre-existing knowledge with the objective reality) as well as in terms of new knowledge acquisition (to be stored in LTM). The *cognitive cycle* corresponds to a set of cognitive processes which collectively handled the internal mental representations, in order to make appropriate decision and then, to act into or on the current environment (like mental representation elaboration, understanding, anticipation, decision-making, or action planning). Lastly, the *cognitive resources allocation cycle* is in charge to dynamically regulate and control the *life cycle* of the cognitive system, in accordance with the attentional resources that are available, on the one hand, and that are required by the cognitive and perceptive functions at a given time, on the other hand.

The central structure supporting to the living cognition in this model is the Working Memory. However, WM described here stems as much from the *operational memory* concept as formulated by Zintchenko (1966), and then the French school

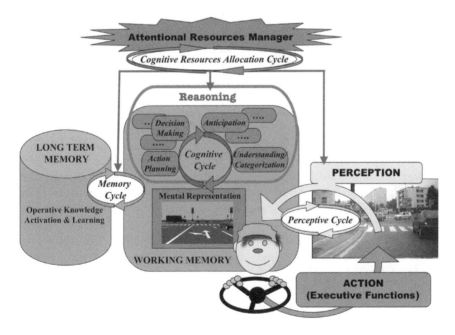

Figure 1.4   Cognitive architecture of the human cognitive system

of ergonomics (for example, Bisseret, 1970), as from Baddeley's Working Memory classical model (1986). For Zintchenko (1966), the operational memory is a mnesic structure whose main function is to *serve the real needs of the activity*. For Bisseret (1970), operational memory should be clearly distinguished from LTM, since the information it encompasses focuses on the operator's current goals. Thus it is a transitory rather than permanent memory. However, it should also be distinguished from Short-Term Memory (the only one mnesic structure able to temporarily store information in the cognitive models of the 1970s; for example, Atkinson and Shiffrin, 1968), in so far as the information it contains remains available for as long as it is useful to perform the activity in progress. According to this view, operational memory far exceeds the storage and processing capacities of Baddeley's WM. It appears to be a kind of *Long-Term Working Memory*, a definition 20 years in advance of the equivalent model formulated by Ericsson and Kintsch (1995). Consequently, the *Working Memory* of the cognitive architecture presented in Figure 1.4 must be understood from this functional interpretation of operational memory, that is, as a structure that hosts active knowledge instantiated through mental representations to serve the activity in progress (contrary to LTM, which stores permanent knowledge in latent state).

3.2 From Operative knowledge to Representation "For Action"

The core data-structure of this dynamic model of self-adaptive regulation, is the functional mental representations built in the Working Memory (Bellet et al., 2009). They correspond to the human operator's understanding of the situation when s/he is immersed, and they also support the human cognitive anticipation of future status of the environment, which depends of operator's activity carried out in the external world. These mental representations form the kernel of complex sequences of cognitive processes, ranging from the perception of events to behaviors implementation, through intermediate steps of decision-making and activity planning (Rasmussen, 1986). However, care is required to avoid taking an over-linear and sequential view of this processing string. Although the perception of an unexpected or critical event sometimes triggers the processing sequence, it is more often the action in progress and the operator's intentions that direct their perceptive exploration and information processing. As explained above in regard with the theory of activity, human operator's mental activities must be considered as an iterative "perception ⇔ cognition ⇔ action" cycle, organized around the operative mental model of the current situation. In this control loop, perception and mental representation are constantly fuelled by actions, which in turn constantly fuel perception and cognitive processes. From this standpoint, such mental representations are not limited to the strict and reductionist definition of "propositional representations" proposed by classical cognitivism (for example, Fodor, 1975), but as an operative mental model dynamically updated and built by using pre-existing operational knowledge activated in LTM, in order to act. Indeed, human beings are not passive observers of the environment, but actors with wills, needs, motivations and goals to be reached, and who are able to transform their environment through their activity. Operative mental representations are *"circumstantial constructions"* formed in a specific context, and for specific ends (Richard, 1990). They are formulated "by" and "for" the action. Therefore they provide *interiorized models of the task* (Leplat, 2005) constructed for the current activity, but which can be stored in LTM and reactivated later in new situations, for future performances of the same task. Thus the role of practical experience is decisive in the genesis of these mental representations: *it is in interaction with reality that the subject forms and tests his representations*, in the same way as the latter govern *the way in which he acts and regulates his action* (Vergnaud, 1985). For this author, the main function of mental representations is precisely to *conceptualize reality in order to act efficiently*. In the next section we will propose a specific formalism, called *"driving schemas"* (Bellet et al., 1999), able to provide a computational model of drivers' mental representations or, to be more precise, to represent the operative knowledge underlying these mental representations when activated (Bellet et al., 2007). However, the predominant idea we wish to emphasize here is that these internal representations are not mental copies of objective reality. They correspond to an explicit and implicit "awareness" one has of the "situation" (Endsley, 1995; Smith and Hancock, 1995; Stanton et al., 2001; Bailly et al., 2003). On the one hand, they only contain a tiny amount of the information available in the environment: they focus in priority on useful information in order to act efficiently, as a function of the situational constraints. On the other hand, they can also convey much more information than that available in perceptible reality (for example, keeping in memory information perceived previously but henceforth hidden, formulating inferences of potential future events based on precursive clues, or anticipating the expected effects of an action in progress). What is more, as illustrated by the work of Ochanine (1977) on *Operative Images*, these representations may lead to functional deformations (due to expertise effects), via the accentuation of certain characteristics (salient and significant) relevant to the activity, but ignoring secondary details with respect to the current driver's goal. As dynamic mental models of the surrounding environment, operative representations are useful for guiding the human performance in interaction with the world. A core function of mental representations is to support cognitive simulations (implicit or explicit) providing expectations of future situational status. Human operators continually updates their occurrent representations as and when they carry out the activity, thereby ensuring the activity permanence through time, with respect to the history of past events on the one hand, and future changes in the current situation on the other. Lastly, one characteristic of humans is their limits in terms of attentional capacities. Therefore, they have to manage their cognitive resources according to the short-term (for example, reacting within a given time to deal with the current situation) and their long-term goals, while taking their experience into account to achieve the task successfully (for example, what they know of their own capacities).

3.3 The Cognitive System "Life Cycle": Levels of Control, Levels of Awareness

We have all undergone the experience of highly automated activity, almost outside the field of one's own awareness, which can be performed under a low level of control and awareness. In this case we can talk of *implicit awareness* of both the external situation and our own activity. On the contrary, we can also all remember situations in which real-time decisions were judged as very complex, difficult, cognitively costly, and even sometimes critical, requiring all our attention in order to carry them out successfully. Activity then based on explicit and voluntary decisions, even if the reasons underlying them may be only partly conscious. In this case we speak of *explicit awareness* of the situation and one's intentions, decisions, and actions. These two levels of awareness, implicit and explicit, co-exist in all our everyday activities. This dichotomy is, moreover, well established in scientific literature, e.g., in the *Psychological Review*, with the distinction put forward by Schneider and Schiffrin (1977) between *controlled processes*, which require attention and which can only be performed sequentially, and *automatic processes*, which can be performed in parallel without the least attentional effort. This is also highlighted by Piaget (1974) who distinguished *pre-reflected* acts on the one hand, and *reflected thought* on the other. This distinction is also classical in Ergonomics since the work of Rasmussen (1986), who distinguishes different levels of activity control according to whether the behaviors implemented rely on; (i) highly integrated sensorial-motor abilities (*Skill-based behaviors*), (ii) well-mastered decision rules for managing familiar situations (*Rule-based behaviors*), or (iii) more abstract and generic knowledge that is activated in new situations, for which the operator cannot call on sufficient prior experience (*Knowledge-based behaviors*). Likewise in the field of Neurosciences, with the Norman and Shallice (1986) model of control of the executive functions or, more recently, with Koch's *zombie agents* theory (2004), bringing to mind somnambulism and animal cognition (Proust, 2003, speaks of *proto-representations* to qualify this level of implicit awareness), in contrast with decisional and volitional acts, oriented towards reaching the subject's explicit aim. Lastly, the field of Artificial Intelligence can be also mentioned with, for example, Smolensky's (1989) distinction between levels of *sub-symbolic* (that is, neuro-mimetic) versus *symbolic* computations. Obviously, every sub-specialities of the cognitive science tend to converge since the last 30 years towards the idea that different cognitive control modes of activity exist, as do by consequence several levels of awareness. Figure 1.5 proposes an integrative model of the human cognitive system combining all these different approach of awareness into a unified way, but that is also fully compatible with the regulation loop approaches of the living cognition, as explored above in Figure 1.4.

In very familiar context, human activity mainly relies on an automatic control mode requiring a low quantity of attentional resource, and thus is essentially based on an *implicit awareness* of the situation. Implicit awareness does not means "unconscious." Although it is not possible for humans to explicitly explain what they feel or what they think at this level, they are nonetheless aware to be involved into the situation they are living. It is a kind of sensorial and proprioceptive awareness, in tune with the environment, as if the subject was "immersed into the world." Dulany (1991) defines this awareness level as a *"feeling of experience."* In this mode *there is no representation of the self as an independent entity* (Pinku and Tzelgov, 2006). According to this last definition, implicit awareness is consistent with the ecological theory of Gibson (1979), who postulates that perception of the self (for example, its spatial location and activity) as embedded within the representation of the environment. This automatic control loop of the executive functions (that is, the lower right circle within the automatic level on Figure 1.4) is inaccessible to the operator's explicit awareness, except the emergent part that can be subject to decisional, intentional, and reflexive cognitive processing. However, if the situation suddenly becomes abnormal or critical, or if we drift too far from the limits of validity framing the routine regulation process (for example,

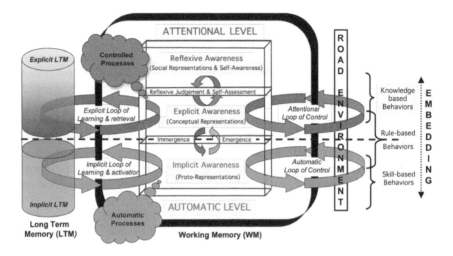

Figure 1.5   Levels of awareness and activity control loops: an integrative model

Source: Adapted from Bellet et al., 2009.

when an action does not bring about the expected effects), then the explicit level of awareness is activated. Indeed, regarding the operational functioning of the human cognitive system, the explicit and implicit levels are intimately embedded. On the one side, even when taking a deliberate decision, a large part of implementing this decision will be done by the way of skill-based behaviors, escaping to conscious control, but nonetheless relying on an implicit form of awareness and activity monitoring to guarantee that the goal defined explicitly is reached. From the other side, when mental activity relies on heavily integrated and automated empirical know-how, this activity as a whole still generally under the control of the subject's *"explicitable" intentions* (that is, likely to become explicit; even if they are not totally currently), that constitutes one part of the explicit cognition in our model. From this point of view, implicit and explicit awareness cannot be seen as two separate entities. As previously said, they are two sides of the same coin. More than as alternative ways, these two cognitive levels are intimately linked through a *dialectic relation*. One of the central processes at work in this dialogue is the *"emergence."* Emergence can occur on two time scales. In the short-term, that is, the temporality of the current situation itself, it corresponds to the irruption (more or less spontaneous) in the field of explicit awareness of information previously not perceived or only taken into account implicitly. In the long-term, that is, in the temporality of permanent knowledge acquisition, emergence is involved in the human operator's elicitation strategies, whether for learning by introspection or self-evaluation of their own abilities (that is, Piaget's *reflected thought*), transmission of one's competences to another operator, or justify one's acts after decision-making. In symmetry with the notion of emergence of conscious thought and conceptual representations, we wish to add the notion of *"immergence"* of this explicit thought to operative know-how and implicit awareness. This is to take into account the embedding process of decisional cognition in operational activity, and to describe the sedimentation phenomenon of explicit thought in implicit knowledge, that is, its operative embodiment in deep-cognition (we could also speak with Anderson (1993) of *compilation*, or the *proceduralization* of knowledge into know-how). The circular nature of this emergence *versus* immergence process makes it possible to unify these two temporalities (short-term and long-term): today's emergences are the result of past immergences, and vice-versa. One is the echo of the other, on nonetheless different levels of awareness. Moreover, in symmetry with the activity control loops (between mental representations and the external environment), it is necessary to add a second regulation loop between the mental representations elaborated in WM and operative knowledge stored in LTM, to take into account both the recovery process (from voluntary recall to implicit activation) and the learning process (from explicit and intentional learning to effortless implicit encoding). This second dual-loop refers directly to the distinction made by Graf and Schacter (1985) between *implicit* memory and *explicit* memory.

Lastly, to this dialectic relation of emergence and immergence of mental representations, it appears necessary to add a third dimension: *reflexivity* (that is, awareness of being aware). This meta-level of "Reflexive Awareness" integrates two main aspects in relation with the explicit awareness: *behavior conceptualization* and *judgment of values*. The issue of conceptualization has been studied in child development by Piaget (1974), and in adults by Vermersch (1994), in the light of the *"prise de conscience"* process (that is, becoming aware) and the elicitation of operative knowledge of one's own actions. According to these authors, this process is based on different steps ranging from *"pre-reflected"* acts to *"reflected thought"* (reflexive and conceptual meta-knowledge allowing understanding of one's own activity as an object of knowledge). However, it is also advisable to incorporate a *value judgment* dimension regarding the situation with this reflexive level, about oneself or one's acts. This topic is more familiar to the field of social psychology (for example, through attitude and social representation concepts) than that of cognitive psychology. In the context of car driving, for example, this dimension of value judgment has been studied in particular from the angles of risk assessment or drivers' attitude in relation to risk taking, for the purposes of deliberate sensation seeking and violation of the Highway Code (for example, Banet et Bellet, 2008). Moreover, the conceptualization of operative activity and value judgments are not independent. On one side, implicit representations cannot be the object of judgments without a certain amount of prior conceptualization in the form of explicit, reflexive and conceptual thinking. On the other side, reflexive judgments (for example, I assess the relevance of an action, its legitimacy, efficiency, or soundness regarding the others and the societal laws), once linked to explicit situational awareness, are liable to be durably immerged in the human's implicit awareness in the form of implicit knowledge incorporating conformity with these social dimensions.

4. MENTAL ACTIVITIES SIMULATION: A FIRST STEP TOWARDS THE "LIVING COGNITION"

By using the cognitive architecture of the integrated model of human cognition presented in Figure 1.5, it becomes possible to investigate the cognitive processes that dynamically regulate the operator's mental life. To be more concrete, this section will mainly consider the mental activities when driving a car, as modeling through a cognitive simulation model developed at INRETS (Bellet, 1998; Bellet et al., 2007). Before presenting this model, it is nevertheless necessary to distinguish two types of cognitive simulation models in the literature: (i) *models of performance* and (ii) *cognitive simulation models*. Even if they both propose computerized models of human operator's cognitive activities, these two approaches are very different in their theoretical foundations as well as in their scientific objectives. The firsts one are predictive models primarily focused on human behavior, and their modeling objective concerning the cognitive processes underlying behavior is only concerned by the model ability to correctly reproduce, or predict, the human operator's performances. By contrast, cognitive simulation models are *explicative models* aiming to explain and simulate internal mental states and cognitive processes carried out when humans think. This distinction between *predictive* versus *explicative* models is very important in terms of epistemology (Thom, 1991). But it also determines the computerized modeling strategy: for a performance model, what is the most important is the final result, irrespective of how the processing is implemented. These models are generally, like cybernetics, limited to a black box whose *inputs* correspond to information coming from the external environment, while the *outputs* correspond to human operator performances. The implementation choices, at the internal level of the black box, are essentially determined by technical criteria like the calculation time, without considering the real nature of the cognitive processes implemented in the natural cognition. Only the similarities between the model and the human performances are considered. On the contrary, cognitive simulation models are not only focused on the probability of occurrence between a situational context and human performance, but the way the computational processing are implemented leads to an isomorphism with the human natural cognition. This approach allows an in-depth understanding of the cognitive system functioning, and is therefore the only adapted way for approaching the *"living cognition."*

4.1 COSMODRIVE: A Cognitive Simulation Model of the Driver

Figure 1.6 describes the driver's mental activities as simulated into the COSMODRIVE (COgnitive Simulation MOdel of the DRIVEr; Bellet, 1998, Bellet et al., 2007) functional architecture of the tactical level.[3] The whole activity of the tactical module is dedicated to the elaboration and the handling of mental representations of the driving situation. Computationally, this module is implemented as a *multi-agent system* based on a *blackboard architecture*: several *Cognitive Agents* process the information in parallel and exchange data (read/write) via common storage structures: the *blackboards*. Cognition is therefore here *distributed*, resulting from cooperation between several cognitive agents. Each agent has only a part of the required expertise to find the solution. As the solving procedure progresses, the product of each agent reasoning is written in the blackboard. It then becomes available to the other agents sharing this blackboard,

---

3   In accordance with Michon (1985) typlology, that distinguishes three levels in the driving task. The strategic level corresponds to the itinerary planning and managing, the tactical level corresponds to the current driving situation management, and the operational level concerns the driving actions carried out to control the car.

and they can then use these results to furthering their own reasoning. They can also modify the content of the blackboard, and thus contribute to the collective solving of the problem. Communication between the cognitive agents of the tactical module can also be done via *messages* sending. Lastly, the complexity and speed of the processes performed are dependent on the cognitive resources allocated to the solving agent by the *Control and Management* Module. The quantity of resources allocated can change according to the number of active processes, and their respective needs. A lower quantity of resources can slow down the agent computation, change the solving strategy, or momentarily interrupt the process underway.

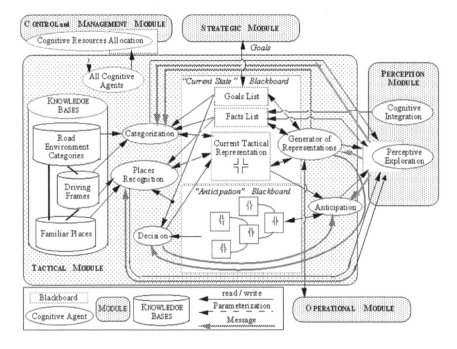

Figure 1.6   Functional architecture of the tactical Module of COSMODRIVE

Source: Adapted from Bellet, 1998.

As represented in Figure 1.6, the tactical module of COSMODRIVE integrates two *blackboards* (representing the human Working Memory), three *knowledge bases* (corresponding to the Long-term Memory), and five *cognitive agents* (implementing the cognitive processes required for managing the driving task at the tactical level).

Regarding the Working Memory, it is simulated in COSMODRIVE through two blackboards: the *Current State Blackboard (CSB)* and the *Anticipation Blackboard*. The CSB contains all information related to the current driving situation. It includes a *goal list*, a *fact list*, and a *Current Tactical Representation*. The *goal list* contains the *"local"* goals to be attained in the current infrastructure (for example, *turn left*), and *"global"* goals to be reached in the more or less long-term (for example, *save time*, because I am late). These goals come from the Strategic Module. The *fact list* contains all information extracted from the road scene. This data comes from the *Perception* module. The

Current Tactical Representation (CTR) corresponds to the driver's situation awareness of the driving situation. It is built from a generic *driving schema* activated in Long-Term Memory, then *instantiated* with data available in the *fact list* and in the *goal list*. In contrast to the *fact list*, which only lists events individually, the CTR specifies the spatial and dynamic relations existing between these objects in the road scene. It provides a visuo-spatial mental model of the road environment. Based on operative knowledge, the *driving schemas*, the CTR provides a functional, simplified and finalized representation of the reality, in accordance with the driver's tactical goal in the current situation (for example, turn on the left). Once generated, the CTR provides an operational plan of the driving activity able to be implemented by the *Operational Module*. It also orients new perceptive information collection and processing, as well as the decision-making. The *Anticipation Blackboard* holds *Anticipated Representations* (AR) derived from the CTR by the *Anticipation* agent. Each AR constitutes a possible evolution of the current driving situation. Anticipated Representations are organized as a tree, whose *root* corresponds to the CTR, *nodes* correspond to the potential future status of this situation (that is, AR), and *links* between AR correspond to the *actions* to be carried out and/or the *conditions* to be complied with, to go from one AR to the next one. Each AR is associated with parameters indicating a *risk-taking* value and a *time Cost/Saving ratio*, to pass from the previous AR to this new one. The *Anticipation* agent is in charge to assess the value of these parameters for each new temporal derivation. This assessment is based on the analysis of *safety zones* conflicts (Kontaratos, 1974) between the own driver's car, on the one hand, and other road users, on the other. Furthermore, as the elaboration of the AR-tree progresses, *Anticipation* computes the overall value of these two parameters for the whole branch that integrate the new derived AR (the whole sequence of AR starting from the RTC-root). These local (from one AR to another one) or global values (for the whole branch) will be then used by the *Decision* agent to select the best action (or sequence of elementary actions) in the current context.

Regarding the Long-Term Memory, it is simulated in COSMODRIVE tactical module through three Knowledge Bases (KB): the *Road Environment Categories* KB, the *Familiar Place* KB, and the *Driving Frame* KB. These different knowledge bases are strongly interconnected and constitute a global network handled by two cognitive agents specialized in information retrieval: *Categorization* and *Place Recognition*. The *Road Environment Categories* KB is a functional typology of the different prototypes of driving environments likely to be encountered by the driver. This KB is hierarchically structured (Bellet, 1998). At the top of the hierarchy are generic categories corresponding to classes of *Driving Contexts* (urban, country, highway). On descending the hierarchy, the knowledge becomes more and more specialized (for example, urban junctions, highway entrance), until reaching precise categorization of the driving context (for example, "crossroads with traffic lights in city center"). The *Familiar places* KB holds specific knowledge of the road sites that are familiar to the driver. This KB is a direct extension of the environment categories base: each familiar place constitutes a specific *instance* of one of the *classes* represented by the road categories. Lastly, the *Driving Frame* KB holds the driver's operative knowledge as they are computationally formalized in COSMODRIVE (Bellet et al., 1999): the "*Driving Schemas.*" Based on both the Piaget (1936) concept of "*operative scheme*" and the Minsky (1975) "*frames theory,*" driving schemas are operative mental models of the driving activity *situated on the road*. They correspond to prototypical situations, actions, and events, learnt from practical experience. Like the piagetian schemes, driving schemas are able of *assimilation* and *accommodation*, giving them a plasticity to fit with reality through a process of instantiation (Bellet et al., 2007). Once activated and instantiated with reality, the active driving schema becomes thus the *Current Tactical Representation* (CTR) of the driver, which will be continually updated as and when s/he progresses into the current road environment.

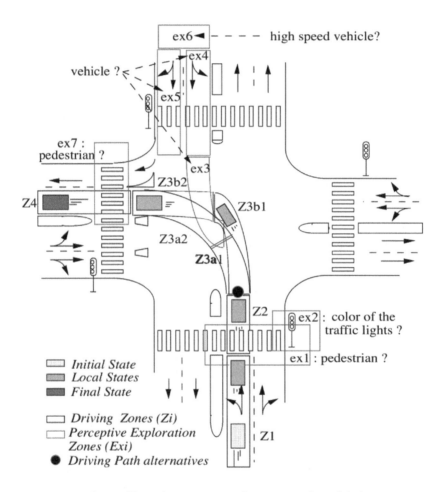

Figure 1.7   A formalism for representing operative driving knowledge: the *driving schemas*

Note: From a formal point of view a driving schema is composed of (i) a functional model of road infrastructure, (ii) a tactical goal (for example, turn left), (iii) a sequence of States and (iv) a set of Zones. Two types of zone are distinguished: Driving Zones (Zi) that correspond to the driving path of the vehicle as it progresses through the crossroads, and the Perceptive Exploration Zones (exi) in which the driver seeks information (for example, potential events liable to occur). Each driving zone is linked to Actions to be implemented (for example, braking or accelerating, in view to reach a given state at the end of the zone), the Conditions of performing these actions, and the perceptive exploration zones that permit checking these conditions (for example, color of traffic lights, presence of other road users). A State is characterized by the vehicle's position and speed. The different sequences of the driving zones make up the Driving Paths that progress from the initial state to the final one (that is, achievement of the tactical goal). In the Left Turn driving schema, Two driving paths are thus possible: Z1, Z2, Z3a1, Z3a2, Z4 or Z1, Z2, Z3b1, Z3b2, Z4.

Regarding the Cognitive Processes implemented by cognitive agents in COSMODRIVE, their collective aim at the tactical level is to generate the mental representation of the situation (that is, CTR). As mentioned above, this representation is built by matching a driving frame with perceptive information extracted from the driving situation. Integration of the perceptive information can be done according to two distinct modes. Either the information is actively sought by the driver (for example, expectations of the probable event occurrence in such area of space), or the information is particularly salient and catches driver's attention (like a red light at night, on a deserted road). The first type of information integration is a *top-down process* performed by the *Perceptive Exploration* agent. Indeed, this agent receives all the perceptive exploration queries from all the model's cognitive agents. According to their level of priority, it defines the visual strategies permitting the best response to these queries, then it positions the glance at the road scene. The second type of information integration is a *bottom-up process* and performed by the *Cognitive Integration* agent. This can be likened to an array of filters that only allows the information of the *Perception Module* having greater physical magnitudes than certain thresholds (for example, size, speed of movement, color, shape, and so on) to pass into the tactical representation. Beyond perceptive processes, five Cognitive Agents cooperate at the tactical level: (1) Categorization, (2) Place Recognition, (3) Generator of Tactical Representation, (4) Anticipation, and (5) Decision. These agents run in parallel and they are potential users of cognitive resources.

Categorization and *Place Recognition* agents are the both processes in charge of driving knowledge retrieval in MLT (respectively corresponding to a generic road category versus a familiar place) and to activate a pre-existing driving schema able to fit with the current driving situation.

The *Generator of Tactical Representations* (GRT) is the orchestral conductor of the tactical module. The main cognitive functions monitored by GRT are; (i) the driving frame instantiation by integration of the current situation characteristics, (ii) integration of new data coming from the *Perception Module*, (iii) monitoring the CTR validity (for example, has the situation changed, is the goal pursued still valid?) and, if necessary, participate in changing it, (iv) activation the *Decision* agent in order to determine what driving action should be taken, (v) transfer this action to the *Operational Module* for its effective implementation, and (vi), checking that the chosen action effectively provides the expected effects when applied.

The *Anticipation agent* is another central process of the living cognition, allowing humans to be more than only "reactive organisms," but to be pro-active and intentional organisms able to project themselves into the future through mental simulations and to anticipate any situational change before it occurs. Such mental simulations are also essential to assess the potential effects of an action and to compare this action with some of its alternatives before applying in order to determine the most appropriate behavior in the current context. This cognitive function is crucial in a dynamic situation: the greater the pressure of time is, the less time there is to act in situation, and the more anticipation plays a decisive role. In COSMODRIVE model, the *Anticipation* agent computes *Anticipated Representation* (AR) from the *Current Tactical Representation* (CTR). The generated ARs are organized as a tree in the *Anticipation Blackboard*, whose root is the CTR, the nodes are the potential ARs, and the inter-AR links correspond to driving schema actions to be taken or conditions required to go from one AR to the next. In other words, Anticipation virtually (that is, mentally) implement of current active driving schema constituting the CTR. Such a mental *"deployment"* of the driving schema at the tactical level can be costly in cognitive resources, and only a limited part of the possible ARs can be examined at this explicit level of awareness. Nevertheless, implicit anticipation abilities also exist in the *Operational Module*, that are based on automatic parallel computations able to identify the specific AR more particularly relevant in the current context, and to induce their emergence at the field of the tactical explicit awareness for focusing the attentional resources.

Then, the *Decision* agent plays a key-role in making a selection from among these AR and in instantiating the CTR of the Current State Blackboard as a consequence. In detail, the decision-making process is supposed: (i) to examine the Anticipated Blackboard for determining what branch of the AR tree is most adapted to the present context, (ii) to select the next AR that immediately succeeds the driving zone currently implemented by the Operational module, (iii) to instantiate in consequence the corresponding driving zone of the CTR (that will be then transmitted to the Operational module by the GTR agent), (iv) to restart the same procedure for the following zones until reaching the tactical goal of the active driving schema. Furthermore, the Decision also plays an active role in the AR derivation procedure. This agent permanently supervises the work done by Anticipation: each new derived AR is examined with respect to decision-making criteria (based on *risk-taking* values and *time cost/saving ratios*) and, according to whether these criteria are satisfied or not, Decision determines the best derivation strategy to be adopted by Anticipation (for a more detailed presentation of the cognitive agents, see Bellet et al., 2007).

4.2 Operational Level: The Hidden Dimension of the Mental Activities

Underlying the tactical cognitive module of COSMODRIVE, that schematically corresponds to the intentional and explicit part of the driving activity, a set of cognitive skills also run in parallel at the operational level, in a more close way to the final implementation of this activity via the executive functions. For an experienced driver, the operational level is mainly based on implicit cognition. That is why we can speak here of a *"hidden dimension"* of the human mental activities, that partially escaping to the driver's explicit awareness. However, as previously argued, these two levels of awareness are continually interconnected and dynamically synchronized through the *emergence* and the *immergence* processes (cf. Figure 1.5). This synchronization is computationally done in COSMODRIVE by messages exchanges between the *Tactical* and the *Operational Modules*. Basically, the *Operational Module* is built as a multi-agent system with a set of autonomous *"operational units"* specialized in implementing three elementary driving subtasks: (i) the steering wheels control, (ii) the speed control, and (iii) the distance maintaining with other road users. From a cognitive standpoint, and according to the Smolensky (1989) definition of these concepts, mental computations are mainly *sub-symbolic* at this level, by contrast with the strategic and the tactical reasoning that are based on *symbolic* computations. Anyway, these operational units cooperate and combine their effort in order to dynamically manage the regulation loop of vehicle control through the executive functions, in accordance with the decisions taken at the tactical level. Then, driving behavior will be practically carried out on the vehicle commands (pedals, steering wheel, and so on), in order to progress along the driving path of the active driving schema, as instantiated in the *Current Tactical Representation*. Moreover, another central function of the operational module is to assess the risk of collision with other road users. A specific reasoning is in charge of identifying a danger and, if necessary, to activate an emergency reaction. This operational regulation process of the car control is based in COSMODRIVE on two main types of *hidden driving abilities* (Mayenobe et al., 2002, 2004): the *"Pursuit Point"* strategy, related to the lateral and longitudinal control of the vehicle, and the *"Envelope Zones"* used to regulate the interaction distances with other roads users and to assess the risks of collision with obstacles.

Synthetically, kinematics models of the vehicles in COSMODRIVE are based on a *"bicycle model"* approach and on a dynamic regulation law of moving related with the distance between the vehicle itself and its *"Pure-Pursuit Point"* (Figure 1.8). The pure-pursuit point method was initially introduced for modeling in a simplified way the lateral and the longitudinal controls of an automatic car along a trajectory (Amidi, 1990), and then has been adapted by Sukthankar (1997) for driver's situational awareness modeling. Mathematically, the pure-pursuit point is defined as the intersection of the desired vehicle path and a circle of radius centered at the vehicle's rear axle midpoint (assuming front wheel steer). Intuitively, this point describes the steering curvature that would bring the vehicle to the desired lateral offset after traveling a distance of approximately l. Thus the position of the pure-pursuit point maps directly onto a recommended steering curvature: $k = -2x/l$, where k is the curvature (reciprocal of steering radius), x is the relative lateral offset to the pure-pursuit point in vehicle coordinates, and l is a parameter known as the look-ahead distance. According to this definition, the operational control of the car by COSMODRIVE can be seen as process of permanently maintaining of the Pursuit Point in the tactical driving path, to a given speed assigned with each segment of the current tactical schema, as instantiated in working memory (that is, the CTR).

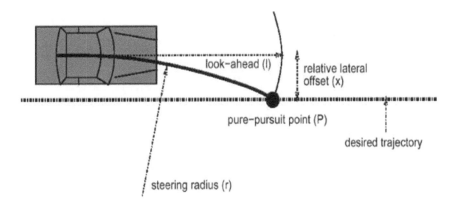

Figure 1.8   The pure-pursuit point method
Source: Adapted from Sukthankar, 1997.

The second hidden dimension of the deep-cognition implemented at the operational level is supported by "*envelope zones,*" that basically correspond to the portion of the driving schema to be occupied by the trajectory of the vehicle in the near future. When jointly combined with the pursuit point, these envelope zones can be used to avoid collision or to comfortably interact with other vehicles. From a theoretical point of view (Bellet et al., 1999), the concept of envelope zones recalls two classical theories in psychology: the notion of *body schema* proposed by Schilder (1950), and the theory of *proxemics* defined by Hall (1966) relating to the distance maintained in social interaction with others. Regarding car-driving activity, this idea can also be found in the notion of *safety margins* (Gibson and Crooks, 1938), reused by different authors. Thus, for example, Kontaratos (1974) defined two *safety zones* (respectively *collision* and *threat*) in which no other road user should enter. If this occurs, the driver systematically performs an emergency reaction. More recently, Ohta (1993) showed how these safety zones come into play when vehicles follow each other. This author defines 3 following distances: a *danger zone* (when the target time headway (that is, *Time-to-Target*) is less than 0.6 s.), a *critical zone* (from 0.6 to 1.1 s.) and a *comfort zone* (from 1.1 to 1.7 s.). Anyway, the envelope zones used in COSMODRIVE can be considered as an extension of the driver's body schema around the car itself that also integrates Hall's *proxemics* rules of interaction. As a hidden dimension of the social interactions at the implicit and operational level of cognition, this "envelope zones" model is not only applied by the drivers to themselves (that is, concerning their own car movement), but is also "mentally projected" onto the other drivers, who currently interact with them. Three envelope zones are distinguished in COSMODRIVE (Figure 1.9): (i) a proximal *danger zone*, in which any intrusion immediately triggers an emergency reaction from the driver, (ii) an intermediate *threat zone*, in which any non-expected intrusion is considered as potentially critical or aggressive, and (iii) a

Figure 1.9   COSMODRIVE *Envelope Zones* and illustration of their use in association with the path of a tactical driving schema for inter-vehicles interaction management

Source: Adapted from Mayenobe et al., 2002.

distant *safety zone*, corresponding to the regulation distance that the driver judges as safe. These zones are called *"relative,"* in contrast to *driving* or *perceptive exploration zones* of schemas (which are qualified as *absolute* zones), in so far as their dimensions are not determined in relation to fixed components of the road infrastructure, but in relation to the dynamics of the driven vehicle. They are effectively based on *Time-to-Target* values (from 0.5 to 1.8 seconds) and therefore directly depend on the vehicle's speed and driving path. The size of these zones may also vary according to the driver's profile (for example, experience, personality traits, aggressiveness), the situational context, the driving strategies currently carried out, and the traffic density.

This "virtual skin" is permanently active while driving, as an implicit awareness of our expected allocated space for moving. As with the body schema, it belongs to a highly integrated cognitive level (that is, implicit regulation loop), but at the same time favors the emergence of critical events in the driver's explicit awareness (that is, in the CTR). Therefore, the envelope zones play a central role in the regulation of social as well as physical interactions with other road users under normal driving conditions (for example, maintaining inter-vehicle distances), and in the risk assessment of path conflicts and their management if a critical situation occurs (commitment of emergency reactions).

4.3 Dynamic Simulation: The Emerging "Living Cognition"

By using the (i) functional architecture of COSMODRIVE described in Figure 1.6, (ii) the cognitive agents that modeling the human cognitive processes, (iii) the driving schemas as pre-existing operative knowledge activated and dynamically updated in the frame of a functional mental representation matched with the road environment, and (iv) the operational skills corresponding to the pure-pursuit point and the

Figure 1.10   **Example of 3-D modeling of the driving schemas *"turn-left at a urban crossroads"* in the COSMODRIVE model**

envelopes zones regulation process, it becomes thus possible to virtually simulate of the human operator "living cognition" as an immersed cognitive system interacting with their surrounding dynamic environment.

The central process that supports the living cognition is the *deployment* of the active driving schema, as instantiated in Working Memory through the current mental representation (that is, CTR). This deployment consists in moving the vehicle along a *driving path* (Figure 1.11), by successively traveling through the different driving zones of the schema, from the initial state (that is, the Z1 entry zone) until reaching the tactical goal (that is, the Z4 exit zone). This deployment process may occurs at two levels: (i) on the representational level (*explicit* and *implicit* mental simulation of the future activity to be carried out), when the drivers anticipate their actions and project themselves mentally in the future, (ii) and through the activity itself, during the effective implementation of the schema while driving the car in the road environment. This twofold deployment process is not performed by a specific agent in COSMODRIVE. It is indeed an *emergent* collective product, resulting from the combined processing of several cognitive agents (for example, anticipation, decision-making, generator of tactical representation), and merged with the computations of the *operational units* based on the *envelope zones* and the *pursuit point* regulation laws. As a result, the deployment process generates a particular *instance* of the current active schema execution, composed of a temporal sequence of occurring mental representations, causally interlinked, and corresponding to the driving situation as it is progressively understood and anticipated, then experienced, and lastly *acted* by the driver, along the driving path progression.

Figure 1.11 gives an example of COSMODRIVE simulation results, permitting to visualize the mental representation evolution of a novice driver (who has the intention to turn on the left), while approaching of an urban crossroads with traffic

Figure 1.11   Example of virtual simulation of a novice driver's mental representation when approaching a crossroads

Note: This is in relation to zone Z1 of the driving schemas presented in Figure 1.7.

lights. In a first time (that is, see the first view on the left, corresponding to the driver's mental representation at a distance of 30 meters of the traffic lights), the driver's situational awareness is mainly centered on the near traffic and on the color of the traffic lights, that directly determines the short-term activity to be implemented. Then, as s/he progresses towards the crossroads, the driver's attention will be gradually focused on the ahead area on the road, and the traffic flow occurring in the intersection center will be progressively considered and partly integrated into the driver's mental representation (that is, second left view, at a distance of 10 meters of the traffic lights).

The advantage of the driving schema formalism—as defined in COSMODRIVE model—is to combine declarative and procedural knowledge in the unified computational structure. When combined with the operational regulation processes linked with the *envelope zones* and the *pursuit point*, it is then possible to use such driving schemas as a structure of control for both monitoring the operative activity, as well as for supervising the mental derivation of the "schema deployment," as this process is implemented by the human cognitive system in order to anticipate future situational status, or mentally explore the potential effects of an action before applied it. In accordance with the operative activity theories presented in the previous sections, these cognitive structures guarantee a continuum between the different levels of (i) awareness (implicit *versus* explicit) and (ii) activity control (tactical *versus* operational), thereby taking full account of the embedding of operative know-how (that is, the level of implementation) in the explicit and decisional regulation loop of the activity.

5. CONCLUSION: "IN SILICO VERITAS!"

After having discussed (in this chapter Introduction and in the first section centered on the Mental Activity Analysis) on the limits of the "*in vitro*" approach for studying human cognition through the natural sciences methods based on artificial laboratory tasks (that is, founded on C. Bernard's *experimental paradigm*), and argued in the third section (dedicated to the Cognitive Modeling) of the necessity to use an ecological "*in vivo*" approach for studying the human operators' mental activities as they are implemented in their everyday life, the last section of this chapter (that is, Cognitive Simulation) was dedicated to an illustration, through a cognitive simulation model of the car driver, of the possibility to design and the necessity to use "*in silico*" simulations for in-depth investigation of the human natural cognition.

Indeed, by considering the challenge of the *living cognition* study, it is needed to apprehend the dynamic functioning of the human cognitive system in interaction with the surrounding environment where s/he is currently immersed. Thus, computational models able to virtually simulate the human mental activities on computer are required. One of the key issues of the living cognition are the mental representations—here considered as pre-existing schemas instantiated with the objective reality—that are dynamically elaborated and continually updated in the working memory of the human operator before (that is, action planning phase) and during their activity (that is, when it is practically carried out). Indeed, mental representations and operative activity are actually intimately connected. In the same way as the human activity fuels itself directly with mental representations, the operator's mental representations are also fuelled "by" the activity, and "for" the activity, according to a double deployment process: cognitive and representational, on the one hand, and sensorial-motor and executive, on the other.

The key mental structure supporting both humans mental representations and their operative activity are *operative schemas*. From a metaphorical standpoint, such operative schemas can be compared to a strand of DNA. They "genetically" contain all the potential behavioral alternatives that allow the human to act within a more or less generic class of situations. Nonetheless, only a tiny part of these "genotypic potentialities" will finally express themselves in the current situation—with respect to the constraints and specific characteristics of reality—during the cognitive (that is, instantiation and deployment of the mental representations), and then executive implementation of this schema (via the effective activity carried out to drive the car). And it is only through this dynamic process of deployment of operative mental representations, involving a collective effort of several cognitive processes that certain of intrinsic properties of the *living cognition* will emerge. From this point of view, the scientific investigation of the living cognition cannot forego the use of computer simulation of the human mental activities, without taking the risk of being largely incomplete.

Therefore, to provide "*in silico*" simulations of the mental activities, considered in their dynamic implementation and by respecting their natural complexity as observed in the everyday life, is the very central, innovative and necessary contribution of the modern cognitive science to the multidisciplinary scientific investigation of the human cognition.

Whether the drunkenness of the truth contained in the silicon is not always as pleasant as the mystery discovered in a good bottle of old wine, it is nevertheless the exciting fate of the researcher in cognitive science to investigate the "*in silico veritas*", for a couple of centuries.

REFERENCES

Amidi, O, 1990. *Integrated Mobile Robot Control*, Technical Report CMU-RI-TR-90–17, Carnegie Mellon University Robotics Institute.

Anderson, J.R.,1993. *Rules of the Mind*. New Jersey: Lawrence Erlbaum Associates, Hillsdale.

Atkinson, R.C., Shiffrin, R.M., 1968. Human memory: a proposed system and its control process. In: K.W. Spence, J.T. Spence (Eds.), *The Psychology of Learning and Motivation*. 2, 89–195, New York: Academic Press.

Baddeley, A.D., 1986. *Working Memory*. Oxford, Clarendon Press.

Bailly, B., Bellet, T., Goupil, C., 2003. Driver's Mental Representations: experimental study and training perspectives. In: L. Dorn (Ed.), *Driver Behaviour and Training*. Ashgate, 359–369,

Banet, A., Bellet, T., 2008. Risk awareness and criticality assessment of driving situations: a comparative study between motorcyclists and car drivers. *IET Intelligent Transport Systems*, 2 (4), 241–248.

Bellet, T., 1998. *Modélisation et simulation cognitive de l'opérateur humain: une application à la conduite automobile*, Thèse de Doctorat, Université René Descartes Paris V.

Bellet, T., Bailly-Asuni, B., Mayenobe, P., Banet, A., 2009. A theoretical and methodological framework for studying and modeling drivers' mental representations. *Safety Science*, 47, 1205–1221.

Bellet, T., Bailly, B., Mayenobe, P., Georgeon, O., 2007. Cognitive modeling and computational simulation of drivers' mental activities. In: P. Cacciabue (Ed.), *Modeling Driver Behaviour in Automotive Environment: Critical Issues in Driver Interactions with Intelligent Transport Systems*. Springer Verlag, 315–343.

Bellet, T., Tattegrain-Veste, H., 1999. A framework for Representing Driving Knowledge. *International Journal of Cognitive Ergonomics*, 3 (1), 37–49.

Bisseret, A., 1970. Mémoire opérationnelle et structure du travail. *Bulletin de Psychologie*, 24 (5–6), 280–294.

Dulany, D.E., 1991. Conscious representation and thought systems. In: R.S. Wyer and T.K. Srull (Eds.), *Advances in Social Cognition*. Hilldale, NJ: Lawrence Erlbaum Associates, 91–120.

Endsley, M.R., 1995. Toward a theory of situation awareness in dynamic systems. *Human Factors*, 37 (1), 32–64.

Ericsson, K.A., Kintsch, W., 1995. Long-term working memory. *Psychological Review*, 102, 211–245.

Fodor, J.A., 1975. *The Language of Thought*, Thomas Y. Crowell (Ed.). New York.

Gibson, J.J., 1950. *The Perception of the Visual World*. Cambridge, MA: Houghton Mifflin.

Gibson, J.J., 1979. *The Ecological Approach to Visual Perception*. Boston, MA: Houghton Mifflin.

Gibson, J.J., Crooks, L.E., 1938. A theoretical field-analysis of automobile driving. *American Journal of Psychology*, 51, 453–471.

Graf P., Schacter, D.L., 1985. Implicit and explicit memory for new associations in normal and amnesic subjects. *Journal of Experimental Psychology: Learning, Memory, and Cognition*, 11, 501–518.

Hall, E.T., 1966. *The Hidden Dimension*. Doubleday, New York.

Johnson-Laird, P.N., 1983. *Mental Models: Towards a cognitive science of language, inference, and consciousness*. Cambridge University Press.

Kontaratos, N.A., 1974. A system analysis of the problem of road casualties in the United States. *Accident Analysis and Prevention*, 6, 223–241.

Koch, C., 2004. *The Quest for Conciousness: A neurobiological approach*. Engelwood: Roberts and Co. Publishers.

Leplat, J., 1985. Les représentations fonctionnelles dans le travail. *Psychologie Française*, 30 (3/4), 269–275.

Leontiev, A., 1977. *Activity and Consciousness*, available online on the web site: http://marxists.org/archive/leontev/works/1977/leon1977.htm.

Leontiev, K., Lerner, A., Ochanine, D., 1961. Quelques objectifs de l'étude des systèmes Homme-Automate. *Question de Psychologie*, 1, 1–13.

Mayenobe, P., 2004. *Perception de l'environnement pour une gestion contextualisée de la coopération Homme-Machine*. PhD thesis, University Blaise Pascal de Clermont-Ferrand.

Mayenobe, P, Trassoudaine, L, Bellet, T. and Tattegrain-Veste, H., 2002. Cognitive Simulation of the Driver and Cooperative Driving Assistances. In: *Proceedings of the IEEE Intelligent Vehicles Symposium: IV-2002*, Versailles, June 17–21, 265–271.

Michon, J.A., 1985. A critical view of driver behavior models: what do we know, what should we do? In: L. Evans, R.C. Schwing (Eds.), *Human Behavior and Traffic Safety*. New York: Plenum Press, 485–520.

Minsky, M., 1975. A Framework for Representing Knowledge. In: P.H. Winston (Ed.), *The Psychology of Computer Vision*. New York: McGraw-Hill, pp. 211–277.

Neisser, U., 1976. *Cognition and Reality: principles and implications of cognitive psychology*. San Fransisco: W.H. Freeman.

Norman, D.A., 1983. Some observations on mental models. In: D. Gentner, A.L. Stevens (Eds.). *Mental Models*. Lawrence Erlbaum, pp. 7–14.

Norman, D.A., Shallice T., 1986. Attention to action: willed and automatic control of behavior. In: R.J. Davidson, G.E. Schwartz, D. Shairo (Eds.), *Consciousness and Self-regulation. Advances in research and theory.* New York: Plenum Press, 4, pp. 1–18.

Ochanine, V.A., 1977. Concept of operative image in engineering and general psychology. In: B.F. Lomov, V.F. Rubakhin, and V.F. Venda (Eds.), *Engineering Psychology.* Science Publisher, Moscow.

Ohta, H. 1993. Individual differences in driving distance headway. In: A.G. Gale (Ed.), *Vision in Vehicles IV.* Netherlands: Elsevier Science Publishers, 91–100.

Ouznadzé, D. 1966. Principes essentiels de la théorie d'attitude. In: A. Léontiev, A. Luria, and A. Smirnov (Eds.), *Recherches Psychologiques en URSS.* Moscou: Editions du Progrès, 244–283.

Piaget, J., 1974. *La prise de conscience,* Presses Universitaires de France, Paris.

Piaget, J., 1936. *La Naissance de l'intelligence chez l'enfant.* Delachaux and Niestlé.

Pinku, G., Tzelgov, J., 2006. Consciousness of the self (COS) and explicit knowledge. *Consciousness and Cognition,* 15, 655–661.

Proust, J., 2003. *Les animaux pensent-ils?* Paris: Bayard.

Rasmussen, J., 1986. *Information Processing and Human–machine Interaction: An approach to cognitive engineering.* Amsterdam, North Holland.

Richard, J.F., 1990. *Les activités mentales: comprendre, raisonner, trouver des solutions.* Paris: Armand Colin.

Schilder, P., 1950. *The Image and Appearance of the Human Body.* New York: International Universities Press.

Schneider, W., Shiffrin, R.M., 1977. Controlled and automatic Human Information Processing I: Detection, search and attention. *Psychological Review,* 84, 1–88.

Smirnov, A., 1966. La mémoire et l'activité. In: A. Léontiev, A. Luria, and A. Smirnov (Eds.), *Recherches Psychologiques en URSS.* Moscou: Editions du Progrès, 47–89.

Smith, K., Hancock, P.A., 1995. Situation Awareness is adaptive, externally directed consciousness. *Human Factors,* 37 (1), 137–148.

Smolensky, P., 1989. Connectionist modeling: Neural computation/Mental connections. In: L. Nadel, L.A. Cooper, P. Culicover, R.M. Harnish (Eds.), *Neural Connections, Mental Computation.* Cambridge MA: The MIT Press, pp. 49–67.

Stanton, N.A., Chambers, P.R.G., Piggott, J., 2001. Situational awareness and safety, *Safety Science,* 39, 189–204.

Sukthankar, R., 1997. *Situation Awareness for Tactical Driving,* Phd thesis, Carnegie Mellon University, Pittsburgh, PA, United States of America.

Thom, R., 1991. *Prédire n'est pas expliquer.* Paris: Eshel.

Vergnaud, G., 1985. Concepts et schèmes dans la théorie opératoire de la representation. *Psychologie Française* 30, (3), 245–252.

Vermersch, P., 1994. *L'entretien d'explicitation (en formation initiale et en formation continue).* Paris: ESF Editeur.

Vygotsky, L.S., 1962. *Thought and Language.* Boston: MIT Press.

Wiener, N. 1948. *Cybernetics or Control and Communication in the Animal and the Machine.* Cambridge, MA: The MIT Press.

Zintchenko P., 1966. Quelques problèmes de psychologie de la mémoire. In: A. Léontiev, A. Luria, and A. Smirnov (Eds,), *Recherches Psychologiques en URSS.* Moscou: Editions du Progrès, 7–46.

2

Psychophysiology and Performance: Considerations for Human-Centered Design

Anil K. Raj, Margery J. Doyle, and Joshua D. Cameron

In our modern information intensive environment, we increasingly rely on man-made technical systems to perform or assist our tasks. Interfaces that represent various system sensors and components, however, often reflect engineering limitations that can create improper representations of information between the system state and our mental models of the system state and expected behavior, creating uncertainty and ambiguity (Sarter and Woods, 1991; Doyle, 2009). These limitations can adversely affect human operator command and control capabilities, particularly when using non-interactive technical interfaces that prevent us from perceiving and correcting mismatches between incoming data and our mental models. This hampers our ability to formulate an understanding of the task and surrounding situation, making us more prone to errors in decision-making that all too often lead to mishaps. Indeed, working under conditions with less than optimal socio-technical systems often forces us to learn new interaction paradigms (that is, work-arounds) in order to adapt (Doyle, 2009; Doyle and Cole, 2008). While automation can assist human operators with task execution, many current designs may actually add to workload and increase user errors (Sheridan, 2002) if automation fails to address the fundamental capabilities and limitations of human cognition and perception (Kirlik, 1993; Parasuraman and Riley, 1997). Understanding human sensory data, the cognitive demands and the task context, as well as their interactions in a specific system, represents the first step toward effective human-centered design of interfaces that optimize operator workload (Kass et al., 2003). Along with cognitive workload, other components of human cognition such as situation understanding (SU) and decision effectiveness (DE) require consideration (Doyle, 2008). While workload and situation awareness (SA) have been modeled rather successfully (Laughery, 2000; Plott, Endsley, and Strater, 2004), models that represent the interaction between workload and SA accurately enough to aid in the design of systems to support human performance have yet to be developed. Because SA and SU both support effective decision-making (Stanners and French, 2005), future models must represent how workload transitions from positive states to negative/inhibitory states and how workload can negatively impact

SA, SU, and decision effectiveness (Doyle, 2008). The field of Augmented Cognition (AugCog) has emerged with a keen focus on developing such models and metrics (Schmorrow and Kruse, 2004). A key element of AugCog concerns the selection and measurement of psychophysiologic changes in the human operator that correlate with various dimensions of cognitive state during a task or mission. With reliable estimates of cognitive state shifts, computational augmentation systems can adjust autonomously to optimize and improve socio-technical team performance (Doyle et al., 2009; Kass et al., 2003).

SITUATION AWARENESS, SITUATION UNDERSTANDING, AND WORKLOAD

Currently, it is possible to model large neuronal networks with biophysically detailed neuronal and synaptic properties that approach the numbers and complexity found in living nervous systems (Silver et al., 2007). However, approaches sufficient for high fidelity modeling will require breakthroughs in our understanding of how to model cognition (National Research Council, 2008). In the interim, modeling the interrelationships between critical elements such as mental workload optimization, SA, SU, and effective decision-making (for example, Adams et al., 1995; Doyle, 2008; Durso and Gronlund, 1999; Endsley and Garland, 2001) can more effectively guide system designers when creating interfaces for specific mission and task domains. Independent but interrelated constructs such as mental workload and SA for example (Endsley, 1993) contribute to task performance. Workload, defined as the portion of limited mental capacity actually required to perform a particular task (O'Donnell and Eggemeier, 1986) and SA, defined as "the perception of elements in the environment within a volume of time and space, the *comprehension* of their meaning, and the *projection* of their status in the near future" (Endsley, 1993), as well as decision effectiveness, can account for as much as 88 percent of human error (Endsley, 1995). Situation awareness, based in sensation perception, differs from situation understanding, which results from a sense-making process (that is, how we understand new information once we have become aware of it). Both SA and SU provide the context needed to decide how or when to act. Human performance models that reliably predict human capabilities and limitations, particularly for SA, SU, and decision-making effectiveness, could assist in the design of novel system interfaces (Doyle, 2008). Complete models must represent the unified SA of both the human and machine members of a socio-technical team (Niklasson et al., 2007). Such models could also drive adjustments to automation assistance in order to preemptively improve system performance and task effectiveness throughout a task, workday or mission.

The flow of information (quantity and quality) needed to provide continuous SA can cause an undesirable increase in cognitive workload (Tsang and Wilson, 1997) even under ideal conditions, and particularly when urgency and sequencing of tasks increases. Meanwhile, degradation of information or bottlenecks due to limited central processing capacity can increase the workload associated with maintenance of SA and SU. Additionally, diverting cognitive assets to manage non-mission related tasks in time critical systems can overwhelm the limited human information processing capacity leading to degraded SA (Wagner, 1976). This occurs when new stimuli (that is, tasking or information-in-need-of-processing) displace current or previous information and potentially weaken previously formed hypotheses driving decision-making processes. While models have proven effective thus far in estimating tasking and SA related operator cognitive workload, they often assume the existence of an optimal cognitive state that supports workload, SA, and effective decision-making. Though multiple-resource theory (MRT) proposes the existence of several different resource pools, each with limited scope but responsible for different types of processing (Wickens, 1980, 1991), current models fail to explain how some individuals maintain decision-making performance even with apparently insufficient information for maintenance of SA.

While workload increases do not always equate to decreases in SA, some impact from the competition for limited resources likely occurs. MRT based modeling separates, for example, cognitive processing of external visual and auditory information into spatial/verbal (text) and spatial/verbal (localizing sound/listening to speech), respectively. Likewise, SA has been successfully modeled using Situation Awareness Global Assessment Technique (SAGAT; Plott, Endsley and Strater, 2004). However, the interaction of workload and SA has yet to be modeled computationally. Variations and discontinuities in components of workload and SA (that is, mental demand, temporal demand, frustration, and so on.) which interact, can lead to uncertainty in SA and impact effective decision-making (Endsley, Bolté and Jones, 2003; Kirlik and Strauss, 2006). Conversely, very low to no workload can also affect SA due to vigilance decrement. The absence of workload differs from degraded SA because very low workload causes the operator to disengage from the task, which requires additional cognitive resources to reacquire SA when anomalies arise or workload increases (Figure 2.1). Figure 2.1a illustrates the general concept where task workload and workload associated with acquiring SA-SU interact, competing for limited mental capacity during complex tasking. Figure 2.1b shows that DE interacts with and depends on SA-SU. Figure 2.1c depicts the state where workload, SA-SU, and DE interact and create an optimal cognitive state that utilizes workload appropriately, supporting maintenance of SA-SU, and therefore, decision-making, or DE. Figure 2.1d illustrates the state where DE competes with SA and task related workload for cognitive capacity.

These interactions will vary as taskload, operator state, mission requirements, environmental factors, and so on, change over time (Figure 2.2). In this hypothetical example, when WL, SA-SU, and DE remain within the upper and lower limits while workload decreases, which frees up cognitive reserve, both SA-SU and DE increase. This crossover within the upper and lower limits, that is, the optimal state, follows from these rules: (a) if WL starts within the upper and lower limits (UL/LL), then when WL increases, SA-SU and DE increase, (b) if WL goes above the UL, then SA-SU and DE decrease, (c) if WL dips below the LL, then SA-SU and DE also fall below LL, (d) when WL, SA-SU, and DE are within the UL/LL *and* WL decreases, SA-SU and DE will increase creating an optimal cognitive state for supporting SA and DE, and (e) if WL rises above the UL and SA-SU decreases, the operator can, sometimes, maintain decision effective (Doyle, 2008).

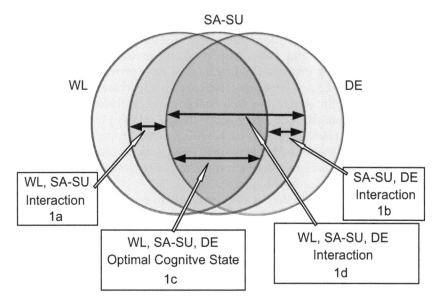

Figure 2.1   The state where DE competes with SA

Notes: From top left to right then bottom left to right: 1a. Workload/SA-SU interaction, SA-SU related workload; 1b. SA-SU/DE interaction, DE dependency on SA-SU; 1c. Optimal cognitive state for WL, SA-SU, DE; and 1d. WL/SA-SU/DE interaction, illustrating co-competiveness and supportiveness of SA-SU and DE for capacity resources.

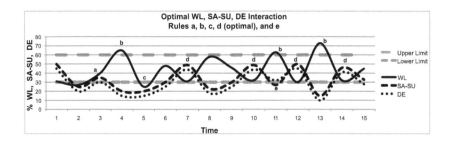

Figure 2.2   Graph representing interactions (hypothetical data) between WL, SA-SU, DE and the optimal cognitive state over time

Source: From Doyle, 2008.

AUTOMATION EFFECTS ON DECISION EFFECTIVENESS

To reduce cognitive workload and improve operator decision-making, technological systems such as software executing on a computer can assume tasks that a human operator would otherwise perform (Wickens, Gordon, and Liu, 1997). Such automated aids and decision support tools control many tasks, including "cognitive" tasks in complex, dynamic environments. In advanced aircraft cockpits, for example, automation would relieve the human pilot of workload associated with detecting and diagnosing system abnormalities, navigation, and calculating fuel-efficient routes (Mosier, Skitka, Heers, and Burdick, 1998). Though simple automation (for example, a wristwatch) or complex automation (for example, the systems that control a nuclear power plant) can each implement various levels or modes, adaptive automation can replace human operator perceptual abilities and assist (or replace) decision-making processes and actions (Parasuraman et al., 1992; Wickens, Gordon, and Liu, 1997). To ensure effectiveness through adaptive automation, however, designers must address issues of automation reliability, operator's level of trust toward the automation, and operator complacency in the presence of automation (Wickens, Gordon, and Liu, 1997).

Functionally, automation assists human operators through management by consent and/or management by exception. In the former, the system suggests courses of action for the operator that it executes only with the operator's approval. In the latter, the system notifies the operator of its intended course of action and executes on its own unless vetoed by the operator. (Billings, 1997; Endsley, 1987; Kaber and Endsley, 2004). Unfortunately, many modern automation systems execute actions without any interaction with or notifications to the operator. While pilots, for example, have said they prefer management by consent, they can miss half of the goal conflicts and all of the presented implementation conflict events (Olsen and Sarter, 2001). Thus, automated decision aids and automation may reduce one class of errors, but may actually introduce another class of errors (Skitka, Mosier, and Burdick, 1999). Because users will often use decision rules of thumb to avoid detailed analysis (Fiske and Taylor, 1994) and tend to expend less cognitive effort when working in a group with human (Karau and Williams, 1993) or computational teammates (Skitka, Mosier, and Burdick, 1999), automation often gets used as another heuristic, leading to errors of omission or commission due to *automation bias* (Mosier, Skitka, Heers, and Burdick, 1998; Skitka, Mosier, and Burdick, 1999). *Omission errors* occur when a decision-maker does not take an appropriate action, despite non-automated indications that a problem exists, sometimes because an automated decision aid does not also indicate that the problem exists. *Commission errors* occur when a decision-maker acts on erroneous or ambiguous directives of an automated device (Mosier and Skitka, 1996) or acts erroneously due to confusion of system state, or system responsibility or responsiveness. While redundancy in such situations might appear to benefit the additional team members, the increased system complexity (Mosier, Skitka, Dunbar, and McDonnell, 2001) can make team situation awareness more difficult to maintain than individual SA (Jentsch, Barnett, Bowers, and Salas, 1999). Time constraints may also increase the tendency to rely on as few cues as necessary, leading teams to use the automation as a decision shortcut (Mosier, Skitka, Dunbar, and McDonnell, 2001). In fact, the presence of automation may disrupt crew coordination (Bowers et al., 1995) by disrupting the hierarchical structure necessary for effective team decision-making (Sarter and Woods, 1997; Wiener, 1989) and decreasing the communication rates between crew members (Costley, Johnson, and Lawson, 1989). When introduced to a system, automated aids can disrupt the pattern of cue utilization and problem evaluation (Layton, Smith, and McCoy, 1994), and users may act on the decision aid directives, even while knowing that the automation lacks an adequate model of the "world" and in the face of conflicting data from other indicators (Mosier, Skitka, Heers, and Burdick, 1998). A decision-maker making such confirmation and assimilation errors may avoid re-evaluation of the situation (Hamilton, 1981; Wickens and Flach, 1988) or erroneously judge conflicting secondary indicators as displaying data in agreement with the automation (Darley and Gross, 1983; Glick, Zion and Nelson, 1988).

Operators who rely heavily on automated devices often loose proficiency (currency) in complex task skills including maintenance of situation awareness and increasing reaction time to correct problems when automation fails (Endsley and Kiris, 1995). This "out-of-the-loop" performance consequence results from the validation of automation (Billings, 1991; Moray, 1986; Wickens, 1992; Wiener and Curry, 1980) and compounds with the loss, typically seen in automated systems, of proprioceptive, kinematic and other subtle sensory cues (Kessel and Wickens, 1992). When operating "out-of-the-loop," the user maintains an inadequate *mental model* of the system which can lead to an increased workload and "automation surprises" (Honeywell, Feary, Polson, and Palmer, 2000) resulting from the failure of the automation-operator system to establish or maintain a shared understanding of the situation, or agree on the correct response to the situation (Norman, 1988; Parasuraman, Mouloua, Molloy, and Hilburn, 1996; Reason, 1987; Sherry and Polson, 1999).

However, automation can benefit situation awareness and keep the operator engaged when used appropriately to manage taskload (Ephrath and Young, 1981), as long as it allows users to distribute their attention, detect system failures and remain active in the decision-making loop (Endsley and Kiris, 1995). Automation can support human operator performance and task reliability by: (a) keeping the human informed, (b) keeping the human current (that is, trained), (c) keeping the operator in the loop, and (d) making automation flexible and adaptive (Wickens, Gordon, and Liu, 1997). Depending on the implementation of these concepts, automation may not actually reduce workload but rather shift the kind of workload experienced, as the operator moves from a role of control to one of monitoring (Billings, 1991; Wiener, 1989). Both partial task automation and adaptive automation strategies that keep the operator in the decision-making loop can avoid some of the pitfalls associated with out-of-the-loop performance (Endsley and Kiris, 1995). For example, automating early-stage functions, such as information acquisition, data fusion and analysis, while reserving decision-making functions for operator supervisory control, facilitates operator situation awareness, trust, and maintenance of skill sets (Parasuraman, Visser, and Cosenzo, 2007). This may preclude, however, achieving the highest levels of automation (Sheridan and Verplank, 1978). Thus, the system designer must determine the most effective levels and type of automation to support the operator based on four stages of human–automation interaction: information acquisition, information analysis, decision, and action selection, and action implementation (Parasuraman et al., 2000).

Though automation can support each of these stages (Sheridan and Verplank, 1978), each stage deals with distinct aspects of information processing. Separation of *information automation* (information acquisition and analysis) and *decision automation* (decision selection and action implementation) enables a reduction in operator workload (Billings, 1997). For example, the Theater High Altitude Area Defense (THADD) ballistic missile interception system has relatively high levels of automation for information acquisition, information analysis, and decision selection with a lower level of action implementation automation, freeing the operator to focus on decisions regarding execution of a specific action (Parasuraman et al., 2007). This leads to a distributed cognition organizing principle (Hutchins, 1995; Hutchins and Klausen, 1992), that changes the unit of analysis from the individual to the socio-technical unit comprised of the human and non-human entities that are interacting, and can enable estimation of cognitive properties not found at the level of either the human or system components of that unit.

Human decision-making performance depends on personality and motivation, level of knowledge, training, and natural abilities. Furthermore, task performance requires strategic thinking and planning and effective use of short and long-term memory, all while avoiding natural biasing tendencies (recent effects, premature closure, anchoring, and so on). Thus, the management of high information and task load systems could clearly benefit from the application of intelligent automated workload and decision-making assistance at many levels. Appropriate real-time task division would reduce cognitive complexity, workload, and short-term memory demands, freeing the operator to think more creatively about strategic, tactical, and operational situation states and potential outcomes. Bias of perception and reasoning can appear from several sources and affect decision effectiveness. Computational procedures, human intuitions, and both transient and long held beliefs for which the facts support alternative views or for which little or no factual support exists (Stoyenko, Laplante, Harrison, and Marlowe, 1994) may impose biases in the process of evaluating certain data objects. Such biases may result from lack of knowledge or awareness about prior probabilities, deciding by similarity or representativeness (conjunctive fallacy), favoring hunches and personal experience, and/or anchoring to fixed beliefs or a limited subset of available information. In addition, temporal bias can manifest, due to the presentation order of data (primacy or recency), hindsight, prejudgment of effects in a data set, premature closure of the analysis (that is, acting before all available data arrives to the user), and/or erroneous extrapolation. These biases contribute to poor performance of human decision-makers, particularly with probabilistic and statistical calculations and mathematical inference. Model-based human-centered adaptive systems designed to improve operational safety, however, can reduce errors associated with making decisions based on probabilistic data, and their contribution to mishaps (Kahneman and Tversky, 1979).

ADAPTIVE AUTOMATION FOR AUGMENTATION OF COGNITION

Neuroergonomics encompasses both the understanding of the neural basis of cognition and behavior, as well as the design, development and operation of technology that utilizes this knowledge (Kramer et al., 2005; Marek et al., 2004), Neuroergonomic, human-centered adaptive automated systems adjust the mode and level of automation assistance dynamically in response to changes in operator workload (Scerbo, 2006; Scerbo, Freeman, and Mikulka, 2000), rather than manual inputs from the operator, which can increase taskload (Wiener, 1989). Adaptive systems that respond to task specific operator psychophysiological feedback reduce the workload associated with manually initiated automated systems (Hancock and Chignell, 1987; Kramer, Trejo, and Humphrey, 1996; Prinzel et al., 2000; Rouse, 1976; Scerbo, 1996; Scerbo, Freeman, and Mikulka, 2000; Scerbo et al., 2001). Such mixed-initiative approaches allow the human and computational systems to each contribute to management of the system, performing the roles that each does best

(Ferguson, Allen, and Miller, 1996). Flexible automation can remain robust to human tendencies of using heuristics to conserve cognitive resources in critical situations (Skitka, Mosier, and Burdick, 1999).

Modern implementations of this neuroergonomic approach to managing adaptive automation use real-time understanding of operator cognitive state along with changes in the mission environment to provide a moment-to-moment adjustment of information flow and automation assistance. These augmented cognition (AugCog) based automation systems non-invasively estimate various dimensions of human cognitive state and use this state information to adapt closed-loop computational systems to the operator's needs (Schmorrow and Kruse, 2004; Schmorrow et al., 2005). For example, if the AugCog system detects a visual working memory overload, it might redirect critical incoming messages to an auditory display (verbal presentation) in order to maximize the capability of cognitive resources. Augmented Cognition goes a step beyond traditional human-centered interface (HCI) techniques to enable adaptation based upon not only the environment and tasks at hand, but also on the real-time assessment of operators' cognitive state (Raley et al., 2004). AugCog platforms have demonstrated success using technologies from many different disciplines, including cognitive science, cognitive engineering, neuroscience, human factors, mathematical modeling, computer science, modeling and simulation, information science, knowledge engineering, socio-technical science and engineering, complex systems science, electrical engineering, mechanical engineering, and systems engineering in order to adapt the presentation of information and task automation to maximize socio-technical team performance over a mission (Marshall and Raley, 2004). These include, but are not limited to tracking changes in electroencephalography (EEG), functional near infrared imaging (fNIR), heart rate variability (HRV), electrocardiogram (EKG), pulse oximetry, postural changes, galvanic skin response/electrodermal response (GSR/EDR), body temperature, electro-oculography (EOG), pupilometry, and gaze tracking. Many of these sensing technologies have been integrated into cognitive state gauges, which give accurate classification of workload and other measures of cognitive state such as fatigue, alertness decrement, inattention, or mental and sensory overload in real-time by tracking changes in human behavioral and physiological patterns (Reeves et al., 2007; Schmorrow and Kruse, 2004). Various research teams have investigated the feasibility of various psychophysiologic and environmental sensors (by evaluating their accuracy, operational relevance, and comfort/wearability) and the effectiveness of novel techniques by which to process sensor data into meaningful gauge information (Matthews et al., 2007; Russell et al., 2005; Snow et al., 2006; St. John, Kobus, and Morrison, 2005; Kass et al., 2003; Doyle et al., 2009). These gauges also take into account the neurological and physiological delays between a firing event in the body and the sensing of this event (Belyavin, 2005; Dorneich et al., 2005; Gerson, Parra, and Sajda, 2005). Using advanced machine learning, algorithms for automated biosignal analyses have been developed (Koska et al., 1997; Trejo et al., 2003), that, for example, require as little as 3.5 seconds of EEG data for a robust multivariate support vector classifier to correctly identify periods of cognitive fatigue in 90 percent of individuals performing a demanding 3-hour task (Trejo et al., 2003, 2004). A number of methods for employing and testing cognitive model prototype AugCog systems have been developed (Schmorrow and Stanney, 2008), which have demonstrated that incomplete models or mismatches in context between the system and model can adversely affect performance despite the human-centered approach (Raj et al., 2006).

MODELING APPROACHES

Task network (TN) modeling, an approach applied in military domains such as ships, aircraft (Scott-Nash et al., 2000) and ground based vehicles (Laughery et al., 1986), can represent these interactions for human-system integration, task, and manpower optimization. TN based models employ activity functional decomposition in a discrete-event modeling approach with high construct, face, and predictive value (Zachary, Campbell, Laughery, and Glenn, 1998). By using procedural documentation such as training manuals and concept of operations (CONOPS) combined with subject matter expert (SME) feedback, TN's provide repeatable, objective, and quantifiable information about operator workload and timing questions. Networks organized by task sequence can interact with dynamic system-of-systems (SOSs) models to create a closed-loop representation of the total system, allowing parameter predictions such as the effectiveness of computer screen real estate utilization, information flow, and peripheral integration or placement. TN models can help analysts predict effects of changes in system configuration, concept of operations and manpower on error rate, task duration, and so on, and be fined tuned using scenario based simulation. In most situations, particularly combat command and control (C2), uncertainty can result from, for instance; (1) lack of good probabilistic knowledge, (2) lack of information, and (3) lack of situation awareness. Often experience and historical knowledge can substitute for the missing information and may include recognition of patterns and trends, analogical reasoning, case-based inference, and evidential deductions (Cooper, 1995; Dagum and Chavez, 1993). Reasoning under uncertainty, however, forces assumptions about the nature, intentions and methods of elements in the environment (Chickering and Heckerman, 1996). If all these elements behaved rationally and predictably then one could regain SA and infer likely system behavior, performance, and future state changes to maximize one's gain and/or minimize losses depending on the conditions. Models of explicit and tacit situation knowledge that have various levels of abstraction include multi-attribute utility theory (MAUT), bootstrapping, and composite judgment models (Cooper, 1995; Doyle and Thomason, 1999; Osherson et al., 1997). Each employs a linear modeling technique and can provide useful types of consistent, reliable advice to decision-makers in a variety of situations. Although each method varies in approach, they each express explicit and tacit knowledge, modeled in a linear fashion using a weighted function based on usefulness (that is, utility) of the information for a given situation.

Other approaches that utilize input from SMEs to guide model development such as Visual, Cognitive, Auditory, and Psychomotor (VCAP) modeling (Aldrich, Szabo, and Bierbaum, 1989) and the Workload Index (W/Index; North, and Riley, 1989) fundamentally rely on MRT, breaking task related workload into four and six channels, respectively. Unlike the VCAP measure of channel utilization, the W/Index uses a conflict matrix computation for total workload based on visual perception, auditory perception, verbal cognition, spatial cognition, manual (that is, psychomotor) response, and speech response channel activity (Bowen, 2005) to expose the relationship between task related workload and SA related workload and their effects on cognitive capacity. W/Index can also provide a measure of backlog related workload, task shedding and operator task overload based on the time frame, priority, and criticality of tasks left in the process queue. Additionally, other "information driven decision-making" architectures with reasonably good predictive qualities (Archer, Warwick, and Oster, 2000), such as SAGAT, represent SA elements and temporal features to model the time related salience factor of the information presented to an operator. Also, the recurrent network method can reflect the short-term memory characteristics of SA by using connections between units to form a directed cycle, which can exhibit dynamic temporal behavior (Engh, Yow, and Laughery, 1997).

By using SAGAT to administer queries pertaining to all three levels of SA, a comprehensive assessment of operator SA related requirements can be determined (Endsley, 1987, 1988, 1995b). This method taps into the operator's direct perceptions rather than behaviors, without requiring that subjects or test personnel make judgments about situation knowledge. SAGAT provides a straightforward score based approach that easily informs human performance based measures of a TN (Plott, Endsley, and Strater, 2004) by briefly interrupting a test scenario to probe operator short-term memory for SA (Endsley, 2000). Compared to other scoring methods such as VCAP or W/Index (North and Riley, 1989), SAGAT reveal changes in SA values over the course of a scenario, identify tasks where an operator would normally update his or her knowledge base to gain or maintain SA, and select points in the TN simulation where SA related probes could be embedded. The SAGAT probe questions relate to task attributes (that is, state of the system, type of threat, speed of threat, and so on) that reflect SA and current memory at a coarse level of granularity. Models built on temporal changes in SAGAT responses have demonstrated high levels of accuracy (Plott, Endsley, and Strater, 2004) and can estimate future SA when used to help design and evaluate new system interfaces and automation components.

Game theory and Bayesian models can manage probabilities to identify stochastic connections between actions and consequences. Bayesian probability (BP) enables reasoning under uncertainty and combines the advantages of an intuitive representation with a sound mathematical basis. BP models can assist, using heuristics and biases, during conditions of uncertainty where decisions must follow from objective goals. The Bayesian probabilities capture many stochastic-process factors that affect the attributes of interest and game theory models. These process factors can then predict the effects that certain attribute changes have on data fusion processes. There are several ways of determining the probabilities for the entities in the Bayesian probabilities (Hanks and McDermott, 1994). One common approach is to use the joint probability distributions of the constituent components. Models that employ Bayesian probability can accommodate both subjective probabilities (elicited from domain experts) and probabilities based on objective data. A Bayesian reasoning process can be initialized with certain background knowledge, either manually or automatically extracted from relevant information sources (Haddawy, 1999). The BP then can readily handle missing data and avoid over-fitting of data in a decision-making process by applying the Dempster-Shafer's rule of evidence combinations to the processing of information with multiple uncertain resources (Barnett, 1991; Bogler, 1987). Adaptive software can interpret, filter and correlate information (for example, track histories) more efficiently and correctly by learning and adjusting Bayesian game models using weight evolution in utility formulae, correlation links, and so on. Similar to neural net learning, this method also operates with significant autonomy of constrained decisions and without a detailed, largely static net. Overall, the data fusion approach for SA could benefit from both evolutionary game models estimating state determinations and solutions of the mappings between the state space and the representation hypotheses, and BP models evaluating sensory and environmental data, quantitatively ranking the action alternatives in terms of cost functions.

Classical neural net and Bayesian classifier "black box" methods, however, suffer from two problems: they often fail to accurately predict cognitive state when the context of the task changes significantly, and they produce cryptic, difficult to interpret models. Dimensionality reduction methods such as principal components analysis (PCA) or independent components analysis (ICA) express data more compactly, but they do not provide much insight into the data's underlying structure, particularly its time-varying structure. Current research using statistical techniques have shown the feasibility of classifying a person's overall cognitive state into a small number of categories from EEG data (Koska et al., 1997; Schmorrow and Stanney, 2008; Trejo et al., 2003), but classification performance suffers dramatically when the data comes from a future point in time where the operational context or environment has changed (Berka et al., 2004; Lan et al., 2005). Understanding and modeling the EEG signal (or SA, workload, and so on) as a collection of independent components, where some components vary with external stimuli and others vary with internal cognitive states, would improve model performance. The data signatures of these separate components vary with time, even with the time frame of a single task, which makes them difficult to identify. While neurons in the brain handle constantly shifting sensory signals without difficulty, learning algorithms that assume a stationary distribution cannot. Such stationary algorithms include statistical regression, hidden Markov model learning (Obermaier et al., 2001; Zhong and Ghosh, 2002), connectionist back propagation, the expectation-maximization (EM) algorithm, support vector machine learning, and other learning algorithms that require large amounts of data to constrain parameters.

Because brain activity associated with processing external stimuli does not remain stationary over time, traditional statistical methods assuming a stationary process can fail. Though stochastic statistical analysis methods such as hidden Markov models do not assume a stationary process, their accuracy depends on the model designer correctly specifying the possible spatial and temporal structure of the underlying process generating the data. An entirely different approach, Finite state machine (FSM) induction, however, models a multidimensional data stream as a collection of independent, time-varying components with computational efficiency, while learning patterns in the data (Hong, Turk, and Huang, 2000). This method can explicitly represent the modeling process and structure visually and in real-time to enhance understanding of the underlying process. The model produces an internal representation, or "memory," by segmenting the time-varying signal in terms of the signal's most frequently occurring parts and detecting temporal relationships between those parts, which may or may not share the same set of spatial variables. In a process similar to data compression, individual neuron-like processing elements come to represent the most frequent components within a signal. FSM induction can quickly partition a multidimensional signal with many variables into groups of correlated variables without any prior information about variable relationships. If the signal represents a collection of independently evolving state trajectories, the algorithm learns to track each trajectory in the group. FSM models can continue tracking changes in cognitive state despite changes in the sensory environment because it can decompose a signal into familiar and unfamiliar parts. The FSM approach has the potential to model brain activity, SA, workload, and so on, as a collection of weakly dependent, stochastic processes, where one or more processes correspond to the socio-technical team internal cognitive state, and other processes map to sensory processing or noise in the signal. By basing the probability of future events on the occurrence of prior events without imposing a limit on how far in the past the prior events have occurred, it can model non-Markov processes such as operator and system cognitive state (Raj et al., 2009). The FSM can remain robust to physiologic perturbations in the system and continue to improve its underlying model over time using new data, as it does not require extended calibrations or closed training sets for operation.

Data and events generated from real-world systems may be sampled or occur at greatly differing time scales. Data sampled at high frequency, for example, may relate to events in a low frequency channel, or some events (that is, anomalies) may occur much more infrequently than others. By representing the brain from the point of view of nonlinear control theory (Cohen and Grossberg, 1983), different neural and behavioral patterns can be recognized as multiple attractors in a multidimensional state/phase space. Activity of these different families of attractors and bifurcations can represent different behaviors (McKenna et al., 1994). Nonlinear data analysis of EEG data (for example) is usually based on the analysis of Lyapunov exponents trying to catch statistically significant changes in degree of chaotic dynamics. Chaotic transitions likely emerge in a wide variety of cognitive phenomena (Bob et al., 2006). Nonlinear observers can improve FSM models of dynamic socio-technical systems by identifying and tracking chaotic attractors corresponding to different mental states automatically. Nonlinear observers not only estimate the state of a nonlinear system, but also can identify mismatches (anomalies) between the model and the actual system. Sliding mode variable structure observers (VSOs) can identify chaotic attractors in the data and augment the FSM of a given model by providing a longer-term memory of anomalous events and structural changes in the underlying system (Drakunov, 1984, 1992; Drakunov and Utkin, 1995). Classical linear observers (also known as Kalman-Bucy or Kalman filters) model systems using additional control inputs to match both the model output and the corresponding real-life system output (that is, the flow of sensor data). For well-known linear models and Gaussian noise distributions with known intensities, this approach can provide optimal estimates of a system state. However, in nonlinear systems, especially those with non-Gaussian noise, nonlinear VSOs with sliding modes perform more effectively. They can update the model when they detect an anomaly, which becomes a known pattern, thus creating a change in the model structure. This property allows reconstructing/ estimating categories of cognitive state that can arise in different situations, such as stress, surprise, uncertainty, and so on, that are not directly modeled but that can be identified or extracted from the data prior to or between tests. An automation system that combines FSM and VSO methods could identify natural variations in human-generated actions and data from background noise, as well as identify infrequent events and shifts in the structure of the system from random perturbations.

HUMAN-CENTERED APPROACHES TO AUGMENTING SOCIO-TECHNICAL TEAM COGNITION AND PERFORMANCE

Modern electronics, radio and computer technology developments have enabled prototype systems that provide the real-time data acquisition and processing needed to support AugCog and adaptive automation in real world, operational environments (Dorneich et al., 2007; Matthews et al., 2007; Raj et al., 2005; Sellers et al., 2009). While earlier adaptive automation approaches required user input to change automation levels (Parasuraman, Sheridan, and Wickens, 2000), current technologies can provide human-centered control of automation that dynamically tracks the status of the human–machine system in order to act as a virtual crewmember (VCM). A VCM adaptively alters multimodal displays and adjusts levels of automated assistance of the system *without* requiring operator intervention (Carvalho, Drakunov, and Raj, 2001; Diethe et al., 2004). For example, a VCM system could automatically take over orientation control of an aircraft to allow a pilot to troubleshoot a multiple system failure, or initiate an emergency descent should the pilot become hypoxic due to loss of cabin pressure. By continuously monitoring the state of the operator and system, and optimizing the interface and level of automated assistance, the VCM would act as an adaptable team member, rather than an independent autonomous control mechanism. By bringing real-time human operator (or operators) sensing into the automation reasoning loop, the VCM can perform more like human crew members when optimizing crew resource management in complex, mundane or emergency control situations, without imposing any additional workload associated with changing automation modes. For VCMs to work in the operational environment, they must exploit management of the operator interfaces to provide a higher level of interaction in order to avoid issues associated with loss of mode awareness (Sarter and Woods, 1995). Such loss can lead the user to assume that the automation will manage certain tasks or that he or she must expend cognitive assets to manage a task that has been automated. Either of these misunderstandings between the socio-technical team can lead to increased workload, poor DE and, potentially, mishaps. By improving the robustness of models of socio-technical team SA, SU and workload (that is, both the human and computational components), the human-centered VCM approach could provide improved workload management to maintain operator engagement, cooperative task sharing, and improved team performance. Indeed, VCMs could encompass systems comprised of many human operators and computational assistants by employing unified models of socio-technical team cognitive state and workload (Niklasson et al., 2007).

With accurate cognitive state detection, the flow of information and level of automation can adjust dynamically to decrease (or increase) operator workload in order to maximize socio-technical team performance based on mission requirements and changes in operator cognitive capacity and reserve. This human-centered approach avoids pitfalls associated with technology-centered approaches to automation typical of many modern systems, which tend to increase operator task load during critical moments when the operator requires the most assistance. Though overly automated systems may lead to vigilance decrement and decreased arousal, adaptive AugCog-based systems can decrease automated assistance to appropriately re-engage the user. The full potential of psychophysiologically driven human-centered systems has not yet transitioned to operational systems, primarily due to limitations in development of robust socio-technical team cognition models and due to transition time for technologies designed for laboratory use to be fielded in real-world environments. Emerging advances, however, in machine learning algorithms can automatically build complex system models from small training sets and operational data in order to continuously learn and tune their underlying models. In addition, advances in physiologic sensing technologies for operational environments will soon allow engineers to incorporate human-centered adjustable autonomy into modern designs to optimize performance of operational human–machine systems.

REFERENCES

Adams, M.J., Tenney, Y.J., and Pew, R.W. (1995). Situation awareness and cognitive management of complex systems. *Human Factors*, 37 (1), 85–104.

Aldrich, T.B., Szabo, S.M., and Bierbaum, C.R. (1989). The development and application of models to predict operator workload during system design. In G. MacMillian, D. Beevis, E. Salas, M. Strub, R. Sutton, and L. Van Breda (Eds.), *Applications of Human Performance Models to System Design*. New York: Plenum Press, pp. 65–80.

Archer, S., Warwick, W. and Oster, A. (2000). *Current Efforts to Model Human Decision-making in a Military Environment*, Paper presented at the Advanced Simulation Technologies Conference, Washington DC.

Barnett, J.A. (1991). Calculating Dempster-Shafer Plausibility, *IEEE Transactions on Pattern Analysis and Machine Intelligence*, 13 (6), 599–602.

Belyavin, A. (2005). Construction of appropriate gauges for the control of Augmented Cognition systems. *Proceedings of the 1st International Conference on Augmented Cognition*, Las Vegas, NV, July 22–27, 2005.

Berka, C., Levendowski, D.J., Cvetinovic, M., Petrovic, M.M., Davis, G.F., Lumicao, M.N., et al. (2004). Real-Time Analysis of EEG Indices of Alertness, Cognition and Memory Acquired with a Wireless EEG Headset. [Special Issue] *International Journal of Human–computer Interaction on Augmented Cognition*, 17(2), 151–170.

Billings, C.E. (1991). *Human-centered Aircraft Automation: A concept and guidelines* (NASA Tech. Memorandum 103885). Moffett Field, CA: NASA Ames Research Center.

Billings, C.E. (1997). *Aviation Automation: The search for a human centered approach*. Mahwah, NJ: Erlbaum

Bob, P., Kukleta, M., Riecansky, I., Susta, M., Kukumberg, P., and Jagla, F. (2006). Chaotic EEG Patterns During Recall of Stressful Memory Related to Panic Attack. *Physiological Research*, 55 (Suppl. 1), S113–S119.

Bogler, P.L. (1987). Shafer-Dempster Reasoning with Applications to Multisensory Target Identification Systems, *IEEE Transactions on Systems, Man, and Cybernetics*, 17 (6), 968–977.

Bowen, S. (2005). *Workload Theories and Models in Task-network Simulations*. Micro Analysis and Design Inc.

Bowers, C., and Deaton, J., Oser, R., Prince, C., and Kolb, M. (1995). Impact of automation on aircrew communication and decision-making performance. *The International Journal of Aviation Psychology*, 5(2), 145–167.

Carvalho, M.M., Drakunov, S.V., and Raj, A.K. (2001). Hierarchical human-in-the-loop control systems: An application for tactile interfaces and adjustable autonomy. *SAE Technical Paper Series* 2001–01–3854.

Chickering, D. and Heckerman, D. (1996). Efficient Approximations for the Marginal Likelihood of Incomplete Data Given a Bayesian Network, *Proceedings of the Conference on Uncertainty in Artificial Intelligence*, 158–168.

Cohen, M. and Grossberg, S. (1983). Absolute stability and global pattern formation and parallel memory storage by competitive neural networks, *IEEE Trans. Syst. Man Cybernet.* SMC-13, 815–826.

Cooper, G.F. (1995). A method for Learning Belief Networks that Contain Hidden Variables. *Journal of Intelligent Information Systems*, 4 (4), 1–18.

Costley, J., Johnson, D., and Lawson, D. (1989). A comparison of cockpit communication B-737-B757. In R.S. Jensen (Ed.), *Proceedings of the Fifth International Symposium on Aviation Psychology* (pp. 413–418). Columbus, OH: Ohio State University.

Dagum, P. and Chavez, R.M. (1993). Approximating Probabilistic Inference in Bayesian Belief Networks, *IEEE Trans. Pattern Analysis and Machine Intelligence*, 15 (3), 246–255.

Darley, J.M. and Gross, P.H. (1983). A hypothesis-confirming bias in labeling effects. *Journal of Personality and Social Psychology*, 44, 20–33.

Diethe, T., Dickson, B.T., Schmorrow, D., and Raley, C. (2004). Toward an augmented cockpit. *HPSAA II conference proceedings* (2), pp. 65–69.

Dorneich, M.C., Mathan, S., Creaser, J., Whitlow, S., and Ververs, P.M. (2005). Enabling improved performance through a closed-loop adaptive system driven by real-time assessment of cognitive state. In *Proceedings of the 1st International Conference on Augmented Cognition*. Mahwah, NJ: Lawrence Erlbaum Associates.

Dorneich, M.C., Whitlow, S., Mathan, S., Ververs, P.M., Erdogmus, D., Adami, A., Pavel, M., and Lan, T. (2007). Supporting Real-time Cognitive State Classification on a Mobile Individual. *Cognitive Engineering and Decision-making (Special Issue on Augmented Cognition: Past, Present, and Future)*.

Doyle J. and Thomason, R.H. (1999). Background to qualitative decision theory, *AI Magazine*, 20 (2), 55–68.

Doyle, M.J. (2008). Modeling the interaction between workload and situation awareness: An overview and future course. In C.A. Ntuen, E. Park and X. Jian (Co-Chairs), *Complex Systems and 2nd Sensemaking of Complex Information: The theory and practice of complexity, human interactions with automation, and making sense of complex information networks*. Symposium conducted at the Human Interaction with Complex Systems and 2nd Sensemaking of Complex Information Annual Conference, Norfolk, VA.

Doyle, M.J. (2009). Decision-making under uncertainty: Trust in automation. In Department of Defense Human Factors Engineering Technical Advisory Group Meeting 61: Unmanned Systems Sub-TAG. Seattle, WA.

Doyle, M.J. and Cole, K. (2008). Impact of automation on decision-making. In C.A. Ntuen, E. Park and X. Jian (Co-Chairs), Complex Systems and 2nd Sensemaking of Complex Information: The theory and practice of complexity, human interactions with automation, and making sense of complex information networks. Symposium conducted at the Human Interaction with Complex Systems and 2nd Sensemaking of Complex Information Annual Conference, Norfolk, VA.

Doyle, M.J., Gould, J.E., Kass, S.J., Raj, A.K., Andrasik, F., and Higgins, J.P. (2009). Psychophysiological Correlates of Cognitive Workload During a Satellite Management Decision-training Task. In *Human Systems Integration: 2+2=22! Greater Than the Sum of Its*

Parts Symposium. Annapolis, Maryland. Sponsored by the American Society of Naval Engineers (ASNE).

Drakunov, S.V. (1984). Adaptive Quasioptimal Filters with Discontinuous Parameters. *Automation and Remote Control,* 44 (9), 1167–1175.

Drakunov, S.V. (1992). Sliding-Mode Observers Based on Equivalent Control Method. In *Proceedings of the 31st IEEE Conference on Decision and Control (CDC),* Tucson, Arizona, December 16–18, pp. 2368–2370.

Drakunov, S.V. and Utkin, V. (1995). Sliding Mode Observers. In *Proceedings of the 34th IEEE Conference on Decision and Control (CDC),* Dec. 13–15, New Orleans, LA, pp. 3376–3378.

Durso, F.T. and Gronlund, S. (1999). Situation awareness. In Durso, F.T., Nickerson, R., Schvaneveldt, R.W., Dumais, S.T., Lindsay, D.S., Chi, M.T.H. (Eds.), *The Handbook of Applied Cognition.* Wiley, New York, pp. 284–314.

Endsley, M.R. (1987). *SAGAT: A methodology for the measurement of situation awareness* (No. NOR DOC 87–83). Hawthorne, CA: Northrop Corporation.

Endsley, M.R. (1988). Situation awareness global assessment technique (SAGAT). *In Proceedings of the National Aerospace and Electronics Conference (NAECON)* (pp. 789–795). New York: IEEE.

Endsley, M.R. (1993). Situation awareness and workload. Flip sides of the same coin. In R.S. Jensen and D. Neumeister (Eds.), *Proceedings of the Seventh International Symposium on Aviation Psychology (pp. 906–911).* Columbus, OH: Ohio State University.

Endsley, M.R. (1995a). Measurement of situation awareness in dynamic systems. *Human Factors,* 37(1), 65–84.

Endsley, M.R. (1995b). Toward a theory of situation awareness in dynamic systems. *Human Factors,* 37 (1), 32–64.

Endsley, M.R. (2000). Direct measurement of situation awareness: Validity and use of SAGAT. In Endsley, M.R., Garland, D.J. (Eds.), *Situation awareness analysis and measurement.* Erlbaum, Mahwah, NJ, pp. 147–174.

Endsley, M.R., Bolté, B., and Jones, D.G. (2003). *Designing for situation awareness: An approach to user-centered design.* Boca Raton, FL. Taylor and Francis.

Endsley, M.R. and Garland, D.J. (Eds.) (2001). *Situation Awareness: Analysis and Measurement.* Mahwah, NJ: Erlbaum.

Endsley, M. and Kiris, E. (1995). The out-of-the-loop performance problem and level of control in automation. *Human Factors,* 37 (2), 381–394.

Engh, T., Yow, A., and Laughery, K.R. (1997). Task Network Modeling of Operator Interaction with an Alarm System. *Proceedings of the Sixth Conference on Human Factors and Power Plants* sponsored by IEEE, June 8–12, 1997, Orlando, FL.

Ephrath, A.R. and Young, L.R. (1981). Monitoring vs. man-in-the-loop detection of aircraft control failures. In J. Rasmussen and W.B. Rouse (Eds.), *Human detection and diagnosis of systems failures* (pp. 143–154). New York: Plenum, pp. 143–154.

Ferguson, G., Allen, J. and Miller, B. (1996). TRAINS-95: Towards a Mixed-Initiative Planning Assistant, Proc. Third Conf. AI Planning Systems (AIPS-96), Menlo Park, CA: AAAI Press, pp. 70–77.

Fiske, S.T. and Taylor, S.E. (1994). *Social Cognition* (2nd. edn). New York: McGraw-Hill.

Gerson, A., Parra, L., and Sajda, P. (2005). Cortical origins of response time variability during rapid discrimination of visual objects. *NeuroImage.* Manuscript under revision.

Glick, P., Zion, C., and Nelson, C. (1988). What mediate sex discrimination in hiring decisions? *Journal of Personality and Social Psychology,* 55, 178–186.

Haddawy, P. (1999). An overview of some recent developments in Bayesian problem-solving techniques. *AI Magazine*, 20 (2), 11–20.

Hamilton, D.L. (1981). *Cognitive processes in stereotyping and intergroup behavior*. Hillside, NJ: Lawrence Erlbaum Associates, Inc.

Hancock, P.A. and Chignell, M.H. (1987). Adaptive control in human–machine systems. In P.A. Hancock (Ed.), *Human Factors Psychology*. North Holland: Elsevier Science Publishers, pp. 305–345.

Hanks, S. and McDermott, D. (1994). `Modeling a dynamic and uncertain world I: symbolic and probabilistic reasoning about change, *Artificial Intelligence*, 66 (1), 1–55.

Honeywell, L.S., Feary, M., Polson, P., and Palmer, E. (2000). Formal method for identifying two types of automation surprises. *Formal Method Auto Surp*, 4, 1–6: Honeywell Publication C69-5370–016.

Hong, P., Turk, M., and Huang, T.S. (2000). Constructing finite state machines for fast gesture recognition. In *Pattern Recognition, 2000. Proceedings. 15th International Conference on*, 3, 691–694.

Hutchins, E. (1995). *Cognition in the Wild*. Cambridge, MA: MIT Press.

Hutchins, E. and Klausen, T. (1992). Distributed cognition in an airline cockpit. In D. Middleton and Y. Engestrom (Eds.), Communication and Cognition at Work. Beverly Hills, CA: Sage Books.

Jentsch, F., Barnett, J., Bowers, C.A., and Salas, E. (1999). Who is flying the plane anyway? What mishaps tell us about crew member role assignment and aircrew situation awareness? *Human Factors*, 41, 1–14.

Kahneman, D. and Tversky, A. (1979). Prospect theory: an analysis of decision under risk. *Econometrics*, 47, 263–291.

Kass, S.J., Doyle, M., Raj, A.K., Andrasik, F., and Higgins, J. (2003). Intelligent adaptive automation for safer work environments. In J.C. Wallace and G. Chen (Co-Chairs), *Occupational health and safety: Encompassing personality, emotion, teams, and automation*. Symposium conducted at the Society for Industrial and Organizational Psychology 18th Annual Conference, Orlando, FL.

Karau, S.J. and Williams, K.D. (1993). Social loafing: a meta-analytic review and theoretical integration. *Journal of Personality and Social Psychology*, 65, 681–706.

Kaber, D.B. and Endsley, M, R. (2004). The effects of level of automation and adaptive automation on human performance, situation awareness, and workload in a dynamic control task. *Theoretical Issues in Ergonomic Science*, 5(2), 113–153.

Kessel, C.J. and Wickens, C.D. (1982). The transfer of failure detection skills between monitoring and controlling dynamic systems. *Human Factors*, 24, 49–60.

Kirlik, A. (1993). Modeling strategic behavior in human–automation interaction: Why "aid" can (and should) go unused. *Human Factors*, 35, 221–242.

Kirlik, A. and Strauss, R. (2006). Situation awareness as judgment I: Statistical modeling and quantitative measurement. *International Journal of Industrial Ergonomics*, 36, 463–474.

Koska, M., Rosipal, R., Konig, A., and Trejo, L. J. (1997). Estimation of human signal detection performance from event-related potentials using feed-forward neural network models. In K. Warwick and M. Kárny (Eds.), *Computer intensive methods in control and signal processing: The curse of dimensionality*. Cambridge. MA: Birkhauser Boston, 129–134.

Kramer A.F. and Parasuraman, R. (2005). Neuroergonomics: application of neuroscience to human factors. In Caccioppo JT, Tassinary LG, Berntson GG (Eds.). *Handbook of psychophysiology* (3rd edn.). New York: Cambridge University Press.

Kramer, A.F., Trejo, L.J., and Humphrey, D. (1996). Psychophysiological measures of human information processing activities: Potential applications to automated systems. In R. Parasuraman and J. Mouloua (Eds.), *Automation and Human Performance: Theory and Applications*. Mahwah, NJ: Lawrence Erlbaum Associates.

Lan, T., Erdogmus, D., Adami, A., and Pavel, M. (2005). Feature selection by independent component analysis and mutual information maximization in EEG signal classification. International Joint Conference on Neural Networks, pp. 3011–3016.

Laughery, R. Scott-Nash, S. Wetteland, C. and Dahn, D. (2000). Task network modeling as the basis for crew optimization on ships. *Proceedings of the Meeting on Human Factors in Ship Design on Automation*, sponsored by the Royal Institute of Naval Architects, London, England.

Laughery, K.R., Drews, C., and Archer, R. (1986). A Micro Saint Simulation Analyzing Operator Workload in a Future Attack Helicopter. In *Proceedings of NAECON Meeting, Dayton, Ohio, May, 1986*.

Layton, C., Smith, P.J., and McCoy, C.E. (1994). Design of a cooperative problem-solving system for en-route flight planning: An empirical evaluation. *Human Factors*, 1, 94–119.

Marek, T. and Pokorski, J. (2004). Quo vadis, ergonomia? — 25 years on. *Ergonomia*, 26, 13–8.

Marshall, L. and Raley, C. (December 2004). Platform-Based Design of Augmented Cognition Systems. Project Report for ENSE623 course at the University of Maryland ISR.

Matthews R, McDonald, N.J., Hervieux, P., Turner, P.J., and Steindorf, M.A. (2007). A wearable physiological sensor suite for unobtrusive monitoring of physiological and cognitive state. *Proceedings of the 29th Annual International Conference of the IEEE Engineering Medicine Biological Society 2007*, 5276–5281.

McKenna, T.M., McMullen, T.A., and Shlesinger, M.F. (1994). The brain as a dynamic physical system. *Neuroscience*, 60, 587–605.

Moray, N. (1986). Monitoring behavior and supervisory control. In K. Boff (Ed.) *Handbook of perception and human performance*. New York: Wiley, pp. 40/1–40/51.

Mosier, K.L., Skitka, L.J., Heers S. and Burdick, M. (1998). Automation bias: Decision-making and performance in high-tech cockpits. *The International Journal of Aviation Psychology*, 8 (1), 47–63.

Mosier, K.L., Skitka, L.J., Dunbar, M., and McDonnell L. (2001). Aircrews and automation bias: The advantage of teamwork? *The International Journal of Aviation Psychology*, 11(1), 1–14.

Mosier, K.L. and Skitka, L.J. (1996). Human decision-makers and automated decision aids: Made for each other? In R. Parasuraman and M. Mouloua (Eds.), *Automation and Human Performance: Theory and Applications*. Mahwah, NJ: Lawrence Erlbaum Associates Inc, pp. 201–220.

National Research Council, Committee on Military and Intelligence Methodology for Emergent Neurophysiological and Cognitive/Neural Science Research in the Next Two Decades (2008). Emerging Cognitive Neuroscience and Related Technologies. National Academies Press. ISBN-10: 0–309–11894–8.

Niklasson, L., Riveiro, M., Johansson, F., Dahlbom, A., Falkman, G., Ziemke, T., Brax, C., Kronhamn, T., Smedberg, M., Warston, H., and Gustavsson, P.M. (2007). A Unified Situation Analysis Model for Human and Machine Situation Awareness. In Koschke, R., Herzog, O., Rödiger, K. -H., and Ronthaler, M. (Eds.), *Trends, Solutions, Applications. Proceedings of SDF 2007*. LNI P-109, pp. 105–110. Köllen Druck and Verlag.

North, R.A., and Riley, V.A. (1989). W/Index: A predictive model of operator workload. In G.R. McMillan, D. Beevin, E. Salas, M.H. Strub, R. Sutton, L. Van Breda (Eds.), *Applications of human performance models to system design. Defense Research Series*, vol. 2, pp. 81–89.

Norman, D.A. (1988). *The Design of Everyday Things*. New York, NY: Doubleday.

Obermaier, B., Guger, C., Neuper, C., and Pfurtscheller, G. (2001). Hidden Markov models for online classification of single trial EEG data. *IEEE Pattern Recognition Letters*, 22 (12), 1299–1309.

Olsen, W.A. and Sarter, N.B. (2001). Management by consent in human–machine systems: When and why they break down. *Human Factors*, 43 (2), 255–266.

O'Donnell, R.D. and Eggemeier, F.T. (1986). Workload assessment methodology. In K.R. Boff, L. Kaufman, and J. Thomas (Eds.), *Handbook f perception and human performance: Volume II. Cognitive processes and performance* (Chap. 42). New York: John Wiley.

Osherson, D., Sharif, E., Krantz, D.H., and Smith, E.E. (January 1997). Probability Bootstrapping: Improving Prediction by Fitting Extensional Models to Knowledgeable but Incoherent Probability Judgments. *Organizational Behavior and Human Decision Processes*, 69 (1), 1–8.

Parasuraman, R., Bahri, T., Deaton, J., Morrison, J.G., and Barnes, M. (1992). *Theory and Design of Adaptive Automation in Aviation Systems*, Naval Air Warfare Center, Warminster, PA, Tech. Rep. NAWCADWAR-92 033–60.

Parasuraman, R., Sheridan, T.B., and Wickens, C.D. (2000). A model for types and levels of human interaction with automation. *IEEE Transactions on Systems, Man, and Cybernetics*, 30, 286–297.

Parasuraman, R., and Riley, V.A. (1997). Humans and Automation: Use, misuse, disuse, abuse. *Human Factors* 39, 230–253.

Parasuraman, R., Mouloua, M., Molloy, R., and Hilburn, B. (1996). Monitoring of automated systems. In R. Parasuraman and M. Mouloua (Eds.), *Automation and human performance: Theory and applications*. Mahwah, NJ: Lawrence Erlbaum Associates, pp. 91–115.

Parasuraman, R., Visser, E. de, and Cosenzo, K. (2007). Adaptive automation for human supervision of multiple uninhabited vehicles: Effects on change detection, situation awareness, and workload. Technical report.

Plott, B., Endsley, M.A., and Strater, L.D. (2004). Integrating SAGAT into human performance models. In D.A. Vincenzi, M. Mouloua, and P. Hancock (Eds.), *HPSAA II, Volume I: Human performance, situation awareness, and automation: Current research and trends*. Mahwah, NJ: Lawrence Erlbaum and Associates, Inc.

Prinzel L.J., Freeman, F.G., Scerbo, Mikulka, P., and Pope A.T. (2000). A Closed-Loop System for Examining Psychophysiological Measures for Adaptive Task Allocation. *The International Journal of Aviation Psychology*, 10 (4), 393–410.

Raj, A.K., Bonnlander, B.V., Drakunov, S.V. and Kitchen-McKinley, S.J. (2009). Brain Activity Modeling of Multisensory Interface Effectiveness. In *Proceedings of the 2009 Chemical and Biological Defense Science and Technology Conference. Dallas, TX*.

Raj, A. K., Carff, R. W., Johnson, M. J., Kulkarni, S. P., Bradshaw, J. M., and Drakunov, S. V. (2005). A Distributed software agent system for operational environments. In: *Proceedings of the 1st International Conference on Augmented Cognition*. Mahwah, NJ: Lawrence Erlbaum Associates.

Raj A.K., Trejo, L., Higgins, J., Kochavi, K., and Matthews, B. (2006). Embedded Real-Time Advisory System (ERTAS) for Crew-Automation Reliability: Task Performance Effects. In *Proceedings of Habitation 2006*, Orlando, FL 5–8 Feb 06.

Raley, C., Stripling, R., Kruse, A., Schmorrow, D., and Patrey, J. (September 2004). Augmented Cognition Overview: Improving Information Intake Under Stress. *Proceedings of the Human Factors and Ergonomics Society 48th Annual Conference*, New Orleans, LA.

Reason, J. (1987). The psychology of mistakes: A brief view of planning failures. In J. Rasmussen, K, Duncan, and J. Leplat (Eds.), *New Technology and Human Error*. John Wiley: New York, NY, pp. 45–52.

Reeves, L.M., Schmorrow, D.D., and Stanney, K.M. (2007). Augmented cognition and cognitive state assessment technology: Near-term, mid-term, and long-term research objectives. In D.D. Schmorrow and L.M. Reeves (Eds.), *Foundations of Augmented Cognition*. Berlin, Springer, LNAI 4565, pp. 220–230.

Rouse, W.B. (1976). Adaptive allocation of decision-making responsibility between supervisor and computer. In T.B. Sheridan and G. Johannesen (Eds.), *Monitoring behavior and supervisory control*. New York: Plenum, pp. 295–306.

Russell, C.A., Wilson, G.F., Rizki, M.M., Webb, T.S., and Gustafson, S.C. (2005). Comparing classifiers for real time estimation of cognitive workload. In *Proceedings of the 1st International Conference on Augmented Cognition*. Mahwah, NJ: Lawrence Erlbaum Associates.

Sarter, N.B. and Woods, D.D. (1991). Situation Awareness: A Critical But Ill-Defined Phenomenon. *International Journal of Aviation Psychology*, 1(1), 45–57.

Sarter, N.B. and Woods, D.D. (1995). How in the world did we ever get into that mode? Mode error and awareness in supervisory control. *Human Factors* 37 (1), 5–19.

Sarter, N.B. and Woods, D.D. (1997). Team play with a powerful and independent agent: Operational experiences and automation surprises on the Airbus A-320. *Human Factors*, 39, 553–569.

Scerbo, M.W. (1996). Theoretical perspectives on adaptive automation. In R. Parasuraman and M. Mouloua (Eds.), *Automation and human performance: Theory and applications*. Mahwah, NJ: Lawrence Erlbaum Associates, pp. 37–63.

Scerbo, M.W. (2006). Adaptive Automation. In R. Parasuraman and M. Rizzo (Eds.), *Neuroergonomics: The Brain at Work (Oxford Series in Human-Technology Interaction)*.

Scerbo, M.W., Freeman, F., and Mikulka, P. (2000). A Biocybernetic System for Adaptive Automation. In R.W. Backs and W. Boucsein (Eds.), *Engineering Psychophysiology*. Mahwah, NJ: Lawrence Erlbaum Associates, Inc, pp. 241–253.

Scerbo, M.W., Freeman, F., Mikulka, P., Parasuraman, R., Di Nocero, F., and Prinzel III, L. (2001). *The Efficacy of Psychophysiological Measures for Implementing Adaptive Technology*. NASA/TP-2001–211018 [Electronic Version] retrieved February 23, 2002. http://aerade. cranfield. ac. uk/subjectlisting/human. html.

Schmorrow, D.D. and Kruse, A. (2004). Augmented Cognition. In W. Bainbridge (Ed.), *Berkshire Encyclopedia of Human–computer Interaction: When science fiction becomes science fact*. Berkshire Publishing Group, pp. 54–59.

Schmorrow, D.D., Stanney, K.M., Wilson, G., and Young, P. (2005). Augmented cognition in human-system interaction. In G. Salvendy (Ed.), *Handbook of human factors and ergonomics* (3rd edn). New York: John Wiley.

Schmorrow, D.D. and Stanney, K.M. (Eds.) (2008). *Augmented cognition: a practitioner's guide*. Santa Monica, CA: Human Factors and Ergonomics Society.

Scott-Nash, S., Carolan, T., Humenick, C., Lorenzen, C., and Pharmer, J. (2000). The Application of a Validated Performance Model to Predict Future Military System Capability. In the *Proceedings of the 2000 Interservice Industry Training Systems Conference*, Orlando, Florida.

Sellers, E.W., Turner, P., Sarnacki, W.A., McManus, T., Vaughan, T.M., and Matthews, R. (2009). A Novel Dry Electrode for Brain-Computer Interface. In J.A. Jacko (Ed.), *Human–computer Interaction*. San Diego: Springer.

Sheridan, T.B. (2002). *Humans and Automation: system design and research issues*. Santa Monica CA: John Wiley and Sons, Inc.

Sheridan, T.B. and Verplank, W.L. (1978). *Human and computer control of undersea teleoperators.* Cambridge, MA: MIT, Man Machine Systems Laboratory.

Sherry, L. and Polson, P. (1999). Shared models of flight management systems vertical guidance. *International Journal of Aviation Psychology- Special Issue: Aircraft Automation.* NY: L. Erlbaum.

Silver, R., Boahen, K., Grillner, S., Kopell, N., and Olsen, K.L. (2007). Neurotech for Neuroscience: Unifying Concepts, Organizing Principles, and Emerging Tools. *The Journal of Neuroscience,* 27 (44), 11807–11819.

Skitka, L.J., Mosier, K.L., and Burdick, M. (1999). Does automation bias decision-making? *International Journal of Human–computer Studies,* 51, 991–1006.

Snow, M.P., Barker, R.A., O'Neill, K.R., Offer, B.W., and Edwards, R.E. (2006). Augmented Cognition in a Prototype Uninhabited Combat Air Vehicle Operator Console. *Proceedings of the 2nd Annual Augmented Cognition International Conference.* San Francisco, CA, Nov. 12–15, 2006.

St. John, M., Kobus, D.A., and Morrison, J.G. (December 2003). DARPA Augmented Cognition Technical Integration Experiment (TIE), available at http://handle. dtic. mil/100. 2/ ADA420147. Last accessed November 20, 2005.

Stanners, M. and H.T. French (2005). *An empirical study of the relationship between situation awareness and decision-making.* Commonwealth of Australia. DSTO Systems Sciences Laboratory.

Stoyenko, A.D., Laplante, P.A., Harrison, R., and Marlowe, T.J. (December 1994). Engineering of Complex Systems: A Case for Dual Use and Defense Technology Conversion. *IEEE Spectrum,* 31 (11), 32–39.

Trejo, L.J., Wheeler, K.R., Jorgensen, C.C., Rosipal, R., Clanton, S., Matthews, B., Hibbs, A.D., Matthews, R., and Krupka, M. (2003). Multimodal neuroelectric interface development. *IEEE Transactions on Neural Systems and Rehabilitation Engineering,* 11(2), 199–204.

Trejo, L.J., Kochavi, R., Kubitz, K., Montgomery, L.D., Rosipal, R., and Matthews, B. (2004). (Submitted to *Psychophysiology* 41:S86). Measures and models for estimating and predicting cognitive fatigue. Paper read at the 44th Annual Meeting of the Society for Psychophysiology at Santa Fe, NM October 20–24, 2004.

Tsang, P.S. and Wilson, G.F. (1997). *Mental workload. Handbook of human factors and ergonomics.* (Chap. 13). New York: John Wiley.

Wagner, A.R. (1976). Priming in STM: An information processing mechanism for self-generated or retrieval generated depression in performance. In T.J. Tighe and R.N. Leaton (Eds.), *Habituation: Perspectives from child development, animal behavior, and neurophysiology.* Hillsdale, NJ: Erlbaum, 1976.

Wickens, C.D. (1980). The structure of attentional resources. In R.S. Nickerson (Ed.), *Attention and performance VIII.* Hillsdale, NJ: Erlbaum, 239–257.

Wickens, C.D. (1991). *Engineering psychology and human performance.* New York: Harper Collins.

Wickens, C.D. (1992). *Engineering psychology and human performance* (2nd edn.). New York: Harper Collins.

Wickens, C.D., Gordon, S.E., and Liu, Y. (1997). *An Introduction to Human Factors Engineering.* New York, NY: Addison-Wesley Educational Publishers Inc.

Wickens, C.D. and Flach, J.M. (1988). Information processing. In E.L. Weiner and D.C. Nagel (Eds.), *Human Factors and Aviation.* San Diego, CA: Academic, pp. 111–156.

Wiener E.L. and Curry, R.E. (1980). Flight deck automation: Promise and Problems. *Ergonomics,* 23, 995–1011.

Wiener, E.L. (1989). *Human factors of advanced technology ("glass cockpit") transport aircraft.* NASA Contractor Report 117528. Moffett Field, CA: NASA Ames Research Center.

Zachary, W., Campbell, G., Laughery, R., and Glenn, F. (1998). *Application of Human Modeling Technology to the Design, Operation, and Evaluation of Complex Systems*: [Technical Memo No. 980727. 9705]; CHI Systems, Inc., Lower Gwynedd, PA.

Zhong, S. and Ghosh, J. (2002). HMMs and Coupled HMMs for multichannel EEG classification. International Joint Conference on Neural Networks 2002, pp. 1154–1159.

3

Automation and Situation Awareness

Anke Popken and Josef F. Krems

INTRODUCTION

The increase in mobility and in use of road transport poses serious safety and environmental challenges on society at the beginning of the twenty-first century. In Europe, the number of cars per thousand people has increased from 232 in 1975 to 460 in 2002. Besides economic and environmental problems (congestion, fuel consumption, emissions), the high number of accidents caused traffic safety to be a key topic on the agenda of the European Commission's actions. 1,300,000 accidents happen on the European roads per year, involving 40,000 deaths and 1,700,000 injuries. In 2001, the European Commission issued a White Paper with the ultimate objective to halve the number of road traffic injuries by 2010. As partial fulfillment of this objective, in 2005, the Commission has launched the Intelligent Car Initiative "Raising Awareness of Information and Communication Technologies (ICT) for smarter, safer, and cleaner vehicles." Such Intelligent Transport Systems (ITS) include various categories of system applications making use of the latest developments in information and communication technologies to interact between the car driver, the vehicle, and the road environment as well as between vehicles (vehicle-to-vehicle communication) and between vehicle and road infrastructure such as traffic management systems (Archer, 2000). Thus, ITS are envisaged to have the potential to increase the overall efficiency and the productivity of the transport system, to use energy efficiently, to reduce environmental pollution, and to improve traffic safety.

Improving traffic and driver safety is the ultimate objective of a specific category of intelligent systems implemented in the vehicle termed "Advanced Driver Assistance Systems" (ADAS). ADAS aim at assisting the driver by providing real-time feedback and (safety) warnings and/or by directly intervening in driving within different time-horizons in order to prevent accidents, for example, by initiating braking in order to avoid a collision or by automating driving subtasks such as headway maintenance or lane keeping. Driven by the fact that human (driver) errors contribute to 93 percent of all accidents and that it is the main underlying cause in three-quarters of these cases (for example, GIDAS database), the rationale behind ADAS is to reduce driver stress and errors, increase driver comfort, and thereby avoid accidents (for example, Brookhuis and De Waard, 2005; Nilsson, 2005; Stanton and Young, 1998).

Thus, today a number of systems and functions are available on the market, as the trend goes towards an increasing automation of functions and assistance in more and more complex driving situations such as lane changes and intersections (for example, Carsten, 2005; Janssen, Wierda, and Van der Horst, 1995; Marchau and Van der Heijden, 2000; Walker, Stanton, and Young, 2001).

This trend towards increasing automation of the driving task shows similarities with technological developments in other transport areas like aviation and air traffic control in the 1980s and 1990s (Hancock and Parasuraman, 1992). There, it became apparent that automation does not simply supplant human activity, but changes the nature of tasks that often leads to unanticipated consequences for human performance and underlying cognitive processes (Parasuraman and Mouloua, 1996; Parasuraman, Sheridan, and Wickens, 2000). Leading researchers have suggested to learn from automation issues in other transport areas and to take the human-factors insights, proactively rather than retroactively, into account in the design of ADAS (Hancock and Parasuraman, 1992). The "human factor" is widely acknowledged nowadays by manufacturers and researchers who foster a "human-centered" or "driver-centered" design of ADAS (for example, Cacciabue and Martinetto, 2004; Goodrich and Boer, 2003; Hancock, Parasuraman, and Byrne, 1996; Tango and Montanari, 2006) albeit some persistent uncertainties regarding the application of concepts and methods (Cacciabue, 2006).

One major concern with regard to automation is the so-called "out-of-the-loop performance" often documented by the difficulty of human operators to detect system malfunctions or automation failures when they do not actively (manually) control a process (Endsley and Kiris, 1995; Kessel and Wickens, 1982; Metzger and Parasuraman, 2005; Molloy and Parasuraman, 1996; Parasuraman, Molloy, Mouloua, and Hilburn, 1996; Parasuraman, Molloy, and Singh, 1993; Parasuraman, Mouloua, and Molloy, 1996; Skitka, Mosier, and Burdick, 2000; Wickens and Kessel, 1981). This difficulty is generally attributed to a lack of involvement of the human operator in the automation-controlled processes inherent in the shift from active to supervisory control (Sheridan, 1997). A number of cognitive and motivational factors accompanying humans' adaptation to the changing task demands are hypothesized to contribute to out-of-the-loop performance, among them vigilance problems associated with excessive system monitoring demands or due to underload and boredom, an inaccurate or incomplete mental representation of the current situation (Situation Awareness), over-reliance on automation, and inappropriate trust in system capabilities. Those adaptation effects are insofar problematic as, despite the sophistication of current technologies, systems often do not meet the requirement of working completely reliable in any type of expected and unforeseen conditions characterizing highly dynamic environments such as road traffic (Parasuraman et al., 2000).

In consideration of the increasing automation of the driving task, over-reliance on a driver assistance system's actions, accompanied by an incomplete mental representation of the current driving situation (Situation Awareness) might cause major safety concerns based on the requirement that drivers must be prepared to intervene appropriately to take manual control in case of a system failure (Brookhuis and De Waard, 2005; Carsten and Nilsson, 2001; De Waard, Van der Hulst, Hoedemaeker, and Brookhuis, 1999; Nilsson, 2005; Stanton and Young, 1998).

In general, reliance on an assistance system is operationally defined as the extent to which a system is used by operators (for example, Dzindolet, Peterson, Pomranky, Pierce, and Beck, 2003; Dzindolet, Pierce, Beck, and Dawe, 2002; Lee and Moray, 1992, 1994; Parasuraman and Riley, 1997; Riley, 1996). Rather than a discrete decision of engaging and disengaging in automation, reliance reflects a graded process of operators allocating control between themselves and a system (Lee and See, 2004). A number of empirical studies have demonstrated the strong influence of system characteristics on operator reliance. The reliability of a system's performance was found to affect human trust in the system (Lee and Moray, 1992; Muir and Moray, 1996), which in turn guided reliance (Muir and Moray, 1996). In general, people tend to rely on systems they trust, and tend to reject systems they distrust. Furthermore, an inverse relationship was found between reliance on a system and operators' monitoring of its behavior (Muir and Moray, 1996). It is hypothesized that high reliance on a system negatively affects operators' Situation Awareness (Sarter and Woods, 1991; Scerbo, 1996) because operators invest less effort in updating an accurate and complete mental representation of the components of a situation controlled by the system.

In the following, existing theoretical accounts and empirical research on reliance and Situation Awareness in the context of automation (mainly in the area of aviation and process control) are summarized. Emphasis is placed on the influence of system characteristics like its performance and the design of the human–machine interaction, especially the level of automation. It is hypothesized that reliance evolves from the dynamic interaction of system, operator, and context characteristics that affect cognitive, motivational, and social processes that in turn influence reliance. After that, empirical studies on drivers' reliance and Situation Awareness when driving with driver assistance systems are reviewed in more detail.

AUTOMATION AND CHANGES IN OPERATORS' LEVEL OF TASK ENGAGEMENT

Automation can be defined as "a system that accomplishes (partially or fully) a function that was previously, or conceivably could be, carried out (partially or fully) by a human operator" (Parasuraman et al., 2000, p. 287). Automation of functions is rarely realized in an all-or-none fashion, but can rather be characterized by a continuum of levels corresponding to varying degrees of computer vs. human operator autonomy (Sheridan and Verplanck, 1978).

According to Parasuraman et al. (2000), automation can be applied to different stages of human information processing and action regulation. According to their model, the following four types of functions can be automated to different degrees: (1) information acquisition; (2) information analysis; (3) decision and action selection; and (4) action implementation. Thus, systems can be distinguished according to the degree to which they automate each of these four functions. For example, an automobile night vision enhancement system may support the driver by presenting an additional infrared-image of the road scene in order to ease the detection of pedestrians at night, corresponding to a high level of information acquisition automation. Alternatively, the system may not provide an extra-image of the road scene, but solely draw the drivers' attention to pedestrians once detected by an internal image processing algorithm, for example, by highlighting them in the windscreen or by presenting an auditory warning. This would correspond to low automation of information acquisition and high automation of information analysis.

Parasuraman et al. (2000) propose to use their model of types and levels of automation as a framework for the decision to which degree particular functions should be automated in a given task context. While it is undisputable that automation is mostly beneficial for human performance when it works properly problems arise from the fact that automated systems are rarely completely reliable. Full automation not only requires the technical ability to deal with all types of known errors, but also the ability to handle unforeseen faults and events. This requirement goes beyond the ability of most intelligent systems. There has been a growing research interest in how humans adapt to automation, given that they have to be able to intervene and to resume manual control in cases of automation failures or malfunctions. Of major concern is the operators' declining level of task engagement as a major hypothesized contributor for the out-of-the-loop performance problem. Parasuraman at al.'s taxonomy and those of others (for example, Endsley and Kaber, 1999) are based on the justified assumptions that the more automation intervenes in the human control processes, the more difficulties will human operators have to stay "in the loop," that is, to maintain a high level of task involvement. Automation applied to higher-level cognitive processes (such as information analysis and decision-making) is expected to be particularly harmful for the operators' ability to stay in the loop and to detect and react efficiently to automation malfunctions (Parasuraman and Wickens, 2008). Two concepts related to the degree of operators' involvement in a task when assisted by an automated system will be the focus of this chapter. The first one is operators' reliance on automation, and the second one is operators' Situation Awareness.

Reliance on automation will be defined here as the deliberate act of allocating varying levels of control to an automated system. Inherent in this conceptualization of reliance is the assumption that to the extent an operator decides to allocate control to a system, she or he will be less likely to actively engage in the respective task (assisted by automation), will increasingly hand over responsibility for maintaining overall performance to the system, and will invest less effort in critically monitoring and examining the appropriateness of the system's actions or behavior. Thus, reliance refers to the operators' efforts to stay actively involved in a task when this task is automated to a lower or greater extent.

There are concerns that operators may increasingly rely on automation when a greater portion of a task is automated, also referred to as over-reliance or misuse of automation (Parasuraman and Riley, 1997; Sheridan and Parasuraman, 2005). Such concerns are supported by empirical studies in which the reliability of an automated system was manipulated. Those studies have shown that operators were more likely to allocate control to a system, invested less effort in system monitoring, and had more difficulties in detecting system malfunctions the higher the reliability of the automated system. Thus, the reduced necessity for manual control or intervention in highly reliable and highly automated systems can be assumed to foster operators' reliance on automation.

The second cognitive psychological concept related to the degree of the operators' involvement in a task is Situation Awareness. *Situation Awareness* refers to the operators' maintenance of a coherent and comprehensive understanding (mental representation) of the current situation (Endsley, 2000b). The availability of a current mental representation of the situation is regarded as prerequisite for the operators' ability to detect and to react to unforeseen critical events such as automation failures. Based on cognitive theoretical frameworks it can be predicted that automation interrupts the cognitive processes necessary to achieve and maintain Situation Awareness.

SITUATION AWARENESS

What is Situation Awareness?

The term Situation Awareness has emerged from aviation psychology in the 1980s in order to account for human errors that occurred in connection with modern aircraft technologies and apparently resulted from pilot's insufficient understanding of the current situation, including a lack of awareness about the state of various automated system components. Situation Awareness (SA) thus is related to the ability of an operator to achieve and maintain a current and comprehensive understanding of the situation while interacting with an increasing number of automated systems. Meanwhile, SA has been applied to many areas in which operators act in complex dynamically changing environments and where automation of task processes becomes more and more prevalent (Durso and Sethumadhavan, 2008; Wickens, 2008). While the intuitive notion of "knowing what is going on around you" (Endsley, 2000b, p. 5) as a prerequisite for successful performance is most widely accepted by human factors researchers; the status of SA as a concept, its definition, and measurement is still subject to an ongoing debate (for example, Dekker and Hollnagel, 2004; Durso, Rawson, and Girotto, 2007; Flach, 1995; Rousseau, Tremblay, and Breton, 2004; Sarter and Woods, 1991; Tenney and Pew, 2006).

The most influencing definition was given by Mica Endsley who defined SA as "the (1) perception of the elements in the environment within a volume of time and space, (2) the comprehension of their meaning and the (3) projection of their status in the near future" (Endsley, 1995b, p. 36). Other definitions of SA have mostly adhered to this conceptual understanding, although they differ in the proposed linkage of SA to other cognitive concepts (such as attention, perception, and working memory) and its integration in existing cognitive psychological theories (such as information processing, decision-making). Maybe the most apparent divergence in conceptual definitions of SA refers to the *product* or *process* aspect of SA, that is, whether SA is regarded as a state of knowledge—a snapshot of the operators' momentary mental representation of the situation (for example, Endsley, 1995b), or as the cognitive processes necessary to achieve and maintain this mental representation (for example, Smith and Hancock, 1995). The view of SA as a product or process has important implications for its operational definition and its measurement. Yet another view is taken by researchers who emphasize the interrelationship between product and process in postulating that the current mental representation affects the process of acquiring and interpreting new information in an ongoing cycle (for example, Adams, Tenney, and Pew, 1995, by referring to Neisser's perceptual cycle). SA could accordingly be defined in line with Sarter and Woods (1991, p. 52) as "the accessibility of a comprehensive and coherent situation representation which is continuously being updated in accordance with the results of recurrent assessments."

The Role of Top-Down and Bottom-Up Attentional Processes in Achieving and Maintaining SA

A central role in this definition has the concept of a dynamic mental representation of the situation, which is also referred to as situation model following Van Dijk and Kintsch's (1983) notion in text comprehension (Baumann and Krems, 2007; Durso and Gronlund, 1999; Durso et al., 2007; Endsley, 1995b). The situation model is dynamic in the sense that it has to be continuously updated through the alternation of top-down and bottom-up attentional processes (Adams et al., 1995; Baumann and Krems, 2007; Durso et al., 2007; Endsley, 1995b, 2000b). The construction of the situational model is based on the perception of new elements in the environment which are then integrated into a coherent mental representation by means of pattern recognition (Durso and Gronlund, 1999; Durso et al., 2007). Pattern recognition happens through the activation of knowledge structures in long-term memory such as mental models and schemata whereby the current situation is connected to prior experiences of similar situations or configurations of elements (Baumann and Krems, 2007). This activation of stored knowledge in long-term memory serves as a basis for the comprehension of the current situation, as a mean for guiding subsequent sampling of the environment, and allows for anticipating of the progress of the current situation. Furthermore, the construction of the situation model is assumed to also activate related action schemata that may directly be implemented based on the recognition of typical situations (Klein, 1993). Baumann and Krems (2007) offer a detailed account of how Situation Awareness may be achieved and maintained while driving and how it may influence action selection by referring to Kintsch's Construction-Integration theory of text comprehension (Kintsch, 1998) and Norman and Shallice's theory of action selection (Norman and Shallice, 1986). McCarley, Wickens, Goh, and Horrey (2002) provide a computational model of SA with particular emphasis on the role of top-down control of attention in achieving and maintaining SA.

The successful alternation of top-down and bottom-up control of attention is seen as a prerequisite for maintaining a high level of Situation Awareness (Adams et al., 1995; Durso et al., 2007; Endsley, 1995b, 2000b). The currency and comprehensiveness of the situation model is necessary for guiding attention to the relevant cues in the environment (top-down control of attention). Similarly, SA requires the sensitiveness for new information (particularly information that contradicts the momentary comprehension of the situation) in order to be able to react to changing situational demands. The successful interplay between top-down and bottom-up processes is especially important in highly dynamic tasks and environments such as driving. In driving, the momentary situation may change possibly in a few seconds depending on the behavior of other traffic participants, demanding adaptive responses from the driver including the reformulation of action goals. Nilsson (2005) described the role of top-down and bottom-up processes while driving: First, "driving includes continuous monitoring of relevant parts of the environment. The driver has to know *where and when* to search (mainly look) for and acquire necessary information" (p. 294). Second, "the driver must be able to distinguish necessary and important information from irrelevant information for the task (trip) at hand. Therefore, car driving includes *selection* of relevant information from a 'noisy' whole, meaning that the driver has to know *what* information is important and of relevance in various occasions and situations" (p. 294). Finally, because driving is a highly dynamic task and depends on the interaction with other road users, there exists a high degree of uncertainty. Therefore, "car driving includes readiness for unexpected situations. The driver has to be prepared to revise and change planned actions, even if they are based on 'correct' predictions and interpretations based on previous knowledge and experience, because situations not always develop accordingly and 'as usual'" (p. 294). Whereas the first two points made by Nilsson highlight the role of expectancies or top-down processes in directing attention, the third point accounts for the importance of bottom-up processes in updating the situation model.

Automation and Situation Awareness

Automation results in changing task demands and therefore affects the human control processes that are normally involved when operators perform a task manually. Because of the goal-driven nature of attention, automation can be also expected to influence the control of attention as a central mechanism that enables humans to perform tasks. Automation may have positive as well as negative effects on operators' SA.

The Enhancement in SA Due To Lower Mental Workload with Automation

The positive effects of automation on SA are generally attributed to its potential to relieve the operator from mental workload. The process of building up and maintaining a high and accurate level of SA can be considered a resource intensive process (Endsley, 1995b; Wickens, 2001). Working memory plays a central role in this regard. As Baumann and Krems (2007) noted, "working memory resources are necessary for associating perceived elements in the environment with knowledge stored in long-term memory, for integrating these new elements in the current situation model, for removing irrelevant elements from the situation model, for keeping the information in the situation model available for the selection of appropriate actions, for monitoring the selection and execution of actions and so on" (p. 259). The limited capacity of working memory therefore acts as a bottleneck in achieving and maintaining a high level of SA. Thus, automation may lead to higher levels of SA by reducing mental workload and enabling the operator to invest more cognitive resources in the maintenance of SA. Empirical evidence for the beneficial effect of automation on SA was for example found in a study by Ma and Kaber (2005) who studied the effects of driving with an ACC system and concurrent cellphone use on drivers' mental workload and SA. A product-oriented, memory-based measure of SA (SAGAT—Situation Awareness Global Assessment Technique, Endsley, 1995a) was used by assessing participants' responses to queries referring to Endsley's three levels of SA after freezing the simulation. Level 1 *(perception)* queries required recalling car locations and colors of traffic signs they had passed. Level 2 *(comprehension)* queries required participants to identify necessary driving behaviors in order to improve the progress of the current situation (for example, acceleration, braking, and so on). Level 3 *(anticipation)* required participants to project times to certain events (for example, time to the next turn and so on). Ma and Kaber (2005) found that driving with ACC reduced drivers' mental workload compared to driving without ACC, and SA accordingly increased across all three levels. This result was interpreted in the way that the ACC decreased demands associated with continuous speed and headway control, and therefore allowed drivers to invest more resources in the maintenance of SA.

Support for the view that reductions in mental workload help operators to maintain higher levels of SA was also found in a study by Endsley and Kaber (1999). Participants reported lower workload when the decision-making aspect of a simulated radar-monitoring task was automated, and their level 2 SA was superior compared to other forms of human–automation control allocations. However, this higher level of SA did not automatically lead to better performance when control was completely returned to participants at different times during the experiment.

However, other research has shown that reduction of mental workload does not necessarily lead to improved SA. Kaber and Endsley (2004) found that improvements in SA with intermediate levels of automation in a dynamic control task were not related to reductions in mental workload. Endsley and Kiris (1995) also found that changes in level 2 SA (situation comprehension) with varying levels of automation in a decision task were unrelated to reported mental workload.

Vigilance-Related Impairments in SA and Motivational Factors

The reduction of mental workload is not necessarily beneficial for human performance. Especially high automation levels and highly reliable systems minimize the demands for manual control and may therefore lead to underload, a decline in arousal, and impair the operators' ability for vigilant monitoring. The maintenance of SA, that is, the need to continuously update the situation model however requires sustained attention. Thus, in the same way as automation may lead to impairments in sustained attention, it may also impair SA.

According to Endsley (1996), over-reliance on automation and/or complacency is the primary cause for vigilance-related impairments in SA. Thus, she assumes that complacency and over-reliance reduce the operators' efforts for vigilant monitoring and for continuously updating the situation model. In other words, the primary reason for vigilance-related impairments in SA is motivational in nature and results from the decision of the operator to invest fewer cognitive resources in maintaining SA than would be optimal. Although it can be assumed that both reliance on automation and complacency may negatively affect SA, the nature of the processes leading to impairments of SA may be different. This argues for keeping the two concepts and its hypothesized causal relation to SA distinct from another. Complacency is an attitude towards automation and may result in high level of reliance that is, in the allocation of a considerable amount of control to an automated system. Whereas the impairment of SA due to a complacent attitude can be considered to be clearly motivational in nature, changes in SA due to reliance can be assumed to be caused both by cognitive and motivational factors. Cognitive factors can be referred to as changes in information processing and attentional control related to the allocation of control to a system. Motivational factors are related to operators' attitudes towards automation that influence their intention to rely on a system (such as trust and complacency).

The impairment of SA due to complacency appears to be a widely acknowledged fact in the literature, although it has been rarely empirically tested. Lower levels of SA are often attributed post-hoc to a high level of trust in a system and as a consequence, to complacency. Normally however, neither trust nor complacency (for example, by assessing operators' system monitoring strategies; cp. Moray, Inagaki, and Itoh, 2000) are tried to be measured directly. Thus, there is little empirical evidence supporting the assumed negative relationship between complacency and SA, although it has some plausibility.

The Impairment in SA Due To Changes In Cognitive Processes

Automation and reliance (as the action of allocating control to a system) can be assumed to influence the operators' cognitive processes underlying performance. Automation changes the operators' task(s) usually from active controlling to monitoring the automated functions. Consequently, automation changes the performance requirements and accordingly, affects humans' information processing and the control of attention as a basic mechanism for resource allocation. It was already mentioned above that the successful alternation of top-down and bottom-up control of attention is a prerequisite for the maintenance of a current and comprehensive situation model.

Changes in information processing and in the control of attention may result from changes in the task goal structure and/or the disruption of control processes under automated conditions.

CHANGES IN THE TASK GOAL STRUCTURE DUE TO AUTOMATION

Automated systems always rely on some sensory input and internal information processing algorithms that are applied to this sensory input. That is, some sort of information analysis is an integral part of all automated systems regardless of which function they are designed to automate. Therefore, automation changes or reduces demands associated with the acquisition and analysis of certain types of information for the operator as these functions are (more or less sufficiently) performed by the system. It can be expected that through these changes in information processing demands the informative value of certain perceptual information (cp. McCarley et al., 2002) changes in that it may become less relevant for performance under automated conditions. For example, when driving with a lane keeping assistance system, perceptual information related to lateral control may become less relevant over time. As a consequence, fewer attentional resources may be allocated to the processing of this information which may in turn hinder appropriate bottom-up control of attention, for example, when unexpected situations occur that demand for the driver's intervention (for example, obstacles on the road that are not recognized by the lane keeping assistance system).

Hoc et al. (2006) performed a driving study in which they investigated whether driving with a Heading Control (HC) system affected drivers' processing of visual information necessary for either lateral or longitudinal control of the vehicle in curves. Specifically, they compared drivers' perception of visual information located either near to the tangent point of a curve (assumed to be critical for lateral control of the vehicle) or located in the straight-ahead visual field (assumed to be critical for speed adjustment). For this purpose, they placed non-familiar advertising logos near to these two interesting points. After having passed the curves, they asked drivers to stop and to give subjective ratings of how sure they were about having seen these logos. Results showed that drivers had higher recognition scores when driving with the HC system than without, which was however mainly attributed to technical problems and an effect of the procedure. (Apparently, certainty judgments were only available for 6 out of 12 drivers who drove first without assistance and then with the HC system. Thus it was assumed that these drivers were more prepared to recall the logos when they encountered the situation a second time while driving with the HC system). Interestingly (although no inferential statistics were reported), when driving with the HC system, participants judged to have seen the logos placed straight ahead with higher certainty than the logos located near to the tangent point. The reverse was found for the manual driving condition, for which certainty scores were higher for logos located near to the tangent point than for logos located straight ahead. Although doubts may be raised regarding the subjective nature of the measurement, results seem to be in accordance with the assumption that active processing of information related to an automated subtask (in this case: lateral control) may be reduced because it is no longer relevant for performance of the remaining task components (in this case: longitudinal control). It must be added that Hoc et al. (2006) attributed this effect not to changes in cognitive processes, but to complacency.

THE DISRUPTION OF CONTROL PROCESSES DUE TO AUTOMATION

On the other hand, automation intervenes in the control processes that are normally involved when operators perform a task manually and therefore interrupts the feed-forward and feed-backward control mechanism that are necessary for keeping an operator actively involved in a task. Recently, the driving task has been described as a set of simultaneous, interrelated, and layered control processes (Engström and Hollnagel, 2007). Within the Extended Control Model (ECOM) four simultaneously active layers of control are distinguished: tracking, regulating, monitoring, and targeting. The outputs of a higher control loop form the objectives (goals, criteria) of a lower control loop. For example, activities initiated at the regulating level (such as lane changes) affect the activities at the tracking control loop (for example, control of speed and headway). In turn, the input of the lower levels is required for efficient control on higher levels. Today's driver assistance systems mostly automate activities at the tracking control loop, such as longitudinal control (ACC) or lateral control (HC). However, the automation of tracking activities is likely to make control on the higher levels more difficult because important information is filtered out from the dynamic control process (Hollnagel and Bye, 2000; Hollnagel and Woods, 2005). As Hollnagel points out, "the efficiency of regulating requires the input from the tracking activities. If these therefore are heavily automated, regulating is likely to suffer, even though the tracking activities themselves may be efficiently carried out by automation" (Hollnagel, 2002, p. 20). The lacking feedback from the tracking control loop may result in failures in bottom-up control of attention, in that information demanding for changing objectives at the higher control levels is not sufficiently processed. Referring to SA and Norman and Shallice's (1986) theory of action selection, the relevant information may not become activated and therefore not available in the situation model and thus, is not able to trigger the appropriate action schemata.

Several studies were carried out in order to investigate the effects of different levels of automation on operators' SA. Those studies have yielded in part conflicting results demonstrating that there is no simple relationship between the degree of task automation and SA, mental workload, and task performance. Results in fact appear highly dependent on the concrete realization of different levels of automation in specific task settings, the experimental procedure (for example, duration of automated vs. manual control periods), the performance requirements (for example, reward structure), and the methods used to assess SA and mental workload for example.

Endsley and Kiris (1995) investigated the effect of increasing levels of automation in a decision-making task on performance, SA, and mental workload. They found that increasing automation of decision-making was related to increasing impairments in level 2 SA (situation comprehension), but not in level 1 SA (situation perception). Although participants seemed to have perceived the relevant information, they did not develop a higher-level understanding of the situation as the automation increasingly relieved them from the evaluation of decision alternatives and from action implementation. The impairment in level 2 SA was mirrored by the time participants needed to reclaim manual control of the task when the automated decision aid failed. For example, longer task times after automation failure were associated with lower levels of SA. Conflicting results were found by Kaber and Endsley (2004) who compared six levels of automation (from full manual control to full automation) with different degrees of computer assistance in four basic task functions (monitoring, generating, selecting, implementing) involved in a simulated radar-monitoring task. They found that computer assistance in monitoring (sensory processing) and action implementation functions of the task resulted in worse (level 2) SA as compared to assistance in decision-making functions and full automation of the task. However, in manual control periods (described as automation failures), performance was better when assistance was previously applied to sensory functions and action implementation (those levels associated with lower SA). Endsley and Kaber (1999) found that computer assistance primarily in action selection and implementation yielded higher level 2 SA, but mostly worse level 3 SA and were associated with relatively long recovery times in manual control periods.

Kaber, Perry, Segall, McClernon, and Prinzel (2006) investigated the effects of automation of different functions (information acquisition, information analysis, decision-making, action implementation) on SA, mental workload, and performance in an air traffic control simulation. Automation of information acquisition resulted in highest level 1 SA (perception) and automation of action implementation resulted in lowest level 1 SA. Performance was best when automation was applied to information acquisition and action implementation, however, during intermediate manual control periods, performance was worse when automation was formerly applied to decision-making and action implementation.

SUMMARY

In summary, research on the impact of automation on operators' SA has not yielded consistent results. It is predicted that automation affects human information processing and disrupts the top-down and bottom-up control of attention. The active processing of information and the successful interplay of top-down and bottom-up attentional processes are however seen as a prerequisite for maintaining an accurate and comprehensive understanding of the current situation. However, research indicates that the effects of automation on cognitive processes are complex and that automation may not necessarily reduce, but also enhance SA. Several reasons may account for these findings. First, "automation" is a broad term and means different things in different task contexts. Performance requirements of particular types and levels of automation may be different across task contexts and even within one particular context, automation may be realized in different ways (for example, different designs of the human–machine interface) associated with different demands for human information processing. Second, knowledge-based and process-oriented measures may be sensitive to qualitatively different aspects of SA or may dissociate under specific conditions. Most research has focused on changes in operators' state of knowledge rather than on the cognitive processes necessary to achieve this state of knowledge. Often it was found that particular types of automation led to improved SA under normal conditions, but led to degraded operator performance (for example, longer recovery times) during intermediate manual control periods. One explanation could be that the cognitive processes involved in the maintenance of SA were disrupted by automation, but in the same vein did automation help operators to maintain an appropriate state of knowledge about the current situation by supporting them in information analysis or providing them with decision support. However, the taking away of this additional support may have led to impaired performance in periods of manual control.

REFERENCES

Adams, M.J., Tenney, Y.J., and Pew, R.W. (1995). Situation Awareness and the cognitive management of complex systems. *Human Factors, 37*(1), 85–104.

Archer, J. (2000). *Fundamental traffic safety issues concerning the use of Intelligent Transport Systems* (No. CTR2000:06). Stockholm: Royal Institute of Technology Publication.

Baumann, M. and Krems, J.F. (2007). Situation awareness and driving: A cognitive model. In P.C. Cacciabue (Ed.), *Modeling driver behaviour in automotive environments: Critical issues in driver interactions with Intelligent Transport Systems* (pp. 253–265). London: Springer.

Brookhuis, K.A. and De Waard, D. (2005). ADAS` acceptance and effects on behaviour: The consequences of automation. In G. Underwood (Ed.), *Traffic and transport psychology: Theory and application. Proceedings of the ICTTP 2004* (pp. 273–278): Elsevier Ltd.

Cacciabue, P.C. (2006). Editorial: CTW special issue on human-centred design in automotive systems. *Cognition, Technology and Work, 8*(3), 159–160.

Cacciabue, P.C. and Martinetto, M. (2004). Driving support and user-centred design approach: The case of the EUCLIDE anti-collision system. *IEEE International Conference on Systems, Man and Cybernetics*, 6465–6471.

Carsten, O.M.J. (2005). Mind over matter: Who's controlling the vehicle and how do we know. In G. Underwood (Ed.), *Traffic and transport psychology: Theory and application. Proceedings of the ICTTP 2004* (pp. 231–242): Elsevier Ltd.

Carsten, O.M.J., and Nilsson, L. (2001). Safety assessment of driver assistance systems. *European Journal of Transport and Infrastructure Research, 1*(3), 225–243.

De Waard, D., Van der Hulst, M., Hoedemaeker, M., and Brookhuis, K.A. (1999). Driver behavior in an emergency situation in the automated highway system. *Transportation Human Factors, 1*(1), 67–82.

Dekker, S. and Hollnagel, E. (2004). Human factors and folk models. *Cognition, Technology and Work, 6*, 79–86.

Durso, F.T. and Gronlund, S.D. (1999). Situation awareness. In F.T. Durso, R.S. Nickerson, R.W. Schvaneveldt, S.T. Dumais, D.S. Lindsay, and M.T.H. Chi (Eds.), *Handbook of Applied Cognition* (pp. 284–314). New York: Wiley.

Durso, F.T., Rawson, K.A., and Girotto, S. (2007). Comprehension and situation awareness. In F.T. Durso, R.S. Nickerson, S.T. Dumais, S. Levendowski and T.J. Perfect (Eds.), *Handbook of applied cognition* (2nd edn., pp. 163–193). Chichester, UK: Wiley.

Durso, F.T. and Sethumadhavan, A. (2008). Situation Awareness: Understanding dynamic environments. *Human Factors: Golden Anniversary Special Issue, 50*(3), 442–448.

Dzindolet, M.T., Peterson, S.A., Pomranky, R.A., Pierce, L.G., and Beck, H.P. (2003). The role of trust in automation reliance. *International Journal of Human–computer Studies, 58*, 697–718.

Dzindolet, M.T., Pierce, L.G., Beck, H.P., and Dawe, L.A. (2002). The perceived utility of human and automated aids in a visual detection task. *Human Factors, 44*(1), 79–94.

Endsley, M.R. (1995a). Measurement of situation awareness in dynamic systems. *Human Factors, 37*(1), 65–84.

Endsley, M.R. (1995b). Toward a theory of situation awareness in dynamic systems. *Human Factors, 37*(1), 32–64.

Endsley, M.R. (1996). Automation and situation awareness. In R. Parasuraman and M. Mouloua (Eds.), *Automation and human performance: Theory and applications.* (pp. 163–181). Hillsdale, NJ, England: Lawrence Erlbaum Associates, Inc.

Endsley, M.R. (2000b). Theoretical underpinnings of situation awareness: A critical review. In M.R. Endsley, M.R. and D.J. Garland (Eds.), *Situation awareness analysis and measurement* (pp. 3–32). Mahwah, New Jersey: Lawrence Erlbaum Associates. (pp. 3–32).

Endsley, M.R. and Kaber, D.B. (1999). Level of automation effects on performance, situation awareness and workload in a dynamic control task. *Ergonomics, 42*(3), 462–492.

Endsley, M.R. and Kiris, E.O. (1995). The out-of-the-loop performance problem and level of control in automation. *Human Factors, 37*(2), 381–394.

Engström, J. and Hollnagel, E. (2007). A general conceptual framework for modeling behavioural effects of driver support functions. In P.C. Cacciabue (Ed.), *Modeling driver behaviour in automotive environments: Critical issues in driver interactions with Intelligent Transport Systems* (pp. 61–84). London: Springer.

Flach, J.M. (1995). Situation awareness: Proceed with caution. *Human Factors, 37*(1), 149–157.

Goodrich, M.A. and Boer, E.R. (2003). Model-based human-centered task automation: A case study in ACC system design. *IEEE Transactions on Systems, Man, and Cybernetics–Part A: Systems and Humans, 33*(3), 325–336.

Hancock, P.A. and Parasuraman, R. (1992). Human factors and safety in the design of intelligent vehicle-highway systems (IVHS). *Journal of Safety Research, 23*(4), 181–198.

Hancock, P.A., Parasuraman, R., and Byrne, E.A. (1996). Driver-centered issues in advanced automation for motor vehicles. In R. Parasuraman and M. Mouloua (Eds.), *Automation and human performance: Theory and applications* (pp. 337–364). Mahwah, New Jersey: Lawrence Erlbaum Associates, Inc.

Hoc, J.-M., Mars, F., Milleville-Pennel, I., Jolly, É., Netto, M., and Blosseville, J.-M. (2006). Human–machine cooperation in car driving for lateral safety: Delegation and mutual control. *Le Travail Humain, 69*(2), 153–182.

Hollnagel, E. (2002). Cognition as control: A pragmatic approach to the modeling of joint cognitive systems. Retrieved December 17, 2008, from www.ida.liu.se/~eriho/images/IEEE_SMC_Cognition_as_control.pdf.

Hollnagel, E. and Bye, A. (2000). Principles for modeling function allocation. *International Journal of Human–computer Studies, 52*(2), 253–265.

Hollnagel, E. and Woods, D.D. (2005). *Joint cognitive systems: Foundations of cognitive systems engineering*. Boca Raton, FL: Taylor and Francis/CRC Press.

Janssen, W., Wierda, M., and Van der Horst, R. (1995). Automation and the future of driver behavior. *Safety Science, 19*(2), 237–244.

Kaber, D.B. and Endsley, M.R. (2004). The effects of level of automation and adaptive automation on human performance, situation awareness and workload in a dynamic control task. *Theoretical Issues in Ergonomics Science, 5*(2), 113–153.

Kaber, D.B., Perry, C.M., Segall, N., McClernon, C.K., and Prinzel, L.J. (2006). Situation awareness implications of adaptive automation for information processing in an air traffic control-related task. *International Journal of Industrial Ergonomics, 36*(5), 447–462.

Kessel, C.J. and Wickens, C.D. (1982). The transfer of failure-detection skills between monitoring and controlling dynamic systems. *Human Factors, 24*(1), 49–60.

Kintsch, W. (1998). *Comprehension: A paradigm for cognition*. New York, NY: Cambridge University Press.

Klein, G.A. (1993). A recognition-primed decision (RPD) model of rapid decision-making. In G.A. Klein, J. Orasanu, R. Calderwood and C.E. Zsambok (Eds.), *Decision-making in action: Models and methods* (pp. 138–147). Westport, CT, US: Ablex Publishing.

Lee, J.D. and Moray, N. (1992). Trust, control strategies and allocation of function in human–machine systems. *Ergonomics, 35*(10), 1243–1270.

Lee, J.D. and Moray, N. (1994). Trust, self-confidence, and operators' adaptation to automation. *International Journal of Human–computer Studies, 40*, 153–184.

Lee, J.D. and See, K.A. (2004). Trust in automation: Designing for appropriate reliance. *Human Factors, 46*(1), 50–80.

Ma, R. and Kaber, D.B. (2005). Situation awareness and workload in driving while using adaptive cruise control and a cell phone. *International Journal of Industrial Ergonomics, 35*(10), 939–953.

Marchau, V.A.W.J. and Van der Heijden, R.E.C.M. (2000). Introducing advanced electronic driver support systems: An exploration of market and technological uncertainties. *Transport Reviews, 20*(4), 421–433.

McCarley, J.S., Wickens, C.D., Goh, J., and Horrey, W.J. (2002). *A computational model of attention/ situation awareness*. Paper presented at the 46th Annual Meeting of the Human Factors and Ergonomics Society, Santa Monica.

Metzger, U. and Parasuraman, R. (2005). Automation in future air traffic management: Effects of decision aid reliability on controller performance and mental workload. *Human Factors, 47*(1), 35–49.

Molloy, R. and Parasuraman, R. (1996). Monitoring an automated system for a single failure: Vigilance and task complexity effects. *Human Factors, 38*(2), 311–322.

Moray, N., Inagaki, T., and Itoh, M. (2000). Adaptive automation, trust, and self-confidence in fault management of time-critical tasks. *Journal of Experimental Psychology: Applied, 6*(1), 44–58.

Muir, B.M. and Moray, N. (1996). Trust in automation. Part II. Experimental studies of trust and human intervention in a process control simulation. *Ergonomics, Special issue: Cognitive Ergonomics V, 39*(3), 429–460.

Nilsson, L. (2005). Automated driving does not work without the involvement of the driver. In G. Underwood (Ed.), *Traffic and transport psychology: Theory and application. Proceedings of the ICTTP 2004* (pp. 273–301): Elsevier Ltd.

Norman, D.A. and Shallice, T. (1986). Attention to action: Willed and automatic control of behavior. In R.J. Davidson, G.E. Schwartz and D. Shapiro (Eds.), *Consciousness and self-regulation: Advances in research and theory* (vol. 4, pp. 1–18). New York: Plenum Press.

Parasuraman, R., Molloy, R., Mouloua, M., and Hilburn, B. (1996). Monitoring of automated systems. In R. Parasuraman and M. Mouloua (Eds.), *Automation and human performance: Theory and applications* (pp. 91–115). Mahwah, NJ: Lawrence Erlbaum Associates.

Parasuraman, R., Molloy, R., and Singh, I.L. (1993). Performance consequences of automation-induced "complacency." *The International Journal of Aviation Psychology, 3*(1), 1–23.

Parasuraman, R. and Mouloua, M. (Eds.). (1996). *Automation and human performance: Theory and applications*. Mahwah, New Jersey: Lawrence Erlbaum Associates, Inc.

Parasuraman, R., Mouloua, M., and Molloy, R. (1996). Effects of adaptive task allocation on monitoring of automated systems. *Human Factors, 38*(4), 665–679.

Parasuraman, R. and Riley, V. (1997). Humans and automation: Use, misuse, disuse, abuse. *Human Factors, 39*(2), 230–253.

Parasuraman, R., Sheridan, T.B., and Wickens, C.D. (2000). A model of types and levels of human interaction with automation. *IEEE Transactions on Systems, Man, and Cybernetics—Part A: Systems and Humans, 30*(3), 286–297.

Parasuraman, R. and Wickens, C.D. (2008). Humans: Still Vital After All These Years of Automation. *Human Factors: Golden Anniversary Special Issue, 50*(3), 511–520.

Riley, V. (1996). Operator reliance on automation: Theory and data. In R. Parasuraman and M. Mouloua (Eds.), *Automation and human performance: Theory and applications* (pp. 19–35). Mahwah, New Jersey: Lawrence Erlbaum Associates.

Rousseau, R., Tremblay, S., and Breton, R. (2004). Defining and modeling situation awareness: A critical review. In S. Banbury and S. Tremblay (Eds.), *A cognitive approach to situation awareness: Theory and application* (pp. 3–21). Aldershot, UK: Ashgate.

Sarter, N.B. and Woods, D.D. (1991). Situation awareness: A critical but ill-defined phenomenon. *The International Journal of Aviation Psychology, 1*(1), 45–57.

Scerbo, M.W. (1996). Theoretical perspectives on adaptive automation. In R. Parasuraman and M. Mouloua (Eds.), *Automation and human performance: Theory and applications* (pp. 37–63). Mahwah, New Jersey: Lawrence Erlbaum Associates.

Sheridan, T.B. (1997). Supervisory Control. In G. Salvendy (Ed.), *Handbook of human factors* (2nd edn., pp. 1295–1327). New York: John Wiley and Sons.

Sheridan, T.B. and Parasuraman, R. (2005). Human-automation interaction. *Reviews of Human Factors and Ergonomics, 1*, 89–129.

Sheridan, T.B. and Verplanck, W.L. (1978). *Human and computer control of undersea teleoperators* (Tech. Rep.). Cambridge, MA: M.I.T., Man-Machine Laboratory.

Skitka, L.J., Mosier, K., and Burdick, MD (2000). Accountability and automation bias. *International Journal of Human–computer Studies, 52*(4), 701–717.

Smith, K. and Hancock, P.A. (1995). Situation awareness is adaptive, externally directed consciousness. *Human Factors, 37*(1), 137–148.

Stanton, N.A. and Young, M.S. (1998). Vehicle automation and driving performance. *Ergonomics, 41*(7), 1014–1028.

Tango, F. and Montanari, R. (2006). Shaping the drivers' interaction: How the new vehicle systems match the technological requirements and the human needs. *Cognition, Technology and Work, 8*(3), 215–226.

Tenney, Y.J. and Pew, R.W. (2006). Situation awareness catches on. What? So what? Now what? In R.C. Williges (Ed.), *Reviews of human factors and ergonomics* (vol. 2, pp. 89–129). Santa Monica, CA: Human Factors and Ergonomics Society.

Van Dijk, T.A. and Kintsch, W. (1983). *Strategies of discourse comprehension*. New York: Acadamic Press.

Walker, G.H., Stanton, N.A., and Young, M.S. (2001). Where is computing driving cars? *International Journal of Human–computer Interaction, 13*(2), 203–229.

Wickens, C.D. (2001). Workload and situation awareness. In P.A. Hancock and P.A. Desmond (Eds.), *Stress, workload, and fatigue* (pp. 443–450). Mahwah, New Jersey: Lawrence Erlbaum Associates.

Wickens, C.D. (2008). Situation Awareness: Review of Mica Endsley's 1995 articles on Situation Awareness theory and measurement. *Human Factors: Golden Anniversary Special Issue, 50*(3), 397–403.

Wickens, C.D. and Kessel, C. (1981). Failure detection in dynamic systems. In J. Rasmussen and W.B. Rouse (Eds.), *Human detection and diagnosis of system failures. NATO Conference Series* (vol. 15, pp. 155–169): Plenum Press.

4

Human Error, Interaction, and the Development of Safety-Critical Systems

Christopher Johnson

This chapter summarizes the theoretical and practical consequences of human error for the design, operation, and maintenance of interactive systems. The focus is on safety-critical applications, in industries ranging from aviation to healthcare. However, human error has an impact on all systems that require human intervention. Individual failures have enormous financial consequences, although most cost less than the 40.5 billion yen that was lost in 2005 when a Japanese trader agreed to sell 610,000 shares for as little as 1 yen each, rather than one share for 610,000 yen (New York Times, 2005). Human error also has a cumulative effect. Less dramatic errors contribute to the frustration that many computer users experience as they work to complete deadlines and make deliveries in everyday working environments (Reason, 1990). If designers, managers, and regulators can identify those situations in which users are likely to make errors then we can help to minimize their impact (Johnson, 2003). This may save lives, avoid financial disaster or simply increase the sense of satisfaction that users experience when they operate complex systems.

PART 1: WHAT IS ERROR?

This opening section summarizes different perspectives on human error. The aim is to distinguish between different types of failure and also to identify the situations or contexts in which they are likely to occur. There is an increasing recognition that part of the responsibility for human error lies with designers and operators and not just with the end users of interactive systems (Hollnagel, 2009). This joint responsibility can be illustrated by a simple example. If an end user selects the wrong item from a menu then we might say that it was "their fault." If the user had read the manual then they would not have made this mistake. Equally, it can be argued that the menu item should have been given a more appropriate label so that the user never had to refer to the manual in the first place. This joint responsibility for error between the user and designer extends beyond the human–machine interface into the working environment. Many regulatory organizations take an increasingly broad view of the contexts in which errors are likely to occur (Kirwan, 1994). Even if end-users are provided with excellent user interfaces, errors will still happen if people are expected to work in noisy environments or cramped conditions against tight deadlines.

Resilience and the Myth of Expert Performance

It is difficult to understand human error unless we first consider the strengths that justify user involvement in complex tasks (Hollnagel, Woods, and Leveson, 2006). It is important to recognize that people are particularly good at coping with failure. We constantly adapt to problems in our working lives. We learn to operate poorly designed human–machine interfaces. The limitations of previous systems have been well documented in the other chapters of this book. These coping mechanisms help to explain why we find so many legacy applications that continue to be used even though they show no evidence of even the most basic human factors involvement in their design.

Over time users learn through their mistakes (Reason, 1990). They find new ways of doing frequent tasks so that they avoid problems in the user interface. Hence, failure is a necessary component of learning. By making mistakes, users develop expertise and so paradoxically, error is a necessary component of expert performance (Rasmussen, 1983). Over time, frequent computer users will develop higher-level coping strategies that help them to reduce the number of errors that they make and hence to learn to use new systems faster. For instance, many graphical user interfaces deliberately encourage users to experiment with different aspects of their functionality. Desktop publishing systems will automatically update font selections as the user scrolls through a list of options. Frequent users quickly learn how to apply "undo" commands to these selections so that they can get back to the previous version of document if they make a mistake. This supports further experimentation that, in turn, increases familiarity with the system and reduced the likelihood of further errors. Hence, it is possible to identify a "virtuous circle" in which experimentation and error lead to learning and the accumulation of expertise. Equally, one can identify a "vicious circle" in which novice users inadvertently change the font of their document but do not know enough about the user interface to be able to undo the change. This may lead them into further problems as they get further and further away from the original version of their document with every subsequent interaction.

A great deal of attention has recently been devoted to the topic of "resilience engineering" (Hollnagel, Woods, and Leveson, 2006). This assumes that we should focus less on the causes of human error and more on the promotion of recovery actions, such as the application of undo in the previous desktop publishing example. Resilience engineering starts from the assumption that humans are not simply the cause of error, they act as a key means of mitigating failure in complex systems. This is a critical observation (Reason, 2008). For many years, developers have responded to the problem of human error in safety-critical systems by attempting to engineer-out the human involvement in these systems (Dekker, 2006). The argument is made that because even experts make mistakes we should minimize the opportunity for operator error to undermine safety. For this reason, engineers have worked hard to develop autonomous spacecraft, such as NASA's DART or the European Space Agency's Autonomous Transfer Vehicle, they have also developed automated systems that intervene for instance to apply automatic braking equipment in rail applications. However, these systems have had very mixed success. For instance, accidents, and collisions have been caused when automated braking systems have been inadvertently triggered. In other words, removing or restricting operator intervention tends to move the opportunity for error to other areas of the development lifecycle (Johnson, 2003). The end user may not be responsible for particular failures; however, errors tend to occur in the design and maintenance of the automated systems that are assuming new levels of control. It seems likely, therefore, that "human error" will remain a significant concern for the development of complex systems.

Slips, Lapses, Mistakes, and Violations

In this chapter we are mainly concerned with "errors" as opposed to deliberate violations. A violation occurs when users knowingly break a rule (Reason, 1990). These rules may take the form of Standard Operating Procedures (SOPs) that govern the interaction with complex systems in the military, aviation or maritime environments. Other rules stem from the operating requirements placed on companies and individuals by regulatory agencies, for instance within the nuclear industry. Violations can also occur in more "every day" settings—for instance when users ignore security policies by sending unencrypted emails or by accessing social networking sites in company time.

The distinction between errors and violations is not always as clear as it might seem. For instance, users can unwittingly violate rules if they are unaware of them or the rule is not clearly expressed. In such circumstances, it can be argues that an error has occurred rather than a deliberate violation. In other words, it is difficult to distinguish between errors and violations because these two forms of failure stem from different intentions even though the observable actions can be identical.

One way of identifying errors is to break down a task into its component steps (Kirwan, 1994). Any departure from those steps can be seen as a potential failure on the part of the user. Unfortunately, this does not really help designers very much. Many recent styles of interface enable the same task to be accomplished in many different ways. For example, this document is being composed on a desktop publishing system that offers at least seven different ways of changing the font associated with a word in the text. This can be done directly by altering the font associated with a selected word through a scroll down menu or through a text input box. It can be done as part of a more complex dialogue by right clicking over the word. It can also be done indirectly by editing the style associated with the word and so on. This leads to immense complexity even over a relatively simple and frequent task. It seems rather harsh to argue that the user committed an error if they inadvertently fail to select precisely the best means of changing the font at any single point during the editing of a document providing that they eventually achieve the desired goal. Very few users ever perform complex tasks in exactly the same way that a designer might envisage. There are also tremendous variations in performance between different users. Hence, what might seem to be an optimal trace of interaction for a novice might be seen as an "error" for more expert users.

Instead of defining errors to be a departure from optimal performance, they might instead be defined as a departure from "normal" operation. This definition acknowledges that we might normally expect tremendous variation between different users. It, therefore, addresses one of the problems that arose in comparing performance with a "perfect approach." What might be a "normal" error to expect from a novice might not be expected for an expert. This definition also recognizes that we might be able to recognize unusual or erroneous performance that differs from expected interaction. However, a number of theoretical and practical problems complicate this approach. For instance, we tend to commit hundreds of small errors every day. This is a consequence of the key role that errors play in learning. As we have seen, most people deploy "coping strategies" so that they can recover from tiny failures within minimum disruption to their higher level tasks (Tversky and Kahneman, 1974). Errors often occur in successful interactions in which the user managed to achieve their goal. In many cases, we may not even realize that an error has occurred.

James Reason has approached the problem of defining error by looking at differences between intentions, actions and consequences (Reason, 1990). If a user has an intention then they act in a manner that is intended to achieve a particular goal. For instance, I might plan to print a double-sided version of this document using my desktop publishing application. Errors of omission can occur when users forget to perform an action—these are known as lapses. This could occur if I select the print dialogue but forget to click on the check-box for double sided printing. Errors of commission occur when users perform an action that does help them to achieve their goal—these are known as slips. For instance, I might inadvertently close the document while scrolling down the File menu. Finally, users may not be able to identify a plan of action that is an appropriate means of achieving their goal— these are known as mistakes. It would be a mistake to try and find the print option in the Edit menu of most publishing applications.

Situation Awareness and Team-Based Interaction

The discussion up to this point has focused narrowly on individual users interacting with particular applications. However, the topic of human error is often associated with the loss of situation awareness that occurs when users fail to identify the consequences of changes in their environment (Endsley, 2004). This is most apparent in safety-critical domains. For instance, if an Air Traffic Controller becomes preoccupied in other tasks then they may fail to hear the Short-Term Conflict Alerts which are issued when two aircraft are in a dangerous proximity to each other. This oversight can lead to a loss of situation awareness that, in turn, can lead a controller to divert one aircraft into the path of another. This loss of awareness not only applies to the user's failure to monitor changes in software systems; it also arises when individuals fail to observe the actions of their colleagues. Hence it is an important aspect of team-based error. For instance, one person might send an email without realizing that their co-worker had just sent exactly the same request moments earlier. In this context, a loss of situation awareness is closely associated with "distributed cognition"—this is the process by which teams work together to achieve collective goals.

Endsley (2004) has developed a number of conceptual models that help us to understand the ways in which a loss of situation awareness can contribute to team-based errors. He argues that in order to interact with complex systems we must first be able to perceive key changes in our environment. If we miss warnings, such as the Short-Term Conflict Alert, then we are likely to make mistakes. At a second level, we may perceive key information but fail to comprehend what those signals mean. For instance, it is unlikely that a lay person would be able to recognize the meaning of an STCA even if they heard the warning. Finally, a loss of situation awareness may contribute to errors if we cannot use the information that we obtain to make accurate predictions about future states. In other words, even if we recognize that a warning has been issues we must be able to identify those aircraft that are in danger.

A number of other researchers have extended this work in different directions. For instance, Klein has developed the ideas of Recognition Primed Decision-Making—this suggests that we do not conduct detailed explicit analysis of the changes in our environment prior to making a plan for action (Klein, 1998). Instead we attempt to approximate a "best fit" between what we see around us and things that we have met in previous interactions. Hence the user of a desktop publishing system does not spend hours reading manuals and experimenting with tutorials before starting to use an application. Instead, they are more likely to have a go by applying analogies and expertise gained in other similar systems. Because these analogies may be misleading, this "best fit" process will inevitably lead to errors that call upon the coping strategies identified within resilience engineering.

Workload and Performance Shaping Factors

A range of factors can affect the likelihood that a user will make an error. These factors also determine whether, having committed an error, we can detect the problem and intervene to resolve or mitigate any adverse consequences. For instance, increasing workload can make a user more likely to make mistakes. Distractions and a number competing priorities can combine to undermine situation awareness (Endsley, 2004). If teams are working to the limit then individuals may not have enough time to update their colleagues on their actions and this can degrade distributed cognition in complex multiuser tasks. It is, however, notoriously difficult to predict the impact of workload on user performance. Some people commit errors in situations where their co-workers continue without any problems. There may be gender differences in the ability to juggle multiple tasks or to gain an overview across many competing priorities. These variations in performance are compounded by the difficulty in defining or measuring workload. One approach is to measure physical effort, for instance in terms of oxygen consumption over time using techniques developed within sports medicine. However, these metrics hardly apply to the mental workload that characterizes most human computer interaction. Subjective approaches have also been used, for example, within NASA's Task Load Index (Hart, 2006). However, great care is required to calibrate these approaches and also to ensure that external influences do not bias the users' answers about their subjective impressions of an interactive system. A further problem is it can be difficult to extrapolate from subjective impressions as a means of predicting future errors under carrying levels of workload.

Alternatively, secondary tasks can assess the impact of workload on errors. It can be difficult to force users to make errors if their primary task is to focus on interaction with a particular user interface. As we have seen, users quickly become skilled at overcoming minor set-backs to achieve their overall task. From this it follows that designers can introduce additional secondary tasks to determine whether increasing workload will have an impact on the frequency and consequences of errors during interaction with a primary system. For example, users might be requested to perform a number of simple mental calculations as they use an interface. Overall performance can be judged both in terms of the number of errors made using the primary system and the number of errors made in the secondary task over time. Workload can be varied by adjusting the difficulty of the calculations or by reducing the time to complete each mental task.

Users react to increasing levels of workload in many different ways. Encysting occurs when individuals become so preoccupied with the details of a particular task that they ignore the bigger picture (Reason, 1990). For example, a user may be so busy trying to alter the font in their title that they no longer have enough time to complete the rest of the report. In contrast, thematic vagabonding occurs when users move from one task to the next without devoting sufficient time to make real progress on any of them. It is important also to see these responses as part of a wider set of psychological mechanisms that users adopt when faced with a broader range of "performance shaping factors" (Hollnagel, 1998). As mentioned previously, users are remarkably resilient to errors. They learn from them and work around them. However, these processes can be undermined by a range of issues including fatigue, distraction, heat, noise, work related stress, domestic stress, alcohol or drug consumption, and so on. These negative performance shaping factors can have such a profound impact on users that they undermine resilience to poor interface design. For instance, traders may continue to use a securities trading system without error until they are forced to make a series of complex trades before the close of business on a Friday afternoon. The additional pressure created by the deadline and the complexity of the transactions may combine to provide the performance shaping factors that lead to error.

Balanced against PSF's such as fatigue or stress, are a number of positive performance shaping factors—these include explicit training that is intended to help individuals and teams of operators understand the causes and consequences of human error. For instance, Crew Resource Management (CRM) techniques have been widely applied in aviation and in healthcare to encourage good practice in communication between groups of co-workers (Civil Aviation Authority, 2006). The aim is to encourage mutual monitoring to support distributed cognition and mutual situation awareness. CRM is also intended to encourage a flexible allocation of tasks between groups as a means of responding to increasing levels of workload. In the previous example, teams of traders might work together to make final checks before a transaction is completed. This cooperation increases the level of mutual resilience against errors that continue to be made even after designers have "optimized" interfaces to reduce the likelihood of erroneous transactions.

Context and Systemic Failures

Very often performance shaping factors are independent of the human computer interface. Stress, heat, noise, distraction, and fatigue are all issues that emerge from the environment or context in which a system is being used (Johnson, 2003). In safety-critical systems this has led to an escalation in the scope of accident investigations. In previous generations, the focus would have been on the system operator as the source of a potential error. Problems might then have been acknowledged in the human factors of complex systems—looking at the design and layout of critical controls as well as the format of information being displayed to the end user. Increasingly, however, the focus has moved to management and regulation to identify the ways in which higher level decisions create the working environment in which an error is more likely to occur. The user may not have been trained properly, they may have been asked to complete tasks with insufficient time to check for potential errors, they may not have access to adequate communications infrastructure to communicate with their colleagues and so on. In such circumstances, we must look at the management of an organization which is responsible for creating the context in which users will make mistakes (Reason, 1997). Many Western countries have acknowledged this change in perspective by enacting legislation dealing with Corporate Killing or Corporate Manslaughter in addition to the Health and Safety Legislation that considers individual violations and errors (Johnson, 2008).

If we trace the links of influence back from the "sharp end" at which an operator makes a mistake we can follow responsibility through middle and senior management. Ultimately, however, we can reach the regulator or government organization that is responsible for supervising the market in which a company can operate. It is for this reason that many regulatory agencies have organized initiatives to address the human factors of error. Crew Resource Management is a requirement for all commercial aircrew within European and North American air space. Individual agencies have gone further—for instance EU-OPS and JAR-OPS 3 Subpart N contain requirements for anyone delivering CRM training. The UK Civil Aviation Authority has issued specific requirements within a document known as CAP 737–"Crew Resource Management (CRM) Training" and a CAA Standards Document 29.

Emotional Aspects of Error

The previous paragraphs might have given the impression that human error was a subject for abstract academic research and of concern to engineers in a narrow range of safety or security related industries. However, it is important to reiterate that error is part of the human condition. The ability to learn from mistakes is a key component of resilience in every form of interaction ranging from the use of spreadsheets through to mobile phones and missile systems. It is also important to stress that there is an emotional aspect to error (Dekker, 2006). The process of learning from previous incidents or accidents can be undermined by the feelings of guilt and blame that are often felt by the individuals who are involved in adverse events. Fear of retribution or sanction can encourage users to destroy logs or other forms of evidence that might be used to avoid future errors—for example by improved training or through redesign. These emotions can also create a situation in which one error can trigger further failures. For instance, users may become so preoccupied with replaying the previous failure "in their head" that they commit further errors. It is for this reason that Air Traffic Control Officers will, typically, be removed from further duties if they have been involved in a near miss incident. In the same way, the users of more general application can experience increasing levels of frustration as time pressure or stress lead from one error to the next.

PART 2: CONSEQUENCES OF ERROR FOR THE DESIGN OF COMPLEX USER INTERFACES

The first part of this chapter has provided an overview of human error—for example by distinguishing between violations, slips, lapses, and mistakes (Reason, 1990). We have also pointed out the remarkable resilience that enables users to overcome and learn from the hundreds of small errors that characterize everyday interaction. In contrast, this second part of the chapter looks at the consequences of error for the design and operation of complex user interfaces. In particular, we look at attempts to model human error and thereby to minimize the likelihood of slips, lapses and mistakes. We also look at the problems that arise when trying to validate predictions of particular errors rates in a given context of use (Bainbridge, 1987).

Simulation and Verification?

One of the problems that complicate the development of interactive systems is that it is hard for designers to anticipate the problems that users will experience. Simply being involved in the development of a complex application will give developers insights that would often never occur to everyday users. These insights can be derived from hours of work on dialogue design, as well as a direct knowledge of implementation mechanisms or the probable error modes that could complicate the use of software systems. It is difficult, therefore, to convey the sense of surprise that development teams often experience when they see users struggling to operate the systems that they have delivered (Norman, 1990).

One reason for the difficulty in anticipating errors is that it can be difficult to reproduce errors under experimental or laboratory conditions. People behave differently if they know they are being watched—they read instructions more diligently and often will obey warnings that would simply elicit an automatic cancel in the workplace. Other problems relate more directly to the practical difficulty of testing for errors. It can be difficult to recreate the full range of performance shaping factors, including stress and fatigue that might be encountered in the workplace— often there are ethical concerns about running these types of evaluations prior to deployment. Serious errors will hopefully be relatively rare events; hence tests may have to run for weeks or months before one is observed. Even if such events are never detected during a test then this may provide developers with little confidence about the eventual reliability of their system. Dijkstra noted that testing only ever established the presence of a design problem but not its absence. If the tests were continued over a longer period, with different input data or with different users then further evidence may be obtained about mistakes, slips, and lapses.

A number of alternate techniques might be recruited to help identify problems of situation awareness, workload or distributed cognition during the development of complex, interactive systems. For example, participatory design techniques recruit potential end-users to development teams. Part of their role can be to alert designers to potential errors that might complicate the operation of the system in the eventual working environment. However, this can be difficult to manage. Over time it can be increasingly hard for end users to disassociate themselves from the development team. By working with a design for a prolonged period of time, it can be increasingly difficult for individuals to place themselves back in the position of one of their co-workers using an interactive system for the first time (Beyer and Holtzblatt, 1998).

User modeling techniques a provide alternative for the development of interactive systems. These try to model some of the cognitive mechanisms that both support resilience but which also lead to errors involving software applications. For instance, they can be used to model the limited capacity of short-term memory or the interference effects from high workload that have been observed as triggers for slips and lapses (Johnson, 1999). This approach can be used not only to predict potential error mechanisms but also to provide an explanation for why those errors might occur. This is important if development teams are to identify potential design solutions. Unfortunately, the application of user modeling creates new challenges. Rather than simply establishing that error predictions are observed in the use of an interactive system, it also becomes important to ensure that the models also provide a valid explanation of the underlying error mechanisms.

Human Reliability Analysis

Risk analysis continues to play a key role in the design of safety-critical systems. This process provides numeric estimates of the likelihood and consequences of the different hazards that can lead to an adverse event. Quantified risk assessments works best for hardware systems for which it is possible to derive statistical estimates of the probability of random failures over time. For example, the US military publish handbooks that contain the probability of failure for a range of components over time (US Department of Defense, 1995). Designers can use this data to calculate the probability of failure for a system that is built from these various individual components. In the same way, Swain and Guttman (1983) have sought to publish handbooks of human reliability that provide high-level estimates for the likelihood of particular types of error. For example, the probability that a user might incorrectly read back a series of figures from a display might be 1 in 200 attempts. This approach has numerous advantages for the engineering of complex systems—the same risk-based approaches can be applied throughout all aspects of the development process.

A number of concerns limit the practical application of human reliability analysis. Firstly, critics of the approach have argued that the probabilities can be difficult to validate (Reason, 1990). If users know that their actions are being observed then they may be less likely to make an error; they will exploit a range of self-monitoring techniques to catch and rectify any mistakes that might jeopardize their tasks.

Secondly, even if accurate data is available for previous errors in similar systems then gross estimates do not take into account a host of more complex cognitive and social factors. Hollnagel (1998) voices this criticism when he describes Human Reliability Analysis as "psychologically vacuous." In other words, this approach often neglects the impact of performance shaping factors on the likelihood of user errors. More recent methodologies have sought to address these criticisms by helping designers to first calculate the base probability for particular errors and then apply deltas or modifying terms to equations that account for the impact of performance shaping factors. If a user is likely to be acting under time pressure then the probability of incorrectly reading back some data is increased. If they have prior training in techniques like Crew Resource Management then a delta may be applied to reduce the probability of such errors. Although these developments help to address caveats about the application of Human Reliability Analysis, they also raise further concerns about the validation of both the base probabilities and also the "fudge factors" that are introduced to account for performance variations.

In less critical domains, it can be difficult to make an appropriate business case to justify the investments that are needed to support human reliability analysis as a means of predicting potential errors with mass-market interactive systems. These techniques have been used in financial software and in other forms of secure applications. The longevity of the approach is certainly surprising given the sustained theoretical objections, mentioned in previous paragraphs.

Incident and Accident Reporting

Incident and accident reports can be used to identify the base probabilities that are used in Human Reliability Analysis (Johnson, 2003). They provide useful evidence about those human errors that have the potential to threaten safe and successful operation. Unlike more heuristic forms of design, they provide a clear and tangible link with operational experience and hence usually provide clear insights into the impact of performance shaping factors, including fatigue, interruptions, and stress. It is important not only to focus on the role of human error in major adverse events. By focusing on the individual errors that led to the loss of billions of Yen, as in the example cited in the opening sections, we might waste resources trying to protect against the last failure rather than preparing for the next. Similarly, we might also neglect the many less significant errors that have a greater cumulative impact on successful interaction over the life time of a system. The Heinrich ratio is widely used to relate the number of accidents to serious and to minor incidents. Typically, this is written as 1 accident to 30 major incidents to 300 minor incidents (Johnson, 2003). The precise figures in the Heinrich ratio remain a focus for considerable debate and they vary between industries. For example, studies of railway maintenance have shown that there is a bi-polar distinction between accidents which tend to be fatal and near-miss incidents that were a long way from resulting in an accident.

In everyday environments, system logs and critical incident diaries provide equivalents of accident and incident reports in safety-related applications. For example, web server logs can be instrumented to monitor for situations in which users decide to terminate a transaction before payment is confirmed. These can then form the focus for other types of usability study based on scenarios that mimic the trajectory of failure that is illustrated in the logs. Critical incident diaries require users to note down any adverse events that arise during their interaction with interactive applications. They may also be prompted to provide evidence about any performance shaping factors that may have influenced the problems that they experienced or which increased the likelihood of an error even if they managed to spot the problem in time.

In spite of these different approaches to eliciting evidence about previous failure, considerable uncertainty remains over the reliability of any information obtained in this way. For example, incident diaries depend upon users being motivated enough to remember to pause after an error which will already have delayed their primary task in order to complete an entry in their diary. In the initial phase after an incident reporting system has been installed, companies can quickly become overwhelmed by a mass of relatively low priority incidents as users learn to report their concerns. After this "confessional phase," the number of incident reports often dries up. Under-reporting remains a problem even in safety-critical industries where staff may be concerned that they will be punished if they confess to particular errors. Management may be worried about subsequent litigation or the loss of operating licenses if they are informed about near-miss incidents. Although automated logs can provide a trace of the interactions that lead to potential failures, they provide relatively few insights into the cognitive mechanisms and performance shaping factors that might have led users to make particular errors (Dekker, 2006).

As one might expect, accident and incident analysis have been profoundly affected by changes in wider research into human error. For example, many previous studies have been conducted to derive estimates for the number of accidents that are caused by mistakes, slips, and lapses (Reason, 1997). These studies have typically been used in one of two ways—either to increase spending on human factors and interface design to reduce operator error or to justify increased spending on automation to entirely remove user input. There is, however, a growing recognition that human error only acts as a catalyst or trigger for underlying problems in the management and operation of complex systems. In this view, we can think of interactive systems being protected by different barriers. If an industry is well regulated, the company is well managed and the operator follows standard operating procedures then an accident is unlikely to occur. If, however, there are ambiguities in the regulatory regime and the management have not provided a suitable working environment or equipment and the user switches off elements of the protection system then we can see how holes appear in each layer of defense. This model is sometimes referred to as Reason's Swiss cheese model, for obvious reasons (Reason, 1990).

It can be difficult to ensure that organizations and individuals act on information about previous errors, even if such insights can be obtained in a reliable manner. For instance, attribution bias is one of several cognitive phenomena that affect the way we determine who was responsible for an adverse event (Johnson, 2003). Salience is a particularly important aspect of this bias because issues that were critical for the person involved in an adverse event may not be apparent to outside observers. This makes it difficult for designers to understand the reasons why an individual might have made a mistake, slip or lapse. Further problems arise when we are quick to condemn the errors of others while we are eager to identify the impact of performance shaping factors in explaining our own failures.

Lifecycle Issues: Design, Operation, Maintenance and Decommissioning

Incident and accident reporting can be used to form a feedback look that is intended to ensure that organizations learn from those failures that do occur. In systems engineering, prospective risk assessments that were used to guide the early stages of development can be validated against the data that is derived about real hazards during the operation of complex, interactive systems. As we have seen, however, these feedback loops will only work if users are encouraged to provide information about the errors that they commit or observe. In addition there also needs to be appropriate mechanisms that enable end user concerns to be communicated back to development teams. This is not as simple as it might sound. Very often the groups who are involved in the design of an interactive system will move to subsequent projects as soon as an application has been delivered. From this it follows that they may never hear about the problems that end users experience in the everyday operation of complex systems (Beyer and Holtzblatt, 1998). Other problems arise when applications are developed for one market place and are then transferred to new user groups with minimal changes in their user interface. For instance, many GPS units that were designed to help private pilots are now being sold into the maritime market. A new crop of navigation errors and accidents have occurred with marine systems because some designers have failed to learn the lessons provided by the initial application of these units within the aviation community.

Further problems arise when the end users of safety-critical systems have to learn to cope not only with design problems in their user interfaces but also with problems in underlying applications. Many accidents have occurred during what are termed "degraded modes of operation" (Johnson, Kirwan, and Licu, 2009). These arise when users struggle to maintain levels of service even though they may have lost key components in their underlying systems infrastructure. Examples include situations in which Air Traffic Controllers have tried to keep aircraft moving in low visibility during a failure of their ground movement radar system or when train drivers have proceeded through red lights without being able to confirm that the track ahead is clear because of faulty communications with signaling staff or systems. Such situations represent particular challenges for the development of complex, interactive systems because designers must consider not simply the errors that can occur with a "perfect application" but also what could happen weeks and months into the future when imperfect maintenance activities lead to degraded modes of operation.

Not only do designers have to consider the problems that arise during the development and maintenance of complex systems, there is also a requirement to consider decommissioning activities. Increasing concerns over the environmental impact of safety-related applications has persuaded regulators to extend a lifecycle approach to the mitigation of operator error. Lessons learned from the decommissioning of nuclear and military installations have been used to persuade the operators of complex systems that they must consider the hazards that can arise from mistakes, slips, and lapses at the end of the working lives of many applications.

Safety Cases and Safety Management Systems

Safety Management Systems have been developed to formalize the processes of organizational learning that are intended to ensure we learn the lessons from previous errors. They, typically, include guidance on the documentation both of risk assessments and of incident reports. They also help to formalize responsibility for ensuring that the concerns of end users are considered and, where necessary, are acted upon. Safety cases are an increasingly important component of safety management systems. These can be thought of as arguments about why a complex system is "acceptably safe" (Johnson, 2003). Safety cases are significant from the perspective of this handbook because they often include assumptions and evidence about operator intervention. For instance, it might be argued that a control system is acceptably safe, in part, because the user can respond to a critical warning by shutting down operations within a fixed time period. This argument might, in turn, be supported by evidence derived from user testing in simulators. The safety case might later be amended to reinforce this argument with further data derived from operational experience with the application. As we have seen, however, the theoretical and practical problems in predicting potential errors makes it difficult to place high levels of confidence in arguments that rest on the ability of operators to meet such requirements. Safety cases must, therefore, often extend arguments about operator intervention to demonstrate that the system will still be acceptably safe even when a user fails to intervene in the manner that might initially be expected.

The processes and products that help to define Safety Management Systems are important from another perspective. They illustrate the extent to which developers must go to mitigate the consequences of human error not simply in the operation of complex systems but in the design, implementation, operation, maintenance, and decommissioning of safety-related applications. Mistakes, slips, and lapses complicate every stage of the lifecycle in human machine systems. This makes it difficult to identify the boundaries of safety-critical applications. For instance, it is obvious that the systems used by clinicians, pilots or nuclear engineers have a direct impact on safety. However, it can also be argued that the user interfaces to the tools that designers employ in the development of aerospace, healthcare, and nuclear systems will also indirectly have an impact on the safety of the final applications. The care and thought that goes into the development of safety-critical systems is often lacking in the design of software and interface development tools. Similarly, the user interfaces of the reporting systems that are often intended to elicit information about previous errors with other systems are often poorly designed. In such circumstances, it can hardly be a surprise that so little is known about the mistakes, slips, and lapses that end users experience in their everyday work.

PART 3: CONCLUSIONS AND LOOKING TO THE FUTURE

This chapter has provided a broad overview of human error in the context of both safety-critical and mass market applications. It is impossible to provide a complete survey of such a vast and active area of research. The continued prevalence of human error as a contributory cause in accidents across many industries also demonstrates that much remains to be learned in this area. However, we have identified key insights that emerge from the application of research ideas in a range of different industries. The distinctions between violations, mistakes, slips, and lapses, the interaction between performance shaping factors and the quantitative predictions of human reliability analysis, the importance of workload and situation awareness, as well as the Swiss cheese model of accident causation have all informed the development and operation of complex interactive systems in domains ranging from healthcare to power distribution, from aviation to the military.

Looking to the future, it seems likely that we will see increasing levels of automation as a potential means of reducing the impact of human error. This is already apparent, for example in the development of autonomous space craft for future manned missions to Mars and the Moon or in proposals to extend the role of Unmanned Autonomous Vehicles into controlled airspace. However, these developments will not reduce the importance of human error. Instead the focus may shift away from the immediate operator of a safety critical system onto the teams that must develop and maintain increasing levels of complexity.

REFERENCES

Bainbridge, L. (1987). Ironies of Automation. In J. Rasmussen, K. Duncan, and J. Leplat, *New technology and human error*. New York: Wiley.

Beyer, H. and Holtzblatt, K. (1998). *Contextual design: Defining customer-centered systems*. San Francisco: Morgan Kaufmann.

Civil Aviation Authority. (2006). *CAP 737: Crew Resource Management Training*. Farnham, UK: UK Civil Aviation Authority.

Dekker, S. (2006). *The Field Guide to Understanding Human Error*. Aldershot, UK: Ashgate.

Endsley, M. (2004). Situation awareness: Progress and directions. In S. Banbury and S. Tremblay, *A cognitive approach to situation awareness: Theory, measurement and application* (pp. 317–341). Aldershot, UK: Ashgate.

Hart, G. (2006). NASA-Task Load Index (NASA-TLX); 20 years later. *Proceedings of the Human Factors and Ergonomics Society 50th Annual Meeting* (pp. 904–908). Santa Monica, CA: Human Factors and Ergonomics Society.

Hollnagel, E. (1998). *CREAM (Cognitive Reliability and Error Analysis Method)*. North Holland: Elsevier.

Hollnagel, E. (2009). *The ETTO Principle: Efficiency-Thoroughness Trade-Off*. Farnham, UK: Ashgate Publishing.

Hollnagel, E., Woods, D., and Leveson, N. (2006). *Resilience Engineering: Concepts and Precepts*. Aldershot, UK: Ashgate.

Johnson, C. (2003). *Handbook of Accidents and Incidents*. Glasgow, Scotland: Glasgow University Press.

Johnson, C. (2008). Ten contentions of corporate manslaughter legislation: Public policy and the legal response to workplace accidents. *Safety Science*, 46:3(349–370).

Johnson, C. (1999). The Application of User Modeling Techniques to Reason about the Human Contribution to Major Accidents. *Proceedings of the 7th International Conference on User Modeling, Banff Canada* (pp. 13–22). New York, US: Springer Verlag.

Johnson, C., Kirwan, B., and Licu, T. (2009). The Interation Between Safety Culture and Degraded Modes: A Survey of National Infrastructures for Air Traffic Management. *Risk Management*, 11:3(241–284).

Kirwan, B. (1994). *A Guide to Practical Human Reliability Assessment*. London, UK: Taylor and Francis.

Klein, G. (1998). *Sources of Power: How People Make Decisions*. Boston, US: MIT Press.

New York Times. (Friday December 9, 2005). Japan rebukes exchange for costly trading error.

Norman, D. (1990). The "problem" of automation: Inappropriate feedback and interaction, not "over-automation." In D. Broadbent, A. Baddeley, and J. Reason, *Human factors in hazardous situations* (p. 585). Oxford: Oxford University Press.

Rasmussen, J. (1983). Skills, rules, and knowledge: Signals, signs, and symbols and other distinctions in human performance models. *IEEE Transactions on Systems, Man, and Cybernetics*, SMC-13, 257–267.

Reason, J. (1990). *Human Error*. Cambridge: Cambridge University Press.

Reason, J. (1997). *Managing the Risks of Organizational Accidents*. Aldershot, UK: Ashgate.

Reason, J. (2008). *The Human Contribution: Unsafe Acts, Accidents and Heroic Recoveries*. Aldershot, UK: Ashgate.

Swain, A.D., and Guttman, H.E. (1983). *Handbook of human reliability analysis with emphasis on nuclear power plant applications*. Washington DC, US: NUREG/CR-1278.

Tversky, A., and Kahneman, D. (1974). Judgment under uncertainty: Heuristics and biases. *Science*, 185, 1124–1131.

US Department of Defense. (1995). *MIL-HDBK-217: Reliability Prediction of Electronic Equipment*. Washington DC, US: US Department of Defense.

5

Operating Documents that Change in Real-time: Dynamic Documents and User Performance Support

Barbara K. Burian and Lynne Martin

A DAY IN THE LIFE OF A PILOT

Nearing the end of the cruise portion of a flight, the airline captain began to prepare for the descent, approach, and landing. After weather and airport information were obtained through an automated radio broadcast and instructions were given by air traffic control, she began to look at the assigned arrival and approach procedures. First, she had to locate the arrival procedures to be used among six different ones for their destination airport. Once found, she then had to search through 23 lines of tiny text on the chart to find the arrival procedures to follow for their assigned runway. On this chart, she noted that for aircraft without a Global Positioning System (GPS), such as theirs, three other ground-based navigation aids had to be operational when flying that arrival. She asked her first officer to check the lengthy list of Notices to Airmen to confirm that the navigation aids they needed were in-service.

The wet runways and poor braking action reported by other pilots at the airport meant that the crew also needed to perform calculations to ensure their assigned runway would be long enough. To do this calculation the captain had to locate the Landing Distance table in a thick manual filled with other tables and checklists, and then find the section for her particular type of aircraft. In the table she located the subsection for the brake and flap settings they would be using along with their anticipated landing speed with "poor" braking action. This yielded a standard landing distance that she had to modify based upon the aircraft's expected weight at landing, the wind speed and direction, temperature, and airport altitude. Finally, after all these calculations, she was able to determine that the assigned runway would be acceptable.

As she completed her review of the arrival, approach, and landing, she reminded herself and her first officer that when it came time to complete the landing checklist, they should remember *not* to arm the speedbrakes as they normally did as a part of that checklist. They had dispatched on that flight with the speedbrakes inoperative, using procedures in their minimum equipment list, and it could be quite dangerous to inadvertently try to use this equipment when it was not operating properly.

This vignette describes typical actions required by pilots who complete thousands of flights every day. They include searching through multiple similar documents and lines of text to locate that which is pertinent, performing complicated calculations using tables and data acquired through multiple sources, and remembering not to perform typical actions even though checklists indicate that those actions should be taken. With the introduction of electronic operating documents, this snapshot of the current life of airline pilots has already begun to change. Indeed, electronic operating documents are now routinely used in a number of professional and industrial settings: nuclear and power plant control rooms (O'Hara, Higgins, and Stubler, 2000; Niwa, Hollnagel, and Green, 1996), ship and submarine bridges (Ronan, Routhier, and Ryan, 2000), airplane cockpits (Air Transport Association, 2002; Boorman and Hartel, 1997), airline operations centers, manufacturing and maintenance facilities (Seamster and Kanki, 2005), and more. Electronic operating documents which are *dynamic*, meaning they are altered in real-time based on specific circumstances that exist at the moment in which they are being used, bring even greater changes to the lives of professionals who work in these settings.

We begin this chapter with an introduction to operational documents and their formats and provide some examples from the world of airline operations. We then identify and examine a number of important issues with regard to the design, development, functionality, and use of dynamic operating documents. These issues are grouped into three main categories: operational considerations, cognitive and human performance considerations, and certification and approval considerations.

Electronic and Dynamic Operational Documents

What are operational documents?

Generally speaking, an operational document is any printed or electronically presented textual, numerical or graphical information[1] relevant for performing actions or interpreting data and displays in operational settings. They include warnings, notes, lists, bulletins, checklists, procedures, performance tables, training and operations manuals, systems descriptions, charts and maps, system synoptic diagrams, alarm codes ... and the list goes on. Some documents might contain just a single line of text, like a caution statement. Other documents, like an inspector's handbook, consist of volumes. Some information included in these documents, such as the location of pressure relief valves in a hydraulics system, will never change. Other information, such as the strength and direction of winds at an airport, can change almost as soon as it is determined.

Operational information and documents currently can be presented in four basic formats: paper, stand-alone electronic, integrated electronic, and dynamic electronic. A stand-alone electronic document is simply the electronic display of static information. It differs from a paper document only in the medium used for presentation. Integrated electronic documents are connected to at least one

---

1   For the purposes of this chapter, the terms "data" and "information" are used interchangeably.

or, more commonly, a system of sensors. Sensor data is used to alter what or how information is displayed. It is sensor data that allows a particular document to be selected for display automatically or automatically indicate that a checklist step has been completed. A dynamic document, as described earlier, is one in which the actual content, specifications, directions, or instructions change in real-time. As with integrated electronic documents, dynamic documents rely upon data from an advanced system of sensors.

In addition to the four basic formats just described, there are also two subtypes within each of the three electronic operational document formats—those that do and do not allow or require the manual input of data by the operator for computation and use with other information (that is, documents with or without an interactive feature). As is summarized in Table 5.1, the functionality, use, development, and maintenance of documents across these formats differ widely.

Although some documents exist solely as one of the seven described in Table 5.1, it is not uncommon for a single electronic document to actually be composed of a combination of the six different electronic format types of information. For example, a procedure might contain some steps that are simply presented and do not change (stand-alone electronic, not interactive), some steps that require the entry of data that is combined with sensor information (integrated electronic, is interactive) and some steps whose content changes when certain conditions are sensed to exist (dynamic, not interactive).

Paper documents are still by far the most common but stand-alone and integrated electronic documents can be found in most operational settings. Integrated electronic documents are found less often though, as they require data from sensors, which may not be installed. Dynamic documents or information are the most rare. Although this chapter focuses on dynamic documents, some of what follows also pertains to integrated electronic documents as well. Our discussion will review types of documents which might be made dynamic and the benefits and limitations of dynamic and other types of electronic documents. Special attention will be given to some of the many challenges in developing dynamic documents with particular focus on human cognitive capabilities that must be considered during their design if they are to truly provide optimal user support. Some worthy topics pertaining to the mechanics of dynamic documentation (for example, hyper-linking, eXtensible Mark-up Language (XML), and data tagging), different electronic document programming formats (pdf, doc, and so on), and display presentation issues (for example, scrolling versus paging) are beyond the scope of this chapter and will not be addressed (for information on these and related topics see Civil Aviation Authority, 2005; Cosimini, 2002, and Hackos, 2002).

To facilitate our discussion of dynamic operational documents, we will use examples from the world of airline operations; however, first we must revisit our definition of the word "document." Prior to the digital age, an operating document was information printed on paper. Clearly, an operations manual was a document whereas aircraft airspeed information displayed in the cockpit during flight was not. Documents contained static information; they could be revised (and reprinted) but otherwise, their content did not change. A significant limitation of paper documents is that information contained in some is not pertinent to the particular operation, or becomes obsolete very quickly due to variable external conditions, such as the weather at a destination airport. Dynamic operating documents, because they can change in

Table 5.1   Operational document formats

Basic Format Type and Sub-type	Example	Functionality	Operator Use	Development
Paper	A table printed on paper located in the performance table chapter of an operating handbook.	Static information exists on paper and is organized according to some predetermined scheme (e.g., single sheet, several page bulletins, chapter in a manual, etc.).	Operators must remember that a paper document with required information exists, and must manually locate the document and desired information at the required time of use.	Information is generated, organized, and printed on paper according to predetermined organizational scheme. Document is then distributed for use.
Stand-Alone Electronic—Without Interactive Feature	A description of the procedure to be followed when changing a tire on aircraft main-gear is in the equipment care and maintenance section of a file saved on a laptop computer.	Static information is available for electronic display and is organized according to some predetermined scheme.	Operators must remember that an electronic document with required information exists, must manually locate the document at the required time, and must cause it to be electronically displayed. Some search or hyperlink feature may be available to assist in locating the desired document or information.	Information is generated, organized, and saved for later presentation on an electronic display according to a predetermined organizational scheme. Document is then distributed for use.
Stand-Alone Electronic—With Interactive Feature	Fuel load, weight of baggage, and number of passengers is entered into a computer, which then calculates aircraft weight and balance information and determines where an aircraft falls within its center of gravity envelope.	Data is manually entered into a computer that uses it to calculate some value and generate other information related to it. This information may or may not be compared against or combined with other information and is then displayed electronically.	Operators must remember that an electronic document exists, must manually locate the document, cause it to be electronically displayed, obtain and manually insert required data in the proper fields at the time of use. Some search or hyperlink feature may be available to assist in locating the desired document or information.	Information is generated, organized, and saved for later presentation on an electronic display according to a predetermined organizational scheme. Fields for operator data entry are determined and programming allows for manipulation of data, presentation, and use with other static information. Saved program including information file, data entry fields and data computation is then distributed for use.

Table 5.1 continued   Operational document formats

Basic Format Type and Sub-type	Example	Functionality	Operator Use	Development
Integrated Electronic—Without Interactive Feature	An electrical bus relay fails and the procedures for handing the failure are automatically displayed for reference.	Static information is available for electronic display and is organized according to some predetermined scheme Sensor information identifies the user's need for static information and it is displayed or queued automatically.	An electronic document is automatically displayed or queued for display and the operator must attend to the display or notice that a document has been queued and then cause it to be displayed.	Information is generated, organized, and saved for later presentation on an electronic display according to a predetermined organizational scheme. Data file is then distributed for use. A system of sensors within the operational environment is connected to the electronic information system so that specified sensor values will cause certain electronic information to be accessed and presented automatically.
Integrated Electronic— With Interactive Feature	While completing a "Motor Failed" procedure, a message is displayed asking if the operator wishes to attempt to restart the motor. The operator selects the "yes" option and all the procedural steps required to restart the motor are then displayed for completion.	Static information is available for electronic display and is organized according to some predetermined scheme Sensor information identifies the user's need for this static information. Data is manually entered into a computer, which uses it to calculate values and generate related info. This information may be compared against static or sensor information and is then automatically displayed or queued for display.	Operator must obtain and manually insert required data in the proper fields at the proper time. An electronic document is automatically displayed or queued for display and the operator must attend to the display or notice that a document has been queued and then cause it to be displayed.	Information is generated, organized, and saved for later presentation on an electronic display according to a predetermined organizational scheme. Fields for operator data entry are determined and programming for manipulation of data, presentation, and use with other information, including that which comes from a system of sensors. Saved program including information file, data entry fields and data computation is then distributed for use. A system of sensors within the operational environment is connected to the electronic information system so that specified sensor values will cause certain electronic information to be accessed and presented automatically.

Table 5.1 continued   Operational document formats

Basic Format Type and Sub-type	Example	Functionality	Operator Use	Development
Dynamic Electronic—Without Interactive Feature	Aircraft readiness for pushback data is combined with its flight priority to determine when and what order aircraft will be given clearances to pushback on a ramp. Schedules for pushback carts are altered accordingly and presented to the dispatcher with a scheduled time.	Real-time data from multiple sources (sensors, up-linked or down-loaded data) are used in combination with each other and with static data to yield other information which is then electronically displayed.	An electronic document is automatically displayed or queued for display and the operator must attend to the display or notice that a document has been queued and then cause it to be displayed.	Information is generated, organized, and saved for later presentation on an electronic display according to a predetermined organizational scheme. Programming for manipulation of data, presentation, and use with other information, including that which comes from a system of sensors, uplinked and down-linked data, is also saved. Program file is then distributed for use within the operational environment is connected to the electronic information system so that specified sensor values will cause certain electronic information to be accessed and presented automatically.

Table 5.1 continued   Operational document formats

Basic Format Type and Sub-type	Example	Functionality	Operator Use	Development
Dynamic Electronic With Interactive Feature	A pilot enters that an aircraft thrust reverser is not to be used into the system. This information is combined with assigned runway and weather information, uplinked to the aircraft from air traffic control and compared with stored aircraft performance and limitations data. Displayed landing procedures are altered to for equipment limitations and environmental conditions.	Real-time data from multiple sources (sensors, up-linked or down-loaded data, data input from operators) are used in combination with each other and with static data to yield other information which is then electronically displayed.	Operator must obtain and manually insert required data in the proper fields at the proper time. An electronic document is automatically displayed or queued for display and the operator must attend to the display or notice that a document has been queued and then cause it to be displayed.	Information is generated, organized, and saved for later combination with other data and/or presentation on an electronic display according to a predetermined organizational scheme. Fields for operator data entry are determined and programming for manipulation of data, presentation, and use with other information, including that which comes from a system of sensors, uplinked and down-linked data, is also saved. Determinations of how various operational documents will be altered in real-time based on these data are made and saved to the program which is then distributed for use. A system of sensors within the operational environment is connected to the electronic information system so that specified sensor values will cause certain electronic information to be accessed and presented automatically.

Notes: Maintenance for all these document systems will consist of updates to their content. Updates and revisions must be performed manually and the revised electronic information must be saved and distributed. In the case of electronic documents, previous versions must be located and overwritten or deleted, for paper documents, previous versions must be located and destroyed.

real time, overcome these limitations. However, the demarcation is now much less clear between information in dynamic operating documents and other operational information, such as aircraft airspeed, which is also dynamic and is also derived through various sensors (Seinfeld, Herman, and Lotterhos, 2002). Although we will continue to use it for the time being, we shall see that the term "document" may cease to be particularly accurate. In this discussion we will consider all operational information, regardless of its source, as existing on a continuum from that which is static and unchanging to that which is dynamic and able to change as contexts change. Current constraints on treating all dynamic information as having equivalent integrity regardless of its source, as we have done below, will be addressed in a later section on limitations in dynamic data.

Dynamic Information (and Documents) on Airline Flight Decks

As with most highly skilled professions, airline pilots use information from many sources during the course of a flight. Information related to flight parameters (for example, airspeed, altitude), systems functioning (for example, engine pressure ratio, cabin pressurization), active automation modes (for example, flight level change, vertical speed), aircraft configuration (for example, gear down, cargo door open), and weather radar, is derived largely through on-board sensor data and is displayed digitally or through the use of gauges or panel indicators located throughout the flight deck. Other information pertaining to navigation and flight management, such as the route and estimated time of arrival at destination, is displayed to the pilots through the flight management system (FMS) display units. The flight management computer derives this information using a combination of data entered by the pilots and data from on-board sensors and databases. Some information originates away from the flight deck and is transmitted to and from the pilots via radio voice communication or digital uplinks of textual data to the aircraft through the use of satellite or radio (that is, data link). This includes information such as current airport weather conditions and air traffic control (ATC) clearances.

Operational information that traditionally existed as paper documents (some of which was carried on-board in pilot flight bags), such as aeronautical charts, airport information, operations manuals, the aircraft minimum equipment list and logbook, performance tables, and normal and emergency checklists, is accessed on the flight deck through onboard databases and manuals. This kind of information, when available in electronic form, is located either in an electronic flight bag (EFB; Gosling, 2002; Wade, 2002) or is displayed on one of the main forward multifunction displays.

An EFB is simply a type of electronic computing and display device, such as a laptop computer or personal digital assistant (Air Transport Association, 2002; Chandra, Yeh, Riley, and Mangold, 2003). There are three different classes of EFB hardware (Federal Aviation Administration (FAA), 2003a) and only the highest level, class 3, will accommodate integrated or dynamic electronic documents. This is because only class 3 EFBs are integrated with airplane databuses and thus allow documents stored on them to respond to sensor data from the aircraft. Therefore, class 3 EFBs are permanently installed aboard the aircraft and are subject to stringent approval and certification requirements (FAA, 2003a). EFB information is typically presented on its own displays which are usually positioned at an angle slightly off to the sides of the main forward flight-deck displays.

Some types of dynamic document information currently exist on airline flight decks. For example, sensors can detect low pressure in the right and center hydraulics systems and cause the "Right and Center Hydraulics Low Pressure" checklist to be automatically displayed. An electronic graphic depicting the hydraulics systems shows the right and center system lines in red, instead of the normal green, and graphically shows pump switches changing from ON to OFF as crews complete checklist steps directing them to complete those actions. Final actions from that checklist that need to be completed later during descent and approach are not presented but are appended to the Descent and Approach Checklist instead.

These are simple but powerful examples of the advantages of dynamic documents over static ones (see Table 5.2). A document, in this case the Descent and Approach Checklist, is lengthened to include steps that must be accomplished at that time to accommodate a non-normal situation. The electronic synoptic display provides immediate feedback to crews as they perform various actions which confirm that their commands are actually being carried out and also increases the likelihood of identifying an error should one be made.

Table 5.2   Benefits and limitations of dynamic operating document systems

Benefits	Limitations
• Change in real-time to reflect exact circumstances in effect at moment they are being used • Eliminate the need to search among multiple documents of the same type (e.g., tables, checklists, etc.) to find the one needed • Eliminate the need to navigate through conditional branches within procedures to locate only those steps that are pertinent at that moment • Combine information and data from multiple sources (some static, some dynamic) • Use data from multiple sources to perform complex calculations • Provide information that is needed when it is needed • Reduce operator workload • Reduce operator memory load (working memory, long-term memory, prospective memory) • Reduce likelihood of errors due to interruptions and distractions • Reduce likelihood of some types of other cognitive and performance errors (e.g., habit capture) • Fewer requirements for manual data entry, error checker for manual data entry • Support more effective and timely operator decisions	• Poor design of interface and displays increases workload and gives rise to operator confusion • Operator loses situational awareness e.g., operator is not aware of what types of information from what sources have been used or combined • Information is not displayed at the correct time to support effective task management • Wrong information is accessed, combined, displayed • Dynamic information is unreliable or incorrect • Operator is unable to evaluate veracity of dynamic information • No procedure for what to do if dynamic documents/information is unavailable or unreliable

Note: Benefits are only possible if the dynamic document system is well designed. Some benefits listed (e.g., reduce operator workload) also exist for some types of integrated electronic document systems. Some limitations listed exist only if the dynamic document system is not well designed (e.g., wrong information is accessed, combined, or displayed).

Returning to our "A Day in the Life of a Pilot" vignette at the beginning of the chapter we can see far greater future possibilities for dynamic operating documents on the flight deck. Current airport weather conditions and ATC instructions could be uplinked to the flightdeck causing the exact assigned arrival procedures (and only those procedures) to be automatically evaluated on-board for suitability; aircraft performance capabilities and equipage data (in our example, the lack of a GPS) would be compared against the performance requirements of the assigned arrival and electronic information confirming the operation of necessary external navigation aids. Suggested landing brake and flap settings could be determined automatically through computation of data from the uplinked weather information and on-board data and presented to the crew for confirmation. The required landing distance, instead of being computed through a complicated printed table and reference to external data, is computed automatically and in the blink of an eye, the assigned arrival and runway would be determined to be acceptable and the arrival procedure queued for display on the flight deck. At the same time, the routing of the arrival procedure would load into the flight management computer awaiting the pilots to press the "Execute" button. Finally, data in the electronic minimum equipment list would be referenced in constructing the approach and landing checklists, and the item "Set Speedbrakes" on the landing checklist would change to read "Do Not Arm Speedbrakes" since the crew dispatched with the speedbrakes inoperative. Thus, actions that once took many minutes to complete, required reference to multiple sources of information, and involved considerable cognitive demand in terms of attention, memory, and mental calculations are reduced to two or three simple and quickly executed steps with the potential for pilot error being significantly lessened.

There are many other possible ways in which dynamic operating documents might be employed on the flight deck. For example, numerous conditional branches are used in checklists for response to emergency and abnormal situations: IF a, THEN do steps x, y, and z; but IF b, THEN do steps q, r, s, and t. Integrated electronic and dynamic checklists, through their use of sensors, can determine which actions are pertinent and required for a particular set of circumstances and only these are presented, thereby eliminating the often confusing task of evaluating, selecting, and navigating through multiple conditional branches and even across multiple checklists (Burian, Barshi, and Dismukes, 2005; Niwa et al., 1996). Another example pertains to customizing procedures which would dynamically alter based on variables, such as wind speed and direction, aircraft weight, and the performance capabilities of specific aircraft equipage; flight management systems and avionics packages developed by different manufacturers vary in performance characteristics and these differences have crucial implications for how certain procedures are flown. As a final example, imagine the utility of an aircraft sensing its low and decreasing altitude and the fact that both its engines have been shut down, combining that with navigation data concerning its precise coordinates, and then automatically presenting only the most essential emergency checklist actions for flight crew completion. Here, the checklist adapts to the exact circumstances and needs of the situation as well as the workload of the pilots.

In the future, information from electronic operating documents, the FMS and data regarding flight parameters, systems functioning, autoflight modes, aircraft configuration, equipage, performance capabilities, on-board radar, external hazard detection, and external information uplinked to the aircraft could be combined and fully integrated to provide powerful support to the flight crew.

Benefits and Limitations of Dynamic Electronic Operational Documents

As illustrated above, there are many benefits to be had by the introduction of dynamic documents in operational settings (see Table 5.2). Workload can be substantially reduced, particularly with regard to combining information from a variety of sources to complete complex calculations, and sorting through reams of information to identify only that which is expected to be pertinent for the specific situation and operational procedure to be conducted. Decreased workload means that tasks become less vulnerable to interruptions minimizing the likelihood that procedural steps will get skipped (Dismukes, Berman, and Loukopoulos, 2007) and there is less demand placed on working[2] and prospective[3] memory. The likelihood of other types of human error, such as those related to habit capture,[4] may also be reduced. Because dynamic documents are typically located and/or presented automatically based on data from sensors, it is significantly less likely that operators will access the wrong document or information. Dynamic documents will also tend to have fewer manual data entry requirements and could contain error checkers to help identify when manually entered data is incorrect. Thus, operational procedures can be simplified and streamlined resulting in great gains in accuracy and enhanced operator performance (Boorman, 2000).

Information from dynamic documents must be displayed however, and the design of clear, comprehensible displays, especially when document information is combined with other operational information, can be challenging. A poor design can actually increase operator workload and give rise to confusion and errors. Further, serious trouble can result if incorrect information is generated (for example, there is a sensor failure), the wrong information is accessed or combined, or even if correct information is presented but at inappropriate times. Determining how to best combine and present information that accommodates situations or conditions that are highly unusual and unexpected is also extremely daunting and, in some cases, may never be fully achievable. Display "real estate" in many operational settings is also limited and it can be cumbersome to toggle among different displays when accomplishing concurrent tasks if separate displays are required (that is, information from the multiple displays is not or cannot be combined). Indeed there are many challenges in designing dynamic document systems and the remainder of this chapter will be devoted to discussing some of them in more detail.

---

2   Working Memory is that part of human memory where information is held and manipulated. It is working memory that allows humans to analyze, plan, and perform mental calculations. The maintenance of information in working memory typically requires some type of rehearsal.
3   Prospective Memory is remembering to perform a task at a later point in time when it is appropriate to do so.
4   A Habit Capture error is the completion of a habitual task when, because of changes in circumstances, it is not appropriate to perform it.

Issues in Designing and Developing Dynamic Operational Documents: Operational Considerations

Philosophy of operations, design, and use

Whether explicitly stated or not, manufacturers design operating work stations, such as airplane cockpits, and documents and procedures in keeping with various philosophies (Boorman, 2000; Chandra et al., 2003). The answers to several questions help to clarify the philosophies that underlie the development, design, and use of dynamic operating documents. What kinds of roles should automation play relative to humans in the performance of different operational tasks? How much information should be made available or be presented to operators? How much control should humans have with regard to what dynamic information gets displayed, in what format, and when (that is, is information automatically dynamically altered, manipulated, and combined or must users request that information and documents behave dynamically)? Is information automatically presented—"pushed"—or do operators have to request or "pull" it? Normal operational demands fluctuate over time and further vary as abnormal or emergency conditions arise. Over the course of these normal and non-normal operations there are many functions that dynamic operating documents might perform (for example, to inform, complete a computation, support decision-making, accomplish or support completion of a task, and so on). For which purposes, tasks, or situations should dynamic information or documents be developed and why? Are there purposes, tasks, or situations for which the development and use of dynamic documents is not appropriate or is contraindicated?

These questions cut across many different areas: automation, workload and information management, communication, non-normal situation response, display design, and fundamental notions about how operations should be performed. Although dynamic operating documents can be quite beneficial, their development should be based upon a well-reasoned, consistent set of principles and stated philosophy rather than developed indiscriminately or haphazardly and driven mostly by serendipitous opportunity afforded by newly available technologies and sensors. Just because one *can* combine information and make a document dynamic does not mean that one *should*.

Advanced sensor technologies make it possible to "package" information for operator use in a variety of ways and developers must be clear at the outset about where on the "document-task demand" continuum their development efforts will be focused. At one end of the continuum, the "document" end, the traditional notion of what constitutes a document is the organizing feature. In other words, information is packaged and displayed as distinct and discrete documents. A dynamic checklist is located with other checklists and is recognizable as a single, coherent, and complete checklist. It is accessed or presented at the appropriate time, accomplished, and then put away. In contrast, at the "task demand" end of the continuum, documents cease to exist as identifiable units during operations. Instead, the information, actions, data, and directions that comprise traditional documents are broken apart (LeRoy, 2002; Ramu, Barnard, Payeur, and Larroque, 2004) and combined with other types of operational data. Entirely new compositions of data are presented to support the operator's task requirements at each moment. Thus, the specific task demands encountered are the feature that drives how information is organized and what is presented. Typically, not all dynamic documents will fall at the same place on the continuum within any single operational setting. Clearly, levels of automation, not to mention philosophy of automation-human roles, and the availability of various types of sensor data will drive some of the decisions about where on the document-task demand continuum the development of dynamic operational information will fall. For ease of reference, we will continue to use the term operational "document" to refer to any dynamically constructed and presented information regardless of where it technically falls on the continuum.

Data sources, reliability, and integrity
In most operational settings there are a large number of sources where data and information might originate for the construction of dynamic documents. Does the information come from databases, sensors, or algorithms? Does it come from sources within or near to the operational work station or is it sent or acquired from afar? How fresh or stale is the information? Is manual entry of some information required or is it generated automatically? Regardless of the source, the degree to which the data are accurate and reliable will be of paramount concern. When data from several sources are combined, bad data from one source affects all the others and renders all resulting dynamic operational information incorrect and untrustworthy. Obviously, it is absolutely essential that underlying algorithms or the manner in which information is combined and yields information is correct throughout all phases of the operation and under normal and non-normal operating conditions.

Operators may find it helpful for the sources of various types of dynamic operational information and the underlying assumptions or algorithms upon which they are based to be transparent (Chandra et al., 2003; National Transportation Safety Board (NTSB), 2007), in addition to having mechanisms whereby sensor errors can be identified and suspect information can be verified. However, operators should not be placed in the role of constantly having to cross-check or verify dynamic operational information; the current philosophy in the airline industry is for the automation to ensure that the information is correct or to not present it at all (Boorman, personal communication, February 19, 2009). When dynamic operational information is not correct or available, operators will need to have a back-up method for acquiring the information necessary for the performance of tasks. Currently, the minimal implementation of dynamic operating documents in most settings is due to the lack of necessary sensors or the complexity of testing and guaranteeing dynamic document reliability and integrity.

Information integration and presentation
The optimal ways to present dynamic operating documents to users, particularly when display space is limited, also poses challenges for developers. Many initial decisions regarding presentation will be driven by decisions made about where on the document-task demand continuum the development effort will be focused. From the development perspective, it is easier to keep documents as identifiable units and only select certain information within them for dynamic behavior. So too, operators are currently used to referring to multiple documents throughout an operational cycle, so maintaining documents as unified wholes requires the least amount of change in their behavior. This approach, however, does not harness the full potential of dynamic information in operational settings and does less to

streamline procedures, minimize information gathering and consolidation activities, and reduce overall workload than development approaches closer to the middle or task demand end of the continuum.

Whatever development approach is used, it is essential that dynamic operational documents and information are compatible and consistent with other systems, information, displays, and technologies to be used by the operators (Chandra et al., 2003). Procedures should be developed for the integrated and coherent use of these multiple systems, displays, and technologies. If the same dynamic information is available in more than one display or through different technologies, developers must ensure that the information presented is the same, regardless of the display on which it is presented (Chandra et al., 2003). Additionally, it should be made clear to operators if back-up systems contain documents that are not dynamic. Procedures must also be in place for the use of these back-up document systems as well as the transition between the dynamic system normally used and the back-up, non-dynamic document system.

Optimal user support
Dynamic operational documents, when well-designed, can greatly enhance operator performance. For this to occur, however, they must be designed with the human user's capabilities and limitations, particularly in the cognitive domain, first and foremost in mind. These considerations are so important that we devote an entire section to them later in this chapter.

Obviously, the organization of dynamic information and documents and modes of accessing them must support the user's operational needs throughout the operational cycle, during periods of high and low workload. Various types of tasks and work analyzes that deconstruct operational (and cognitive) demands can be useful in guiding the development of dynamic systems (Boy, 1998; Diaper and Stanton, 2004; Seamster, Redding, and Kaempf, 1997; Vicente, 1999). Dynamic documents must support both operational tasks that are commonly performed as well as those that are rarely performed (Boorman, 2000) and thus, operational demand analyzes must consider both normal and non-normal operations. During periods of high workload especially, dynamic operational documents should support and enhance user performance rather than serve as a distracter or increase workload demands (Chandra et al., 2003). Additionally, the right information should be presented or made available at the time it is needed. Alternate methods for locating operational information should be available to support users who desire information which cannot be anticipated by an automated dynamic operating document system. An extreme example of this would be during a non-normal event that has not manifested itself before. In this case, because the non-normal operating condition had not been previously predicted, the system will not be programmed to select the right documents or the right steps to address the problem. The default settings that the system falls back to should follow the basic guidelines above—to assist rather than hinder the user through the information it provided.

When manually input data are required, the type and format of the information needed must be clear to the operator. Additionally, operators should only be asked to enter and confirm the manually entered data once, even if this information is used by multiple operational systems and technologies (Chandra et al., 2003). Workload is not reduced if operators have to enter the same information in multiple locations or if they have to guess at what data are required or how it should be formatted for entry.

In most complex operational settings, it is rare for only one task to be completed at a time. Instead, multiple tasks are typically interwoven and accomplished concurrently (Loukopoulos, Dismukes, and Barshi, 2009). Developers will need to consider whether the same technologies, interfaces, or displays (for example, EFB) will be required for accomplishing these multiple concurrent tasks and eliminate or at least minimize the amount of toggling among displays required. Indeed, one of the significant advantages of dynamic operating documents and information over other systems is the combination and integration of operational information that reduces the need to shift among displays and multiple sources of information. Further, it is essential that the behavior of dynamic operational document systems is consistent, predictable, and transparent to users. Some of the greatest confusions for pilots on the flight deck are caused by the unexpected behavior of automated systems (Sarter and Woods, 1995).

Cognitive and Human Performance Considerations

Situation awareness and maintaining operator understanding

Generally speaking, situation awareness, as applied to operational documents, can be thought of as an operator's perception of information, knowledge of the origin of that information, and understanding the meaning or implications that information has for operations both at the current moment but also in the near future (Endsley, 1995). It can be easy for operators to lose situation awareness in several different ways when documents are presented electronically, and particularly when they are dynamic. For example, when an electronic document is not presented automatically, cues may be necessary to remind the operator that a needed document is available so it can be manually accessed. Operators can also lose orientation or perspective (a particular problem when graphic images are presented on displays that cannot accommodate their complete size), or lose track of their progress when using electronically presented textual information. Readers are referred to Boorman (2000), Civil Aviation Authority (2005), Cosimini (2002), and Hackos (2002), for a more in-depth review of document presentation issues and various design solutions (for example, paging versus scrolling, using color to indicate step completion, and so on).

The integration of information from multiple sources can also be rather disorienting, particularly for users who are used to dealing with separate distinct documents or sources of data. Experts' knowledge is cognitively represented in a well-tested schema, which is a mental representation used to structure and organize information (Bartlett, 1979). With practice, users adapt and refine their schema until they can utilize it for organizing and understanding every aspect of their work tasks, which leads to quick and efficient performance. Klein (1993) has emphasized the degree to which experts rely on well-honed schema to recognize and react to time-critical and stressful situations. So, changing a significant aspect of operators' routines, such as the source and format of the information they use, can force them to reorganize their cognitive schema. Additionally, when some of that information changes dynamically, as was illustrated in the revised "A Day in the Life of a Pilot" above, users can easily lose track of what calculations have been performed automatically, what information went into those calculations, and the original sources of that information (Berman, personal communication, March 23, 2009). Knowledge of these things becomes particularly important if an automated calculation is suspected of being incorrect. Therefore, developers must devise ways to ensure the transparency of not only the underlying philosophy, algorithms, and organization of dynamic documents, as discussed earlier, but also the information sources when data are integrated, combined, or used in automated calculations.

Memory load and workload

Despite their intended use as memory aids or memory replacements, static (that is, non-dynamic) documents can place a heavy memory demands and workload on users. This is caused, in part, by users having to navigate within the documents to locate only that information that is pertinent at that time and simply remembering which documents to turn to if there are multiple tasks to complete. Assisting operators by integrating information from multiple sources, performing complicated computations, and presenting only that information which is needed are some of the great advantages of dynamic documents over all other formats.

A related advantage is that dynamic documents can present information at the exact time that it is needed, thereby reducing memory load and helping to minimize prospective memory failures, that is, failing to remember to perform a task when its execution must be delayed until a later point in time. For example, in 1996, a Continental DC-9 landed gear up because the crew missed the "Hydraulics on High" item on the In-Range Checklist and then in the ensuing confusion, forgot to complete the Landing Checklist (NTSB, 1997). Had the In-Range Checklist automatically remained on the display until all items were completed and had the Landing Checklist automatically been presented, it is much less likely that the error chain would have occurred as it did.

Because of the advantages just described, almost by definition dynamic operating documents reduce user workload. It is possible, however, to design a dynamic operating document system that actually increases a user's workload, such as when the interface for accessing documents is not intuitive and simple; when unnecessary, inaccurate, or incomplete information is presented; when users cannot easily locate documents, or information is not automatically presented or queued for presentation; or when the system requires that a great deal of data be manually input by the user. As stated earlier, workload is not reduced when users must manually input the same data in multiple places or must guess at the format in which the data must be entered. A user's workload will also not be lessened when only a small fraction of the possible information is made dynamic and users must still access and integrate information from multiple sources.

Information overload

A question facing the designers of all documents is how much information to make available to potential users of a system beyond the items that require user input. An increasingly prevalent problem resulting from efficient microchip storage (where a small chip can contain terabytes of data) is that a physically small system can provide more data than a person can possibly assimilate. Given more information to sift through than can be organized cognitively, users can experience information overload (Edmunds and Morris, 2000), where they cannot pull out the relevant key items of information required to make a decision or to act. Hiltz and Turoff (1985) describe information overload arising first as a "problem" and then growing into a "constant challenge to be overcome," underlining that people can become drawn into information management to the detriment of the task at hand. Set against this is the benefit of making larger amounts of information available for those who might need it.

Thus, there are two issues that a dynamic document developer has to consider. First, archives and instructions need to be easily obtained without creating clutter in the main flow of activity. Second, if steps in a workflow are not necessary in a particular situation, should they be left in but marked as non-applicable in some way, such as graying out the text, or should they be deleted entirely (the hallmark of dynamic documents)? There are advantages but also costs to both approaches. As discussed earlier, deleting non-applicable information reduces the length of documents, decreases workload, and streamlines procedures. However, retaining but graying out non-applicable steps may assist a user in maintaining better situation awareness and, as noted above, reduce confusion if the user needs to refer to paper or non-dynamic electronic documents in the event that the dynamic operating document system is unavailable.

Interruptions, distractions, concurrent task management, and operator attention
As mentioned earlier, in most professional and industrial settings, operators must accomplish multiple tasks within the same time period. Quite often, steps comprising these multiple tasks are interwoven or interleaved requiring the operator to constantly shift focus among these multiple tasks, performing a few steps for one task before moving to a different task and then back again (Loukopoulos, Dismukes, and Barshi, 2009). The management of these multiple concurrent tasks is not an easy feat, however, and being interrupted or distracted during the performance of these tasks makes operators in all settings vulnerable to errors such as forgetting a step related to a task or getting fixated on one task and forgetting to shift attention and execute the others (Loukopoulos, et al., 2009). Because dynamic operating documents can streamline procedures, the amount of concurrent task management required is reduced as several tasks can be integrated into one. Also, as already discussed, by reducing operator workload and the amount of time required to execute tasks, dynamic operating documents also reduce the likelihood of operator error due to interruptions and distractions. Electronic tools, such as place-holders and moving highlighting or color changes upon task completion can help users combat those interruptions that do occur and avoid memory-related errors when using dynamic and other types of electronic documents.

There are some demands on a user's mental resources that cannot be minimized by making documents dynamic—the amount of attention an operator should pay to any given document is one of these. However, the functionality available for dynamic documents can help users not only focus their attention where they need to but also reduce the amount of time spent looking at irrelevant documents. If the system offers the correct document for a task, users do not spend time and mental resources looking for what they need. For this to happen, the dynamic system has to sense aspects of the situation that allow it to select the correct document. This logic is relatively straightforward if one document must follow another but in less defined situations where there are many possible options, the logic guiding document presentation is far more complex and is correspondingly more difficult to validate (Boorman, 2000).

Thus, how and when to present electronic documents and information are not easy decisions for developers. It is important to provide or make available the information necessary to support efficient operator performance throughout all phases of the operational cycle under both normal and non-normal operating conditions but not in a manner that is in itself distracting or takes the operator's attention from other more critical tasks. A great deal of testing and validation of dynamic and electronic operating document systems is required to ensure that all of these criteria are met.

Limitations in dynamic data and indicating degrees of uncertainty
Integrated electronic and dynamic documents are often developed in response to a number of the common errors that operators make when using paper-based documents (see for example Boorman, 2000). However, as should be obvious by now, the development of a sound, reliable, and accurate dynamic operating document system poses many challenges and designers must take care that they do not introduce new error modes as they try to reduce the likelihood of old error modes common with less technically advanced document formats (Boorman, 2000).

Another development issue, particularly related to dynamic operating documents used in aviation and similar fields, pertains to the fact that information from various sources has different levels of fidelity and is certified or approved according to different standards (see below). Thus, there is the potential that some information may not be as accurate as other information with which it is integrated. In aviation, document developers believe that in a paper-based world, when users turn from one document to another, they should be aware that the content of the documents they are using may have different levels of accuracy, especially if the sources from which they were drawn have different certification or approval requirements (Boorman, personal communication, February 19, 2009). However, users of complex systems tend to trust automation they are familiar with (Lee and See, 2004; Parasuraman and Riley, 1997) even if it makes occasional errors. So, indicating the trustworthiness of dynamic information to users is important. A design challenge for the developer of dynamic operating documents then, is to communicate these confidence levels to users without distracting them. In other words, when using a system, the user should be aware that, although all the documents available dynamically function in the same way (that is, they have the same "look and feel"), they should not be viewed with the same level of confidence. Two approaches to address this would be to allow users to drill down to access information's confidence levels or to display an indicator of the level of uncertainty to remind operators that the information may not be completely reliable or accurate. A third approach is to simply decide that information from sources which have lower levels of integrity will not be integrated or combined with that from sources of higher integrity.

Training new skills
Training operators to use dynamic documents should be easier than training them to use paper-based documents because much of the knowledge about where to find information and manipulating it will be performed by the automation. This eases the users' mental loads—memory and reasoning—thus reducing the number of

skills that need to be trained. However, training will have to expand in other areas. One addition to the curriculum will be explanations of how the dynamic operating document system works, sources from which the information is drawn, and how it is integrated or combined. One key aspect of this training will be to make users aware of how much, and when, information varies in reliability, accuracy, and fidelity, when information of varying levels of integrity have been combined, and educate users about the implications these variations have for how the information, and the dynamic operating document system as a whole, are to be used.

Certification and Approval Considerations

Certification for any product confirms that it meets certain performance and quality requirements. Performance criteria may include efficiency or a product's suitability for its intended use. In the case of safety-critical systems like some dynamic documents, certification may include the degree to which safety criteria are met and testing results are robust. Certification is usually achieved through an assessment by an agent or organization outside of the design and production company—in the field of aviation in the United States this organization is the Federal Aviation Administration (FAA). Thus, certification demonstrates that a third, disinterested party considers that the product meets certain specified criteria.

An electronic document can be seen as having two parts, the database of information that is displayed to the user and the software that drives the look and functionality of the system, giving the data its dynamic capabilities. The database of information must be correct and the software driving the system must function appropriately and be designed with the human operator in mind for users to obtain the information they require at the appropriate time. Users are most concerned with the contents of the documents they are using (and the functionality makes it more or less easy to access the information desired). Although both parts of an electronic document are important to a certifier, in aviation certifiers typically place a greater emphasis on ensuring appropriate software functioning because that software must link to other aircraft systems in order to allow the electronic documents to behave dynamically.

Database approval
The information in a set of documents, the database, needs to be checked for its accuracy when it is initially developed and at any later point after editing, in addition to when the equipment is certified. It is possible that, post-certification some or all of this information may change based on new findings or circumstances. For example, if an element in a system is redesigned, the procedures for using that element may change too, and the procedure-related information for this element will need to be updated in the documentation. (This is the "information maintenance process" described in Table 5.1.) Therefore, the certification process needs to allow for the resubmission and approval of changes to the information in documents (of all formats) on at least a semi-regular basis.

In aviation within the United States, the database for electronic documents is classified as operational information and requires only FAA regulatory approval (rather than full certification) under Federal Aviation Regulations Part 121 (see Advisory Circular (AC) 120–64). Information included in electronic databases has to adhere to the same approval criteria as information in paper manuals (see Federal Aviation Regulation 121.133) because the information in both media is the same. Hence, airlines are able to make updates and changes to electronic document databases when they need to just as they would do in a paper manual, as described in Table 5.1.

Provision for the use of electronic database information for electronic checklist systems is outlined in AC120–64, and includes criteria for training and retraining flight crews in its use.

Software certification
The functionality of electronic document systems should not change as regularly as their content, if at all. Certification needs to verify that document functions—access of documents for display, links, sensor inputs, software-driven reformatting, automatic computations, and so on—are predictable, consistent, accurate, and operate as intended. Currently the software, or functionality, of electronic checklists and documentation developed in aviation under US jurisdiction, is certified as "avionics software" according to AC 20–145 and the Radio Technical Commission for Aeronautics document 178B (RTCA DO-178B). DO-178B states that the software for aviation electronic documents of any kind will be held to the same criteria and treated in the same way with respect to certification as the flight management system or any other computer-driven system on the aircraft. Thus, aviation electronic software must be certified (rather than just approved) under Federal Aviation Regulation Part 25, subpart F.

Prior to certification, software developers will run multiple tests to work out as many system bugs as possible and system checking will be continuous throughout development starting even before any code has been written. There are multiple methods for testing software, ranging from running the system and assessing it based purely on its output, to testing function points, which are derived from user requirements (Albrecht, 1979). However, developing software is an iterative and evolving process. A software developer starts with an analysis of a dynamic document's requirements, and then testing begins with the first program and with each evolution of the dynamic functions until each meets pre-specified exit criteria (Pan, 1999). In the development of some equipment, such as the designing and building of a new aircraft, systems are incrementally constructed and tested. At appropriate points, dynamic documents are integrated into their host systems and tested in-situ. The certification process for the entire aircraft begins when all of these various systems have been integrated and tested together.

The focus of the certification process for some equipment and systems, such as aircraft or air traffic control and processing plant operating stations, is primarily on safety rather than a variety of other factors such as efficiency, weight, or other factors that are of concern to the designer. To meet certification requirements, the designer has to specify all the intended functions of the system and how it will be used and then specify all possible hazards or failures—instances where a system might not operate as intended—and give an account of the effects these failures could have (that is, a Failure Modes and Effects Analysis, FMEA). For example, what possible effects could there be if a checklist gives a flight crew the wrong guidance? If this results in the aircraft gear being left down rather than retracted during flight, then the outcome would be reduced fuel efficiency and possible damage to the gear. However, if the incorrect guidance results in the gear being retracted when it should be left down, then the outcome could be a wheels-up landing, which has many safety implications and could constitute a far greater hazard. The design team works to remove the possibility of these hazards or failures arising. For certification in aviation, the third party regulator (for example, the FAA) has to concur with all the hazard categories developed and analyzes performed by the design team and to agree that functionality of all systems meet their intended objectives.

In aviation, the steps that precede and form the certification process of electronic document software are time consuming, but essentially consist of studying and testing that the system performs its stated functions as specified and ensuring that the listed hazards are avoided or create only the errors specified (and agreed upon) in prior analyzes. It is accepted that there are extremely rare, as-yet unseen, events for which a system may not function as desired but that it is impossible to predict these events. A system will pass certification scrutiny if it is demonstrated to function safely during all possible known events.

The rules governing the approval or certification of electronic documentation systems in other industries (for example, process control, maritime, nuclear, and so on) will likely differ in some respects from those described above and developers of such systems will need to become intimately familiar with the rules that apply to their industry. An illustration of the approval and certification process in the aviation industry is described below to give novice developers of electronic documentation systems a more complete picture of the kinds of steps that might be required.

Electronic Document System Approval and Certification

An illustration

In aviation, because safety is a critical consideration, the process of system checking and certification begins at the outset of design. The FAA, as the aviation regulatory body, certifies aircraft, and all their systems, in a four phase process. These phases are; (1) formal application, (2) design assessment, (3) performance assessment, and (4) administration to issue the final certificates, that is, Part 25 Certification and Part 121 Approval (FAA, 2008). For the formal application, aircraft designers have to submit all the manuals that will accompany the aircraft. This means that any dynamic document content that involves, or is involved in, aircraft procedures has to be scoped and developed prior to the first FAA certification phase. However, aircraft manufacturers begin to design and test electronic documents long before this, as other aircraft systems are being designed.

To take a specific example, the Boeing Company began work to design the electronic checklists (ECL) for their B777 aircraft more than four years before the airplane was certified. Developers created the checklists in three phases prior to certification and a fourth phase that followed certification. In the first development and review phase the preliminary ECL system and database were scoped. The second, validation, phase had two stages. The first stage began with paper and pencil evaluations of checklist procedures and ramped up to testing using simple simulators. The findings from this stage were used to inform the next stage of validation and also to develop relevant portions of the aircraft's Flight Crew Operations Manual and flight crew training.[5] At this point, Boeing developers had the electronic checklist materials they needed to begin their application to the FAA for certification. The second validation stage repeatedly tested the checklists in simulators with increasing fidelity and culminated in flight tests in the first B777 aircraft itself. The ultimate test for an aircraft display system was (and is) a diversion to airport not originally intended as a destination, as might be needed during an emergency. This scenario maximizes the demands on the display functions. After the FAA certified the aircraft (and the checklists) Boeing designers worked with their customers to ensure that they understood how permissible modifications could be made to the checklist database.

Treating dynamic documents as two parts makes their ongoing revision possible. Boeing releases content updates approximately twice a year, and each airline customizes the generic checklists they receive from Boeing to fit their own policies and procedures, but these must also meet the instructions and requirements in AC120–64.

CONCLUSION

In the future, designers will be able to take advantage of advances in software and integrated system design to convert paper documents, not only to an electronic facsimile, but also to interactive dynamic documents that collect and manipulate data to present real-time information to the user. Thus, user workload with respect to document manipulation will be minimized. In the aviation world, advances in this direction are already being made with electronic flight bags, integrated navigational maps, and electronic checklists, to name a few. While stand-alone electronic documents reduce the "paper mountain," integrated electronic documents make the operator's task easier by using sensor data to facilitate progression through and use of the documents. Dynamic documents go one or two steps further—they integrate information from a wide variety of sources and manipulate these data, taking advantage of the ability to pare information presented down to just that which has expected relevance at that time, thereby providing more timely and better support to the system users.

ACKNOWLEDGEMENTS

We would like to express our thanks to Guy A. Boy for his helpful editorial assistance. We would also like to express our deep appreciation to Ben Berman, Dan Boorman, and John Hajdukiewicz for their thoughtful reviews, helpful suggestions, pertinent examples, and willingness to share their extensive expertise as we wrote this chapter.

---

5   FAA Certification also has to consider the user. The certification process has to include an implementation plan and this has to include a plan for pilot training to proficiency.

REFERENCES

Air Transport Association. (2002). Displaying data on the flight deck. In *Proceedings of the FAA/ NASA Operating Documents Meeting*, San Diego, CA.

Albrecht, J. (1979). Measuring Application Development Productivity, *Proceedings of the Joint SHARE, GUIDE, and IBM Application Development Symposium*, Monterey, California, October 14–17, IBM Corporation, pp. 83–92.

Bartlett, F.C. (1932). *Remembering: An Experimental and Social Study*. Cambridge: Cambridge University Press.

Boorman, D. (2000). Reducing flight crew errors and minimizing new error modes with electronic checklists. In *Proceedings of the International Conference on Human–computer Interaction in Aeronautics*, 57–63, Polytechnic International Press, Toulouse, France.

Boorman, D. and Hartel, M. (April–June 1997). The 777 electronic checklist system. *Boeing Airliner Magazine*. Seattle, WA: The Boeing Company.

Boy, G.A. (1998). *Cognitive function analysis*. Stamford, CT: Ablex Publishing Corporation.

Burian, B.K., Barshi, I., and Dismukes, K. (2005). *The challenge of aviation emergency and abnormal situations*. NASA Technical Memorandum, NASA/TM-2005–213462.

Chandra, D.C., Yeh, M., Riley, V., and Mangold, S.J. (2003). *Human factors considerations in the design and evaluation of electronic flight bags (EFBs), Version 2*. DOT/FAA/AR-03/67.

Civil Aviation Authority (2005). *CAP 708: Guidance on the design, presentation and use of electronic checklists*. London: Civil Aviation Authority, United Kingdom.

Cosimini, G. (2002). Structure of information in the future. In T.L. Seamster and B.G. Kanki (Eds.), *Aviation information management: From documents to data* (pp. 37–49). Aldershot, Hampshire, England: Ashgate.

Diaper, D. and Stanton, N. (Eds.). (2004). *The handbook of task analysis for human–computer interaction*. Mahwah, NJ: Lawrence Erlbaum Associates.

Dismukes, R.K., Berman, BA, and Loukopoulos, L.D. (2007). *The limits of expertise: Rethinking pilot error and the causes of airline accidents*. Aldershot, Hampshire, England: Ashgate.

Edmunds, A. and Morris, A. (2000). The problem of information overload in business organizations: a review of the literature. *International Journal of Information Management, 20*, pp. 17–28.

Endsley, M.R. (1995). Toward a theory of situation awareness in dynamic systems, *Human Factors, 37*, 32–64.

FAA (2009) *Title 14: Aeronautics and Space, Part 25-Airworthiness Standards: Transport Category Airplanes*. e-CFR. http://ecfr.gpoaccess.gov.

FAA. (2008). Air Carrier Certification Process, 14CFR Part 121, Washington, D.C.: Author.

FAA. (2003a). *Guidelines for the certification, airworthiness, and operational approval of electronic flight bag computing devices*. Advisory Circular 120–76A.

FAA. (2003b). *Guidance for Integrated Modular Avionics (IMA) that implement TSO-C153 authorized hardware elements*. AC 20–145. Washington, D.C.: Author.

FAA. (1996). Operational use and modification of electronic checklists, Advisory Circular 120–64. Washington, D.C.: Author.

Gosling, K. (2002). Electronic flight bag: Enabling a safe and efficient global air transportation system. In *Proceedings of the FAA/NASA Operating Documents Meeting*, San Diego, CA.

Hackos, J.T. (2002). *Content management for dynamic web delivery*. New York: John Wiley and Sons, Inc.

Hiltz, S.R. and Turoff, M. (1985). Structuring computer-mediated communication systems to avoid information overload. *Communications of the ACM, 28 (7)*, 680–689.

Klein, G.A. (1993). A recognition primed decision (RPD) model of rapid decision-making. In G.A. Klein, J. Orasanu, R. Calderwood, and C.E. Zsambok, *Decision-making in Action: Models and Methods* (pp. 138–147). New Jersey: Ablex.

Lee, J.D., and See, K.A. (2004). Trust in automation: Designing for appropriate reliance. *Human Factors, 46*(1), 50–80.

LeRoy, W.W. (2002). Structured information for the cockpit. In T.L. Seamster and B.G. Kanki (Eds.), *Aviation information management: From documents to data* (pp. 93–105). Aldershot, Hampshire, England: Ashgate.

Loukopoulos, L.D., Dismukes, R.K., and Barshi, I. (2009). *The multitasking myth: Handing complexity in real-world operations*. Aldershot, Hampshire, England: Ashgate.

Niwa, Y., Hollnagel, E., and Green, M. (1996). Guidelines for computerized presentation of emergency operating procedures. *Nuclear Engineering and Design, 167*, 113–127.

NTSB (2007). *Safety Recommendation A-07–58*. Downloaded from www.ntsb.gov/Recs/letters/2007/A07_58_64.pdf.

NTSB (1997). *Continental Airlines DC-9–32, Houston, Texas, February 19, 1996. Report no. NTSB/AAR-97/01*. Washington: Author.

O'Hara, J.M., Higgins, J., and Stubler, W. (2000). Computerization of nuclear power plan emergency operating procedures. In *Proceedings of the IEA 2000/HFES 2000 Congress*, San Diego, CA.

Pan, J. (1999). Software Testing (18–849b Dependable Embedded Systems), *Topics in Dependable Embedded Systems*, Electrical and Computer Engineering Department, Carnegie Mellon University.

Parasuraman, R. and Riley, V. (1997). Humans and automation: Use, misuse, disuse, abuse. *Human Factors, 39* (2), 230–253.

Ramu, J.-P., Barnard, Y., Payeur, F., and Larroque, P. (2004). Contextualized operational documentation in aviation. In D. de Waard, K.A. Brookhuis, and C.M. Weikert (Eds.), *Human factors in design* (pp. 1–12). Maastricht, the Netherlands: Shaker Publishing.

Ronan, D, Routhier, T, and Ryan, J. (2000). Electronic navigation on the Coast Guard's medium-endurance cutters. *Navigation, 47* (1), 51–64.

RTCA (1992). *Software Considerations in Airborne Systems and Equipment Certification, RTCA/DO-178B*. RTCA.

Sarter, N.D., and Woods, D.D. (1995). How in the world did we ever get into that mode? Mode error and awareness in supervisory control. *Human Factors, 37* (1), 5–19.

Seamster, T.L., and Kanki, B.G. (2005). Human factors design of electronic documents. In *Proceedings of the 12th International Symposium on Aviation Psychology*. Dayton, OH: Wright State University.

Seamster, T.L., Redding, R.E., Kaempf, G.L. (1997). *Applied cognitive task analysis in aviation*. Aldershot, Hants, England: Avbury Aviation.

Seinfeld, R.D., Herman, R., and Lotterhos, L. (2002). *A pilot information display for the paperless cockpit and more*. In Proceedings of the SPIE Conference, vol. 4712, pp. 8–13.

Vicente, K.J. (1999). *Cognitive work analysis: Toward safe, productive, and healthy computer-based work*. Mahwah, NJ: Lawrence Erlbaum Associates.

Wade, D.R. (2002). Display of electronic information in the cockpit. In T.L. Seamster and B.G. Kanki (Eds.), *Aviation information management: From documents to data* (pp. 147–160). Aldershot, Hampshire, England: Ashgate.

6

The Authority Issue in Organizational Automation

Guy A. Boy and Gudela Grote

INTRODUCTION

Automation is one of the main topics in engineering and human factors. In engineering, several approaches, techniques and tools were developed during the second half of the twentieth century. They range from cybernetics, Laplace transfer functions, Kalman filtering, to further advanced mathematical and computational approaches. In human factors, researchers followed the engineering trend trying to rationalize the way people coped with automation. Human operator models ranged from very simple transfer functions to very sophisticated multi-agent simulations. However for a long time, research efforts were concentrated on a single agent interacting with a machine. During the eighties, we started to be interested in cognitive issues related to human–computer interaction. *Cognitive engineering* was born during this period (Norman, 1982; Hollnagel, and Woods, 1983, 2005; Boy, 1998, 2003).

Since Fitts's report on human engineering for an effective air-navigation and traffic-control system, published in 1951, no significant work has been done to better understand the way humans and machines can fit together, even if the famous Fitts's list was heavily commented and even criticized (Dekker and Woods, 2002). Fitts and his colleagues drafted possible roles of the human operator in future air-traffic control and navigation systems. They developed principles and criteria to design and assess the division of *responsibility* between human operators and machines, as well as among human operators themselves. They anticipated issues in decision-making, the nature of information, the form that information may take (that is, encoding), the rate of flow of information, its storage, perturbation, redundancy, and related research problems. They mostly focused on visual and voice communication problems. This preliminary work led to several lists of strengths and weaknesses of human operators and automated machines (Chapanis, 1965; Swain and Guttman, 1980; Sheridan, 1987). They were called MABA MABA, that is, "Men Are Better At—Machines Are Better At." This was an easy but very limited way to provide guidelines for automation design (Parasuraman, Sheridan, and Wickens, 2000). Later on, Hollnagel and Woods (2005) based their approach on the fact that joint cognitive systems (humans and machines) are dynamic and therefore complex, and need to cope with this kind of complexity at both individual and organizational levels. This approach is descriptive and requires operational developments.

Function allocation cannot be only addressed from a static point of view; it can also be highly dynamic. It can be dynamic because underlying processes are dynamic; it would be better to talk about real-time function adaptation, even if this is often referred to as dynamic function allocation (Corso and Maloney, 1996; Hildebrandt and Harrison, 2003). It can also be dynamic because cognition is distributed (Hutchins, 1995; Wright, Fields, and Harrison, 2000). Distributed cognition investigates the way cognitive issues could be thought in a multi-agent environment. It is not surprising that anthropologists were among the first to introduce this very important human factors perspective (Hutchins, 1995).

What drastically changes today in air traffic management (ATM) is the magnitude of the air capacity, that is, the number of aircraft is tremendously more important than in 1951. Consequently, the conceptual model shifts from a single agent approach to a multi-agent approach. It is no longer possible to analyze each agent in the system independently of the others because the interrelations are far more important than before. Technology is information intensive and organizational setups need to be revisited. Furthermore, agents are no longer only human operators, but also automation in the form of various kinds of software agents dedicated to specific tasks. For that matter, function allocation cannot be thought as an a priori process, but as an evolutionary process. The separability of human–automation sub-systems has become a real issue. The overall ATM system is becoming like a multi-agent biological entity where *complexity* is as much in the links between agents as in agents themselves. This is why function allocation among a set of interconnected agents is a difficult problem.

In order to reach our objective, we will first describe how authority issues emerge from automation. We will define what we mean by authority in human and machine safety-critical systems, and describe the evolution of automation issues, especially in the context of increasingly pervasive computing systems. Then, we will provide a socio-cognitive model that addresses the issue of authority sharing. This model is based on various processes dealing with authority. It should be useful for anticipating possible surprises early enough before they become catastrophic. It will be described as a metaphor of an orchestra. Of course, organizational automation is much broader than classical automation where a single human agent faces an automated machine. We will uncover the difficult issues of emergence, organizational changes, and regulatory developments. The proposed models are presented to support the rationalization of organizational automation where people will have to learn from experience, and technology will have to be adapted accordingly. We are talking about co-adaption of people and technology together within evolutionary organizational changes also. A discussion will be started on the generic aspects of this approach as well as its specificities. The global issue of product maturity and maturity of practices will be described and discussed as a major endeavor for the next decade. Finally, authority in socio-technical systems cannot be really understood without discussing expertise and human involvement, as well as economical constraints and financial philosophies.

AUTHORITY ISSUES THAT EMERGE FOR AUTOMATION

Many authors agree (for example, Boy, 1998; Grote et al., 2000; Hauss and Timpe, 2002; Hollnagel and Woods, 2005; Waterson et al., 2002; Ulich, 1994) that limits to automation are not only determined by technical feasibility and societal acceptance, but to a large part by the necessity to maintain human authority over system goals and their attainment, including all positive and negative (side) effects. Authority involves both control over systems as well as responsibility and accountability for system functioning. Human control over technical systems, including transparency, predictability, and sufficient means of influencing the systems, is considered to be the main prerequisite responsibility and accountability. As Hollnagel and Woods (2005) point out, control not only concerns the ability to achieve desired outcomes, but also the ability to recover from disturbances and disruptions. The increasing complexity of automated systems, for instance, through increasing application of "autonomous" and "learning" systems, renders it more and more difficult to meet the conditions for human control, and thereby also raises the question of whether human operators can still be held accountable for the functioning of these systems.

In order to discuss issues of authority properly, it is important to point out that every automated system is a socio-technical system, independent of its degree of automation, as the workerless factory, the driverless subway, or automated money transfer systems have been developed by humans for humans. Therefore, technical systems should never be looked at in isolation, but always as part of a socio-technical system, which includes humans operating the system and the formal and informal structures and processes within which they work. Furthermore, it is necessary to include in the system definition all those organizations and organizational units, which are in charge of system design and maintenance, as well as those that are responsible for rules and regulations controlling system design and operation. This much broader framework helps to reframe questions on the distribution of authority in complex socio-technical systems (Baram, 2007).

Despite the many system design methods which have been developed with the core tenet of human control over technology (for example, Boy, 1998; Grote et al., 2000; Hollnagel, 2003; Hollnagel and Woods, 2005; Timpe et al., 2002), there still is ample evidence especially in accident and incident analyses of an unfortunate coupling of human and technology. One example is the accident involving a Lufthansa Airbus A320 in Warsaw on September 14, 1993 (Main Commission Aircraft Accident Investigation Warsaw, 1994), where the automatic algorithm (with no manual override) for braking the aircraft after touchdown on the runway was instigated too late. This algorithm is released only when there is a pre-specified amount of pressure on both back wheels, which in this case did not happen immediately after touchdown due to a slight tilt of the aircraft and the resulting unequal pressure on the wheels. The delay in braking the aircraft resulted in the aircraft overrunning the runway and crashing into a mound of earth. The aircraft caught fire immediately and two people were killed. As a consequence of this accident, Lufthansa pilots were informed in more detail about the technical definition of the landing procedure and some technical improvements of the Lufthansa Airbus aircraft were implemented. The fully automatic control of reverse thrust and of the brakes during landing was left unchanged. Informing the pilots was meant to re-establish conditions for keeping them responsible, without actually changing the distribution of authority between human and technology.

The problems resulting from removing control from the human operator in this way have been described very well by Amalberti (1992, 1993). He assumes that human operators act on the basis of an "ecological risk management," which allows pilots to deal with their resource limitations by anticipating different courses of action, prioritization of actions, and active control forcing the actual situation to follow the anticipated one. He further argues that this way of dealing with risk is rendered more difficult by automation as transparency and flexibility are lost. Pilots react to this difficulty by trying either to outwit the technical system—for example, they may enter non-existent wind into the computer in order for the computer to calculate a different, that is, the desired, approach angle—or by fully ceding responsibility to the technical system.

For technology to support the pilots' ecological risk management, system designers would have to consider human situated problem-solving strategies more, instead of assuming prescriptive optimal strategies. This would require acknowledging the human as being at least as much a safety factor as a risk factor. By viewing the human mainly as a risk factor and assigning the majority of functions to technology as the presumed safety factor, the human is turned into a risk factor instead. A self-fulfilling prophecy is created.

The importance of implicit or explicit assumptions concerning the role of humans and technology in the overall socio-technical system for selecting allocation criteria in system design has been pointed out by Bailey (1989). He distinguished five such assumptions and described their consequences for decisions on function allocation (see Table 6.1). Methods like KOMPASS (Grote et al., 2000; Wäfler et al., 2003) support design teams by systematically reflecting upon their basic assumptions regarding the role of human and technology in bringing about system performance. Specifically, they aim to change designers' assumptions about the nature of humans and technology when necessary, in order to support the human as a resource and safety factor.

Table 6.1   Criteria for human–machine function allocation and underlying assumptions

Allocation criterion	Implicit assumptions about the nature of	
	Humans	Technology
Cost efficiency: The allocation to human or technology is solely determined by who can do the job cheaper	Both are cost producing factors	
Leftover: As many functions as possible are automated, the rest are allocated to the human	Disturbance and risk factor	Effectiveness and safety factor
Performance comparison: Human and technological capabilities are compared and the presumably better performing agent is allocated the respective function	Both are competing factors	
Humane tasks: Functions are allocated so as to create meaningful, motivating tasks for the human	Valuable resource	Support for human operator
Flexible allocation: Functions are allocated redundantly to the joint human-technology system in order to be able to decide on the actual function allocation flexibly according to situational demands	Both are valuable resources	

Source: From Grote, 2009; adapted from Bailey, 1989.

A SOCIO-COGNITIVE MODEL THAT SUPPORTS AUTHORITY SHARING

Authority can be distributed among a set of agents. The hierarchical model is certainly the most well known and used for a long time. At the top, there is a president, a director or a general. There are several levels down to the "atomic" agent who is typically called an employee, a worker or a soldier. The hierarchical model is a priori and rigidly structured, and information flows are essentially vertical, mainly downwards. Authority is also going upwards, that is, an agent at a given level L reports to an agent at level L-1. However, deliberate hierarchical authority is not necessarily accepted when it does not reflect enough competence, empathy, as well as appropriate control and responsibility. On top of deliberate hierarchical authority is emergent authority that is really recognized by people. When the same agent owns both, he or she is at the right place, that is, the right cognitive function is allocated to the right agent. The hierarchical model assumes vertical dependencies among agents, but affords very few interactions horizontally, or laterally. This creates ignorance among lateral agents. At the same time, when two agents want to interact between each other and do not know about each other, they need a great deal of supervision. This leads to the first important model of interaction that is *supervision*. In human–machine interaction, when people do not know how to use a machine, they need a knowledgeable person who will be able to help them to interact and eventually recover from errors or failures. This knowledgeable person is called a supervisor. Supervisors have recognized authority because they are competent and can support multi-agent interactions. Note that operational documentation often replaces external supervision. Human operators use such operational documentation to support their tasks. We then can see operational documentation, and today intelligent assistant systems, as a kind of supervision.

Authority can be shared by several agents. The blackboard model was taken in artificial intelligence (AI) to represent a common knowledge base that can be iteratively updated by various agents. The blackboard was used to support the elaboration of a problem statement and the iterative construction of a solution. Various specialist agents can work together without knowing each other, but are able to share and understand their productions mediated by a set of well-organized blackboard constraints. The blackboard is a mediating support enabling multi-agent interactions. It was originally designed as a way to handle complex and ill-defined problems. AI researchers who extensively worked on blackboard systems talk about knowledge sources instead of agents. They see the generic blackboard as a sort of dynamic library of agents' contributions on a specific issue. The Web can be seen as a blackboard for example. Meeting environments can also be seen as blackboards that require moderators, facilitators or mediators. This leads to the second important model of interaction that is *mediation*. In human–computer interaction, WYSIWYG (what you see is what you get) user interfaces are very good examples of mediating environments that enable humans and machines to interact easily. A good desktop user interface usually does not require additional operational documentation to support user interaction. We could consider that mediation is a step ahead of supervision in the sense that agents are "automatically" mediated, and consequently leads to easier interaction. Office automation and human computer interaction communities have contributed a great deal in the development of such a model. Mediation involves the concept of common frame of reference because any agent needs to be able to understand what the others are "saying," and eventually doing.

Authority can be delegated from one agent to other agents. Anytime a task is too complicated and overloads the human being, Agent-1, who executes it, a part of it is usually delegated to someone else, Agent-2, in order to perform it correctly. The way this delegation is performed is crucial. For example, Agent-1 may supervise Agent-2, or Agent-1 and Agent-2 may work together, reporting to each other cooperatively. We have already seen in the supervision model that the supervisor, Agent-1 for example, has the authority. But in the cooperation model, Agent-1 and Agent-2 need to have a common understanding of what each other is doing. We call this model *cooperation by mutual understanding* (Boy, 2002). This means that cooperative agents must understand what the others are doing, why, when, and how, in order to anticipate their own actions. Human beings interacting between each other typically use this model. More generally, when people use computing media, they need to understand the behavior of this media in reaction to their own actions and the feedback from the environment. The more we introduce interconnected machine agents, that is, automation, the more people interacting with them must understand emerging behaviors. Conversely, saying that machine agents must understand human operator's behavior means that designers and engineers must understand it in order to implement the right functions in them. This is extremely difficult because designers and engineers cannot anticipate all situations and contexts in which human operators will use the software agents that they are designing. Consequently, the model of cooperation by mutual understanding is build incrementally by trial and error, putting the overall human–automation system at work. It is important to understand that anytime someone delegates a task (or a sub-task) to someone else, he or she looses direct control of the delegated task. He or she needs to manage the coordination between what the delegate performs and his or her own performance. The overall control is now a question of management and not longer direct control of the delegated actions performed by the delegate. As already said above in a different way, authority is either deliberately assigned to a supervisor, or emerges from the construction of a common frame of reference shared by all interacting agents. The management of this common frame of reference could be supported by contracts established by the various agents. The way these contracts are established is also a matter of policy (Bradshaw et al., 2005); it could be done deliberately by a leader, or cooperatively by reaching consensus.

Authority can be traded among agents. This means that authority is not allocated to one or several agents forever; it could be reallocated with respect to context. Trading involves planning and therefore reduction of uncertainty, that is, static function allocation. It also involves real-time problem-solving and therefore flexibility, that is, dynamic function allocation. Authority trading may be handled globally at the level of the entire organization to reduce uncertainty by solid planning, or locally within a subset of the organization to insure flexibility for rapid adjustments. Global trading and local trading may be conflicting processes. Both are typically performed according to principles and criteria such as safety and performance. Authority trading involves *negotiation*. Negotiation is the fourth interaction model. It involves at least two agents trading for the establishment of appropriate contracts, eventually used by them to cooperate by mutual understanding. Negotiation involves work on information flows between agents. In the air space system, information flows relate to trajectories of aircraft.

Today, we would like to be able to anticipate everything. This is of course impossible, but knowing in which interaction model we are supports the anticipation of potential surprises. Our behavior will not be the same if this model is supervision, mediation, cooperation by common understanding or negotiation. In the supervision model, the supervisor is in charge of everything, and therefore needs to anticipate at any time. In the mediation model, the shared database or blackboard is responsible for such *anticipation* and warn agents of potential hazards and important events. In the consensual cooperation by common understanding model, anticipation is often the result of a well-organized distribution of cognition among agents. In the negotiation model, anticipation results from the best compromise between planning and flexibility.

Let's take a concrete example. To date, air traffic controllers (ATCO) have full authority for sending orders to aircraft in order to fix flight levels and clearances; that is typically the supervision model. One exception was introduced when the Traffic-alert and Collision Avoidance System (TCAS) was installed on board aircraft. When two planes are getting close to each other, each TCAS provides an alert: one requests the pilot to climb and the other requests to descend. These orders are coordinated. Whenever a TCAS alert occurs, aircrew must take action to avoid collision with the other aircraft by descending or climbing, and sending resolution advisory information to the ground. Consequently, authority is delegated to pilots in this particular case; that is typically the cooperation by common understanding model. This means that both air crew and ATCO must share the same frame of reference with the same information instantiating it.

THE ORCHESTRA MODEL

There is a vast amount of work done in the domain of shared (or not shared) mental models (Kanki and Foushee, 1989; Walz et al., 1993; Malone and Crowston, 1994; Faraj and Sproull, 2000; Mathieu et al., 2000). Even though, there is still a large amount of research to be carried out on the difficult problem of representing and simulating interaction among agents. The Orchestra model was designed and proposed as a metaphoric framework to rationalize authority sharing in the highly computerized evolution of human–machine systems (Boy, 2009). Indeed, information technology is mainly responsible for making information flows more horizontal, that is, people may communicate using telephone, email and Internet with almost anyone with few hierarchical constraints. In addition, people and groups have become more expert and autonomous, that is, there are more specialists whether they are individual contributors in the organization or sub-contractors and external suppliers. Today, practices within the organization are very similar to musicians' practices within an orchestra. Playing a beautiful symphony requires four types of pillars: music theory, scores for musicians, a conductor and the musicians themselves.

Today, some companies are more multifunctional, multinational, and distributed among large networks of employees, suppliers, and clients. The various agents in the product life cycle need clear definitions of data, information, and knowledge used in the domain, as well as the relations among them. All agents as "musicians" need to share a common "music theory." In industry where organizational automation is integrated, music theory is the ontology of the domain, for example, the concepts and vocabulary used in aeronautics or medicine. We could talk about a common frame of reference that supports communication, cooperation, coordination, and, more generally, authority sharing and consequently a common frame of reference.

Each agent (as a musician) has a specific score to perform his/her part (of the symphony), that is, a prescribed task to perform. The functional "score" represents far more than the musical sheet in front of the performer. It extends to the culture and traditions of music and orchestral work, the rules and regulations of a particular orchestra company, the formal and informal lines of authority, the established "good manners" of the performers in relation to each other, and so forth. Each agent is an expert and knows how to play his/her part in the symphony, but needs to cooperate with the others to perform the symphony. Consequently, all scores must be coordinated in the orchestra. In addition to the norms and regulations of being in an orchestra, this is usually the job of the composer. In industry, this is what planning, programming, and culture are all about. We can see that we strongly need composers in industry today, and that these composers should have broader competences than finance. This is where authority distribution enters into play.

The conductor takes care of the synchronization of the musicians during performance. The conductor has specific skills that include knowing music theory, scores, and the way to coordinate the performing musicians. The conductor articulates work performed by the right agents at the right time. We could say that the conductor takes care of the delegation issue.

Each musician has his or her own competence and role. Each of them knows how to play an instrument. Musicians also know how to adjust (adapt) their play according to the play of the others, that is, they know how to articulate the relevant part of the symphony that they are in charge of playing in coordination with others. In addition, they are accountable for their performance. Using the terms defined above, each good musician has trading information to play with other players. This is even more obvious for jazz musicians. Musicians need to share mental models.

Until recently, an industrial organization was typically managed as an army. CEOs were generals who sent orders to their lieutenants and so on until the soldiers executed the basic tasks they were employed to execute. The typical organization structure was a tree. Each node of the tree was characterized by a cognitive function, that is, a role, a context of operations and appropriate allocated resources. As already explained, such a cognitive function should be considered as a society of cognitive functions. These cognitive functions were understood as being hierarchically organized. If such a hierarchy is vertically represented, information flows were always vertical and very seldom horizontal. Thomas Landauer describes this phenomenon as "organization of organizations" where the hierarchy of authority is flattened. He described the evolution of jobs done by "highly valuable specialists who must be given adequate authority and access to the parts of the organization that depend on them. In turn, the increased flexibility and directness of the communication tools that information technology provides make obsolete the deep hierarchical command and control structures that originated in pre-electronic military organizations" (Landauer, 1996, p. 122).

The evolution from army to orchestra is not straightforward. Even if in many cases emergent practices, resembling orchestra-type practices, have become very clear, most old structures persist. There are still many issues yet to be addressed in this recent evolution. Today, companies barely have the four pillars of the orchestra that we have just described, and in many cases they are not perceived and understood as useful and relevant. Structures of most companies are still army-type based, with emerging orchestra-type practices. The issue is then structure-practices matching.

In current industrial organizations, the major problem is that music theory turns out to be finance theory, scores are spreadsheets, conductors are finance-driven managers, and musicians have very specific functions, that is, very specific roles, highly limited and constrained context of operations, and limited resources. This is why we need to examine this concomitant finance-driven evolution of the way organizations are managed.

RECENT EVOLUTIONS IN AUTOMATION

After decades of trying to develop theories and methods to affect a change in perspectives on the interplay between humans, technology, and organization in order to support better system design, one may start to question the basic assumption of human control over automation itself (Dekker and Hollnagel, 2004; Dekker and Woods, 2002; Parasuraman et al., 2008). What if the insufficient human control of technology is not caused by normative assumptions about humans, technology, and organizations, but by factual limitations of human control and, even more basically, human imagination, due to the ever increasing complexity of technology? Then, either technology development has to be stopped—which is no real option—or the (partial) lack of control has to be accepted. Technically, this acceptance is equivalent to the determination of unmanaged residual risks. On the human side, there is hesitance to admit to a lack of control due to problems of unmanaged accountability. The human operator is kept in the system as a backup where all problems come together and have to be dealt with. The fallibility of this approach and its abuse by system developers and the organizations operating the systems in order not to have to admit to the lack of control has been pointed out by Bainbridge (1982) with utmost clarity.

Polemically one could argue that the current interest in research on trust in technology at the level of human–machine interaction (for example, Lee and See, 2004; Muir, 1994; McGuirl and Sarter, 2006; Moray et al., 2000; Rajaonah et al., 2006) has its roots in the fact that—while still acknowledging that control would be better than trust—trust is all that is left to the human operator. Experiments have shown that technology is trusted most when trust in one's own competences is low (for example, Lee and Moray, 1992, 1994). From general psychology we know that self-confidence is strongly related to perceived personal control (Bandura, 2001). Trust may therefore be a consequence of lack of control. This agrees with sociological definitions of trust as a mechanism to cope with uncontrollable uncertainties (for example, Luhmann, 1979, 1988). In the system design literature, however, trust is often understood as a desirable user attitude based on familiarity with the system and confidence stemming from high transparency, predictability, and reliability of systems, thereby actually providing essential prerequisites for control (Lee and See, 2004; McGuirl and Sarter, 2006; Muir, 1994). To explore further the sociological notion of trust as substitute for control, might prove valuable in supporting system design based on the assumption of only partial controllability of technical systems.

Current concepts of automation in future air traffic management are a good example of new potential for producing ironies of automation, despite an increasing awareness of human factors issues (for example, Wickens et al., 1998; Hoekstra, 2001; Boy and Grote, 2009; Federal Aviation Administration, 2007; SESAR consortium, 2008). The Traffic Alert and Collision Avoidance System (TCAS) is used as an illustration of these fundamental automation issues. The tragic flight accident over Überlingen in July 1, 2002, has instigated a heated debate on the design of air traffic control systems, in particular the Traffic Alert and Collision Avoidance System (TCAS) (for example, Weyer, 2006). TCAS is a warning system for avoiding mid-air collisions with which all modern aircraft are equipped. When the radar-based system detects a possible conflict with another aircraft, a warning is issued 40 seconds prior to the predicted collision and 15 seconds later the pilots are instructed usually to either climb or descend in order to resolve the conflict. When both aircraft involved in the conflict are equipped with TCAS, the instructions given to the pilots are coordinated and a collision should definitely be avoided. In parallel, aircraft are monitored by Air Traffic Control (ATC), which has raised the issue of assigning priority to either system. With current technology, TCAS information is not directly available to ATC, but has to be transmitted verbally by the pilots. Therefore, it is not unlikely that TCAS and ATC will issue contradictory instructions to the pilots. In the final phase of the Überlingen accident, the collision was caused by the pilots of both aircraft following the rules of their airlines on whom to give priority to. The US crew followed the TCAS instruction to descend, the Russian crew followed the ATC instruction to descend, after having received a TCAS instruction to climb.

After the Überlingen accident, an international standard was released stating that TCAS instructions have priority over ATC and that it is the pilot's responsibility to follow TCAS instructions. Hidden within this standard is the problem that TCAS is not 100 percent reliable and that, consequently, the pilot has to make the final decision on whether to follow TCAS. Interestingly, the TCAS instructions are also not called instructions as such, but advisories. In the current discussions by aircraft designers about automating TCAS, that is having the TCAS advisory automatically carried out without any action required from the pilot, a manual override is foreseen in order to keep the pilot in charge and also, responsible for executing TCAS instructions. The role of ATC remains unclear. Through automatic data link technology, air traffic controllers will be informed immediately of the TCAS warnings and instructions, but are not to intervene in any way. Collision avoidance, a core ATC task, is therefore delegated more clearly to the pilots and thereby decentralized in these situations, while at the same time it is more automated with less *de facto* control of the humans involved.

The current situation, as well as the future scenarios for collision avoidance, contains an inadequate distribution of uncertainty and of resources for uncertainty handling. Pilots are to consider TCAS as a completely reliable decision-maker during collision avoidance. At the same time, the availability of a manual override function indicates that pilot input may be required due to TCAS problems and that the responsibility stays with the pilot. The uneven distribution of information between pilots and ATC will be alleviated through data link technology, but ATC is not to use the information for any of its own actions, but leave collision avoidance to pilots and TCAS completely. It remains to be seen whether non-intervention by air traffic controllers in the case of wrong decisions by TCAS and/or pilots will really remain uncontested.

If one assumes that technology cannot be controlled fully by human operators, however hard system designers and operators try, the criteria for system design have to be changed (Grote, 2009; Grote, 2009). The main purpose of such new design guidelines would be to free human operators of their impossible role of trying to fulfil stop-gap and backup functions in complex socio-technical systems. Methods supporting adaptive system design indicate a move in a similar direction by allocating control fully and without human influence to the technical system in very stressful situations (for example, Inagaki, 2000; Moray et al., 2000). However, the crucial issue of assigning responsibility and accountability is usually not dealt with in these design methods.

According to Kornwachs (1999) the main prerequisites for taking on responsibility are the freedom to make choices and to act in a chosen manner. If people are forced to act in a particular way they cannot be held accountable unless they have brought this situation upon themselves. Also, he argues that all necessary knowledge concerning the action, its purpose and its consequences has to be available and attainable. He emphasizes that automation attempts to reduce complexity for the human operator in order to achieve these preconditions, but that at the same time, new complexities are created which may violate these conditions.

In order to provide the necessary preconditions for taking on responsibility, and thereby also control, the limits of control should be defined as clearly as possible. In those areas which are classified as outside the control of human operators, they cannot be held responsible. Taking the braking procedure in the Airbus A320 as an example, this would mean that the irreversible automation of the essential braking functions should be taught in pilot training and should also be indicated in the cockpit during landing. If mistakes happen in the execution of these functions, the system developer, or possibly the organization operating the system, should be held responsible, but not the pilots. Only if the pilots—in line with Kornwachs' definition—can be proven to have induced this situation deliberately or carelessly (for example, as a consequence of insufficient competencies) might they have to assume some of the responsibility. Even in such cases, the responsibility might lie more with the airline, especially if a particular pilot's lack of ability or knowledge has already surfaced earlier, for instance, during simulator training, and no action has been taken.

Issues of authority have also become increasingly prevalent due to technologies described as pervasive computing (Satyanarayanan, 2001). Pervasive computing refers to tiny devices, possibly embedded in almost any type of object imaginable, including cars, tools, appliances, clothing, and other consumer goods, all communicating through increasingly interconnected networks. During a recent workshop on the opportunities and risks of pervasive computing, it was postulated that lack of transparency and inherent uncertainty in these technical systems should be made explicit (Meier, 2005). This could imply, for instance, that when switching on an RFID (radio frequency identification) application—such as the milk bottles in our refrigerator that autonomously order new milk when their use-by-date has passed—the user is informed about which network connections have been established and which of those are part of an unprotected network. Such indications do exist already for some Internet applications. If the user still has the choice not to use the connection, the responsibility would rest with him or her. In cases where we are forced to use such connections, we would take note of the insecure status and consequently, lack of control, without being able to influence the situation, but also without being held responsible.

In a similar vein, Bellotti and Edwards (2001) have argued that in the design of context-aware systems, issues of intelligibility and accountability must be addressed. Context-aware systems are an important element of pervasive computing as they are able to identify different contexts and change their behavior accordingly, for instance, allowing or prohibiting connections with other systems. Availability for personal contact in work teams, as an example, might be signaled on the computers or mobile phones of members of these teams based on each of them being in their office and not currently speaking with anybody. Bellotti and Edwards argue that context-aware systems need to be intelligible for users, which necessitates that these systems, before acting upon what they infer about the context must be able to represent to their users what they know, how they know it, and what they are about to do about it. Additionally, accountability must be ensured by providing explicit mechanisms that enforce user identification and action disclosure and by effective user control. The latter does not necessarily imply that the user is intimately involved in task execution but that the desired outcome is attained through an appropriate interaction between system and user.

In order to design socio-technical systems according to such guidelines, existing methods for describing and assessing technical, human, and organizational risks should be extended to clearly indicate zones of uncontrolled risks for both the organizations operating the system and the human operators at the sharp end. Analyzing uncertainties with which the system is confronted and different ways of handling these (reducing, maintaining, or increasing) should be an important element of such methods (Grote, 2009). Once zones of uncontrollable risks have been identified, it would have to be decided whether or not functions in such zones could be fully automated and whether human operators can in any way be supported in acting appropriately despite their reduced level of control. Given the unpredictabilities in the defined zones of limited or no control, support for operators could only be in the form of heuristics. Process rules as suggested by Hale and Swuste (1998) could be such heuristics, that is, rules which do not specify a concrete action nor only specify the goal to be achieved, but provide guidance on what to do in order to find out what the right action is in a given situation. This could concern, for instance, information sources to be used, other actors to be involved, or definition of priorities.

At the same time, in these zones of limited control the responsibility for the safe operation of the system would remain with the system developer and potentially the organization operating the system, but not the human operator. The pressure to keep these zones small and thereby maximize control for the human operator would increase. Something similar is achieved already by US law allowing system operators to sue the system developer when his or her own erroneous action can be proven to be a consequence of bad system design (Baram, 2007).

A method for risk analysis that could be helpful for identifying zones of no or limited control is Hollnagel's (1998) CREAM (Cognitive Reliability and Error Analysis Method), which has recently been developed further into an Extended Control Model (Hollnagel and Woods, 2005). In Hollnagel's model four modes of control are distinguished: scrambled (choice of next action is close to random), opportunistic (choice of next action driven by narrow focus on current situation), tactical (choice of action based on following a known procedure), and strategic (choice of action determined by higher-level goals with longer time horizon). Control may concern anticipatory or compensatory action with each involving more specific activities of targeting, monitoring, regulating, and tracking. The four modes of control are assigned human error probabilities which are used to determine the overall probabilities of human error in event sequences potentially involving several switches between the different modes. By analyzing possible event sequences for a particular human–machine system and the different control modes involved, zones of no or scrambled control can be identified and appropriate measures taken to handle processes in these zones. As an example of such an approach which already exists, one might take the 30 minute rule in nuclear power plants. This rule demands that after the occurrence of major non-routine events the process control systems in these plants are capable of keeping up a sufficiently safe level of operation for as long as 30 minutes without human intervention, thereby giving the human operators time to recover from a state of confusion and scrambled control and to regain tactical or strategic control. Also, different stages of action regulation have to be distinguished, that is, information seeking, decision-making, execution of decided actions, feedback on effects of action, and corrective actions. The lack of control may only concern some of these stages and also, may affect different stages differently. The outcome of a CREAM based analysis would help to make decisions on full or partial automation more systematically, aiming at a very deliberate match between control and responsibility. Also, instead of pretending that systems are safer than they are, in particular due to their increasing embeddedness in complex networks, it may be much better to regain overall control by admitting to areas of opaqueness and uncertainties in the system. Only then can the ability to cope with uncertainty and loss of control be trained and supported systematically.

AUTOMATION, AUTHORITY AND ADAPTATION

Autopilots have been used since the 1930s onboard commercial airplanes. They represent the first layer of automation where human functions were transferred to the aircraft, for example, basic tracking tasks. Flight management systems were introduced during the 1980s. They represent a second layer of automation, which should be better called computerization instead, where human functions for the navigation task were transferred to the aircraft. They were typically modeled using operation research and optimization algorithms. Human modeling shifted from control theory to artificial intelligence approaches. Today, we are attacking another layer of automation, which is the interaction between airplanes, as well as airplanes and ground. Corresponding onboard systems range from collision avoidance systems, to data link systems, to cockpit display of traffic information ... to an integration of all of the above! The major issue today is also, and mainly, an integration of air and ground systems. This of course involves the emergence of new organizational socio-technical models.

What is really new is the emergence of *organizational automation* that results from the massive use of information technology. Any time there is an important change in a society, a new type of complexity needs to be explored, understood and managed. Hollnagel et al. opened a new field of research that they called "resilience engineering." Resilience engineering stands for the view that failure is the flip side of the adaptations necessary to cope with the complexity of the real world, rather than a breakdown or malfunctioning as such (Hollnagel et al., 2006). Human and organizational adaptations are always necessary to cope with evolving environments where, in particular, machines take important roles to support work and more generally life. Today, most machines are computer driven and enable hyper-connectivity. Adaptation in a highly connected agent network is very likely to take time; when the speed of change is too important, people and organizations have difficulty to adapt. The crucial issue here is to find the right pace that facilitates human and organizational adaptation, as well as in turn technology adaptation. Adaptation can be evolutionary, that is, step by step, or revolutionary, that is, in a big jump. It is difficult to figure out what type of adaptation we are in when we develop, deliver and use new technology. Even when we think that we are in an evolutionary type of adaptation, we may suddenly discover that socio-technical practice drastically changes; we usually talk about emergent practice. This phenomenon was nicely described by Hoffman and Hanes (2003).

It is difficult to figure out interactions, coordination, and synchronization among a set of agents in a rapidly changing environment. Automation not only transforms individual tasks but also the overall interactions, coordination, and synchronization in an organization. Organizational complexity and dynamicity increase the difficulty of the rationalization of emerging phenomena in real time, that is, when things are constantly changing. As a general statement, automation modifies the relationships between people, may induce sources of conflicts and generate problems of trust. This is why cognitive function analysis (Boy, 1998, 2010) has become very important where people and automation, as agents, need to interact, coordinate, and synchronize. In particular, when there are goal or role conflicts, the problem of authority becomes crucial because people have to make decisions and take actions, often quickly. In addition, authority needs to be assigned with the most *appropriate expertise*, which is very difficult in rapidly changing environments. However, a cognitive function analysis cannot be done properly without observing human and machine activity, that is, what people and machines really do together within an organization, as opposed to task analysis where the analyst typically stays at the prescription level and not at the effective execution or performance level. A cognitive function is first defined as the transformation of a task into an activity (logical definition), but it can also be defined as by its role (teleological definition), for example, the function or role of a transport pilot is to bring a set of passenger from A to B; this is a high-level cognitive function. Another cognitive function of the pilot is to manage automated systems during flight; this is a lower-level cognitive function. We will say that when a cognitive function, that is, a role in a given context with a set of appropriate resources, is allocated to an agent, it provides this agent with a specific authority. The context of validity of a cognitive function is important because it bounds its role, that is, when corresponding agents use their role, and therefore authority, outside of this context, they override their authority. This is why it is crucial to accurately define the context of validity of a cognitive function. Such definition is obviously performed incrementally because it emerges for the most appropriate maturity of practice. Finally, the resources attached to a cognitive function are important because they empower the agent with the necessary means to accomplish its role. The difficulty comes with the fact that these resources may be distributed among several agents. There may be intertwined networks of cognitive functions distributed among many agents; they are first statically allocated at design time, and further dynamically allocated from emergent practice.

People and organization adapt incrementally to changes involved from automation. Such adaptation is heavily constrained by change resistance. People always need references that could be messed up by a new way of working being introduced too rapidly. People may not understand these new methods and techniques. Those need to be carefully explained, and their values easily demonstrated. They also need to address people's current activity. The appropriation process usually takes time in order to reach an acceptable level of technology maturity and associated maturity of practice. In fact, people need to construct different references. This reconstruction process can be tedious and substantially long. In addition, when someone has an authority, it is difficult to remove this authority without problems.

This chapter is about function integration in the design of complex safety-critical systems with a specific focus on computer-driven operations. Function allocation is a very complex process because once we transform an original working organization into a new one, there are several emerging functions that need to be discovered and taken into account in the design itself. If automation is considered as a multi-agent process where some functions previously performed by humans are transferred to a machine, then there are inevitably new human functions that naturally emerge from new types of interactions. An important question is: how do we make these emerging functions explicit? Can we discover them during design and development processes? Knowledge of such emerging functions is crucial to ensure the maturity of the overall human–machine system when it is actually in operations.

How can we combine a holistic approach of function integration and a socio-cognitive function-allocation approach? In order to address this question, we need to further articulate an epistemological approach of automation. The atomist approach recommends that we divide the world into small pieces that are easy to understand and handle, transfer appropriate functions from humans to machines, and then reassemble the pieces into a human(s)–machine(s) system. This approach may work locally, but is very brittle globally. It makes the very strong assumption of separability, because it is easier to solve supposedly separable problems, but the approach often fails at re-integrating the pieces into a whole, especially when this whole is a complex dynamic socio-technical system.

Conversely, the holistic approach recommends that we take the human(s)–machine(s) system as a whole phenomenon and investigate the various symbiotic interactions. Unfortunately, this phenomenological approach assumes that we already have a developed system like the living systems that biologists study. But, this is not the case in the design of artifacts. It is very difficult to observe any phenomenon before the system is actually in service. We then need to make compromises and work on successive mockups, that is, approximations of the final system, which are formally evaluated. For that matter, participatory design is crucial, that is, all actors, especially end-users, should be deeply involved in design and development processes. They all need to figure out the stories that the product being developed will induce at operations time. Storytelling can be an excellent support to a phenomenological approach of design. A large literature now covers this storytelling aspect in the context of scenario development to support analysis, design and evaluation. For example, Gary Klein claimed that we "organize the cognitive world—the world of ideas, concepts, objects, and relationships. We link these up into stories. By understanding how this happens, we can learn to make better use of the power of stories" (Klein, 1998, p. 178).

In addition, anytime there is a change, people do not learn functions and attitudes at the same speed and may not have the *same understanding and/or interpretation* of these functions and attitudes according to their initial cultures. This, of course, deals with the maturity of emerging practice, and therefore appropriate cognitive functions.

In the Überlingen accident for example, there was a confusion coming from the Euro-American culture that is different from the Russian culture concerning the TCAS. In Europe like in the US, the TCAS provides orders that pilots are required to follow (that is, climb or descent!), even if they know TCAS shortcomings. Russian pilots who were involved in the accident relied on air traffic control (ATC) because of these shortcomings. ATC was more redundant and therefore more reliable for them. This kind of confusion is partly due to the fact that these two systems, ATC and TCAS, are not interconnected. There is no feedback from the TCAS to the ground, that is, there is no common frame of reference and information sharing … an obvious lack of redundancy. In the Überlingen accident, the crew of the DHL cargo Boeing aircraft followed the American standard operating procedures, that is, obey the TCAS, and the crew of the Russian Tupolev followed what the ATC said. Both information items were contradictory! *Redundancy* is a crucial socio-cognitive support to the various ATM agents.

In addition to a design-induced lack of redundancy coming from the TCAS, there was also only one controller on duty in Zürich on July 1, 2002 at 23:35:32. He took care of both airplanes for a few minutes, and realized the conflict only 43 seconds before the collision. He reacted after both TCAS reactions. He did not have the authority over these artificial agents, that is, TCASs. Both TCASs reacted perfectly, the Russian one asking to climb, the US one asking to descend. The problem is that the controller asked the Russian aircraft to descend, that is, opposite order to the TCAS. An accident does not happen with only one cause; in this case, the Short-Term Conflict Alert (STCA) system was partly operational, but the controller did not know this. The STCA is the counterpart of the TCAS for the controller. In addition, the telephone line was out of order for a few minutes. Finally, the controller had to take care of another airplane, leaving the first two airplanes autonomous for a while. This is the reason why he realized too late the occurrence of the conflict. As Weyer said, is it a human error or an organizational failure? This kind of failure relies on complexity management, tight coupling of independently-designed systems (TCAS and ATC), different cultures, lack of awareness of non-operational systems and interruption management.

CONCLUSION

It is crucial to clearly understand chains of authority in a socio-technical system, that is who is in charge (control), responsible, and accountable for a given task at any level of granularity of the overall organization. Since current, and even more future, socio-technical systems are interconnected, understanding interconnectivity, and information flows becomes tremendously important. We have proposed the concept of authority in the context of socio-technical system together with processes and models that support related appropriate analyzes and investigations toward the design and development of software-intensive technology and organizational setups.

We mainly discussed these issues and concepts in the framework of aeronautics, but this applies to other industrial sectors where safety-critical systems need to be designed and used.

Overall, technological automation tends to lead to organizational automation where agents need to better understand what other agents are doing in order to react and plan appropriately. Automation does not remove human expertise; it may actually move the nature of this expertise. This is why we need to be careful to keep an appropriate standard of human expertise during the whole life cycle of a product. We tend to observe that finance-driven organization tend to minimize human technical expertise in order to reduce costs, but safety constraints should prevail. There is no authority without enough recognized technical expertise in any domain, at any level of granularity in the organization. In addition, authority sharing and distribution cannot be fully understood without appropriate rationalization of emergent behaviors. This is why human-in-the-loop simulations are required during the whole life cycle of a safety-critical product.

REFERENCES

Amalberti, R. (1992). Safety in process-control: An operator-centred point of view. In: *Reliability Engineering and System Safety*, 38, pp. 99–108.

Amalberti, R. (1993). Safety in flight operations. In: B. Wilpert and T. Qvale (Eds.), *Reliability and safety in hazardous work systems*. Hove: Lawrence Erlbaum, pp. 171–194.

Amalberti, R. (2001). *From little incidents to the big one*. EURISCO International Summer School on Design for Safety, Saint-Lary, France.

Bailey, R.W. (1989). *Human performance engineering* (2nd edn.). London: Prentice-Hall International.

Bainbridge, L. (1982). Ironies of automation. In: G. Johannsen and J.E. Rijnsdorp (Eds.), *Analysis, design and evaluation of man–machine systems*. Oxford: Pergamon, 129–135.

Bandura, A. (2001). Social cognitive theory: an agentic perspective. *Annual Review of Psychology*, 52, pp. 1–26.

Baram, M. (2007). Liability and its influence on designing for product and process safety. *Safety Science*, 45, pp. 11–30.

Bellotti, V. and Edwards, K. (2001). Intelligibility and Accountability: Human Considerations in Context Aware Systems. *Human–computer Interaction*, 16 (2), pp. 193–212.

Boy, G.A. (1998). *Cognitive function analysis*. Westport, CT, US: Ablex/Greenwood.

Boy, G.A. (2002), Theories of Human Cognition: To Better Understand the Co-Adaptation of People and Technology, in Knowledge Management, Organizational Intelligence and Learning, and Complexity. In: L. Douglas Kiel (Ed.), *Encyclopedia of Life Support Systems (EOLSS)*, Developed under the Auspices of the UNESCO. Oxford, UK: Eolss Publishers, www.eolss.net.

Boy, G.A. (2003). *L'Ingénierie Cognitive: Interaction Homme-Machine et Cognition (The French Handbook of Cognitive Engineering)*. Lavoisier, Paris: Hermes Sciences.

Boy, G.A. (2009). The Orchestra: A Conceptual Model for Function Allocation and Scenario-based Engineering in Multi-Agent Safety-Critical Systems. *Proceedings of the European Conference on Cognitive Ergonomics*, Otaniemi, Helsinki area, Finland; September 30–October 2.

Bradshaw, J.M., Jung, H., Kulkarni, S., Johnson, M., Feltovich, P., Allen, J., Bunch, L., Chambers, N., Galescu, L., Jeffers, R., Suri, N., Taysom, W., and Uszok, A. (2005). Kaa: Policy-based Explorations of a Richer Model for Adjustable Autonomy. *AAMAS'05*, July 25–29, 2005, Utrecht, Netherlands. ACM 1–59593–094–9/05/0007.

Chapanis, A. (1965). Words, words, words. *Human Factors*, 7, pp. 1–17.

Corkill, D.D. (2003). Collaborating Software: Blackboard and Multi-Agent Systems and the Future. In: *Proceedings of the International Lisp Conference, New York*. New York, October.

Corso, G.M. and Moloney, M.M. (1996). Human performance, dynamic function allocation and transfer of training. In: Koubek and Karwowski (Eds.), *Manufacturing Agility and Hybrid Automation-I. Proceedings of the 5th International Conference on Human Aspects of Advanced Manufacturing*. Louisville, KY: IEA Press.

Dekker, S.W.A. and Woods, D.D. (2002). MABA-MABA or Abracadabra? Progress on Human-Automation Coordination. *Cognition, Technology and Work*, 4(4), pp. 240–244.

Dekker, S.W.A. and Hollnagel, E. (2004). Human factors and folk models. *Cognition, Technology and Work*, 6, 79–86.

Engelmore, R.S. and Morgan, A. (Eds.). (1988). *Blackboard Systems*. Addison-Wesley.

Erman, L.D., Hayes-Roth, F., Lesser, V.R., and Reddy, D.R. (1980). The Hearsay-II Speech-Understanding System: Integrating Knowledge to Resolve Uncertainty. *Computing Surveys*, 12(2), June, pp. 213–253.

Faraj, S. and Sproull, L. (2000). Coordinating Expertise in Software Development Teams. *Management Science*, 46(12), pp. 1554–1568.

Federal Aviation Administration. (2007). Joint planning and development office: actions needed to reduce risks with the next generation air transportation system. Report Number: AV-2007–031. FAA, Washington DC.

Fitts, P.M. (Ed.). (1951). Human engineering for an effective air navigation and traffic control system. Washington, D.C., National Research Council.

Grote, G., Ryser, C., Wäfler, T., Windischer, A., and Weik, S. (2000). KOMPASS: A method for complementary function allocation in automated work systems. In: *International Journal of Human–computer Studies*, 52, pp. 267–287.

Grote, G. (2009). *Management of uncertainty: Theory and application in the design of systems and organizations*. London: Springer.

Grote, G., Weichbrodt, J., Günter, H., Zala-Mezö, E., and Künzle, B. (2009). Coordination in high-risk organizations: the need for flexible routines. In: *Cognition, Technology and Work*, 11, pp. 17–27.

Grote, G. (2009). Die Grenzen der Kontrollierbarkeit komplexer Systeme. In: J. Weyer and I. Schulz-Schaeffer (Hrsg.), *Management komplexer Systeme — Konzepte für die Bewältigung von Intransparenz, Unsicherheit und Chaos* (pp. 149–168). München: Oldenbourg-Verlag.

Hale, A. and Swuste, P. (1998). Safety rules: procedural freedom or action constraint? *Safety Science*, 29, pp. 163–177.

Hauss, Y. and Timpe, K.P. (2002). Automatisierung und Unterstützung im Mensch-Maschine-System. In: Klaus-Peter Timpe et al. (Eds.), *Mensch-Maschine-Systemtechnik — Konzepte, Modellierung, Gestaltung, Evaluation*. Düsseldorf: Symposion, pp. 41–62.

Hildebrandt, M. and Harrison, MD (2003). PaintShop — A microworld experiment investigating temporal control behavior. Technical report, DIRC.

Hoekstra, J.M. (2001). Designing for Safety: the Free Flight Air Traffic Management Concept. NLR TP-2001–313. http://hosted.nlr.nl/public/hosted-sites/freeflight/main.htm.

Hoffman, R.R. and Hanes, L.F. (2003). The boiled frog problem. *Intelligent Systems*, IEEE, 18, 4, Jul–Aug, pp. 68–71.

Hollnagel, E. and Woods, D.D. (1983). Cognitive System Engineering: New Wine in New Bottles. *International Journal of Man-Machine Studies*, 18, pp. 583–600.

Hollnagel, E. (1998). *CREAM — Cognitive Reliability and Error Analysis Method*. Oxford: Elsevier.

Hollnagel, E. (Ed.) (2003). *Handbook of Cognitive Task Design*. Mahwah, NJ: Lawrence Erlbaum.

Hollnagel, E. and Woods, D.D. (2005). *Joint Cognitive Systems: Foundation of Cognitive Systems Engineering*. New York: Taylor and Francis.

Hollnagel, E., Woods, D.D. and Leveson, N. (2006). *Resilience engineering; concepts and precepts*. Farnham, UK: Ashgate Publishing Co.

Hutchins, E. (1995). *Cognition in the wild*. Cambridge, MA: The MIT Press.

Inagaki, T. (2000). Situation-adaptive autonomy for time-critical takeoff decisions. *International Journal of Modeling and Simulation*, 20, pp. 175–180.

Kanki, B.G. and Foushee, H.C. (1989). Communication as Group Process Mediator of Aircrew Performance. *Aviation, Space, and Environmental Medicine*, 20(2), pp. 402–410.

Klein, G. (1998). *Sources of Power: How People Make Decisions*. Cambridge, MA: MIT Press.

Kornwachs, K. (1999). Bedingungen verantwortlichen Handelns. In: K.P. Timpe and M. Rötting (Eds.), *Verantwortung und Führung in Mensch-Maschine-Systemen*. Sinzheim: Pro Universitate, 51–79.

Laudeman, I.V., Shelden, S.G., Branstrom, R. and Brasil, C.L. (1998). *Dynamic Density. An Air Traffic Management Metric*. California: National Aeronautics and Space Administration, Ames Research Center, NASA/TM-1998–112226.

Lee, J. and Moray, N. (1992). Trust, control strategies and allocation of function in human–machine systems. *Ergonomics*, 35, pp. 1243–1270.

Lee, J. and Moray, N. (1994). Trust, self-confidence, and operators' adaptation to automation. *International Journal of Human–computer Studies*, 40, pp. 153–184.

Lee, J.D. and See, K.A. (2004). Trust in Automation: Designing for Appropriate Reliance. *Human Factors: The Journal of the Human Factors and Ergonomics Society*, 46: 50–80.

Luhmann, N. (1979). *Trust and power*. Chichester: Wiley.

Luhmann, N. (1988). Familarity, confidence, trust: problems and alternatives. In: Gambetta, D. (Ed.), *Trust making and breaking cooperative relations*. New York: Blackwell, pp. 94–107.

Malone, T., and Crowston, K. (1994). The Interdisciplinary Study of Coordination. *ACM Computing Surveys*, 26(1), March, pp. 87–119.

Mathieu, J., Goodwin, G.F., Heffner, T.S., Salas, E. and Cannon-Bowers, J.A. (2000). The Influence of Shared Mental Models on Team Process and Performance. *Journal of Applied Psychology*, 85(2), pp. 273–283.

McGuirl, J. and Sarter, N.B. (2006). Supporting Trust Calibration and The Effective Use of Decision Aids by Presenting Dynamic System Confidence Information. *Human Factors*, 48(4), pp. 656–665.

Muir, B.M. (1994). Trust in automation, part I: Theoretical issues in the study of trust and human intervention in automated systems. *Ergonomics*, 37, pp. 1923–1941.

Norman, D. (1982). Steps toward a Cognitive Engineering: Design Rules Based on Analyses of Human Error. *Proceedings of the 1982 conference on Human factors in computing systems (CHI'82)*, Gaithersburg, Maryland, US, pp. 378–382.

Hayes-Roth, B. (1985). A blackboard architecture for control. *Artificial Intelligence*, 26, pp. 251–321.

Main Commission Aircraft Accident Investigation Warsaw. *Report on the Accident to Airbus A320–211 Aircraft in Warsaw on 14 September 1993*. Warsaw, Poland, March 1994. Web version prepared by Peter Ladkin, URL: www.rvs.uni-bielefeld.de/publications/Incidents/DOCS/ComAndRep/Warsaw/warsaw-report.html.

Meier, K. (2005). *Stakeholder-Dialog über Pervasive Computing — Überall und unsichtbar*. St. Gallen: Stiftung Risiko-Dialog.

Moray, N., Inagaki, T., and Itoh, M. (2000). Adaptive automation, trust, and self-confidence in fault management of time-critical tasks. *Journal of Experimental Psychology: Applied*, 6, pp. 44–58.

Parasuraman, R., Sheridan, T.B., and Wickens, C.D. (2000). A Model for Types and Levels of Human Interaction with Automation. *IEEE Transaction on Systems, Man, and Cybernetics — Part A: Systems and Humans*, 0, 3, May, pp. 286–296.

Parasuraman, R., Sheridan, T.B., and Wickens, C.D. (2008) Situation awareness, mental workload, and trust in automation: viable, empirically supported cognitive engineering constructs. *Journal of Cognitive Engineering and Decision-making*, 2, pp. 140–160.

Rajaonah, B., Anceaux, F., and Vienne, F. (2006). Trust and the use of adaptive control: A study of a cut-in situation. *Cognition, Technology and Work*, Springer, London, 8, 2, June, pp. 146–155.

Satyanarayanan, M. (2001). Pervasive Computing: Vision and Challenges. IEEE Personal Communications, 8, 4 (August) www.stanford.edu/class/cs444n/handouts/pcs01.pdf.

SESAR consortium (2008). *SESAR master plan*. Brussels: Eurocontrol.

Sheridan, TB. (1987). Supervisory Control. In: G. Salvendy (Ed.), *Handbook of Human Factors*, New York: Wiley.

Swain, A.D., and Guttman, H.E. (1980). *Handbook of human reliability analysis with emphasis on nuclear power plant applications* (NUREG/CR-1278). Washington, DC: US Nuclear Regulatory Commission.

Timpe, K.P., Jürgensohn, T. and Kolrep, H. (Eds.) (2002). *Mensch-Maschine-Systemtechnik — Konzepte, Modellierung, Gestaltung, Evaluation*. Düsseldorf: Symposion.

Ulich, E. (1994). *Arbeitspsychologie* (3. Aufl.). Zürich: Verlag der Fachvereine; Stuttgart: Schäffer-Poeschel.

Wäfler, T., Grote, G., Windischer, A. and Ryser, C. (2003). KOMPASS: A method for complementary system design. In: Erik Hollnagel (Ed.), *Handbook of Cognitive Task Design*. Mahwah, NJ: Lawrence Erlbaum, 477–502.

Walz, D.B., Elam, J.J. and Curtis, B. (1993). Inside a Software Design Team: Knowledge Acquisition, Sharing, and Integration. *Communications of the ACM*, 36(10), pp. 63–77.

Waterson, P.E., Gray, O. and Glegg, C.W. (2002). A sociotechnical emthod for designing work systems. *Human Factors*, 15, pp. 34–45.

Weyer, J. (2006). Modes of governance of hybrid systems. The mid-air collision at Überlingen and the impact of smart technology. *Science, Technology and Innovation Studies*, 2, Nov. ISSN: 1861–3675, pp. 127–149.

Wickens, C.D., Mavor, A., Parasuraman, R., and McGee, J. (1998). *The future of air traffic control: Human operators and automation*. Washington, DC: National Academy Press.

Wright, P., Fields, R., and Harrison, M. (2000). Analysing Human–computer Interaction As Distributed Cognition: The Resources Model. *Human Computer Interaction journal*, 51(1), pp. 1–41.

PART II

Design

7

Scenario-Based Design

John M. Carroll and Steven R. Haynes

INTRODUCTION

Scenario-based design is a family of techniques in which the use of a future system is concretely described at an early point in the development process. Narrative descriptions of envisioned usage episodes are then employed in a variety of ways to guide the development of the system. Scenario-based design changes the focus of design work from defining system operations (that is, functional specification) to describing how people will use a system to accomplish work tasks and other activities.

Scenario-based design elaborates a traditional theme in human factors and ergonomics, namely, the principle that human characteristics and needs should be pivotal considerations in the design of tools and artifacts. In scenario-based design, descriptions of usage situations become more than orienting examples and background data, they become first-class design objects. Scenario-based design takes literally the adage that a tool is what people can do with it, and the consequences for them and for their activities of using it.

ORIGINS: STRATEGIC PLANNING AND STRATEGIC MANAGEMENT

During the early years of the Cold War, strategic planners came to rely on scenarios to anticipate and analyze future contingencies. The situations they were concerned with were complex and unfamiliar. Scenarios facilitated vivid and broad-scope analyses that encouraged consideration of contextual details and temporal dynamics that were sometimes overlooked in more formal contingency planning. The simple rubric of time facilitated comprehension and integration of the many interacting elements in a problem situation, while emphasizing to analysts that circumstances are constantly changing. Scenarios were found to stimulate imagination, helping analysts generate new contingencies and relationships. Finally, scenarios reduced the perceived costs of considering more alternatives. The "accidental war scenario," in which a mistaken launch of a single tactical missile somewhere in Europe triggers a cascade of events, culminating in all-out global war, was discovered through scenario analysis and became a touchstone of strategic planning for a generation. Prior to the late 1940s, no planner had ever considered such escalating contingencies (or cataclysmic outcomes).

Beginning in the 1970s, scenario-based methods were widely adopted and developed in corporate strategic management. Scenario analysis was credited with Royal Dutch Shell's success during the mid-1970s oil crisis. Since 1980, scenario-based techniques have developed in key areas of computer system and software design—requirements engineering, human–computer interaction, and software design. These separate lines of methodological development have begun to converge around the proposal that various scenario-based practices can be mutually leveraged throughout the system development process.

WHAT IS SCENARIO-BASED DESIGN?

In scenario-based design, key situations of use in established work practice are enumerated and described in schematic narratives. Each narrative depicts one or more actors, a defining goal and possibly several ancillary goals, a context of tools and other artifacts, and a sequence of actions and events through which the defining goal is achieved, transformed, obstructed, and/or abandoned. Figure 7.1 describes the use of a handheld, portable maintenance device (PMD) for Marine Corps light armored vehicle mechanics. At an early phase of design, this might be an envisioned scenario, vividly conveying a new system concept, or, if this type of system is already in use and being refined, this might be an observed scenario, summarizing typical use and current design challenges (for example, how to get users to carry out practice exercises). In either case, the scenario guides the development of requirements and prototypes, and the specification of system functions. Subsequently, it could guide the development of training and documentation, and the design of evaluation tasks.

Sgt. Garcia is diagnosing a fault with a Marine Corps light armored vehicle (LAV). He connects his personalized portable maintenance device (PMD) to a port on the LAV's onboard computer (OBC). The OBC sends the PMD information on the exact configuration of the vehicle, its maintenance history, recent location and use history, and information its current "health". This last piece of information suggests that the fault may relate to one of the vehicles planetary hubs, which appears to have been overheating. The mechanic's PMD opens the device's integrated electronic technical manual, which automatically navigates to the pages on planetary hubs, their common faults, and related diagnostic trees. In separate windows on the PMD he sees both an exploded view of the planetary assembly and an animation showing the planetary in operation. This latter view includes the flow of lubricant through the hub and suggests how overheating can occur and lead to a specific component failure mode. Using the PMD's built-in speech annotation system, Sgt. Garcia records his notes on the diagnostic process and result.

Figure 7.1   A scenario of use for a Marine Corps portable maintenance device (PMD)

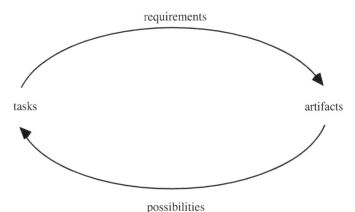

Figure 7.2   The task-artifact cycle

Note: Tasks help articulate requirements for new technology that can support them; designed artifacts create possibilities (and limitations) that redefine tasks.

The ability of scenarios to vividly depict both current and future situations has encouraged their use as working representations in a wide variety of disciplines, from strategic management and operations research to requirements engineering, object-oriented design, and human–computer interaction. In the large, work and technology co-evolve: people engage in tasks and activities. They make discoveries and encounter difficulties; they experience insight and satisfaction, frustration and failure. At length, their tasks and experiences help to define requirements for future technology. Subsequent technological tools, in turn, open up new possibilities for tasks and activities, new ways to do familiar things, and entirely new things to do. They entrain new skills to learn and perform, new opportunities for insight and satisfaction, and new pitfalls of frustration and failure. Ultimately, the new tasks and new technology become a new baseline, helping to evoke requirements for further technology development. Scenarios have been proposed as an integrative representation of work and technology for managing this pattern.

HOW DOES SCENARIO-BASED DESIGN WORK?

Scenario-based design addresses five key technical challenges in the design of technology: Scenarios evoke reflection in the content of design work, helping developers coordinate design action and reflection. Scenarios are at once concrete and flexible, helping developers manage the fluidity of design situations. Scenarios promote work-oriented communication among stakeholders, helping to make design activities more accessible to the great variety of expertise that contributes to design, and addressing the challenge that external constraints designers and clients often distract attention from the needs and concerns of the people who will use the technology. Scenarios afford multiple views of an interaction, diverse kinds and amounts of detailing, helping developers manage the many consequences entailed by any given design move. Finally, scenarios can be abstracted and categorized, helping designers to recognize, capture, and reuse generalizations, and to address the challenge that technical knowledge often lags the needs of technical design.

Design Action can Undermine Reflection: Scenarios Evoke Reflection in Design

Constructing scenarios of use as focal design objects inescapably evokes reflection in the context of doing design. The scenario in Figure 7.1 succinctly and concretely conveys a vision of student-directed, multimedia instruction. It is a coherent and concrete vision, not an abstract goal, not a list of features and functions. Elements of the envisioned system appear in the scenario embedded in the interactions that will make them meaningful to people using the system to achieve real goals—perhaps revelatory, perhaps cryptic, but definitely more than just technological capabilities. For example, the role of natural language query is exemplified as a means of locating further case studies that illustrate the principles of harmonic motion.

The scenario emphasizes and explores goals that a person might adopt and pursue, such as watching the film clips twice, or skipping the exercises. Some of these goals are opportunistic, such as investigating the Tacoma Narrows collapse because of experience with a totally unrelated bridge collapse, or deciding to branch from bridge failures to flutes. The scenario implicitly articulates the usage situation from multiple perspectives: the student stores and annotates a video clip with speech, raising specific requirements for user interface tools and presentation as well as for particular data structures and memory. The scenario impels the designer to integrate the consideration of such system requirements with consideration of the motivational and cognitive issues in education that underlie the person's actions and experiences.

Design Problems are Complex and Fluid: Scenarios are Concrete but Flexible

Scenarios reconcile concreteness and flexibility. They are concrete in the sense that they simultaneously fix an interpretation of the design situation and offer a specific solution: the scenario in Figure 7.1 specifies a particular usage experience that could be prototyped and tested. At the same time, scenarios are flexible in the sense that they are deliberately incomplete and easily revised or elaborated: in a few minutes, a piece of the scenario could be re-written (for example, stipulating a system-initiated prompt for the associated course module on harmonic motion) or extended (for example, the objects in the scenario could be described as anchors for a variety of link types).

Scenarios embody concrete design actions and evoke concrete move testing on the part of designers. They allow designers to try things out and get directive feedback. But their flexibility facilitates innovative and open-ended exploration of design requirements and possibilities, helping designers to avoid premature commitment. This is especially critical in that design problems are ill defined: they can always be understood and approached in multiple ways. Interactively exploring design problems often helps to reveal more about them.

The power of scenarios to convey concreteness through tentative and sketchy descriptions derives from the way people create and understand stories. Like the strokes of an expressionist painting, scenarios evoke much more than they literally present. The human mind seems especially adept at overloading meaning in narrative structures, both in generation and interpretation, as illustrated by the remarkable examples of dreams and myths. Indeed, dreams and myths are universal tools for coping with uncertainty. Part of their power stems from being recalled and discussed throughout a community. In a more modest scale, design teams do this too: Sharing and developing scenarios helps to control the uncertainties inherent in the work, while strengthening the team itself.

Design is Constrained by External Factors: Scenarios Promote Work Orientation

Scenarios are work-oriented design objects. They describe systems in terms of the work that people will try to do as they make use of those systems. A design process in which scenarios are employed as a focal representation will ipso facto remain focused on the needs and concerns of prospective users. Thus, designers and clients are less likely to be captured by inappropriate gadgets and gismos, or to settle for routine technological solutions, when their discussions and visions are couched in the language of scenarios, that is, less likely than they might be if their design work is couched in the language of functional specifications. Design work is often constrained by various external factors in the development organization and the marketplace (policies, standards, competitive products, past and planned products, schedules, resource budgets). Scenarios help keep attention focused on the work activity to be supported.

Scenarios help to integrate the variety of skills and experience required in a design project by making it easier for different kinds of experts to communicate and collaborate. They support the direct participation of users and other client stakeholders, helping to anticipate organizational impacts of new technology. Scenarios also ease problems associated with handoffs and coordination in the design process by providing all groups with a guiding vision of the project goal to unify and contextualize the documents and partial results that are passed back and forth.

Scenarios directly support the development of summative evaluation tasks. But perhaps more importantly, maintaining work-oriented scenarios throughout the development process allows formative evaluation walkthroughs to be carried out continuingly.

Design Moves have many Effects and Side-Effects: Scenarios have many Views

Scenarios are multifarious design objects; they describe designs at multiple levels of detail and with respect to multiple perspectives. A scenario briefly sketches tasks without committing to details of precisely how the tasks will be carried out or how the system will enable the functionality for those tasks. The portable maintenance device scenario in Figure 7.1 is at an intermediate level, with some detail regarding task flow; it could be elaborated with respect to Sgt. Garcia's moment-to-moment thoughts and experiences in order to provide a more elaborated cognitive view, or with respect to individual interactions to provide a more detailed functional view. Alternatively, the scenario could be presented from the point of view of a novice LAV mechanic watching Sgt. Garcia, perhaps in order to learn how to operate the PMD. It could be elaborated in terms of hardware and software components that could implement the envisioned functionality in order to provide a system view. Each of these variations in resolution and perspective is a permutation of a single underlying use scenario.

Scenarios can leave implicit the underlying causal relationships among the entities in a situation of use. For example, in Figure 7.1 the envisioned speech annotation capability allows adding personal, context-sensitive comments on the diagnostic task without the overheads of opening an editor and typing text. However, the annotation is non-coded, and thus cannot be edited symbolically. These relationships are important to the scenario, but often it is enough to imply them. This is an aspect of the property of being concrete but rough that we discussed above.

Sometimes it is useful to make these relationships explicit. For example, in another scenario Sgt. Garcia may wish to revisit his verbal comments on an earlier repair, one that was particularly complex and difficult. Unfortunately, his non-coded voice annotations cannot be searched by string. Thus, this new scenario would end in failure. To understand and address the variety of desirable and undesirable consequences of the original annotation design move, the designer might want to make explicit the relevant causal relationships in these two scenarios. Doing so provides yet another view of the envisioned situations, as shown in Figure 7.3.

Scenarios help designers manage trade-offs. For example, the data structures for the PMD's mechanic voice annotation functionality might differentiate between annotated and non-annotated items, allowing annotated items to be retrieved and browsed as a subset. This would not allow Sgt. Garcia to directly retrieve the set of items with a particular annotation, but it would still simplify the search. Alternatively, the search problem might be addressed directly by speech recognition or audio matching, or by including the option of text annotation. Each of these alternatives would entrain different elaborations for both the annotation scenario in Figure 7.1 and the search scenario discussed immediately above. These elaborations could then be explored for further consequences and interdependencies.

Animated views of LAV component operations:
  provide a visual portal into otherwise hidden vehicle component processes
  evoke curiosity and self-initiated learner exploration in novice mechanics
  but are expensive and time-consuming to create and update

Speech annotation of a diagnostic repair task:
  allows easy attachment of contextual data (mechanic, vehicle serial number and
    maintenance history)
  but does not support indexing or search of metadata

Figure 7.3   Consequences associated with the LAV component animation and the speech annotation capability in the diagnosis and repair task

Scientific Knowledge Lags Design: Scenarios can be Abstracted and Categorized

Scenarios exemplify particular themes and concerns in work and activity situations. Earlier we discussed two scenarios for Marine Corps personal maintenance device. In one (Figure 7.1), a person is at first exploring an information structure, but eventually adopts a particular theory about a diagnosis that guides the rest of his exploration. In the other, a person wishes to search and organize information that has previously been browsed. Described at this level of generality, these are not scenarios unique to personal maintenance devices, or even to computers. They are general patterns for how people work with information. Therefore, it is likely that some of the lessons learned in managing the "guided exploration" pattern or the "searching under a description" pattern in the design of any given situation might be applicable in the subsequent design of other situations. Such a taxonomy of scenarios provides a framework for developing technical design knowledge.

Scenarios can also be classified in terms of the causal relations they comprise. In Figure 7.1, for example, providing speech annotation simplifies the actions needed to personalize and augment a piece of information. In this causal relation, the consequence is the simplification of organizing and categorizing—a general desideratum in designing interactive systems. Generalizing the relation in this way allows the feature associated with the consequence (in this example, speech annotation) to be understood as a potential means for that consequence, and employed to that end in other design contexts. There is of course no guarantee that the generalization is correct, that can only be settled by trying to use it and succeeding or failing. The point is that such candidate generalizations can be developed from scenario descriptions.

The generalization of the causal relations comprising scenarios can also be carried out across features: speech annotation of data helps people create a personalized view of their information, and allows capturing the knowledge gained for undertaking specific tasks (such as an LAV repair) in context. But this relation holds independent of whether the data is annotated by speech, by text or by handwriting. Understanding the relation more generally allows designers to consider any medium for annotation as a potential means of facilitating a personalized data view.

Scenarios can also be taken as exemplars of model scenarios; for example, Figure 7.1 illustrates a model of guided exploration. Sgt. Garcia follows the "advice" of the personal maintenance device only because he is reasonably confident of the accuracy and effectiveness of the device. The system was designed to support this style of use; to that extent it embodies a model of guided exploration. Other models are possible of course; many diagnostic systems would require a maintainer to follow a specified diagnostic tree, even if that meant following branches that an experienced mechanic knows to be irrelevant to the current component fault. Seeing the scenario in Figure 7.1 as a guided exploration scenario allows the designer to benefit from prior knowledge pertaining to this model and to contribute further design knowledge of the model based on the current project.

HOW IS SCENARIO-BASED DESIGN USED?

One of the strengths of scenario-based methods is that while they are centered on a single representation, the scenario, they are able to use this representation in a multitude of ways at different points in the systems development lifecycle.

Requirements Engineering

Requirements engineering is the process of identifying and articulating needs for new technology and applications. It involves a wide range of activities including interviews with potential customers and future users of new systems, observations of workplace activity that new systems are intended to support, and participatory workshops involving direct collaboration among various stakeholder constituencies (users, their managers and co-workers, system developers, documentation designers, user interface specialists).

Several kinds of scenarios are used in the requirements process. Routine workflow scenarios describe typical episodes of the human activity that the new system must support. By describing work practices vividly, scenarios help to keep developers focused on the user's needs. Problem scenarios describe episodes of breakdown in workflow, including difficulties in usability and threats to safety. They concretize outcomes that the new system must avoid. Envisionment scenarios describe possible alterations of extant situations. They can be taken as initial design proposals, sometimes called paper prototypes, and at the same time be used instrumentally to evoke further requirements and analysis from users and developers. They encourage "what if?" reasoning.

As an example, a problem scenario might describe obstacles a Marine Corps light armored vehicle commander encounters in determining the parts block (the number and type of spare parts) required for an overseas deployment. A related envisionment scenario might describe how such a task might be carried out using a predictive simulation and modeling tool, as in Figure 7.4.

Scenarios help to integrate the requirements engineering process by providing a single type of representation to evoke, codify, and analyze various sources of requirements information. The trade-offs implicit in the scenarios can be articulated as an a priori design rationale, guiding design work rather than merely describing its outcomes. For example, the new predictive simulation and modeling tool may increase the accuracy of parts planning, as well as reduce planning time and cost, but it may result in over-reliance on technology that may not always be available to the Marine commander.

Such an explicit design rationale can help to clarify the root concepts for the system early in the development process, promoting more elegant design solutions. The accessibility of scenarios to non-technologists facilitates greater participation by users. Scenarios can be created by the users themselves, or created by designers and shared with users to identify and prioritize requirements.

The flexibility of scenarios facilitates management of emergent requirements—the new design goals that often become apparent during system development. Requirements scenarios can be modified continuously to provide an overall view of the most current understanding of the goals for the system.

Major Positano is planning the overseas deployment of a Marine Corps Light Armored Reconnaissance Battalion. Among the more difficult questions to answer concerns what spare parts the battalion needs to take to ensure continuity of operations in a harsh desert environment. He reviews records from prior deployments, talks to the maintenance chief about the kinds of repairs most common on their last deployment, and considers some of the upgrades that have since been made to the vehicles they will be taking. He also considers the specific requirements of the mission they will undertake on this deployment, and the microclimate in the area of operations. Another important input to the parts planning process is the state of the parts resupply pipeline, and difficulties they are currently experiencing with their new enterprise resource planning (ERP) system.

The Major also has at-hand a new predictive simulation and modeling software tool that constructs a suggested parts block using some of the same data sources as inputs to a sophisticated planning algorithm derived from ideas in artificial intelligence, specifically, evolutionary computing and genetic programming. He enters information describing some of the parameters of the mission including environmental variables, the potential for combat operations, and current resupply lead times, and then presses the "run" button. Within under two minutes the system produces three recommended courses of action differentiated by risk and cost.

Figure 7.4   Envisionment scenario, "planning an LAR deployment parts block"

Human–Computer Interaction

Human–computer interaction involves the design and evaluation of systems as they are experienced and used by people. It includes understanding and modeling the perception, cognition, behavior, and social interaction of work activity, and developing user interface displays and interaction devices, and associated documentation and training to support human characteristics and preferences.

Human–computer interaction forces a strongly task-oriented perspective on defining systems and their use. Human–computer interaction designers use scenario walkthroughs to develop transparent and consistent rubrics for the appearance and behavior of displays and controls, sometimes called user interface metaphors. Scenario walkthroughs are used to ensure that the information displayed by the system in any given state suggests appropriate actions and interpretations to users, and that error recognition, diagnosis, and recovery information is available, accurate, and easy to employ. Training, online help, and other system documentation now typically presents information in a task context, that is, as a scenario description.

In the system development process, human–computer interaction closely couples design and evaluation. Envisionment scenarios can be detailed in terms of specific goals for user performance and experience, for example, how quickly on average users will be able to perform routine tasks, like scheduling a community meeting, with what error rates, and with what levels of satisfaction. Such explicit usability goals can become part of the design scenarios for the system, and subsequently can be assessed with test subjects.

Such evaluation work goes on throughout the development process. Early in development, the performance and experience of subjects in test scenarios can be used as formative evaluation to refine the original goals for the system. Later in the development process, similar scenarios can be used as summative evaluation to verify that development goals were met.

Object-Oriented Software Engineering

Scenario-based approaches to requirements engineering and human–computer interaction have been dramatically integrated in the past decade by scenario-based approaches to software development. The key bridging insight is that the people and things described in requirements scenarios, and the user interface display objects and controls of human–computer interaction scenarios, can correspond to the same software objects. This insight derives from the distinction between software models and views in object-oriented software: software models describe underlying functionality, views describe the presentation of the functionality.

Scenario-based approaches to object-oriented software engineering suggest taking the nouns and verbs of an envisionment scenario as a first approximation object model: the nouns are the objects, the verbs are the methods (capabilities) of the objects. In the parts block planning example, vehicle (LAV), component, plan, repair, and the operating environment would be part of the initial object model. A vehicle can be repaired, a spare part can be consumed, a plan can be computed, and so on.

Scenarios are then "run" as simulations on such object models, successively elaborating the models in terms of what each object is responsible for (what data it holds, what methods it uses) and how objects collaborate (share data to enable one another's methods). For example, running the community meeting scenario against the initial object model suggests that the meeting object creates the form to gather user data, that it works with the room to schedule itself, that it holds its own topic, date/time, and location, and that it creates the notice.

A stronger scenario-based software development method is use cases. A use case is a set of system event traces that accomplish a particular scenario goal within a given system model. A simple example is the "Get Cash" use case in an ATM machine. The set of event traces gives the software designer a precise way of verifying how the use case scenario has been implemented in the software.

Scenario-Based Evaluation

Scenarios are also useful as test cases for prototypes or production systems. Trade-offs identified in scenario-based design can later be employed as criteria or metrics in evaluation activities. Especially in cases where scenarios are used early in the development lifecycle, they can serve as a sort of contract between stakeholders and the development team. They couch system requirements in a form and vocabulary that both understand, so can help reduce the ambiguities and miscommunication that can result when more abstract and technical representations are used as the basis for the development of system capabilities.

We evaluate systems framed by the tasks those systems were designed to enhance. Scenario-based methods emphasize this relationship, creating and maintaining task narratives throughout the system development process. Scenarios are available and referred to throughout all phases of the development process, enabling early upstream formative evaluation, coherently evolving into focused and efficient summative evaluation. Even guideline-driven analytic evaluation can be carried out more easily and more thoughtfully if framed by realistic domain tasks. Any kind of empirical evaluation must start with consideration of the tasks that participants will be carrying out. Evaluation task scenarios are a natural place for productive contact between designers and users: the users are engaged by the system as framed in the tasks they understand, perform, and will perform with the system. This is also where the users have critical expertise to share.

The trade-offs we illustrated in Figure 7.3 above analyze scenario narratives into constitutive causal relationships. Such trade-offs are useful criteria for understanding the behavior of people carrying out evaluation scenarios: For example, with respect to Figure 7.3, do participants easily perform and appreciate capabilities for gathering contextual data, do they seem frustrated with respect to search?

Scenarios as a Fulcrum in the System Lifecycle

Scenario-based practices currently span most of the software development lifecycle: Requirements development and analysis, envisionment and design development, user interface design and prototyping, software development and implementation, documentation and training development, formative and summative evaluation.

Surveys of contemporary development methods indicate that the use of scenarios is pervasive but not systematic. Developers say they would like more comprehensive methods and better tool support. An underlying tension in this is that a key property of scenarios as planning and design tools is that they seem quite concrete to the analyst/designer, while actually leaving most details unfixed. This has the effect of engaging greater imagination and critical reflection in system development work. It will be interesting to see how the tension between the benefits of roughness and the need for explicit engineering methods is resolved during the next decade.

MOVING FORWARD WITH SCENARIO-BASED DESIGN

Scenario-based design provides a framework for managing the flow of design activity and information in the task-artifact cycle. Scenarios evoke task-oriented reflection in design work; they make human activity the starting point and the standard for design work. Scenarios help designers identify and develop correct problem requirements by being at once concrete and flexible. They help designers to see their work as artifacts-in-use, and through this focus to manage external constraints in the design process. Scenarios help designers analyze the varied possibilities afforded by their designs through many alternative views of usage situations. And scenarios help designers cumulate their knowledge and experience in a rubric of task-oriented abstractions. This is depicted in Figure 7.5.

In current practice, scenario-based design techniques are widely used in human–computer interaction. Many new methods for capturing, generating, and classifying scenarios are emerging. For example, scenarios can be directly negotiated with end-users (participatory design), generated by systematically instantiating the signature phenomena of theories of human activity (theory-based design), or by various heuristic brainstorming techniques, like question generation and analogy. Scenarios can be applied in a wide variety of ways in system development. Besides their direct roles as descriptions of current or envisioned system use, they can be employed as

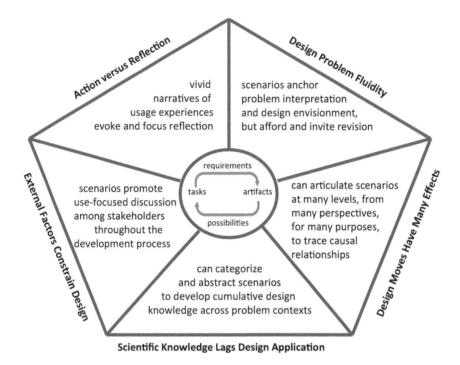

Figure 7.5   Challenges and approaches in scenario-based design

bounding contexts for developing design rationales, for theories of human–computer interaction, and for software development (for example, as use cases).

A key challenge is to more systematically leverage this wide variety of scenario-based activity within the development process. The most promising recent developments involve closer integration of practice in human–computer interaction with the development of standard schemata, and support for libraries and reuse frameworks developed in requirements engineering.

REFERENCES

Carroll, J.M. (Ed.) 1995. *Scenario-based design: Envisioning work and technology in system development*. New York: John Wiley and Sons.

Carroll, J.M. 2000. *Making use: Scenario-based design of human–computer interactions*. Cambridge, MA: MIT Press.

Jacobson, I., Christerson, M., Jonsson, P., and Overgaard, G. 1992. *Object-oriented software engineering: A use case driven approach*. Reading, MA: Addison-Wesley.

Jarke, M., Bui, X.T., and Carroll, J.M. 1998. Scenario management: An interdisciplinary approach. *Requirements Engineering*, 3(3–4), 155–173.

8

Socio-Cognitive Issues in Human-Centered Design for the Real World

Saadi Lahlou

ABSTRACT

In order to avoid resistance and hidden costs in the deployment and maintenance phase of complex socio-technical systems, we developed a participative technique which addresses the deployment and maintenance issues early in the design process: "experimental reality." It enables realistic stakeholders' involvement at an early stage of design, by developing the new system in actual context of use. This approach implies a different way of managing development projects, and in contrast highlights some shortcomings of current practice.

This chapter provides; (1) a framework, installation theory, to sort out and address the problems encountered by design projects for complex socio-technical systems, (2) a quick presentation of activity theories, and (3) an illustration of our design technique in the domain of information technology systems supporting collaborative work in a large industrial organization.

1. INTRODUCTION: DESIGNING FOR REAL-WORLD SYSTEMS

Although we design for the future, this future is supposed to start at the end of the design project. This is usually pretty close, and by the time the new system starts it will still have to be compatible with a lot of the current world-as-is-now. This chapter addresses this issue.

The world in which we design comes with some already installed basis: physical (equipment, devices), social (laws, customs, norms), and cognitive (habits, education). Even the users are "second-hand": they are not new to the system being designed in the sense that they have already been educated and trained within the current system. The designer will have to cope with this pre-existing installation. *Installation theory* (section 1) provides a framework for comprehensive design and a checklist of the three levels of reality which the designer should address.

If we want to design in a user-centric way, we must be on the user's side. But observing what users do is not enough. Current behavior of the users is a biased indication of what the users want, precisely because current behavior is framed by present installation. User-centric design should focus on what the users actually want: their motives, their goals. We found Russian Activity Theory to be the most efficient for complex system design among the variety of theories we tried. Section 2 presents a remix of this theory, adapted for design purposes with some additions of current distributed cognition and psychology.

In section 3 we address the case of designing Information Technology (IT) systems. These are specific because they are by nature communicating with the rest-of-the-world—hence they must adapt to the fast-changing technological context. The need to support openness and connectivity confronts their design with the Sisyphean "never-endingness" of continuous upgrade. We present a design technique, "experimental reality," tailored for this problem. This is illustrated by the example of conference rooms.

2. DESIGN AND CHANGE MANAGEMENT: MAKING NEW IN THE OLD CONTEXT

Designers of a single object or service may (sometimes) find it possible to draw the limit of the problem-space they should address and work with a clear set of specifications to redesign on a blank sheet. But designers of large socio-technical systems are often cornered into "upgrading" a previous system and keeping some continuity with the current state of things. This is because of the complexity (relations between parts of the system) and the impossibility of the redesign of some of the parts. For example, a new IT system, a new transportation system, a new plant and even a new building must take for granted a series of limiting socio-technical specifications. They must fit into the existing frameworks of the environment which surrounds them (the organization, the transportation network, the trade, the city, and so on). Designers must then cope with existing users, installed basis, and existing rules.

Subsection 2.1 introduces installation theory taking inspiration on how the global society deals with these issues to generate some design guidelines. Subsection 2.2 provides some indications to involve users in a realistic design process.

2.1 Installation Theory

This section introduces "installation theory," a general framework describing the evolution of socio-technical systems. Although installation theory is general in scope, it is useful for practical applications as it clearly delineates three levels where action should by taken to ensure acceptability of change, smooth operation, and future evolution. These levels are:

- the physical level of artifacts where we design affordances;
- the psychological level of representations and practices where users are trained to acquire adapted competence;
- the institutional level where rules will be created and externalities controlled in order to keep the system running and updated.

The existence of these three layers has direct implications on the process of design, and especially on the way the users and other stakeholders should be involved in this process. Designers should always think of the system as a *socio-technical* system: human operators and users, and the rules, are functional parts of the system, just as is the physical installation of machines and software. The view that we design "a technical system operated by humans" is naïve: what is designed is a socio-technical system where the physical parts are operated by human parts (and in fact sometimes also vice-versa, physical parts operate human parts). This means, in the design process, that operator's training should be planned for as well as hardware maintenance.

Considerable work in social science has been devoted to the study of how social systems are created, maintained, and how they evolve. To make a long story short, fit socio-technical systems (those which survive) are continuously recreated by their own users, at local level and during normal operation. This is true for a production plant, the Internet, or society at large. All these systems are social constructions (Berger and Luckmann, 1966), in which the new users are educated and trained in such a way that they will use, and maintain in the course of use, the existing system. Giddens (1984), in his *structuration theory*, showed how the structure of a system has the dual property of being the result of continuous reconstruction by the practice of participants, and of producing these practices.

When one thinks of any concrete example, this somewhat abstract statement becomes clearer. For example, a company, a workflow, or even an aircraft will continue being operated, maintained, and slowly upgraded as the result of the practices of the professionals who use them. Their very role as professionals is in fact to maintain and operate the system. This illustrates the fact that usage reconstructs structure. Rules of practice or norms which format the system are built from practice. It is less trivial for hardware but examination of how hardware is maintained and redesigned shows that it is precisely tailored to be inserted in the fabric of practice, in the light of experience. Classic design guidelines always insist on this feed-back loop.

Conversely, user's behaviors will be elicited, guided, and constrained by the surrounding cultural system. Installation theory (Lahlou, 2008) addresses this aspect by distinguishing three major layers in the "installation of the world" which determine individual behavior. At a given moment, the world can be considered as an *installation* (in the artistic sense of assembling patterns in space to modify the way we experience this situation). This installation guides subjects into their activity track, at three levels: physical, psychological, and institutional.

At the *physical level*, artifacts have affordances which both limit some behaviors and call for some other. A classic example is the door handle (Norman, 1988), which (usually) signals how it should be handled and turned, and also affords only these movements. In the same vein, a workflow will prompt for specific entries at specific places in the screen, and will accept only "relevant" ones. The *physical level* is the one which is most classically addressed by designers.

But the physical level cannot be used by humans unless they have in their mind and body the adequate cognitive installation to interpret this physical level. For example, there are many possible ways of (mis)using even a door handle, and someone who has never used one may well stay trapped in the room even if the door is not locked. This does not happen often in our societies precisely because users have been educated to use doors. They have a mental model of what "a door" is and how it should be operated. This mental model is shared by the population: it is a "social representation" (Moscovici, 1961; Abric, 1994) that has been adapted to the actual collection of doors in the society by a double mechanism of adaptation (Lahlou, 1998): people learn how to use doors, and designers make doors according to the representation of doors. People experience difficulties in interpreting new "things" for which there is no social representation. In such cases, they tend to create a new representation by "anchoring" (Moscovici, 1961) on something they believe is similar, and try to apply existing interpretation schemes from "similar" objects to the new one. This is why designers should be extremely cautious when giving new things a form factor or name: what is evoked may serve as a basis for anchoring. *Social representations are the world's user's manual. These representations are installed in the user's minds, just like the artifacts are installed in the Physical environment.* They constitute a large installed basis, which is very powerful and inert considering the efforts one must make to train users.[1]

So the second level of determination of behavior by the installation of the world is the embodiment of representations and practice in users, which have also been designated as *skills* (Rasmussen, 1983, 1985), *competencies*, and so on. The cost of installing adequate skills in the users of a system is often several orders of magnitude greater than the cost of the hardware itself because there are installation costs: knowledge cannot be distributed over a population as a commodity; learning is an interactive process. Installation costs should also include (although this is never counted) the time and effort spent by users and other stakeholders of the system in order to implement the proper psychological installation in the user population. It is worth noting that while physical installation is usually within the sole control of the owners of the system, psychological installation is inevitably a co-construction with users.

Of course, since using a system is using both the artifacts and the skills, it is good practice to reuse existing skills; this is called *designing for cognition* (Lahlou, Nosulenko et al., 2002, Lahlou, 2009). This is a way to turn around the issue of installation costs. A good example of leveraging the power of an installed basis of skills can be found in the design of web-services, which tend to use common conventions of interaction with the mouse and keyboard, or the navigation in virtual worlds (World of Warcraft, Second Life, and so on) which all use similar keyboard conventions for moving the avatars.

As said earlier, and especially in large populations of users, the installation cost (persuasion, training, evaluation of skills) is often too high to be even considered seriously in the design project. The designer must then integrate in the design some kind of device which will gradually install these skills as the system is used. Viral dissemination of practice and skills is ideal from the designers' perspective, because

---

1   Note that just as representations are embodied, practice also is. Enacting and interpretation (e.g., using a door, entering a password) is embodied both as a cognitive level (mental interpretation: this is a door) and at motor level (the very motor action of opening the door).

the costs are outsourced to users. Users may have a different point of view, though, so designers should be careful. Since many designers take this approach, users are confronted with an unbearable cognitive load to learn *all* systems, and end up not reading *any* user's manuals.

In any case, this installation at psychological level should be considered and a solution proposed at designed stage, otherwise the user organization will incur massive costs.

Let us look now how change monitoring happens in real ecologies (societies) to see how that installation takes place. This will introduce the third layer of determination, institutions.

In a society, representations and objects follow a co-evolution process: representations are constructed by the practice people have of objects. Conversely, objects are made after the pattern of their representation: ladders are made to look like ladders; firemen are trained to behave as firemen; email software is built after the representation of email. And this is the reason why representations match with objects (Lahlou, 2008).

A first lesson to learn here is that if we want new systems to be usable and sustainable, we have to make sure the representations that designers have of the system are informed by the actual representations of the system among users. If the system follows the user's mental model, it will be used more easily. Designing for cognition means finding among the user's existing (cultural) portfolio of skills and representations the ones which could be readily reused for this specific system and tailor the system accordingly. Conversely, the differences between the new system and previous representations should be highlighted in order to avoid misunderstanding.

This seems trivial, and of course designers do usually try to take into account users' representations. Nevertheless, in practice, the designers often delegate this investigation to "specialists" (ergonomists, ethnographers, social psychologists, marketers or other social scientists), and, however skilled these intermediaries may be, something is lost in translation. We strongly advise that designers, on top of these surveys done by someone else, and after them, do engage in *direct* informed discussions with the users to make sure they have correctly understood the users' representations and expectations. We will see in section 3 that we have ourselves adopted an even more radical approach, inspired by the Russian psychology of engineering, where designers, social scientists, and users discuss the design together.

Coming back to societies, at a social level, the co-evolution of objects and representations is monitored by domain-local communities of interest (users, providers, public authority, and so on) who set the patterns of objects, the rules of practice and so on. Because these stakeholders know the field from the inside, objects, representations and rules are adapted to behaviors. These stakeholders create *institutions*, which are both sets of rules to be applied to keep order and cooperation, and communities of interest aware that they play in the same game. So, institutions set common conventions which enable cooperation (for example, people should all drive on the same side of the road, not send massive attachments to large mailing lists, and so on). Conversely, they control potential abuse or misuse, and minimize social costs (Coase, 1960) also called "negative externalities." Many of the rules are already contained in the normative aspects of representations, but institutions are special in their capacity to enforce behavior, by social pressure or more direct means.

In the process of negotiation between institutions, stakeholders are involved on the basis of their implication in the system, they engage in negotiation processes in order to defend their interests or simply to fight against externalities. This complex interplay between institutions is not a market for information; rather it is a multi-party, sometimes a bit anarchic, series of trials and errors, and of local negotiation. There is no such thing as a general initial consensus conference or general negotiation: stakeholders get into the process as they become aware of the potential impacts of the system on them, which impacts are sometimes very indirect or unexpected. Some stakeholders help, and some oppose. But, as the sociology of translation (Akrich, Callon et al., 2006) notes, the projects succeed only if they manage to convene a sufficient mass of supporters.

What is to be learned at this stage is that there must be some organized authorities (institutions) who explicitly regulate the system, and especially its reproduction, by preventing abuse and misuse; and these institutions should have some capacity of coercion. The question to ask is "Who will sanction misuse and abuse?" Usually, the system should have an explicit "owner," but other regulatory bodies may have their word to say because they will have to be in charge of coercion. *These stakeholders should be consulted at some point, not too late.* Once again this seems obvious, but in practice the head of the design project is often taken as the single referent; which is hazardous because she will often not be the one in charge of the actual system. Also, he/she has his or her own interest, among which finishing the project in time and delay which means a bias towards overlooking issues which may be too long or expensive to solve within allocated resources.

Another take-away point from this observation of natural systems is that it is very difficult to predict beforehand who will be impacted by externalities. A reality test recruits relevant stakeholders on the basis of actual impact, and they come motivated to solve the issue because they have become aware of this impact. One way to mimic this recruitment effect in the design process, which we apply in experimental reality, is to make sure a real test will be carried long enough so as to observe these externalities. As externalities surface, the parties concerned get involved into the design process to solve the issues before the final system is launched. Otherwise, the new system will encounter "resistance," which means costs and delay. Resistance is a signal of pain in the organization and should be treated as a warning symptom rather than be fought against (Bauer, 1991).

So, at a given moment, individual behavior is determined by this distributed installation of the world: artifacts installed in the physical environment, interpretive systems installed in humans, and institutions installed in society. The co-evolution between artifacts and representations is done under continuous monitoring and control of stakeholder communities, which use institutions as social and economics tools to safeguard their interests. This is a factor of stability of this normative framework.

The designer of a new system should ideally set up such a distributed installation so that his system is sustainable and regulated. As it is a trial and error process, this takes time, and is never fully stabilized, so the need of a system designer remains throughout the life of the system. Unfortunately, the designer usually withdraws from the scene when the project is over; she is replaced by maintenance, management, consultants and subcontractors, or sometimes R&D, to fix the local problems ... until a deep redesign is needed. This is fine for rather stable systems. But some other systems continue to undergo evolution, especially the ones which use fast-evolving technological bricks. For such systems, we advise that a specific unit remains which continuously explores DOME[2] possible improvements (Lahlou, 2005), tests them locally, and upgrades the system when a good solution is found. Keeping alive such a unit which capitalizes considerable knowledge (technical, social, organizational) can be a cheaper and more efficient way to keep the system updated than consulting or designing a fix only when badly needed, because in the latter case the designers will have to rediscover the system, and may have less organizational agency to mobilize the stakeholders. Section 3 gives an example of such a unit with the "mother room" of conference rooms at EDF.

2.2 Involving Users

Users are usually more conscious than anyone else of the shortcomings of the current system; so they can become, if they are made aware of what the new system could bring them, strong allies for the designers.

When using the system, the users focus on their local, current goals, and will try to cope with what is there as the "conditions given" within which they will try to attain their goal. In these moments, users will make no effort to cure the system, simply because it is not their current goal, unless a quick and local fix will enable them to make sufficient satisfaction. This is why we cannot expect too much from users alone. And this is why the organization calls for designers whose goal is precisely to make the system better.

Another issue with involving the users and stakeholders (as we advocate) is that these participants are usually bound within the current system. Especially, they will be quick to seize or imagine ways in which the new system will cause problems to some of their existing habits or privileges.

What we advise here is threefold: focus on activity, use the subcam and recruit friendly users.

On the one hand, design should focus on the user's activity, seen from the user's perspective. In doing so, the designer (and the rest of the project team) will be able to communicate better with the user, in his own language, and the user will feel involved in the problem. Technically, we use the Subcam (Lahlou, 1999, 2006), a miniature wide-angle video camera which the users wear at eye level (on glasses, a helmet, a bandana ...) during their daily activities (Figure 8.1). The subcam records what the subject sees, does, where the attention is focused; the sound track provides not only records of verbal interaction or talk-out-loud, but also cues of emotional state such as voice tone/pitch and breathing. It is a dive in the subjects' phenomenological tunnel.

Analyzing the Subcam tapes with the users themselves and focusing on the problems they encounter provides designers with an insight into the actual activity. It proved to be an extremely efficient way to produce solutions with the users. For analysis, we use Russian activity theory, which will be described in section 2.

The subcam is a precious help because the users can wear it in their usual context, in the absence of the design team. It provides a situated view, from the best point of

---

2   DOME: Dissemination, Operations, Maintenance, Evolution.

Figure 8.1   Subject wearing a subcam, 1998 version (left), frame from a subcam (right)

observation possible. Beyond a merciless account of what the actual activity is, the subcam enables setting up protocols supporting activity analysis. As we shall see in section 2, activity analysis is very powerful but it requires knowing the goals of the operator at every moment. Because the subcam provides a situated recording, the capacity of subjects to remember their intentions at each moment when they watch the tape is far better than in any other techniques; sometimes it is stunningly accurate even months after the fact.[3] Therefore, we use the tapes not only to spot the problems, but to collect, during self-confrontations of subjects with their subcam tapes, the goals and emotions of the subject as he was performing the task; which will then be a critical element in the activity analysis. As a side effect, the subcam enables designers to get a deep insight into what the user actually does, without the social filters and the mediations of language.

For the recruitment of subjects, we do not try to be representative in a statistic sense. Most users experience some difficulties in participating in a design process, especially since it does come on top of their normal work. Although most users would actually be able to provide valuable input in the design process, some, for one reason or another, are more motivated, more ready to verbalize their experience and collaborate. We call these "friendly users" (Lahlou, 2009; Jégou, 2009); they may be technology fans, friends of the project members, interested stakeholders, or simply curious people who are happy to test something new and participate in innovation. In our experience, a couple of motivated "friendly users" who will follow the project all the way bring more usable input than a large sample of "standard" subjects. This is especially true for the early phases of design, when a lot of compliance and good will is needed on the part of users to actually use a system in infancy, with a poor user interface and hazardous functionalities. Some of these friendly users can be involved to the point they participate regularly to design meetings, and serve as

---

3   We have the capacity to judge whether what the subject remembers of his state of mind at one moment is accurate, because when we watch the tape with the subject, and ask him "What you did next?", or "What were you up to then?", it is quite easy to verify if the subject is correct simply by watching what actually happened next on the tape. Reliving one's phenomenological trajectory in the world tends to re-prompt the same state of mind: look how, when moving around your house, you suddenly realize you forgot why you had just come into this specific room; usually, returning to the previous location and walking the path again will make you remember.

brokers or scouts with more distant users and stakeholders. As the system grows in quality along the design process, the team can involve less and less friendly users, until finally the system could stand the tests of unfriendly users.

3.2 A Quick Presentation of Activity Theories

Being user centric has rightly become a claim of modern design. There are different ways of being user-centric, though. One is to focus on the user as an object of study, and to analyze his interaction with the system. Another, more radical, for which we advocate, is the anthropocentric approach; which considers the human as the central element in the system (not just as a part of it or as a source of usability constraints for design), and designs the system from the perspective of the user. The difference is easily illustrated by the stand of the designer: in the latter, the final user is considered to be the legitimate source of specifications for the system, that is, "the client" (rather than the sponsor who is the client of "the project"); the designer works to help the users attain their goals, within the constraints given by the project and other stakeholders (for example, budget).

This may be a source of conflict with the official sponsor of the project, or the project manager, who consider *they* are the clients. But in the end, even though the project sponsor pays for the system, the users have to buy it. Therefore, for the sake of the system's success, the final user's voice should be taken *really* seriously. Too often, even though the design process claims to be user-oriented, the final user's voice is listened to only as long as it does not cause major problems to the project (for example, substantially increased costs or delays). More often than not, overlooking the user's voice at design phase will result in increased costs in the system's DOME (Deployment, Operation, Maintenance, Evolution). These costs are externalities for the project manager, and sometimes even for the project sponsor (who may be in the end of his carrier in the organization, or in a subdivision of the organization that will not be in charge of DOME; for example, procurement or R&D), but these costs will be incurred by the user organization anyway.

During design phase the anthropocentric approach often seems to be biased towards more user comfort and freedom that would seem strictly necessary for the system to operate in theory, but in the end, the anthropocentric approach pays because the users will be supportive of the system, and palliate its shortcomings. In fact, many goals of the users, which seem unnecessary or abusive to short-sighted functional design, often appear crucial to enable the flexibility and informal adaptation of the system in real conditions, therefore overlooking them can be disastrous, as we learned the hard way ourselves (see example of our design failures in conference rooms in Lahlou, 2009).

In practice we take an anthropocentric perspective by adopting activity theory approach, which is to study the activity of the operators. Activity is very different from behavior. Behavior is the sequence of actions described objectively by an external observer; activity is the sequence of intentions and actions as seen by the user.

Humans are specific in that they have motives, goals, plans; actual behavior is only one possible path that the operator took to reach his goals in the conditions given. For example, while "taking the bus" may be behavior, the activity would be to travel to a given destination. What is most important is not the means of transportation, but reaching a given destination on time with minimum cost and effort: if the operator finds another means of transportation that has better efficiency than the bus that day, he will probably switch to that mode of transportation. In that case, making a better system is not necessarily designing a better bus, but understanding the transportation bottlenecks of the population concerned and addressing the issues, which may be a matter of interconnection with other transport, modifying the location of bus stations, training users. When we talk about "the conditions given," this means not only the affordances of the physical layer, but also the sets of institutional rules. As another illustration, in the domain of accounting Suchman (1983) showed, with an ethnographic approach, that the nature of activity is rather to reach the goal (for example, pay an invoice) with the constraint of respecting the rules, than to follow a rigid procedure.

While in the West clinical psychology and analysis of individual subjects were developed, in Russia considerable progress took place on the analysis of groups at work. The success of the Russian orbital missions testifies to this advance (Nosulenko and Rabardel, 1998). In fact, the history of Russian psychology on the whole is focused on the problem of activity. Activity design was especially developed in the "psychology of engineering" analyzing the activity of the human operators of complex technical systems (Leontiev and Lomov, 1963; Lomov, 1977; Zavalova, Lomov et al., 1986). As underlined by Lomov, the pioneer of the Russian psychology of engineering (Lomov, 1963; Nosulenko and Rabardel, 1998) who coined the concept of activity design, the design should address both the tools and the human subject of work (Lomov, 1977).

Designing activity differs from designing objects. In activity design, one seeks to set up an environment allowing the subject to carry out his activity and to achieve his goal. Here, the artifact which is the initial object of the design (for example, a product, a software and so on) is only a small portion of the system considered. The rules and procedures, the representations, operator training, maintenance, and diffusion within the organization of the central artifact are also in the scope of the design and are not considered as intangible givens, but as aspects of the environment which could possibly be re-installed. A central element of the system is the operator himself. Theories of activity, originated in Russia (Rubinstein, 1940; Leontiev, 1974; Nosulenko and Samoylenko, 1998), are an essential source of renewal and development of current psychology and ergonomics (for example, Wertsch, 1981; Engeström, 1990; Bödker, 1991, 1996; Kaptelinin, 1996; Nardi, 1996; Bedny and Meister, 1997; Daniellou and Rabardel, 2005; Nosulenko and Rabardel, 2007; Nosulenko and Samoylenko, 2009). One must also be aware that there is no such thing as one single theory of activity: a considerable number of authors have proposed variants over a period that spans nearly 70 years. Analyzing activity is done with a couple of conceptual tools which are sometimes apparently close yet deeply different from concepts used in Western psychology, and the history of the concept is in itself a domain of research in Russia. Also, activity theory per se has a series of shortcomings for design. We present here our own short "remixed" digest which is what we use in practice.

Activity theory is *anthropocentric*: it considers activity from the perspective of the subject, where action is always intentional (it is aimed towards a goal, and directed towards objects-of-the-world).

A goal is a conscious representation the subject has of the future situation to be reached. A goal is a local means of satisfying one or several more general motives.

Motive is some perceived need; it refers to a state of dissatisfaction *internal to the subject*; while a goal is rather some state of the environment including the subject. For example, hunger will be a motive and dining at the restaurant a goal; self-esteem will be a motive and getting promoted is a goal.

Although the difference between motives and goals is essential to understand, and to get the gist of activity theory, it is often unclear in literature. Motives are an internal, psychological state, and goals are a means to satisfy these motives. There may be different ways of satisfying the same motive (for example, there are many ways of gaining self-esteem, there are many ways of satisfying hunger). In a workplace context, there may be many ways to fix a machine, foster a decision, and even to process an invoice, each being a specific trade-off between for example, speed, risk, cost, and quality; depending upon the situation, one may be better than another. So, subjects may change their goals on an opportunistic basis to satisfy the same motive, for example, buy a sandwich if the restaurant is closed, or subcontract a task if local resource is lacking.

Also a subject may carry several motives (for example, sociability and hunger) and will tend to choose goals which can satisfy several motives (for example, go to lunch with a colleague). Finally, there are many ways to reach a goal (for example, one can walk to the restaurant or take the bus). Hence, subjects will choose their trajectory to the goal in a trade-off involving functional efficacy (availability of resources, efficiency, hazard reduction, or cognitive cost) but also considering the motivational benefits which can be cropped along the trajectory (for example, walking is good for health, displaying professional proficiency is good for self-esteem, being compliant to hierarchy is good to avoid stress and so on).

As we can see, activity theory enables a detailed and realistic account of life, and activity analysis evidences the many layers of determination of behavior, while classical mere functional analysis will tend to overlook the subjective aspects involved in individual performance. When we redesign a system, understanding what features will actually feed motivation of the operator is crucial. Usually, satisfying the objectives of the system as a worker (say, keep a good standard of quality, enhance safety, and so on) are, from the subjective perspective of the operator, goals to satisfy personal motives (own self-esteem, wealth, health, recognition by group of peers, sociability and so on). Failing to connect the system's goals to individual operator's motives results in low motivation, minimal ("satisficing") performance of operators, and need of external control; while connecting goals to individual motives enables increased performance, mindful contribution, creativity, self-regulation, and good social climate.

Let us now go in more detail in activity analysis. Motives and goals are rather general levels of determination. In practice, to reach the goal the subject will have to create a trajectory from current state (conditions given) to desired state (the goal). To do so the subject goes through steps ("tasks"); each one having its own aim (sub-goal). For example, to operate an electric valve, the subject may have to first check actual state of valve and compare with expected state as given by his instruction sheet, connect the motor of the valve to the mains, operate the controls, check the valve has attained desired value, report, consignate valve, disconnect from mains. And each task may break into subtasks (for example, checking state of valve starts by checking one is in front of the right valve by checking valve reference number).

Execution of some tasks might reveal problems, and need conscious monitoring of motor and mental actions by the subject; while for some others a routine sequence of automatic actions is sufficient. When actions are automatic and are applied beyond conscious control (for example, changing gear when driving a car, turning on the cooker, typing a password, and so on) they are called "operations."

So activity appears as an oriented trajectory from a given state ("conditions given") to a consciously represented expected state ("goal"). Attaining the goal satisfies the motives of the subject. The trajectory of activity is a succession small problems to be solved of ("tasks"), which can each be seen as reaching a local sub-goal. The operator solves each task by taking actions (consciously controlled motor or mental moves) and operations (automatic, routinized moves taking place beyond threshold of consciousness). At each moment, the subject is confronted with the possibility of taking a different local route to reach the final trajectory, and may do so opportunistically in consideration of the local conditions given at this point.

A good design will result in offering the operator trajectories which are legible, efficient, and enjoyable because they feed his motives.

From the designer's perspective, the number of variables is enormous, and the tree of possibilities too big to be fully explored. It is simpler to fix a "one best way" that the operator should rigidly follow. This tailorist design strategy is applicable where the conditions are stable, for example, in a production line for material products. The one best way approach is more difficult to apply in complex systems where the configuration of the problem space may change during operation, or have a large array of possible states which must be regulated (transportation networks, aircraft, power plant). It is almost impossible to apply to systems in continuous transformation where some creative input from the operators or users is expected (managerial chain, information workflows, client-fed systems for example, web 2.0). In these more flexible systems, what stays stable are the motives and goals rather than the procedures to attain them, because the latter change opportunistically with the state of the system.

In these complex systems it is advisable to have a goal-oriented design. Any part of the process should be explicitly marked with respect of what is its specific goal in the global framework. This enables the operator to make sense of her activity to take the appropriate decision and evaluate results in the light of what is the goal to be attained. As in complex systems there is considerable labor division; the local goals of a task or procedure may not always be clear to the operator, especially if they are aimed at obtaining a distant effect (for example, avoiding externalities in some distant department), or at some long-term or distributed consequences such as risk management or overall quality control. If such sensemaking is not facilitated, local decisions may be taken to stick too rigidly to a procedure, or operators may choose what seems to be a locally acceptable decision but is fact is a less efficient route to reach the higher order goals. Not only does this goal-directed design enable operators to take better informed decisions and makes them feel empowered and participating, but it also helps to connect their activity to higher goals which may fuel their motivation.

This goal-oriented design unfolds from general goals of owners of the system (informed by customers' and end-users' perceived quality) and is subdivided at lower levels of the system as labor division takes place when these supraordinate goals are broken down into sub-goals. In practice, during design, trace of the goals at higher level must be kept explicit when the subsystem is designed. For example, to take again the example of the valve described earlier, the goals of comparing current state with instruction sheet, and reporting final state after operations, both aim at tracing an accurate state of current installation, checking the information system is accurate, and feeding the predictive maintenance system (which will trigger preventive maintenance on all similar valves in plant if systematic drift is observed). These tasks have minor use in the current operation, but have an important impact on overall safety: knowing this will motivate the operator to perform them with attention because they make his gesture contribute to important collective goals, rather than resent them as cumbersome overhead done for some distant quality control bureaucrat or anonymous computer system. An action without a goal is meaningless for the operator. It will therefore tend to be overlooked or poorly performed.

Also the subject must have a way to evaluate if the goal has been reached. Therefore a system should provide feed-back to enable the user turn to next action. In the example provided, this could simply be the fact of ticking a cell in a report sheet; electronic information systems can provide richer feedback including a "thank you" and a check that value is within range.

While documenting functional goals, making them explicit, and designing feed-back is a matter of good organization of the design project (which is similar to the good practice of comments in code in software development), it may seem a daunting task to collect individual goals, and motives of operators and users. In practice it is feasible only when the system as a prototype has reached a threshold of usability sufficient for it to be given for test to actual operators. Then, local goals can be made explicit with a talking-out-loud technique during performance, or a subcam capture followed by interview during self-confrontation of the operator with the tapes. One must note that if such protocols have been applied on a current version of the system before redesign started, usually many an interesting insight will have been already captured, which have informed design, and made explicit many tricks of the trade, expert shortcuts, and seasoned operator's criteria for evaluating their action.

When dealing with end-users who are not professional operators, which is often the case in "2.0" systems, we advise using the "perceived quality" technique (Nosulenko, Parizet et al., 1998; Nosulenko and Samoylenko, 1997, 1999, 2009). Perceived quality approach is an operationalization of activity theory, mitigated with communication theories and theory of mental image. Elements of activity are described (goals, motives, aims, actions, operations), and to each is attributed their subjective evaluation by the individual. Then, statistical techniques are used to characterize "objectively" the elements of activity (for example, physical measurement) and match them with their subjective evaluation. In contrast to classical techniques, the perceived quality approach begins with identifying the aspects of the object or system that are salient or valuable for a certain individual in the course of the given activity. Subjective evaluations which might appear at first sight intractable for the designers (for example, "good, "clear," "difficult," "disagreeable") are by this process gradually quantified, and attributed to objective criteria which can be modified in design.

In a nutshell, this method consists:

1. Obtaining a verbal description of what the user thinks (in very open terms) of performing the activity with the system to be evaluated; the verbatim are obtained by asking subjects to describe their activity as they perform it, usually by comparing the present situation with another (comparing two or more systems successively for the same activity, or comparing the "new" system with what their usual practice, and so on);

2. Extracting from the verbatim individual evaluations (for example, "this one is faster than the one I have") and finding out all dimensions used for evaluation (for example, fast/slow; light/heavy; clear/cluttered and so on);
3. Constructing a database where each evaluation is attributed to a specific element of activity (object, operation, and so on);
4. Statistical analysis of the database using evaluation dimensions as variables (for example, "verbal portrait" giving quantified profile of an object of activity on all characteristics; comparison of objects, comparison of operations on different objects, and so on).

This description of the perceived quality of activity is useful in comparing different systems or versions of the same system with quantitative measures. It also enables discovering which dimensions are relevant for the user, and spotting the problems. For example, we discover for which sub-goal or operation the artifact produces an impression of slowness in use. And it will then become obvious what technical affordances are at stake. The next step is redesigning the system to modify this affordance in order to better support the local goal.

In the course of "activity design," by focusing on creating the proper support environment to help the operator attain his goals, the designer will encounter several challenges for redesign. As predicted by installation theory, these challenges will be at the level of the technical system, the representations and practice, and the institutional setting.

As designing large socio-technical systems is complex, we find it easier to proceed by trial and error with friendly users, fixing problems as they emerge with the prototype in real use, and as stakeholders come to join the design process with their own requirements. This means setting up a design process, which enables this continuous and fruitful hands-on collaboration between designers and uses.

Our design approach, *experimental reality*, consists in implementing a continuous design cycle, taking place in a real setting, integrated in the normal processes of the larger organization. It operates in continuous process mode rather than in project mode. In a way, it is a step back from the current fashion of project mode management.

3. EXPERIMENTAL REALITY: A SYSTEM FOR CONTINUOUS DESIGN ADDRESSING NEVER-ENDINGNESS OF *IT* INNOVATION

This section describes experimental reality and illustrates it with the Mother Room system that was set up at the EDF Laboratory of Design for Cognition (3.1, 3.2). Then it lists the set of design targets for usability of information systems which we gradually came to adopt (3.3). Finally, we draw some lessons learned about the development cycle of IT systems (3.4), and describe some principles we found useful.

3.1 Experimental Reality

Experimental reality as a design technique has been extensively described elsewhere (Lahlou, Nosulenko et al., 2002; Lahlou, 2009) so this section will only provide a short illustrated overview.

Participative design is a method of action-research in which the experimenters voluntarily take part in focusing, in a constructive dialog with the designers (Ehn, 1992; Kyng and Mathiassen, 1997). This is usually done in a spiral design cycle where user consultation alternates with new design iteration, the user being given a version 1 to evaluate, then a version 2, and so on.

Experimental reality started one step further: we enabled continuous and direct contact between social scientists, designers, and users in a long-term process. In a nutshell, the idea is to install in a small unit a "next generation of work environments." This unit serves a continuous experimentation of possible improvements of the current system. The approach is specific in that this unit is not simply a living lab; it is actually functional and carries "normal work" in the organization. But it does so using the "next" versions of hardware, software, rules, and so on. As members of this unit experience specific problems because they test new systems but still must be compatible with the rest of the organization, they have a specific highly skilled maintenance and support team, and the benefit of extended clearance for external help, subcontracting, procurement, and exception to some internal rules—and of course of top equipment and cutting-edge technology. In exchange for which they are continuously monitored, report, and propose new solutions on the basis of their own experience.

What we can learn at the contact zone between the new and the old system in actual operation is obviously a major added value of the approach. The problems which occur there are a preview of deployment and future operations issues.

In practice, we constructed a living laboratory, a large vivarium (the K1 building of some 400 m^2: Figure 8.2) which is the arena where the team lived for such interaction: the team ended as a new organizational concept. The idea was to have a realistic test bed where future environments could be tested by real users, while their activity could be fully monitored. We wanted to monitor everything in order to capture systemic and emerging effects, especially in the process of adoption, for basic research purposes.

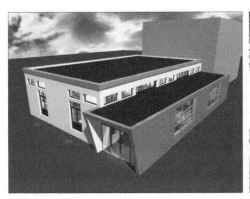

Figure 8.2   The K1 building at EDF R&D: CAD view and real view

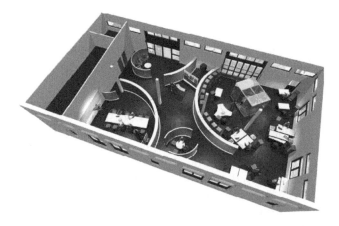

Figure 8.3   The project space and the RAO Mother Meeting Room (lower left corner)

In experimental reality, proximity with users enables taking shortcuts because the possible iterations are discussed with users without a heavy formal evaluation systematically taking place. For example, designers would discuss possible improvements with users as the latter are using the system or reporting problems: "What if we designed it like this?"

In these discussions the users can propose modifications and explore possibilities with some quick prototyping tools, sketches, mock-ups and so on and get immediate feed-back of technical feasibility from the designers; while designers can test ideas and get feed-back on their acceptability by the users. Jégou (2009) provides examples of "quick and dirty" design techniques which empower such hands-on discussions.

Not only the idea proved useful for basic research since a lot was learned about innovation processes, but also the experiment was so productive (several innovations were successfully disseminated in the company) that the laboratory, initially created for a period of three years (2000–2002), was transformed into a permanent facility hosting the "mother room" of augmented conference rooms for the company.

As this concept of mother room illustrates best the nature of experimental reality and how it can be implemented in practice in large organizations we shall describe it in more detail.

3.2 The Mother Room

To study "augmented" meetings (with videoconferencing, online collaborative tools and so on) we provided a comfortable meeting room (Figures 8.3 and 8.4) which could be reserved for free, in an industrial facility housing more than 2,000 office workers (engineers, scientists, and administrative personnel). This provided a large flow of volunteer users (over 200 meetings per year used this room), which enabled systems-tests in many configurations. This "mother room," called RAO, is used to test new versions of room communication systems before they are disseminated in the company; as technology evolves, so as to keep the fleet of rooms up-to-date and nice-to-use.

Figure 8.4   The RAO Mother Meeting Room in 2002

The infrastructure of the room is oversized, with high bandwidth networks of various protocols (WLAN, Bluetooth, RF-ID, CPL, GSM, GPRS, IRDA, EDI, and so on), sensors, and so on, deep raised floors and a technical ceiling to enable relocating within moments any resource (data, power, voice, sensors, and fluids including HVAC since the plenum is pressurized. Clever plug-and-play infrastructure designed by our colleagues of the Intelligent Workplace at Carnegie-Mellon University (Hartkopf, Loftness et al., 2009) empower users to do all these manipulations themselves, and they actually do modify them up to several times a day. As all the furniture is foldable, stackable, and/or wheeled, the room can be instantly adapted by the users to the configuration desired for each meeting. Configuration of the digital resources (videoconferencing, displays, lights, and so on) is done with ServiceTags: users simply have to select the card with the desired action and put it on a (RFID) tag reader (Figure 8.5). A vast array of technologies is made available to the team of users and designers, with a rather open budget, and most important, clearance to buy non-standard equipment and service.

The whole building, and especially the meeting room, is instrumented for continuous observation and recording. Subjects may wear subcams. What happens in the room is continuously recorded by a series of video cameras: a dozen Offsats (time-lapse cameras with automatic movement recognition (Lahlou, 1999), classic digital video cameras and screen recorders which record not only what happens in the room but also on the giant screens, and logs.[4] This continuous monitoring

---

4   Because of this continuous observation, participation in the experiments requires acceptance to take part in sometimes invasive and continuous protocols of observation, and considerable trust of users in the innovative unit. These issues and how they were solved are described in detail in Lahlou et al. 2002, 2009. The participants are voluntary. They are informed of our approach and are interested in its results. They take part in the construction of the system of observation and with its maintenance; nothing is hidden from them. The key of the device resides in the psychological contract which produces their participation, by taking into account their own interests (and not only those of the researcher and those of the organization which funds it). The observation is possible and productive because the observers are

Figure 8.5   RFID ServiceTags on a reader

Note: On the left notice the 1€ coin for scale.

provides material for discussing the issues with users, documenting the changes, measuring the impact (for example, the time spent, number of errors, and so on), and evaluate the number of resources needed (for example, bandwidth) or the level of actual load on the systems. This measurement is an indispensable basis to evaluate the actual hidden costs and the return on investment. For example, we could measure precisely how much time, delay, transports costs and CO_2 were spared with multiplex IP videoconferencing, based on actual use and this fed the decision to deploy in the corporation. Tracing and measuring is also a critical resource in the incurring discussions with the relevant services and decision-makers when it comes to change the institutional rules and negotiate who will pay for what (cf. infra): nothing is more convincing than actual examples in such discussions.

Beyond this oversized and flexible infrastructure, the RAO room is served by two full-time highly skilled "wizards" who are in fact system engineers with a multidisciplinary training in informatics, networks, telecom and multimedia; and had the capacity to draw specialists in a large array of scientists of the R&D division, for example, for cutting-edge security issues, virtual reality, sensing, communication networks, parallel processing, and so on. Observation is supervised by social psychologists and cognitive scientists on permanent or long-term contract.

Experience shows that permanent staffing with several wizards is a critical requirement for success. Several (at least two) wizards are needed, because wizards also go on holidays, and when one is programming, daily or emergency maintenance must be attended to anyway. In our experience, the limitation of many university labs or under-funded industry "user labs" comes from the fact that there are not enough support personnel to ensure the smooth operation of real work. It would be unthinkable that a group who has reserved the RAO room for a videoconference could not perform the meeting properly because there is no wizard to help solve a

---

trusted: they are in the same team, they work within a few meters of them, and the subjects know what will be done with the data, and more still, that they have an immediate interest so that these data are of good quality in order to improve their experimental environment. The situation is similar to that of the patients taking part in experimental protocols which aim at discovering drugs which could cure them.

technical issue: the Mother Room is used for real operations. This is precisely what enables it to tackle real world-problems, involve real stakeholders, and to prove that the technology being developed is efficient and robust.

3.3 Usability Design Criteria

We set up a set of design criteria for usability of information systems:

- Zero training "no time to learn": use pre-existing user cognitive skills and representations (design for cognition).
- Zero configuration: users have "no time to install".
- Zero user maintenance, it is not manageable: provide instant hotline support.
- Zero impact on user workstation, because often users' workstations are locked: no specific client should be needed.
- Zero complication, two clicks maximum to get result, trivial GUI: the technology should disappear; in activity based-design only the goals of the user are relevant for the user, the system's goals should be transparent.
- Zero euro, "or, anyway, not on my budget": all costs are taken care of on the server side, paid by the owner of the system, not by the user.
- Immediate benefit for individual end-user "and God bless you if it's good for the group": again design focuses on user's real motives.
- High security and privacy level compliant with corporate rules: NO compromise with security.

Although these "zero" requirements seem tough, they are possible to meet especially with web services which need only a very light client, and have, with web 2.0 and sensing techniques, the capacity to offer a situation-adapted GUI. Still, the reality test is extremely severe, and many sophisticated items which seemed at first to be good solutions were abandoned, for example, various types of touch displays, early blue-tooth systems, and so on because, although they could be used by experts or friendly users, they would not stand the reality test of normal users in normal conditions. Lahlou (2005) lists a series of such practical issues.

3.4 Lessons Learned

Continuously keeping in-house a running beta-version of the future organization is costly but has many advantages. The first is that it enables testing in real conditions how far new solutions are usable within the local company culture and socio-technical infrastructure. Inter-operability at technical level is one obvious issue; but even more complex to evaluate are the integration issues of new modes of conducting activity with the new system. For example, the Laboratory of Design for Cognition was the place where in 2000 the nomadic workstation concept was tested within the company, with VPN secure access to the highly-protected company intranet. This enabled measuring the pros and cons of having company staff working in nomadic ways, including legal aspects and family life impacts, the actual costs and volumes of connection, and so on. The same was done with wireless infrastructure;

PDAs; reconfigurable meeting-rooms; upgrading to the next Windows OS; IP videoconferencing, online synchronous collaborative platforms; various types of biometric access; IP telephone; virtual architectures for servers; augmented reality with RF-ID tokens, online video-editing, to mention the most prominent technologies which were tested than disseminated. Most of these reality experiments were simply using commercial-off-the-shelf physical components as advised by Johansson, Fox et al. (2009); the challenge was in fact to create the adequate adaptations of the two other layers: representations and institutions.

Most of the time, the technical layer "worked" within a few weeks, but it took usually three to seven years for the other layers to be co-constructed with the rest of the organization, in a continuous struggle.

The development cycle usually followed the following phases:

1. In the beginning, the team spots a potentially interesting technology, and manages to source it (get a working version and a direct "R2R"—Research to Research—connection with the laboratory, start-up, R&D of provider). At this stage, the technology is considered as, at best, a useless gadget—if not a potential safety, security, organizational, or economic threat by most people especially the middle management, IT services, corporate security, and the procurement division. Unless the experimental unit manager has full clearance and coverage by the highest level of the top management (a blank check, basically), the experiment would stop before it can even start. Getting direct connection with the source is essential because at this stage the system may be unstable, changing fast, poorly documented and needing adaptations to the specific context of the organization, or simply "not yet really" on the market.[5]

2. During test phase, the unit must not only manage to make the system work internally, but involve powerful allies within the organization, and convince, on an individual, and often friendly and informal basis, the crucial gatekeepers, especially finance, top management and maintenance. It is crucial that members of the unit have a large and powerful network, and enough official support to access gatekeepers. A lot of what is done at this stage is informal, and the formal reports only reflect a minor part of what is actually tested, because the rest may be in contravention with current formal corporate rules.

3. When it becomes obvious that the technology is mature, stable, useful and profitable, a plateau occurs, where the use is tolerated but not officially part of corporate policy. During this phase which can be excruciatingly long, while nothing seems to happen on the surface, the technology expands informally and small lobbies of users try to get official access. A series of battles and benchmarks take place redundantly in many units against other systems and especially the current official solution, which is defended by internal lobbies, administration and external providers. At this step, defenders of the current solution fight with desperate energy to maintain the existing organization and routine, and will often put strong and indirect organizational pressure on the innovation unit to de-credibilize the new solution or even try to remove it with its source; for example, by financial blocks or accusation of jeopardizing security.

---

5   In our experience, vendors are often exceedingly optimistic in their presentations of their products, especially about the dates of release of a stabilized usable version.

4. Finally, the solution is taken over by the official structures. The frustrating part at this stage is that the work of the innovating unit is then completely forgotten or minimized: after all, this is (by the time the innovation is adopted) a solution that is commercially available off the shelf, so what? The non-technical aspects of the innovation problem-solving are hardly acknowledged, except by a few top managers.

It is the nature of innovation to "effract" the existing structures, and cause some level of resistance, fear, and conflict. It is also a general rule that the innovation will deploy only if users and stakeholders adopt it, and this means that the origin of the innovation must be forgotten. Therefore, such innovating units should not expect much official recognition. It was rather unexpected that ours finally obtained a permanent status. More often than not, the innovators' destiny is exhaustion and organizational death (Alter, 1993), while their innovations survive.

But, on the other hand, we got some strong support from powerful users; and a lot of informal recognition as "the place where new things are" and word of mouth was enough publicity so that, after a couple of years of existence, the unit was the place where naturally, and informally, innovators converged with a solution and users with an exotic problem, both in search of someone to talk to. At this stage, the unit, fueled by this continuous source of offers and demands, could operate as a reactor by enabling and supporting people who came with a problem and volunteered to test some of the solutions in the unit's portfolio.

One interesting feature of experimental reality organization-wise, which counterbalances its apparent subversive aspect, is that it has the remarkable property of enabling quite tight risk control. On the budget side, the costs of the unit are known in advance because they do not vary much with the projects, and there is considerable elasticity in the amount, size, and type of projects that can be monitored simultaneously by such a unit. On the administrative side, the perimeter of the enclosure where "non-standard" procedures take place is also quite well known, specific audit and control procedures can be implemented; and by the very nature of continuous observation, documentation and tracing of what happens is easy.

4. CONCLUSION

Current techniques of development and innovation, because they take place in the framework of "project management," tend to focus on local technical design issues and to overlook the socio-cognitive impact of the new system on the rest of the organization. This enables cutting down design costs and saving time; but tends to generate severe problems and costs when the system and the general organization have to adapt to each other at later stages, during dissemination, operation, maintenance and evolution (DOME).

The theoretical framework of *installation theory* describes the three layers of reality (physical, mental, and institutional) in which the designer must monitor changes by installing distributed devices of guidance and control for the new system. As these three layers are complementary and sometimes redundant, the designer is given some freedom for opportunistic choice, by addressing in priority the layer which gives the best efficiency/cost leverage. Experience shows that technology is not always the best angle to approach the problem.

It appears that, in large socio-technical systems, the complexity is such that it is extremely difficult to predict actual impacts of the innovation in the system, and especially its negative externalities upon distant domains in the organization and on the user side, where the system messes an already installed ecology of technical devices, mental habits, and institutional regulations. These externalities might mean massive future costs (for example, in employee resistance, training, maintenance cost and so on) which of course the project tends to overlook.

Experimental reality consists in testing the new system in a limited domain fully integrated in the rest of the organization (for example, a small service or operation). Beyond the usual benefits of participative design, experimental reality enables testing the compatibility with the rest of the system and the ways in which adaptation and dissemination is possible. It is therefore possible to anticipate future problems in a realistic way, explore solutions, and dimension costs and added value. By meeting the DOME issues at the interface of the new and the old system, it is possible, to some extent, to integrate preventive features at design stage. Furthermore, keeping the innovative unit alive along the life of the system in connection with the departments in charge of Operations and Maintenance (for example, using it to design the evolution of the future system) enables keeping alive the organizational memory and having a continuously updated system.

The method was successfully applied in a large corporation of the energy sector. We described in detail how this was done (especially in the case of videoconference rooms). We provided the list of our design criteria for usability, and also a series of principles and lessons learned in operating several innovations.

The experimental reality approach we advocate goes against the current mainstream trend of managing innovation "in project mode." It does not apply to all cases. Still, we believe that in many cases, especially in large and complex organizations like the one we described, because this approach solves problems before they occur on a large scale and at irreversible design stages, it can save a considerable amount of time, costs, and produce both happier users and a smoother organization.

REFERENCES

Abric, J.-C. (1994). *Pratiques sociales et représentations*. Paris, PUF.

Akrich, M., M. Callon, et al. (2006). *Sociologie de la traduction: textes fondateurs*. Paris Mines Paris, les Presses.

Alter, N. (1993). "La lassitude de l'acteur de l'innovation." *Sociologie du travail* (4): 447–468.

Bauer, M.W. (1991). "Resistance to change: A monitor of new technology." *Systems practice* 4 (3): 181–196.

Bedny, G. and D. Meister (1997). *The Russian Theory of Activity: Current Applications to Design and Learning*. Mahwah, New Jersey, Lawrence Erlbaum.

Berger, P. and T. Luckmann (1967). *The Social Construction of Reality*. New York, Doubleday.

Bödker, S. (1991). Activity theory as challenge to system design. *Information system research: contemporary approaches and emergent traditions. Proceedings of the IFIP TC 8/WG 8.2 Working Conference*. H.-E. Nissen and Sanström, Elsevier: 551–564.

Bödker, S. (1996). Applying Activity Theory to Video Analysis: How to Make Sense of Video Data in Human–computer Interaction. *Context and Consciousness: Activity Theory and Human–computer Interaction*. B.A. Nardi. Cambridge, The MIT Press: 147–174.

Coase, R. (1960). "The Problem of Social Cost." *Journal of Law and Economics* (3): 1–44.

Daniellou, F. and P. Rabardel (2005). "Activity-oriented approaches to ergonomics: some traditions and communities" *Theoretical Issues in Ergonomics Science* 6(5): 353–357.

Ehn, P. (1992). Scandinavian Design: On Participation and Skill. In: *Usability: Turning technologies into tools*. P.S. Adler and T.A. Winograd. New York, Oxford University Press: 96–132.

Engeström, Y. (1990). *Learning, working and imaging: Twelve studies in activity Theory*. Helsinki, Orienta-Konsultit.

Giddens, A. (1984). *The constitution of society: Outline of the theory of structuration*. Cambridge: Polity.

Hartkopf, V., V. Loftness, et al. (2009). Towards a global concept of collaborative space Designing User Friendly Augmented Work Environments. In: *From Meeting Rooms to Digital Collaborative Spaces*. S. Lahlou. London: Springer, 63–85.

Jégou, F. (2009). Co-design Approaches for Early Phases of Augmented Environments: Designing User Friendly Augmented Work Environments. In: *From Meeting Rooms to Digital Collaborative Spaces*. S. Lahlou. London: Springer, 159–190.

Johansson, B., A. Fox, et al. (2009). The Stanford Interactive Workspaces Project Designing User Friendly Augmented Work Environments. In: *From Meeting Rooms to Digital Collaborative Spaces*. S. Lahlou. London: Springer, 31–61.

Kaptelinin, V. (1996). Computer mediated activity: functional organs in social and developmental contexts. In: *Context and consciousness, activity theory and Human Computer Interaction*. B. Nardi. Cambridge, MIT Press.

Kyng, M. and L. Mathiassen, Eds. (1997). *Computers and design in context*. Cambridge, MA, MIT Press.

Lahlou, S. (1998). *Penser manger: Alimentation et représentations sociales*. Paris, PUF.

Lahlou, S. (1999). Observing Cognitive Work in Offices: Cooperative Buildings. In *Integrating Information, Organizations and Architecture*. N. Streitz, J. Siegel, V. Hartkopf and S. Konomi. Heidelberg, Springer, *Lecture Notes in Computer Science*, 1670: 150–63.

Lahlou, S. (2005). "Cognitive Attractors and Activity-Based Design: Augmented Meeting Rooms." Proceedings of Human Computer Interaction Conference.

Lahlou, S. (2006). "L'activité du point de vue de l'acteur et la question de l'inter-subjectivité: huit années d'expériences avec des caméras miniaturisées fixées au front des acteurs (subcam)." *Communications* (80): 209–234.

Lahlou, S. (2008). L'Installation du Monde. De la représentation à l'activité en situation. Aix-en-Provence, Université de Provence. *Habilitation à Diriger des Recherches en Psychologie*: 375.

Lahlou, S. (2009). Experimental Reality: Principles for the Design of Augmented Environments. Designing User Friendly Augmented Work Environments. In: *From Meeting Rooms to Digital Collaborative Spaces*. S. Lahlou. London, Springer: 113–158.

Lahlou, S., V. Nosulenko, et al. (2002). "Un cadre méthodologique pour le design des environnements augmentés." *Informations sur les Sciences Sociales* 41(4): 471–530.

Leontiev, A.N. (1974). "The problem of activity in psychology." *Soviet Psychology* 13(2): 4–33.

Leontiev, A.N. and B.F. Lomov (1963). "Tchelovek i tekhnika (L'homme et la technique)." *Voprosy psykhologii (Questions en psychologie)* 5: 29–37.

Lomov, B.F. (1963). *Tchelovek i tekhnika (L'homme et la technique)*. Moscou, Sovetskoe radio (Radio Soviétique).

Lomov, B.F. (1977). O putyakh postroeniya teorii inzhenernoj psikhologii na osnove sistemnogo podkhoda (Les perspective de la conception d'une théorie de la psychologie de l'ingénierie dans le cadre de l'approche systémique). In: *Inzhenernaya psikhologiya (La psychologie de l'ingénierie)*. B.F. Lomov, V.F. Rubakhin and V.F. Venda. Moscou, Nauka: 31–54.

Moscovici, S. (1961). *La psychanalyze son image et son public*. Paris, PUF.

Nardi, BA (1996). Studing Context: A Comparison of Activity Theory, Situated Action Models, and Distributed Cognition. In: *Context and Conscious: Activity Theory and Human Computer Interaction*. B. Nardi. Cambridge, MIT Press: 69–102.

Nosulenko, V., E. Parizet, et al. (1998). "La méthode d'analyze des verbalizations libres: une application à la caractérization des bruits de véhicules." *Informations sur les Sciences Sociales* 37(4): 593–611.

Nosulenko, V. and P. Rabardel (1998). Ergonomie, psychologie et travail dans les pays de l'ex-URSS. (Historicité et spécificité du développement). In: *Dés évolutions en ergonomie ...* M.F. Dessaigne and I. Gaillard. Toulouse, Octarès: 13–28.

Nosulenko, V. and P. Rabardel, Eds. (2007). *Rubinstein aujourd'hui. Nouvelles figures de l'activité humaine*. Toulouse–Paris, Octarès — Maison des Sciences de l'Homme.

Nosulenko, V. and E. Samoylenko (2009). Psychological Methods for the Study of Augmented Environments: Designing User Friendly Augmented Work Environments. In: *From Meeting Rooms to Digital Collaborative Spaces*. S. Lahlou. London, Springer: 213–236.

Nosulenko, V. and E. Samoylenko (1997). "Approche systémique de l'analyze des verbalizations dans le cadre de l'étude des processus perceptifs et cognitifs." *Informations sur les Sciences Sociales* 36(2): 223–61.

Nosulenko, V. and E. Samoylenko (1998). Activité, Cognition, Interaction, Communication: Certains aspects des approches élaborées en Russie. Paris, EDF/ANVIE/MSH: 1–40.

Nosulenko, V. and E. Samoylenko (1999). Synthèse des fondements de l'approche élaborée pour l'étude de la qualité perçue des produits et services (résumés et extraits des travaux publiés). Paris, CNET/ANVIE/MSH: 1–182.

Rasmussen, J. (1983). Skills, rules, knowledge; signals, signs, and symbols, and other distinctions in human performance models. *IEEE Transactions on Systems, Man and Cybernetics* 13: 257–266.

Rasmussen, J. (1985). The role of hierarchical knowledge representation in decision-making and system management. *IEEE Transactions on Systems, Man and Cybernetics* 15: 234–243.

Rubinstein, S.L. (1940). *Rubinstein aujourd'hui. Nouvelles figures de l'activité humaine*. V. Nosulenko and P. Rabardel. Toulouse — Paris, Octarès — Maison des Sciences de l'Homme: 129–140.

Suchman, L. (1983). Office Procedure as Practical Action: Models of Work and System Design. *ACM Transactions on Office Information Systems* 1(4): 320–328.

Wertsch, J., Ed. (1981). *The Concept of Activity in Soviet Psychology*. Armonk, NY, M.E. Sharpe.

Zavalova, N.D., B.F. Lomov, et al. (1986). *Obraz v sisteme psykhitcheskoj regulya tsii deyatel'nosti (L'image dans le système de régulation mentale de l'activité)*. Moscou, Nauka.

9

Cognitive Function Analysis in the Design of Human and Machine Multi-Agent Systems

Guy A. Boy

INTRODUCTION

Cognitive function analysis (CFA) started to be articulated during the 1990s in the framework of the active development of cognitive engineering (Boy, 1998). This was an alternative to the "conventional" cognitive task analysis (Crandall, Klein, and Hoffman, 2006; Schraagen, Chipman, and Shalin, 2000). From the start, CFA is based both on the distinction between task, that is, what has to be performed, and activity, that is, what is effectively performed, and on a multi-agent approach of human–machine interaction, that is, cognitive functions can be organized into interactive networks. Indeed, when the work place is the playground of people and software-intensive machines, a multi-agent approach needs to be taken.

Ergonomics is the science of work and the work place. Up to now, the co-adaptation of jobs and tools was done locally and the notion of human–machine interaction was thought between a human and a machine. CFA is consistent with the evolution of our industrial world that moves from local ergonomics to *global ergonomics*. Today, the problem has become more complex in the sense that the co-adaptation includes various levels of organization. Human–machine interaction needs to be thought more broadly between three types of agents: humans, technologies and organizations. A machine agent has capabilities that enable it to act on its environment in a similar way, as a human agent would do. In addition, the very notion of agent needs to be considered not only at the local level of an individual interacting with a machine, but also at the global level of an organization and even between organizations that now include sophisticated machines empowered with their own authority. An agent is also an agency of agents (Minsky, 1985), that is, organizations themselves are agents. This is why the cognitive function paradigm was forged to support this evolution, that is, it is both working for the local level and the global level of interaction.

A cognitive function is defined by three attributes that are its role, context of validity and a set of resources. Therefore each agent has at least a cognitive function, and more specifically a role. For example, postmen are agents belonging to a postal service organization, that is, an agency, and their role is delivering letters. They also represent postal services, that is, they are responsible for what they do and accountable to someone within the organization (see the chapter on authority issues in this handbook). The *role* of cognitive function is then strongly related to responsibility and accountability of the agent owning it. However, this responsibility and accountability is limited to a predefined or emerging *context*. For example, postmen are responsible for letter delivery from 8:00 AM to noon and 2:00 PM to 5:00 PM from Monday to Friday (at least in France); this is a specified definition of a temporal context. Context may take various forms. It could define space limits such as the neighborhood where the postman is responsible for delivering letters. Both of these contexts, that is, defined and in time and space, can be predefined. However, in some situations, they can emerge from necessity; for example, a postman is sick and his colleagues take some parts of his/her neighborhood, therefore extend their own space context and consequently extend their time context also. When such emergence is infrequent, context can be qualified being dynamic. However, when it is persistent, the agency needs to be redefined; for example, a new postman has to be hired, or predefined time and space contexts have to be redefined. Context could be nominal, that is, as normal situations, or off-nominal, that is, as abnormal or emergency situations. Finally, a cognitive function empowers an agent with control to execute related assigned tasks. This control is only possible when appropriate *resources* are available to the agent. Resources can be physical or cognitive. For example, postmen have bags, bicycles or cars to carry letters; they also have cognitive resources such as pattern matching to appropriately associate the name of the street on the envelope and a street nameplate, the number of the house or apartment, and finally the name of the addressee. Note that cognitive resources are cognitive functions themselves. Therefore, cognitive functions have a recursive property, that is, there are cognitive functions of cognitive functions. In addition, other agents could own cognitive resources. For example, in the case of a strike, since the number of postmen is significantly lower than usual, postmen who remain on duty have longer hours and bigger neighborhood, that is, this off-nominal context is different from the nominal one and implies different responsibility, accountability, and control. As far as control is concerned, since context is different, postmen on duty may have to delegate some of their tasks to other people, students for example. In this off-nominal context, delegation is now a cognitive resource that can be decomposed into a set of cognitive functions such as training, supervision, and management. It is interesting to notice that a cognitive function that is owned by an agent can lead to a set of similar cognitive functions distributed among a set of other agents; these cognitive functions are created (trained), supervised, and managed by the initial cognitive function. Consequently, carrying out a cognitive function analysis turns out to be the development of a cognitive function network over a set of agents.

Cognitive function networks are incrementally developed through the generation of cognitive functions in both the resource space and the context space (Figure 9.1). The development of such cognitive function networks is guided by several properties of cognitive functions themselves. These properties will be described in this chapter, as well as the processes that put them at work.

In the resource space, configuration scenarios are described to improve the rationalization of the allocation of physical and cognitive functions to appropriate and available agents. In the context space, event scenarios (for example, chronologies

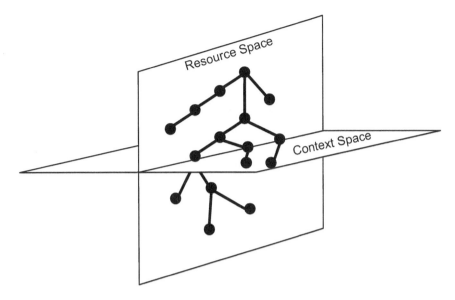

Figure 9.1   A cognitive function network view in both context and resource spaces

in temporal contexts) are described to improve awareness of procedural connections between cognitive functions. Consequently, a cognitive function is also defined as a process that transforms a task into an activity (Figure 9.2).

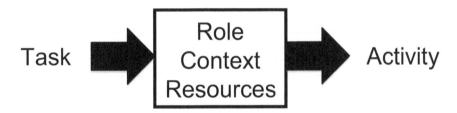

Figure 9.2   A cognitive function as a transformation of a task into an activity

Both task (what is planned to done) and activity (what is effectively done) can be described using the same representation, called an *interaction block* (*i-Bloc*), which involves five attributes (Figure 9.3): a context of validity, a goal to be reached (a normal final condition of the process), a set of triggering conditions that enable to start the process, a context of validity that supersedes the triggering conditions (contextual conditions are more permanent than triggering conditions), a set of actions (typically organized into an algorithm), and a set of abnormal final conditions (in the case of failures).

Consequently, cognitive function analysis (CFA) can be carried out in two complementary ways by describing: the resource space through *declarative configuration-driven scenarios*, and the context space through *procedural event-driven scenarios*. We already saw that cognitive resources are cognitive functions themselves.

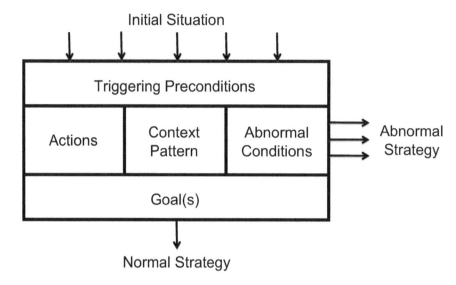

Figure 9.3   Interaction block representation
Source: Boy, 1998.

Therefore, the resources space is the space that supports the elicitation of all cognitive functions in the form of cognitive function networks. In a similar way, a context of an i-Block is an i-Block itself. Consequently, i-Blocks are organized in the form of information flows by contexts, sub-contexts, sub-sub-contexts and so on. Performing a cognitive function analysis consists in articulating cognitive function networks (the resource space) and i-Blocks information flows (the context space). In the next sections, we will develop a case in order to show the applicability of CFA.

When these two representations were designed, they were not targeted toward the same objective; i-Blocks were designed to represent operational procedures. Cognitive functions were designed to represent human and machine cognitive processes; i-Blocks were designed to better understand interaction between human and machine agents. Cognitive functions were designed to better understand how a task is transformed into an activity, as well as how they can be described in terms of role, context and resources; i-Blocks are external representations of interactions, and cognitive functions are internal representations of agents' cognitive processes. To a certain extent, we could say that if i-Blocks are used to represent prescribed procedures, they are inputs of cognitive functions; in contrast, if i-Blocks are used to rationalize agents' activities, they are outputs of cognitive functions. When a cognitive function network is developed, cognitive functions are teleologically described in the resource space, and logically connected through i-Blocks in the context space.

More properties of human and machine agents' cognitive functions will be presented in the next sections of this chapter. After its initial publication (Boy, 1998), CFA has been used extensively and successfully in many research and industrial projects. Examples will be taken in the aerospace domain, but CFA is also useful in any life-critical system analysis, design, and evaluation.

PROPERTIES OF THE RESOURCE SPACE

There are two types of cognitive function's resources:

- cognitive resources that can be an agent or a cognitive function; and
- physical resources that are neither agents nor cognitive functions, and are typically used by a cognitive function of an agent.

For example, let's take the *Traffic alert and Collision Avoidance System* (TCAS) of current commercial aircraft. The TCAS monitors the airspace surrounding the aircraft by interrogating the transponder of other aircraft. TCAS, transponders, and aircraft are represented as machine agents equipped with cognitive functions. TCAS has a first high-level cognitive function that has a role, that is, "get information from transponders around," a context of validity, that is, the range of the signals between TCAS and transponders (in practice the range may vary from 40 nm to 80 nm with respect to the type of TCAS), and a set of resources, that is, software that calculates: the bearing/range to the intruder; the closure rate; the relative altitude difference and the vertical speed of the intruder (under some conditions).

If the TCAS predicts that the separation is below safe boundaries, then a *traffic advisory* (TA) message is triggered and informs the crew that the intruder is in the vicinity (this is another machine cognitive function). The crew should always attempt to visually clear the airspace before maneuvering the aircraft in response to a TA (this handled by a human cognitive function). The purpose of the TA is to advise the crew to attempt to get visual contact with the intruder. No evasive action should be solely based on the TA.

If the TCAS predicts a collision threat then a *resolution advisory* (RA) is triggered to maintain a safe separation between the aircraft. The RA is coordinated between the aircraft and the intruder; the RAs are thus complementary. The crew is then required to follow the RA promptly and smoothly. The crew should never maneuver in the opposite direction of the RA since maneuvers are coordinated. This is what the task says, but it may happen that the activity could be different such as in the Überlingen accident.

To further develop the resource space of the high-level "collision avoidance" cognitive function, that is often called the configuration space, there are three kinds of configurations that may be useful to describe:

- (Configuration-1) the two conflicting airplanes are not equipped with TCAS that are independent of *air traffic control* (ATC), that is, traffic (collision) alert is only available to the *ATC controller* (ATCO) who typically uses radar information (R) (Figure 9.4);
- (Configuration-2) airplanes are equipped with TCAS, and in addition, ATCO may use the ground-based *Short-Term Conflict Alert* (STCA) system, which currently warns en-route ATCO when two airplanes are dangerously close to one another (Figure 9.5); and
- (Configuration-3) a data-link connection exists between TCAS and STCA; this could be a future possibility (Figure 9.6).

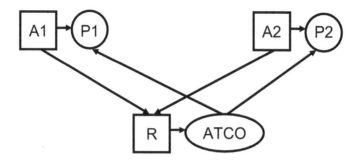

Figure 9.4   Configuration-1: Current situation where ATCO uses radar information to anticipate possible conflicts and control separation between airplanes

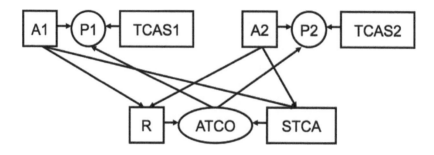

Figure 9.5   Configuration-2: Using TCAS onboard and STCA on the ground

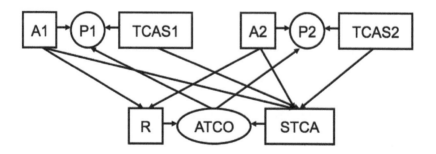

Figure 9.6   Configuration-3: Using TCAS connected to STCA

What is the configuration space? In Configuration-1, main agents are the pilot (P1) of airplane 1 (A1), the pilot (P2) of airplane 2 (A2) ATCO and STCA. In Configuration-2, there are the same agents, as well as TCAS1 for A1 and TCAS2 for A2. In Configuration-3 that does not exist today, TCAS and STCA are able to talk between each other.

PROPERTIES OF THE CONTEXT SPACE

Continuing on the collision avoidance problem, let's assume that two airplanes converge toward each other. As already described in the resource space, below a specific separation distance, there should be a traffic alert that triggers an abnormal situation. This is interpreted in terms of cognitive functions as follows: the set of cognitive functions belonging to a "normal" context are replaced by the set of cognitive functions belonging to the "traffic alert" context. In this new context, the highest cognitive function's role, or goal, is to go back to a normal context.

In Configuration-1, ATCO is the only agent to have the authority to separate A1 and A2. ATCO manages the separation using radar information and sends requests to P1 and P2 according to the situation, that is, whenever a conflict is detected, ATCO is in charge. Therefore, in terms of i-Blocks, the first triggering condition is the detection by ATCO of a possible conflict; the goal is to change A1 and/or A2 trajectories in order to solve this conflict. ATCO sends requests to pilots, for example, "climb" to P1 and "descent" to P2. Possible abnormal conditions are, for example, radio transmission failures and pilot inattention to radio messages. On the pilot side, actions have to be taken (another i-Block) that leads to another i-Block on ATCO side for the monitoring and acknowledgement of appropriate pilots actions and finally effective conflict resolution. The i-Block network is pretty simple, and provides a very clear explanation of ATCO-centered authority.

In Configuration-2, each TCAS monitors the airspace around the airplane for another TCAS transponder. It warns the pilot when it detects the presence of another TCAS. TCAS sends a traffic alert (TA) requesting the pilot to "climb" or "descend." Then, the pilot sends to ATCO a resolution advisory (RA) after a period of time $t_{RA} - t_{TA}$ (Figure 9.7). After the conflict is cleared, ATCO sends a "clear of conflict notification." The main problem comes from the fact that during $t_{RA} - t_{TA}$, ATCO, who does not know about TCAS TA, could possibly send conflicting requests to P1 and/or P2. This is clearly explained by the fact that pilots' and ATCO's conflict resolution i-Blocks are not connected. This issue is solved in Configuration-3, that is, ATCO knows about both TCAS traffic alerts. If this kind of analysis would have been performed at design time, the probability of accidents such as the mid-air collision that occurred at Überlingen in 2002 would have been significantly decreased. In particular, abnormal conditions could be generated only by analysis, that is, the development of such analytical scenarios could generate the emergence of such absence of links between crucial i-Blocks. In addition, the use of i-Block networks linking agents between each other in a dynamic way affords to figure out the way displays and controls should

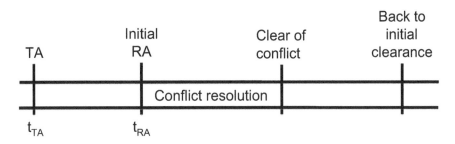

Figure 9.7   **Timeline of TCAS alert and conflict resolution**

be designed. Therefore, in this specific aviation case, "collision avoidance" displays provided to both pilots and ATCOs should be coordinated. The link between TCAS and STCA for example is a new resource and generates new contexts shared by both pilots and ATCOs.

By definition, a context of i-Blocks is an i-Block itself (see Figure 9.8). Therefore, i-Block construction may be done alternatively from inside-out or outside-in, that is, developing bottom-up and top-down task analysis. The former attempts to induce generic i-Blocks from experience data; the latter attempts to decompose high-level i-Blocks into more specific i-Blocks. In practice, both approaches are used to mutually bootstrap each other.

Consequently, developing an i-Block network is like "making a house with prefabricated blocks." Note that this construction, typically made in the context space, should be carried out concomitantly with the construction of the related cognitive function network in the resource space. Let's concentrate on this analogy. In order to get a beautiful house, an architect is strongly needed in the first place to provide professional directions based on experience and knowledge. This is the same for the design and development of an i-Block network, experience, and knowledge of an i-Block architect is required. This type of architect is called a *cognitive engineer*. Obviously, cognitive engineers base their activity on domain actors, for example, railway engineers and train drivers or aerospace engineers and pilots. They know for example that the more an i-Block network is linear, that is, a chain of i-Blocks going from one to another on a normal strategy only, is better than an i-Block network that would have too many transversal abnormal strategy branches. They also know that a too linear i-Block network is a "theory" that would break when put into the real world. Therefore, i-Block networks are able to suggest what kind of experiments should be performed to elicit relevant normal or abnormal strategies.

We already introduced the concepts of normal, or nominal, and abnormal, or off-nominal, contexts, strategies and i-Blocks. Normality is a notion that can be static, that is, domain-dependent, and/or dynamic, that is, context-dependent. But even in the

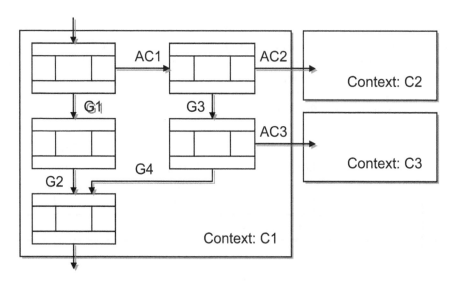

Figure 9.8   **Contexts of i-Blocks**

former notion, the domain may evolve, normality is sensitive to technology maturity as well as maturity of practice. This issue of maturity will be further discussed later in this chapter. The latter notion of normality is adaptable according to context. This adaptable normality concept is essential to better understand the distinction between weak and strong abnormal conditions. A weak abnormal condition (for example, AC1 in Figure 9.8) leads to a set of i-Blocks that have the same context pattern, that is, the generated abnormal strategy stays within the same context. A strong abnormal condition (for example, AC2 and AC3 in Figure 9.8) leads to a set of i-Blocks that do not have the same context patterns, that is, the generated abnormal strategy does not stay within the same context of the initial i-Block.

GENERAL PROPERTIES

Emerging Cognitive Functions

A cognitive function can be defined a priori; in this case, it is a *deliberate* cognitive function. Deliberate cognitive functions can be implemented in a machine, usually in the form of software, or learned by a human being. However, it may happen that a new technology or the way work is organized among different interacting agents induces the *emergence* of new relevant cognitive function, that is, cognitive functions that are not defined a priori. For example, text-processing tools that we use today have two important functions, that is, copy and paste, which emerged from the technological possibilities provided by graphical displays and interactive computers. These functions were not specifically developed to support text-processing tools in the first place. Text-processing tools were designed to enable people to write text without needing an external resource, such as a secretary, to type written reports, papers, or books. However, the copy and paste functions naturally emerged because it was easy to implement them using graphical displays and interactive technologies such as the mouse. These functions are both cognitive and physical because their resources are both cognitive and physical. On the cognitive side, we shifted from linear writing to nonlinear writing. Indeed, in the past, we wrote manually using paper and pencil; our thinking was forced to be linear. This is why we learned in primary school to design an outline of the text, and then we were writing chapters, paragraphs, and sentences linearly. Today, we have several tools that enable us to write in a nonlinear way an introduction, a conclusion and everything that is in between. It is possible to backtrack as many times as we want on what has been already written and modify it easily. We use "copy," "cut," and "paste" machine cognitive functions ... In other words, the global cognitive function of linear writing has been totally modified into a global emerging cognitive function of nonlinear writing. This took a decade or so to see the emergence of this new cognitive function, and stabilize the related maturity of practice.

An emergent cognitive function, or emerging cognitive function, can be implemented within a technology, for example, "copy" and "paste" within text processing and beyond in desktop applications. It can also stay at the level of practice and anchor itself into the organizational environment. Office automation emerged as a technology and a practice; it contributed to remove secretary's traditional functions, and in many cases secretaries themselves.

Therefore, an emergent cognitive function is a cognitive function that naturally emerges from the use of a new tool or the implication of an agent into a new organization. An emergent cognitive function can become mature in a variable amount of time. This time is very difficult to predict. For example, MP3 uploading mainly emerged from the use of iPods even if we believed that CDs were there to stay as the major music support. The notion of cognitive function is thus related to the notion of practice, like the practice of CDs or MP3. In general, a cognitive function emerges because resources that are associated to it are easier to implement and use, and also because the context of this implementation is appropriate. Note that fashion phenomena could also drive this emergence. The obsolescence or persistence of the resulting cognitive function is then a question of robustness and resistance to new competing emergent cognitive functions.

Complexity Analysis

In multi-agent systems, complexity mainly results from the multiple links between agents. Highly connected multi-agent systems behave like biological systems. Many definition of complexity may be taken to assess complexity. Complexity can be expressed in terms of the number of (possibly interconnected) problems to be solved at a given time for a given human agent. For an ATCO, complexity can be expressed as the number of relevant aircraft to be managed per appropriate volumetric zone (AVZ) at each time. An AVZ is calculated with respect to the type of flow pattern, for example, aircraft crossing, spacing, and merging. The definition of such an appropriate volumetric zone requires the assistance of operational ATC controllers. From a socio-cognitive perspective in ATM, complexity should be considered together with capacity. This is what the COCA (COmplexity and CApacity) project investigated (Athènes et al., 2002; Cummings and Tsonis, 2006; Hilburn, 2004; Laudeman et al., 1998; Masalonis et al., 2003). This can be expressed in terms of cognitive functions and available resources in context. When the airspace capacity increases for example, the number of resources should also increase. This is why it is crucial to carry out a cognitive function analysis to investigate the relevance and appropriateness of cognitive function allocation to software. Criteria, such as workload and situation awareness acceptability, should be defined to assess such allocation. In any case, it is always useful and often mandatory to run human-in-the-loop simulations (HITLS) in order to further elicit, validate, and verify cognitive function networks. This complexity analysis is carried out concurrently in both resource and context spaces.

Socio-Cognitive Stability Analysis

In highly connected multi agent systems, such as our evolving airspace with a constant growth of interdependencies among agents, it is necessary to be able to assess socio-cognitive stability (SCS). SCS can be derived from various contributions, including Latour's account on socio-technical stability (Callon, 1991; Latour, 1987), emerging cognitive functions (Boy, 1998), distributed cognition (Hutchins, 1995), and socio-cognitive research and engineering (Hemingway, 1999; Sharples et al., 2002). In previous work, we made a distinction between local and global SCS (Boy and Grote, 2009). Local SCS is related to agent's workload, situation awareness, ability to make appropriate decisions and, finally, correct action execution. It can be supported by appropriate redundancies and various kinds of cognitive support such as trends, relevant situational information and possible actions, that is, cognitive function resources. Global SCS is concerned with the appropriateness of functions allocated to agents, pace of information flows and related coordination, that is, an improved understanding of the context space. It is very similar to the level of synchronization of rhythms in a symphony. Globally, socio-cognitive support could be found in a safety net that would take into account the evolution of interacting agents and propose a constraining safety envelope in real time.

Flexibility Analysis

Flexibility is defined as the ease of modification of a contract between two or several agents in real-time, for example, an air-ground contract that specifies the trajectory of an aircraft. Flexibility assessments should guide cognitive function allocation in both resource and context spaces, for example, in the ATM of the future, resource allocation mainly means human-centered automation and context definition; and management means organizational setting. As already said, increasing capacity also increases complexity and uncertainty, which need to be managed by finding the right balance between reducing uncertainties through centralized planning, that is, compiling cognitive functions and their interconnections, and coping with uncertainties through decentralized action. The main problem comes from the fact that the more we reduce uncertainty by planning, the more flexibility becomes an issue. Loose coupling is required for actors to use their autonomy in accordance with system goals (Grote, 2004).

ACTIVITY ANALYSIS AND HUMAN-CENTERED DESIGN

Understanding and Taking into Account People Experience in Design

Human factors and more specifically cognitive engineering have been recently concentrating on taking into account human issues in design and development of both technology and emerging societal practices. *Human-centered design* (HCD) is about designing technology tailored to people. I prefer to talk about people and not about users because it is a broader concept, even if in many cases we will still use the term "user." Users deal with tools. Users are often customers. People deal with life. This is why the concept of life-critical systems is crucial here.

Technology has multiple facets; it can be used, maintained, repaired, and eventually dismantled. In other words, there will be people who will use, maintain, repair, or dismantle technology. This is true for houses, cars, airplanes, and nuclear power plants, for example. A main objective is to design and develop for people who are not immediately perceived as obvious customers. Therefore, when we talk about human-centered design, we need to be careful to focus on all people who will interact with the technology being produced, as much as possible. Consequently, cognitive functions that we will be trying to elicit and rationalize will concern all possible agents dealing with the product being designed.

On the one hand, if too much emphasis on current practice should not guide the design of a novel interface, it is crucial to understand the constraints and requirements that people have when they perform their work now. It is important to understand why they cannot accomplish their work properly or, conversely, perform it very well in a wide variety of situations. Both positive information and negative information on work practice are equally good to consider and analyze. People experience cannot be separated from the tools, methods, and organizational setups that go with it. The difficult part is to access the right people, and not intermediary people who would synthesize their views on what should be the requirements for the design team. Obviously, all users cannot be accessed in all possible situations. However, by experience, selecting appropriate sets of users is much better than nothing! We need to remember that resulting acquired information is partial. This is why we need to have conceptual models that support interpretation and extrapolation in some cases. These conceptual models may be very loose and provided by domain experts in the form of narratives or simply active explanations of acquired information. Cognitive functions, as a mediating representation between human operators and designers, provide such a model.

On the other hand, it is possible to analyze some parts of possible future people experience from experts, but there are situations, configurations or initiatives that will never be possible to anticipate and therefore only a prototype-based approach will enable the elicitation of possible operational patterns. First, there are behaviors that are standard and could be anticipated because they are related to a style of interface, for example. The more the interface conforms a standard, the more behaviors will be predictable. Standardization is therefore a great incentive for future people experience prediction. Nevertheless, when new kinds of systems and user interfaces are designed and developed, usability predictability is no longer possible without an experimental protocol that involves a set of users facing a prototype.

This is why both current-activity analysis (present) and emerging-activity analysis (future) require a mediating representation in the form of cognitive functions. The former is based on the observation of what is being done today, and the latter is based on human-in-the-loop simulations and related activity observation and analysis. As a matter of fact, activity analysis should be a constant effort carried out during the life cycle of a life-critical product.

Designing for Maturity

When a chef is cooking a memorable dish, his or her experience and expertise play a crucial role, and incremental testing is a must. We do not insist enough on this necessary capacity of domain experts to be involved and concentrated during the design process. We often talk about latent human errors (Reason, 1990) that are committed during the design and development process and re-appear at use time, sometimes viciously. If we take a positive approach of this problem, latent errors deal with product maturity.

Product maturity is a matter of constant testing by experts. In an ideal world, we would have to test the product and its former prototypes in all situations in order to make sure that it will be fully mature at delivery time. This is obviously impossible, but designers and engineers must remember that the more situations they will experience in the use of the product, the better. This is a practice that happens to disappear with our current industrial way of managing projects. Indeed, engineers need to fill in spreadsheets and report all the time instead of fully concentrating on their design and development tasks. It seems that reporting has become more important than actual design and development! Motivation must be kept and creativity must remain the main asset of human-centered design teams. For that matter, reporting could be used in a different way that would effectively and significantly improve design. At this stage, it is important to make a distinction between reporting for work FTE (full-time equivalent) justification and writing for improving design.

A technology becomes mature when it is useful, usable, and acceptable, that is, is socially accepted, meets legal requirements, and answers relevant commercial issues. Appropriate people experience must be taken into account to enhance maturity in engineering approaches. All actors involved in the life cycle of the product, for example, end-users, customers, maintainers, trainers, and designers, must be taken into account, as well as the repercussions on other people of its use and eventually the deconstruction of the product. In the early stages of a technology, products are driven by the needs of technically sophisticated consumers, but these needs should be reevaluated when the technology matures.

The operational life cycle of a technology can be divided into two periods that are characterized by different maturity criteria: (period 1) technology and performance; (period 2) ease of use, reliability, and price. We need to take into account that people behavior changes when they are using such technology. For example, in the early stages of computer industry development in the 1970s, computers were big and mostly used by highly skilled engineers. Computer use was a matter of technical performance. Microcomputers emerged and democratized the use of information technology to the point that most people have a computer at home today. Microcomputers arrived during the first half of the 1980s. Many engineers at that time did not want to use such a new technology because they thought that it was made for technically low-skilled users. The transition from period 1 to period 2 was being reached at that point. Today, computers are becoming invisible, integrated within the most familiar tools such as the telephone, automobile, or microwave. This is another transition point. We will say cognitive functions changed.

At such transition points, maturity is an issue. The best way to master maturity is to improve the period 0 that includes design and development of the product. The main issue here is that it is very difficult and almost impossible to predict the future without relevant data. Experience feedback and expert knowledge are often required to make appropriate design and development decisions. Instead of periods 0, 1 and 2, it is much better to work on periods n, n+1 and n+2. This assumes that we work on a family of products. This product family issue is crucial and has emerged for many industrial products including aerospace, software, and telecommunication. Thus n-1 knowledge is incrementally used in period n. The incremental development of cognitive function networks is an important support for understanding and managing various human–machine interactions, and therefore deciding potential changes in either technology or people practices.

CFA-Based Design

Design and development are typically organized top-down. Everything starts with an idea, for example, building a new aircraft that will be able to transport 800 people. Then, technical experts meet to examine this very high level requirement and the current technological possibilities. Usually, there are various kinds of technological innovations that may need to be experimented to develop an appropriate solution. However, the initial top-down goal-driven approach must be cross-fertilized by an event-driven approach also, that is, solutions must be incrementally tested on appropriate scenarios. From a human factors point of view, scenarios are key in a human-centered design process. They are difficult to develop and I advise the reader to refer to the chapter on scenario-based design included in this handbook. The development of scenarios and their use in human-in-the-loop simulations are a good way to elicit cognitive functions involved in the interactions between humans and technology. In the introduction of this volume, I introduced the AUTOS pyramid as a conceptual tool to guide human-centered design. AUTOS supports the analysis and synthesis of cognitive functions into five generic categories related to Artifacts (that is, the technology being designed and developed), Users (that is, people who will interact one way or another with this technology), Tasks (that is, things that needs to be accomplished using this technology), Organizations (that is, the various ways people are interconnected), and Situations (that is, environment status and events).

There are many ways to describe agents' activities. In this chapter, I will take two distinctive categories, declarative and procedural descriptions. These distinctions are not new and were used in artificial intelligence for a long time. For example, a cognitive function can be represented in a declarative way by specifying three attributes: a role, a context of validity, and a set of resources; and i-Blocks support the procedural description of information flows between agents and more specifically cognitive functions.

DISCUSSION

CFA is one of the many approaches useful for analyzing, designing, and evaluating interactive systems in a human-centered way. Unlike previous approaches that were based on a single-agent human operator model (Rasmussen, 1983; Endsley, 1988; Vicente and Rasmussen, 1992), CFA straightaway provides a very usable and useful framework for socio-technical and organizational analysis, because it is multi-agent by construction.

Cognitive work analysis (CWA), for example, is commonly based on domains that are incrementally redesigned (Vicente, 1999). CWA typically starts with an analysis of social and organization factors but does not have any multi-agent formalism to support the description of such analysis. The first formal step of CWA is the work domain analysis (WDA) that consists in the identification of all the goals and purposes of the system being studied. WDA is based on data, information and knowledge from existing documentation and expert elicitation results. WDA is performed using either the abstraction-decomposition method (Rasmussen, 1985) or the abstraction hierarchy method. The former method includes a sequence of five steps that consist in determining goals, priority measures, general functions, processes, and objects.

The latter method is very similar but attempts to answer questions such as "Why" and "How" for each provided piece of information. The second formal step of CWA is the control task analysis, which involves the identification of the control tasks that are performed within the system being analyzed. A control task analysis is used to determine what tasks are undertaken within the system being analyzed, regardless of how they are undertaken or who undertakes them. Decision ladders are used for the control task analysis component of CWA. The third step consists in analyzing strategies. This phase involves identifying and representing the strategies that actors within the system being analyzed use when they perform the control task identified during the control task analysis phase. Information flow maps are used for the strategies analysis component of CWA. In the fourth step, we could see the social organization and cooperation analysis of CWA as the identification of how control tasks are allocated among agents and artifacts within the system. It uses the abstraction-decomposition hierarchy, decision ladders and information flow maps previously developed, but does not involve any specific modeling tool. The last step involves the identification of the cognitive skills required for the performance of the control task. Rasmussen's *Skill, Rule, Knowledge* (SRK) framework is used to categorize these activities.

Another approach is the *Goal-Directed Task Analysis* (GDTA) that focuses on the production of situation awareness requirements (Endsley et al., 2003). Situation awareness is typically decomposed into three levels: (1) perception of elements in the environment; (2) comprehension of the current situation; and (3) projection of future status (Endsley, 1988). GDTA attempts to break down a specific work domain into various goals and sub-goals that have specific SA requirements that can be elicited. First a goal hierarchy is produced from previous appropriate knowledge and information. This hierarchy is typically limited to three levels. Like in CFA, GDTA requires that the goal or role of each function should be explained. Then a set of secondary interviews is carried out in order to validate the first elicited hierarchy. The resulting structure is then used to generate appropriate questions that address situation awareness requirements. Finally, feedback is conducted to validate the resulting GDTA structure until a high level of consistency, coherence, and completeness has been achieved.

More recently, a new technique that combines CWA and GDTA was proposed (Humphrey and Adams, 2009), the *Cognitive Information Flow Analysis* (CIFA). The authors put to the front that GDTA focuses on part-whole relationships, as CIFA and CWA focus on producer-consumer relationships. This distinction is essential. The part-whole relationship denotes the teleological nature of functions. The producer-consumer relationship denotes the logical nature of functions. In CFA, there are two planes of interconnectivity, the teleological one (that is, using part-whole relationships that connect functions between each other) and the logical one (that is, using producer-consumer relationships that connect i-Blocks from one to another). In addition, the notion of function in CFA is somehow different than in CIFA because CFA takes into account the concept of role, and therefore authority, as a basic attribute. CFA intrinsically includes the notion of control and accountability (and responsibility).

What these other approaches do not include at all is the notion of context. Context is crucial because it is the unifying link between the teleological nature and logical nature of cognitive functions. The co-development of cognitive function networks and i-Block networks results in chains of accountability in the sense of functional and operational traceability and reliability. In addition, these networks provide a very good framework for verification and validation, and more importantly test the degree of maturity of both technology and practice.

Furthermore, CFA is a system-level framework that differs from a user-interface-level framework such as GOMS (Card, Moran, and Newell, 1983; Irving et al., 1994). CFA make a distinction between task-content-related cognitive function and interaction-related cognitive functions (Boy, 1997). The part-whole nature of CFA provides the analyst with enough relief to represent the task content part of a high-level function and the interaction part of a low-level function. In a sense, when it comes to describe interaction cognitive functions, CFA cognitive functions could be modeled as GOMS methods.

The more agents are interconnected, the more the resulting multi-agent systems is complex, and the more it is difficult to isolate part to study them locally. The separability issue imposes a global approach of multi-agent systems. This is why both resource and context spaces need to be considered and developed in concert. Both local and global socio-cognitive stability need to be assessed to figure out where real problems are. If analytical studies using CFA are useful to start a design process of a multi-agent system, HITLS are necessary to observe and discover emerging cognitive functions and further rationalize resulting cognitive function networks. Consequently, CFA needs to be used incrementally during the life cycle of a multi-agent systems. This leads to the maturity issue that was presented earlier in the chapter.

CONCLUSION AND RESEARCH PERSPECTIVES

This chapter presents an evolution of the cognitive function analysis from the perspective of developing both resource and context spaces using the properties of both cognitive functions and i-Blocks. Contexts are difficult to define a priori during design unless experience and expertise is heavily used. In fact, they emerge from incremental refinement of cognitive function and i-Block networks first generated analytically and eventually refined experimentally from the results of human-in-the-loop simulations (HITLS). Understanding contexts of use is crucial in order to maximize the anticipation of possible surprises. It is then important to elicit persistent operational patterns to reduce uncertainty during subsequent operations. However, it is also important to be careful to understand the product resulting from automation, that is, the integration of these patterns into software and systems, and the emergent cognitive functions resulting from this automation. Cognitive function and i-Block representations are useful to support both the discovery of progressive emergence and consolidation of generic contexts. The development of cognitive function and i-Block networks helps in the rationalization of the design and evaluation of multi-agent systems by better understanding the various assigned roles in appropriate contexts of operations with the provision of relevant and available resources.

SUMMARY

The cognitive function representation is used to describe the role of a human, a machine or an organization in a given context, involving a set of resources. *Cognitive function analysis* (CFA) is an approach and a method that enables the description of cognitive function allocation among human and machine agents in highly-automated life-critical systems. It consists in incrementally describing both intentionally-created, as well as emerging, cognitive functions. CFA can be typically carried out from the first idea during the design phase to the obsolescence of the system itself. Cognitive functions are elicited at the same time as interaction blocks (i-Blocks) that links them between each other. Each i-Block is described in a procedural way by specifying a quintuplet (goal, triggering conditions, context, actions, and abnormal conditions). Both cognitive function and i-Block formalisms enable the description of declarative configuration-driven scenarios and procedural event-driven scenarios, which guide formative evaluations of the system being designed.

REFERENCES

Athènes, S., Averty, P., Puechmorel, S., Delahaye, D., and Collet, C. (2002). ATC complexity and Controller Workload: Trying to bridge the gap. *Proceedings of HCI-Aero'02*, J. Hansman, S. Chatty, and G. Boy (Eds.), Boston, US.

Boy, G.A. (1997). Cognitive function analysis: an example of human-centered redesign of a flight management system. *Proceedings of the 13th Triennial Congress of the International Ergonomics Association*, June 29–July 4, Tampere, Finland.

Boy, G.A. (1998). *Cognitive function analysis*. Ablex. Distributed by Greenwood Publishing Group, Westport, CT, US. ISBN 1567503764, 9781567503760.

Boy, G.A. and Ferro, D. (2003). Using Cognitive Function Analysis to Prevent Controlled Flight Into Terrain. Chapter of the *Human Factors and Flight Deck Design Book*. Don Harris (Ed.), Farnham, UK: Ashgate.

Boy, G.A. and Grote, G. (2009). Authority in Increasingly Complex Human and Machine Collaborative Systems: Application to the Future Air Traffic Management Construction. In the *Proceedings of the 2009 International Ergonomics Association World Congress, Beijing, China*.

Callon, M. (1991), Techno-economic networks and irreversibility, in Law, J. (Ed.), *A sociology of monsters: essays on power, technology and domination*. London: Routledge, pp. 132–161.

Card, S., Moran, T., and Newell, A. (1983). *The Psychology of Human–computer Interaction*. Hillsdale, NJ: Lawrence Erlbaum Associates.

Crandall, B., Klein, G., and Hoffman, R.R. (2006). *Working Minds: A Practitioner's Guide to Cognitive Task Analysis*, Cambridge, MA, US: Bradford Book/MIT Press.

Cummings, M.L. and Tsonis, C.G. (2006). Partitioning Complexity in Air Traffic Management Tasks. *International Journal of Aviation Psychology*, Volume 16, Issue 3, July 2006, pp. 277–295.

Endsley, M. (1988). Design and evaluation for situation awareness enhancement. *Proceedings of the Human Factors Society 32nd Annual Meeting, Human Factors Society, Santa Monica*. pp. 97–101.

Endsley, M., Bolté, B., and Jones, D. (2003). *Designing for situation awareness: An approach to user-centered design*. New York: Taylor and Francis.

Grote, G. (2004). Uncertainty management at the core of system design. *Annual Reviews in Control*, 28, pp. 267–274.

Hemingway, C.J. (1999). Toward a Socio-cognitive Theory of Information Systems: An Analysis of Key Philosophical and Conceptual Issues, *IFIP WG 8.2 and 8.6 Joint Working Conference on Information Systems: Current Issues and Future Changes*. Helsinki, Finland: IFIP, pp. 275–286.

Hilburn, B. (2004). Cognitive complexity in air traffic control: A literature review. Project COCA—COmplexity and CApacity. EEC Note No. 04/04.

Humphrey, C.M. and Adams, J.A. (2009). Cognitive Information Flow Analysis. *Cognition, Technology and Work*.

Hutchins, E. (1995). How a Cockpit Remembers its Speeds. *Cognitive Science*, 19, pp. 265–288.

Irving, S., Polson, P., and Irving, J.E. (1994). A GOMS analysis of the advanced automated cockpit. *Proceedings of CHI'94*. Boston, MA: ACM Press.

Latour, B. (1987). *Science in action: how to follow scientists and engineers through society*. Cambridge, MA: Harvard University Press.

Laudeman, I.V., Shelden, S.G., Branstrom, R., and Brasil, C.L. (1998). *Dynamic density. An air traffic management metric*. California: National Aeronautics and Space Administration, Ames Research Center.

Masalonis, A.J., Callaham, M.B., and Wanke, C.R. (2003). Dynamic Density and Complexity Metrics for Realtime Traffic Flow Management. Presented at the *ATM 2003 Conference, 5th EUROCONTROL/FAA ATM R&D Seminar (Budapest, Hungary)*.

Midkiff, A.H., R.J. Hansman, and T.G. Reynolds (2004). *Air carrier flight operations. Report No. ICAT-2004–3*. MIT International Center for Air Transportation. Department of Aeronautics and Astronautics, MIT, Cambridge, MA, US.

Rasmussen, J. (1983). Skills, Rules and Knowledge: Signals, Signs and Symbols, and other distinctions in human performance models. *IEEE Transactions on Systems, Man and Cybernetics*, vol. 13, pp. 257–266.

Rasmussen, J. (1985). The role of hierarchical knowledge representation in decision-making and system management. *IEEE Transactions on Systems, Man and Cybernetics*, vol. 15, pp. 234–243.

Reason, J. (1990). *Human error*. New York: Cambridge.

Sharples, M., Jeffery, N., du Boulay, J.B.H., Teather, D., Teather, B., and du Boulay, G.H. (2002). Socio-cognitive engineering: A methodology for the design of human-centered technology. *European Journal of Operational Research*, Volume 136, Issue 2, January, pp. 310–323.

Schraagen, J.M., Chipman, S.F., and Shalin, V.L. (Eds.). (2000). *Cognitive task analysis*. Mahwah, NJ, US: Lawrence Erlbaum Associate.

Vicente, K. (1999). *Cognitive work analysis. Toward safe, productive and healthy computer-based work*. Mahwah, NJ: Erlbaum.

Vicente, K. and Rasmussen, J. (1992). Ecological interface design: Theoretical foundations. *IEEE Transactions on Systems, Man and Cybernetics*, vol. 22, pp. 589–606.

10

Authority and Cooperation between Humans and Machines

Patrick Millot, Serge Debernard, and Frédéric Vanderhaegen

INTRODUCTION

In the human–machine field of research, the term *machine* refers not only to computers, but also to diverse control devices in complex dynamic situations, such as industrial processes or transportation networks. Human activities are mainly oriented toward decision-making, including monitoring and fault detection, fault anticipation, diagnosis and prognosis, and fault prevention and recovery. The objectives of this decision-making are related to human–machine system performance (production quantity and quality), as well as to overall system safety.

In this context, human operators may have a double role: a negative role in that operators may perform unsafe or erroneous actions affecting the process, and a positive role in that they are able to detect, prevent, or recover an unsafe process behavior caused by another operator or by automated decision-makers. In both cases, the operators can be the victims of an erroneous action affecting the process.

This multidisciplinary study combines two approaches to human–machine systems: a human engineering approach, aimed at designing dedicated assistance tools for human operators and integrating them into human activities through human–machine cooperation, and an approach centered on cognitive psychology and ergonomics, which attempts to analyze the human activities in terms of the need for and use of such tools.

The influence of these two approaches, one proposing technical solutions and the other evaluating the ergonomic acceptability of these solutions for the human operators, is apparent throughout this chapter. First, the main parameters influencing human–machine system performance and safety are described. Then, human–machine cooperation is defined particularly concepts such as coordination, authority, task allocation and a framework for implementing this cooperation is proposed.

PARAMETERS INFLUENCING AUTOMATED SYSTEM PERFORMANCE AND SAFETY

Human–machine system safety depends on three kinds of parameters: technical parameters, human parameters, and parameters related to the interaction of the first two. This section focuses on some of the parameters in the last category.

Managing System Complexity

Technical failures and human errors generally increase with the size and/or the complexity of the system (that is, the number of interconnections between the controlled variables and their degree of interconnection). For instance, large systems, such as power plants or transport networks, can have several thousand interconnected variables that need to be supervised. In order to manage the resulting complexity, the human supervisor must be able to understand the system's behavior. This understanding can be facilitated by defining dedicated analysis methods, based on systemic approaches (Lemoigne, 1984).

For that purpose two complementary ways for analyzing the system and then breaking its complexity do exist:

- The system decomposition can be guided by technical and organizational view-points as Multilevel Flow Modeling one's (MFM) developed by M. Lind (1990, 2003).
- The decomposition can be guided by classifying the tasks through an abstraction hierarchy according to several levels: strategic, tactical and operational ones (Sheridan, 1985; Millot, 1999).

With MFM the global system is decomposed along two axes, the means-ends axis, and the whole-part axis (Figure 10.1).

- The means-ends axis is composed of four model levels: the higher the level, the more global and abstract the model, and conversely, the lower the level, the more concrete and detailed the model. Each level corresponds to a different kind of model: goal models (for example, a financial point of view of the system), functional models (for example, symbolic or graphic relationships) behavioral models (for example, differential equations), and technical models (for example, mechanical or electrical components). Each level's model is the means of attaining the higher-level model and is the ends (goal) of the lower-level model.
- The whole-part axis is linked to the decomposition imposed by the means-ends axis. At the highest level, the system is analyzed at a very global level (that is, without details), making it possible to take the whole system into account. At the lowest level, the analysis is very detailed, providing a view of each component and looking at only one part of the system at a time.

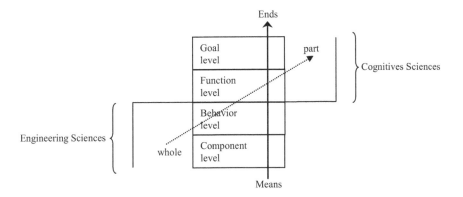

Figure 10.1   Multilevel decomposition of a system
Source: Lind, 1990, 2003.

This modeling method seems promising, as it tends to associate cognitive sciences and engineering sciences in a complementary manner that allows complex systems to be modeled.

In a more "human–machine approach," Sheridan (1985) proposed a four-level hierarchical organization (Figure 10.2):

- The lower level is the process to be controlled or supervised, decomposed into subsystems.
- The second level is composed of the local control units of these subsystems.
- The third one is the coordination of the local control units, including DSS.
- The upper supervision level composed by the human team.

Millot added three scales to Sheridan's Supervisory Control structure (Figure 10.2) (Millot, 1999):

- A scale related to the nature of the information, with the precise numerical information towards the bottom of the scale and the symbolic and global information towards the top.
- A scale related to the level of abstraction, with the means towards the bottom and the objectives towards the top (similar to MFM hierarchy).
- A scale related to the temporal horizons, with the activities to be performed in real time (for example, the subsystem control tasks) towards the bottom and the long-term activities (for example, planning or strategic decision-making) towards the top.

Indeed sorting the tasks according to these three scales facilitates the definition of the nature of the task and the expected task performance for each level. Human abilities are best suited to processing symbolic information and planning and anticipating decisions about global objectives rather than specific means, and this on a middle- or long-term horizon. For this reason, activities towards the bottom of the scale are not well suited to human capabilities, and this can lead to human errors. Such assumption is confirmed by problem-solving pathway models issued from the cognitive psychology field.

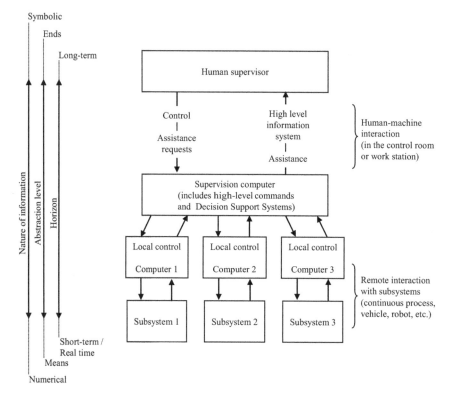

Figure 10.2   Supervisory Control

Source: Adapted from Sheridan (1985) and completed by Millot (1999).

Understanding Human Complexity

Modeling human problem-solving in supervision tasks is another difficult objective for controlling Human–Machine systems. A lot of models have been proposed, among them the well-known Rasmussen's ladder (Rasmussen, 1983, revisited by Hoc in 1996), Figure 10.3. This functional model gathers four major functions: (1) abnormal event detection; (2) situation assessment by perceiving information for identifying (diagnosis) and/or predicting (prognosis) the process state; (3) decision-making by predicting the consequences of this state on the process goals, defining targets to be achieved and breaking these targets down into tasks and procedures; and finally (4) performing the resulting tasks and procedures to affect the process. Since the early 1980s, a strong parallel has been drawn with the artificial intelligence used to model and implement some of these functions in machines.

Hoc has introduced revisions that provide more details about the cognitive mechanisms for assessing situations (for example, hypothesis elaboration and testing) and about certain temporal aspects of the process (that is, diagnosis of the present state, prognosis of the future state, expected evolution of the process or projections regarding the appropriate instant for performing an action or for perceiving information).

This model has three behavioral levels, which enhances its effectiveness:

- *A skill-based behavior* is adopted by a trained operator, who performs an action in an automatic manner when perceiving a specific signal.
- A *rule-based behavior* is adopted by an expert operator, who, faced with a known problem, reuses a solution learned in the past.
- A *knowledge-based behavior* is adopted by an operator faced with an unknown problem, who must find a new solution; in this special case, the operator needs to be supported either by other operators or by a decision-support system in order to understand the process situation and make the right decision.

The second and third levels involve cognitive mechanisms.

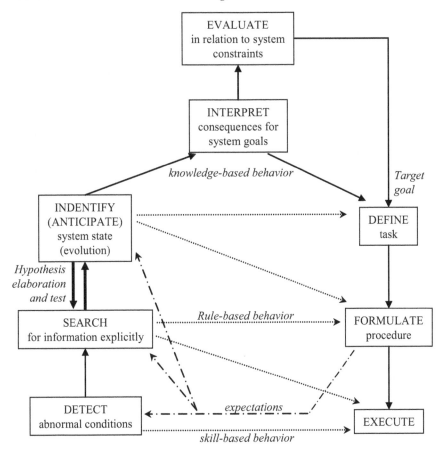

Figure 10.3   Rasmussen's step-ladder

Source: Revisited by Hoc (1996).

This model also served as starting point for understanding human error mechanisms (Reason, 1993) and for providing barriers for preventing and/or managing these errors. For instance, an erroneous action can be the result of either the incorrect application of a right decision or the right application of an inappropriate decision. The erroneous decision itself can either produce a wrong solution based on a correct situation assessment or a sound solution based on an incorrect situation assessment, and so on.

Reason divides human errors into two categories: non-intentional and intentional. These categories are further sub-divided into *slips* and *lapses* for non-intentional actions, and *mistakes* and *violations* for intentional decisions/actions. Thus, Reason imagines a total of four kinds of human errors. Violations differ from mistakes in that the decision-maker is conscious of violating the procedure, with either negative intent (for example, sabotage) or positive intent (for example, preventing an accident). Amalberti (1996) tries to explain the production of certain violations through the need for human operators to reach a compromise solution for three joint, sometimes contradictory, objectives: performance standards, imposed either by the organization or by the individual operator; system and/or operator safety; and the cognitive and physiological costs of attaining the first two objectives (for example, workload, stress). For Rasmussen, the dimensions of these three objectives are limited, and thus they constrain the field of human actions, Figure 10.4 (Rasmussen, 1997). An action that crosses the limits can lead to a loss of control, and subsequently, an incident or an accident. Barriers or defenses can then be designed to prevent human operators from crossing these limits (Polet et al., 2003).

Technical, organizational or procedural defenses can aim at remedying faulty actions or decisions. Thus, several risk analysis methods have been proposed for detecting risky situations and providing such remedies (Fadier et al., 1994; Hollnagel, 1999; Vanderhaegen, 1999; Polet et al., 2002; Van der Vlugt et al., 2003). Usually, risk management involves three complementary steps, which must be anticipated when designing the system:

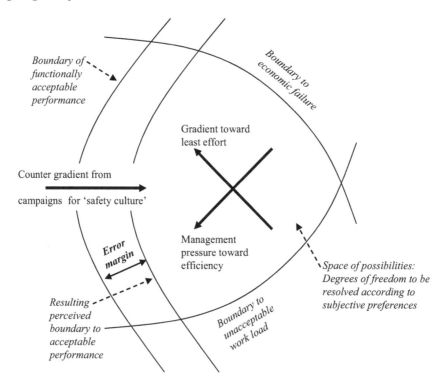

Figure 10.4   Three boundary dimensions constraining human behavior
Source: Rasmussen, 1997.

- *Prevention:* the first step is to prevent risky behaviors. Unexpected behaviors should be anticipated when designing the system, and technical, human and organizational defenses should be implemented to avoid these behaviors (for example, norms, procedures, maintenance policies, supervisory control).
- *Correction:* if prevention fails, the second step allows these unexpected behaviors to be detected (for example, alarm detection system in a power plant) and corrected (for example, high speed train brakes).
- *Containment:* if the corrective action fails, an accident may occur. The third step attempts to deal with the consequences of a failed corrective action, by intervening to minimize the negative consequences of this accident (for example, roadside emergency care).

These three steps offer prevention, correction or recovery tasks that can be performed, some by the human operators and some by the machine. Several questions must then be asked in order to allocate the tasks:

- Should (or could) these tasks be shared between the human and the machine and performed separately?
- In that case who should coordinate the task sharing?
- Should the task be performed by both the human and the machine together?
- In that case, could the task be decomposed into subtasks, and who should coordinate the decomposition and the subtask allocations?

The answers involve the concepts of cooperation.

Degrees of Automation

The influence of the human role and the degree of human involvement on overall human–machine system performance (production, safety) has been studied since the early 1980s. Sheridan (1984) defined the well-known degrees of automation and their consequences.

In a fully manual controlled system, safety depends entirely on the human controller's reliability.

At the opposite in a fully automated system the human operator is absent of the control and supervision loops. This degree of automation can lead to a lack of vigilance and a loss of skill of the operators involved in the supervision, which prevents them from assuming their responsibility on the system. Consequently, the system safety is almost fully dependent on the technical reliability.

Between these two extremes, an intermediate solution consists in establishing supervisory control procedures that will allow task-sharing between the human operators and the automated control systems. In addition, dedicated assistance tools (for example, DSS: Decision Support Systems) can be introduced into the supervision and control loop in order to enhance the human ability to apply the right decision and/or to manage the wrong decisions.

Sheridan (1992) has defined 10 levels of automation, as shown in Table 10.1. Levels 1 and 10 do not concern human–machine cooperation as each of the agents performs the tasks alone. Levels 2 to 4 correspond to a static allocation where the human operator has the control of the system but where a machine (a computer) proposes solution(s). So the human operator has the authority for controlling the system, can implement its own solution but can also choose the solution provided by the machine. At these levels, interactions between both agents are developed at a tactical level, for performing the task and in accordance with several modes of human machine cooperation.

At levels 5 and 6, the approach differs due to the integration of strategic aspects dealing with authority allocation for performing the task.

Levels 7 to 9 correspond to a static allocation where the machine has the authority for implementing the solutions. These levels differ in the kind of feedback provided to the human operator.

This 10-degree scale mixes tactical and strategic aspects, that is, performing a task, allocating a task. Some authors proposed to add intermediate levels of automation especially for copping with particular contexts. For instance, in case of emergency Inagaki (2006) defines the level 6.5 where "the computer executes automatically upon telling the human what it is going to do." At this level, the machine performs the actions on the system for safety reasons, but informs human operator in order to reduce the automation surprise and to maintain situation awareness.

Parasuraman et al. (2000) proposed to extend this approach through a simplified version of the Rasmussen's ladder in four steps: *information elaboration*, *identification*, *decision-making* and *implementation of the decision*. For each step the scale of automation is applied, allowing a better representation of the interactions between the agents, an allocation of subtasks (static and dynamic), and the sharing of authority between the agents for performing and also for allocating a task. Let us see below further developments of these ideas.

Table 10.1   Scale of levels of automation

1	The computer offers no assistance, human must do it all
2	The computer offers a complete set of action alternatives, and
3	Narrows the selection down to a few, or
4	Suggests one, and
5	Executes that suggestion if the human approves, or
6	Allows the human a restricted time to veto before automatic execution, or
7	Executes automatically, then necessarily informs human, or
8	Informs him after execution only if he asks, or
9	Informs him after execution if it, the computers, decides to
10	The computer decides everything and acts autonomously, ignoring the human

Source: Sheridan, 1992.

CRITERIA FOR SHARING THE TASKS BETWEEN OPERATOR AND MACHINE

Identifying the Tasks to Be Shared Between Humans and Machines

Human–machine task-sharing decisions should be made according to two criteria: *technical feasibility* and *ergonomic feasibility* (Figure 10.5).

The technical feasibility criterion is used to divide the initial task set into two classes:

- TA tasks, which are technically able to be performed automatically by the machine.
- TH tasks, which cannot be performed automatically due to lack of information or due to technical or even theoretical reasons, and thus must be allocated to human operators.

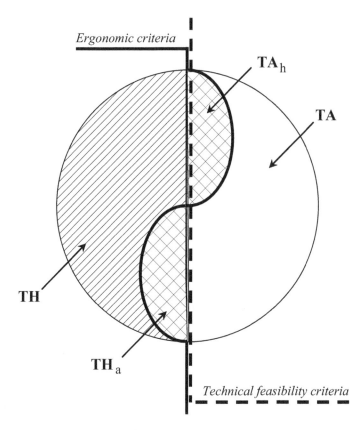

Figure 10.5   Human–machine task-sharing

Source: TA: automatizable tasks; TH: tasks that cannot be automated and thus must be performed by humans. TAh: tasks that can be performed by both humans and machines. THa: tasks that cannot be performed by machines or humans working alone.

The ergonomic feasibility criterion is applied to both subsets, TA tasks and TH tasks, to evaluate the human tasks in terms of global system safety and security:

- In the subset TA tasks, some automated tasks TAh can also be performed by humans, and allocating them to the human operators can allow these operators to better supervise and understand the global system and the automated devices. The subset TAh is thus the set of the shareable tasks used in a form of human–machine cooperation (that is, the dynamic task allocation presented below).
- In the subset TH tasks, some subtasks THa are very complex, or their complexity is increased by a very short response time. Humans performing such tasks could be aided by a Decision Support System or a Control Support System. The subset THa can thus be the basis of another form of human–machine cooperation.

The ergonomic feasibility criterion is based on human operator models that define the potential human resources, as well as the intrinsic limits of the operators (perceptual and/or physical) when performing the related actions. Human cognitive resources depend on the context, and human physical resources can be determined through ergonomic guidelines (Reason, 1993, 1986; Hoc, 1996; Amalberti, 1996).

Provisions for the Design of Cooperative Human–Machine Systems

Despite the existence of the automation, human operators must still master the process and the situation they manage (Goettl, 1991; Riera and Debernard, 2003), and they must remain active in the control and supervisory loop of the human–machine system. Nevertheless, the use of automated systems can increase the interaction between both the human and machine decision-makers and the workload related to this interaction.

Technical progress has increased machine decisional capabilities so that human–machine systems have increasingly become complex cognitive systems in which interactions between the human and artificial agents increase as the systems deal with more complex and cognitive tasks (Hollnagel, 2003). For this reason, human operators must control not only the process but also the artificial agents. One major problem is linked to the respective roles allocated to the agents involved in the system, and thus to the definition of their responsibilities (Debernard and Hoc, 2001). Human operators who are responsible for complete system operations may thus have some doubts about interacting with a machine if they do not feel that they can control it completely. Even when the machine has the responsibility for making the decisions and taking the actions according to the choices of the designer, the human operators can nevertheless intervene when they perceive a problem related to the system safety. This is for instance the case in aeronautics with on-board anti-collision systems (Rome et al., 2006).

Allocating the responsibility between human and machine relates to the general problem of *sharing the authority* and thus involves human parameters, such as *self confidence* and *trust (to the machine)* (Muir, 1987). Rajaonah (2006, 2008) has described the confidence construction mechanisms and their impact on the relationship between the human and artificial agents.

Through an evaluation of computerized decision support systems, Barr and Sharda (1997) highlighted the positive and negative effects of their use by human operators. These authors pointed out, that using Decision Support Systems; (1) increases the human operators' understanding of the problems to be solved, (2) improves operator information processing times, and (3) boosts operator confidence in the final decision, by allowing the operators to focus on the strategic aspects of the problem to be solved. However, at the same time, using these computerized decision-making systems can make the users passive, leading them to refuse to try to understand the situation, specifically because they do not know which information led to the final decision produced by the system. Since their behavior depends on the system's decisions, that passivity generally reduces their efficiency.

Human machine cooperation is a way for preserving human–machine safety.

HUMAN–MACHINE COOPERATION AND AUTHORITY

Defining Cooperation

In the field of cognitive psychology, Hoc (1996) and Millot and Hoc (1997) proposed the following definition: "two agents are cooperating if (1) each agent strives towards goals and can interfere with the other, and (2) each agent tries to detect and process such interference to make the other's activities easier."

Two classes of cooperative activities can be derived from this definition. They relate to the so-called *know-how-to-cooperate* (KHC) as defined by Millot (1998) and Millot and Lemoine (1998):

- The first activity class, *Managing Interference* (MI), requires the ability to detect and manage interference between goals. Such interference can be positive (for example, common goal or sub-goal) or negative (for example, conflicts between goals or sub-goals or about common shared resources).
- The second activity class, *Facilitating Goals* (FG), requires the ability to make the achievement of the other agents' goals easier.

MI corresponds to *coordination abilities*, while FG involves a more benevolent kind of agent behavior. Providing an agent with MI capabilities and the relevant KH allows it/him *authority for sharing the tasks*. Before specifying the exact abilities required for MI and FG, the organizational aspects of cooperation must first be considered.

Defining an Agent

Decision Support Systems (DSS) provide assistance that makes the human operator's tasks easier and helps to prevent erroneous actions. Both the DSS and the human operator are called agents. Both the human and machine agents can be modeled according to three classes of capabilities: Know-How, Know-How-to-Cooperate, and Need-to-Cooperate.

Know-How (KH) is applied to solve problems and perform tasks autonomously, while acquiring problem-solving capabilities (for example, knowledge sources, processing abilities) and communicating with the environment and other agents through sensors and control devices.

Know-How-to-Cooperate (KHC) is a class of specific abilities needed for Managing Interference between goals (MI) and for Facilitating other agents' Goals (FG) with respect to the definition of cooperation given above (Millot and Hoc, 1997).

Need-to-Cooperate (NC), proposed by Millot and Debernard (2007), is a new class that combines:

- The *Adequacy* of the agents' personal KH (that is, knowledge and processing abilities) in terms of the task constraints.
- The *Ability to perform* the task (that is, the workload (WL) produced by the human agents' tasks, perceptual abilities, and control abilities).
- The *Motivation-to-Cooperate* of the agents that is, motivation to accomplish the task, self-confidence, trust (Moray et al., 1995), and confidence in the cooperation (Rajaonah et al., 2008).

For that, let us analyze the know-how-to-cooperate according to the different forms of human–machine cooperation.

Authority

Let us consider an agent AG_x doted with a know-how KH_x and a know-how-to-cooperate KHC_x; this agent is within a structure.

Authority relates to the *decisional independence* of an agent. Such an agent can decide and act alone on the process without requiring other agents for validating this decision or action. For that purpose the agent must have *coordination abilities*, a *relevant KH* for performing the task or sharing the tasks between other agents and *have a position in a structure which allows it to decide or act in an autonomous manner*.

In a human–machine cooperative organization the machine KHC has generally an uncompleted MI, especially for technical feasibility reasons. Therefore the human agent becomes naturally the coordinator and the machine must then have been designed with fully FG abilities in order to assist the human in his/her coordination tasks. Then allowing *the position of authority* in a structure to one of the agents (human or machine) needs this agent be provided with authority abilities: MI and KH. Examples of implementation are given bellow.

Cooperative Forms

The objective is to specify KHC_x using MI_x and FG_x in the different cooperative situations that can be encountered (or built). This can be done by adapting and using the generic typology of cooperative forms proposed by Schmidt (1991): augmentative, debative, and integrative.

Augmentative Form

Cooperation is *augmentative* when agents have similar know-how, but multiple agents are needed to perform a task too demanding for only one agent. Thus, task T must be divided into similar subtasks ST_i. Interference between the agent activities can result when common resources must be shared or when agents have conflicting goals or sub-goals stemming from their individual ST_i. Thus, KHC must allow; (1) the decomposition of task T into independent ST_i before the task is performed in order to prevent these conflicts, (2) the management of residual conflicts (for example, about common resources) during ST_i execution, and (3) the recomposition of the results afterwards if the ST_i did not result in an action, or the rebuilding of the task context. These activities can be performed by a third agent called the coordinator, or by either AG_x or AG_y, which will then play the double role of coordinator and agent.

The coordinator's KH includes the abilities needed to acquire the task context, to build a global plan for the task, and to decompose it into sub-plans to accomplish ST_i. The coordinator's KHC includes the abilities needed to acquire other agents' KH (or to infer them from a model), workloads (WL) and/or resources for sub-task allocation, to control and recompose the results or the contexts after each ST_i has been performed, and to manage conflicts about shared common resources. All these KHC abilities are related to MI. The non-coordinator agents' KHC abilities consist of answering the coordinator's requests and are related to FG.

Debative Form

Cooperation is *debative* when agents have similar know-how and are faced with a single task T that is not divided into ST_i. Each agent solves the task and then debates the results (or the partial results) with the other agents. Conflicts can arise, and the KHC must allow these conflicts to be solved through explanations based on previous partial results along the problem-solving pathway and on a common frame of reference, for instance (Millot and Hoc, 1997).

Before task execution, each agent's KH consists of its ability to acquire the task context and build a plan (that is, establish a goal, sub-goals, and means). Each agent's KHC consists of acquiring the other agents' KH either by inferring the other agents' KH models or by asking the other agents for their KH. These inferences and/or requests are part of MI capabilities. The other agents' responses to these requests constitute FG capabilities.

After task execution (complete or partial), each agent transmits its own results to the others, receives results from the other agents and compares them to its own results. In addition to MI (for example, asking for results from others) and FG (for example, transmitting its own results) capabilities, this process requires that each agent have specific competencies for understanding the others' results, comparing them to its own results, and deciding whether or not to agree with the others' results. These competences are all included in MI.

In case of conflict, each agent must be able to ask the other one for explanations (for example, the other agent's view of the task context, its partial results, its goal and/or sub-goals) in order to compare these explanations with its own point of view and to decide whether or not the conflict should continue. In addition, each agent must be able to acknowledge its own errors and learn the lesson needed to avoid such errors in the future. This last ability can have important consequences on agent KH.

Integrative Form

Cooperation is *integrative* when agents have different and complementary know-how and the task T can be divided into complementary sub-tasks ST_i related to each KH. As in the augmentative form of cooperation, a third agent can play the role of coordinator; however, this role could also be played by one of the agents, AG_x or AG_y. The coordinator's KHC must allow; (1) the elaboration of a common plan (goal and means) and its decomposition into complementary sub-plans (ST_i, sub-goals) related to each of the respective agents' KH, (2) the control of the partial results or the evolving context throughout the agents' execution of the ST_i, and (3) the recomposition of the results afterwards if the results of the ST_i were not an action, or the rebuilding of the task context. The integrative form of cooperation is similar to the augmentative form, except that during ST_i execution, the possibility of conflictual interactions between the different ST_i requires that the coordinator be capable of checking each partial result and of ordering corrections, if needed.

A more general and complex case can be imagined, in which both agents, AG_x and AG_y, must cooperate in order to build a shared common plan and then must share the authority. This case is often studied in the field of Distributed Artificial Intelligence. In such a situation, each agent plays the role of coordinator, first seeking to establish a common frame of reference with respect to the task context and each agent's KH (Millot and Hoc, 1997) and then working to develop its own comprehensive common plan and comparing it with those of the other agents in debative cooperation. Examples of this case can be found in multidisciplinary studies of Human-Human cooperation, for instance.

Human–Human Cooperation Examples

As mentioned above, these three forms already exist in human-human organizations and are sometimes naturally combined. An example of the augmentative form of cooperation can be observed in banks; when the line in front of a window is too long, a second window is opened, thus cutting the line in half and reducing the first teller's workload. An example of the debative form is found in the mutual control established between the flying pilot and the co-pilot in the plane cockpit. An example of the integrative form can be seen in the coordination of the different tasks required to build a house. The innovation lies in implementing these forms in human–machine systems. Grislin and Millot (1999) have shown that these three forms are generic to all kinds of cooperation.

Cooperation forms are suitable for sharing the authority in particular conditions and with regard to the know-how-to-cooperate of the cooperative agents. For implementation purposes an agent must be integrated in a structure.

Structures for Cooperation

In an organization, the agents play roles and perform tasks, combining the different activities needed to acquire and process information and to make decisions. The decisions may, or may not, result in actions. Defining the organization has often been seen as a way to prevent or resolve decisional conflicts between agents, especially in human engineering in which agents may be human or machine (for example, artificial DSS). This perspective is also studied in the field of Distributed Artificial Intelligence.

Implementing a structure is the way to connect the inputs and outputs of each agent to the inputs and outputs of the other ones and to the sensors and actuators of the machine to be controlled. But it is also the way to affect the authority to one of the agents or to share it between them.

Two generic structures exist: vertical (that is, hierarchical) and horizontal (that is, heterarchical) (Millot et al., 1989; Grislin and Millot, 1999).

In the *vertical structure* shown Figure 10.6, the human agent is at the upper level of the hierarchy and is responsible for all the decisions. If necessary, he/she can call upon the other agent, which can give advices. So, here, the human agent has the final authority for selecting a solution and implementing it. An efficient use of this authority needs this human agent be provided with coordination abilities MI associated with the relevant KH.

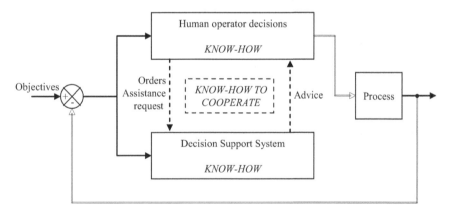

Figure 10.6   Vertical Structure for human–machine cooperation

In the *horizontal structure* shown Figure 10.7, both agents are on the same hierarchical level and can behave independently if their respective tasks are independent. Otherwise, they must manage the interferences between their goals using their MI and FG abilities. Here, each agent has *the authority for performing* their own tasks. A coordinator introduced at an upper level has the *strategic authority for sharing these tasks* between them. Then we see here two kinds of authorities: one for sharing the tasks and one for performing the tasks. In a human machine horizontal structure sharing the tasks is implemented by a task allocator which can be human (explicit mode), or artificial (implicit mode); that is, in both explicit and implicit modes no agent is allowed to modify the allocation. In this structure too, both authorities, tactical and strategic, need the related agents be provided with the coordination abilities and the relevant KH.

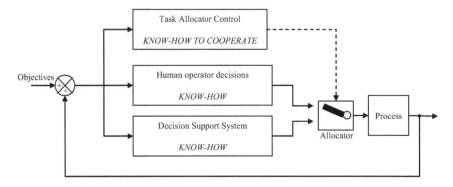

Figure 10.7   Horizontal structure for human–machine cooperation

Several combinations of both structures are also possible by decomposing the task into several abstraction levels (Rasmussen, 1991) and assigning a dedicated structure to each level. (An example will be given below.) However, evaluating these structures, both the generic and the combined, with realistic experimental platforms has shown that choosing a cooperative structure is not sufficient to allow real cooperation between a human and a machine or, more generally, between two agents (Millot and Hoc, 1997). It is necessary to introduce a complementary framework for describing the nature of the cooperative activities and for specifying the agents' KHC.

A Common Work Space as a Foundation of Know-How-To-Cooperate

Characterizing human–machine cooperation starts with the implementation of the agent's know-how. According to Rasmussen's model (1985), the human decision-maker provides different states of the problem to be solved along the solution path. In order to manage situations, the human agents build a frame of reference that contains different attributes: *information* from information elaboration activities, *problems* from identification activities, *strategies* from schematic decision-making activities, *solutions* from precise decision-making activities, and *commands* from solution implementation activities (Pacaux-Lemoine and Debernard, 2002).

When several human operators supervise and control the same process, they elaborate and maintain a *Common Frame Of Reference* (COFOR), which is a common representation of the environment and the team resources (Decortis and Pavard, 1994). The COFOR contains common goals, common plans, role allocation and representations of the process, among other things. (Carlier and Hoc, 1999). To cooperate, human agents exchange information, problems, or strategies, for example, in order to share their own frame of reference. In this way, they build a cognitive support for managing the content of their COFOR.

The characterization of a cooperation can then be derived from this COFOR and the three generic Schmidt's forms of cooperation (that is, augmentative, integrative, and debative). However, a poor verbal communication of one agent may lead to an incorrect interpretation of the frame of reference of another agent. One manner to avoid this is to support the cooperation by implementing the COFOR using what is called *Common Work Space* (CWS), which depends on the domain and the tasks to be achieved (Pacaux-Lemoine and Debernard, 2002). Using a CWS not only generates some new activities for the human agent, but also some new functions for the assistance tool. These new activities correspond to the know-how-to-cooperate capability. These activities (or functions) must allow:

- The COFOR to be updated, starting with the activities/functions for updating each COFOR attribute from the agents' individual frames of reference.
- The COFOR to be controlled using activities/functions for comparing the COFOR and the agents' individual frames of reference; these activities/functions correspond to a mutual control and allow the detection of interferences for one or more attributes, especially information perception.
- The interferences to be managed first by detecting these interferences through a diagnosis of the differences between the CWS and an agent's frame of reference and then by resolving the interferences using dedicated activities.

Three forms of resolution may be used by the agent (Pacaux-Lemoine and Debernard, 2002): *negotiation*, *acceptance*, or *imposition*. These forms imply different cognitive and communication costs. Negotiation aims to reduce the differences between the CWS and an agent's frame of reference by modifying one of them based on agent explanations. Acceptance updates the frame of reference from the CWS and is chosen when the cost of a negotiation is too high or when an agent wants to facilitate the activities of the other agent. The imposition is the opposite of the acceptance.

Implementing a CWS between an artificial agent and one or more human agents provides some constraints, particularly when engaging a negotiation. When two human agents negotiate, they may use very efficient symbolic explanations. An artificial agent needs an explicit explanation based on operational information. For this reason, it is currently very difficult to provide an artificial agent with real negotiation capabilities to be used with human agents. Furthermore human agents can be reticent to accept a solution given by an artificial agent if they cannot modify this solution later.

Modeling and allocating all these cooperative activities/functions in order to perform the tasks requires the use of the three Schmidt's generic forms of cooperative agent interaction. In the debative form (Figure 10.8-a), all the agents supply the CWS with new data for one task and for one activity/function; if interference appears, the agents can negotiate. In the integrative form (Figure 10.8-b), only one agent supplies data for the CWS, and the other one takes this data into account when performing the next activity/function. In the augmentative form (Figure 10.8-c), the agents perform the same activity/function and they mutually update the CWS but for different tasks, depending on the task allocation.

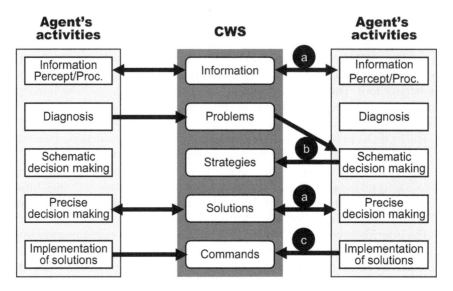

Figure 10.8   Cooperative interaction between agents through the CWS:
a. debative form; b. integrative form; c. augmentative form

IMPLEMENTATION OF A HUMAN–MACHINE COOPERATION

Human-Centered Automation Methods

Implementing human–machine cooperation must be set back in the global context of automation, and with *a human centered approach of automation* (Riera et al., 2003) which takes into account the next points:

1. The main objective is the improvement of the global performance of the human–machine system and not only the technical system.
2. Consequently, induced effects of the artifact must be taken into account. For that purpose, the human–machine system is studied, taking into account human characteristics as well as technical aspects.
3. Alternative approaches to technical centered automation must be proposed. Human machine cooperation and Dynamic Tasks Allocation are examples of solutions.
4. After the design of the human–machine system including a human machine cooperation is achieved, an evaluation step is needed involving technical as well as human criteria. The latter are difficult to perform due to the lack of "observability" of HO's cognitive behavior.

Millot (1999) has proposed a methodology for defining the roles of human operators and allocating their tasks.

- First, the technical constraints (for example, dynamics, safety) with respect to the different predictable system operational modes need to be extracted. The functional and dysfunctional system analysis methods proposed for instance respectively by Fadier (1990) and Villemeur (1988) can be used to deduce (or induce) the tasks to be performed.
- Then, these tasks must be allocated to the human and/or the machine, according to their respective capabilities. To do so, the tasks must be specified in terms of their objectives, acceptable means (for example, sensors, actuators) and functions.
- At this point, the designer must implement the automated processors for managing future automated tasks and the human–machine interfaces that will facilitate future human tasks and support the cooperative activities between the agents.
- Finally, the entire system must be evaluated in terms of technical and ergonomic criteria.

The main stage is of course the allocation of tasks. Billings (1992) has proposed several principles related to human centered automation. These principles had been enhanced by Boy (1999) by taking into account the problematic of situation awareness. A human agent who interacts with an artificial agent must be awareness of what it did, what is doing and why, and finally what it will do.

Several methods exist for choosing the allocation of tasks (Dearden et al., 2000; Grote et al., 1995) which consist first in defining a static allocation, and then a dynamic allocation. That needs to take several aspects of human–machine cooperation into account such as (1) How implementing a dynamic task allocation in terms of command and responsibility? (2) How defining a feed-back which allows the human operator to control the system? (3) How supporting cooperative activities in order to enhance the global human–machine system? (4) How implementing know-how-to-cooperate in the machine? (5) How make the agent position in a structure consistent with his/its authority abilities?

Cooperative Forms and Structures in Human–Machine Cooperation

This section presents an analysis of the kind of structure that should be chosen to support the different cooperative forms; the recommended forms are illustrated with examples.

Augmentative form and structure, the example of Air Traffic Control

In this example, both agents have similar KH, and each performs a subtask STi resulting from the division of task T into similar subtasks. In order to prevent conflicts between the agents, the coordinator must decompose T into independent subtasks.

In Air Traffic Control (ATC), the objectives consist of monitoring and controlling the traffic in such a way the aircraft cross the air space with a maximum level of safety. The air space is divided into geographical sectors, each of them controlled by two controllers. The first one is a tactical controller, called *Radar Controller* (RC), who supervises the traffic using a radar screen and dialogues with the aircraft pilots. The supervision task entails detecting possible traffic conflicts between planes that may violate separation norms, resulting in a collision, and then solving them. Conflict resolution usually consists in asking one pilot to modify his/her flight level, heading, or speed.

The second controller is a strategic controller, called the *Planning Controller* (PC). PC coordinates the traffic in his/her own sector with the traffic in other sectors in order to avoid irreconcilable conflicts on the sector's borders. They are also supposed to anticipate traffic density and regulate the workload of the RC. In addition, in traffic overload conditions, the PC assists the RC by taking responsibility for some tactical tasks. To support the RC, a dedicated DSS called SAINTEX has been developed. In this system, each agent (that is, the RC and SAINTEX) is allowed to perform actions affecting the traffic, and the tasks are dynamically distributed between these two agents based on performance and workload criteria.

To accomplish this dynamic task allocation, a task allocator control system is introduced at the strategic level of the organization (Debernard et al., 1992; Vanderhaegen et al., 1994), which can be:

- A dedicated artificial decisional system with the ability to assess human workload and performance, in which case the dynamic task allocation is called implicit.
- The human operator, who plays a second role dealing with strategic and organizational tasks, in which case the dynamic task allocation is called explicit.

So, in both approaches, the authority is decomposed into tactical and strategic levels. At the strategic level, the allocator (human in explicit *mode*, artificial in implicit *ones*) controls the allocation of shareable tasks, whereas at the tactical level the controller and SAINTEX solve the conflict in an autonomous way.

These two task allocation modes were implemented on a realistic Air Traffic Control (ATC) simulator and evaluated by professional Air-Traffic Controllers. A series of experiments implemented both implicit and explicit dynamic task allocation between the radar controller and SAINTEX (Debernard et al., 1992; Lemoine and Debernard et al., 1996). The task allocation depended on the know-how (KH) of the two decision-makers. The SAINTEX KH was limited to simple aircraft conflicts (that is, between only two planes). The RC's know-how was only limited by the workload. Evaluation criteria were defined in terms of performance: the overall traffic safety as the rate of non-solved conflicts and the fuel traffic consumption. The experiments showed a better performance, as well as a better regulation of the RC's workload, in the implicit allocation mode than in the explicit one. However, the responses to questionnaires showed that professional Air Traffic Controllers would not easily accept implicit allocation in real situations because (a) the different tasks were not completely independent, and (b) they had no control over the tasks assigned to SAINTEX, but retained total responsibility for all tasks.

Thus, it seems that if AGx and AGy are both provided with all the KH and KHC capabilities of a coordinator, a purely horizontal structure like the ones used in Distributed Artificial Intelligence must be envisaged. However, if only one agent, for instance AGx, is assigned the capabilities needed to be a coordinator, the result is a *de facto* hierarchy in which AGx has the *strategic authority* and manages the cooperation. AGy will then have FG abilities and become an assistant in the cooperation. This situation is quite realistic in Human–Machine Cooperation, and the dynamic task allocation aiming for this form of cooperation can be analyzed from this perspective. In the ATC experiment involving only RC and SAINTEX, there was an asymmetry between the KHC of both agents, creating a *de facto* hierarchy in which the RC naturally held the higher position. Therefore in the explicit mode, this natural hierarchy was consistent with the authority given by the structure, but in implicit mode, the authority was reversed to the intrinsic agent abilities, which could explain the RC's refusal of this type of organization.

In addition, the sub-tasks were not really independent since solving some traffic conflicts increased the risk of creating new ones. Thus, the cooperative form was not purely augmentative; a purely augmentative form would have required SAINTEX to have other KHC related to the other cooperative forms.

Debative form and structure, the example of supervision of a power plant
In this example, both agents have similar KH and are faced with a single task T that is not (or cannot be) divided into sub-tasks. After each agent performs the task, they compare the results (or the partial results), and when there is a conflict, they debate.

If both agents are given all the KH and KHC abilities, a purely horizontal structure can be imagined. The ability to recognize and acknowledge errors may then depend on trust and self-confidence (Moray et al., 1995). On the other hand, giving only one agent full KHC results in a *de facto* hierarchy in which this agent is provided with a strategic authority; if such a hierarchical structure is chosen, the conflict resolution process can be aided (or perturbed) by the hierarchy. This situation is realistic in human–machine cooperation, because the machine capabilities can be reduced to FG capabilities. In this case, the designer of the machine must have simulated the human user's conflict resolution pathway so as to allow the machine to help the human to cooperate with it.

In a study aiming to integrate a DSS into the supervision loop of a continuous power plant, a justification graphic interface was designed for that purpose by Millot, Taborin, and Kamoun (1989). The conflict resolution process was simulated by running both decisional pathways (human and DSS) in parallel, with both paths being inspired by Rasmussen (1983).

In this study, the conflict resolution consisted of looking for "consensus points" in the common deductions of each decision-maker (Figure 10.9). For instance, in a conflict resulting from each decision-maker proposing a different procedure, the first consensus point would be the previous common deduction, or in other words, each decision-maker's diagnosis. A second consensus point would be the set of variables used by each decision-maker to make this diagnosis.

Integrative form and structure, the example of diagnosis in a telecommunication network
In this example, both agents have different and complementary KH, and each performs a subtask Sti resulting from the division of T into complementary subtasks. The task can be decomposed and managed by the coordinator, which can be a third agent or one of the two original agents, all with KHC capabilities.

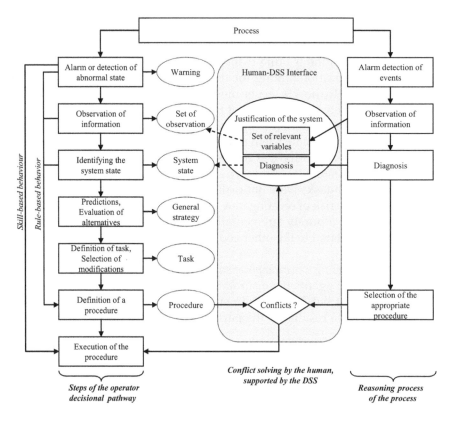

Figure 10.9   Synthesis of the decisional conflict resolution pathway in a debative form of cooperation

As in the other cooperative forms, a horizontal structure, in which each agent has all KHC capabilities, can be imagined. This is generally the case in Human-Human Cooperation, for instance between the pilot and the co-pilot in the plane cockpit. When the KHC capabilities of one agent are only partial, as is usually the case in Human–Machine Cooperation, the structure is a *de facto* hierarchy, either for reasons of competency or legal responsibilities, or both as is the case in ATC. Thus, the designer must respect this hierarchical organization and the natural authority involvement when creating the structure.

Let us consider the form of cooperation found in the diagnosis task, in which two main tasks are essential for quickly focusing on the failures affecting the system:

- The first task is to interpret the data collected on the system and to generate a set of failure hypotheses. The hypotheses are then cross-analyzed to determine a minimal failure set that explains the effects observed.
- The second task is to check the consistency of the hypotheses at each step in the reasoning, according to the system model.

The first task requires a flexible overall view of the system in order to quickly generate consistent failure hypotheses. The necessary Know-How is best suited to human abilities and thus is allocated to the human operator. The second task requires calculating power in order to check the consistency of the hypotheses and to consider multiple alternatives rapidly. The KH needed is best suited to machine abilities and thus is allocated to the machine (Figure 10.10). After the task allocation, a main problem remains: the definition of the means for coordinating both decision-makers' activities during the diagnosis process because, in fact, the partial results must be aggregated. As the tasks are shared, the decision-makers must exchange data and interpret them. Furthermore, both decision-makers must share knowledge about the process (for example, external data); a shared workspace is also needed for coordinating the reasoning processes of the human operator and the machine (Pacaux-Lemoine and Debernard, 2002). The shared knowledge can be represented as a causal network of links between the symptoms and the causes of failure.

An example of a diagnosis task was studied in domestic phone network. Customers having difficulties with their phone call a "hotline" service, and an operator must make a diagnosis. The problem can come from the hardware, or a customer mistake, or from a combination of the hardware and the line itself. A DSS was built to assist the operators of such hotlines and was evaluated in well-defined experimental conditions: in the experimental protocol, the network could have 49 possible phone system failures; these failures were linked to 150 symptoms. The result was a causal network with 500 possible links. In less than three minutes, hotline operators must find one diagnosis among the possible 49, using knowledge of the actual symptoms among 150 possible ones. Operators gather information about the symptoms through direct dialogue with the customer and through test devices. The experiments showed that using integrative cooperation with the DSS, the average number of good correct diagnoses increased from 64 percent to 82 percent (Jouglet and Millot, 2001; Vanderhaegen, Jouglet and Piechowiak, 2004).

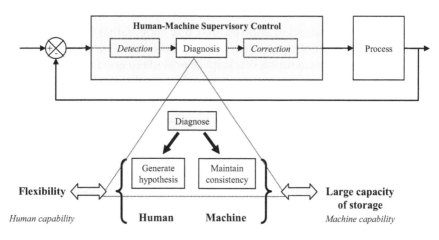

Figure 10.10　Task allocation in human–machine diagnosis

Complex real case, an example in air traffic control
Generally, pure cooperative forms do not exist in the real world; most often, a combination of the three forms is encountered. This is the case in Air Traffic Control (ATC). The AMANDA (Automation and MAN-machine Delegation of Action) project has studied a new version of cooperation between Human Controllers and a

new tool called STAR in the ATC context (Debernard et al., 2002). The objective of the project was to build a Common Frame of Reference, so called Common Work Space (CWS), using the support system STAR (Pacaux-Lemoine and Debernard, 2002). STAR is able to take controller strategies into account in order to calculate precise solutions and then transmits the related commands to the aircraft. The Common Frame of Reference of the air traffic controllers was first identified experimentally by coding their cognitive activities (Guiost et al., 2003).

Here, the human controllers keep the strategic authority to delegate some activities to the system. He/she can delegate a problem to solve to the machine with some constraints represented by his/her strategies for solving a conflict, and can control the machine with the feed-backs that STAR introduce in the CWS.

The CWS was implemented on the graphic interface of the AMANDA platform (Guiost, Debernard, and Millot, 2003). The CWS plays a role similar to a blackboard, displaying the problems to be solved cooperatively. As each agent brings pieces of the solution, the CWS displays the evolution of the solution in real time.

The cooperation between STAR and the human controller can take the three forms (Figure 10.11):

- Debative for building the problems. Here, the problem is called a cluster, and is a set of conflicting aircraft (that is, at least two aircraft in a duel situation (binary conflict) and other aircraft that can interfere with this duel).
- Integrative for resolving a problem using a strategy given by the air traffic controllers. Here, the strategy is modeled as one or several "directives," and a directive can be, for example, "turn AFR365 behind AAL347."
- Augmentative for implementing the calculated solution using the integrative form of cooperation.

The experimental evaluation showed that this cooperative organization allows the controllers to better anticipate air traffic conflicts, and then increasing the level of safety. In addition, the Common Work Space provides a good representation of air traffic conflicts and thus appears to be a good tool for conflict resolution. Furthermore,

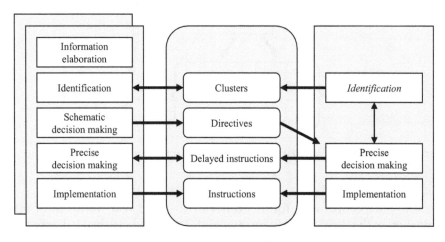

Figure 10.11   AMANDA's Common Work Space

this organization provides a better task sharing between both controllers (RC and PC), which results in a better regulated workload (Guiost, Debernard, Poulain, and Millot, 2003 and 2004).

CONCLUSION

This chapter has proposed a review of the objectives of human engineering and the methods used to enhance the safety of automated systems, focusing on the parameters related to human–machine cooperation—degree of automation, system complexity, and the richness and complexity of the human component—among the different classes of parameters that influence safety. An important way of solutions consists in implementing cooperation between human operators and DSS. This chapter proposes a framework for designing human–machine cooperative systems. To do so, the system needs to be able to deal with the KH and respective KHC of the different agents (human or machine). Three forms of cooperation and the notion of a common frame of reference (COFOR) have been introduced to describe the activities that make up each agent's KHC. These activities can be divided into two groups: MI activities, which correspond to coordination activities, and FG activities, which correspond to a benevolent behavior that facilitates the other agent's goals. In addition, the designer needs to choose the appropriate cooperative structure to accomplish the cooperation. An appropriate MI and KH and a relevant position in a structure provide an agent with the authority: strategic authority if he/it is allowed to share the tasks between the agents, tactical authority if he/it can perform the task in an autonomous manner. For each form of cooperation, we presented several examples related to diverse fields of application: Air Traffic Control, power plant supervision and telecommunication networks. An example of COFOR implementation through a Common Work Space was also presented. The ability of a machine to accomplish coordination tasks in cases of human–machine cooperation was discussed for each example. More generally an agent needs to possess the full authority abilities (MI and KH) to be in an appropriate position of authority in a structure and then perform its tasks efficiently.

REFERENCES

Amalberti, R. (1996). *La conduite des systèmes à risques*. Paris, PUF.

Barr, S.H., Sharda, R. (1997). Effectiveness of decision support systems: development or reliance effect? *Decision Support Systems*, 21, October 2, pp. 133–146.

Billings, C.E. (1992). *Human-centered aircraft automation: A concept and guidelines* (NASA Techn. Mem. 103885). NASA-Ames Research Center.

Boy, G. (1999). Human–computer interaction in aeronautics: a cognitive engineering perspective. *AirandSpace Europe*, 1, 1, January, pp. 33–37(5).

Carlier, X., Hoc, J.M. (1999). Role of a common frame of reference in cognitive cooperation: sharing tasks in Air-Traffic-Control. CSAPC'99. Villeneuve d'Ascq, France, September.

Dearden, A., Harrison, M., Wright, P. (2000). Allocation of function: scenarios, context and the economics of effort. *Int. J. of Human Computers Studies*, 52, 2, February, pp. 289–318.

Decortis, F., Pavard, B. (1994) Communication et coopération: de la théorie des actes de langage à l'approche ethnométhodologique. In Pavard, B. (Ed.), *Systèmes Coopératifs de la modélization à la conception*. Toulouse, France, Octarès.

Debernard, S., Vanderhaegen, F., Millot, P. (1992). *An experimental investigation of dynamic task allocation between air traffic controller and AI system*. 5th IFAC/IFIP/IFORS/IEA Symposium on Analysis, Design and Evaluation of Man-Machine Systems. The Hague, the Netherlands. June 9–11, 1992.

Debernard, S., Hoc, J.-M. (2001). Designing Dynamic Human–Machine Task Allocation in Air Traffic Control: Lessons Drawn From a Multidisciplinary Collaboration. In M.J. Smith, G. Salvendy, D. Harris, R. Koubek (Eds.), *Usability evaluation and Interface design: Cognitive Engineering, Intelligent Agents and Virtual Reality*, volume 1. London: Lawrence Erlbaum Associate Publishers, pp. 1440–1444.

Debernard, S., Cathelain, S., Crevits, I., and Poulain, T. (2002). *AMANDA Project: delegation of tasks in the air traffic control domain*. In M. Blay-Fornarino, A.-M. Pinna-Dery, K. Schmidt, P. Zarraté (Eds.), *Cooperative Systems design*. pp. 173–190. IOS Press. (COOP'2002).

Fadier, E. (1990). Fiabilité humaine: Méthodes d'analyse et domaines d'application. In J. Leplat et G. de Terssac (Eds.), *Les Facteurs humains de la fiabilité dans les systèmes complexes*. Edition Octarès, Marseille (1990).

Fadier, E., Actigny, B. (1994). Etat de l'art dans le domaine de la fiabilité humaine. Ouvrage collectif sous la direction de E. Fadier, Octarès, Paris.

Goettl, B. (1991). *Attention, Workload, and Automation*. NATO ASI series. vol. F73. Automation and Systems Issues in Air Traffic Control. pp. 293–297.

Grote, G., Weik, S., Wäfler, T., Zölch, M. (1995). Criteria for the complementarity allocation of functions in automated work systems and their use in simultaneous engineering projects. *Int. Journal. of Industrial Ergonomics*, 16, October 4–6, pp. 367–382.

Grislin, E., Millot, P. (1999). *Specifying artificial cooperative agents through a synthesis of several models of cooperation*. Seventh European Conference on Cognitive Science Approaches to Process Control, Villeneuve d'Ascq, 21–24 September 1999, France, pp. 73–78.

Guiost, B, Debernard, S., Millot, P. (2003). Definition of a Common Work Space. In 10th International Conference of Human–computer Interaction, Crete, Greece, January 442–446.

Guiost, B., Debernard, S., Poulain, T., Millot, P. (2003). Evaluation of Human-Human Cooperation to design a support tool for Air-Traffic Controller. 22nd European Conference on Human Decision-making and Manual Control, Proceedings of EAM 2003, University of Linköping, Swedish, June 2–4, 2003 (pp. 167–174).

Guiost, B., Debernard, S., Poulain, T., Millot, P. (2004). Evaluation of a new ATC support system based on human machine task delegation. IFAC—HMS 2004, Atlanta, GA—US, September, 7–9.

Hoc, J.M. (1996) Supervision et contrôle de processus: la cognition en situation dynamique. *Presse Universitaire de Grenoble, Collection Sciences and Technologie de la connaissance*.

Hollnagel, E. (1999). *Cognitive Reliability and Errors Analysis Method: CREAM*. Elsevier, Amsterdam.

Hollnagel, E. (2003). Prolegomenon To Cognitive Task Design. *Handbook of Cognitive Task Design*, Erik Hollnagel (Ed.), Lawrence Erlbaum Associates, Publishers, London, 2003, pp. 3–15.

Inagaki, T. (2006). Design of human—machine interactions in light of domain-dependence of human-centered automation. *Cognition, Technology and Work*, 8, 3, pp. 161–167, ISSN:1435–5558.

Jouglet, D., Millot, P. (2001). Performance improvement of Technical diagnosis provided by human–machine cooperation. IFAC Human–Machine Systems: Analysis Design and Evaluation of Human–Machine Systems, Kassel, Germany, September.

Lemoigne, J.L. (1984). *La théorie du système général, théorie de la modélization*. PUF, Paris (re-edited 1994).

Lemoine, M.-P, Debernard, S., Crévits, I., Millot, P. (1996) Cooperation between humans and machines: first results of an experimentation of a multilevel cooperative organization in air traffic control. *Computer Supported Cooperative Work: The journal of Collaborative Computing*, 5, 2–3, pp. 299–321.

Lind, M. (1990). Representing Goals and Functions of Complex Systems: an Introduction to Multilevel Flow Modeling, Technical Report 90-D-381 TU Denmark.

Lind, M. (2003). Making sense of the abstraction hierarchy in the power plant domain. *Cognition Technology and Work*, 5, 2, 67–81.

Millot, P. (1998). Concepts and limits for Human–Machine Cooperation, IEEE SMC CESA'98 Conference, Hammamet, Tunisia, April.

Millot, P., Lemoine, M.P. (1998). An attempt for generic concept toward human–machine cooperation. Paper Presented at IEEE SMC'98. San Diego, US.

Millot, P. (2003). Supervision et Coopération Homme-Machine: approche système. In G. Boy (Ed.) *Ingénierie Cognitive IHM et Cognition*, chapitre 6, pp. 191–221, Paris Hermés.

Millot, P., Debernard, S. (2007). An Attempt for conceptual framework for Human–Machine Cooperation. IFAC/IFIP/IFORS/IEA Conference Analysis Design and Evaluation of Human–machine Systems Seoul Korea, September.

Millot, P., Hoc, J.M. (1997). Human–Machine Cooperation: Metaphor or possible reality? European Conference on Cognitive Sciences, ECCS'97, Manchester UK, April.

Millot, P. (1999). Systèmes Homme-Machine et Automatique. Journées Doctorales d'Automatique JDA'99, Conférence Plénière, Nancy, septembre.

Millot, P., Taborin, V., Kamoun, A. (1989). Two approaches for man-computer Cooperation in supervisory Tasks. 4th IFAC Congress on Analysis Design and Evaluation of Man–Machine Systems, XiAn China, September.

Moray, N., Hiskes, D., Lee, J., and Muir, B. (1995). Trust and Human Intervention in automated Systems." in Hoc, Cacciabue, Hollnagel (Eds.), *Expertise and Technology cognition and Human Computer Interaction*. Lawrence Erlbaum Publ.

Muir, B.M. (1987). Trust between humans and machines, and the design of decision aids. *International Journal of Man-Machine Studies*, 27, pp. 527–539. Academic Press.

Pacaux-Lemoine, M.-P., Debernard, S. (2002). Common work space for human–machine cooperation in air traffic control. *Control Engineering Practice*, 10, 571–576.

Pacaux-Lemoine, M.-P., Debernard, S., Crévits, I., Millot, P. (1996). Cooperation between humans and machines: first results of an experimentation of a multilevel cooperative organization in air traffic control. *Computer Supported Cooperative Work*, 5, pp. 299–321.

Parasuraman, R., Sheridan, T.B., Wickens, C.D. (2000). A Model for Types and Levels of Human Interaction with Automation. *IEEE Transactions on System, Man and Cybernetics*, 30, 3 (May), pp. 286–297.

Polet, P., Vanderhaegen, F., Wieringa, P.A. (2002). Theory of Safety-related violations of a System Barriers, *Cognition Technology and Work*, 4, 171–179.

Polet, P., Vanderhaegen, F., Amalberti, R. (2003). Modeling Border-line tolerated conditions of use (BTCUs) and associated risks. *Safety Science*, 41, 111–136.

Rajaonah, B. (2006). Rôle de la confiance de l'opérateur dans son interaction avec une machine autonome sur la coopération homme-machine. Thèse de doctorat de l'Université Paris 8. 27 février 2006.

Rajaonah, B., Tricot, N., Anceaux, F., Millot, P. (2008). Role of intervening variables in driver-ACC cooperation, *International Journal of Human Computer Studies*, 66, 185–197.

Rasmussen, J. (1983). Skills, Rules and Knowledge: signals, signs and symbols and other distinctions in human performance models: *IEEE Transaction on Systems, Man and Cybernetics* SMC, 3.

Rasmussen, J. (1985). The role of hierarchical knowledge representation in decision-making and system management. *IEEE Transaction on Systems, Man and Cybernetics*, SMC-15, 2.

Rasmussen, J. (1991). Modeling distributed decision-making. in Rasmussen J., Brehmer B., and Leplat J. (Eds.), *Distributed decision-making: cognitive models for cooperative work*, pp. 111–142, John Willey and Sons, Chichester, UK.

Rasmussen, J. (1997). Risk management in a dynamic society: a modeling problem. *Safety Sciences*, 27, 2/3, 183–213.

Reason, J. (1986). Intentions, errors and machines: a cognitive science perspective. *Aspects of consciousness and awareness*, Bielefeld, W. Germany, December.

Reason, J. (1993). *Human error.* Cambridge University Press. (1990.Version française traduite par J.M. Hoc, *L'erreur humaine*, PUF.)

Riera, B., Debernard, S. (2003). Basic Cognitive Principles Applied to the Design of Advanced Supervisory Systems for Process Control. In *Handbook of Cognitive Task Design*, Erik Hollnagel (Ed.), London: Lawrence Erlbaum Associates, Publishers, pp. 255–281.

Rome, F., Cabon, P., Favresse, A., Mollard, R., Figarol, S., Hasquenoph, B. (2006). Human Factors Issues of TCAS: a Simulation Study. International Conference on Human–computer Interaction in Aeronautics (HCI–Aero 2006), Seattle, Washington, September 20–22.

Schmidt, K. (1991). Cooperative work: a conceptual framework. In J. Rasmussen, B. Brehmer, and J. Leplat (Eds.), *Distributed decision-making: cognitive models for cooperative work*. Chichester, UK: John Willey and Sons, pp. 75–110.

Sheridan, T.B. (1984). Supervisory Control of Remote Manipulators, Vehicles and Dynamic Processes: Experiments in Command and Display Aiding. *Advances in Man-machine Systems Researches*, 1.

Sheridan, T.B. (1985). Forty-Five Years of Man-Machine Systems: History and Trends. 2nd IFAC Conference Analysis, Design and Evaluation of Man-Machine Systems, Varese, September.

Sheridan, T.B. (1992). *Telerobotics, Automation, and Human Supervisory Control.* MIT Press: Cambridge, MA.

Van der Vlugt M., Wieringa P.A. (2003). Searching for ways to recover from fixation: proposal for a different view-point. Cognitive Science Approach for Process Control CSAPC'03, Amsterdam, September.

Vanderhaegen, F. (1999). APRECIH: a human unreliability analysis method-application to railway system. *Control Engineering Practice*, 7, 1395–1403.

Vanderhaegen, F. (2001). A non-probabilistic prospective and retrospective human reliability analysis method—application to railway system. *Reliability Engineering and System Safety*, 71, pp. 1–13.

Vanderhaegen, F., Crévits, I., Debernard, S., Millot, P. (1994). Human–machine cooperation: toward an activity regulation assistance for different air traffic control levels. *Int. J. Human–Computer Interaction*, 6, pp. 65–104 (Salvendy, Smith, Oshima (Eds.) Norwood, NJ: Ablex Publishing Corporation).

Vanderhaegen, F., Jouglet, D., Piechowiak, S. (2004). Human-reliability analysis of cooperative redundancy to support diagnosis. *IEEE Transactions on Reliability*, 53, pp. 458–464.

Villemeur, A. (1988). *Sûreté de fonctionnement des systèmes industriels: fiabilité, facteur humain, informatization.* Eyrolles: Paris.

11

Formal Description Techniques for Human–Machine Interfaces: Model-Based Approaches for the Design and Evaluation of Dependable Usable Interactive Systems

David Navarre, Philippe Palanque, Célia Martinie,
Marco A.A. Winckler, and Sandra Steere

While a significant effort is currently being undertaken by the Human–Computer Interaction community in order to apply and extend current User Centered Design methodologies, very little has been done to improve the reliability of software offering these kinds of interaction techniques. As these new interaction techniques are currently more and more used in the field of command and control safety critical systems, possibilities of incidents or accidents increase. In addition, at design time, the non-reliability of interactive software can even jeopardize usability evaluation activities by producing unexpected or undesired behaviors. This is critical as this activity is at the center of design processes of usable interactive systems. Lastly, iterative design processes promote multiple designs through evolvable prototypes in order to accommodate requirements changes and to incorporate results from usability evaluations. Such iterative processes reduce reliability of the final system by lack of global and structured design. This chapter presents a multi-perspective approach for the design of interactive safety-critical systems called the "Generic Integrated Modeling Framework" (GIMF). The goal is to propose techniques, methods and tools for model-based design of interactive systems while taking into account human and system-related erroneous behavior. Our research proposes a model-based approach for supporting the representation of multiple viewpoints on the socio-technical context of safety critical interactive systems. The multiple views include operators' tasks, entire system graphical and behavioral descriptions, training program, incidents, and accidents descriptions. The objective of the tools supporting the GIMF is to allow designers to assess the compatibility of the various views and to support the scalability issues raised by real size systems.

INTRODUCTION

The design of a usable, reliable, safe, and error-tolerant safety-critical interactive system is a goal that is hard (actually impossible totally, because we cannot guarantee either of these characteristics) to achieve because of the unpredictability of the humans involved, but can be more closely attainable by taking into account information from previous known situations. One such usually available and particularly pertinent source is the outcome of an incident or accident investigation.

With the objective of increasing safety, in safety-critical interactive systems, previous research in the field aimed at trying to eliminate the error completely by identifying its source. It has now been widely accepted however that human "errors" are inevitable due to the idiosyncratic nature of humans and we must instead try to manage errors. The perspective of blame has also changed from isolating an individual operator to having a wider outlook on the organization as a whole. However, the broader the perspective, the more information has to be gathered and thus making it more complex not only to organize it but also to reason about it.

Beyond that central aspect of human error (work such as [35] report that 80 percent–90 percent of accidents in industry are attributed to human error) other aspects are playing the role of contributing factors and thus must be dealt with accordingly. Amongst them, the most prominent ones are the usability of the system, its dependability, and the training of operators.

The design and implementation of such systems requires the definition of specific methods, able to deal with usability, dependability and safety. For many years, research in human–computer interaction engineering intended to offer such methods for systems involving simple interaction techniques. The most prominent method for designing for usability is called User Centered Design (UCD) and promotes systematic involvement of users both in the design and evaluation phases. In extension to these UCD approaches and in order to deal with these complex combinations of factors and systems, we promote the use of formal methods and model based design as a way of representing these components and their interrelations whether it is during design, construction, or investigation.

This chapter proposes a multidisciplinary generic integrated modeling framework for the design of safety critical interactive systems. The goal is to propose means (such as model based design techniques, notations, tools, and methods) that allow people involved in the process to take into account and manage erroneous human and system behavior. While designing interactive systems, the use of formal description techniques (FDT) is of great help because it provides non-ambiguous, complete, and concise descriptions. The advantages of using such a FDT is widened if it is provided by formal analysis techniques that allow to prove properties about the design, thus giving an early verification to the designer before the application is actually implemented.

This is not a new goal for the field, and, in order to tackle these issues, modeling processes and techniques have been defined and applied widely in the field of safety critical systems. Model-based development (MBD) is a developing trend in the domain of software engineering (MDA Guide version 1.0.1 2003) advocating the specification and design of software systems from declarative models [1]. It relies on the use of explicit models and provides the ability to represent and simulate diverse abstract views that together make up a "system", without the need to fulfill its implementation. It is widely accepted within the community that models are needed for the design of safety critical interactive systems; this is to be able to understand issues such as safety and resilience and to think about how safety can be ensured, maintained, and improved [17].

We have developed an approach that supports the integration of information relating to human and system-related erroneous behavior in models (principally the task and system models) by feeding models with information from human error analyses, incident and accident investigation analyses and barrier analysis. Incorporating such data significantly increases the size of the models, thus we also define model patterns for error tolerance as a means of dealing with these complexities. Furthermore, we have also developed techniques and tools for dealing with interactive systems dependability and representation of operators tasks. Lastly, we also include the training program development process in this approach, as it closes the loop between the models and the users of the system, by educating them, in a personalized way. Such training takes full advantage of the other models thus connecting tasks, system, and previous failures. We believe this perspective extends the general boundaries of model based development (MBD), by taking into account additional information related to previous experiences of failure. The ultimate goal is improvement of the design process with the aim of producing safer, more reliable, and more usable safety-critical interactive systems.

The first section presents in details the problems that have been briefly introduced above and identifies key challenges we are trying to address. The second section proposes the generic integrated modeling framework, while the third section illustrates the framework on an interactive cockpit application called WXR which stands for Weather Radar System. The conclusions are presented in the last section together with the identification of the limitations and the perspectives to this work.

PROBLEMS TO BE ADDRESSED

According to the recurring desire of increasing the bandwidth between the interactive system and the users, more sophisticated interaction techniques are continuously being proposed. Such proposals are usually presented in conferences such as ACM CHI (Human Factors in Computing Systems) or UIST (User Interfaces Software and Technology) with a focus on the innovation and on the usability evaluation of interactive systems proposing such interaction techniques. Researchers presenting those interaction techniques usually have to build their own user interface tools to be able to implement the interaction technique they want to design and evaluate.

For this reason, they also present prototypes of User Interface Tools (often also called User Interface Management Systems) to show what language and development environment are needed to develop the proposed interaction technique.

Once published, it remains a long way for these innovative interaction techniques to reach the maturity level required for dissemination in industry as several problems remains to be solved. These problems are detailed in the following sections.

- The first problem is related to the scalability issue where research contributions must be able to go from demonstrational prototypes to real-size applications.
- The second problem is related to the reliability issue, that is, to find ways to guarantee the correct functioning of the interactive system. Issues such as verification, validation, and exhaustive testing are the only possible ways to solve this problem.
- The third problem is related to the link between User Interface tools and the development process of interactive systems. The issue is here to be able to integrate such tools within development processes and other software development tools currently used in industry.
- The last problem is related to lessons learned and, on one hand, how to systematically explore options when building an interactive system and, on the other hand, how to provide way justifying choices made at design or implementation time.

This remaining of this chapter presents with additional details the set of requirements that UI tools have to meet to be applicable in the field of safety critical interactive software.

Scalability Issue

Providing the entire specification of an interactive application is now increasingly considered as a requirement in the field of software for safety critical systems due to their increasing use as the main control interface for such systems. As the user interface part of command and control systems may represent a huge quantity of code, User Interface Tools must provide ways to address this complexity. Support only dealing with code management is not enough and there is thus a critical need for addressing this complexity at a higher level of abstraction.

This chapter argues that one possible way to deal with these issues is to follow the same path as in the field of software engineering where modeling activities and model-based approaches take the lead with standards like UML. In the field of human computer interaction model-based approaches have been heavily criticized. For instance, at a panel at UIST 94 [38] Dan Olsen wrote *"There have been two major problems with this approach [model based ones]. The first is that we always seem to be modeling the interface styles of the previous generation of user interfaces. The second is that the models developed in some way limit the kind of user interface that is possible."*

Recent contributions in the field of model-based approaches have been explicitly addressing this issue of coping with new interaction technique (such as the so-called Post-WIMP [19]) and can be found, for instance, in the proceedings of Design Specification and Verification of Interactive Systems (DSVIS) conference series such as DSVIS 2008 for instance [12].

Reliability

It is now widely agreed upon that, in order to build easier to use and easier to learn systems, generic, and specific functionalities have to be offered to the users of such systems. However, increasing the number of functionalities by adding, for instance, undo/redo mechanisms and WYSIWYG facilities, increases the likelihood of system crashes. In particular, the current reliability level of software suites proposed by main software companies clearly show that building reliable interactive software is still a challenge for software development teams.

While rebooting the systems is the most reasonable action in order to recover from a software crash this is totally unacceptable in real-time safety critical systems where people life is at stake.

The reason for putting some effort in the use and the deployment of formal description techniques lies in the fact that they are the only means for both modeling in a precise and unambiguous way all the components of an interactive application (presentation, dialogue, and functional core) and to propose techniques for reasoning about (and also verifying) the models.

Applying formal description techniques can be beneficial during the various phases of the development process from the early phases (requirements analysis and elicitation) to the later ones including evaluation (testing).

Verification techniques aim at providing ways for ensuring systems reliability prior to implementation. User Interface Tools that would provide such capabilities would empower developers by offering means for reasoning about their systems at a higher level of abstraction. For instance, verification techniques over a formal description technique make it possible to assess properties, such as whatever state the system is in, at least one interactive object is enabled; mutual exclusion of actions; attainability of specific states [28].

Model-based approaches [1] featuring formal description techniques can provide support to developers in the later phases of the development process where the intrinsic nature of interactive systems makes them very hard to address properly otherwise. For instance, the event-based nature of interactive systems makes them impossible to test without tool support for the generation of the possible test cases. Work in this field is still preliminary but contributions are available for WIMP interaction techniques providing means for regression testing [1] and coverage criteria [22].

Development Process

The User Interface is only one component of an interactive system. Research in the field of HCI has been contributing to development processes but mainly addressing the UI of such systems. For instance, development processes promoted by HCI community as the ones presented in [8] pp. 206–207 or in [16] pp. 102 only deal with the user interface part. Prototyping is now recognized as a cornerstone of the successful construction of interactive systems as it allows making users at the center of the development process. However, iterative or incremental prototyping tends to produce low quality software as no specification or global design and understanding is undertaken. User Interface tools should be able to support this incremental and iterative prototyping activities by making as simple as possible for developers to modify their prototypes. Certification is a phase of the development process specific to safety critical systems. Developers of such systems are in charge of demonstrating that the system is "acceptably safe" before certification authorities grant regulatory approval.

Without adequate integration within development processes dealing with such as the one described in DO-178B [10] that explicitly states the various stages to be followed throughout development process to prepare the certification phase, User Interface Tools would be inadequate to deal with the new challenges offered by safety critical interactive software.

Design Rationale

Systematic exploration of options and traceability of choices made throughout the development process have to be supported. Current User Interface tools mainly focus on the result of the process, that is, the actual system to be built. We believe that tools supporting argumentation about why a given option has been selected or rejected would significantly improve reusability and reliability of designs.

However, our experience with the development of safety critical interactive systems has shown that, in order to be more efficient, Design Rationale must be heavily tool-supported. We have already proposed notations and tools to support such rationalizing activities in the context of safety critical interactive systems [32] and [20] but we don't address that in this chapter due to space constraints.

A GENERIC INTEGRATED MODELING FRAMEWORK

Our research on a multi-perspective method for the design of safety critical interactive systems aims at proposing model based design techniques that allow taking into account and managing erroneous human and system behavior. The general idea is to bring together, in a unified framework, four complementary aspects for building reliable interactive systems design:

- Human factors issues (including human performance models, human error, task analysis, and modeling) within a User Centered Design framework [15].
- A formal description of the system (including the interactive and the non-interactive part of the system as well as the barriers that might have been added to it).
- Incidents/accidents representation.
- The training programme.

One of the key aspects of the approach is to support consistency between these multiple perspectives. Indeed, task modeling and system modeling are often performed by experts from different disciplines. It is unlikely that a human factors specialist will design the task model and go on to design the system model. Therefore, it is probable that there will be a mismatch between the two; that is, a task may have been incorporated into the task model that cannot be performed with the system model. We therefore define mechanisms for ensuring consistency between models. For tasks and system models this allows designers, for instance, to check the system complacency and ability to handle all human tasks necessary for achieving a given goal. For incidents models and system models it supports the activity of assessing that a previous accident or incident cannot re-occur [1].

We present a generic integrated modeling framework to attain this goal. By generic, we mean that the approach can be applied to safety-critical interactive systems other than those used for our research (for example the mining domain or cockpit application design).

Figure 11.1 illustrates the generic integrated modeling framework which presents as a summary and in a single diagram, the set of information, data, and processes required for the design of safety safety-critical interactive systems.

The framework represents a cyclic and iterative process for design. The process can commence from either the requirements capturing phase, the system modeling phase, or the task modeling phase. The emboldened arrows illustrate the iterative procedure that is to be followed though additional processes such as qualitative evaluation and the safety modeling phase can be used to inform the procedure. The training program development process is also included in the framework as a step of the whole framework. The solid lines represent processes while the dotted/dashed lines represent information. The only-dotted lines represent processes including information.

The following paragraphs are based on the five principle phases of the framework. The sixth phase (labeled 6 in Figure 11.1), requirements capturing, has been included in the framework as it is also an important modeling phase of systems design, as well as for safety-critical interactive systems design. However, requirements' modeling is a research field within itself and is considered out of scope of our current research contribution and we use any "standard" notation such as temporal logics for describing them.

The following paragraphs provide an overview of the four main phases with larger diagrams of each phase for increased legibility. The arrows connecting various phases and specific analyses cannot be explained here until the full contents of the phases have been explained.

System Modeling

Phase 1 System Modeling (Figure 11.2). For the system modeling we use the PetShop environment [5] and the Interactive Cooperative Objects (ICO) formalism [29]. The phase is divided into two parts: the modeling of functional behavior and of safety-related behavior. After modeling the system, we perform a socio-technical barrier analysis [3] based on accident report data and a technical barrier analysis based on user interaction hazard analysis on the system model to eventually reduce the possibility of erroneous events. This coupling of barriers and system and what it brings to increase the reliability of an interactive system can be found in [3]. The main point is that it supports fast integration of changes in the system behavior without redesigning it completely.

ICO notation
ICO (Interactive Cooperative Objects) is a formal description technique devoted to the specification of interactive systems. It uses concepts borrowed from the object-oriented approach (dynamic instantiation, classification, encapsulation, inheritance, client/server relationship) to describe the structural or static aspects of interactive systems, and uses high-level Petri nets to describe their dynamic or

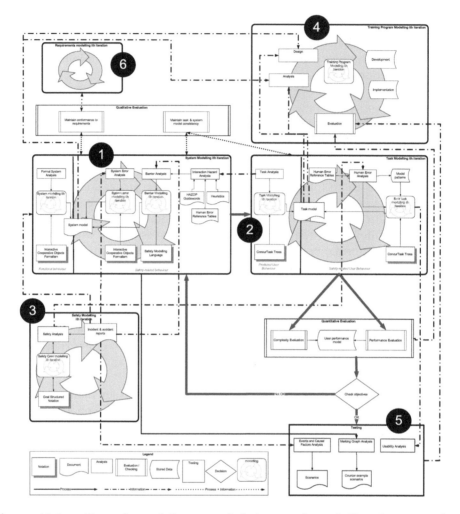

Figure 11.1   Overview of the generic integrated modeling framework

Note: Phases are detailed later.

behavioral aspects. ICOs are used to provide a formal description of the dynamic behavior of an interactive application. An ICO specification fully describes the potential interactions that users may have with the application. An ICO description encompasses both the "input" aspects of the interaction (that is, how user actions impact on the inner state of the application, and which actions are enabled at any given time) and its "output" aspects (that is, when and how the application displays information relevant to the user).

In ICO, an object is an entity featuring four components: a cooperative object which describes the behavior of the object, a presentation part, and two functions (the activation function and the rendering function) which make the link between the cooperative object and the presentation part. A more detailed description of the notation and the tool can be found in [26].

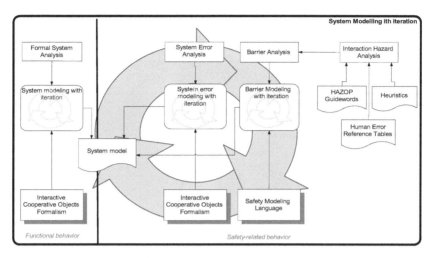

Figure 11.2   System modeling phase of the generic integrated modeling framework

Task Modeling

Phase 2 Task Modeling (Figure 11.3). This phase is also divided in two: the first describes the predicted behavior of the user and results in an analysis of user tasks and activities. The second concerns the modeling of user deviations with respect to predicted behavior. For this phase, we use the HAMSTERS (Human-centered Assessment and Modeling to Support Task Engineering for Resilient Systems) notation presented at the beginning of the case study (see section 5). To take into account erroneous user behavior, our task modeling is extended by reusable subtasks (called error patterns) resulting from human error analyses. The method for integrating "standard" task models and task models representing potential deviations are described in [28]. We present here HAMSTERS with more details than the other notations as it has not been presented in other papers. Prior to defining it we used CTTE [33] which, unfortunately, was not possible to integrate with our system model.

HAMSTERS (which stands for Human-centered Assessment and Modeling to Support Task Engineering for Resilient Systems) is a task-modeling language with a supporting tool. It is widely inspired by existing notations and tools and takes advantages from all of them (as illustrated by its meta-model in Figure 11.4).

In HAMSTERS, tasks are special nodes in a hierarchical structure that can be of different types (as illustrated by Figure 11.5):

- Abstract task is a task that involves sub tasks of different types.
- System task describes a task performed by the system only.
- User task is an abstract task performed by the user. It has the following specialization Motor task (a physical activity), Cognitive task (calculation, decision-making, analysis ...), Perceptive task (perception of alert for instance).
- Interactive task describes an interaction between the User and the System, which can be refined into Input task when the user provides input to the System, Output task when the system provides an output to the user and Input Output task is a mix of both but in an atomic way.

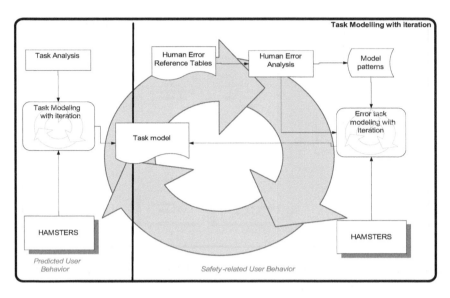

Figure 11.3   Task modeling phase of the generic integrated modeling framework

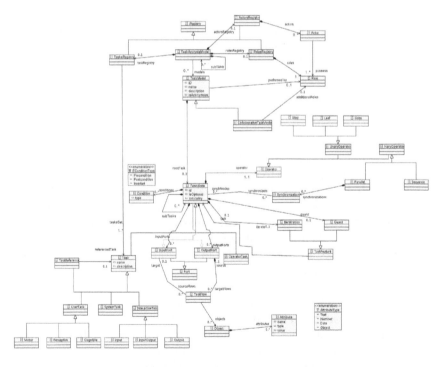

Figure 11.4   Meta-model of the HAMSTERS notation

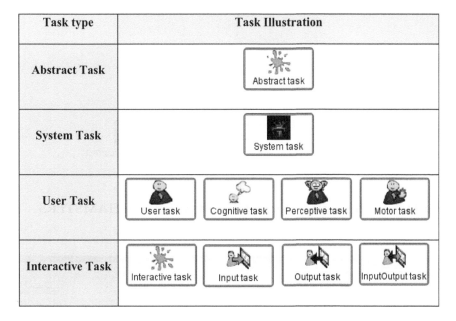

Task type	Task Illustration
Abstract Task	Abstract task
System Task	System task
User Task	User task · Cognitive task · Perceptive task · Motor task
Interactive Task	Interactive task · Input task · Output task · InputOutput task

Figure 11.5   Illustration of the task type within HAMSTERS

Each task model in HAMSTERS is associated with a well defined role which can in turn have multiple models describing the different tasks it can perform. Roles are also mandatory to describe collaborative models.

In HAMSTERS, the notion of objects (defined through a set of attributes as illustrated by Figure 11.6) represents part of the world handled by tasks. Tasks are defined to execute a set of actions that aims basically at manipulating those objects. Objects are defined by a set of attributes.

HAMSTERS offers two types of relationships between tasks: the first one describes how tasks are related to other tasks and the second one represents the information flow between tasks (as illustrated by Figure 11.7) where the PIN entered in the first task is conveyed to the next task by means of input and output ports).

Similarly to MAD [36] and CTT [33], qualitative time is expressed using LOTOS-like temporal operators attached to the parent node. Quantitative time is represented by expressing task duration (such as with CTT) and delay before tasks availability.

The implementation of HAMSTERS was done with the objective of making it easily extendable and it results in a CASE tool that contributes to the engineering of task models. In a nutshell, HAMSTERS is open source, featuring a task simulator and provides a dedicated API for observing editing and simulation events. It results in a CASE tool, illustrated by Figure 11.8 that contributes to ease engineering task modeling.

Figure 11.6   Illustration of objects within HAMSTERS

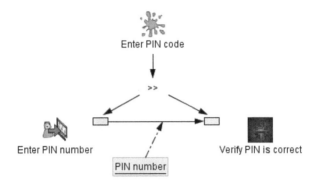

Figure 11.7   Illustration of task relationship within HAMSTERS

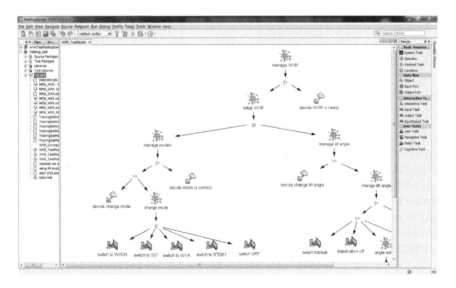

Figure 11.8   Illustration of the HAMSTERS CASE tool

Safety Modeling

Phase 3 Safety Modeling (Figure 11.9). In this phase, we propose a safety analysis by exploiting the Safety Cases using the Goal Structuring Notation (GSN) [9] in order to inform the system model. Phase 3 exploits further information including incident and accident reports. It is clear from the number of arrows (4) exiting the incident and accident report block of the framework, that this information is central to our proposed approach since a significant aspect of safety is to make sure successive versions of a system do not allow the same incidents or accidents to be reproduced.

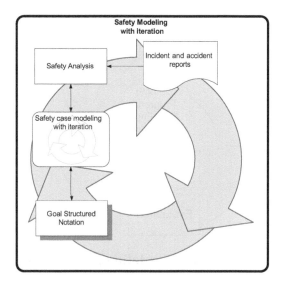

Figure 11.9 **Safety modeling phase of the generic integrated modeling framework**

Training

Phase 4 Training Program Design (Figure 11.10). In this phase, we propose to follow an instructional design process because it has proven to produce effective training programs, usually applied for safety critical systems. Instructional Design and Technology uses a systematic approach to analyze, design, implement, evaluate, and maintain training programs as detailed in [1] and [37]. Among the many methods and processes that are currently in use, the first one to be widely exploited was Instructional Systems Development (ISD) [40] [23] [34] which has been further developed in many ramifications such as, for instance, the process called Systematic Approach to Training (SAT) [39] [23] [27] (see [1] for a detailed explanation of the relationship between ISD and SAT). Most of them are based on a detailed process called the Analyze Design Develop Implement Evaluate (ADDIE) model. A complete description of the ADDIE steps in Figure 11.10 can be found in [1].

The first phase is the Analysis that encompasses analysis of both the system and the tasks. One of the key features of these training approaches is the importance of Instructional Task Analysis [14], particularly the decomposition of a job in tasks and sub-tasks in order to decide what knowledge and skills must be acquired by the trainee. This fits well with the model-based approach, which relies on the system and task models and allows reusing them for the training analysis purpose. The Analysis phase also includes the selection of performance measures and instructional settings.

The second phase is the Design of the training program with the development of objectives and tests, the identification of learning steps and prerequisites, and the training structuring. All of these parts also rely on the system and task models. Development is the third phase of the process and completes the training platform. The fourth phase is the Implementation of the training program and comprises the execution of the training. These different phases provide information for the Training Program evaluation, which is performed throughout the entire process.

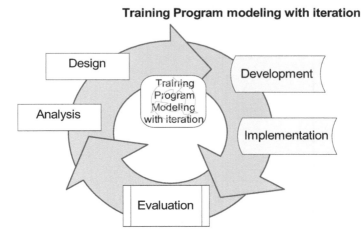

Figure 11.10   Training program modeling phase of the generic integrated modeling framework

Furthermore, our integrated framework and associated tools enable the co-execution of the system and task models (detailed in the Illustration section). It is a value-added input for the entire Training Program development process. PetShop and HAMSTERS tools (described in previous sections and put in action in the Illustration section) enable to co-execute both the system and tasks models for a given scenario. They allow to experience a particular scenario of interaction with the system and to record a log of the simulated interaction, in order to analyze a posteriori the sequence of played system and user actions (interleaved or not) during the session. As a matter of fact, this co-execution is able to contribute to the Analysis and Design phases by providing information to estimate the definition of team structure and size, the cognitive, perceptive, and motor resources consumption (fatigue, team organization hand over, on call duty), but it is also able to contribute to the Evaluation phase by logging this session executed by the trainee. Data extracted from the simulation and from its observation can be processed into different kind of metrics which will be reused to enhance the framework.

Testing

Phase 4 Testing (Figure 11.11). This phase concerns the verification of prototypes and models. We use incident and accident reports to perform events and causal factors analyses. We also use the ICO system models to perform marking graph analyses. The graphs are used to systematically explore all of the possible scenarios leading to an accident which described in terms of states in the system model. The techniques serve two purposes. First, to ensure that "modified" system model does not allow the same sequence of events that led to the accident, and second, our approach can be used to reveal further scenarios that could eventually lead to non-desirable system states.

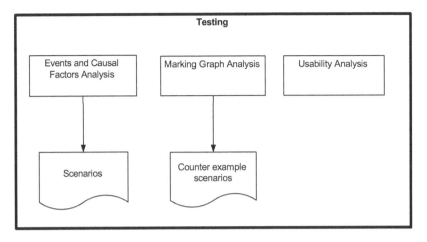

Figure 11.11   Testing phase of the generic integrated modeling
                framework

ILLUSTRATION OF THE FRAMEWORK

To illustrate our approach, we use the example of an interactive cockpit application (see Figure 11.12) called WXR (for Weather Radar System) that allows the crewmembers to manage the weather radar.

Figure 11.12   Snapshot of the WXR application in civil commercial
                aircrafts

The lower part of Figure 11.12 is dedicated to the adjustment of the weather radar orientation (called tilt selection), while the upper part allows the crew members changing the mode of the weather radar (independently from the tilt selection).

This example is firstly used to illustrate the two notations we use within our framework (HAMSTERS for task modeling and ICO for system modeling) and lastly it illustrates how it provides this framework with basic bricks to support co-modeling activities. Obviously, the work presented here may be extended to other system and task notations provided that they allow an equivalent level of description.

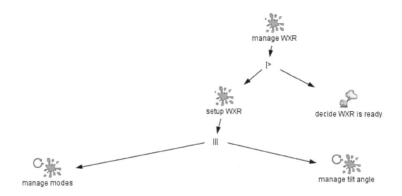

Figure 11.13   High-level set of tasks for weather radar management

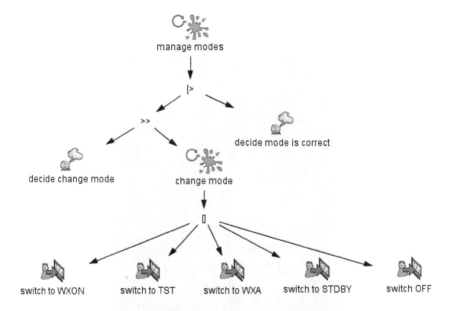

Figure 11.14   Detailed set of subtasks for "manage modes" task

Task Modeling Using HAMSTERS for WXR Application

As shown in Figure 11.13, the high-level tasks for managing the weather radar (that is, "manage WXR") are decomposed into two tasks, "setup WXR" and "decide WXR is ready." Task "setup WXR" represents the two activities of adjusting the weather radar orientation and mode, while task "decide WXR is ready" may interrupt it at any time. The rounded arrows, one at the left of task "manage modes" and one at the left of "manage tilt angle," indicate that these tasks are iterative and that they can be performed repeatedly until task "decide WXR is ready" interrupts them. The two abstract tasks "manage modes" and "manage tilt angle" are detailed in Figures 11.14 and 11.15. In Figure 11.14, the iterative task "manage modes" is activated by the cognitive task "decide change mode" to represent the decision activity performed by the crew members before interacting with the system. The crew members can switch between five modes of the weather radar itself (on, test, focus alert, standby, and off).

The cognitive task "decide mode is correct" may interrupt the iterative process of changing the mode at any time.

As shown in Figure 11.15, the crew members may adjust the orientation (the tilt angle) of the weather radar when required (the main idea being to use this feature only if necessary as, most of the time, the default behavior is the correct one). The cognitive task "decide change tilt angle," which represents the decision activity performed by the crew members, activates the task "change tilt angle." There are three possible modes for tilt angle selection: auto adjustment, auto-stabilization and setting up manually the tilt angle (represented by the three tasks "select manual," "stabilization off" and "angle editing"). These modes can only be accessed sequentially. Indeed, for changing the tilt angle manually the pilot must first disable the auto mode ("select manual"), then disable stabilization ("stabilization off") and finally edit the angle ("angle editing").

The task "edit angle" is the activity of modifying the tilt angle and may be interrupted at any time by the task "stabilization on," which turns the weather radar back to the auto stabilization mode. Modifying the tilt angle manually implies three sub-tasks:

- Cognitive task "decide angle" is the choice of a value by the crew members.
- Interactive input task "edit angle" is the interaction for editing the value in the aircraft system.
- Interactive output task "check updated value" provides crew members with output from the system to check that the entered value has been taken into account.

System Models Using ICO

This section refers to the system modeling phase (see Figure 11.2) of the proposed generic integrated modeling framework.

Modeling the WXR system using ICO is quite simple as interactive applications in the area of interactive cockpits are of type WIMP. This means that interaction takes only place through a set of widget. Hereafter we present the ICO modeling technique including the dialog part and the presentation part (according to *Arch* model [27]) and two functions (the activation and the rendering functions) that are connecting these two parts.

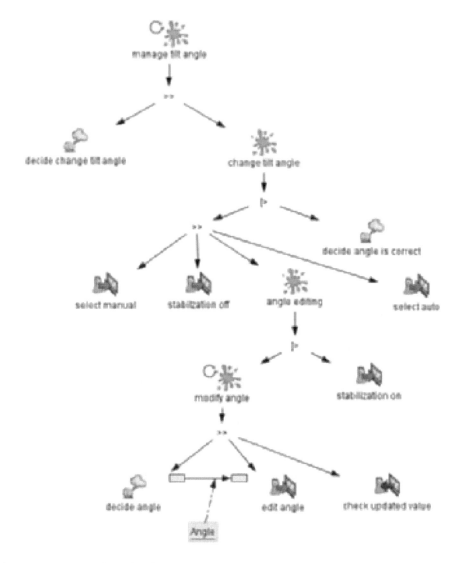

Figure 11.15   Subtasks for "manage tilt angle" abstract task

Dialog part as an interactive cooperative object
In ICO, the dialog part encompasses the following features:

- Links between user events from the presentation part and event handlers from the Interactive Cooperative Objects.
- Links between user events availability and event-handlers availability, that is, the availability of widgets on the user interface.
- Links between state changes in the Interactive Cooperative Object and rendering of that state on the user interface.

Figure 11.16 shows the entire behavior of page WXR which is made of two non-connected parts:

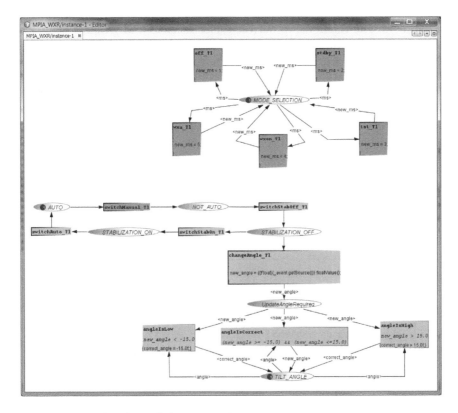

Figure 11.16   Behavior of the page WXR

- The upper part of the Petri net handles events received from the 5 CheckButtons (see Figure 11.12 for the presentation part). Even though they are CheckButtons, the actual behavior of that application makes it only possible to select only one of them at a time. The current selection (an integer value from 1 to 5) is stored in the token of place MODE_SELECTION and corresponds to one the possible selected CheckButtons (OFF, STDBY, TST, WXON, WXA). The token is modified by the transitions (new_ms = 3, for instance) using variables on the incoming and outgoing arcs as formal parameters of the transitions.
- The Petri net in the lower part handles events from the 2 PicturePushButton and the EditBoxNumeric. Interacting with these buttons will change the state of the application. In the current state, this part of the application is in the automatic state (that is, a token is in place AUTO and a token is place TILT_ANGLE).

Linking dialog to presentation part
The Presentation part of an object corresponds to its visual appearance. In a WIMP interface the Presentation consists of set of widgets organized in a set of windows. Each widget is a mean for the user to interact with the interactive system (*user → system interaction*) and/or a mean for the system to provide feedback to the user (*system → user interaction*).

When considering WIMP interfaces, user → system interaction (inputs) only takes place through widgets. Each user action on a widget may trigger one of the ICOs event handlers. The relationship between user services and widgets is fully stated by the activation function that associates each event from the presentation part to the event handler to be triggered and to the corresponding rendering method for representing the activation or the deactivation.

When a user event is triggered, the Activation function is notified and requires the ICO to fire the corresponding event handler embedding the value received in the user event. When the state of an event handler changes (that is, becomes available or unavailable), the Activation function is notified (via the observer and event mechanism presented above) and calls the corresponding activation rendering method from the presentation part embedding the values from the event handler.

The activation function is expressed through a mapping to an ICO behavior element. Figure 11.17 shows the activation function for page WXR.

User Events	Event handler	Activation Rendering
asked_off	Off	setWXRModeSelectEnabled
asked_stdby	Stdby	setWXRModeSelectEnabled
asked_tst	Tst	setWXRModeSelectEnabled
asked_wxon	Wxon	setWXRModeSelectEnabled
asked_wxa	Wxa	setWXRModeSelectEnabled
asked_auto	switchAUTO	setWXRTiltSelectionEnabled
asked_stabilization	switchSTABILIZATION	setWXRTiltSelectionEnabled
asked_changeAngle	changeAngle	setWXRTiltSelectionEnabled

Figure 11.17   Activation Function of the page WXR

Each line in this table describes the three objects taking part in the activation process. The first line, for instance, describes the relationship between the user event ask_off (produced by clicking on the CheckButton OFF), the event handler off (represented in the model by transition off_t1) and the activation rendering method setWXRModeSelectEnabled from the presentation part. More precisely:

- When the event handler off becomes enabled, the activation function calls the activation rendering method setWXRModeSelectEnabled providing it with data about the enabling of the event handler. On the physical interaction side, this method call leads to the activation of the corresponding widget (that is, presenting the checkButton OFF as available to the user).
- When the button OFF of the presentation part is pressed, the presentation part raises the event called asked_off. This event is received by the activation function which requires the behavior part to fire the event handler off (that is, the transition off_T1 in the Petri net of Figure 11.16).

System → user interaction (outputs) present to the user the state changes that occur in the system. The rendering function maintains the consistency between the internal state of the system and its external appearance by reflecting system states changes on the user interface. Indeed, when the state of the Interactive Cooperative Object changes (for example, marking changes for at least one place), the Rendering function is notified (via the observer and event mechanism) and calls the corresponding rendering method from the presentation part with tokens or firing values as parameters. In a similar way as for the Activation function, the Rendering function is fully expressed as an ICO class.

Figure 11.18 presents the rendering function of the WXR application in a table where each line features the objects taking part in the rendering process. For instance, the first line shows the link between the place MODE_SELECTION, the event linked to this place (a token enters the place) and the rendering method showModeSelection from the presentation part component. It can be read as follows: when a token enters the place MODE_SELECTION, the rendering function is notified and the rendering method showModeSelection is invoked with data concerning the new marking of the place that is used as parameters of the rendering method.

ObCS Node name	ObCS event	Rendering method
MODE_SELECTION	token_enter	showModeSelection
TILT_ANGLE	token_enter	showTiltAngle
AUTO	marking_reset	showAuto
AUTO	token_enter	showAuto
AUTO	token_remove	showAuto
STABILIZATION_ON	marking_reset	showStab
STABILIZATION_ON	token_enter	showStab
STABILIZATION_ON	token_remove	showStab

Figure 11.18   Rendering Function of WXR page

Demonstration of Co-Execution

In this section we illustrate the synergistic modeling framework using the WXR example. We present the correspondence edition between the models and then the co-execution of these models exploiting that correspondence. Then we discuss validation and verification possibilities of this framework.

The Correspondence Editor

On the task side, the integration relies on the HAMSTERS environment that provides a set of tools for engineering task models (edition and simulation of models). Similarly, on the system side, the integration relies on the ICO environment (PetShop) that provides means for editing and simulating the system model:

- From the tasks specification we extract the set of interactive tasks (input and output tasks) representing a set of manipulations that can be performed by the user on the system and outputs from the system to the user.
- From the ICO specification we extract the activation and rendering function that may be seen as the set of inputs and outputs of the system model.

The principle of editing the correspondences between the two models is to put together interactive input tasks (from the task model) with system inputs (from the system model) and system outputs (from the system model) with interactive output tasks (from the task model). Setting up this correspondence may show inconsistencies between the task and system model such as interactive tasks not supported by the system or rendering information not useful for the tasks performance. The correspondence edition process is presented on Figure 11.19 where each tool feeds the correspondence editor with information from the API in order to notify it with modifications are done both in the task model and in the system model.

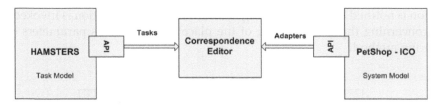

Figure 11.19   Correspondence Edition Phase

The edition of correspondences between the two models are done by a dedicated editor (see Figure 11.20) enabling to putting together interactive input tasks (from the task model) with system inputs (from the system model) and system outputs (from the system model) with interactive output tasks (from the task model).

The left-hand side (labeled 1) contains a tree structure with the relevant items from both the task model and the system model (interactive input and output tasks, activation and rendering adapters). The case study only features one role (only one task model) and only one ICO model; but the editor is able to handle larger set of models at a time. The top right-hand side (labeled 2) is made up with two tables representing the current state of the editing of the correspondence:

- The table on top represents the input correspondences for example, the link made between an input task and an activation adapter (a user event). In the example, five tasks are already connected to five user events (for example, "switch_off" is connected to user event "Off").
- The bottom table represents the output correspondences for example, the link made between an output task and a rendering adapter. In the example, two tasks are already connected to two rendering events ("verify_mode" has changed is connected to rendering event Token enters SELECTION_MODE and "verify_angle" has changed is connected to rendering event Token enters TILT_ANGLE ...).

The bottom right-hand part (labeled 3) represents the current status of the editing of correspondences. It is made up with a progress bar showing the current coverage of task and system items by the edited correspondences (that is, the rate of used items: the current editing of Figure 11.20 shows 14 items used among 26). Below the progress bar, a set of warnings are displayed, showing how many tasks and system items are not currently used (for instance, three at the bottom of Figure 11.20).

At any time, the co-execution of models may be launched (via a tool bar icon), even if correspondence editing is not completed.

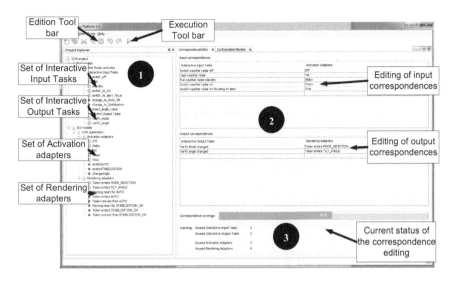

Figure 11.20   Snapshot of the correspondence editor

The co-execution monitoring interface
Our framework allows the co-execution of task and system models controlled by both the execution of the system model and the execution of the task model as shown in Figure 11.21 where the top part represents the correspondence edition presented in Figure 11.19.

Figure 11.21 highlights the two ways communication allowed by the services embedded within the four APIs:

- Through an API, HAMSTERS notifies the Simulation controller of changes in the current scenario.
- Through another API, the Simulation controller fires the corresponding activation adapter (according to the correspondence provided by the Correspondence editor).
- Through an extended API, PetShop interpreter notifies the Simulation controller of the evolution of the current execution of the system model (it notifies rendering changes that comes from both rendering and activation functions).
- Through an extended API, the Simulation controller performs the corresponding task (according to the correspondence provided by the Correspondence editor), simulating the user manual action on HAMSTERS simulator.

When the task simulator controls the execution of the system model, the framework behaves as follows: while building a scenario, if the task performed within the scenario is one of the identified interactive input tasks within the correspondence editor, an event is sent to the activation function (simulating the corresponding user event on the user interface), resulting in a user action on the interactive application (from the execution of the model). As a scenario describes a sequence of tasks and as we are able to define a correspondence between an interactive input task and an activation adapter, it is now possible to convert the scenarios into a sequence of firing

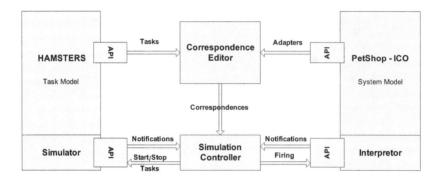

**Figure 11.21   Global architecture of the framework for the co-execution
of task and system model**

of event handlers in the ICO specification. In other words, a scenario performed from
these tasks can be converted into a sequence of firing of event handlers that directly
drive the execution of the ICO specification in exactly the same way as user actions
on the user interface would have triggered the same event handlers.

Symmetrically, when the execution is controlled by the execution of the system
model, user actions are directly linked to the corresponding tasks from the task model
and the user's action on the user interface of the application change the current state
of the task model simulation.

The execution of models in the framework can start either by task models or system
models. When the co-execution is launch from the correspondence editing, a new set
of components allows to control and to monitor this co-execution as presented by
Figure 11.22 which can be decomposed in three parts:

- The left-hand part (labeled 1 and detailed in Figure 11.16) is a set of tabs
  containing the ICOs involved in the co-execution showing their evolution
  during the execution (one tab per model).
- The upper central part (labeled 2) contains on its top part a view of the task
  model and at the bottom part the simulation controller of HAMSTERS with an
  empty panel on its right side that contains when necessary means to provide
  values for the task execution (that is, numerical values typed in a text field, or
  more complex objects selected using a list box).
- The lower central part (labeled 4) allows interacting with the ongoing
  simulation and is detailed in Figures 11.23, 11.24 and 11.25.
- The right-hand part (labeled 3) contains a table featuring a logging for events
  occurring during the execution and their counter partner input or output
  correspondences.

Additionally, the window of the executed application (WXR) is visible at the
bottom of Figure 11.22 (labeled 5), ready to react to user events.

Task models execution controlling the system execution
The execution of a task model produces a sequence of tasks including interactive
(input and output) tasks. Non-interactive tasks are not related to the system execution
as they involve user without interaction with system or system without feedback to

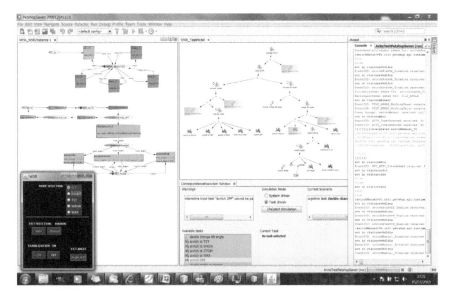

Figure 11.22   Snapshot of the co-execution monitoring interface

the user. Using the correspondences identified within the correspondence editor, it is now possible to convert the sequence of interactive tasks into a sequence of user event triggering within the ICO specification, controlling the system execution as if the scenario played were a user.

For the case study, when the co-execution monitor starts, the initial set of available tasks contains "decide change tilt angle," "decide change mode," "decide mode is correct" and "decide WXR is ready" (as shown on Figure 11.23). To execute one of these two tasks, one must select the corresponding task, double-click it or use the button "Perform Task."

Task "decide tilt angle" is a cognitive task and means that the user decides to setup the weather radar orientation. Such task does not change the system state as it is not related to any user event. Performing this task makes available the interactive input task "select manual" and the cognitive task "decide angle is correct."

The execution of the system model driven by the task model is performed task after task within the HAMSTERS simulation controller until it reaches the end of the scenario. If no system item corresponds to one of the available tasks then the co-execution monitor will display a warning (such as illustrated by Figure 11.24 where tasks "switch OFF" is available and corresponding user event is disabled until the user press the CTRL button). Such case could be normal as it would correspond to sequence of actions forced by the system for safety purpose, for instance.

In Figure 11.25, task "decide angle" has an output port that represents the value the user wants to set the tilt angle with. Performing this task activates the interactive output task "edit angle" that receives the tilt angle value through its input port. If the corresponding user event for task "edit angle" is enabled (that is, the editing of the tilt angle using the edit box), performing the interactive task requires runtime information. Such values may be system values (values within the system model) or free values (such as numbers). When performing such task, the co-execution monitor provides means to enter or select the corresponding value. The identification of the value type is done according to the artifact description attached to the output port of the corresponding interactive task within the HAMSTERS model and the corresponding activation adapter.

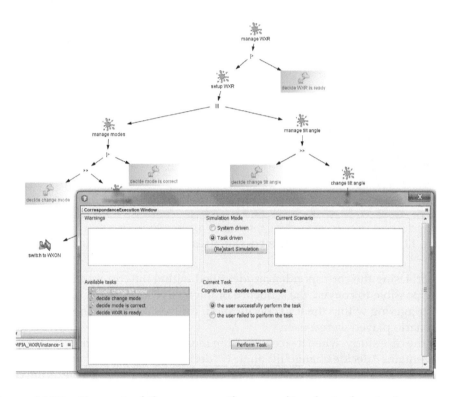

Figure 11.23   Excerpt of the co-execution monitor featuring task availability. (A) Available tasks

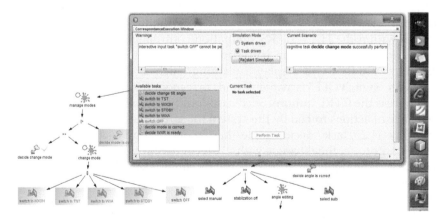

Figure 11.24   Excerpt of the co-execution monitor featuring task availability. (B) Unavailable tasks

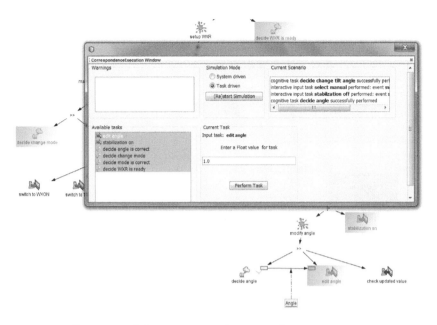

Figure 11.25   Excerpt of the co-execution monitor

Note: Presented in Figure 11.22 with object editing.

If none of the available task can be executed on the system model, the simulation is stopped and an error is notified. The simulation ends when there is a no more available interactive task.

When system execution controls the task execution

A sequence of actions on the user application (played using the ICO model) is able to control the execution of a task model according to the edited correspondences, as each user action may be related to an interactive input task (see Figure 11.26 where task "stabilization off" is highlighted on the task model after the user has pressed the button CTRL).

While interacting with the system, it is possible to point out which task from the task model is performed. This allows tracing the system execution within the task model. Ambiguity in pointing tasks may appear if there is more than one task with the same name within the task model. In the current design of the framework, when such ambiguities appear, the co-execution monitor triggers warnings showing the set of potential corresponding tasks.

This policy of co-execution allows knowing at any time where a user is with respect to the described activity within the task model. Knowing this, it is possible to provide the user with a contextual help such as in [31].

Another possible use of the execution of task driven by the system model could be to determine if going from one interactive task to another (according to the system execution) is possible, using path analysis on the task model. An interesting output of such work is that it allows finding inconsistencies such as sequences of user actions allowed by the system model and forbidden by the task model.

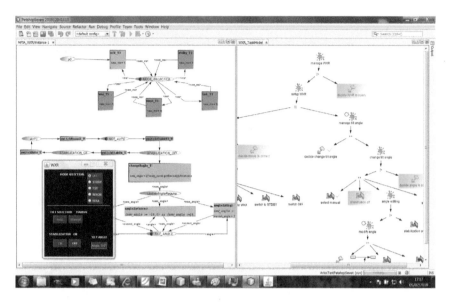

Figure 11.26   Interaction between task model execution and system model

Systematic Approach to Training Exploiting PetShop and HAMSTERS

During the Analysis phase of the training program, the WXR task model described using HAMSTERS allow designers to represent the tasks that have to be performed by the crew members. The business and general objectives of the training program, as well as the targeted audience are also set during this phase. Exploiting these objectives and the tasks representation, the Design phase determines the pre-requisites for the training and the knowledge and skills they will have to learn.

For example, with respect to "modify angle" subtask presented in Figure 11.15, the trainees will have to be able to change manually the Tilt mode. It implies that the crew member in charge of that task will have to be able to decide the angle value, insert and verify it. According to the individual needs recorded during the Analysis phase, the crew member will have to be trained on how to decide the value of the angle to be entered in the system. Then they will have to be trained on how to use the application to insert the value and where in the application they can check that the entered value is correct. During the Execution phase of the training, they will be able to experiment the way to change the Tilt angle manually by using the PetShop-HAMSTERS co-execution framework presented in the previous section. The output of this simulation will lead to evaluating if the training objectives are met and to the evaluation of the performances. It will be possible to ensure that the trainees are able to change the Tilt angle value and how much time it takes for them to perform this action. Beyond that, it is possible to store information about the models execution and check how much the training program covers the possible interactions on the system and the tasks that have been modeled in HAMSTERS.

This process helps ensuring that: the training is in line with the system and its environment and that each trainee is prepared for the job. Furthermore, as a complement path to testing phase, it can help to discover interaction problems that might have been overlooked during the usability evaluation phase or during the prototyping phase.

CONCLUSION

This chapter presented a set of issues for the research community working on User Interface tool to address the specific concerns raised by user interfaces for safety critical systems. We propose to extend research in a different direction that the one taken by main stream research in the field of UI tools. Indeed this main stream focuses on new interaction techniques including (how to interact with novel physical devices, how to bridge the physical and electronic worlds, …).The proposed direction is to have a bi-focus that is, to deal with new and innovative interaction techniques (as currently done) but also to deal with consolidation work, that is, to provide ways of delivering reliable interaction techniques and thus to go form demonstration prototypes to interaction techniques reliable enough to be exploited in operations and in a safety critical domain.

The contribution is mainly based on PetShop [5] that embodies the results of several years of research about the formal modeling of interactive systems, on HAMSTERS that solves identified problems with task modeling (such as connection of the tasks with the system and representation of the information flow in the task models) and lastly on the coupling of these two models. Its main application domain is safety-critical interactive applications such as air-traffic control or military command and control systems. PetShop stands apart from most formal-based tools since it supports and promotes an iterative and user-centered design process, and also stands apart from most model-based tools since it goes beyond WIMP interfaces and deals with post-WIMP interaction techniques including direct manipulation and multimodal interfaces [1, 11].

Beyond the tool, the proposed framework advocates the use of models for the design of interactive safety critical systems. It claims that the issues raised by the design of such systems require the use of systematic ways to support the gathering, refinement and storage of data. This data is, by nature, multidisciplinary and thus requires a multi-notation approach to support individually each discipline.

However, this multi-notation approach calls for additional means in order to support additional activities such as verification of models consistency. Besides, in order to alleviate the burden for developers and designers, software tools supporting their activities are also at the core of the applicability of such an approach.

We have studied and propose methods for integrating the necessary models for safety-critical interactive systems design. We have devised approaches for integrating task models and system models while using various techniques to take into account erroneous human and system behavior. Our approach relies heavily on scenarios to bridge the main modeling phases and on tools to support scalability aspects and thus making possible to address real-life applications.

The framework provides support for the gathering, refining, and embedding of multi-source and multi-type data while tolerating experts of their multiple domains to perform analyses and use techniques they are accustomed to. All of these components, we believe, are essential for the design of safety-critical interactive systems design.

REFERENCES

1. Basnyat, S., Chozos, N., and Palanque, P. (2006). Multidisciplinary perspective on accident investigation. *Reliability Engineering and System Safety*, 91, 12, December, pp. 1502–1520.

2. Basnyat, S., Palanque, P., Bernhaupt, R., Poupart, E. (2008). Formal Modeling of Incidents and Accidents as a Means for Enriching Training Material for Satellite Control Operations, Joint ESREL and 17th SRA-Europe Conference. September 22–25, Valencia, Spain.

3. Basnyat, S., Palanque, P., Schupp, B., Wright, P. (2007). Formal socio-technical barrier modeling for safety-critical interactive systems design. *Safety Science*, 45, June 5, ISSN: 0925–7535.

4. Bass L., Pellegrino, R., Reed, S., Sheppard, S., Szczur, M. (1991). The Arch Model: Seeheim Revisited, Proceedings of the User Interface Developers' Workshop at CHI'91.

5. Bastide, R., Navarre, D., and Palanque, P. (2002). A Model-Based Tool for Interactive Prototyping of Highly Interactive Applications. Full demonstration, ACM CHI 2002 conference on Human Factors for Computing Systems. Minneapolis, US, April 20–25.

6. Bastide, R., Navarre, D., Palanque, P., Schyn, A., and Dragicevic, P. (2004). A Model-Based Approach for Real-Time Embedded Multimodal Systems in Military Aircrafts. Sixth International Conference on Multimodal Interfaces (ICMI'04) October 14–15, Pennsylvania State University, US.

7. Bodart, F., Hennebert, A.-M, Leheureux, J.-M., and Vanderdonckt, J. (1993). "Encapsulating Knowledge for Intelligent Automatic Interaction Objects Selection." In *Human Factors in Computing Systems INTERCHI'93*, Addison Wesley, 424–29.

8. Clark, D.R. (2004). Instructional System Design Concept Map. Retrieved January 26, 2010 from http://nwlink.com/~donclark/hrd/ahold/isd.html.

9. Dix, A., Finlay, J., Abowd, G., and Beale, R. (1998). *Human Computer Interaction*. Second edition, Prentice Hall.

10. DO-178B: "Software Considerations in Airborne Systems and Equipment Certification," Radio Technical Commission for Aeronautics, Inc. Http://www.rtca.org/.

11. Dragicevic, P., Navarre, D., Palanque, P., Schyn, A., and Bastide, R. (2004). Very-High-Fidelity Prototyping for both Presentation and Dialogue Parts of Multimodal Interactive Systems. DSVIS/EHCI 2004 joint conference 11th workshop on Design Specification and Verification of Interactive Systems and Engineering for HCI, Tremsbüttel Castle, Hamburg, Germany, July 11–13, Lecture Notes in Computer Science (to appear).

12. DSV-IS. (2008). Interactive Systems. Design, Specification, and Verification 15th International Workshop, DSV-IS 2008, Kingston, C.A.N. Graham and P. Palanque (Eds.), vol. 5136, 2008.

13. European cooperation for space standardization, space engineering, ground systems and operations— part I: principles and requirements, ecss-e-70 part IA, April 2000.

14. Gagné, R. (1985). *The conditions of learning and the theory of instruction* (4th edn.). New York: Holt, Rinehart, and Winston.

15. Gulliksen, J., Bengt, G., Boivie, I., Blomkvist, S., Person, J., and Cajander. (2003). A. Key principles for user-centered systems design. *Behavior and information technology*, November–December, 22, 6, 397–409.

16. Hix, D., and Hartson, R. (1993). *Developing User Interfaces: Ensuring Usability Through Product and Process*. New York, NY: John Wiley and Sons.

17. Hollnagel, E, Woods, D., and Leveson, N. (2006). *Resilience Engineering Concepts and Precepts*. Ashgate.

18. International Atomic Energy Agency, Experience in the use of Systematic Approach to Training (SAT) for Nuclear Power Plant Personnel, Technical Report, IAEA-TECDOC-1057.

19. Jacob, R. (1999). A Software Model and Specification Language for Non-WIMP User Interfaces. *ACM Transactions on Computer-Human Interaction 6*, 1, 1–46.

20. Kleppe, A., Warmer, S., Bast, W. (2003). *MDA explained: The model-driven architecture Practice and promise*, p. 192. Addison-Wesley, Reading.

21. Lacaze, X., Palanque, P., Barboni, E., Bastide, R., Navarre, D. (2006). From DREAM to Realitiy: Specificities of Interactive Systems Development with respect to Rationale Management. In *Rationale management in software engineering*, Allen H. Dutoit, Raymond McCall, Ivan Mistrik, Barbara Paech (Eds.), Springer Verlag, Springer-Verlag/Computer Science Editorial, p. 155–172.

22. Memon, A.M., and Soffa, M.L. (2003). Regression testing of guis. In Proceedings of the 9th European software engineering conference held jointly with 10th ACM SIGSOFT international symposium on Foundations of software engineering, pp. 118–127.

23. Memon, A.M., Soffa, M.L., Pollack, M.E. (2001). Coverage criteria for GUI testing. In proceedings of the 8th European software engineering conference held jointly with 9th ACM SIGSOFT international symposium on Foundations of software engineering, pp. 256–267.

24. Myers, P.M., Watson, B., Watson, M. (2008). Effective Training Programs Using Instructional Systems Design and E-Learning. *Process Safety Progress*, 27, 2, pp. 131–138.

25. Navarre, D., Palanque, P., Bastide, R., Paternó, F., and Santoro, C. (2001). A tool suite for integrating task and system models through scenarios. In 8th Eurographics workshop on Design, Specification and Verification of Interactive Systems, DSV-IS'2001, June 13–15, Glasgow, Scotland, Lecture notes in computer science, no. 2220, Springer 2001.

26. Navarre, D., Palanque, P., Ladry, J., and Barboni, E. (2009). ICOs: A model-based user interface description technique dedicated to interactive systems addressing usability, reliability and scalability. *ACM Trans. Comput.-Hum. Interact.* 16, 4 (Nov.), pp. 1–56.

27. Neitzel, D.K. (2006). How to develop an effective training program. *IEEE Industry Applications Magazine*, May–June.

28. Palanque, P., and Basnyat, S. (2004). Task Patterns for taking into account in an efficient and systematic way both standard and erroneous user behaviors. HESSD 2004 Conference co-chair (with Chris Johnson) 6th International Working Conference on Human Error, Safety and System Development, August 22–27, Toulouse, France (within the IFIP World Computing Congress WCC 04).

29. Palanque, P., and Bastide, R. (1993). Interactive Cooperative Objects: an Object-Oriented Formalism Based on Petri Nets for User Interface Design. Proceedings of the IEEE/System Man and Cybernetics 93 "Systems Engineering in the Service of Humans," Le Touquet, 17–20 October.

30. Palanque, P. and Bastide, R. (1995). Verification of an Interactive Software by analysis of its formal specification Proceedings of the IFIP Human–computer Interaction conference (Interact'95) Lillehammer, Norway, June 27–29, p. 191–197.

31. Palanque, P., Bastide, R., Dourte, L. (1993). Contextual Help for Free with Formal Dialogue Design. In Proc. of HCI International 93, North Holland. Orlando, US, August 8–15, 1993.

32. Palanque, P., and Lacaze, X. (2007). DREAM-TEAM: A Tool and a Notation Supporting Exploration of Options and Traceability of Choices for Safety Critical Interactive Systems. In Proceedings of INTERACT 2007, Rio, Brazil, September, Lecture Notes in Computer Science, Springer Verlag.

33. Paterno, F., Mancini, C., Meniconi, S. (1997). ConcurTaskTrees: A Diagrammatic Notation for Specifying Task Models. Proceedings of the IFIP TC13 International Conference on Human–computer Interaction Pages, Interact'97, pp. 362–369, July 1997, Sydney, ISBN:0–412–80950–8, Chapman and Hall.

34. Reiser, R.A. (2001). A History of Instructional Design and Technology: Part II: A History of Instructional Design. *Educational Technology Research and Development*, 49, 2, pp. 57–61.

35. Salminen, S., and Tallberg, T. (1996). Human errors in fatal and serious occupational accidents in Finland. *Ergonomics*, 39 (7), pp. 980–988.

36. Scapin, D. and Pierret-Golbreich, C. (1989). Towards a Method for Task Description: MAD. Work with Display Units WWU'89, Amsterdam: Elsevier Science Publishers, pp. 27–34.

37. Scott, D.W. (2009). Growing a Training System and Culture for the Ares I Upper Stage Project, NASA Technical Report, Number: IEEEAC Paper 1550.

38. Sukaviriya, P.N., Kovacevic, S., Foley, J.D., Myers, B.A., Olsen Jr., D.R., and Schneider-Hufschmidt, M. (1994). Model-Based User Interfaces: What Are They and Why Should We Care? In Proceedings UIST '94, November, pp. 133–35.

39. US Army Field Artillery School. (1984). A System Approach to Training (Course Student textbook). ST—5K061FD92.

40. US Department of Defense Training Document. (1975). Pamphlet 350–30. August 1975.

12

Designing Human–Automation Interaction

Amy Pritchett and Michael Feary

When we look at human–automation interaction, what is it that we "design"—the human, the automation, or the interaction? We don't design the humans—indeed, a good design generally minimizes dependency on personnel selection and training. An emphasis on designing the automation is likely to make a technology that complies with specifications but, if history is a guide, brittle to the unexpected and opaque to its human compatriot. Thus, our perspective in this chapter is to examine the *interaction* as the construct of interest, formally modeling it from several perspectives, and noting how implications for training the humans and specifying the technology can then be articulated.

How do we describe "interaction" sufficiently to create effective human–automation interaction? The richness of the behavior observable in human–automation interaction (HAI) and the depth of behavior underlying it—suggest that several constructs must be created and coordinated at varying levels of abstraction:

- At the highest level of abstraction, a construct centered on *authority* needs to examine if accountability for outcomes is designated to those agents with the capability to enact them.
- A construct centered on *teams* examines how the human(s) and automated system(s) coordinate their specific functions to perform their work, including considerations taken from human teams such as shared situation awareness and team maintenance.
- A construct centered on *work* examines the patterns of activity required across all agents to meet their collective goals. This construct is used as a mid-level abstraction that accommodates the range of feasible joint activities independent of specific interfaces.
- A construct centered on *representations* examines how humans abstract specific behaviors or aspects of the environment, in order to construct automation around these abstractions so that its behaviors are comprehensible to, and interactable with, humans.
- At the most tangible, detailed level, a construct centered on *interface mechanisms* then examines the specifics of information that a specific automated system and its human operator convey to each other, and the actions required by each on the other to enact desired behavior.

Ideally, in a "blue skies" approach where any design is allowed, a design process would step from the highest level of abstraction to the most detailed. In many situations, however, such as introducing an updated flight management system to an established flightdeck, only certain aspects of the system are fully under the designer's control, such as training, procedures and the interface; in such cases, the ability to articulate the other constructs ensures that the available interventions can support the established features of the system, in some cases even correcting for problematic characteristics.

This chapter steps through these constructs, identifying the contributions of a variety of domains including models of organizations, work, teams, and specific information processing mechanisms. The chapter concludes with a discussion of how these constructs can coordinate and contribute to each other.

AUTHORITY

As described by Boy elsewhere in this volume, true authority exists when accountability for an outcome within an organization is demanded of an agent with the capability to enact it. The challenge is to ensure that true authority exists—that accountability for all outcomes is unambiguously designated, that it is designated to agents with corresponding capability, and that these designations will hold across the full dynamics of operations. Thus, creating effective human–automation interaction within an organization from the autonomy perspective requires an intersection of technology design (what capability does the machine provide, and how is it executed?) and policy (who's accountable?).

In the context of managing an organization, an agent's autonomy may be generally defined as its ability to perform a task, no matter how simple, and report problems in time for the organization to take corrective action. This corresponds to progressive delegation of true authority—a delegate is both capable and accountable—and by this definition increased autonomy corresponds to a decreased requirement for supervision. However, the common parlance used to describe machine autonomy often conflicts with the needs of the organization by focusing on its capability within intended operating conditions ("boundary conditions"). Thus, increased autonomy may create technological capability with no accountability, thus requiring constant supervision lest it break or operate outside its boundary conditions—yet its human supervisor may not have the capability or information to comprehend whether its myriad functions are correct and appropriate to the immediate situation.

An operator's willingness to delegate functions to automation is often described as "reliance." Parasuraman and Riley (1997) noted how this reliance can be correct (in their terms, appropriate "use") or incorrect ("misuse") depending on whether the automation is capable of the action delegated to it. They also note situations where operators don't rely on automation ("disuse"). Inappropriate reliance on automation is often described as a human (supervisor) error without attributing the same fault to the machine subordinate that a human subordinate would receive.

Lack of reliance on automated systems, or overly attentive supervision, is often attributed in the literature to a "lack of trust." As with human teams, trust is generally defined as the belief that the automation is capable, sometimes including the resulting reliance in the definition (for example, Lee and See, 2004, Riley, 1996). However, a human's trust in automation is not symmetric: automation has no motivation to live up to its obligations, does not experience shame or embarrassment, and cannot be assessed for attributes such as loyalty, benevolence and agreement in values. Thus, Lee and See (2004) caution that "care must be exercised in extrapolating findings from human-human trust to human–automation trust," beyond the extent that automation embodies the intentions of its designer, even as "people may attribute intentionality and impute motivation to automation as it becomes increasingly sophisticated." Instead, variables which determine trust in automation include the human's perception of the automation's performance and reliability, time, the automation's feedback to the human about its functioning, and cultural and organizational factors, where the human's perception of these variables may or may not be accurate. A prediction of reliance is made by contrasting trust in automation with the human's self-confidence in performing the same task; this self-confidence is often driven by similar factors as trust, as well as skill, workload, and fatigue, and has the same problem with accurate perception (Lee and Moray, 1994; Pritchett, 2001; Riley, 1996).

However, we would argue that, where the human doesn't trust automation, creating effective human–automation interaction is not as simple as "giving the operator the right trust level." Instead, poor trust is a symptom of deeper problems with delegating authority, especially given the asymmetric trust relationship between human and automation. Over-reliance and misplaced trust corresponds to a case where authority is delegated to automation that lacks autonomy—it cannot identify and report back from situations where it lacks capability, instead requiring human supervision. Such supervision may not be sustainable due to workload or, even when the human is actively involved, he or she can be "cognitively railroaded" by a lack of information and resources into accepting the automation's behavior without true oversight, or the automation may unduly shape the human's judgment of the environment or representation of decision options, an effect generally known as automation bias (Bass and Pritchett, 2008). Under-reliance result in the same situation when the human, recognizing the difficulties and dangers, chooses to not delegate to the automation.

How do we then appropriately delegate functions to automation within the organization? This ongoing challenge is only partly addressed by methods for function allocation. For example, Price (1985) summarized strategies based on "mandatory allocation" (that is, those based on fundamental limitations or regulatory issues), "balance of value" (that is, those valuing and contrasting the performance of human and automation at a function, such as the expected-value analysis proposed by Sheridan and Parasuraman (2000) for failure-response tasks), "utilitarian and cost-based" (that is, those valuing and contrasting the cost of assigning a function to human and to automation), and "affective or cognitive support" (that is, those considering the automation's ability to support the human (for example, Wei, Macwan, and Wieringa, 1998)). As a different construct for function allocation, Parasuraman, Sheridan, and Wickens (2000) examined allocating functions via a finer characterization of the automation's capabilities referenced to a model of human information processing, allowing for inclusion of a broader range of automated functions and for direct comparison to its human operator's activities. While such methods address "capability," the construct of "accountability" is not explicitly addressed.

Likewise, broad-based categorizations, such as "level of automation" (for example, Billings, 1997; Sheridan, 1992), are limited in their ability to describe accountability. For example, a "high" level of automation may automatically execute actions, yet it contributes little if accountability concerns drive its human supervisor to override its output; conversely, a "low" level of automation may only suggest a course of action yet the human may be "cognitively railroaded" into following its output exactly (Pritchett, 2001). Thus, descriptions of automation's functioning via categorizations such as levels of automation do not delineate the humans' involvement in and responsibility for the associated work (for example, Dekker and Woods, 2002).

All these concerns are especially profound when accountability is changed dynamically. Such dynamics can be instigated exogenously to the human or automation—for example, the issuing of an authoritative Traffic alert and Collision Avoidance System (TCAS) resolution advisory is triggered by a developing conflict between aircraft. Other function allocations may be dynamic, that is, the automation may be "adaptive" (changing its function allocation automatically) or "adaptable" (allowing its human operator to change its function allocation) (for example, Kaber, Wright, Prinzel, and Clamann, 2005; Miller and Parasuraman, 2007); this mirrors the "organizational flexibility" and "dynamic allocation of tasks" noted in high-reliability (human) teams (Rasmussen, Pejtersen, and Goodstein, 1994). Dynamic function allocation for adaptive automation may be based on performance (that is, in response to an actual performance decrement), psychophysiological assessment (that is, in response to estimates of physiological stressors experienced by the human), performance modeling (that is, in response to a model-based prediction of a performance decrement), and critical-events logics (that is, in response to environmental occurrences pre-identified as warranting a change in execution). While some current automated systems may minimally fit within these definitions (for example, an alerting system that detects some critical event), research into adaptive automation is examining more complex function allocations. Likewise, research into adaptable automation is examining sometimes-intricate function allocations that can be described coherently (for example, the "playbooks" described by Miller and Parasuraman, 2007) or that mirror changes in human cognitive control in response to task demands (for example, Feigh and Pritchett, 2010). As with strategies for more static function allocation, the focus of these methods is often on assessing relative capability without explicitly articulating accountability.

TEAMS

Within the broad range of definition of "team" provided in the literature, Salas et al., provide a generally accepted definition of teams as a collection of (two or more) individuals working together inter-dependently to achieve a common goal (1992). This definition specifies an entity that is more than just a group—shared work goals bind it together, instill a vested interest in each other's performance, and reduce self-centered actions (Klimoski and Mohammed, 1994). Within this definition, teams may range from highly structured and interdependent to those whose members interact infrequently from a shared group context. Their work demands interdependence and coordination, including intricate social and cognitive aspects. Thus, our discussion in this section goes beyond the accountability concerns just addressed to consider "how does the team interact?"

Several automation studies have gone further in describing automation as a team member. For example, Muir (1994) related models and measures of trust from the social sciences to human trust in automation; Bass and Pritchett (2008) modified social judgment theory to quantitatively model human interaction with automated judges; Pritchett (2001) proposed framing human interaction with alerting systems in terms of the same type of "role" descriptions used within human teams; and Sarter and Woods (2000) explicitly described flight path automation as a "team member" (albeit often a poor team member!). More explicitly, Woods and Hollnagel (2006) suggested that "good" automation should create a diverse joint human–machine cognitive system. Likewise, the strategy of "complementation" seeks to form a heterogeneous team where automation and humans work together cooperatively, each contributing their strengths (Schutte, 1999), and Miller and Parasuraman's "playbook" metaphor for assigning functions to automation is specifically described using delegation in human teams as a metaphor (2007). Thus, comparing human teams with teams of humans and automated systems is well-grounded in the research community.

Teamwork processes include, but are not limited to: acceptance of suggestions or criticisms, adaptability, communication (both verbal and non-verbal), cohesion, cooperation, coordination, leadership, decision-making, giving of suggestions or criticisms, group spirit, synchronization, load balancing, consensus formation, conflict resolution, monitoring and critiquing, confirming, and even interpersonal interactions such as reassurance. Outputs include not only team performance but also team longevity and team maintenance. The lack of team maintenance skills' is an obvious comparative weakness of automation (at least at this time): automation is focused solely on its own functions, without team maintenance as a supporting objective.

Teamwork is supported by a *shared mental model*, with similar constructs commonly called "team knowledge", "shared situation awareness", "complementary mental model" and "transactive memory". Sperling (2005) defined a complementary mental model as the condition in which: (1) Each team member has the knowledge necessary to conduct his/her tasks; (2) Each team member knows which information is known by the other team member should he/she need to seek it; and (3) Each team member knows which information is needed from them by other team members and when (for related definitions see Cannon-Bowers et al., 1993). Similarly, three forms of cooperation have been defined for human teams (Schmidt, 1991): (1) Augmentative cooperation, when agents have similar skills but divide the volume of work into similar subtasks due to workload considerations; (2) Integrative cooperation, when agents have different, complementary knowledge and integrate their contributions to achieve a task; and (3) Debative cooperation, when agents with similar skills compare their results, especially in unfamiliar circumstances.

Teams with members that share similar knowledge structures communicate more effectively and perform better than teams whose members do not share such knowledge, especially in high workload environments (see Heffner, 1997 for a review). Mental models guide team interactions, and help team members form accurate expectations of the task and each other. Consequently, the development of shared mental models among team members is a common goal of training programs (for example, Cannon-Bowers et al., 1998) and, in some cases, system design (for example, Sperling, 2005).

Coordination and communication are tightly coupled with shared mental models, creating an evolving knowledge structure (for example, Cannon-Bowers, Salas, and Converse, 1993). Communication affects the cognitive processes within each group member by influencing one another's perceptions, judgments, and opinions, and serves as the vehicle for "social cognition" by which group members' perceptions, judgments, and opinions are combined to arrive at a single solution to a given problem. Communication is also the means by which teams coordinate resources and activities. However, some communication patterns can be disruptive; therefore, it is important to have a combination of team structure and shared mental model that enables team members to predict each others' information needs and provide information at useful, non-interruptive times.

Exchange of information and direction of action are generally recognized as the purpose of automation interfaces, but is only part of effective communication and coordination. For example, situation awareness is often described as the purpose of human–automation interfaces, yet with a crucial difference: rather than being shared, the automation's mental model and situation awareness are fixed to the automation designer's representation of the work environment and task, rather than a shared construct created through a dialectic. Likewise, the reflection of thoughts (including "integrative" and "debative" forms of coordination) between humans is an opportunity to examine the representation of concepts relative to their immediate situation, including generating new abstractions in new contexts; this is currently beyond machine reasoning. The problems thus caused are then reflected in the interface, as discussed later in this chapter.

Thus, rather than contributing to team communication, automation's introduction often creates new requirements for communication and coordination amongst the human team members. For example, new automation in the cockpit generally necessitates new crew resource management strategies and coordination protocols, such as the need for explicit communication and cross-check between captain and first officer following any new command to the autoflight system (for example, Helmreich, Merritt, and Wilhelm, 1999). The challenge for human–automation-interaction, then, is to incorporate the insights of team dynamics into actionable guidance for automation designers to better support (if not fully anticipate) the needs of the team.

WORK

Work may be succinctly defined as "purposeful activity." The word "purposeful" implies that the activity has a broader effect outside of its internal machinations, such as a tangible impact on the broader environment. Going further, work requires patterns of activity as needed by goals and as driven by inherent dynamics within the worker's environment. For example, flying an aircraft requires a certain pattern of activity mirroring the aircraft's response to control surface commands, the physics of which can be described. Work may span several disparate tasks which themselves need to be deliberately scheduled, interleaved or prioritized.

What may be more interesting is what we do not include here in our abstraction of "work"—we do not include descriptions of activity specific to particular interfaces. Such abstractions risk losing sight of the broader patterns defining work regardless of specific system or interface, and are not well suited to examining significantly different, equally capable strategies for performing work. Thus our conception of work can not be captured by, for example, a task analysis that describes button presses on a specific interface or spanning only one of many required activities.

This broader viewpoint of work is useful for addressing fairly fundamental design decisions—given an understanding of the work required to meet goals in a given environment, the abstraction of work is useful for examining "what needs to happen" and "who will do what." Descriptions of work can inform answers to such questions while remaining unbiased by the specific mechanisms currently used to perform such work, and while capturing the multiplicity of tasks and goals that may need to be met simultaneously. How do we represent work? Two cognitive engineering methods are worth mentioning here. First, cognitive work analysis provides a progression of modeling approaches, starting with a work-domain analysis of the successively detailed abstract functions, general functions and physical functions that need to happen in the environment for work goals to be achieved (see, for example, Vicente, 1999). Subsequent strategies analysis examines potential patterns of activity required for a human or automation to initiate and regulate those functions. These are valuable insights, although in our experience there are also some limitations. In terms of modeling, cognitive work analysis is well-suited to modeling the physical environment in terms of the affordances and constraints it provides, but it is not well-established how to capture the affordances and constraints created by the organizational and procedural aspects of the environment. For example, a typical analysis of driving a car would recognize the physical constraint of a curb demarcating the shoulder of the road but not the procedural constraint restricting crossing a solid painted line; depending on how shallow the curb is and whether a police car is driving just behind, the former physical constraint might be considered a lesser constraint than the latter procedural one. Second, organizational analysis within cognitive work analysis generally represents different actors as acting on different "parts" of the environment—this is useful when their functions are so divided, but doesn't provide insight into function allocations where multiple actors (human and automated) inter-leave activities on shared aspects of the environment.

Contextual design (see, for example, Beyer and Holtzblatt, 1998) develops explicit models of work from five perspectives: "flow" of information and artifacts between actors; "cultural" influences within an organization (including the social aspects of teams noted in the previous section); use of the "physical environment" to support work; use of specific "artifacts" to support work; and specific activity "sequences" to enact the work. Contextual design was developed to design information technology for relatively static domains such as business administration. Extending it to environments with varying demands on its workers suggests the need to recognize the different patterns of activity as applicable to the immediate context (for example, Feigh and Pritchett, in press). Likewise, extending such representations of work to environments with inherent dynamics suggests the need to include, at a minimum, the mission task and associated purpose, objectives and success criteria, utility function (including key trade-offs such as speed-accuracy trade-offs), event triggers, task criticality, timing and ordinality considerations in the order of steps conducted, and boundary conditions for the procedure (Billman et al., 2010; Ockerman and Pritchett, 2001).

During design it is important to recognize that the work itself can be designed and redesigned to be more efficient, effective or robust. For example, the newer air traffic procedure "Continuous Descent Approach" (CDA) allows aircraft to fly their optimal vertical profile down to landing. While this procedure takes advantage of new technology, such as autoflight systems, it demanded a redesign of the work of each air traffic controller to allow "hand-offs" of aircraft to the controller in the neighboring section at varying altitudes and speeds. Thus, the technology redesign was minimal—the big difference was in the procedures used to enact the work, leading to dramatic reductions in aircraft noise and emissions. Once the work is redesigned, then new technology can be envisioned to support the work—rather than introducing new technology and then trying to figure out how to work around it!

Poor human–automation interaction can result from a number of problems well captured by the abstraction of work. Some of these problems are generally lumped together as problems with human–automation "function allocation" beyond those with authority noted earlier. Most obviously, what if the automation doesn't execute the right functions to meet work goals? Additionally, what if the human's contribution to the combined work is spread across diffuse, incoherent activities? For example, the relative capabilities of humans and automation have long been used as a basis for function allocation, as formalized in the famous (some might say infamous) Men Are Better At/Machines Are Better At list (Fitts, 1951). While the authors of this list recognized several caveats in its application, subsequent designers often found it all too seductive to apply broadly; resulting function allocations can be piece-meal and incoherent. Such incoherence can quickly show up on a graphical depiction of work if the human's contributions are highlighted in, say, a particular color—if this color is sporadically spread across the entire model, perhaps providing inputs where the automation does not have sensors, monitoring for situations where the automation is not appropriate, and generally filling in on disparate functions where the automation is not capable, then the human's work is likely fragmented and difficult. The final problem of note here also introduces the construct to be discussed next—when the "work" as represented by the human is not easily translated into the representations used by the automation to explain its actions and by which it can be commanded.

REPRESENTATIONS

The construct of "representations" a common dictionary definition: "the presentation to the mind of an idea, image or concept." The choice of representation in designing human–automation interaction, then, focuses on the concepts, ideas, and images used to frame the work and environment. Zhang and Norman (1994) noted that external representations (such as displays and interfaces) can anchor and structure cognitive behavior, change the nature of a worker's task, and, ideally, provide information that can be directly perceived and used without being interpreted and formulated explicitly. Thus, representation aiding (and similar strategies) seeks to enhance or leverage human cognitive and perceptual processes in support of problem-solving (see Smith, Bennet, and Stone, 2006, for a review).

Representation aiding, however, has generally been viewed as unrelated to "automated solutions." We instead argue that automation interacting with (or supervised by) humans is dependent on shared representations—the only automation that need not represent its work is that capable of executing its component of the collective work with neither input, nor supervision, nor inter-leaved tasks with humans. Specifically, human–automation interaction involves these multiple representations:

- First, the automation itself has an internal representation of the functions needed to perform the work, and of associated aspects of the work environment (Riley describes the similar concept of automation's "functional logic," 2001). Depending on the automation's purpose and its designer's training, this representation may be best described as control loops, as a finite state machine, as an expert-system's series of event-triggers to established rules, and so on.
- Second, the human similarly has an internal representation of the collective work. Such a representation may be the most detailed for the functions assigned to him or her—but, as noted earlier, he or she generally needs some knowledge of team-mates' functioning to understand their requirements and activities.
- Third, an explicit representation may be displayed to the human of the automation's output and, perhaps, processes. (Similarly, some types of automation build a representation of the human's output and processes).
- Finally, an explicit representation is generally made to the human of the other aspects of the environment. For example, a pilot's instruments shows the state of the aircraft in terms of airspeed, altitude, heading and attitude, even as the autoflight system controls these parameters, and the autoflight system's targets may be shown explicitly on the instruments and/or shown separately.

Examining pairwise combinations of these representations, several potential problems in human–automation interaction are quickly identified:

- What if the automation's external representation doesn't accurately or completely mirror the internal representation driving the automation's behavior, or depends on subtle or confusing distinctions? This condition is that sometimes described as "opaque" or "unobservable" (for example, Sarter and Woods, 2000). Here, then, the focus is on the *observability* of the automation's functioning.
- What if the human's internal representation of the automation's internal functioning (as mediated by external representations in the human–automation interface) is erroneous or incomplete? Javaux (2002) described, for example, a model of humans assembling their representation of automated functions via frequential reasoning (they often see a behavior so they have the opportunity to make a correct representation of it) and inferential reasoning (they infer the automation performs a function in a similar manner to other similar functions). By this model, "mode surprises" arise when the human encounters a rare or unusual automated function. Here, then, the focus is on the *complexity* of the automation's functioning—can a human ever internally represent it?
- What if the automation's functioning conflicts—or appears to conflict—with other representations of the work environment? Here, the focus is on the *consistency* of the automation's functioning relative to the other aspects of the environment.

Within this construct, design guidance based on the abstraction of "representations" is fairly clear. The external representation of the automation's functioning should be correct relative to the automation's internal functioning. The complexity of the automation's functioning should be limited so that it can be comprehensible to the human, and it should be consistent with the other aspects of the work environment.

These demands can be addressed in large part by explicitly considering the need for a common construct underlying the representations. One such common construct can often be a representation of the work, as discussed in the previous section. This notion has been hinted at by similar approaches in the community. For example, Work Centered Design approaches (for example, Butler et al., 2007) focus on modeling the work construct, developing interfaces which match the characteristics identified in the work structure, and evaluating the performance of the human–automation system in performing the work and achieving the work goals. Thus, the construct of work is additionally important because it may itself be a representation used by the human operator and, if the automation's internal functioning mirrors the inherent structure of "the work", then its behavior can be externally represented via a construct known and valued by the human.

INTERFACE MECHANISMS

Let's review what automation does and doesn't do well according to the constructs examined so far. By the construct of an organization, automation may be technically capable of specific functions yet not have accountability for its actions, requiring a human supervisor to monitor and, perhaps second-guess and override its functioning.

By the construct of a team, automation rarely participates well in the team-maintenance activities required of all team members, notably including communication and coordination towards the development of a shared mental model and efficient teamwork processes. Instead, automation tends to communicate either raw data or commands rather than intermediate interpretations contributing to a dialogue; likewise, automation often provides this information in formats or representations conflicting with the human's information needs and, often, disparate with other information sources. Rather than being framed in terms of the human's information needs, the automation's communication is typically based on its information availability; it is generally framed by a static representation inherent to its internal logic and isolated to specific tasks, leading to problems such as "mode confusion".

By the construct of work, automation may take on isolated functions within the broad tasking given to a team, leaving its human team members to pick-up on the disparate and incoherent collection of functions not covered by the automation. Then, by the construct of representations, automation may frame its knowledge, functioning and output via abstractions that do not easily translate to those represented in its displays, to those used (and needed) by the human operator relative to their work, and to other information displays.

These conceptual issues become manifest when the human interacts with automation through an interface. Thus, although the design and evaluation of an interface is many times limited to the look and feel of the displays and controls the pilot interacts with, the problems that present themselves as interface problems are many times symptoms of larger, underlying interaction issues.

Of course, some interface issues are driven by current interface technology. Computer displays can well represent spatial information and provide a persistent portrayal of detailed information; communicating the other way, however, machines can not comprehend a human's sketches except for some technologies' recognition of a small number of constructs. Verbal communication is increasingly possible, but again is currently limited to established constructs, often using a structured language and specific vocabulary. Gestures as communication is a field still in its infancy relative to operational needs. One-way modes of communication generally not examined in human-human communication include tactile displays, three dimensional picture of the physical environment, haptics (for example, to provide force feedback constraints and affordances relative to directions of motion) and, of course, the common human–automation interface consisting of buttons, switches, keyboards, and other input devices for the human to enter commands and specifications into the automation. Compared with the easy of communication within human teams, these interfaces already limit automation's ability to act as a team member; indeed, use of these interfaces may disrupt or be redundant with human team members' communication. However, other interface issues can be addressed by integrated tools that consider factors in the organization, team, work, and representation, as well as interface capabilities and human information processing.

Ideally, methods and tools for the design of human–automation-interaction would allow us to; (1) learn about a work domain in terms of both desired performance metrics and "utility functions" describing competing performance trade-offs, (2) place what we have learned into an appropriate representation, (3) design a prototype interface by matching the work representation to a library of interface objects, and (4) use computational automation and human performance analysis tools to rapidly evaluate prototypes early in the design process, and optimize the performance of the interface against the utility functions and performance metrics. Although no comprehensive methods or tools exist, let's examine the current state of the art.

While there really is no way to automate the process of knowledge elicitation from domain experts, we can focus on methods for only collecting a minimum set of information (Sherry and Feary, 2004). For example, Riley (2001) provides a case study of how to go from mission goals to the design of an interface. The Cockpit Control Language was constructed from a thorough analysis of pilot work domain, specifically focusing on clearances received from air traffic control. The interface allowed the user to directly specify these commands to the automation using the same representation of work the pilots appeared to rely on. Evaluation of the interface showed a large reduction in training time with the new interface.

Similarly, there are no automatic tools for generating representations from work domains; however, there are methods that will suggest the types of interface objects and graphics for specific types of data and themes in a work domain. Casner (1991) has automatically generated appropriate graphic displays for certain types of data specified in a task analysis. Similarly, Zhang's (1994) representational analysis produces a mapping between the type of data (ordinal, ratio, and so on) and the most appropriate display. Jorgensen (2009) has generated graphics which present continuous and discrete data as a pattern language which enables trends and transient events more clearly, and Degani et al. (2009) have identified different types of geometric patterns for the display of complex information.

Once we have generated interface objects, we do have formal analyses of Human—Automation Interaction properties, including some of the HAI difficulties mentioned earlier, such as Armed, automatic, and inhibited behaviors, as well as interface error states (Bolton et al., under review). We also have accurate models for analysis of some aspects of human performance; however, we face challenges when modeling cognitive performance (Howes et al., 2009). New approaches are trying to resolve this problem by focusing on cognitive architectural constraints and Human—Automation Interaction strategies (Howes et al., 2009).

An additional challenge for the use of human performance modeling in automation design is the difficulty in creating implementable models that are usable during the design process. Recent research has focused on the creation of tools to help solve this problem. One example, Cogtool (John et al., 2004) allows users to specify a task, import different interface representations, and analyze the performance of the task on the interface using a computational human performance model. Cogtool has also been connected to models of visual search and semantic interpretation (Teo et al., 2008), allowing the computational human performance model to "learn," and to analyze the process of learning how to perform work via a given interface (John et al., 2009), and allows different human performance models to be applied.

CONCLUSIONS

As we, the research and design community, get closer to establishing methods and tools for the detailed design of human–automation interfaces, we will find that larger issues also need to be addressed spanning multiple constructs. Indeed, the interface is where problems with human–automation interaction are revealed. Whether the interface is able to resolve the problem depends on the problem's origin—if it stems from fundamental concerns with accountability within the organization, communication, and coordination within the team, design of work and allocation of functions to conduct it, or conflicting representations of work between human and automation, then this is more than "just" an interface problem and designers need to do more than relegate its solution to the interface.

Insights into effective human–automation interaction may be garnered from examining high-performing human organizations and teams. Such insights cannot be taken too literally, however, as automation cannot act as a fully functional human holding accountability, demonstrating leadership and joining in dialectic to form and reform a mental model across the team. Perhaps instead a more reasonable goal is to recognize and design-out predictable disruptions to the team, and to build-up where effective human–automation interaction can be fostered within the limitations of the machine according to each of the constructs described here.

REFERENCES

Bass, E.J., and Pritchett, A.R. (2008). Human-automated judgment learning: A methodology to investigate human interaction with automated judges, *IEEE Transactions on Systems, Man and Cybernetics, 38*(4), 759–776.

Beyer, H., and Holtzblatt, K. (1998). *Contextual design: Defining customer centered systems.* San Francisco, CA: Kaufmann.

Billings, C.E. (1997). *Aviation automation: The search for a human-centered approach.* Mahwah, NJ: Lawrence Erlbaum.

Billman D., Feary, M., and Schreckenghost, D. (2010) Needs Analysis: The Case of Flexible Constraints and Mutable Boundaries, 28th ACM Conference on Human Factors in Computing Systems (CHI2010), April 10–15, Atlanta, GA. (in press).

Bolton, M.L., Bass, E.J., Siminiceanu, R.I., and Feary, M. (Under Review). Applications of Formal Verification to Human–automation Interaction: Current Practices and Future Developments, *Human Factors.*

Butler, K.A., Zhang, J, Esposito, C, Bahrami, A, Hebron, R., and Kieras, D.E. (2007). Work-centered design: a case study of a mixed-initiative scheduler. Proceedings of ACM CHI 2007 Conference on Human Factors in Computing Systems 2007. pp. 747–756.

Cannon-Bowers, J.A., Salas, E., Blickensderfer, E., and Bowers, C.A. (1998). The impact of cross-training and workload on team functioning: A replication and extension of initial findings, *Human Factors, 40,* 92–101.

Cannon-Bowers, J.A., Salas, E., and Converse, S. (1993). Shared mental models in expert team decision-making. In N.J. Castellan, Jr. (Ed.), *Current Issues In Individual And Group Decision-making* (pp. 221–246). Hillsdale, NJ: Erlbaum.

Casner, S.M. (1991). A task-analytic approach to the automated design of graphic presentations, *ACM Transactions on Graphics,* 10 (5), 111–151.

Degani, A., Jorgensen, C., Iverson, D., Shafto, M., Olson, L. (2009). *On Organization of Information: Approach and Early Work.* NASA Technical Memorandum #215368. Moffett Field, CA: NASA Ames Research Center.

Dekker, S.W.A., and Woods, D.D. (2002). MABA-MABA or Abracadabra? Progress on Human—Automation Coordination, *Cognition, Technology and Work, 4*(4), 240–244.

Feigh, K.M., and Pritchett, A.R. (2010). Modeling work for cognitive work support system design in operational control centers, *Journal of Cognitive Engineering and Decision-making.* 4, 1 , pp. 1-26

Fitts, P.M. (1951). Human engineering for an effective air navigation and traffic control system. Washington, DC: National Research Council.

Heffner, T (1997). *Training teams: The impact of shared mental models and team performance.* Published Doctoral Thesis. Pennsylvania State University Graduate School.

Helmreich, R.L., Merritt, A.C., and Wilhelm, J.A. (1999). The evolution of Crew Resource Management training in commercial aviation, *International Journal of Aviation Psychology, 9*(1), 19–32.

Howes, A., Lewis, R. L., and Vera, A. H. (2009). Rational adaptation under task and processing constraints: Implications for testing theories of cognition and action, *Psychological Review, 116*(4), 717–751.

Javaux, D. (2002). A method for predicting errors when interacting with finite state systems: How implicit learning shapes the user's knowledge of a system, *Reliability Engineering and System Safety, 75*(2), 147–165.

John, B.E., Blackmon, M.H., Polson, P.G., Fennell, K., and Teo, L. (2009). Rapid Theory Prototyping: An Example of an Aviation Task. Proceedings of the Human Factors and Ergonomics Society 53rd Annual Meeting (San Antonio, Texas, October 19–23, 2009).

John, B., Prevas, K., Salvucci, D., and Koedinger, K. (2004). Predictive Human Performance Modeling Made Easy. Proceedings of CHI, 2004 (Vienna, Austria, April 24–29, 2004) ACM, New York.

Jorgensen, C. (2009). Visual Coding of Monotonic Signals and Closed Functions for Development of Advanced Displays. Proceedings of the 2009 International Conference on Modeling, Simulation and Visualization Methods, pp. 293–299, WorldComp 2009, July 13–16, 2009.

Kaber, D.B., Wright, M.C., Prinzel, L.J., and Clamann, M.P. (2005). Adaptive automation of human–machine system information-processing functions, *Human Factors*, 47(4), 730–741.

Klimoski, R., and Mohammed, S. (1994). Team mental model: Construct or metaphor? *Journal of Management*, 20, 403–437.

Lee, J. D., and Moray, N. (1994). Trust, self-confidence, and operators' adaptation to automation. *International Journal of Human–computer Studies*, 40, 153–184.

Lee, J.D., and See, K.A. (2004). Trust in automation: Designing for appropriate reliance, *Human Factors*, 46(1), 50–80.

Miller, C.A., and Parasuraman, R. (2007). Designing for flexible interaction between humans and automation: Delegation interfaces for supervisory control, *Human Factors*, 49(1), 57–75.

Muir, B.M. (1994). Trust in automation: I. Theoretical issues in the study of trust and human intervention in automated systems, *Ergonomics Special Issue: Cognitive Ergonomics*, 37(11), 1905–1922.

Ockerman, J.J., and Pritchett, A.R. (2001). A review and reappraisal of task guidance: Aiding workers in procedure following, *International Journal of Cognitive Ergonomics*, 4(3), 191–212.

Parasuraman, R., and Riley, V. (1997). Humans and automation: use, misuse, disuse, abuse, *Human Factors, 39*(2), 230–253.

Parasuraman, R., Sheridan, T.B., and Wickens, C.D. (2000). A model for types and levels of human interaction with automation, *IEEE Transactions on Systems, Man and Cybernetics, 30*(3), 286–297.

Price, H.E. (1985). The allocation of functions in systems. *Human Factors, 27*(1), 33–45.

Pritchett, A.R. (2001). Reviewing the roles of cockpit alerting systems, *Human Factors in Aerospace Safety, 1*(1), 5–38.

Rasmussen, J., Pejtersen, A., and Goodstein, L. (1994). *Cognitive systems engineering*. New York: Wiley.

Riley, V. (1996) Operator reliance on automation: Theory and data. In R. Parasuraman and M. Mouloua (Eds.), *Automation and human performance: Theory and applications* (pp. 19–35). Mahwah, NJ: Erlbaum.

Riley, V. (2001). "A New Language for Pilot Interfaces." *Ergonomics in Design*, 9(2), 21–26.

Salas, E., Dickinson, T.L., Converse, S.A., and Tannenbaum, S.I. (1992). Toward an understanding of team performance and training. In R.W. Swezey and E. Salas (Eds.), *Teams: Their training and performance* (pp. 3–29). Norwood, NJ: Ablex.

Sarter, N.B. and Woods, D.D. (2000). Team play with a powerful and independent agent: A full-mission simulation study, *Human Factors*, 42(3), 390–402.

Schmidt, K. (1991). Cooperative work: A conceptual framework. In J. Rasmussen, B.Brehmer, and J. Leplat (Eds.), *Distributed decision-making: Cognitive models for cooperative work* (pp. 75–110). Chichester, UK: John Willey.

Schutte, P.C. (1999). Complementation: An alternative to automation, *Journal of Information Technology Impact, 1*(3), 113–118.

Sheridan, T.B. (1992). Telerobotics, automation and human supervisory control. Cambridge, MA: MIT Press.

Sheridan, T. and Parasuraman, R. (2000). Human vs. automation in responding to failures: An expected value analysis. *Human Factors, 42*, 403–407.

Sherry, L., and Feary, M. (2004). Task Design and Verification Testing for Certification of Avionics Equipment. The 23rd Digital Avionics Systems Conference, 2004 (DASC 04), vol. 2., pp. 10.A.3–101–110, 24–28 Oct., Salt Lake City, UT, US.

Sherry, L., Feary, M., Polson, P., Mumaw, R., and Palmer, E. (2001). *A Cognitive Engineering Analysis of the Vertical Navigation (VNAV) Function*, NASA Technical Memorandum 2001–210915. NASA Ames Research Center, Moffett Field, CA, US.

Smith, P.J., Bennett, K.B., and Stone, B.R. (2006). Representation aiding to support performance on problem-solving tasks, *Reviews of Human Factors and Ergonomics, 2*, 74–108.

Sperling, B.K. (2005). *Information distribution in complex systems to improve team performance.* Doctoral thesis, Georgia Institute of Technology. (http://smartech.gatech.edu/handle/1853/6975).

Teo, L. and John, B.E. (2008). Towards Predicting User Interaction with CogTool-Explorer. Proceedings of the Human Factors and Ergonomics Society 52nd Annual Meeting (New York City, New York, Sept 22–26, 2008).

Thimbleby, H. (1990). *User interface Design*. Wokingham, England: Addison-Wesley.

Vakil, S. (2000). Analysis of Complexity Evolution Management and Human Performance Issues in Commercial Aircraft Automation Systems. PhD Thesis, Massachusetts Institute of Technology, Cambridge, MA, US.

Vakil, S., and Hansman, R.J. (1997). Predictability as a Metric of Automation Complexity, *Human Factors and Ergonomics Society 41st Annual Meeting*, September, p. 70–74.

Vicente, K. (1999). Cognitive Work Analysis, Toward Safe, Productive and Healthy Computer-Based Work. Mahwah, NJ: LEA.

Wei, Z-G, Mcwan, A.P., and Wieringa, P.A. (1998). A quantitative measure for degree of automation and its relation to system performance and mental load, *Human Factors, 40*(2), 277–295.

Woods, D.D. and Hollnagel, E. (2006). *Joint cognitive systems: Patterns in cognitive systems engineering*. Boca Raton, FL: CRC Press.

Zhang, J. (1994). A Representational Analysis of Relational Information Displays, *International Journal of Human–computer Studies, 45*, pp. 59–74.

Zhang, J. and Norman, D.A. (1994). Representations in distributed cognitive tasks, *Cognitive Science, 18*, 87–122.

13

Human–Agent Interaction

Jeffrey M. Bradshaw, Paul J. Feltovich, and Matthew Johnson

INTRODUCTION

The concept of automation—which began with the straightforward objective of replacing whenever feasible any task currently performed by a human with a machine that could do the same task better, faster, or cheaper—became one of the first issues to attract the notice of early human factors researchers. Pioneering researchers such as Fitts attempted to systematically characterize the general strengths and weaknesses of humans and machines [28]. The resulting discipline of *function allocation* aimed to provide a rational means of determining which system-level functions should be carried out by humans and which by machines (Figure 13.1).

Obviously, however, the suitability of a particular human or machine to take on a particular task may vary over time and in different situations [36]. Hence, early research in adaptive function allocation and adjustable autonomy was undertaken with the hope that shifting of responsibilities between humans and machines could be made dynamic. Of course, certain tasks, such as those requiring sophisticated judgment, could not be shifted to machines, and other tasks, such as those requiring ultra-precise movement, could not be done by humans. But with regard to tasks where human and machine capabilities overlapped—the area of variable task assignment—a series of software-based decision-making schemes were proposed to allow tasks to be allocated according to the availability of the potential performer (Figure 13.2).

Eventually, it became plain to researchers that things were not as simple as they first appeared. For example, many functions in complex systems are shared by humans and machines; hence the need to consider synergies and conflicts among the various performers of joint actions. Moreover, it has become clear that function allocation is not a simple process of transferring responsibilities from one component to another [5]. Automated assistance of whatever kind does not simply enhance our ability to perform the task: it changes the nature of the task itself [15; 50]. For example, those who have asked a five-year-old child help them by doing the dishes know this to be true—from the point of view of an adult, such "help" does not necessarily diminish the effort involved, it merely effects a transformation of the work from the physical action of washing the dishes to the cognitive task of monitoring the progress (and regress) of the child.

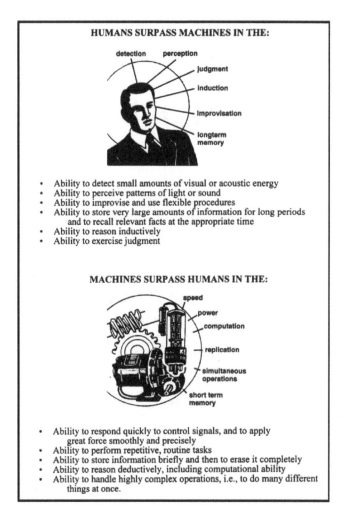

HUMANS SURPASS MACHINES IN THE:

- Ability to detect small amounts of visual or acoustic energy
- Ability to perceive patterns of light or sound
- Ability to improvise and use flexible procedures
- Ability to store very large amounts of information for long periods
  and to recall relevant facts at the appropriate time
- Ability to reason inductively
- Ability to exercise judgment

MACHINES SURPASS HUMANS IN THE:

- Ability to respond quickly to control signals, and to apply
  great force smoothly and precisely
- Ability to perform repetitive, routine tasks
- Ability to store information briefly and then to erase it completely
- Ability to reason deductively, including computational ability
- Ability to handle highly complex operations, i.e., to do many different
  things at once.

Figure 13.1   The Fitts HABA-MABA (humans-are-better-at/machines-are-better-at) approach

As automation becomes more sophisticated, the nature of its interaction with people will need to change in profound ways. In non-trivial interaction of this sort, the point is not to think so much about which tasks are best performed by humans and which by automation but rather how tasks can best be shared by both humans and automation working in concert [36]. Licklider called this concept *man-computer symbiosis* [43]. In the ultimate form of such symbiosis, human capabilities are transparently augmented by cognitive prostheses—computational systems that leverage and extend human intellectual, perceptual, and collaborative capacities, just as a steam shovel is a sort of muscular prosthesis or eyeglasses are a sort of visual prosthesis [11; 30; 35]. To counter the limitations of the Fitts' list, which is clearly intended to summarize what humans and machines each do well on their own, Hoffman has summarized the findings of Woods in an "un-Fitts list" [38] (Table 13.1), which emphasizes how the competencies of humans and machines can be enhanced through appropriate forms of mutual interaction.

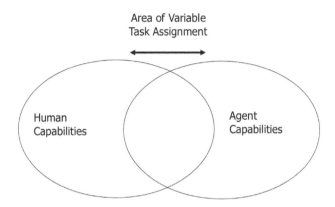

Figure 13.2   Perspective of early research in adaptive allocation and adjustable autonomy

Table 13.1   An "un-Fitts" list [38], © 2002 IEEE

Machines	
Are constrained in that:	Need people to:
Sensitivity to context is low and is ontology-limited	Keep them aligned to context
Sensitivity to change is low and recognition of anomaly is ontology-limited	Keep them stable given the variability and change inherent in the world
Adaptability to change is low and is ontology-limited	Repair their ontologies
They are not "aware" of the fact that the model of the world is itself in the world	Keep the model aligned with the world
People	
Are not limited in that:	Yet they create machines to:
Sensitivity to context is high and is knowledge- and attention-driven	Help them stay informed of ongoing events
Sensitivity to change is high and is driven by the recognition of anomaly	Help them align and repair their perceptions because they rely on mediated stimuli
Adaptability to change is high and is goal-driven	Effect positive change following situation change
They are aware of the fact that the model of the world is itself in the world	Computationally instantiate their models of the world

The Concept of Agents

Though machines that demonstrate superhuman strength, rapid calculation, or extreme agility have proven indispensable in their own right, one of the greatest dreams of scientists and ordinary people has always been a non-human agency whose capabilities might begin to approach those of their fellow beings. The word *robot*, derived from the Czech word for drudgery, captured the public imagination following Karel Capek's 1921 play *RUR: Rossum Universal Robots* (Figure 13.3).

Figure 13.3   Scene from Capek's 1921 play, *Rossum Universal Robots*

Though automata of various sorts have existed for centuries, it is only since World War II, with the development of computers and control theory, that anything resembling modern agent technology has begun to appear. Computer visionary Alan Kay provided a thumbnail sketch tracing the more recent roots of the idea:

> The idea of an agent originated with John McCarthy in the mid-1950s, and the term was coined by Oliver G. Selfridge a few years later, when they were both at the Massachusetts Institute of Technology. They had in view a system that, when given a goal, could carry out the details of the appropriate computer operations and could ask for and receive advice, offered in human terms, when it was stuck. An agent would be a "soft robot" living and doing its business within the computer's world. [41]

Since the idea of agents was first introduced, people have debated the meaning of the term. The debate on the definition of agenthood will probably never be fully settled: one person's "intelligent agent" is another person's "smart object"; and today's "smart object" is tomorrow's "dumb program" [6, p. 5]. However, by whatever names and definitions we adopt, the systems we interact with a few decades from now will be different in fundamental ways, and will bring new questions to the fore.

"Agents occupy a strange place in the realm of technology," argues Don Norman, "leading to much fear, fiction, and extravagant claims" [51, p. 49]. By their ability to operate independently in complex situations without constant human supervision, agents can perform tasks on a scale that would be impractical or impossible for fully human-in-the-loop approaches to duplicate. On the other hand, this additional autonomy, if unchecked, also has the potential of effecting severe damage if agents are poorly designed, buggy, or malicious. Because ever more powerful intelligent

**Figure 13.4   The concept of agents has evoked fear, fiction, and
                   extravagant claims**

Source: Kelly Freas, *The Gulf Between*, with permission.

agents will increasingly differ from software that people are accustomed to, we need
to take into account social issues no less than the technical ones if the agents we
design and build are to be acceptable to people.

Norman continues:

> The technical aspect is to devise a computational structure that guarantees that from the
> technical standpoint, all is under control. This is not an easy task.

> The social part of acceptability is to provide reassurance that all is working according to
> plan … This is also a non-trivial task. [51, p. 49]

The Emergence of Human-Agent Interaction Research

Much of the early work of researchers in software agents and robotics was motivated
by situations in which autonomous systems were envisioned to "replace" human
participation, thus minimizing the need to consider the "social" aspects of acceptability.
For example, one of the earliest high-consequence applications of sophisticated agent
technologies was in NASA's Remote Agent Architecture (RAA). RAA was designed to
be used in situations where response latencies in the transmission of round-trip control
sequences from earth would have impaired the satellite's ability to respond to urgent
problems or take advantage of unexpected science opportunities [49]. However, in
contrast to autonomous systems that are designed to take humans out of the loop, an
increasing number of efforts are being specifically designed to address requirements
for close and continuous interaction with people [1; 7; 44; 55].

Specific approaches to human-agent interaction (HAI) have been explored in many forms and with somewhat divergent perspectives. For example, research communities have formed around the topics of interface agents and assistants [16; 21; 39; 44; 45], adjustable autonomy [9; 10; 22; 23; 33; 46; 47], mixed-initiative systems [2; 3; 9; 12; 27], human-agent teamwork [46; 58], and collaboration theory [34; 53].

In this chapter, we will examine the elements of successful HAI from the perspective of joint activity theory [25; 42], a generalization of Herbert Clark's work in linguistics [18, p. 3]. We will not attempt to provide detailed recommendations or a survey of the voluminous literature, but rather will outline some of the most important principles of HAI based on our own experience.

A JOINT ACTIVITY PERSPECTIVE ON HAI

The essence of joint activity is interdependence. In a joint activity, the parties involved must intend to produce something that is a genuine joint product—as Woods writes, "It's not cooperation if either you do it all or I do it all" [61].

In order to carry out the joint activity, the parties effectively enter into what we call a "Basic Compact"—an agreement (usually tacit) that all parties will support the process of coordination. If there is no need for substantive coordination among the various parties as they carry out their actions, then this is parallel—not joint—activity.

Joint activity is a *process*, extended in space and time. There is a time when the parties enter into joint activity and a time when it has ended. These are not "objective" points of time that would necessarily be agreed on by any "observer-in-the-world," but most importantly are interpretations arrived at by the parties involved [18, p. 84]. In some circumstances the entry and exit points may be very clear such as when two people play a classical duet; the same would probably not be said of musicians involved in a jam session or of participants in a mass demonstration.

The overall *structure* of joint activity is one of embedded sets of actions, some of which may also be joint and some of which may be accomplished more or less individually. All these actions likewise have entry and exit points, although as we have mentioned earlier, these points are not epistemologically "objective." Synchronizing entry and exit points of the many embedded phases involved in complex joint activity is a major challenge to coordination.

Types of Joint Activity

As mentioned previously, interdependence is the essence of joint activity. Thus, it should not be a surprise that different kinds of joint activity can be distinguished according to the types of interdependencies involved.

Co-allocation: This is characterized by interdependence among necessary resources only. Parties have independent goals, and there is no functional coupling of methods. Examples include two groups trying to schedule a conference room they both need to use on a certain day, or simultaneously sharing a wireless network. In sharing, constraints on resource allocation require negotiation.

Cooperation: In cooperation—perhaps better rendered here as "co-operation"—there is interdependence of activities but not of motivations and goals. Often there is also interdependence of resources. Following the last example, two groups trying to conduct their own meetings within the same room at the same time would be a cooperation. So also, interestingly, are competitive games, such as football, where the two teams' actions are clearly interdependent while their aims are not the same and even contrasting.

Collaboration: Shared objectives are the hallmark of collaboration. Teamwork can be seen as a particular form of collaboration. All parties are trying to achieve the same end (mutually defined), and there is also usually interdependence of actions (often involving different roles) and resources. Team members within one team in a football game (or a relay team in track and field) fit this description, as does a group of scholars working together to produce a genuinely multiauthored article on a topic of mutual interest. The more sophisticated collaboration roles—for example, those involving negotiation of complex goals and meanings—are more adeptly handled by humans than by agents. Today's agents, however, have begun to participate in the relatively simpler roles of collaboration support. Notwithstanding the many challenges involved, adult humans and radically less-able entities (for example, small children, dogs, video game characters) have shown themselves capable of working together effectively in a variety of situations where a subjective experience of collaboration is often maintained despite the magnitude of their differences [37]. Generally this is due to the ability of humans to rapidly size up and adapt to the limitations of their teammates, an ability we would like to exploit in the design of approaches for HAI.

The Challenge of Human-Agent Coordination in Joint Activity

In a very real sense, the cumulative success of research on agent autonomy can be seen as fueling its own demand for more sophisticated HAI. For example, human interaction with simple teleoperated robotic platforms is confined to whatever actions are necessary to direct the robot from one place to another. The final destination—and, more importantly, the reasons behind the journey—remain completely in the mind of the operator, who stays in more or less continuous contact with the platform. However, the more that navigation and reasoning about how to meet mission objectives are delegated to the robotic platform itself, with the operator providing only intermittent supervisory feedback, the greater the need for effective coordination. This need dramatically increases when there are multiple parties—humans, software agents, and robots—involved.

Clark observes that "a person's processes may be very different in individual and joint actions, even when they appear identical" [18]. For example, he contrasts playing a musical solo versus playing a duet. A major difference between the two is the need for coordination. Malone and Crowston [48] defined coordination as "managing dependencies between activities." For example, any sort of teamwork, which by definition implies interdependence among the players, therefore requires some level of work for each party over and beyond the carrying out of task itself in order to manage its role in coordination. Part of that "extra" work involves each party doing its part to assure that relevant aspects of the agents and the situation are observable at an appropriate level of abstraction and using an effective style of interaction [8].

Although coordination is as much a requirement for joint activity among groups of software agents as it is in HAI, the magnitude of the representational and reasoning gulfs separating humans from agents is much larger [50]. Moreover, because the agent's ability to sense or infer information about the human environment and cognitive context is so limited, agent designers must find innovative ways to compensate for the fact that their agents are not situated in the human world. Brittleness of agent capabilities is difficult to avoid because only certain aspects of the human environment and cognitive context can be represented in the agent, and the representation that is made cannot be "general purpose," but must be optimized for the particular use scenarios the designer originally envisioned. Without sufficient basis for shared situation awareness and mutual feedback, coordination among people and agents simply cannot take place, and, as argued above, this need for shared understanding and feedback increases as the size of the group and the degree of autonomy of the agents increase. This increase in size and complexity changes the very nature of the task and the relationships among participants.

Requirements for Effective Coordination

Joint activity theory highlights three major requirements for effective coordination: interpredictability, common ground, and directability [42]:

- *Interpredictability:* In highly interdependent activities, it becomes possible to plan one's own actions (including coordination actions) only when what others will do can be accurately predicted. Skilled teams become interpredictable through shared knowledge and idiosyncratic coordination devices developed through extended experience in working together. On the other hand, bureaucracies with high turnover compensate for such experience by substituting explicit, predesigned structured procedures and expectations relative to formal organizational roles.
- *Common ground:* Common ground refers to the pertinent mutual knowledge, beliefs, and assumptions that support interdependent actions in the context of a given joint activity [17]. This includes whatever common ground is already shared prior to engaging in the joint activity as well as mutual knowledge of shared history and current state that is obtained while the activity is underway. Unless I can make good assumptions about what you know, we cannot effectively coordinate.
- *Directability:* Directability refers to the capacity for deliberately assessing and modifying the actions of the other parties in a joint activity as conditions and priorities change [15]. Effective coordination requires adequate responsiveness of each participant to the influence of the others and the requirements of the situation as the activity unfolds. When things go wrong we want to feel assured that there is a mutual commitment to resolve problems in a timely manner.

Following the lead of pioneering researchers such as Geertz [32, pp. 44–46, 67], we have argued that people create and have created cultures and social conventions—albeit in many disparate forms across mankind that can be hard for outsiders to understand—to provide order and predictability that lead to effective

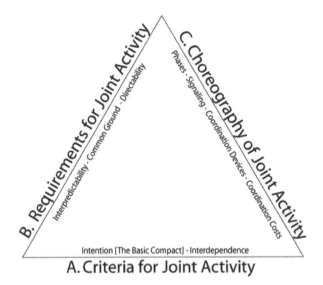

Figure 13.5   Criteria, requirements, and choreography of joint activity

coordination [24; 25], including ongoing progress appraisal [26].[1] Order and predictability may have a basis in the simple cooperative act between two people, in which the parties "contract" to engage together in a set of interlinked, mutually beneficial activities. From this simple base, in humans at least, there are constructed elaborate and intricate systems of regulatory tools, from formal legal systems, to standards of professional practice, to norms of proper everyday behavior (along with associated methods of punishment or even simple forms of shaming for violations of these). Such diverse regulatory mechanisms can be exploited in HAI to support coordination of complex, interdependent activity [25], as can additional mechanisms discussed next.

The Choreography of Coordination

People coordinate through signals and more complex messages of many sorts (for example, face-to-face language, expressions, posture). Human signals are also mediated in many ways—for example, through third parties or through machines such as telephones or computers. Hence, direct and indirect party-to-party communication is one form of a "coordination device," in this instance coordination by *agreement*. For example, a group of scientists working together on a grant proposal, may simply agree, through email exchanges, to set up a subsequent conference call at a specific date and time. Besides agreement, there are three other common coordination devices [18; 42]:

---

1   Even simple forms of animal cooperation seems to bear out such a thesis [56], and we would argue that the more autonomous the agents involved, the more need there is for such regulation and the wider the variety of forms it might take.

- *Convention*: Often, prescriptions of various types apply to how parties interact. These can range from rules and regulations, to less formal codes of appropriate conduct such as norms of practice in a particular professional community, or established practices in a workplace. Coordination by convention depends on structures outside of a particular episode of joint activity.
- *Precedent*: Coordination by precedent is like coordination by convention, except that it applies to norms and expectations developed within an episode of the ongoing process of a joint activity (or across repeated episodes of such activity if the participants are a long-standing team that repeats conduct of some procedure): "That's the way we did it last time."
- *Salience*: Salience is perhaps the coordination device that is most difficult to understand and describe. It has to do with how the ongoing work of the joint activity arranges the workspace so that next move becomes highlighted or otherwise apparent among the many moves that could conceivably be chosen. For example, in a surgery, exposure of a certain element of anatomy, in the course of pursuing a particular surgical goal, can make it clear to all parties involved what to do next. Coordination by salience is a sophisticated kind of coordination produced by the very conduct of the joint activity itself. It requires little or no overt communication and is likely the predominant mode of coordination among long-standing, highly practiced teams.

Roles, Regulations, and Organizations in Joint Activity

Roles can be thought of as ways of packaging rights and obligations that go along with the necessary parts that people play in joint activities. Of course, multiple roles can be played by the same actor in a given activity. Knowing one's own roles and the roles of others in a joint activity establishes expectations about how others are likely to interact with us, and how we think we should interact with them. Shoppers expect cashiers to do certain things for them (for example, total up the items and handle payment) and to treat them in a certain way (for example, with cheerful courtesy), and cashiers have certain expectations of shoppers. When roles are well understood and regulatory devices are performing their proper function, observers are likely to describe the activity as highly coordinated. On the other hand, violations of the expectations associated with roles and regulatory structures can result in confusion, frustration, anger, and a breakdown in coordination.

Collections of roles are often grouped to form organizations. In addition to regulatory considerations at the level of individual roles, organizations themselves may also add their own rules, standards, traditions, and so forth, in order to establish a common culture that will smooth interaction among parties.

Knowing how roles undergird organizations and how rights and obligations undergird roles helps us understand how organizations can be seen as functional or dysfunctional. Whether hierarchical or heterarchical, fluid or relatively static, organizations are functional only to the extent that their associated regulatory devices and roles generally assist them in facilitating their individual responsibilities and their work in coordinating their actions with others when necessary.

The lesson here for human-agent interaction is that the various roles that different parties assume in their work must include more than simple names for the role and algorithmic behavior to perform their individual tasks. They must also, to be successful, include regulatory structures that define the additional work of coordination associated with that role.

Norms and Policies in Joint Activity

The order needed for agents to engage in joint activity is typically implemented in terms of formalized social regulations. The idea of building strong social regulation into intelligent systems can be traced at least as far back as the 1940s to the science fiction writings of Isaac Asimov [4]. Shoham and Tennenholtz [54] introduced the theme of social "laws" into the agent research community, where investigations have continued under two main headings: *norms* and *policies*. Drawing on precedents in legal theory, social psychology, social philosophy, sociology, and decision theory [60], *norm-based* approaches have grown in popularity [52; 59]. In the multi-agent system research community, Conte and Castelfranchi [20] found that norms were variously described as constraints on behavior, ends or goals, or obligations. For the most part, implementations of norms in multi-agent systems share three basic features:

1. they are designed offline; or
2. they are learned, adopted, and refined through the purposeful deliberation of each agent; and
3. they are enforced by means of incentives and sanctions.

Interest in *policy-based* approaches to multi-agent and distributed systems has also grown considerably in recent years (see, for example, www.policy-workshop.org/). While sharing much in common with norm-based approaches, policy-based perspectives differ in subtle ways. Whereas in everyday English the term *norm* denotes a practice, procedure, or custom regarded as typical or widespread, a *policy* is defined by the American Heritage Online dictionary as a "course of action, guiding principle, or procedure considered expedient, prudent, or advantageous." Thus, in contrast to the relatively descriptive basis and self-chosen adoption (or rejection) of norms, policies tend to be seen as prescriptive and externally-imposed entities. Whereas norms in everyday life emerge gradually from group conventions and recurrent patterns of interaction, policies are consciously designed and put into and out of force at arbitrary times by virtue of explicitly-recognized authority. These differences are generally reflected in the way most policy-based approaches differ from norm-based ones with respect to the three features mentioned above. Policy-based approaches:

1. support dynamic runtime policy changes, and not merely static configurations determined in advance;
2. work involuntarily with respect to the agents, that is, without requiring the agents to consent or even be aware of the policies being enforced; thus aiming to guarantee that even the simplest agents can comply with policy; and
3. wherever possible they are enforced preemptively, preventing buggy or malicious agents from doing harm in advance rather than rewarding them or imposing sanctions on them after the fact.

Figure 13.6   **Policies constitute an agent's "rules of the road," not its "route plan"**

Policy management should not be confused with planning or workflow management, which are related but separate functions. Planning mechanisms are generally *deliberative* (that is, they reason deeply and actively about activities in support of complex goals), whereas policy mechanisms tend to be *reactive* (that is, concerned with simple actions triggered by some environmental event) [31, pp. 161–162]. Whereas plans are a unified roadmap for accomplishing some coherent set of objectives, bodies of policy collected to govern some sphere of activity are made up of diverse constraints imposed by multiple potentially-disjoint stakeholders and enforced by mechanisms that are more or less independent from the ones directly involved in planning. Plans tend to be relatively comprehensive, while policies, in our sense, are by nature piecemeal. In short, we might say that while policies constitute the "rules of the road"—providing the stop signs, speed limits, and lane markers that serve to coordinate traffic and minimize mishaps—they are not sufficient to address the problem of "route planning."

Norms and policies can, of course, be combined in agent systems. Typically, however, agent system designers tend to gravitate toward one approach or the other, based on the kinds of agents they are defining and the kinds of problems they are trying to solve. A norm-based approach is always useful when:

- a primary purpose of the agent system is to model the learning and adaptation of norms;
- the norms are not arbitrary constraints, but have a rational basis in repeated experience;
- the results of deliberate violations of regulation is relatively inconsequential.

Implementing regulation through policy is most useful when:

- the application requires predictability and repeatability with respect to the specific agent behavior being regulated;
- the agents themselves are not capable of learning;
- compliance with regulation within a specified tolerance is essential.

COACTIVE DESIGN

The term "coactive design" was coined by Johnson as a way of characterizing an approach to HAI that takes *interdependence* as the central organizing principle among people and agents working together in joint activity [40]. Besides implying that two or more parties are participating in an activity, the term "coactive" is meant to convey the reciprocal and mutually constraining nature of actions and effects that are conditioned by coordination. In joint activity, individual participants share an obligation to coordinate, sacrificing to a degree their individual autonomy in the service of progress toward group goals. Below we sketch some of the important considerations that play into coactive design.

- *Teamwork vs. task-work*. Coactive design complements task-focused approaches to HAI such as function allocation, adjustable autonomy, and mixed-initiative interaction. It is more focused on teamwork than task-work. For example, the task-work of playing soccer includes kicking to a target, dribbling, tackling, and tracking the ball and the goal. By way of contrast, the teamwork of soccer focuses on things like allocating players to roles, synchronizing tactics, and sharing information.
- *Mutual affordances and obligations*. Software agents are often described in terms of their role as assistants to people. While this one-way relationship between assistant and the one who is assisted sometimes may be a helpful, it is inadequate for describing joint activity of humans and agents working together. Joint activity, by its nature, implies the greater parity of *mutual* assistance, enabled by intricate webs of complementary, reciprocal affordances and obligations. Human speech would be useless without the complementary affordance of hearing. Likewise a software agent designed to assist with ongoing human needs for navigation help is useless unless its navigation algorithm allows for outside guidance.
- *Soft dependencies*. Coactive design emphasizes the importance of both "hard" and "soft" dependencies in coordinating related activities. Hard dependencies are necessary, or the joint activity could not happen in the first place. An example of a hard dependency is the passing of a baton in a relay race—the second runner simply can't begin until the first runner completes the handoff. Soft dependencies are not strictly necessary but are *helpful*. Attending to soft dependencies is a subtle, but no less significant process—in fact, it is what generally distinguishes great teams from mediocre ones. For instance, the first runner may shout something to the second runner before or during the handoff to convey a warning about a slippery section of track or to share other kinds of relevant information. If the approach of the first runner were difficult to confirm visually, progress appraisal would be in order ("I'll be there in about five seconds!"). Of course, none of the first runner's signals would be of any use unless the second runner were monitoring for such communications. Soft

dependencies may go beyond the sharing of information when, for example, a person or agent suspends its current activity in order to help another member of the group perform their task.

- *Joint goals*. Multi-agent teamwork research typically has held a simple view of joint goals, based on the unification of symbols common to all parties [19; 57]. However, Cartwright and Zander [13] point out the necessity of a more sophisticated view when humans are involved in joint activity. Apart from the problem of establishing and maintaining common ground on complex goals and the best means to achieve them, they emphasize that team goals are sometimes in competition with goals that individuals have for themselves and for the team [55].

- *Mixed-initiative opportunities in all phases of the sense-plan-act cycle*. Mixed-initiative interaction, where the roles and actions of people and agents are opportunistically negotiated during problem-solving [2], has typically been limited to the planning and command generation aspects of human-agent interaction. To these, Fong [29] perceptively added the aspects of perception and cognition. Coactive design extends this earlier work in all phases of the sense-plan-act cycle, consistent with Castelfranchi's contention that "any needed resource and power within the action-perception loop of an agent defines a possible dimension of dependence or of autonomy" [14]. Coactive design the mutual interdependence of the all parties instead of merely focusing on the dependence of one of the parties on the other. It recognizes the benefits of designing agents with the capabilities they need to be interdependent.

SUMMARY

With all these considerations in mind, we might formulate the characteristics of a good agent—human or artificial—with regard to joint activity in the following simple maxims:

1. A good agent is *observable*. It makes its pertinent state and intentions obvious.
2. A good agent is attuned to the requirement of *progress appraisal*. It enables others to stay informed about the status of its tasks and identifies any potential trouble spots ahead.
3. A good agent is *informative* and *polite*. It knows enough about others and their situations so that it can tailor its messages to be helpful, opportune, and appropriately presented.
4. A good agent *knows its limits*. It knows when to take the initiative on its own, and when it needs to wait for outside direction. It respects policy-based constraints on its behavior, but will consider exceptions and workarounds when appropriate.
5. A good agent is *predictable* and *dependable*. It can be counted on to do its part.
6. A good agent is *directable* at all levels of the sense-plan-act cycle. It can be retasked in a timely way by a recognized authority whenever circumstances require.
7. A good agent is *selective*. It helps others focus attention on what is most important in the current context.
8. A good agent is *coordinated*. It helps communicate, manage, and deconflict dependencies among activities, knowledge, and resources that are prerequisites to effective task performance and the maintenance of "common ground."

REFERENCES

1. Allen, J., N. Chambers, G. Ferguson, L. Galescu, H. Jung, M. Swift, and W. Taysom. "PLOW: A Collaborative Task Learning Agent." In *Proceedings of AAAI 2007*. 2007.

2. Allen, J.F. "Mixed-initiative interaction." *IEEE Intelligent Systems*, September–October 1999, 14–16.

3. Allen, J.F. and G. Ferguson. "Human–machine collaborative planning." Presented at the Proceedings of the NASA Planning and Scheduling Workshop, Houston, TX 2002.

4. Asimov, I. "Runaround." In *I, Robot*, edited by I. Asimov, 33–51. London, England: Grafton Books. Originally published in *Astounding Science Fiction*, 1942, pp. 94–103, 1942/1968.

5. Boy, G. *Cognitive Function Analysis*. Stamford, CT: Ablex Publishing, 1998.

6. Bradshaw, J.M. "An introduction to software agents." In *Software Agents*, edited by J.M. Bradshaw, 3–46. Cambridge, MA: AAAI Press/The MIT Press, 1997.

7. Bradshaw, J.M., M. Sierhuis, Y. Gawdiak, R. Jeffers, N. Suri, and M. Greaves. "Teamwork and adjustable autonomy for the Personal Satellite Assistant." Presented at the Workshop on Autonomy, Delegation and Control: Interacting with Autonomous Agents. Seventeenth International Joint Conference on Artivicial Inelligence (IJCAI-2001), Seattle, WA, August 6, 2001.

8. Bradshaw, J.M., M. Sierhuis, A. Acquisti, P. Feltovich, R. Hoffman, R. Jeffers, D. Prescott, N. Suri, A. Uszok, and R. Van Hoof. "Adjustable autonomy and human-agent teamwork in practice: An interim report on space applications." In *Agent Autonomy*, edited by H. Hexmoor, R. Falcone, and C. Castelfranchi, 243–280. Kluwer, 2003.

9. Bradshaw, J.M., P. Feltovich, H. Jung, S. Kulkarni, W. Taysom, and A. Uszok. "Dimensions of adjustable autonomy and mixed-initiative interaction." In *Agents and Computational Autonomy: Potential, Risks, and Solutions. Lecture Notes in Computer Science, vol. 2969*, edited by M. Nickles, M. Rovatsos, and G. Weiss, 17–39. Berlin, Germany: Springer-Verlag, 2004.

10. Bradshaw, J.M., H. Jung, S. Kulkarni, J. Allen, L. Bunch, N. Chambers, P.J. Feltovich, L. Galescu, R. Jeffers, M. Johnson, W. Taysom, and A. Uszok. "Toward trustworthy adjustable autonomy and mixed-initiative in KAoS." Presented at the Proceedings of the Autonomous Agents and Multi-Agent Systems (AAMAS) 2004 Trust Workshop, New York City, NY, July 19, 2004, 9–20.

11. Bradshaw, J.M., N. Suri, M.R. Breedy, A. Canas, R. Davis, K.M. Ford, R. Hoffman, R. Jeffers, S. Kulkarni, J. Lott, T. Reichherzer, and A. Uszok. Updated and expanded version of an article that originally appeared in IEEE Intelligent Systems, July 2001, pp. 49–56. "Terraforming cyberspace." In *Process Coordination and Ubiquitous Computing*, edited by D.C. Marinescu and C. Lee, 165–185. Boca Raton, FL: CRC Press. Updated and expanded version of an article that originally appeared in IEEE Intelligent Systems, July 2001, pp. 49–56, 2002.

12. Burstein, M.H. and D.V. McDermott. "Issues in the development of human–computer mixed-initiative planning." In *Cognitive Technology: In Search of a Humane Interface*, edited by B. Gorayska and J.L. Mey. Elsevier Science, 1996.

13. Cartwright, D. and A. Zander. *Group Dynamics: Research ant Theory*. Third edn. New York City, NY: Harper and Row, 1968.

14. Castelfranchi, C. "Founding agents' "autonomy" on dependence theory." Presented at the 14th European Conference on Artificial Intelligence (ECAI 2000), Berlin, Germany, August 20–25, 2000, 353–357.

15. Christofferson, K. and D.D. Woods. "How to make automated systems team players." In *Advances in Human Performance and Cognitive Engineering Research, vol. 2*, edited by E. Salas. JAI Press, Elsevier, 2002.

16. Clancey, W.J. "Roles for agent assistants in field science: Understanding personal projects and collaboration." *IEEE Transactions on Systems, Man, and Cybernetics — Part C: Applications and Reviews 32*, no. 2 (2004).

17. Clark, H.H. and S.E. Brennan. "Grounding in communication." In *Perspectives on Socially Shared Cognition*, edited by L.B. Resnick, J.M. Levine, and S.D. Teasley. Washington, D.C.: American Psychological Association, 1991.

18. Clark, H.H. *Using Language*. Cambridge, UK: Cambridge University Press, 1996.

19. Cohen, P.R. and H.J. Levesque. "Teamwork." Menlo Park, CA: SRI International, 1991.

20. Conte, R. and C. Castelfranchi. *Cognitive and social action*. London, England: UCL Press, 1995.

21. Cypher, A. (Ed.). *Watch What I Do: Programming by Demonstration*. Cambridge, MA: MIT Press, 1993.

22. Dorais, G., R.P. Bonasso, D. Kortenkamp, B. Pell, and D. Schreckenghost. "Adjustable autonomy for human-centered autonomous systems on Mars." Presented at the Proceedings of the AAAI Spring Symposium on Agents with Adjustable Autonomy. AAAI Technical Report SS-99–06, Menlo Park, CA 1999.

23. Falcone, R. and C. Castelfranchi. "Adjustable social autonomy." (2002).

24. Feltovich, P., J.M. Bradshaw, R. Jeffers, N. Suri, and A. Uszok. "Social order and adaptability in animal and human cultures as an analogue for agent communities: Toward a policy-based approach." In *Engineering Societies in the Agents World IV. LNAI 3071*, edited by A. Omicini, P. Petta, and J. Pitt. Lecture Notes in Computer Science, 21–48. Berlin, Germany: Springer-Verlag, 2004.

25. Feltovich, P., J.M. Bradshaw, W.J. Clancey, and M. Johnson. "Toward and Ontology of Regulation: Support for Coordination in Human and Machine Joint Activity." In *Engineering Societies in the Agents World VII. Lecture Notes in Computer Science*, edited by G. O'Hare, A. Ricci, M. O'Grady, A. Ricci, and O. Dikenelli, 175–192. Heidelberg, Germany: Springer-Verlag, 2007.

26. Feltovich, P., J.M. Bradshaw, W.J. Clancey, M. Johnson, and L. Bunch. "Progress appraisal as a challenging element of coordination in human and machine joint activity." In *Engineering Societies for the Agents World VIII. Lecture Notes in Computer Science*, edited by A. Artikis, G. O'Hare, K. Stathis, and G. Vouros, 124–141. Heidelberg, Germany: Springer-Verlag, 2008.

27. Ferguson, G., J. Allen, and B. Miller. "TRAINS-95: Towards a mixed-initiative planning assistant." Presented at the Proceedings of the Third Conference on Artificial Intelligence Planning Systems (AIPS-96), Edinburgh, Scotland 1996, 70–77.

28. Fitts, P.M. (Ed.). Human Engineering for an Effective Air Navigation and Traffic Control System. Washington, D.C.: National Research Council, 1951.

29. Fong, T.W. "Collaborative Control: A Robot-Centric Model for Vehicle Teleoperation. Technical Report CMU-R1-TR-01–34." Carnegie Mellon University, 2001.

30. Ford, K.M., C. Glymour, and P. Hayes. "Cognitive prostheses." *AI Magazine 18*, no. 3 (Fall 1997): 104.

31. Fox, J. and S. Das. *Safe and Sound: Artificial Intelligence in Hazardous Applications*. Menlo Park, CA: AAAI Press/The MIT Press, 2000.

32. Geertz, C. *The Interpretation of Cultures*. New York, NY: Basic Books, 1973.

33. Goodrich, M.A., D.R. Olsen Jr., J.W. Crandall, and T.J. Palmer. "Experiments in adjustable autonomy." Presented at the Proceedings of the IJCAI_01 Workshop on Autonomy, Delegation, and Control: Interacting with Autonomous Agents, Seattle, WA, August 20–25, 2001.

34. Grosz, B.J. "Collaborative systems." *AI Magazine 17*, no. 2 (Summer 1996): 67–85.

35. Hamilton, S. "Thinking outside the box at IHMC." *IEEE Computer* (January 2001): 61–71.

36. Hancock, P.A. and S.F. Scallen. "Allocating functions in human–machine systems." In *Viewing Psychology as a Whole*, edited by R. Hoffman, M.F. Sherrick, and J.S. Warm, 509–540. Washington, D.C.: American Psychological Association, 1998.

37. Helton, W.S. *Canine Ergonomics: The Science of Working Dogs*. Boca Raton, FL: Taylor and Francis, 2009.

38. Hoffman, R., P. Feltovich, K.M. Ford, D.D. Woods, G. Klein, and A. Feltovich. "A rose by any other name … would probably be given an acronym." *IEEE Intelligent Systems*, July-August 2002, 72–80.

39. Horvitz, E. "Principles of mixed-initiative user interfaces." Presented at the Proceedings of the ACM SIGCHI Conference on Human Factors in Computing Systems (CHI '99), Pittsburgh, PA, May, 1999.

40. Johnson, M., J.M. Bradshaw, P. Feltovich, C. Jonker, B. van Riemsdijk, and M. Sierhuis. "Coactive design: Why interdependence must shape autonomy. Submitted for publication." 2010

41. Kay, A. "Computer Software." *Scientific American 251*, no. 3 (1984): 53–59.

42. Klein, G., P.J. Feltovich, J.M. Bradshaw, and D.D. Woods. "Common ground and coordination in joint activity." In *Organizational Simulation*, edited by W.B. Rouse and K.R. Boff, 139–184. New York City, NY: John Wiley, 2004.

43. Licklider, J.C.R. "Man-computer symbiosis." IRE Transactions in Electronics. New York: Institute of Radio Engineers. (1960): 4–11.

44. Lieberman, H. (Ed.). *Your Wish is My Command: Programming By Example*. San Francisco, CA: Morgan Kaufmann, 2001.

45. Lieberman, H. and T. Selker. "Agents for the user interface." In *Handbook of Software Agents*, edited by J.M. Bradshaw. Cambridge, MA: AAAI Press/The MIT Press, 2002.

46. Luck, M., M. D' Inverno, and S. Munroe. "Autonomy: Variable and generative." In *Agent Autonomy*, edited by H. Hexmoor, C. Castelfranchi, and R. Falcone, 9–22. Dordrecht, the Netherlands: Kluwer, 2002.

47. Maheswaran, R.T., M. Tambe, P. Varakantham, and K. Myers. "Adjustable autonomy challenges in personal assistant agents: A position paper." In *Computational Autonomy*, edited by M. Klusch, G. Weiss, and M. Rovatsos, in press. Berlin, Germany: Springer, 2004.

48. Malone, T.W. and K. Crowston. "What is coordination theory and how can it help design cooperative work systems?" Presented at the Conference on Computer-Supported Cooperative Work (CSCW '90), Los Angeles, CA, October 7–10, 1990, 357–370.

49. Muscettola, N., P.P. Nayak, B. Pell, and B.C. Williams. "Remote Agent: To boldly go where no AI system has gone before." *Artificial Intelligence 103*, no. 1–2 (August 1998): 5–48.

50. Norman, D.A. "Cognitive artifacts." In *Designing Interaction: Psychology at the Human–computer Interface*, edited by J.M. Carroll, 17–38. Cambridge: Cambridge University Press, 1992.

51. Norman, D.A. "How might people interact with agents?" In *Software Agents*, edited by J.M. Bradshaw, 49–55 (see also How might people interact with robots? www.jnd. org/dn.mss/how_might_humans_int.html). Cambridge, MA: The AAAI Press/The MIT Press, 1997.

52. Penserini, L., H.M. Aldewereld, F.P.M. Dignum, and M.V. Dignum. "A formal specification for organizational adapation." Presented at the Proceedings of the Tenth International Workshop on Agent-Oriented Software Engineering (AOSE-09) 2009.

53. Rich, C., C. Sidner, and N. Lesh. "COLLAGEN: Applying collaborative discourse theory." *AI Magazine* (2001).

54. Shoham, Y. and M. Tennenholtz. "On the synthesis of useful social laws for artificial agent societies." Presented at the Proceedings of the Tenth National Conference on Artificial Intelligence, San Jose, CA 1992, 276–281.

55. Sierhuis, M., J.M. Bradshaw, A. Acquisti, R. Van Hoof, R. Jeffers, and A. Uszok. "Human-agent teamwork and adjustable autonomy in practice." Presented at the Proceedings of the Seventh International Symposium on Artificial Intelligence, Robotics and Automation in Space (i-SAIRAS), Nara, Japan, May 19–23, 2003.

56. Smith, W.J. *The Behavior of Communicating*. Cambridge, MA: Harvard University Press, 1977.

57. Tambe, M., W. Shen, M. Mataric, D.V. Pynadath, D. Goldberg, P.J. Modi, Z. Qiu, and B. Salemi. "Teamwork in cyberspace: Using TEAMCORE to make agents team-ready." Presented at the Proceedings of the AAAI Spring Symposium on Agents in Cyberspace, Menlo Park, CA 1999.

58. Tambe, M., D. Pynadath, C. Chauvat, A. Das, and G. Kaminka. "Adaptive agent architectures for heterogeneous team members." Presented at the Proceedings of the International Conference on Multi-Agent Systems (ICMAS 2000) 2000.

59. Vecht, B.v.d., F.P.M. Dignum, J.-J.C. Meyer, and M. Neef. "Coordination, organizations, institutions, and norms in agent systems." In *Proceedings of COIN*. Lecture Notes in Computer Science 4870, 83–96. Berlin, Germany: Springer Verlag, 2007.

60. Verhagen, H. "Norms and artificial agents." Presented at the Sixth Meeting of the Special Interest Group on Agent-Based Social Simulation, ESPRIT Network of Excellence on Agent-Based Computing, Amsterdam, Holland, December 4–5, 2001.

61. Woods, D.D. "Steering the reverberations of technology change on fields of practice: Laws that govern cognitive work." Presented at the Proceedings of the Annual Meeting of the Cognitive Science Society, August 10, 2002.

PART III

Evaluation

14

From Usability to User Experience with Interactive Systems

Jean-Marc Robert and Annemarie Lesage

UX STORY #1: BIXI RENTAL BICYCLES

Since spring 2009, the city of Montreal offers a public bike service. Citizens and visitors have access to batches of bicycles located on different street corners all over the city. They can rent a Bixi (the name of the bicycle) for their short trips and leave it in one of the numerous parking lots set up in the city. Evaluating the UX of the cyclists goes beyond usability evaluation. Of course, the bike is expected to be reliable, easily usable and comfortable and the support organization should help one find a bike, pay, and contact help in case of problems, and so on. But there is more: the pleasure of going cycling, the satisfaction of doing an activity that helps keep in shape, that is in harmony with one's values (healthy living, prevent pollution), that reinforces self-image (as active and strong), and that makes one participates to large societal movements (closer to our bodies and the environment).

UX STORY #2: THE WII CONSOLE

Older people are using the Nintendo Wii console to exercise. This console uses a haptic control called Wiimote, which can detect movements and rotations in three dimensions. These movements done in coordination with dynamic scenes of a game environment showed on a screen allow one to virtually play tennis, bowling, golf, and so on. Here, evaluating the usability of the product is far from being sufficient if one is interested in the experience with it. The UX of people using this system includes the fun of playing, the satisfaction of being physically active, the development of abilities for coordination and concentration, the pleasure of interacting with other people who observe, encourage, keep score, and comment on the performance, and the improvement of the self-image (being active, dynamic, and cool).

Figure 14.1   A Montrealer about to pull away on a Bixi

Figure 14.2   Older couple playing with a Wii

UX STORY #3: AIR TRAVELERS

The travelers' experience is negatively affected by national security requirements and airlines financial stress. The enchantment of air travel has nowadays given way to a laborious and compromised experience: there are luggage issues, long security procedures, and tight economy class seating. Interestingly, some airlines have opted to equip each seat with a monitor allowing the traveler to watch movies or programs of his/her choosing at his/her own pace. This basic interactive technology gives the traveler a small measure of empowerment in the traveling experience. Watching a movie with a headset creates a strong immersive experience that alters the traveler's sense of time and space, offering an escape from the physical discomfort and making the journey appear shorter. Although technology here does not address the root causes (some of which are out of the airlines control), it doctors up a situation to the point where most travelers feel OK about their trip, partly reversing what is an otherwise mitigated experience. Here again, the usability of the system does not capture the essence of the interaction with it. The system is an efficient mean to make us forget about discomfort and even have some enjoyable moments.

Figure 14.3   **Passengers plugged into their monitor during flight**

1. INTRODUCTION: A RAPID START

These stories illustrate different facets of User eXperience (UX). They show how the concept looks rich, inclusive, holistic, applicable to different systems, and in a better position than usability to capture the global experience of system use. UX has received a rapid acceptance in the fields of HCI (Human Computer Interaction) and interaction design. The concept appeared in the literature in the second half of the 1990s (Alben, 1996) and since then, researchers and practitioners of different disciplines involved in the analysis, design, and evaluation of interactive systems have readily adopted it.

Yet, although well received, UX is still theoretically incoherent and methodologically immature (Law et al., 2007). The serious reader of UX research may feel that the field is like a construction site with many interesting beginnings and little in the way of a general view. This chapter is the first of two addressing fundamental issues of UX. Its goal is to present the state of knowledge on the nature, characteristics, and process of UX. It is structured as follows: in section 1, we go back over some historical pointers of UX; in section 2, we define the scope of UX; in section 3, we present definitions and several characteristics of UX; in section 4, we describe the role of emotions in UX; and in the conclusion, we propose some promising research avenues about UX.

Historical Pointers

The precursors of UX: 1970s–1980s

Paying attention to the user is not a new idea. As far back as 1971, Hansen proposed engineering principles for the design of interactive systems. His first principle was: Know the user. He was not referring to a UX, but UX is tributary of this early orientation. Several other authors from the HCI community in the 1970s, 1980s and 1990s underlined the importance of paying attention to the user to design good systems. They focused on the anthropometric, motor, perceptual, cognitive, cultural, social, and attitudinal characteristics of the user.

Also in the 1970s, in Japan, Nagamachi (see later publication, 2002) and others (for example, Yamamoto, 1986) developed the field of Kansei Engineering. Although this had little impact on western HCI until the last decade (for example, Grimsaeth, 2005), this field shares exactly the same concerns as UX. It is a method for translating feelings and impressions into system properties, and to deliver predictable emotions.

The 1980s have seen a growing appreciation for Csikszentmihalyi's (1975) notion of Flow as a framework to understand positive user interactions. Flow is a complex psychological state that describes a perceived optimal experience characterized by engagement in an activity with high involvement, concentration, enjoyment, and intrinsic motivation.

New games and new toys

Parallel to the development of the personal computer and the new concerns about the user, the 1970s saw the beginning of computer games such as Pong created in 1972 and of new toys, like Sony's portable audio cassette player, the Walkman (1979). The Walkman followed in the steps of the portable transistor radio of the 1960s, and was a revolution that eventually led to the iPod. These leisurely tools questioned the work-related approach to interface design.

In our opinion, nothing questioned the work-related approach more than games. Video and computer games' popularity and the strong involvement of the players drew the attention of various HCI researchers and interaction designers. In 1983, Thomas Malone completes a doctoral thesis titled: "Heuristics for designing enjoyable user interfaces: Lessons from computer games." He points to surprise, challenge, and difficulty levels as important factors to keep the user's interest. He meant to transpose these factors to workplace interactive systems, so that users would be more incline to adopt them. Game design has developed into a field of its own. Salen and Zimmerman (2004), reviewing the theoretical and practical literature on games since the mid-thirties, identified the corner stone concept of *meaningful play*.

Beyond usability

When computers migrated from the office to the home and on to different interactive systems, our interactions with them diversified. In an article on quality of experience, Alben (1996) asks: how does effective interaction design provide people with a successful and satisfying experience? With this new wave of technological products, it became apparent that the parameters of usability were not enough to help fashion interactions that offered fulfilling experiences outside of work-related activities.

Hygiene vs. motivator factors
Usability is one of those things that is first understood in the negative. By that I mean it is often easier to know when something isn't usable than when it is [a]. This assertion with which we agree is closely akin to a major critique about usability concerning the absence of positive. During decades, the HCI community acted as if it had equated system quality to the absence of problems (for example, errors, user frustration) instead of striving for the presence of positive elements in the system (for example, self-development, fun) (Robert, 2008). Interestingly, this critique can be put in relation with a well-known model of job satisfaction: the American psychologist Frederick Hertzberg's two factor model which is sometimes called the Motivator-Hygiene model (Hackman and Oldham, 1976). Herzberg investigated the factors that were responsible for the satisfaction at work of employees from different organizations. He discovered that they could be classified in two categories: hygiene factors and motivators. The former, which includes working conditions, company policies and administration, supervision (technical), relations with peers, and relations with superiors do not cause any encouragement or satisfaction, but instead they cause dissatisfaction when they are not met. The latter, motivators which include achievement, recognition, work itself, responsibility, and advancement, encourages people's performance and satisfaction. So by transposing the two-factor model of Herzberg to HCI, it is tempting as Schaffer (2009) does to see usability as a hygiene factor rather than a motivator. Motivators have the real power to create positive UX.

Emotions
By the end of the 1990s, in reaction to the limits of usability and in search for positively motivating factors, a large field of research has developed to better understand the impact of non-instrumental qualities of systems and personal factors that affect the UX. The research looked at three general topics: beauty, pleasure, and emotions. Clearly no single aesthetic appreciation or emotional response can explain UX as a whole, but the great variety of specific emotional responses does point to the importance of understanding the user's emotions as the key to understanding the UX.

2. THE SCOPE OF UX

When we think of UX, images of video games, new technology, and intense experiences come to mind. But really UX does not refer to new human activities, it is a new lens through which interactive system designers see and understand human activity, and from which they can conceive better relationship between the user and the interactive systems. To understand the concept of UX, it is necessary at first to define the concept of experience and examine different types of human experiences.

Human Experience

The *Merriam Webster* (2002) *Dictionary* defines experience as the fact of having been affected by or gained knowledge through direct observation or participation. To experience is to learn by experience. This general definition makes a distinction between the psychological effect ("having been affected by") and the cognitive effect of experience ("gained knowledge"), and between two types of people's engagements ("direct observation or participation").

Categories of Systems

We can have an experience with or without a system, and if it is with a system, our relation with it will be different depending on how we engage with it and on the type of system at hand. We propose the following classification (see Table 14.1).

Table 14.1   Examples of experiences according to the system and the type of engagement

		Engagement of the person having the experience					
		Active users (possible modes of engagement)			Passive users (possible modes of engagement)		Not a "user"
		Pro-active	Creative	Receptive	Witnessing	Receiving information	
System	No system is used	Visiting a friend in need	Brainstorming	Being told a story	Watching a sunset	Getting the gossip	Not a UX
	slightly or not adjustable, not interactive	Consulting an atlas	Playing the cello	Riding a chairlift	Watching a ski competition	Listening to a report on tramways	
	adjustable	Driving a car	Doing photography	Taking a workshop on digital photography	Seeing Bixis go by	Seeing a DVD system advertisement	
	interactive	Online shopping	Designing an interactive exhibit	Visiting an interactive exhibit	Overhearing cell phone conversations in public	Listening to news report on the new smartphone	

Experience without a system
We can live experiences without using a system. For instance, watching the sunset, visiting Paris, brainstorming, helping someone cross the road, walking on the Great Wall of China, or being in love, are all real life experiences where no system is involved; the person having the experience is not a "user," so it is inappropriate to talk of UX.

Experience with non-interactive systems
Some often fairly high-tech systems are designed to offer a user experience where there is no interactivity: for instance, a city bus or the chairlift at a ski resort. People use these, but have no control on the operation of the systems, which is not say that there is no UX; the interaction scenario is just simpler.

Experience with adjustable systems
Some mechanical and digital systems (for example, office chair, mountain bike, radio, Blue-Ray player) are to be adjusted in the course of their use. These adjustments vary in frequency (sometimes, it is only once at the very beginning, and sometimes it is continuous during the usage) and range from simple adjustments (for example, on the office chair) to more complex ones (for example, on the mountain bike).

Experience with interactive systems
To be called interactive, a system must enter an action dialog with the user that goes beyond the kind of exchange one has with adjustable systems. According to Rafaeli (1988) to be considered "interactive," an exchange between a system and a user must sustain three or more exchanges, responding to each other, and referring to previous exchanges (for example, searching for information on the Web). The level of interactivity varies widely from one system to another. Interactivity can be seen on a continuum going from low interactivity (for example, on a bank teller) to high interactivity (for example, on a video game).

Categories of Engagement of the Person Having the Experience

Active users
Active users are the people for whom a system was created, the primary users or target users. It appears that there are different modes of user engagement within the active user category. There are differences in engagement between the user of commercial exchange applications (for example, from online banking to eBay), the visitor of an interactive museum exhibit, and the designer using software to design the interactive exhibit. In the first, the user travels along interactive scripted paths; we see this user as proactive. The museumgoer paces the rate at which s/he receives the exhibit's information, which makes him/her something of an interactive spectator in an actively receptive mode. Whereas the designer is a creative user, producing open-ended results, using interactive tools. There are perhaps other modes of engagements such as the social-networker, the collaborators, and so on. The user engagement applies to all three types of systems: non-interactive, adjustable, and interactive.

Passive users
We can have experiences vicariously through observing others around us. Even though we do not use the system, we get a second hand or passive UX. These experiences involve the same types of systems we use ourselves. At least two categories of experiences fall in this category depending on the way we relate to the system:

- Systems we experience through the media: through publicity, critical journalism or set in the narrative frame of a movie, for example. All these will shape how we perceive a system. Efficient publicity positively influences our perception and our actions. Experiential marketing (Schmitt, 1999) makes sure we get a sense of the product experience ahead of time. Critical reporting also modulates our mental pictures and thus our expectations. Through repetitive media exposure, we end up getting a UX by proxy even though we do not use the device ourselves. For instance, think of young people dancing on the music of an iPod. Through the media, the potential user is receiving information.

- Systems used in our close environment may positively or negatively affect us. For instance, the bad experience of having to endure people continuously talking on their cellphone in our close environment may influence our opinions about this product. Another example is the Bixi, Montreal's rental bike mentioned in the opening story. The city of Montreal operates a park of 3,000 bikes. The citizens of Montreal are affected by the users of these bikes because they see them, hear them, and deal with them in traffic on a daily basis. If these bikes were ugly, rusty, noisy, often broken, and parked everywhere the passive UX would be strongly negative. Passive users experiencing through direct observation are, in our opinion, in witness mode.

In this chapter we will concentrate on experiences involving system use, whether active or passive (in grey in Table 14.1). The active experience is regarded as the core of UX, the actual interaction, while the passive experience usually folds into the UX as part of the expected UX.

3. DEFINING UX

In the expression "this was quite an experience," there is an underlying sense that something is new or different, special, exciting, surprising, or outstanding. This colloquial reference to experience reveals that the user is aware that something is going on. The experience may be due to some external event occurring in the world the person is aware of, or to a particular state of mind of this person. Without this awareness there is no experience, there would be only automatic behavior.

There is a need for a commonly agreed and shared UX definition; this would be beneficial for teaching, doing research, and managing UX (Roto, 2007). A definition reflects a common understanding of the nature and scope of the concept, and it provides a solid basis for evaluation. In 2004, Forlizzi and Battarbee asserted that the term UX was associated with a wide variety of meanings. It is still true today. Here are several definitions of UX:

> All the aspects of how people use an interactive product: the way it feels in their hands, how well they understand how it works, how they feel about it while they're using it, how well it serves their purposes, and how well it fits into the entire context in which they are using it. (Alben, 1996)

> "User experience" encompasses all aspects of the end-user's interaction with the company, its services, and its products. (Nielsen-Norman Group, 2009) The overall experience, in general or specifics, a user, customer, or audience member has with a product, service, or event. In the Usability field, this experience is usually defined in terms of ease-of-use. However, the experience encompasses more than merely function and flow, but the understanding compiled through all of the senses. (Shedroff, 2001)

Shedroff goes on to define what is an experience:

The sensation of interaction with a product, system, service, or event, through all of our senses, over time, and on both physical and cognitive levels. The boundaries of an experience can be expansive and include the sensorial, the symbolic, the temporal, and the meaningful. (Ibid.)

Every aspect of the user's interaction with a product, service, or company that makes up the user's perceptions of the whole. User experience design as a discipline is concerned with all the elements that together make up that interface, including layout, visual design, text, brand, sound, and interaction. UE works to coordinate these elements to allow for the best possible interaction by users. (UPA, 2006)

The term user experience, most often abbreviated UX, but sometimes UE, describes the overarching experience a person has as a result of his/her interactions with a particular product or service, its delivery, and related artifacts, according to their design. (Wikipedia, online October 2009)

A consequence of a user's internal state (predispositions, expectations, needs, motivation, mood, and so on), the characteristics of the designed system (for example, complexity, purpose, usability, functionality, and so on) and the context (or the environment) within which the interaction occurs (for example, organizational/social setting, meaningfulness of the activity, voluntariness of use, and so on). (Hassenzahl and Tractinsky, 2006)

We agree with these definitions which identify several characteristics of UX:

- UX is concerned with every aspect of the interaction with a system, related artifacts, the services, and the company;
- UX is an overall effect over time on the person;
- UX depends on four elements: the user (what s/he brings to the interaction, and how s/he interacts), the context, the quality of the system, and the activity done with the system;
- UX has several levels or dimensions (the text in quotes in this paragraph comes from the definitions above): functional ("how well it serves their purposes"), physical ("the way it feels in their hands"; on both physical ... levels"), sensorial ("through all of the senses"), cognitive ("on both ... and cognitive levels"), and psychological ("how they feel about it").

Our Definition and Explanations

We propose a new definition in light of the ones above because it seems essential to mention that UX is a construct and is multidimensional. Here is the new definition:

UX is a multidimensional construct that defines the overall effect over time on the user of interacting with a system and service in a specific context.

UX is a construct, meaning that it is a theoretical object corresponding to some reality. Different constructs are necessary in several disciplines: for example, workload in human factors engineering or social classes in sociology. In each discipline, the definition of a construct is a challenge. UX is no exception.

UX is multidimensional since it is the combination of different types of experiences (hence the dimensions) such as they are perceived by the user. The dimensions are: functional, physical, perceptual, cognitive, psychological, and social. There are two meta levels which relate to each dimension: sense making and aesthetic. Note that we added the functional and social dimensions to the ones already mentioned by the authors. Because of space constraints, the dimensions are defined in Robert and Lesage, Chapter 15).

A single interaction may serve two different and concurrent sets of goals and needs: extrinsic and intrinsic, delivering two different and concurrent sets of results, all of which participate to the user's perception of the whole.

UX depends of four basic elements, centering on the User as s/he interacts with a System for doing an Activity in a specific Context (USAC).

Here are brief explanations about how each of the following terms relates to UX: user, system, activity, context, granularity, expected UX, in-progress UX, overall UX, extrinsic and intrinsic goals, instrumental and non-instrumental qualities.

The user

"UX happens inside the person" (Roto, 2007), it is a subjective feeling about the system. A UX is ultimately personal because each user will have a unique experience according to his/her background. The UX is strongly affected by what users bring to the interaction in terms of mood, interests, goals, values, previous experience, needs, and expectations. Consequently a positive UX for a first user could be neutral for a second user and negative for a third one. This being said, the design team cannot design for 100 percent of the experience. Designers can only set the stage for an ideal UX for a specific type of users, based on their profile. Although UX is personal, it makes sense to think of "team UX" when users collaborate together to achieve some activities, when a part of the experience comes from interactions, competition, or comparison with others, and when people have fun together. So far little work has been done on team UX.

The system

As in any good design, the interactive system is expected to have several basic qualities: appropriate functionality, reliability, usability, and so on. To use Herzberg's word, in all cases there is a basic "hygiene" level that needs to be achieved to access a good UX. Indeed it would be hard to imagine that poor functionality would attract and keep the users, that a non-reliable system would lead to a positive UX, and that poor usability would satisfy the users. Each system has instrumental qualities (for example, appropriate functionality, security, efficiency, usability, good design) that allow one to do activities (for example, register to a conference through Internet) and reach some external goal (be registered on time). Some systems also have non-instrumental qualities (for example, beauty, pleasant look and feel, smoothness of the interaction, novelty, values they represent) which bring pleasure, satisfaction, pride, sense of belonging to a community, and so on. Note that some qualities (for example, pleasant "look and feel", smoothness of the interaction) may also be instrumental when they are used to increase user performance and satisfaction. The innovation with UX is to consider that both instrumental and non-instrumental qualities of the system contribute to the UX.

The activity
At the center of a UX, there is a user interaction with a system, implying that there is an activity. In a UX perspective, we prefer to step back from the "task" and talk of activity, be it related to work, leisure, transport, or daily chores. It is essential to take into account the specifics of the activity in terms of location, time pressure, social interaction, security issues, quality requirements, inputs and outputs, and so on. If an activity is misunderstood or looked at out of context, the designed system however efficient, will not be appropriate to deliver a positive UX.

UX should cover the related activities as well. These are essential or normal behavior with good use of the system. These should also be done safely, easily, and efficiently. The frontier may be fuzzy between the central activity and related activities. For example, the central activity with a camera is to take pictures; the related activities are to be transported, transfer photos to a computer, connect to a TV, change batteries, share the pictures with friends and relatives, make prints, archive the pictures, and so on. This example shows how some related activities potentially have a thread of intrinsic experience running through them, for example, the satisfaction of manipulating personal material that makes sense and creates emotions, and of connecting with relatives and friends.

The context
We refer here to the wider human and environmental factors that end up coloring the UX, such as social, cultural, political, linguistic, economic, or environmental factors. These influence all three other elements of the USAC group, that is, the User, the System and the Activity. For example digital devices require high compatibility with other digital devices of their specific technological ecosystem. Likewise, it is now a sign of good environmental stewardship to design systems with their full life cycle in mind, including the disposal of their parts after the life of the system no matter what purpose the system actually serves.

Granularity of the UX
As mentioned by Roto (2007), UX can be analyzed at different levels of granularity. The analysis conducted at each level will provide useful information to different groups of shareholders (for example, the management, the designers). These levels are not rigid, they are defined in relation to one another.

At a high level, the UX rests upon the interaction of the user with the whole infrastructure or organization that supports the system or the service. For example, the overall UX of the traveler with the airport will include his/her interactions with a multitude of systems and services, such as parking services, transport between terminals, registration service, security checks, duty free shops, money exchange, and so on. The overall UX will result from an accumulation of smaller UX with each of the systems or services that the user interacted with.

At a mid-level, the UX rests upon the interaction of the user with the specific system or service that supports a significant activity. For instance, the interaction with the registration desk of the carrier, the security check, or the airport service to handicapped people each corresponds to a UX.

At a low level, the UX rests upon the interaction of the user with specific components of a system that partly supports an activity; for instance, the use of visual displays for information on arrival and departure flights, and the use of various icons and symbols used in an airport fall into this level.

Expected UX

There are important differences between the three UX periods: expected, in-progress, and overall UX (Roto, 2007). Each period brings a significant and different input to our mental construction of UX. Figure 14.4 shows the relations between them and various inputs of information.

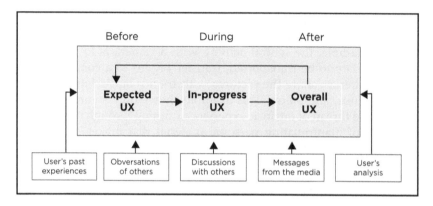

Figure 14.4   Relations between expected UX, in-progress UX and overall UX

An expected UX may exist before the initial use of a system and is renewed by each period of use. It rests on expectations built from different sources of information, such as:

- our past experience with a similar or previous version of the system, systems of the same family or same company, and so on;
- comments from different people around us;
- observations from direct encounters, seeing people around us use the system;
- messages from different media;
- our own analysis of the system.

After each session of use:

- our renewed personal experience with the system.

User's expectations are not static; they evolve continuously with each new input of information. Information cumulates in the user's mind with possibly points of convergence and/or divergence. The expected UX does not rely only on the system designers but also on those involved in creating the brand image of a system (marketing department and communication designers) and those who directly serve the users (sale and after-sale services).

The evaluation of UX should take into account what is brought by the users in terms of comparisons with other systems, past experience, product images, attitudes, goals, needs, interests, and values. It is not enough to make sure through strong brand appreciation that the expected UX is positive, designers and researchers still need to know the specifics of what the users are expecting and why. Such an evaluation will be based on the usual interviews, questionnaires, focus groups, and communication analysis.

In-progress UX
This UX happens during interaction. Because the system may allow the user to achieve extrinsic goals as well as intrinsic goals, the actual interaction may be both a means toward an external end as well as an end in itself.

Evaluating the UX while it is in-progress is unavoidable. It could be based on verbal and non-verbal behavior observations, physiological measures (this is the only period where their use makes sense), and subjective evaluations. However the user may not have sufficient distance to evaluate the entire UX, especially if the last session was problematic.

Overall UX
This UX happens as a result of having interacted with the system. Here the user steps back from the system, reflects on it, and judges the overall UX in light of his/her own experience and of all the information received. S/he is likely to have a holistic impression of the experience even though it is multidimensional.

The evaluation of the UX at this period of time is appropriate because it covers all. It will be based on data collected during the interaction and afterwards through interviews, questionnaires, focus groups, and verbalizations.

Extrinsic and Intrinsic Goals and Needs, Instrumental and Non-Instrumental Qualities of the Device

Hassenzahl (2007) has researched and written extensively on the concurrent strands of experience, which he refers to as pragmatic and hedonic dimensions. In his research, he has found that people perceive interactive products along these two dimensions, and that they perceive them as distinct from one another. The pragmatic dimension focuses on the product's instrumental quality, its utility and usability in relation to the primary activity and extrinsic goals, and the hedonic dimension focuses on the product's non-instrumental quality and how they support intrinsic goals.

Many authors have identified different intrinsic needs and goals, such as self-actualization, esteem, and relatedness (Maslow, 1943), or the need for novelty and change, personal growth and/or self-expression (for example, Ryan and Deci, 2000, see Sheldon et al., 2001 for general lists of human needs). Hassenzahl (2003) distinguishes three kinds of needs: Stimulation (novelty and change, personal growth), identification (communication of identity to relevant others, relatedness), and evocation (provoking memories, symbolizing). This list is by no means exhaustive, and we agree with Hassenzahl that there is no set hierarchy of needs but rather a variable situation-dependent set of goals, some situations leaning heavily towards the intrinsic (like playing games) and some towards the extrinsic (like flying an airplane).

4. THE EMOTIONS

Figure 14.5 shows the process of UX over the three periods of time described above and how the intrinsic and extrinsic goals weave through the experience. These dynamic aspects of the experience do not explain what fuels the experience. Numerous authors have looked at different emotions such as pleasure (for example, Jordan, 2000), appreciation of beauty (for example, Tractinsky et al., 2000), play (for example, Gaver, 2002), fun (for example, Blythe et al., 2004) or at the emotions in general to find the motivational factor at the heart of the UX.

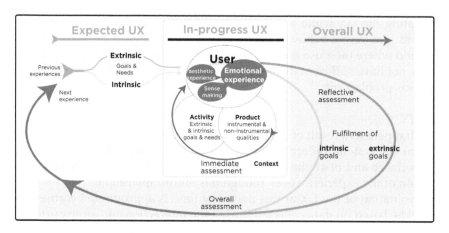

Figure 14.5   The process of UX over time

Desmet and Hekkert (2007) propose that the emotions act as a subjective motor driving people to action. They base their model on experimental psychology (Bradley and Lang, 1994). Emotions are stimulated by perceptual information from the senses and by cognitive processes. Some percepts will evolve into aesthetic experience, while the cognitive processes will deliver sense making, and both will provoke an appraisal and emotional response. For instance, as we come across the latest model of a favorite car, we might appraise it as novel and revolutionary, and the corresponding emotional response might be surprise and enchantment.

Smith and Kirby (2001) see emotions as coherent systems, organized and functional. Their purpose is to establish our position in our environment by attracting to us some things and pushing away others. In the UX story #2 about older people playing with a Wii, the social networking they get by exercising with a Wii is valued enough to keep them playing, or have them come back another day.

User's Levels of Processing

The user appraises devices at several levels. Norman (2004) proposes three levels of processing: visceral, behavioral, and reflective. At the visceral level we make rapid judgments (such as good or bad, safe or dangerous) and a signal is sent to the motor system and to the brain. These judgments could be enhanced or inhibited by the reflective level. The visceral level is seen as the start of affective processing.

The behavioral level controls the different user's actions: use the device, try new functionalities, upgrade it, connect it to other devices, show to friends and colleagues, and so on.

The reflective level watches over, reflects upon, aiming at influencing the behavioral level. Based on information coming from the other levels and on one's knowledge, experience, culture, values, and so on, the reflections about the product will be positive, neutral, or negative. The reflective assessment may happen during or after the interaction, and it will bring different kinds of emotional responses. For instance, after a major effort, one might feel proud or shaken, or feel more competent.

5. SUMMARY OF WHAT MAKES UX

In light of the literature and our own work (Lesage and Dorta, 2008; Robert, 2008; Robert and Lesage, 2010), we can extract the following highlights of UX:

- UX is multidimensional and holistic; its six dimensions are: functional, physical, perceptual, cognitive, social, and psychological; two meta-levels are related to each of them: sense making and aesthetics. Each experience has as unique and coherent set of dimensions meeting together according to variable ratios.
- UX is subjective: it partly depends on what the user brings to the interaction with the system in terms of moods, sensitivity, attitudes, prejudice, interests, knowledge, motivation, and so on. This is the basis for sense making and for attributing weigh to each dimension of UX. It also partly depends on the subjective emotional response to the interaction with the system. All this sets the stage for having an aesthetic experience.
- UX is an overall effect on the user (hence the overall UX): it cumulates the effects (in terms of knowledge and emotions) experienced at each point of contact with the system, the services and related artifacts. Furthermore it cumulates the (perceived) results of activities which are made of two concurrent strands, one answering to extrinsic needs and goals, the other to intrinsic needs and goals.
- UX spans in and over time (so it is not static): it covers the expected UX that built up to the actual use of system and the in-progress UX; these two cumulate in an overall UX.
- UX depends on four basic elements: the *User* interacting with a *System* for doing an *Activity* in a specific *Context*.
- UX is situated in a specific context (or is context-dependent): it depends on the characteristics of the context in terms of location, time, people, opportunities and constraints, technology, incidents, stakes, and so on.
- UX applies to an individual or a team.
- UX can be considered at different granularity levels.

6. CONCLUSION

Usefulness, efficiency, and usability of interactive systems, although essential, are insufficient for capturing the essence of our interaction with systems. The UX movement in the HCI and interaction design communities is an invitation to go beyond instrumental qualities of interactive systems and the achievement of extrinsic goals. Designers are encouraged to strive for the integration of non-instrumental qualities of system as well as the achievement of users' intrinsic goals. Both types of system qualities and goals make sense for users and contribute to the UX.

We need to better understand the relations between design elements, sense making, emotions, and UX. To go beyond the definition and the model of UX process presented in this chapter, our next step will be to carry out empirical research on how the UX builds up for different people, doing different work and non-work activities, with different types of systems, in different contexts, and for different periods of time.

REFERENCES

[a] http://blogs.oracle.com/usableapps/2008/01/a-developers-confessions-about.html [accessed: July 23, 2009].

Alben, L. 1996. Quality of Experience: Defining the Criteria for Effective Interaction Design. *Interactions*, 3(3), 11–15.

Blythe, M., Overbeeke, C., Monk, A.F., and Wright, P.C. (Eds.). 2004. *Funology: From Usability to Enjoyment*. Dordrecht: Kluwer Academic Publishers.

Bradley, M.M. and Lang, P.J. 1994. Measuring Emotion: the Self-Assessment Manikin and the Semantic Differential. *Journal of Behavior Therapy and Experimental Psychiatry*, 25(1), 49–59.

Csikszentmihalyi, M. 1975. *Beyond Boredom and Anxiety: Experiencing Flow in Work and Play*. New York: Harper Collins.

Desmet, P. 2003. A multilayered model of product emotions. *The Design Journal*, 6(2), 4–13.

Desmet, P. and Hekkert, P. 2007. Framework of Product Experience. *International Journal of Design*, 1(1). Available at: www.ijdesign.org/ojs/index.php/ijdesign/article/view/66/15.

Dumas, J.S. 2003. User-based Evaluations, in *The Human–computer Interaction Handbook: Fundamentals, Evolving Technologies and Emerging Application*, J.A. Jacko and A. Sears (Eds.). LEA, Mahwah, NJ, 1093–1117.

Experience Design. Available at: http://en.wikipedia.org/wiki/Experience_design, [accessed: 14.10.2009].

Forlizzi, J. and Ford, S. 2000. The Building Blocks of Experience: An Early Framework for Interaction Designers. *Proceedings of DIS 2000: Designing interactive systems: processes, practices, methods, and techniques, New York, NY*.

Forlizzi, J. and Battarbee, K. 2004. Understanding Experience in Interactive Systems, in *Proceedings of the 5th conference on Designing interactive systems: processes, practices, methods, and techniques*, ACM. Cambridge, US.

Gaver, B. 2002. Designing for homo ludens. *i3 magazine*, June, 2–5.

Grimsaeth, K. 2005. Linking Emotions and Product Features. *Kansei Engineering*. Department of Product Design, Norwegian University of Science and Technology. 1–45.

Gould, I.D., and Lewis, C. 1985. Designing for Usability: Key Principles and What Designers Think. *Commun.* ACM 28(3), 300–311.

Hackman, J.R. and Oldham, G.R. 1976. Motivation through Design at Work. *Organizational Behavior and Human performance*, 16, 250–279.

Hassenzahl, M. 2007. The Hedonic/Pragmatic Model of User Experience, in *Proceedings of COST294-MAUSE Workshop, Lancaster, UK*, April 2007. 10–14.

Hassenzahl, M. and Tractinsky, N. 2006. User Experience: A Research Agenda. *Behavior and Information Technology*, 25(2), 91–97.

Hassenzahl, M. 2003. The Thing and I: Understanding the Relationship between User and Product, in *Funology: From Usability to Enjoyment*, M. Blythe, C. Overbeeke, A.F. Monk, and P.C. Wright (Eds.). Dordrecht: Kluwer Academic Publishers, 31–42.

Jordan, P. 2000. *Designing Pleasurable Products*. London: Taylor and Francis.

Lang, P.J. 1980. Behavioral Treatment and Bio-Behavioral Assessment: Computer Applications. In *Technology in Mental Health Care Delivery Systems*, J.B. Sidowski, H. Johnson and T.A. Williams (Eds.). Norwood, NJ: Ablex Publishing, 119–137.

Law, E., Roto, V., Vermeeren, A., Kort, J., and Hassenzahl, M. 2007. Towards a Shared Definition of User Experience. *Proceedings of the COST_MAUSE workshop at the CHI 2007 Conference, Lancaster, UK*, September 3, 2007.

Lesage, A. and Dorta, T. 2008. Au-delà de l'Utilisabilité: L'Autotélie, in *20 ans d'Interaction Homme-Machine Francophone: de l'Interaction à la Fusion entre l'Humain et la Technologie*, E. Brangier, G. Michel, C. Bastien, and N. Carbonell (Eds.). IHM 2008, Metz, France, September 3–5, 2008, 147–150.

Malone, T.W. 1984. Heuristics for Designing Enjoyable User Interfaces: Lessons from Computer Games, in *Human Factors in Computer Systems*, J.C. Thomas and M.L. Schneider (Eds.). Norwood, NJ: Ablex Publishing, 1–12.

Maslow, A.H. 1943. A Theory of Human Motivation. *Psychological Review*, 50, 370–396.

Nagamachi, M. 2002. Kansei Engineering as a Powerful Consumer-Oriented Technology for Product Development. *Applied Ergonomics*, 33(3), 289–294.

Nielsen-Norman Group, *Our Definition of User Experience*. Available at: www.nngroup.com/about/userexperience.html. [accessed: 8.11.2009].

Norman, D.A. 2004. *Emotional Design. Why we Love (or hate) Everyday Things*. New York: Basic Books.

Rafaeli, S. 1988. Interactivity: from New Media to Communication. *Sage Annual Review of Communication Research*, 110–134.

Robert, J.-M. 2008. Vers la plénitude de l'expérience utilisateur. *Actes du colloque IHM 2008, ACM International Conference Proceedings Series, Metz, 3–5 septembre 2008*, 3–10.

Robert, J.-M., Lesage. 2010. Designing and Evaluating User Experience. (this book).

Roto, V. 2007. User Experience from Product Creation Perspective, Paper in *COST294-MAUSE, Lancaster, UK, April 2007*, 31–34.

Ryan, R.M. and Deci, E.L. 2000. Self-Determination Theory and the Facilitation of Intrinsic Motivation, Social Development, and Well-Being. *American Psychologist*, 55, 68–78.

Salen, K. and Zimmerman, E. 2004. *Rules of play: Game Design Fundamentals*. Cambridge, MA, US: MIT Press.

Schaffer, N. 2009. Verifying an Integrated Model of Usability in Games. *Thesis dissertation*. Troy, New York: Rensselaer Polytechnic Institute.

Sheldon, K.M., Elliot, A.J., Kim, Y., and Kasser, T. 2001. What is Satisfying about Satisfying Events? Testing 10 Candidate Psychological Needs. *Journal of Personality and Social Psychology*. 80(2), 325–339.

Schmitt, B. 1999. *Experiential Marketing: How to Get Customers to Sense, Feel, Think, Act, Relate*. New York: Free Press.

Shedroff, N. 2001. *Experience Design 1*. New Riders. Available at: www.nathan.com/ed./book1/ index.html. [accessed: 20.11.2009].

Smith, C.A. and Kirby L.D. 2001. Toward Delivering on the Promise of Appraisal Theory, in *Appraisal Processes in Emotion*, K.R Scherer, A. Schorr and T. Johnstone (Eds.). New York: Oxford University Press, 121–138.

Tractinsky, N., Katz, A.S. and Ikar, D. 2000. What is beautiful is usable. *Interacting with computers*, 13, 127–145.

UPA (Usability Professionals' Association): *Usability Body of Knowledge*. Available at: www. usabilitybok.org/glossary. [accessed: 8.11.2009].

W3C, *World Wide Web Consortium*. Available at: www.w3.org/. [accessed: 20.1.2010].

Wright, P. and McCarthy, J. 2004. *Technology as Experience*. Cambridge, MA, US: MIT Press.

Yamamoto, K. 1986. *Kansei Engineering-the Art of Automotive Development at Mazda*, Special Lecture at the University of Michigan.

15

Designing and Evaluating User Experience

Jean-Marc Robert and Annemarie Lesage

STORY #1: MOM AND BOY

A phone is ringing. She picks it up from her desk. Him again. Hey. A boyish voice comes through loud and clear, laughing with someone before he realizes that she had answered. It's her son, cheerfully shouting in her ear because his buddies are teasing him. He should be home for supper in 30 minutes. By the way, the presentation went well; even Mr Kim thought so. See! There and then, she receives a picture of her son standing proud beside a patient looking teacher. Silly boy! She folds the phone back into her hand. How amazing, she thinks, that such a small object, that otherwise looks cool, professional, and low key—all qualities she identifies with—can erupt into life, taking on the voice and carrying the boisterous presence of a 12-year-old boy. She smiles. Here UX is not only the result of interactions between a person and a system. Actually, the system often has a support role in a human play, where human relationships are the central issue (see Wright and McCarthy, 2004). In this case, the cellphone supports their relationship, augments the sense of presence, acts as "a virtual elastic band" and allows her to follow his coming and going.

UX STORY #2: THE STOCKBROKER

A stockbroker returns a call to one of his regular customers interested in selling stocks. As a top broker for a big bank, he uses an up-to-the-second stock information application that pools all data (stock performance, quarterly results, industry reviews, and so on) from the 10 best securities brokerage firms. While on the phone with his customer, he can quickly question someone on his team through the application's internal chat window. He has streamlined the application with shortcuts of his own for surveying portfolios, checking specific stocks, filling up forms. The thrill of making the right moves and making big gains for himself and his clients all depends on information. This application feeds him timely pertinent information, making his job a little less stressful and enabling him to really play the market with some confidence (limiting the gamble). Here evaluating usability does not capture the essence of the interaction with the application. One should take into account the satisfaction of interacting with a high-performance system that empowers the user, the thrill of betting along with the assurance of being well informed, the sense of being competent and the satisfaction of being recognized as such by his peers.

UX STORY #3: MOUNTAIN BIKER

JP is a serious cross-country (XC) cyclist, the most common discipline of mountain biking. He enjoys XC for the fun of giving it all he's got: the sheer physical effort required by the climbs and the dare of crazy fast technical downhill trails (some so hard, he would be scared after the fact, looking at them from below). In the midst of the action, his bike becomes a smart, well-engineered extension of himself. The pride, fascination, and gratefulness for the extreme fun this high-tech bike provides are obvious. But JP's true reward comes from meeting harder challenges every time. The initial frustration of not achieving a technical pass only makes its mastery more satisfying. He specifically enjoys those short challenging segments that require all his attention, physical abilities and wits, for minutes on end; and lead him to total, exhilarating exhaustion after two hours or so. The usability of the bike, although essential, is obviously just a part of the interaction with the device. UX is more a question of extreme fun, strong emotions, hard challenge, pride, intense physical effort, acquisition of abilities, and self-accomplishment.

Figure 15.1   Cyclist biking through rough terrain joyfully

1. INTRODUCTION

These stories illustrate the wide variety of User eXperiences (UX) and reveals the rich and complex reality that goes far beyond the strict functional aspect of a system. They are not only about interacting with a system, but also about doing things that make sense in our life, that bring pleasure and satisfaction and relate to our emotions, interests, motivations, values, lifestyle, in short, all that make us human. Although the Human–computer Interaction (HCI) and the interaction design communities have readily accepted UX, their ability to design for and evaluate it is limited by the lack of consensus on what is UX and how it is created, and the lack of design methods and evaluation tools adapted to UX.

A brief review of key elements of UX is necessary as a start. In light of several definitions of UX (Alben, 1996; Shedroff, 2001; Hassenzahl and Tractinsky, 2006; UPA, 2006; Nielsen and Norman, 2009; Wikipedia, 2009) and because we deemed essential to mention some characteristics of UX, we proposed the following definition of UX:

> UX is a multidimensional construct that defines the overall effect over time on the user of interacting with a system and service in a specific context.

Here are comments on some terms of the definition and a summary of the characteristics of UX (same as those in the "Summary of what makes UX" in Robert and Lesage, 2010):

- UX is multidimensional and holistic; its six dimensions are: functional, physical, perceptual, cognitive, social, and psychological; two meta-levels are related to each of them: sense making and aesthetics. Each experience has as unique and coherent set of dimensions meeting together according to variable ratios.
- UX is subjective: it partly depends on what the user brings to the interaction with the system in terms of moods, sensitivity, attitudes, prejudice, interests, knowledge, motivation, and so on. This is the basis for sense making and for attributing weigh to each dimension of UX. It also partly depends on the subjective emotional response to the interaction with the system. All this sets the stage for having an aesthetic experience.
- UX is an overall effect on the user (hence the overall UX): it cumulates the effects (in terms of knowledge and emotions) experienced at each point of contact with the system, the services and related artifacts. Furthermore it cumulates the (perceived) results of activities which are made of two concurrent strands, one answering to extrinsic needs and goals, the other to intrinsic needs and goals.
- UX spans in and over time (so it is not static): it covers the expected UX that built up to the actual use of system and the in-progress UX; these two cumulate in an overall UX.
- UX depends on four basic elements: the *User* interacting with a *System* for doing an *Activity* in a specific *Context*.
- UX is situated in a specific context (or is context-dependent): it depends on the characteristics of the context in terms of location, time, people, opportunities and constraints, technology, incidents, stakes, and so on.
- UX applies to an individual or a team.
- UX can be considered at different granularity levels.

This chapter consists of two main sections. The first one (section 2) is about designing for UX; we show how a user-centered system design (UCSD) approach, with some adjustments, can be used to design for UX. Section 3 is about UX evaluation; it covers two topics: UX dimensions and emotions. In the conclusion, we propose some promising research avenues to improve the design and evaluation of UX.

2. DESIGNING FOR UX

We cannot design a UX because it is internal to the user, yet we can design for a UX. It remains a challenge to design for UX because our understanding of the relations between design elements, sense making, emotions and UX is still incomplete. Yet to have a framework for research as well as an overview, we propose a model of the inputs and outputs of UX (see Figure 15.2). It will help focusing the discussions on specific aspects of UX, and hopefully make progress. In this section we present four design elements of UX and their relationships, and we show how a user-centered system design (UCSD) approach can help designing for UX.

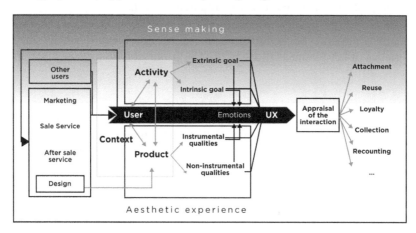

Figure 15.2   The inputs and outputs of UX

Design Elements

We consider four design elements of UX: the user, the system, the activity, and the context, and we examine the control the design team has over.

- *The user*: the design team selects the human factors aspects that will be taken into account into design and decides about the type and level of user participation into design;
- *The system*: the design team exerts full control on the system functionalities and qualities;
- *The activity*: through system functionalities and related artifacts, the design team exerts a control on what the user can do with the system and how s/he does it; to a certain extent, through the functionalities that are offered, it has also an influence on when, with whom and where the system can be used;

- *The context:* the design team is influenced by the context as well as it exerts an influence on it through its innovations.

The design team is not the only unit of an organization having an input on UX; Figure 15.2 shows four of them:

- the design team through its work on design elements;
- the marketing through information about the system presented to users in the media;
- the sale service through information about the system presented to the future users;
- the after-sale service through the quality of assistance, training, maintenance, … offered to users.

Also:

- the management through its culture, values, strategies, policies, and programs that affect the users; its influence on the user filtrates through the different units of the organization.

In this chapter, we only focus on the input of the design team.

Even though several authors (including ourselves Lesage and Dorta, 2008; Robert, 2008) talk of a paradigm change when we pass from usability to UX, we do not see a rupture in the work to be done when designing for UX. We rather see a continuity in the activities of analysis, design, and evaluation that are required for designing good interactive systems, with an opportunity of enrichment. So our approach is to build on well-established knowledge, and propose enrichments where there are needed.

Coming from the disciplines of human factors, HCI and the industrial design, we have access to a large pool of knowledge (for example, theories, models, approaches, principles and guidelines, best practices, methods, tools) for designing good quality interactive systems. In the next paragraphs, we present the central part of this knowledge, that is, the UCSD approach with its principles and activities, and its application to UX.

User-Centered System Design

In the first half of the 1980s, Gould and Lewis (1985) set the foundation of a UCSD approach that has always been a solid reference in the field of HCI. It encompasses four design process principles:

- early—and continual—focus on users (and on their task and context) [N.B.: the text in parenthesis is ours];
- empirical measurement;
- iterative design;
- integrated design—wherein all aspects of usability evolve together.

These principles are at the heart of the UCSD or usability engineering process of several authors in HCI (for example, Pagulayan et al., 2003; Wixon and Wilson, 1997), and their underlying philosophy is now part of the norms ISO 13407 and ISO 18529. The reader can refer to Gould et al. (1997) for a detailed presentation on what they consist in and how to apply them.

In the next paragraphs, we show what adjustments are necessary to use the UCSD approach to design for and evaluate UX.

User

For obvious reasons, the emphasis of HCI on the importance of knowing the user remains highly relevant for UX. In HCI, seven categories of human factors were to be taken into account:

- anthropometric: for example, the size of keys on a keyboard, of a touch on a screen;
- motor: for example, typing speed, reaction time;
- perceptual: for example, visual information presentation;
- cognitive: for example, situated cognition, decision-making, situation awareness;
- social: for example, communication, sharing, and teamwork through collaborative technologies;
- cultural: for example, international and intercultural interfaces;
- psychological: for example, opinions, attitudes, satisfaction.

With UX, two additional categories of factors are to be taken into account:

- motivational: for example, social encounters, curiosity, recognition by others, self-identity, self-achievement, pleasure, value;
- emotional: for example, fun, pride, attachment, enchantment.

With UX, there are also new objects of interest for design, namely aesthetics and sense making; they are discussed below.

In the UCSD approach, depending on the project, the user participates to the design process in different manners, at different moments, for different periods of time, with different level of involvement, and with different levels of participation to decisions. Robert (2003) defined four different roles of the user which correspond to four levels of participation to the design process (the first three levels can be cumulative):

- Informative: the user participates to interviews, observations, or surveys in order to define system requirements: here his/her involvement is low, at the very beginning of design, for a short period of time, and with no participation into decisions;
- Consultative: the user evaluates interfaces through walkthrough and usability tests: here his/her involvement is low or medium, during the design process, for a short period of time, and with no participation into decisions;
- Participative: the user participates to the design of the system; his/her involvement is high, during all the design process, for a long period of time, and s/he participates to decisions;

- Designer: the user designs him/herself the system for his/her own usage. This often happens for sophisticated tools used for instance in research.

In the UX approach, the participation of the user is expected to cover the three first levels. See Muller (2003) for a review of the advantages and critics of different forms of user participations in design.

Finally, traditional HCI is mainly (but not exclusively) associated to serious users operating in work or study environments whereas UX, from its very beginnings, also includes discretionary users doing all kinds of activities (for example, work, leisure, travel, daily life chores).

System
Several qualities are expected to be present in good interactive systems. They are the following:

- usefulness (or appropriate functionality) to do our activities and reach our goals; it includes the functionalities for doing primary as well as related activities;
- reliability: it permits the user to count on the product over time and develop trust;
- security: it is essential in various domains such as transport, medicine, process control, and defense;
- efficiency (and capacity): we are used to interact with more and more high-performance systems in terms of response time, memory space, screen resolution, and so on;
- accessibility for handicapped people, for people with little education, for people equipped with previous versions of applications;
- compatibility (connectivity) with different versions of a software application, different products of a same manufacturer and of different manufacturers;
- usability for the ease of learning and ease of use, and the user satisfaction;
- good design for the look and feel, the smoothness of the interaction, the beauty, the novelty.

It is essential to continue insuring these qualities for UX. To guide us, there are standards, guidelines, methods, and tools available for several of them: for instance, on accessibility, see W3C (2005, 2008); on usability, see Dumas (2003), ISO 9241, Rubin (1994); on good design, see Cross (2006), and on the reflexive approach, see Schön (1983).

All these qualities are instrumental for obtaining objective results and are likely to be perceived as such by the user. For instance, adequate functionality, to do different activities; efficiency, to do them rapidly; accessibility, to be able to do them even with a handicap; usability, to do them with a system that is easy to learn and use; good design, to increase user performance and satisfaction. One of these qualities, good design, is also non-instrumental because it could be appreciated for itself by the user. Indeed, a user may have great pleasure, satisfaction, or pride to use a system that is beautiful, cool, classy, original, well-designed, at the cutting edge of technology, full of intelligence, and so on.

Activity

There are at least four important differences between traditional HCI and UX concerning the user activity.

- First, the change of terms. Historically, HCI has been mainly associated to work (done at the office), and this explains why the term task was used. In UX, the term activity is deemed more appropriate because it is more inclusive. It covers all kinds of activities (work, education, leisure, daily life chores) done in all kinds of settings (office, home, school, transport, outside, and so on). That being said, one should continue to use the term task in UX when it is question of work.
- Second, in traditional HCI, we mostly take into account the attainment of extrinsic goals, that is, that are external to the person. Objective measurements of the result may be taken: for example, user execution time, number of errors, number of requests for help, and so on. Here the user is fully conscious of the goals. Note that in HCI we also consider the user satisfaction with the system. In the UX, in addition to the extrinsic goals, we also take into account the attainment of intrinsic goals, that is, that are internal to the person; for instance, have fun, learn, make progress, have the inner satisfaction of doing an activity in harmony with own values, reinforce self-image, and so on. The user may not be fully conscious of all these goals. The relation between these extrinsic and intrinsic goals contributes to the creation of sense making by the user, and to the aesthetic experience.
- Third, in traditional HCI, the focus is mostly on the use of the system for doing the "tasks" for which the system was designed. In the UX domain, since the overall UX depends on each single experience the user has at each point of contact with the system, we consider the user activities during the entire lifecycle of the device. This means designing for related activities as well; for example, carrying, installing/de installing, learning, connecting/disconnecting, operating, upgrading, doing the maintenance, repairing, cleaning, and so on. So the span is much larger.
- Fourth, in traditional HCI, the input of the marketing service to the design of the system is rarely mentioned in the literature. In the UX domain, since the overall UX also depends on expected UX, the marketing plays a significant role. The images and messages about the system that will be presented in the media to the future users have an impact of expected UX, and therefore on overall UX.

The quality of analysis of the user activities is important for designing good interactive products. There is an abundant literature on task analysis for interactive system design (for example, Hackos and Redish, 1998, Hollnagel, 2003). And over the last 15 years or so, ethnography and ethnomethodology have also greatly contributed. They have much to offer with their global approach, their consideration of the context, their studies "in the wild," and the participant-observation activities (Button, 2003, Nardi, 1997). The input of these disciplines is important for UX.

Context

The careful analysis of the context (for example, technological, economic, social, environmental, and so on.) is essential for good system design; so it is with UX. The difference between traditional HCI and UX is that the latter does not only depend on the impact of the quality of system design on the users. It also depends on the impact of numerous other factors that determine the context of usage of the system once it is designed and is used in the field. For example, the design of the Bixi (the public bike service in the city of Montreal) could be great. But the UX with the Bixi could be globally negative if there was a financial scandal about the Bixi, if the users knew the service in charge of the operation was controlled by the Mafia, if they learned that Bixi components came from companies that hire children, if the location was deemed too expensive, or if the maintenance service was insufficient, and so on. So to optimize the UX, both the context for design and the context of usage of the product must be taken into consideration.

3. UX EVALUATION

Evaluation is part of the design process since it provides feedback to designers for making corrections and improvements. It is highly demanding because it requires having a clear understanding of the object of interest as well as sound criteria, methods, and tools. In practice, there are good reasons to evaluate the UX:

- designers will have a portrait of the UX in the pre-design situation and will use it as comparison with the improved post-design UX;
- designers will know if their decisions about different design elements have a positive, neutral, or negative impact on the UX, and if the level of UX with the new system is satisfying; and
- the management will know if its decisions made in different phases of the lifecycle of the system have a positive, neutral, or negative impact on UX.

Evaluation will make it possible to compare the UX with different versions of a system, different systems, on different groups of users, at different periods of time, and in different contexts.

On a research ground, the evaluation of UX offers the opportunity to:

- define and validate evaluation criteria;
- develop evaluation methods and tools; and
- provide empirical data on the relations between design elements, sense making, emotions, and UX.

Like any other measures of human states, the methods and tools used to measure UX should satisfy several criteria:

- validity: really measure the UX, all the UX and only the UX;
- reliability: the measures should be the same if taken in the same conditions at two different moments with the same user; (N.B.: this is difficult to apply because UX evolves with time);

- sensitivity: the measure is sensitive to the change of level of UX in time;
- diagnosticity: the measure reveals the categories of causes that are involved in the UX;
- selectivity: the measure indicates which aspects of the causes are at work in UX;
- obstruction: the use of the tool does not change the UX;
- span: the tool rapidly provides a measure of UX.

Furthermore, in order to be widely used, measures of UX need to be acceptable for the users, standardized, easy and rapid to use, and easy to interpret (low cognitive complexity).

At least three challenges will be faced when attempting to evaluate UX:

- evaluate the UX for a system that does not exist yet; indeed, it could be relatively easy to evaluate the UX with an existing system, but a real challenge with a concept of system, a non-interactive mock-up, or a low-level prototype;
- evaluate the UX for the mid- and long-term; since UX evolves with time, it is necessary to try anticipating UX over time;
- averaging the evaluations coming from different people; even though UX is subjective, no one designs a product for a single user, so there must be a way to aggregate several evaluations.

A major difference between traditional HCI and UX concerning evaluation is that in the former, the quality of a system is evaluated in terms of usefulness, efficiency, and usability. In the latter, we go beyond that and include sense making, aesthetics, and emotions. In the next paragraphs we focus on the dimensions of UX which are at the basis of sense making and aesthetics, and on emotions which are at the heart of UX.

The Dimensions of UX

When one analyzes the three UX stories presented in this chapter and the three others in Robert and Lesage (2010 (this book), one discovers that the overall UX is not homogeneous, it is rather a combination of different types of experiences for the user (hence the multidimensional nature of UX). We extracted six dimensions of UX and two meta-levels; Table 15.1 shows them with the kinds of user motivation that might be behind each dimension from our UX stories. These dimensions are not mutually exclusive and their relative weigh vary from a UX to the next, depending on the user's perception, to the point that some dimensions may be absent for some users.

Here is a description of the dimensions. Each of them may be perceived as negative, neutral, or positive by the user. There is no tool yet to evaluate them.

Functional: This UX dimension is grounded in the system and is inevitably part of every UX. The user is aware of the instrumentality of the system s/he is using for doing activities and achieving extrinsic or intrinsic goals. There are situations where the user may not perceive anything special besides doing what s/he has to do with the system; in this case s/he has a neutral functional experience. There are also situations where the number, intelligence, or novelty of functionalities may be remarked and either highly appreciated or criticized by the user; in this case s/he has a great or deceiving functional experience.

Table 15.1   Dimensions of UX involved when doing activities with various systems

User's Motivations	Dimensions of UX	Story 1 Bixi users*	Story 2 Wii players*	Story 3 Air travellers*	Story 1 Mom & boy	Story 2 Stock broker	Story 3 Mountain biker
Get an objective result (e.g., move from A to B, make a phone call, follow a therapy)	Functional	4		4	4	4	3
Exercise	Physical	2	4				3
Have fun	Psychological	2	3		3	1	3
Have the satisfaction of using a system that is well-designed and looks cool	Perceptive	2	2		3	2	1
Do an activity in harmony with my values (health, environment, money)	Psychological	2	1		1	2	2
Meet with other people	Social		2		4	1	1
Learn about the system/ consolidate knowledge about the system	Cognitive	1	1			1	
Learn how to do an activity / consolidate competence	Cognitive		1				1
Participate to a movement or interest group (e.g., societal, extreme sport)	Cognitive Social	3	3				3
Reinforce my self-image (as young, active, urban, bright, good parent, good citizen ...)	Psychological	1	2	1	2	2	3

Scale: Nothing—not significantly present; 1—a little; 2—average; 3—strong; 4—very strong.

Source: The first three stories can be found in Robert and Lesage (2011) in this book, the last three, in this chapter.

Physical: The user may have to make significant physical efforts for doing the activity and interacting with the system: for example, when going cycling, playing with the Wii console, using a haptic control device. These efforts which deal with postures, displacements, and movements vary in terms of muscular sites involved, magnitude, frequency, duration, and coordination requirements.

Perceptual: This dimension is present in every UX because the point of contact of the user with the system is inevitably through the senses (visual, auditory, gestural, touch, and so on). Although perception is required in every other dimension, it pertains mainly to the "look and feel," which includes sound and surfaces, the smoothness of the interaction, and the beauty of the system.

Cognitive: This dimension responds to the activities of analysis, appraisal, reflection, learning, and creation which allow one to understand, accumulate knowledge and experience, make progress, consolidate competence, and create through the interaction with the system. It also addresses the desire to develop oneself and grow. This dimension is essential for making sense of an experience, and for living an aesthetic experience.

Psychological: The user does activities that may be due to or have a significant impact on his/her psychological state, that is, on mood, attitudes, opinions, motivation, self-image, self-identity, feeling of belonging, well-being, and so on. The pleasure of doing an amusing activity and the satisfaction of doing an activity in harmony with one's values or that contributes to self-development are good examples.

Social: The user may work or meet with and relate to other people through the interaction with the system and these encounters may contribute significantly to the overall UX. They could even be the primary reason for doing an activity with the system. The computer-mediated social interaction between gamers, the belonging to a virtual group or network, the participation to a societal movement as well as blogging and twitting are all opportunities of social interactions.

We consider sense making and aesthetics as meta levels, the former because it is a basic requirement for every other dimension (it is difficult imagining a positive experience for a meaningless physical or social activity), and the latter because for some users, it acts as higher octave of one or several dimensions at a time, and because researchers have observed users referring to it as an expression of their overall UX.

Sense making (meta level): This meta level runs through all dimensions, since we are constantly processing information, interpreting in order to understand our experience. Many authors in psychology (for example, Bruner, 1990) see the urge we have to interpret and understand our experience as one of the characteristics of being human. Game designers Salen and Zimmerman (2004) have set this meta level up as their guiding principle by establishing that meaningful play is the primary objective of game design: "play is more than a mere physiological phenomenon-or psychological reflex. ... It is a significant function—that is to say, there is some sense to it. In play there is something 'at play' which transcends the immediate needs of life and imparts meaning to the action. All play means something" (Huizinga, 1955, as cited by Salen and Zimmerman, 2004, p. 32).

Designing and evaluating such a wide spread and holistic phenomenon as sense making are a challenge. Wright and McCarthy (2004) have developed an analysis framework that considers six processes participating to sense making. They warn that there is no linear causal relationship between each process, as they can be paired any which way. They are:

- anticipation (the continuous process of expectation);
- connecting (the immediate, pre-conceptual and pre-linguistic sense of a situation encountered);
- interpreting (an unfolding experience involving discerning the narrative structure, the agents and action possibilities, past and future);
- reflecting;
- appropriating (making an experience our own); and
- recounting (telling the experience over).

Aesthetics (meta level): Beyond the basic perceptual experience that comes from the senses, there is the possibility for the user of having an aesthetic experience when the overall experience based on one dominating dimension or several dimensions at a time is perceived as particularly rich, intense, pleasant, stimulating, and so on. The level of aesthetic experience can be found in the UX literature, based on the aesthetic philosophic tradition. Wright and McCarthy (2004) state, following Dewey (1934) and Bakhtin (1990) that the aesthetic experience is the key to understand how rich all experience can be. They argue that it is in the aesthetic experience that our need for sense of the meaningfulness and wholeness of our action is fulfilled (Wright and McCarthy, 2004, p. 57). Here is an example of aesthetic experience: a colleague, needing to do some calculations, pulls out his iPod calculator. The vertical brings up a basic calculator, which was too basic for the job; he flips the iPod sideways, and gets a full-blown scientific calculator on the horizontal screen. This for him was beautiful. He was won over by the elegance of the design thinking that made a digital device rely not on menus and commands, but on direct, intuitive physical movement to deliver two very acceptable alternatives. This beauty owed little to the look and feel.

Table 15.1 clearly shows that several dimensions are simultaneously present in any UX. The presence and relative weigh of a dimension will depend on the user's perception at a certain time. If one dimension stands out significantly, either because it is clearly dominant or the others around are weak, this UX will take the color of that dimension and could be named after it. So one could talk, for instance, of a functional, or physical, or cognitive, or social UX. If at least two dimensions stand out significantly at the same time and with similar weighs, the overall UX will take the mixed colors of these dimensions and could be named differently: for instance, a technological experience.

The six dimensions defined above will have to be validated with a larger number of UX stories in order to know if they are complete and refined enough. Depending on the UX story, some of them can be easily (or objectively) identified by the designer (for example, the physical dimension of the UX with the mountain bike, the social dimension of the UX in the Mom and son story) whereas others can only be pinpointed by the user since they depend on his/her perception. These dimensions, in our view, not only are a pertinent way to understand what goes on in the UX, but they could be the foundation of an evaluation tool for UX, to be developed in future research.

Emotions

Emotional reactions are an essential part of the UX so they should be taken into account when designing for UX. To do so we need to identify and name emotions, define their characteristics, understand their relationship with the experience in each dimension, and be able to evaluate them.

Humans have access to a large variety of emotions. Although the concept of emotion appears to be understood, unfortunately, there is no common definition and the name, number, characteristics, and categories of emotions vary from one author to another. This may have an impact on the choice of the methods used for collecting data on the emotional state of the person. We examine a few categories of emotions.

Several authors adopt the basic emotion theory, which assumes the existence of a certain number of universal (culture independent) emotions that can be distinguished clearly from one another (Ekman, 1992). These are anger, disgust, fear, happiness, sadness, and surprise. Another approach is to classify emotions on two or three dimensions: Valence (positive/negative), Arousal (high/low), and Dominance. For instance, Russell (1980) and Lang (1995) proposed two-dimensional models that vary along the axes of hedonic valence (pleasure/displeasure) and arousal (sleepy/activated). These are seen are relevant dimensions for rapid evaluation of emotions. Other authors distinguish primary and secondary emotions. Primary emotions allow us to make rapid judgments of what is good or bad, safe or dangerous, and send appropriate signals to the muscle (for fight or flight) and to the rest of the brain; they correspond to the visceral level of Norman's (2004) model. Secondary emotions include the full range of emotions, such as happiness, sadness, anger, trust, fear, surprise, contentment, and so on (Damasio, 1994). For his part, Desmet (2003), who developed the evaluation tool PrEmo, defines two categories of emotions:

- seven are pleasant: desire, surprise, inspiration, amusement, admiration, satisfaction, fascination;
- seven are unpleasant: indignation, contempt, disgust, unpleasant, surprise, dissatisfaction, boredom.

Several psychological theories emphasize the multifaceted character of emotions. This appears in Scherer's (1984) model, the one mostly used on the HCI context, which encompasses five components (see Figure 15.3). At the center of the model is the "the emotion triad" of Izard (1977) which comprises three components: subjective feelings, physiological reactions, motor expressions; the two other components are cognitive appraisals and behavioral tendencies. This model shows two important characteristics of emotions: they influence our behaviors as well as they are the results of actions, and they influence our cognitive appraisals as well as they are the results of these appraisals. Three other characteristics of emotions that do not show in this model are worth mentioning because of their relevance for UX: they are situated in context, they are ephemeral or transient (they last a short period of time), and the emotional episodic memory appears to be nonlinear. Indeed there is a "peak and end" effect (Kahneman, 1999) according to which a measure of emotion reaction taken just after an interaction with a system is not an average of the emotions felt at each moment of that interaction. The experience of the peak emotion and of the emotion felt at the tail end of the interaction strongly influences final assessments.

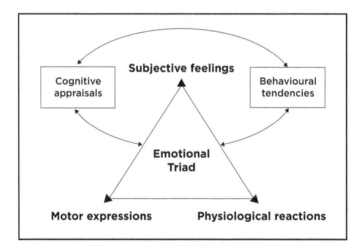

Figure 15.3   The component model of emotions according to Scherer (1984)

There is no standard way to measure emotions. Yet the components of Scherer's model suggest five categories of measures based on the types of data collected. These are the following:

- Physiological reactions: heart rate, electromyography, electrodermal activity (EDA), pupil dilatation, systolic and diastolic blood pressure, breathing rate, facial expressions (measured through muscle contractions). Mahlke and

Minge (2008) see the measure of EDA as the most promising way to determine emotional connotations. Physiological reactions are to be measured during the interaction with the system (otherwise they do not make sense) and provide moment-to-moment ratings.

- Motor expressions: these are related to facial and body expressions, gestures and speech characteristics. The relation between emotions and facial expressions (for example, smiling, frowns) has been studied extensively. Some of the speech characteristics studied in relation with emotions are its speed, intensity, melody, and loudness. Motor expressions are to be observed during the user interaction with the system and also provide moment-to-moment ratings.
- Behavioral tendencies: their role is to prepare for reactions (Scherer, 1984). They include speed of reaction, accuracy of reaching a goal, number of errors, and number of creative ideas. The subject's intentions of use and for instance of purchase, which can be collected by interviews or questionnaires, are indicators of behavioral tendencies.
- Cognitive appraisals: since cognition plays a role in the development of emotions, the assessments of cognitive appraisals by the individual are deemed relevant for evaluating emotions. Quantitative methods can be used: for instance the Geneva appraisal questionnaire of Scherer covers the five dimensions of Scherer's cognitive appraisal theory: intrinsic pleasantness, novelty, goal/need conduciveness, coping potential, norm/self compatibility. Qualitative methods can also be used to gain appraisal-related information: for instance, the thinking aloud method where the individual is encouraged to describe every emotional reaction s/he feels during the interaction with the system.
- Subjective feelings: for example, feeling amused, annoyed, excited, engaged in flow of action, and so on. The postulate behind these measures is that the individual is the best source of information on the emotions s/he experiences. Several self-assessment scales are available: for instance, the SAM scales (Self-Assessment Manikin) introduced by Lang (1980), which consists of pictures of manikins for each of the dimensions valence, arousal and dominance. The manikins represent five emotional states (for example, from happy to unhappy) with which individuals rate their feelings. Csikszentmihalyi's flow is a complex psychological state that describes a perceived optimal experience characterized by engagement in an activity with high involvement, concentration, enjoyment and intrinsic motivation. It is an example of known and measurable positive psychological experience. It is characterized by clear goals and quick feedback, focused attention, loss of self-consciousness, altered sense of time, a sense of control, a merging of action and awareness, a match between participants skills and the activity's challenges. Flow state is determined by the balance between challenges and skills (Csikszentmihalyi and Larson, 1987). The relation between perceived skills and challenges gives eight possible dimensions (Massimini and Carli, 1988): apathy, worry, anxiety, arousal, flow, control, boredom, and relaxation. The evaluation of the user's psychological states can serve as a barometer, reflecting on the perceived success of the activity from the point of view of the user, thus avoiding the subjective pitfall of evaluating the quality of the end results. Experience Sampling Method (ESM) (Csikszentmihalyi and Larson, 1987) is a trusted method to measure the flow and neighboring states.

4. CONCLUSION

In this chapter, we presented a definition and a summary of what makes UX; we proposed a model of inputs and outputs of UX that gives an overview of the process of UX; we suggested to adopt the USCD approach to design for UX but with adjustments to take into account the new context of UX; we suggested evaluating UX through six dimensions of UX and two meta levels, and we showed how the evaluation of emotion, which is considered essential in UX, can be approached. Theoretical and empirical research is still necessary to better understand the relations between design elements, sense-making, emotions and UX; this would help knowing what variables manipulate for increasing UX. Furthermore, we need to develop evaluation methods and tools: to identify the elements of a user's activity and interaction with the device that lead to sense making, the subjective weight of each dimension of UX, the presence and type of aesthetic experience, and the overall UX with the possibility of knowing how expected UX and in-progress UX combine.

REFERENCES

Alben, L. 1996. Quality of Experience: Defining the Criteria for Effective Interaction Design. *Interactions*, 3(3), 11–15.

Bakhtin, M. 1990. *Art and Answerability: Early Philosophical Essays*. Austin: University of Texas Press.

Bruner, J. 1990. *Acts of Meaning*. Cambridge, MA, US: Harvard University Press.

Button, G. 2003. Studies of Work in Human–computer Interaction, in *HCI Models, theories and frameworks*, J.M. Carroll (Ed.). San Francisco: Morgan Kaufmann. 357–380.

Cross, N. 2006. *Designerly Ways of Knowing*. London, Springer.

Csikszentmihalyi, Mihaly and R. Larson. 1987. Validity and Reliability of the Experience Sampling Method. *Journal of Nervous and Mental Disease*, 175(9), 526–36.

Damasio, A.R. (1994). *Descartes' error*. New York: Putnam.

Desmet, P. 2003. A multilayered model of product emotions. *The Design Journal*, 6(2), 4–13.

Desmet, P. and Hekkert, P. 2007. Framework of Product Experience. *International Journal of Design*, 1(1). Available at: www.ijdesign.org/ojs/index.php/ijdesign/article/view/66/15.

Dewey, J. 1934. *Experience of Art*. New York: Pedigree.

Dumas, J.S. 2003. User-based Evaluations, in *The Human–computer Interaction Handbook: Fundamentals, Evolving Technologies and Emerging Application*, J.A. Jacko and A. Sears (Eds.). LEA, Mahwah, NJ, 1093–1117

Ekman, P. 1992. Are There Basic Emotions? *Psychological Review*, 99, 550–553

Experience Design. Available at: http://en.wikipedia.org/wiki/Experience_design, [accessed: 14.10.2009].

Gould, J.D., Boies, S., J. and Ukelson, J. 1997. How to Design Usable Systems, in *Handbook of Human–computer Interaction*, M.G. Helander, T.K. Landauer, and P. Prabhu (Eds.). Amsterdam: Elsevier, 231–254.

Gould, I.D., and Lewis, C. 1985. Designing for Usability: Key Principles and What Designers Think. *Commun. ACM* 28(3), 300–311.

Hackos, J.T. and Redish, J.C. 1998. *User and Task Analysis for Interface Design*. New York: John Wiley and Sons.

Hassenzahl, M. 2007. The Hedonic/Pragmatic Model of User Experience, in Proceedings of *COST294-MAUSE Workshop*, Lancaster, UK, April 2007, 10–14.

Hassenzahl, M. 2004. The Interplay of Beauty, Goodness and Usability in Interactive Products. *Human Computer Interaction*, 19, 319–349.

Hassenzahl, M. and Tractinsky, N. 2006. User experience: A research agenda. *Behaviour and Information Technology*, 25(2), 91–97.

Hollnagel, E. (Ed.). 2003. *Handbook of Cognitive Task Design*. Mahwah, NJ: LEA.

International Organization for Standardization. 1998. ISO 9241–11:1998. *Ergonomic Requirements for Office Work with Visual Display Terminals (VDTs)* — Part 11: Guidance on Usability.

International Organization for Standardization. 1999. ISO 13407:1999. *Human-Centred Design Processes for Interactive Systems*.

International Organization for Standardization. 2000. ISO 18529:2000. *Ergonomics--Ergonomics of Human-System Interaction--Human-Centred Lifecycle Process Descriptions*.

Izard, C.E. 1977. *Human Emotions*. New York: Plenum Press.

Jordan, P. 2000. *Designing Pleasurable Products*. London: Taylor and Francis.

Kahneman, D. (1999). Objective Happiness, in *Well-Being: the Foundations of Hedonic Psychology*, D. Kahneman, E. Diener and N. Schwarz (Eds.). New York, NY: Russell Sage Foundation, 3–25.

Lang, P.J. 1980. Behavioural Treatment and Bio-Behavioural Assessment: Computer Applications. In *Technology in Mental Health Care Delivery Systems*, J.B. Sidowski, H. Johnson and T.A. Williams (Eds.). Norwood, NJ: Ablex Publishing, 119–137.

Lang, P.J. 1995. The Emotion Probe: Studies of Motivation and Attention. *American psychologist*, 50(5), 372–385.

Lesage, A. and Dorta, T. 2008. Au-delà de l'Utilizabilité: L'Autotélie, in *20 ans d'Interaction Homme-Machine Francophone: de l'Interaction à la Fusion entre l'Humain et la Technologie*, E. Brangier, G. Michel, C. Bastien, and N. Carbonell (Eds.). IHM 2008, Metz, France, 3–5 September 2008, 147–150.

Mahlke, S. and Minge, M. 2008. Consideration of Multiple Components of Emotions in Human-Technology Interaction, in *Affect and Emotion in Human–computer Interaction*, C. Peter and R. Beale (Eds.). Berlin: Springer, 51–62.

Massimini, F. and Carli, M. 1988. The Systematic Assessment of Flow in Daily Experience, in *Optimal Experience: Psychological Studies of Flow in Consciousness*, M. Csikszentmihalyi and I.S. Csikszentmihalyi. Cambridge, MA, US: Cambridge University Press, 266–287.

Muller, M.J. 2003. Participatory Design: The Third Space in HCI, in *The Human–computer Interaction Handbook: Fundamentals, Evolving Technologies and Emerging Application*, J.A. Jacko and A. Sears (Eds.). Mahwah, NJ: New York: LEA, 1051–1068.

Nardi, B.A. 1997. The Use of Ethnographic Methods in Design and Evaluation, in *Handbook of Human–computer Interaction*, M.G. Helander, T.K. Landauer, and P. Prabhu (Eds.). Amsterdam: Elsevier, 361–366.

Nielsen-Norman Group, *Our Definition of User Experience*. Available at: www.nngroup.com/about/userexperience.html. [accessed: 8.11.2009].

Norman, D.A. 2004. *Emotional Design. Why we Love (or hate) Everyday Things*. New York: Basic Books.

Pagulayan, R., Keeker, K., Wixon, D., Romero, R., and Fuller, T. 2003. User-Centered Design in Games, in *The Human–computer Interaction Handbook: Fundamentals, Evolving Technologies and Emerging Application*, J.A. Jacko and A. Sears (Eds.). Mahwah, NJ: New York: LEA, 883–905.

Robert, J.-M. 2008. Vers la Plénitude de l'Expérience Utilizateur. In *20 ans d'Interaction Homme-Machine Francophone: de l'Interaction à la Fusion entre l'Humain et la Technologie*, E. Brangier, G. Michel, C. Bastien, et N. Carbonell (Eds.). IHM 2008, Metz, France, 3–5 September 2008, 3–10.

Robert, J.-M. 2003. Que faut-il savoir sur les utilizateurs pour réaliser des interfaces de qualité? *Ingénierie Cognitive: IHM et Cognition*. Paris: Hermès science publications, 249–283.

Robert, J.-M., Lesage, A. 2010. From Usability to User Experience with Interactive Systems. (This book).

Roto, V. 2007. User Experience from Product Creation Perspective, Paper in *COST294-MAUSE*, Lancaster, UK, April 2007, 31–34.

Rubin, J. 1994. *Handbook of usability testing: how to plan, design and conduct effective tests*. New York: John Wiley and Sons.

Russell, J. 1980. A Circumplex Model of Affect. *Journal of personality and social psychology*, 39, 1161–1178.

Salen, K. and Zimmerman, E. 2004. *Rules of play: Game Design Fundamentals*. Cambridge, MA, US: MIT Press.

Schaffer, N. 2009. Verifying an Integrated Model of Usability in Games. *Thesis dissertation*. Troy, New York: Rensselaer Polytechnic Institute.

Sheldon, K.M., Elliot, A.J., Kim, Y., and Kasser, T. 2001. What is Satisfying about Satisfying Events? Testing 10 Candidate Psychological Needs. *Journal of Personality and Social Psychology*, 80(2), 325–339.

Scherer, K.R. 1984. On the Nature and Function of Emotions: A Component Process Approach. In *Approaches to Emotion*, K.R. Scherer and P. Ekman (Eds.). Hillsdale, NJ: Erlbaum, 293–317.

Schön, D.A. 1983. *The Reflective Practitioner: How Professionals Think in Action*. London: Temple Smith.

Shedroff, N. 2001. *Experience Design 1*. New Riders. Available at: www.nathan.com/ed./book1/index.html. [accessed: 20.11.2009].

Tractinsky, N., Katz, A.S. and Ikar, D. 2000. What is beautiful is usable. *Interacting with computers*, 13, 127–145.

UPA (Usability Professionals' Association). *Usability Body of Knowledge*, available at: www.usabilitybok.org/glossary. [accessed: 8.11.2009].

W3C, *World Wide Web Consortium*. Available at: www.w3.org/. [accessed: 20.1.2010].

Wixon, D. and Wilson, C. 1997. The Usability Engineering Framework for Product Design and Evaluation, in *Handbook of Human–computer Interaction*, M.G. Helander, T.K. Landauer, and P. Prabhu (Eds.). Amsterdam: Elsevier, 653–688.

Wright, P. and McCarthy, J. 2004. *Technology as Experience*. Cambridge, MA, US: MIT Press.

16

Eye Tracking from a Human Factors Perspective

Alexandre Lucas Stephane

INTRODUCTION

Eye Tracking (ET) already induced a wide field of applications and investigations. It is used in ET-based applications development, Human Computer Interaction, Virtual Reality, usability testing (Bruneau, Sasse, McCarthy, 2001; Jacob and Karn, 2003), advertising (PRS, 2000; Duchowski, 2003), media and entertainment (McCarthy, Sasse, Miras, Riegelsberger, 2003; Duchowski, 2003), and even art (Santella and DeCarlo, 2002).

Research in ET-based applications utilize ET as a direct control medium, or pointing device (Jacob and Karn, 2003; Hinckley, Jacob, Ware, 2003; Ohno, Mukawa, Yoshikawa, 2002; Sibert, Jacob, Templeman, 2001; Zhai et al., 1999). These ET-based applications are useful especially for disabled people (Majaranta and Räihä, 2002), but can be also utilized in multimodal intelligent user interfaces (Vertegaal, 2002; Duchowski, 2003).

The two main utilizations of Eye Tracking Devices are summarized as follows:

1. Evaluation of Human Machine Interaction;
   - exploration: build design options based on how users gather information on the visual scene,
   - validation: use Eye Tracking as a mean to validating design options.

2. Interaction;
   - Eye Tracking is utilized as an input device in the interactive system (that is, gaze cursor).

The chapter starts by presenting the various fields of application of Eye Tracking. Then follows a section related to basic physiological understanding of the Human Visual System and especially of the eyes' characteristics that are necessary to consider when performing ET experiments. Visual attention is directly linked to eye movements. Thus, the main models of attention and visual attention are presented.

Then, principles and implementation of Eye Tracking devices are described.

Up to this point, the chapter follows the structure of *Eye Tracking Methodology: Theory and Practice* (Duchowski, 2003) that is a recommended complete reference on the topic.

The last sections focus on Eye Tracking Data Analysis and Metrics relates specifically to Human Factors. Beyond commonly used methods, the importance of *Visual Patterns* is emphasized as an optimal solution that enables the linking of eye movements to higher cognitive processes (for cognitive modeling, refer to other chapters in the book). The analysis steps are illustrated by an experiment.

Eye Tracking Research in the Field of Human Machine Interaction

Taking into account eye movement analysis together with activity and task analysis leads to more accurate design and evaluation of Human Machine Interaction (HMI) in general, and of visual systems in particular. Furthermore, in Human Factors (HF), assessment methods used for workload or situation awareness are mostly based on subjective data, while ET analysis contributes with objective data related to cognitive processes, not necessarily to performance. Combining ET with standard HF methods leads to more accurate evaluations and design.

ET data analysis can be top-down, guided either by a cognitive model or a design hypothesis, or bottom-up, based only on observation (Jacob and Karn, 2003).

Examples of each approach are given below:

- top-down based on a cognitive model: longer fixations on an object of the visual scene reflect subject's difficulty to understand that object (or the objects' features);
- top-down based on a design hypothesis: users will easier understand color objects than gray ones;
- bottom-up: users are taking much longer than anticipated making selections on this screen. We wonder where they are looking.

In the first case, because ET contributes with very precise data, a precise behavioral or cognitive model is necessary for the analysis and interpretation of data. If the model is not accurate enough, the use of ET may lose its benefits.

For example, a study performed at EURISCO[1] used ET to evaluate the concept of Procedural Interfaces. Procedural Interfaces integrate the procedure in the interface and are based on the concept of affordance (Boy, 2002; Albrechsten et al., 2001). This study used a top-down based analysis, and combined ET with two situation awareness assessment methods: Cognitive Compatibility-Situation Awareness Rating Technique (Taylor et al., 1997) and Situation Awareness Global Assessment Technique (Endsley and Garland, 2000; Endsley et al., 2003). Seven subjects participated to the experiment. The results obtained with the ET system were very interesting and contributed to the validation of the Procedural Interface concept.

---

1   European Institute of Cognitive Sciences and Engineering.

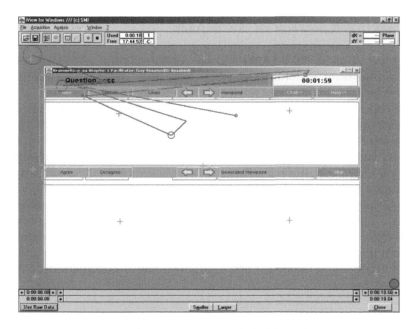

Figure 16.1   Visual scanpath on a Procedural Interface

Eye Tracking and Internet

The main field of investigations for Graphic User Interfaces is currently Internet. Since Internet users are repeatedly exposed to visual displays of information, website designers and advertising companies use ET as a mean for identifying consumer behavior while surfing on the Internet (Josephson and Holmes, 2002). ET studies were also performed on the e-Commerce topic (Sasse, 2003a; Sasse, 2003b).

ET used in Virtual Reality focuses on 3-D perception, 3-D object manipulation and 3-D navigation. Topics such as eye movements in 3-D visual scenes (Duchowski et al., 2002) and 3-D objects level of detail rendering (Alm, 2001) are also very important.

Eye Tracking Research in Automotive

Automotive industry mainly uses ET for the assessment of fatigue and vigilance. Several studies were performed and even the integration of an ET system in the car cockpit as a vehicle-based capability to continuously monitor driver drowsiness/fatigue (Carroll, 1999). Meanwhile, distracting non-driving tasks, such as the use of In-Vehicle Information Systems (IVIS), that is, cell phones, laptop and palmtop computers, radios, CD players, navigation systems and so on, can reduce driver safety (Sodhi et al., 2002).

Eye Tracking Research in Aerospace

Among other studies, ET was used in Air Traffic Control (ATC) to assess both individual and team situation awareness (Hauland, 2002), and visual scanning differences between experts and novices (Källqvist, 1999).

In the cockpit, ET was used with pilots. One of the first experiments using ET techniques involved 40 military pilots during aircraft landing approaches, and measured on each area of interest the gaze rate, gaze duration mean, gaze proportion of time on each area of interest, and established the transition probability between areas of interest (Fitts, Jones, and Milton, 1950). Eighteen military pilots were involved in an experiment in which they had to fly and monitor a threat display containing varying number of symbols (Svensson et al., 1997). ET was used to analyze symbols on the display.

Another interesting experiment was conducted in an A330 Full Flight Simulator with Scientific Research Facility. Sixteen professional pilots were involved in the experiment that aimed to assess situation awareness during approach and landing under CAT I conditions (Anders, 1999). Figure 16.2 shows an example of data analysis for this experiment.

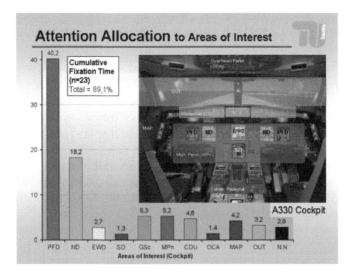

Figure 16.2   Analysis of ET data
Source: Anders, 1999.

HUMAN VISUAL SYSTEM

A complete description of the complex Human Visual System is beyond the scope of this chapter. Thus, only information related to Eye Tracking will be provided. Eye movements are correlated to information processing. Thus, based on observing the eyes, the motivation of using ET is to identify which cognitive processes are involved in specific situations, and to estimate the appropriation of the visual scene in the activity context of the human operator. The main objective is to identify the various processes that connect eye movements to more elaborated cognitive or emotional processes. Visual information perception, detection, and gathering are triggers for actions that, by modifying the visual scene become triggers for information gathering. Thus, as considered in this chapter, Eye Tracking is intended to be performed from an *"active vision"* and *"vision for action"* perspective (Findlay, Gilchrist, 2003).

Spatial Vision

Since one degree visual angle corresponds to approximately 300 µm, the foveola, which is the central part of the fovea, subtends about 2° visual angle, the fovea subtends about 5° visual angle and the macula subtends 16.7° about visual angle. Cone and rod density are illustrated in Figure 16.3.

The entire visual field corresponds to an ellipsoid. The horizontal axis subtends 180° visual angle, and the vertical axis subtends 130° visual angle.

The diameter of the highest acuity region corresponding to the central vision subtends from 1.2° (foveola) to 4° or 5° (parafovea). Beyond the parafovea, detail perception becomes fuzzy and acuity drops. Beyond 25°, the visual field is used for detecting motion, either ego-motion (vection) either targets that enter the visual field (Duchowski, 2003; Holland, 2001). Cones enable to perceivecolor information in photopic vision (luminance level from 1 to 106 cd/m²) with high visual acuity. Rods enable to perceive monochrome information in scotopic vision (luminance level under 10–2 to 10–6 cd/m²).

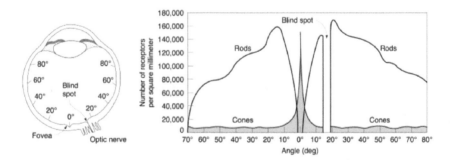

Figure 16.3   Density distributions of rod and cone receptors across the retinal surface: visual angle

Source: Adapted from Cornsweet (1970) (as cited in Lindsay and Norman, 1980).

The distribution of specialized retinal cells provides a better understanding of eye movements. Thus, for detail perception, eyes have to be moved in order to center the object of interest on the retina.

Temporal Vision

Temporal vision is related to the perception of motion. Image refresh frequency has to be tuned with respect to the physiological characteristics of the HVS. The *persistence of vision* and the *phi phenomenon* are essential for the visual response to motion. Both are exploited in television, computer displays, cinema, and graphics.

The *persistence of vision* is directly related to the sampling rate of the HVS. The retina is not able to sample rapidly changing intensities. Flashing frequency of a stimulus together with contrast and luminance conditions determine the Critical Fusion Frequency (CFF) for which the flashing stimulus is perceived as steady.

The *phi phenomenon* corresponds to the threshold above which the HVS detects apparent movement or stroboscopic motion. The delay between successive light flashes should be about 62 Hz in order to create the illusion of motion (Duchowski, 2003).

Perception of Motion

Motion sensitivity of the specialized retinal cells is different. The foveal region is more receptive for slow motion, while the periphery is more receptive for fast motion, although motion is perceived uniformly in the visual field.

For slow and very slow motion, sensitivity to target motion decreases monotonically with retinal eccentricity. A moving target appears slower in the periphery than in the fovea.

Motion detection is the major task of the periphery, because the periphery detects easier moving targets than stationary ones.

Furthermore, for directional motion, the retinal periphery is approximately twice as sensitive to horizontal-axis movement as to vertical-axis movement (Duchowski, 2003).

Color Vision

Three types of retinal cone photoreceptors are involved in color perception. The distribution of retinal cones and rods is responsible for the visual fields of color vision (Figure 16.4). Poor distribution of cones in the retinal periphery suggests that color vision is quite poor in the periphery.

TAXONOMY AND MODELS OF EYE MOVEMENTS

There are two general classes of responses that the eye can make: those in which the eyes themselves do not move (blinking, accommodation, and pupillary responses) and those in which the eyes do move (saccades, pursuit, nystagmus, vestibulo-ocular reflex and vergence).

The first four types of eye movements are termed *conjugate eye movements*—both eyes rotate in the same direction; the last type of eye movement cited above is termed *disconjugate eye movements*—the eyes rotate in opposite directions (that is, towards or away from each other).

Even though it is not mandatory to take into account all types of eye movements when performing ET experiments, it is useful to know them in order to better understand the relationship between the HVS and the visual scene (for a complete description, see Duchowski, 2003).

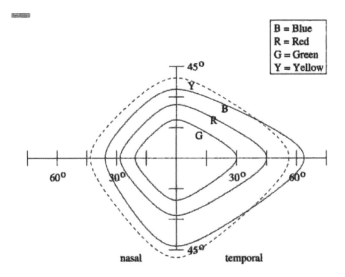

Figure 16.4   Visual fields for monocular color vision (right eye)

Source: Adapted from Boff and Lincoln (1988) (as cited in Duchowski, 2003).

Blinking (blinks are eyelid movements) primary role is to moisten the front surface of the eyeball (cornea) and protects the eye against approaching objects—blinks also often occur as part of a "startle" response to an unexpected stimulus.

Rates of blinking could provide insight into the cognitive state of the person, since blink rates increase with anxiety levels or fatigue and decrease when people are especially alert. Blinks take about 200 ms to complete.

Accommodation is the process that allows images to be focused on the retina through changes in the shape of the lens determined by the state of contraction of the ciliary muscles.

Relaxation of the ciliary muscles pulls on the lens, flattens it out, and allows it to focus on far objects—contraction of the ciliary muscles releases the pull on the lens and allows it to regain its curvature and focus on near objects. The shape of the lens is useful in corneal reflection-based ET.

Pupillary responses are the constriction and dilation of the pupil that determine the amount of light getting into the eye—bright light causes the pupil to constrict—dim light causes the pupil to dilate.

Pupillary responses normally occur in both eyes even if only one eye is exposed to the bright or dim stimulus.

Pupil size is also an indication of the person's cognitive state—the greater is the degree of mental effort required to accomplish a task the greater the size of the pupil. Pupil size could also provide an indication of the amount of interest a person shows in a particular subject. However, pupil size can be taken into account as a reliable indicator only if the lighting conditions are controlled. It can't be a reliable indicator in natural environments where lighting conditions vary.

Eye movements correspond to three dimensions of eye rotations: horizontal, vertical, and torsional (clockwise and counterclockwise). Moving the eye away from the straight ahead by less than 10–15 degrees occurs as a result of an increase in tension in the appropriate set of extraocular muscles. For movements greater than 10–15 degrees the agonist muscles must fire maximally for longer periods of time.

To maintain the eye at the new position there must be a new balance between agonist and antagonist activity. Taken together, this means that a change in eye position is controlled by both force and timing variable in the agonist and antagonist muscles.

Saccades are high-velocity (600–700 deg/s, 10 to 100 ms) movements generally from one stationary target to another, although they can also occur between moving targets. Saccades do not necessarily require a target to be made since it is possible for example to make saccades in the dark.

Saccadic latency depends on several factors such as target eccentricity, target predictability, attentional disengagement, and the number of saccades in a sequence.

Saccade programming is spatially accurate during eye movements. Saccades made to targets flashed during the execution of a prior saccade are accurate despite the fact that the target is not visually present during the saccade and that the saccade direction and amplitude differ from the direction and amplitude of information provided by the flashed target—this implies that the saccadic system can keep track of the position of the eyes in space.

The relationship between saccadic eye movements and attention is not always direct, because attention can be shifted to different parts of space without moving the eyes to those locations. This is considered as *covert* visuospatial attention, opposite to the *overt* visuospatial attention for which attention is directly linked to eye movements.

Smooth pursuit eye movements are slower velocity eye movements that attempt to match the velocity of a moving target. The accuracy of smooth pursuit is given by smooth pursuit gain (eye velocity/target velocity). Perfect pursuit results in a gain of 1.0—in general normal pursuit responses have a gain slightly less than 1.0. This value decreases as target velocity increases.

For target velocities above about 100 deg/s pursuit is impossible and the saccadic system takes over.

Saccadic eye movements are often interspersed within the pursuit response to correct for any positional error between the eye and target.

Unlike saccades, it is very difficult to initiate smooth pursuit without a visual target or in the dark.

Like saccades, smooth pursuit can be influenced by the cognitive state of the subject—when the subject knows that a target will move at a certain time in a certain direction and at a certain speed, target motion will be anticipated and actually start producing a small pursuit response before even the target starts to move.

Optokinetic nystagmus (OKN) is the alternation of smooth pursuit and saccades that occur when people attempt to look at items that pass by them as they ride in a car or train. The slow phase is the smooth pursuit portion and is associated with the visual tracking of the objects—the fast phase is the saccadic portion and is associated with the movement of the eyes to the next selected item in the visual scene. The resulting pattern of eye movements resembles a "sawtooth."

The pursuit and saccadic responses produced during OKN have the same characteristics as pursuit and saccades produced separately. OKN can therefore be viewed as a response that requires precise coordination between these two different eye movement systems.

Vestibulo-ocular reflex (VOR) is the process by which eye position is maintained in space during head rotations. The eyes counter-rotate with respect to the head so that fixations can be maintained on a stationary visual scene item. Head movements are sensed by the vestibular apparatus in the inner ear.

Vergence eye movements are disconjugate eye movements in which eyes rotate towards (convergence) or away (divergence) from each other. The primary stimulus for vergence is retinal disparity: the image of an object falling on different (non-corresponding) places of each eye. Vergence movements can also be triggered by sudden changes in the focus of objects by the accommodation reflex. Thus accommodation and vergence are tightly linked.

As a matter of fact, bi-ocular eye trackers have to be used o take into account vergence eye movements.

The following table summarizes the main eye movements that are studied in common ET experiments.

Table 16.1   Eye movements

Fixations	Gaze at a point
Saccades	Eye movement between fixations
Smooth Pursuit	Involved when visually tracking a moving target
Vergence	Occur during fixation — inward movement
Vestibular Nystagmus	Occur during fixation — rotation of eye to compensate for head movement
Optokinetic Nystagmus	Pursuit interspersed with saccades invoked to compensate the retinal image of the target
Drifts	Occur during fixation — slow movements of eyes due to oculomotor imperfections
Micro-saccades	Special type of saccade — short eye movements to correct drifts from fixation points

VISUAL ATTENTION

Visual attention theories are necessary to analyze and understand eye movements. Several aspects of visual attention are presented below.

Where: visual attention is concerned with a small region of space. Although visual attention can be consciously directed to peripheral objects without moving the eyes, eye movements reflect the will to inspect these objects in fine detail, providing evidence of overt visual attention (Von Helmoltz, 1925, as cited in Duchowski, 2003).

What: visual attention is akin to cognition, and can be defined as the identity, meaning, or expectation associated with the focus of attention. The emphasis is on the active and voluntary aspects of attention (James, 1981, as cited in Duchowski, 2003).

How: visual attention is centered on intention. The emphasis is on the "how" to react behavior based on the viewer's advance preparation, preconceptions or attitude. The intention to react can vary while the expectation of the stimulus is fixed, or conversely, the intention of reaction is fixed while the expectation of the stimulus varies (Gibson, 1941, as cited in Duchowski, 2003).

Selective Filter: attention is seen as a selective filter responsible for regulating sensory information to sensory channels of limited capacity. Information enters in parallel but is then selectively filtered to sensory channels (Broadbent, 1958, as cited in Duchowski, 2003). The filter is applied at recognition level, and the sensory channels have only to process the selected items. Activating the filter at recognition level is thus efficient, because it is not process consuming (Broadbent, 1958, as cited in Reed, 1999).

Importance weightings: it is not attention as such, but the combination of pertinence and sensorial activation ("importance weightings") preset at central high levels that have a causal role in attention, and determine the selection of items in the visual scene (Deutch and Deutch, 1963 as cited in Duchowski, 2003). In this model, the semantic selection is activated after the recognition level. From the recognition level to the semantic selection level, attention is shared between several items, and is thus resource consuming (Deutch and Deutch, 1963 as cited in Reed, 1999; Norman, 1968, as cited in Reed, 1999). In this late selection, due to attention sharing, performance may decrease dramatically (Cherry, as cited in Weil-Barais, 1993).

Scanpaths: in order to recognize and understand the scene, several serial (sequential) viewing patterns are necessary. A coherent picture of the visual field is constructed piecemeal through the assembly of serially viewed regions of interest. Scanpaths, the "*what*," correspond to regions of interest selectively filtered by foveal vision for detailed processing. Scanpath characteristics such as their order of progression can be task dependent (Yarbus, 1967, Noton and Stack, 1971, as cited in Duchowski, 2003).

Spotlight: the orientation of attention is done in parallel and precedes detection. Orientation, the "where," may be an entirely central aspect of attention, and is not always dependent on eye movements. Detecting is context-sensitive, requiring contact between the attentional beam and the input signal (Posner et al., 1980, as cited in Duchowski, 2003).

Glue (Feature Integration Theory): attention provides the glue that enable to integrate separated features in a particular location so that the conjunction is perceived as a unified whole. Attention has to focus on a stimulus before synthesizing its features into a pattern. Attention selects features from a master (mental) map of locations showing *where* all the feature boundaries are located, but not *what* those features are. The feature map also encodes simple and useful properties of the scene, such as color, orientation, size, and stereo distance (Treisman and Gelade, 1980, as cited in Anderson, 2000; Duchowski, 2003).

Window: the attentional window is responsible for selecting patterns in the "visual buffer." The attentional window is scalable (can be adjusted incrementally) and may be related to mental imagery, that is, mental maps. A mental map can be defined as "the mental invention or recreation of an experience that in at least some respects resembles the experience of actually perceiving an object or an event, either in conjunction with, or in the absence of, direct sensory stimulation" (Kosslyn, 1994, as cited in Duchowski, 2003). The diameter of the "Spotlight" (searchlight) as a visual angle determines the "Window" or Useful Field of View (UFOV), and eye movements control the spotlight direction beam (Ware, 2000). The UFOV function seems to be far larger for detecting moving targets than for detecting static targets (Peterson and Dugas, 1972, as cited in Ware, 2000).

Furthermore, two other classifications of visual attention are useful when performing ET experiments: the first one consists in classifying visual processes in bottom-up or top-down models; the second one considers serial versus parallel visual process models.

Bottleneck Models

A well-known phenomenon related to cognition called "bottleneck" corresponds to the saturation of an information channel or of a cognitive resource by too many information, or by incompatible tasks having to be performed on the same channel.

Several locations and ways to deal with the bottleneck were proposed. The ways to deal with the bottleneck depend on the bottleneck location: at the recognition level or after the recognition level.

Top-down models such as Broadbent filter (Broadbent, 1958 in Reed, 1999) and attenuation theory (Treisman, 1960, in Reed, 1999) consider that attention or high cognitive levels guide perception, and thus the bottleneck is situated at the recognition level. The filter allows only relevant data to be processed. The attenuation theory proposes a filter and an activation threshold; the perception of a stimulus is attenuated when the attention is not focused on. The filter can also be applied to different input channels (Cherry, 1953, in Weil-Barais, 1993).

When situated at the recognition level, the bottleneck is efficient because only relevant information is processed.

In the bottleneck model, interference is due to the use of the same mechanism for several incompatible tasks. Interference is specific and depends on the degree of similarity between the used mechanisms.

Mixes between *top-down* and *bottom-up* models place the bottleneck after the recognition level. In these models, pertinence and sensorial activation are combined (Deutch and Deutch, 1963 in Reed, 1999; Norman, 1968 in Reed, 1999).

When placed after the recognition level, the bottleneck is equivalent to semantic selection, and thus resource consuming.

Attention Resource Models

Attention resource models complete the bottleneck models. Resource theories focus resources needed to perform a task or a set of tasks. In the Attention and Effort model (Kahneman, 1973 in Reed, 1999), resources have an activation threshold. The activation is the physiological state that influences the distribution of cognitive resources among several tasks. The choice of the activity to maintain is determined by two categories of attention features: stable dispositions and momentary intentions. Stable dispositions influence the orientation of attention in a non-voluntary way. Momentary intentions are the conscious decisions to distribute the attention on particular tasks or particular aspects of the environment.

In resource models, interference is due to the limited resource capacity. Interference is non-specific, and depends on the set of requirements of a task.

Flexible attention model combines the bottleneck model and the resource model, showing that the selection stage (filter) can be adapted depending on the attention mode required by the task (Johnston and Heinz, 1978 in Reed, 1999). This model confirms that an early selection (at recognition level) is more efficient and less resource consuming than a late selection level (after the recognition level).

An important aspect of resource allocation is the degree of automatism of the task.

Posner and Sydner (Posner and Sydner, 1975 in Reed, 1999) defined three criteria for automatism:

1. automatism happens without intention;
2. automatism does not trigger a conscious attention;
3. automatism does not interfere with other mental activities.

When the automatism becomes too important, trying to control it may be very difficult (Shiffrin and Schneider, 1977 in Weil-Barais, 1993) and causes interferences in the task performance (Stroop, 1935 in Weil-Barais, 1993).

Simple Serial Models

In simple serial models, items are scanned one by one at a time. The scan classifies the item as a target or a distractor. A distinction was made (Treisman and Gelade, 1977, in Bundesen, 1996) between feature search and conjunction search. In *feature* search, the target differs from distractors by a simple physical feature, which is not possessed by distractors. In *conjunction* search, the target differs from distractors by a conjunction of physical features, but the target is not unique by any of the component features of the conjunction. In this model the conjunction search is serial. However, the feature search within non-overlapping groups of items may be parallel, but depends on the degree of discrimination between the target and the distractor.

Selective Serial Models

In selective serial models, items are attended one by one at a time, but the scan order depends on their status as targets or distractors. When a target and a distractor compete for attention, the target is more likely to win. Visual search is a two stages process (Hoffman 1979 in Bundesen, 1996). The first step is fast and parallel and the target filtering is an overall measure of similarity. Probable targets are identified, but this step is prone to errors. The second step is slow and serial: an exhaustive serial comparison against targets is performed.

Parallel Models

The *Independent Channels Model* (Eriksen, 1966 in Bundesen, 1996) is based on the perceptual independence, which means that items presented to different foveal areas are processed in parallel and independently up to and including the level of form identification.

In the *Limited Capacity Model* (Atkinson, 1969 in Bundesen, 1996) a limited processing capacity is added to the independent channels model.

In the *Optimal Capacity Allocation Model* (Shaw, 1978 in Bundesen, 1996), attention can be split among noncontiguous locations in the visual field.

In the *Zoom Lens Model* (Eriksen and Webb, 1989 in Bundesen, 1996), the attentional field can vary in size from 1° to the entire visual field. Due to limitations of the processing capacity, the amount of processing capacity allocated to a given attended location decreases as the size of the attentional field increases. However, the attentional field cannot be split among non-contiguous locations.

In the *Race Models of Attention* (Bundesen, 1987 in Bundesen, 1996) attention selection is made of those items that finished processing first. It is assumed that the processing of targets is faster than the processing of distractors.

Visual Attention and Eye Movements

The effective control of eye movements depends on a combination of sensory and cognitive influences. Attention selects the target for both smooth eye movements and saccades, while lower-level sensory oculomotor mechanisms compute the precise trajectory of eye movements. Trajectory computation is influenced by a combination of immediate visual cues about target position, shape or motion on the retina, combined with cognitive signals, specifically expectations about future target motion (Kowler, 1999).

EYE GAZE PATTERN AND INTEREST

Eye movements can be classified into three types of looking related to the situations in which they occur (Glenstrup et al., 1995):

Spontaneous looking
The subject is just watching the scene, with any specific task in mind. The eyes tend to be attracted to those parts of the scene that contain the most information.

Task-relevant looking
The subject views the scene with a specific question or task in mind. In this case, the subject may only gather information from the scene, or have the intention to manipulating something in the scene.

Orientation of thought looking
The subject is not paying much attention to the scene, but is attending some inner thought. The eye movements are not related to the scene.

EYE TRACKING TECHNIQUES

Several ET techniques were set-up and used during the years. Such techniques are: Electro Oculography (EOG), Scleral Contact Lens/Search Coil, Photo Oculography (POG)/Video Oculography (VOG), Video-Based combined Pupil/Corneal Reflection and Computer-based video software systems. The most commonly used techniques are the last two.

VIDEO-BASED COMBINED PUPIL AND CORNEAL REFLECTION

To provide point of regard measurement, two ocular features have to be measured: the corneal reflection and the pupil center. These two features enable to disambiguate head movement from eye movement. The positional difference between the pupil center and corneal reflection changes with pure eye rotation, but remains relatively constant with minor head movements. The corneal reflections, known as Purkinje reflections, of the light source (typically infra-red) are measured relative to the location of the pupil center. Eye anatomy enables four Purkinje reflections. Video-based trackers are capable to measure the first one. Generation V eye trackers—dual Purkinje image (DPI)—are capable to measure also the fourth Purkinje image, and so they separate translational and rotational eye movements. The first and fourth reflections are identical for eye translations but they move through different distances for eye rotations. Head stabilization may be required for DPI eye trackers.

This last technique is the most appropriate for ET studies in the field of HCI and aeronautics.

There are two techniques of lightening the pupil: the dark pupil technique and the bright pupil technique. They differ by the angle between the camera that records the eye and the infrared light beam projected on the eye (Figures 16.5 and 16.6).

Dark Pupil technique is usable with any kind of light (artificial or natural), and it is quite stable with large changes in ambient illumination. The advantage is that for any pupil size (especially when the pupil is very small), it is possible to distinguish the dark pupil from the bright corneal reflection. Thus, Dark Pupil technique can be used in ecologic experiments, indoor or outdoor, that is, simulators or real cockpits.

Bright Pupil is usable only with artificial light. It is sensitive to large changes in ambient illumination. When the pupil is very small, it can be mismatched with the

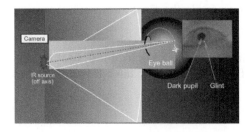

Figure 16.5   Dark Pupil technique

Source: Zhai et al., 1999.

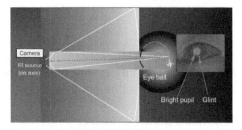

Figure 16.6   Bright Pupil technique

Source: Zhai et al., 1999.

corneal reflection that is equally bright. Moreover, Bright Pupil can be used only indoors, that is, on simulators only.

Eye Tracking Systems

Video based pupil and corneal reflection ET devices are composed as follows: a camera that records the eye, an infrared source that projects an infrared beam onto the eye, and a scene camera, that records the visual scene as seen by the subject.

The infrared beam projected onto the eye is than reflected by the eye on the objects of the visual scene. A pointer (crosshair or circle) is associated with the infrared beam, and thus the eye tracker can be assimilated to a pointing device.

The gaze pointer is overlaid on the scene video, and thus provides real time gaze position.

Video data provided by the eye camera can also be used for blinks and pupil diameter analysis.

It is important to notice that the eye tracker alone only gives analog video data.

Eye trackers can be head mounted or remote. The remote eye trackers are usually utilized for single screen evaluations. The subject should not move the head in order that the eyes stay in the remote camera field. The head mounted eye trackers are not constrained and are usually used for multiple screens (planes) or outdoor evaluations.

Magnetic Head Trackers

ET systems can be combined with magnetic head tracking devices. The use of a head tracker depends on the evaluation context. A magnetic head tracker is composed of a magnetic field generator and a head sensor. The magnetic field generator is the origin of a 3-D space. In this 3-D space referential, object coordinates are measured. Up to 16 planes corresponding to screens, command panels, and so on can be measured. Up to 16 areas, or zones of interest can be defined for each plane. A zone of interest can be associated to an object or set of objects belonging to a plane, that is, instrument 1 of command panel 3. It is thus possible to build a quite complete 3-D model of the physical context.

Eye Trackers Combined with Magnetic Head Trackers

The head sensor provides the precise position of the head in the 3-D model. The distance between the head sensor and both the scene camera and the eye are also entered in the 3-D model. The first distance is needed for the scene camera calibration. The second one is needed for the eye tracker calibration. Head position data are combined with gaze position data and allows a maximum accuracy. Figure 16.7 describes an eye tracker combined with a magnetic head tracker. Data obtained from this combination is digital.

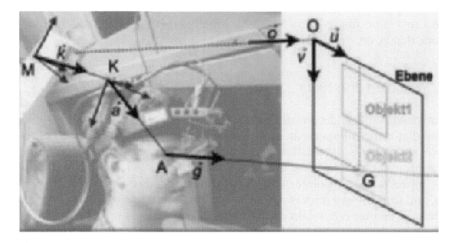

Figure 16.7   Eye tracker combined with a magnetic head tracker

Note: M: magnetic head tracker, K: head-mounted magnetic sensor, A: ET system, O: plane origin, G: gaze point on the plane.

Source: Anders, 1999.

COMPUTER-BASED VIDEO SOFTWARE SYSTEMS

A recently emerging trend in the ET systems marketplace is video (image) processing not only for the eyes, but also for the entire user face. As an improvement of video-based pupil and corneal reflection, video processing does not need anymore corneal reflection. An important benefit of not using corneal reflection anymore is the improved usability of such systems in variable lighting conditions, ET data being more robust in outdoor situations. For specific ET purposes, eyes features (iris, eyelids, eye opening) are detected and analyzed by the software system. Using two remote cameras, the system processes both eye information and associates 3-D vectors to gaze direction (Figure 16.8).

Furthermore, such systems detect also head movements, so there is no need to use head trackers. The accuracy improved over time and is quite the same for the last version of FaceLAB as the accuracy of video-based combined pupil and corneal

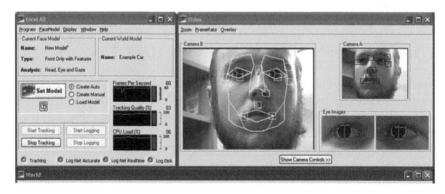

Figure 16.8   FaceLAB gaze detection

Source: Thompson and Park, 2005.

reflection (typical static accuracy of gaze direction measurement 0.5–1° rotational error). All data obtained with these systems is digital.

However, these systems are only remote and thus could be utilized in situations where users sit in front of their visual scene (that is, cockpits and computer screens).

EYE TRACKING DATA ANALYSIS AND METRICS

Commonly, the following data is captured by eye trackers and then analyzed with dedicated software:

1. *Eyelid movements*: blinks/eyelid opening. Blinks are fast eyelid movements, and the two standard types of metrics are the *Percentage of Closure Over Time* (Perclos) (Knipling, 1998) and the *Average Eye Closure/Opening Speed* (AECS). Eyelid opening can also be analyzed (Figure 16.8 bottom right, Figure 16.9). Blinks and eyelid opening are used to assess fatigue and vigilance.

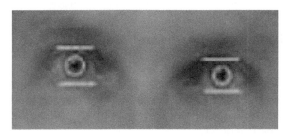

Figure 16.9   Eyelid opening for both eyes (SMI)

2. *Pupillary responses*: The pupillary response analysis is not very reliable, because the pupil diameter varies with ambient luminance changes. Studies focusing emotional states of the subject can be conducted indoor only, where luminance can be precisely defined.
3. *Eye movements*: fixations, saccades, smooth pursuit, drifts. Eye movement analysis may need a video based encoding tool or can be automatic.

If the visual scene is fixed (that is, screen user interfaces, command panels, images), then automatic analysis is possible, based on the previous definition of Regions and Areas of Interest.

If the visual scene is moving (that is, videos, animated screens), than the automatic analysis becomes tough. There are workarounds to mix automatic analysis with video based analysis, provided especially by computer-based video software systems, since visual items detection in the visual scene is possible (that is, pedestrians, road signs, and so on).

For 3-D scenes generated by 3-D simulators, it is possible to synchronize 3-D data with ET data, but further plug-ins have to be set-up.

Automatic analysis computes fixation rates and durations, percentages of fixations in the zones of interest, scanpaths and hot-spots (Figure 16.10).

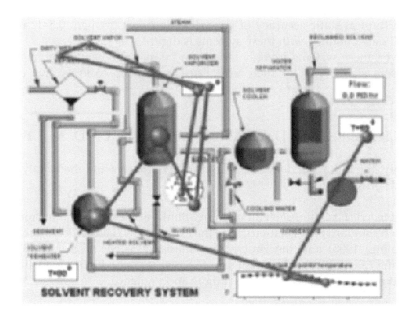

Figure 16.10   Fixations, scanpaths and zones of interest

Whatever the ET system and analysis, it is mandatory to assign behaviors related to the objects of the visual scene, in order to be able to understand detected fixations and scanpaths. Behaviors are defined by task analysis and cognitive modeling, and should be prior to the use of ET.

Because eye movements are not always related to overt visual attention, analysis performed by an expert is in general more accurate than automatic analysis but more time consuming.

EYE TRACKING EXPERIMENT EXAMPLE

The experiment goal was to validate an ET system usability in terms of accuracy, as well as for data analysis and interpretation. The target application was the 3-D Synthetic Vision System (SVS) and ET was used together with Situation Awareness in order to evaluate the new concept of the 3-D SVS.

The experiment was performed with 4 pilots. The 3-D SVS was displayed on a computer LCD screen, standalone. At this stage we didn't need the 3-D SVS to be integrated with the other cockpit instruments, since the 3-D SVS was not yet operational. The size of the 3-D SVS was 6×6 inches. Subjects were asked only to view the pre-recorded 3-D dynamic scene, with no command manipulation. Three scenarios of 15 to 20 minutes presenting difficult approach and landing contexts were presented to each pilot. The dependent variable was the understanding of the scene by the pilots based on the SVS elements (aircraft mockup, trajectories, symbols, relief).

The eye-tracker enabled to follow the gaze path of the pilots on various items of the 6×6 inch visual scene with high accuracy, so the usability of the system was validated.

EYE TRACKING RESULTS: HISTOGRAMS AND VISUAL PATTERNS

Because the 3-D SVS displays a dynamic scene, automatic analysis of ET data, based on zones of interest, could not be used.

Noldus *The Observer,* a video-encoding software, was used instead. All the variables of the experimental protocol were transferred into the software. Once the encoding of ET videos was completed, result analysis was performed at two stages. The first stage provided statistics on the most looked-at visual items. For the second stage, an additional software (Noldus *Theme*) was used. This second stage enabled to link visual items together and thus to obtain *visual patterns*. Visual patterns express in particular visual attention as a cognitive flow related to the whole visual scene where all items are co-dependent. Thus, visual patterns are a step beyond quantitative results expressed as statistic histograms of *individual items,* expressing meaningful structures of *items tied to each other*.

VISUAL PATTERNS

Theme is a professional system for the detection and analysis of hierarchical time dependent patterns called T-patterns (Magnusson, 2000). *Theme* was developed for studying real-time structures of behavior using a time based behavior organization model.

The input for the program is a particular kind of real-time behavior record in which it then searches for particular types of repeated real-time patterns.

A visual pattern is a structured sequence of several Items of Gaze (IOG) that repeats identically at least once during the observed period. Inside patterns, IOG are linked by the user via eye movements, to construct a meaning out of the specific visual scene. Furthermore, atomic behaviors such as the type of eye movement (that is, fixations, sweeping or smooth pursuit) may be added to each IOG in order to obtain refined patterns.

Therefore, visual pattern properties are:

- the *length*, that is the number of IOG that comprise a pattern,
- the *level*, in terms of hierarchical levels of composition of sub-patterns (a complex pattern can be composed of several sub-patterns),
- the *frequency* of the pattern that is the number of times the pattern occurs during the specified period of time.

Pattern Selection: Quantitative Aspects

Within *Theme*, patterns can be selected by their quantitative and structural properties.

Patterns that are selected fit within all the parameter values that are selected.

The following parameters are available:

N—The number of occurrences of patterns: search patterns that are observed at least or at most N times.

Length—The number of event types in the patterns: search only patterns of lengths that are within the given value.

Level—The number of hierarchical levels: search only patterns with more/less than X levels.

Actors—The number of actors in the pattern: search only patterns containing at least/at most X actors.

For our experiment, we used only single actor features of the software. However, *Theme* may be used in experiments that focus on multi-actor communication, such as Pilot Flying and Pilot Not Flying communication and activity.

Pattern Selection: Qualitative Content Aspects

Theme enables as well pattern selection by content. For example, patterns that include specific actions, specific actors, or specific combinations of these may be utilized.

According to the behavior definition and cognitive model contained in *The Observer*, incremental pattern extraction is allowed. Moreover, *Theme* enables to search for specific patterns for a single pilot or for several pilots. Complex pattern extraction is a very powerful feature that is not possible without using the software. The following analysis was fully performed with *The Observer* and *Theme*.

The following sections describe data and patterns detected by *Theme*, based on video encoding.

This analysis was performed incrementally, as described below.

Consistent Visual Patterns

In a first step, we searched the visual items according to their relevance for the pilots. The degree of relevance is based on the number of gaze occurrences on a visual item. In this first step we performed a statistical analysis of each IOG on the visual scene elements (Figure 16.11).

In a second step, we searched the visual patterns based on the main IOG as they appear for each pilot. For these first patterns, we did not consider the behavior type (that is, fixations or sweeping/smooth pursuit) associated to the IOG (Figure 16.11).

Finally, we added pilot visual behaviors (that is, fixations, sweeping or smooth pursuit) to each OG, and we obtained more complex patterns. In this step, we selected only patterns that include the patterns found in Step 2 (Figure 16.12).

STEP 1: WHAT ARE THE VISUAL ELEMENTS TAKEN INTO ACCOUNT BY PILOTS?

*b_* and *m_* prefixes stand for *background* and *middle-ground* (that is, b_left_peaks means background left peaks)
*fp_* prefix stands for *flight path*
*ac_* prefix stands for *Air Craft*

For this first scenario, we can observe that the most important element seems to be the *flight path end*. This corresponds to the Projection component of Endsley's Situation Awareness model.

Figure 16.11 shows a comparison between the relevance accorded by two pilots to the IOG.

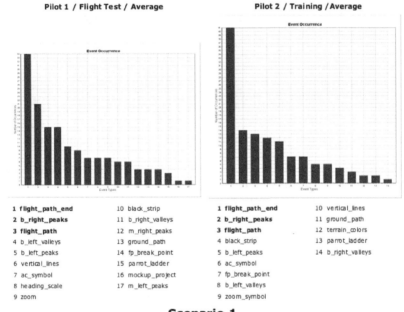

Pilot 1 / Flight Test / Average

1 flight_path_end	10 black_strip
2 b_right_peaks	11 b_right_valleys
3 flight_path	12 m_right_peaks
4 b_left_valleys	13 ground_path
5 b_left_peaks	14 fp_break_point
6 vertical_lines	15 parrot_ladder
7 ac_symbol	16 mockup_project
8 heading_scale	17 m_left_peaks
9 zoom	

Pilot 2 / Training / Average

1 flight_path_end	10 vertical_lines
2 b_right_peaks	11 ground_path
3 flight_path	12 terrain_colors
4 black_strip	13 parrot_ladder
5 b_left_peaks	14 b_right_valleys
6 ac_symbol	
7 fp_break_point	
8 b_left_valleys	
9 zoom_symbol	

Scenario 1

Figure 16.11   Most looked-at visual items: comparison between two pilots

STEP 2: HOW AND WHEN PILOTS GROUP VISUAL ITEMS INTO VISUAL PATTERNS

Figure 16.12 shows on the top the visual pattern that was used by the same pilot at two moments of the scenario, corresponding to the two snapshots on the bottom.

On the top-left, the pattern is represented as the sequence of visual elements looked at by the pilot. Vertically, the number of elements determines the pattern *length,* which is 5 in this case. The pattern *level* is the horizontally nesting structure of

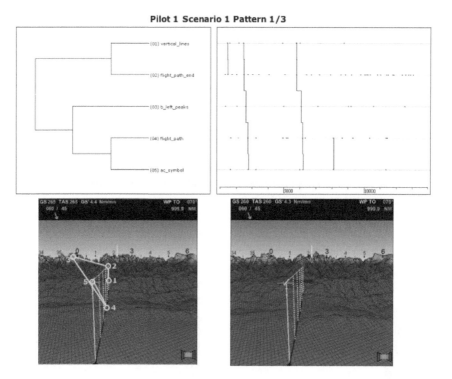

Figure 16.12   A visual pattern and the situations where it occurs

the different sub-patterns. Here, the pattern level is 3. Elements (1) and (2) are sub-patterns of level 1, as well as elements (4) and (5).

On the top-right, a timeline corresponds to each IOG. The dots on each timeline are the gaze occurrences on the specific IOG. Following the vertical links between gaze occurrences on various IOG on these timelines, we can notice that the first sub-pattern [(1), (2)] occurs three times (first and second timelines), and that the second one [(4), (5)] occurs also three times (fourth and fifth timelines). Combined with element (3), the sub-pattern [(4), (5)] becomes a sub-pattern of level 2 [(3), (4), (5)] that occurs two times (timelines 3, 4, 5). Finally, the five elements are combined into a pattern of level 3.

On the left bottom snapshot, the IOG have been highlighted, as well as the specific ordered gaze path from the first to the last IOG.

STEP 3: HOW ARE PILOTS LOOKING AT VISUAL ELEMENTS AND WHAT ARE THE NEW PATTERN STRUCTURES WHEN VISUAL BEHAVIORS ARE ADDED

In this step of pattern analysis, we added behaviors associated to each visual element. Based on the eye movement types, implemented as variables within *The Observer*, behavior (eye movements) classes considered here are static and dynamic, containing respectively short and long fixations, and sweeping and smooth pursuit.

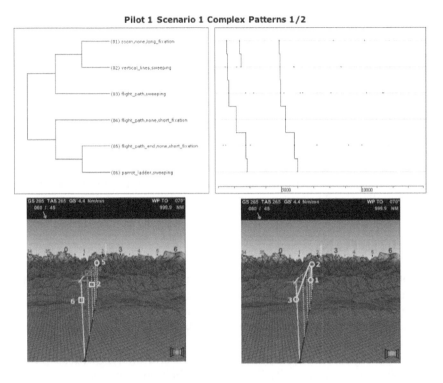

Figure 16.13   Complex pattern with added behaviors

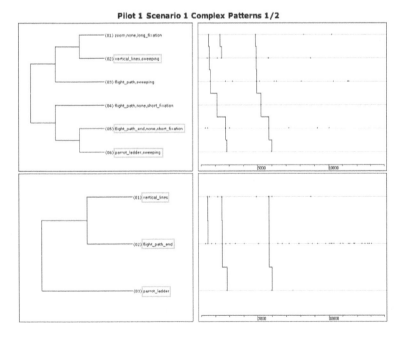

Figure 16.14   Pattern nesting

By adding behaviors to the gaze occurrences on IOG, we obtained refined visual patterns. For analysis consistency, in the new pattern set we selected only those patterns that include the patterns found in Step 2 (the patterns containing only the visual elements without the associated visual behaviors).

Figure 16.13 shows a pattern of length 6 and level 3 that occurs twice entirely, and the sub-pattern [(1), (2)] that occurs three times alone.

The elements of the entire pattern are highlighted on the bottom left snapshot. Circles represent fixations and squares represent sweeping. The pattern without behaviors (obtained in Step 2) is highlighted in the bottom right snapshot.

Figure 16.14 shows the pattern obtained in Step 3 on the top, and the initial pattern obtained in Step 2 on the bottom. The initial pattern is highlighted. The right graphs show the timelines and occurrences of both patterns.

CONCLUSION

This chapter provided a general overview of ET use in Human Factors. As a *technique*, Eye Tracking is quite complex and in order to take the full benefits it should be used according to the specific goals of each experiment. This means that different types of ET devices have to be considered and/or adapted according to each experiment specificities and constraints.

As a *method* Eye Tracking enables to observe and analyze crucial information related to the way users visually interact with their environment. It could be used for validation as well as for discovery purposes.

By contrast with subjective assessment methods (surveys, questionnaires, rating scales), Eye Tracking is an *objective assessment* method meaning that data collected during the experiment is real-time and provides a mean to analyze what actually happened during the experiment. As a *method*, Eye Tracking should be integrated and synchronized with several other assessment methods (subjective as well as objective, that is, Workload, Situation Awareness, Emotion Assessment; audio-video recording, spyware) in order to satisfy the analysis of the complete interaction loop (that is, vision as trigger for action and action as trigger for vision). For example, during an ET experiment, video cameras should be used for recording all the user actions (the cameras provided by the ET device are generally not sufficient to record all the user gestures and movements). Audio recording should be also used. At the same time, rating scales and questionnaires should be administrated at specific points of the scenario. When possible, ET devices should be plugged and synchronized with the experimental simulators or devices. The final analysis should be performed using all the synchronized and integrated data collected during the experiment.

In some experimental contexts manual encoding of the video recordings obtained using ET is necessary instead of the automatic encoding. Manual encoding is time consuming (the eyes move all the time and quite fast, so the manual encoding is performed generally in slow video motion). Thus, Eye Tracking *use-cases* should be identified before the experiment, that is, in which particular part of the scenario Eye Tracking should be employed.

As cognitive structures, *Visual Patterns* that is possible to obtain only with Eye Tracking contribute in a major and refined way to cognitive modeling that is performed in Human Factors.

REFERENCES

Albrechsten, H., Andersen, H.H.K., Bødker, S., Pejtersen, A.M. (2001). *Affordances in Activity Theory and Cognitive Systems Engineering*. Risø-R-1287(EN). Pitney Bowes Management Services Denmark A/S.

Alm, T. (2001). How to put the Real World into a 3-D Aircraft Display. *Proceedings, People in Control Conference*, Manchester, June 2001.

Anders, G. (1999). *Eye Tracking Research in an A330 Full Flight Simulator*. Berlin University of Technology, Institute of Aeronautics and Astronautics.

Anderson, J.R. (2000). *Cognitive Psychology and Its Implications*, Fifth Edition. Worth Publishers and W.H. Freeman.

Boy, G.A. (2002). Interfaces Procédurales. *Proceedings IHM 2002, Poitiers, France,* pp. 81–88. *ACM Press, New York.*

Bruneau, D., Sasse, A., McCarthy, J. (2001). The Eyes Never Lie: The use of ET Data in HCI Research. *CHI'2001.*

Bundesen, C. (1996). Formal Models of visual Attention: A Tutorial Review. In Kramer, A.F., Coles, M.G.H., and Loman, G.D. (Eds.), *Converging Operations in the field of Visual Attention*. American Psychological Association.

Carroll, R. (1999).*Eye-Activity Measures of Fatigue and Napping as Fatigue Counter measure*. Federal Highway Administration, April 1999, Publication No. FHWA-MCRT-99–010.

Duchowski, A.T., et al. (2002). 3-D Eye Movement Analysis. *Behavior Research Methods, Instruments and Computers.*

Duchowski, A.T. (2003). *Eye Tracking Methodology: Theory and Practice*. Springer-Verlag London Limited.

Endsley, M.R., Garland, D.J. (2000). *Situation Awareness Analysis and Measurement*. Laurence Erlbaum Associates, London.

Endsley, M.R. et al. (2003). *Designing for Situation Awareness: An approach to User-Centered Design*. Taylor and Francis, London.

Findlay, J.M., Gilchrist, I.D. (2003). *Active Vision: The Psychology of Looking and Seeing*. Oxford University Press, US.

Fitts, P.M., Jones, R.E., Milton, J.L. (1950). Eye movements of aircraft pilots during instrument-landing approaches. *Aeronautical Engineering Review*, 9(2), 24–29.

Glenstrup, A.J., Engell-Nielsen, T. (1995). *Eye Controlled Media: Present and Future State*. University of Copenhagen, DIKU (Institute of Computer science) Universitetsparken 1, DK-2100 Denmark.

Hauland, G. (2002). *Measuring Team Situation Awareness in Training of En Route Air Traffic Control, Process Oriented Measures for Experimental Studies, Risø-R-1343(EN)*. Pitney Bowes Management Services Denmark A/S.

Hinckley, K., Jacob, R.J.K., Ware, C. (2003). Input/output Devices and Interaction Techniques, in *The Computer Science and Engineering Handbook,* Second Edition (Ed.) A.B. Tucker, CRC Press.

Holland, D.A. (2001). Peripheral Dynamic Visual Acuity Under Randomized Tracking Task Difficulty, Target Velocities and Direction of Target Presentation. PhD. Virginia Polytechnic Institute and State University© Dwight A. Holland.

Jacob, R.J.K., Karn, K.S. (2003). "Eye Tracking in Human–computer Interaction and Usability Research: Ready to Deliver the Promises (Section Commentary)," in *The Mind's Eye: Cognitive and Applied Aspects of Eye Movement Research* (Eds.) J. Hyona, R. Radach, and H. Deubel, pp. 573–605, Amsterdam, Elsevier Science.

Josephson, S., Holmes, M.E. (2002). Visual Attention to Repeated Internet Images: Testing the Scanpath Theory on the World Wide Web. *Eye Tracking Research and Applications Symposium 2002.*

Källqvist, C. (1999). Eye Movements and Visual Scanning in Simulated Air Traffic Control, A Field Study, Master Thesis. Lund University of Cognitive Science, Sweden.

Knipling, R. (1998). *PERCLOS: A valid Psychophysiological Measure of Alertness As Assessed by Psychomotor Vigilance.* Federal Highway Administration, October 1998, Publication No. FHWA-MCRT-98–006.

Kowler, E. (1999). What Movements of the Eye Tell us about the Mind. In *What is Cognitive Science?* Lepore, E. and Pylyshyn, Z. (Eds.), Blackwell Publishers.

Lindsay, P.H., and Norman, D.A. (1980). *Traitement de l'informationetcomportementhumain.* Vigot.

Magnusson, S.M. (2000).Discovering hidden time patterns in behavior: T-patterns and their detection. *Psychonomic Society: Behavior Research Methods, Instruments and Computers,* 2000, 32 (I), 93–11O.

Majaranta, P., Räihä, K.J. (2002). Twenty Years of Eye Typing: Systems and Design Issues. *Eye Tracking Research and Applications Symposium 2002.*

McCarthy, J., Sasse, A., Miras, D., Reigelsberger, J. (2003). How low can you go? User acceptance of video quality for sports coverage on small screens. *CHI'2003.*

Ohno, T., Mukawa, N., Yoshikawa, A. (2002).FreeGaze: A Gaze Tracking System for Everyday Interaction. *Eye Tracking Research and Applications Symposium 2002.*

PRS (2000). The PRS ET Studies: Validating Outdoors' Impact in the Marketplace. Perception Research Services Inc. 2000.

Reed, S.K. (1999). *Cognition: Théorieset applications,* 4ème édition. DeBoeckUniversité.

Santella, A., DeCarlo, D. (2002). Abstracted Painterly Renderings Using ET Data. *International Symposium on Non Photorealistic Animation and Rendering (NPAR) 2002,* pp. 75–82.

Sasse, A. (2003a). Eye-Catcher or Blind Spot? The Effect of Photographs of Faces on E-Commerce Sites. *CHI'2003.*

Sasse, A. (2003b). Trust at First Sight?A Test of Users' Ability to Identify Trustworthy e-Commerce Sites. *CHI'2003.*

Sibert, L.E., Jacob, R.J.K., J.N. Templeman. (2001). *Evaluation and Analysis of Eye Gaze Interaction.* NRL Report NRL/FR/5513--01–9990, Naval Research Laboratory, Washington, D.C.

Sodhi, M., et al. (2002).On-Road Driver Eye Movement Tracking Using Head Mounted Devices. *Eye Tracking Research and Applications Symposium 2002.*

Svensson, E. et al. (1997). Information complexity: mental workload and performance in combat aircraft. *Ergonomics,* 40, 362–380.

Taylor, R. et al. (1997). CC-SART: Validation and Development. *Presented to NATO Research Group 24, Human Engineering Testing and Evaluation, Workshop on Emerging Technologies in Human Engineering Testing and Evaluation,* June 24–26, NATO Headquarters, Brussels, Belgium.

Thompson, P.M., Park, G. (2005). Are You Fatigued? Background and Motivation for the Use of Facelab Sensor Technology. DC213 Conference, July 15, 2005, Los Angeles, CA.

Vertegaal, R. (2002). Designing Attentive Interfaces. *Eye Tracking Research and Applications Symposium 2002.*

Zhai, S., Morimoto, C., Ihde, S. (1999). Manual and Gaze Input Cascaded. *CHI'99.*

Ware, C. (2000). *Information Visualization: Perception for Design.* Morgan Kaufmann Academic Press.

Weil-Barais, A. (1993).*L'homme cognitif.* Presses Universitaires de France.

17

Operator Fatigue: Implications for Human–Machine Interaction

Philippa Gander, Curt Graeber, and Gregory Belenky

ABSTRACT

Operator fatigue is a catch-all term for impairment that commonly occurs if people continue working when they have not fully recovered from the demands of prior work and other waking activities. Fatigue-related impairment can accumulate across a work period where breaks are insufficient to allow short-term recovery from task demands. Fatigue-related impairment also occurs if operators do not obtain sufficient recovery sleep between work periods. The effects of inadequate sleep are cumulative, with performance becoming increasingly impaired to the point where an operator can slip uncontrollably in and out of attentional lapses and microsleeps, during which he or she is unresponsive to task demands or other environmental stimuli. Functional degradation due to fatigue is more likely during times in the circadian body clock cycle when physiological sleep drive is high and performance capacity is sub-optimal. (The circadian body clock is a light-sensitive neural pacemaker that modulates physiological and behavioral functioning in step with the day/night cycle, to facilitate sleep at night.)

Operator fatigue results in systematic changes in physical and mental performance, and in complex behaviors such as situation awareness, decision-making, and communication. It is increasingly being identified as a causal factor in accidents and incidents, as a result of improved scientific understanding and more systematic investigation methods. Thus, the dynamics of fatigue accumulation and recovery need to be integrated into human-centered design.

Fatigue risk has traditionally been addressed at the regulatory level through prescriptive limits on hours of work and rest. Increasingly, Fatigue Risk Management Systems (as an integrated part of safety management systems) are being promulgated as a regulatory alternative. The "defenses-in-depth" paradigm is being applied to identify strategies to reduce the likelihood of fatigue-related errors, to trap such errors when they occur, and to mitigate their consequences at multiple levels in an organization.

At a minimum, fatigue risk reduction strategies should be incorporated into the design of human–machine systems where operator fatigue can be expected to have an impact on safety. Systems that are designed to be resilient to the effects of operator fatigue are also more likely to provide efficient and reliable overall human–machine interaction.

INTRODUCTION

In occupational safety, particularly in transportation, operator fatigue is a widespread and long-standing concern. Traditionally, fatigue was viewed as a simple consequence of the amount of time spent working on a given task—a view that is most applicable to muscle fatigue resulting from physical work. The traditional regulatory approach to managing operator fatigue was to impose prescriptive hours of service limits. Typically, these specify the maximum length of a duty period, minimum rest periods within and between duty periods, and in some cases, the maximum total amount of duty in a week, month or year. For example, long-standing hours of service regulation in the US include the Railroad Hours of Service Act (first enacted in 1907), motor carrier hours-of-service regulations (introduced in 1937), and limits for aviation operators introduced in the Civil Aeronautics Act of 1938 (1).

In the second half of the twentieth century, scientific evidence began accumulating that implicated other causes of operator fatigue in addition to time-on-task, particularly in 24/7 operations. The most significant new understanding concerns the vital importance of adequate sleep in restoring and maintaining all aspects of waking function, and the modulation of performance capacity and sleep propensity by the daily cycle of the circadian pacemaker (biological clock) located in the brain, where the optic nerves cross over in the hypothalamus.

The proportion of safety incidents and accidents in which operator fatigue is a contributing factor is difficult to determine, and is likely to be underestimated. There is no assay (equivalent to an alcohol or drug test) for estimating the level of fatigue-related impairment, so a case must typically be built upon indirect or circumstantial evidence. It is therefore often difficult to conclude unequivocally that fatigue was implicated (1, 2, 3). Despite these investigative difficulties, mitigation of operator fatigue has been on the US National Transportation Safety Board (NTSB) list of "Most Wanted Transportation Safety Improvements" since the list's inception in 1990 (1). Two decades later, it remains on the Federal Most Wanted List for aviation, marine, and pipeline industries (rail was removed from the list with the enactment of the Railroad Safety Improvement Act of 2008; 4).

A search of all Part 121 air carrier accidents and incidents in the NTSB aviation accident database for the 20 years 1989–2008, using the search keywords pilot fatigue and crew fatigue, identified two incidents and one fatal accident (one fatality) where fatigue was identified as a contributing factor (0.22 percent of all Part 121 reports during that period). A similar search of all airplane general aviation accidents and incidents identified 51 accidents or incidents, of which 25 resulted in 52 fatalities. This represents 0.16 percent of all airplane general aviation reports in that time period. In contrast to the ultra-safe aviation system (5), a rigorous case-control study has estimated that motor vehicle crashes resulting in injury could be reduced by 19 percent on a major metropolitan road network if drivers did not drive when they felt sleepy, or when they had slept five hours or less in the last 24 hours, or between 0200 and 0500 h (6).

Beyond the transport sector, fatigue of medical practitioners is also attracting increasing attention, with calls for restrictions on work hours as well as for more comprehensive approaches to managing the risk that fatigued doctors pose both to patients and to themselves (7, 8). In New Zealand, for example, representative nationwide surveys (8, 9) indicate that fatigue-related errors in clinical practice in the last 6 months are recalled by 32 percent of anesthetists (survey response rate, 70 percent), and by 42 percent of junior doctors (survey response rate, 63 percent). A quarter of junior doctors could recall falling asleep at the wheel driving home from work, since becoming doctors (8).

A web-based survey in the US (2,737 interns provided 17,003 monthly reports) examined the safety consequences of extended duration shifts. Compared to months without extended shifts, on months with at least five extended shifts interns were 7.5 times more likely to report fatigue-related significant medical errors, 7.0 times more likely to report fatigue-related preventable adverse events (10), and 2.4 times more likely to report falling asleep while driving or while stopped in traffic (11). Reports of motor vehicle crashes were 2.3 times more likely after an extended shift, and every additional extended shift worked per month increased the risk of reporting a motor vehicle crash after the shift by 16.2 percent (11). Reports of percutaneous injuries were 63 percent more likely during extended shifts than during non-extended shifts, and were twice as likely at night compared to daytime shifts. (12).

The impact of scheduling on error rates was graphically demonstrated in a prospective, randomized control trial conducted by the Harvard Work Hours, Health and Safety Group. Twenty interns working in intensive care took part in the trial that compared a traditional schedule with every third night on call (resulting in shifts of 24 hours or more and an average of 85 hours work per week) and an intervention schedule with a maximum shift length of 16 hours and an average of 65 hours work per week. On the intervention schedule, interns averaged 5.8 hours more sleep per week and had less than half the rate of attentional failures, as measured by continuous electro-oculography during work hours (13). The rate of serious medical errors was reduced by 26 percent, the rate of serious medication errors by 17 percent, and the rate of serious diagnostic errors by 82 percent (14).

To manage the complexities of operator fatigue risk, Fatigue Risk Management Systems (FRMS), are being developed and implemented as part of Safety Management Systems (for example, 15,16). An FRMS is designed to be data driven, monitoring where fatigue risk occurs and where safety may be jeopardized, and having a layered system of defensive strategies to mitigate measured operator fatigue risk (17,18).

Surprisingly little explicit attention has been given to the implications of operator fatigue for human–machine interaction, or to the potential for design-level strategies to minimize operator fatigue and/or mitigate its consequences. This chapter aims to stimulate the interdisciplinary dialogue that is needed to advance these areas. It reviews current understanding of the causes of operator fatigue and the scientific principles that underpin FRMS. It also considers regulatory changes that are facilitating the implementation of FRMS, and thereby opening up exciting possibilities for design-level fatigue risk management strategies.

CAUSES OF OPERATOR FATIGUE

Fatigue-related *performance impairment* implies that an operator would normally be expected to be able to function at the required level, but is (temporarily) unable to do so. Fatigue-related factors known to impair performance capacity include:

- The daily cycle of the circadian biological clock—mental and physical performance capacity typically reach a minimum in the early hours of the morning.
- Increasing time on task—the rate of decline in performance across a period of continuous work is influenced by the intensity of work demands (workload).
- Increasing time awake—as the duration of wakefulness increases, performance degrades (relative to performance with less time awake at that particular time in the circadian cycle).
- Restricted sleep—which causes a cumulative, dose-dependent reduction in performance capacity.

Controlled laboratory experiments cannot address all aspects of workplace safety risk. However, they have the advantage of being able to systematically evaluate the different factors contributing to fatigue-related performance impairment and their interactions. Figure 17.1 illustrates the variation in performance on a standardized 10-minute psychomotor vigilance task (PVT) across a 40-hour experiment with *total sleep deprivation* (19). Participants began the experiment fully rested.

The performance measure is reaction speed (higher values indicate better performance). Lines connect successive 1-minute averages across the 10 minutes of each test, for 50 healthy volunteers who completed the protocol. The following key features of fatigue-related impairment are illustrated.

- Response speed declined cross the 10 minutes of each test session (time-on-task fatigue). Time-on-task effects were evident when volunteers were well-rested (1st day: 0800–2200 hours) and were amplified by increasing time awake and changing circadian phase (2nd day: 0600–1600 hours).
- Response speed declined across the usual sleep time, reaching its lowest around 0800 (after a night with no sleep). It then improved again, but not to the level seen at the corresponding time on the previous day (after a night with normal sleep).
- The fact that performance does not return to its original level on the second day of the study reflects impairment due to sleep loss.
- The (partial) recovery in response speed across the second study day reflects increasing stimulation of wake-promoting centers in the brain by the circadian biological clock, across the morning hours.

The circadian biological clock in mammals is a neural pacemaker located in the suprachiasmatic nuclei (SCN) of the hypothalamus, which endogenously generates a rhythm in firing rate that is close to, but not exactly 24 hours. The SCN receive a direct input from dedicated cells in the retina (separate from the visual system) that monitor environmental light intensity (20). This enables the SCN pacemaker to be reset by the day/night cycle to establish a periodicity of exactly 24 hours, as well as providing sensitivity to seasonal changes in day length.

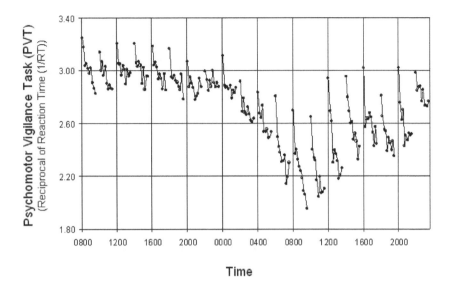

Figure 17.1   Laboratory sleep deprivation experiment illustrating
factors contributing to fatigue-related performance
impairment (19)

The SCN pacemaker has projections to sleep-promoting and wake-promoting centers in the brain, to regulate the timing of the sleep/wake cycle. Thus, sleep at night is not only a social convention but also a genetically-determined physiological preference. The 24/7 society places many people in conflict with this innate temporal pattern. The circadian pacemaker of night workers, for example, does not adapt physiologically to their reversed sleep/wake pattern (for example, 21). As a consequence, they are trying to work when the circadian pacemaker is promoting sleep (and they are therefore least functional) and trying to sleep when the circadian pacemaker is promoting wakefulness (leading to shorter, less restorative sleep). From a physiological perspective, any work pattern that requires the displacement of sleep constitutes shift work. This includes early morning starts and late finishing evening shifts.

The experimental protocol in Figure 17.1 involved *total sleep deprivation*. In 24/7 operations, *chronic sleep restriction* is more common than total sleep deprivation. Figure 17.2 illustrates a different type of experimental protocol where participants have their sleep restricted for 7 consecutive nights (22). The same 10-minute PVT performance test was used as in Figure 17.1, and once again the measure shown is response speed. However, in Figure 17.2, response speed is averaged across four 10-minute tests per day, for the 66 healthy volunteers who completed the protocol.

The experimental protocol in Figure 17.2 began with three days with 8 hours time in bed (TIB), to ensure that participants were well rested. This was followed by seven experimental days (E1–E7) during which groups had either 9 hours TIB (n=16), or 7 hours TIB (n=16), or 5 hours TIB (n=16), or 3 hours TIB (n=18). All groups then had three recovery days (R1–R3) with 8 hours TIB. Figure 17.2 clearly illustrates that the effects of restricted sleep are cumulative and dose-dependent (more rapid performance decline with shorter nightly sleep).

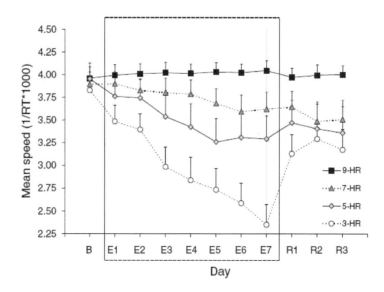

Figure 17.2   Laboratory sleep restriction experiment illustrating cumulative and dose-dependent effects of sleep loss (22)

Experiments such as this confirm another key feature of fatigue-related impairment. Participants rate themselves as feeling increasingly sleepy across the first few days of three hours TIB, but then their self-reported sleepiness stabilizes. However, their performance continues to decline. Thus with severe sleep restriction, people become increasingly unreliable at assessing their own functional status.

Recovery from total sleep deprivation is typically complete with one to two days of unrestricted sleep (23). However, Figure 17.2 suggests that the performance of all the sleep restricted groups failed to recover fully after three nights with eight hours time in bed per night. This suggests that recovery from chronic sleep restriction may take longer and/or that eight hours in bed may not have been sufficient to allow full recovery sleep for some participants. A more recent study (24) suggests that there may be adaptive or accommodative responses to chronic sleep restriction that have a time course of days to weeks. In this later study, one group of participants were allowed to spend their habitual sleep duration in bed (mean = 7.1 hours per night) for eight days before undergoing a week of sleep restriction (three hours time-in-bed per night), followed by five eight-hour recovery nights. The other group had ten hours time-in-bed for eight days prior to the same sleep restriction and recovery protocol. The group who had previously been allowed ten hours in bed maintained better psychomotor vigilance performance and higher objective alertness across the week of sleep restriction, and recovered more rapidly afterwards.

Findings such as these, and the protocol depicted in Figure 17.2, have direct implications for shift work scheduling. Unrestricted nights of sleep must be scheduled periodically to permit recovery from the cumulative effects of sleep restriction caused by shift work. These recovery breaks need to occur more frequently when daily sleep restriction is greater, because of the more rapid accumulation of impairment. The usual recommendation is for a minimum of two nights of unrestricted sleep to allow for recovery. Note that this is not the same as a 48-hour break, since a 48-hour

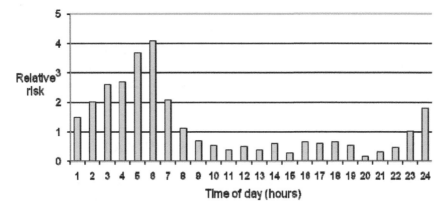

Figure 17.3   Relative risk of a fatigue-related fatal truck crash as a function of time of day (25)

break starting at midnight will only allow one unrestricted sleep opportunity for most people. Sleep restriction experiments such as Figure 17.2 suggest that these recommendations may be conservative with regard to the amount of time needed for full recovery of waking function.

To illustrate the effects of the factors contributing to fatigue-related impairment in safety data requires large numbers of incidents or accidents, making this difficult in ultra-safe systems such as aviation (5). Figure 17.3 illustrates the relative risk of a fatigue-related fatal truck crash as a function of time of day (as a surrogate measure of time in the circadian pacemaker cycle), based on data from all reported fatal truck crashes on US roads in 1991–1996 (25). This relationship is similar across different types of trucking operations and different categories of trucks. The relative risk is greatest in the early hours of the morning, when the circadian sleep drive is maximal and performance is sub-optimal. (In simulators, as drivers become sleepier, their lane deviations increase and speed control becomes more erratic. Decision-making and risk-taking behaviors also degrade with sleep loss. Thus, falling asleep at the

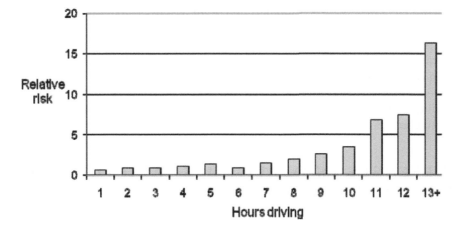

Figure 17.4   Relative risk of a fatigue-related fatal truck crash as a function of hours driving (25)

wheel is the endpoint of a progressive degradation in driving performance that accompanies increasing sleepiness.)

Figure 17.4 illustrates the relative risk of a fatigue-related fatal truck crash as a function of hours of driving, based on the same data set as Figure 17.3 (25). This relationship is attributable to both increasing time awake and the cumulative effects of work demands across the work period.

INDIVIDUAL FATIGUE VERSUS OPERATIONAL RISK

The relationships between individual fatigue and operational risk are complex and depend on the type of task, equipment design, operator expertise and experience, time pressure, other hazards in the environment, and the risk mitigation strategies in place.

Experimental studies indicate that more complex cognitive tasks such as decision-making and communication are more severely affected by sleep loss than simpler tasks (26,27). Positron emission tomography (PET) studies also suggest that the brain regions involved in higher order complex cognitive performance are most affected by sleep deprivation and have the greatest need for sleep-mediated recuperation (28–31).

A rail simulation study comparing the performance of 20 locomotive engineers under varying levels of fatigue found that not all types of performance showed a linear increase in impairment with increasing fatigue levels (32,33). Extreme speed violations and penalty brake applications were highest when drivers were operating with high levels of fatigue, and they had particular difficulty remaining within speed restrictions after moderate-to-heavy descending grades. These findings were attributed to cognitive disengagement from the simulation task at high fatigue levels. On the other hand, fuel use, draft (stretch) forces, and braking errors were found to be greatest at intermediate fatigue levels. The authors of the study proposed that this could be interpreted as efficiency being sacrificed (at intermediate fatigue levels) before safety (at high fatigue levels).

Relationships between individual fatigue and operational risk are even more complex when operators work in teams. An aviation study of 67 experienced international crews flying a simulated line flight in a B747–400 full-motion airplane simulator demonstrated that sleep loss increased the total number of errors made by a two-person cockpit crew (34). Paradoxically however, greater sleep loss among first officers improved the rate of error detection. On the other hand, greater sleep loss among captains led to a higher likelihood of failure to resolve errors that had been detected. Greater sleep loss was also associated with changes in decision-making, including a tendency to choose lower risk options, which would help mitigate the potential impact of fatigue-related impairment.

A DEFENSES-IN-DEPTH APPROACH TO FATIGUE RISK MANAGEMENT

Fatigue risk management is here defined as:

the planning and control of the working environment, in order to minimize, as far as is reasonably practicable, the adverse effects of fatigue on workforce alertness and performance, in a manner appropriate to the level of risk exposure and the nature of the operation.

A fatigue-related incident/accident can be viewed as the final point of a causal chain of events or "hazard trajectory" that penetrates all the defenses present in the system to control that hazard (17,18). Figure 17.5 summarizes a multilayered system of defensive strategies for fatigue risk management (adapted from ref. 18). An attraction of this conceptualization is that it helps clarify where different types of design-level strategies could be developed.

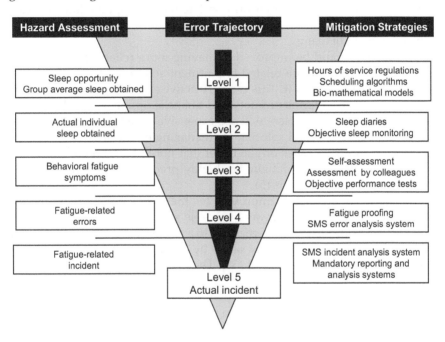

Figure 17.5   A defenses-in-depth approach for fatigue risk management (18)

Source: Adapted from ref. 18.

Level 1 Defenses

One type of Level 1 defenses address the planning of work schedules to ensure that operators are provided with adequate opportunities for sleep. This requires taking into account the placement of rest periods within the circadian pacemaker cycle. For example, a rest period of ten hours between 22:00 and 08:00 provides a much greater sleep opportunity than a rest period of ten hours between 08:00 and 18:00. Level 1 is the focus of traditional hours of service regulations that seek to protect time available for sleep and other non-work activities by prescribing minimum rest breaks between work periods. However, they typically fail to take into account the modulating effects of the circadian pacemaker on the amount of sleep that can be obtained in a given rest period.

Bio-mathematical models are increasingly being used at this level to try to predict and compare sleep and/or fatigue-related impairment across different work schedules. The models seek to simulate the main physiological processes underlying changes in sleep drive and make a series of assumptions relating this to self-rated fatigue and performance. Current limitations of these models include that they predict a single measure of fatigue and do not account for that fact that some tasks are more sensitive to fatigue than others; typically they only predict groups average values, not individual behavior; and they do not accurately capture cumulative impairment with ongoing sleep restriction (illustrated in Figure 17.2), or the process of recovery from it. In addition, they only seek to model fatigue-related impairment of individuals, whereas many safety critical work environments depend upon the coordinated activity of teams.

Level 1 defenses could be improved by having more reliable predictive models of the accumulation of fatigue-related impairment across work schedules, and the time course of recovery from it. This is a very active and potentially very profitable area of research, both in terms of safety and financial opportunity. However, there is an inherent risk that end users will see expensive schedule evaluation software as a stand-alone technological solution for managing operator fatigue. This single-layer defensive approach relies on the belief that not only the occurrence, but also the consequences of operator fatigue are highly predictable, which is not the case particularly in ultra-safe systems (5).

Level 1 defenses are being improved by the development of more flexible regulatory frameworks, moving away from "one-size-fits-all" prescriptive rules and towards permitting industry to self-regulate to a greater or lesser extent. It is argued that this fosters greater ownership of safety by industry and that "those that create the risk are best placed to manage it" (35). The evolution of regulatory strategies is discussed in more detail below.

Another type of Level 1 defense aims to improve the amount and quality of sleep that operators are able to obtain on a given work schedule. Education about personal strategies to improve sleep is a vital defense of this type. In some environments, the provision of rest/sleep facilities at work is important, for example on-board crew rest facilities in long range and ultra-long range aircraft. Better design of such facilities, and of sleep environments generally, would contribute to Level 1 defenses.

Level 2 Defenses

Level 2 defenses in Figure 17.5 require methods for confirming that adequate sleep is being obtained by operators. Among existing sleep monitoring methods, reliability is directly related to cost and to the intrusiveness of the method (36). Continuous monitoring of brain activity (electroencephalogram or EEG) and a variety of other physiological variables (polysomnography) is considered the clinical and laboratory standard for assessing sleep quantity and quality, but is generally too expensive and inconvenient to use on a regular basis to confirm that operators are getting enough sleep. However, it is currently used in situations where a high level of risk is suspected, or where uncertainty is high. For example, polysomnographic monitoring of in-flight sleep of flight crew has been undertaken by Boeing to evaluate on-board rest facilities (36), and when Singapore Airlines launched the first commercial ultra-long-range operations (flights scheduled to be longer than 16 hours), between Singapore and Los Angeles or New York (37).

A second widely-used sleep monitoring methodology is actigraphy, in which the operator wears a watch-sized device that continuously monitors and records movement of the non-dominant wrist (an actiwatch). Minute-by-minute total activity counts, recorded for weeks to months, can be downloaded to a computer and scored for sleep or wakefulness, using an algorithm validated against polysomnography. This methodology is less intrusive and cheaper than polysomnography and gives objective data on sleep patterns over long periods of time, although it does not reveal the internal structure of sleep and does not yield reliable measures of sleep quality (36). Factors that currently limit the usability of actigraphy as a Level 2 defense include the cost of devices and the time and expertise required to score the activity records (although considerably less than is required for manual scoring of polysomnography). The person being monitored also needs to keep a sleep diary that is subsequently used to identify which sections of the actigraphy record should be analyzed as sleep periods, and periods when the actiwatch was not being worn.

Subjective reports on when and how well people sleep (either retrospective questionnaires or prospective sleep diaries) are cheap and easy ways to obtain information for Level 2 defenses. However, they are not as reliable for measuring sleep as either polysomnography or actigraphy (36).

Level 2 defenses could be improved by the development of cheaper, validated objective methods for monitoring sleep. For example, improved methods of EEG monitoring, or better algorithms for automated EEG artifact screening and sleep staging, could reduce the cost and facilitate the use of polysomnography as a Level 2 strategy. (In the clinical context, such improvements could also have a significant role in reducing the cost and increasing the availability of diagnostic services for sleep disorders). Further refinement of surrogate measures of sleep, such as actigraphy, would enhance their usability for Level 2 defenses. New technologies that monitor combinations of other readily-monitored physiological signals might also provide systems for tracking sleep/wake cycles, for example heart rate variability, thermoregulatory changes, and postural changes.

Level 3 Defenses

Level 3 defenses address detection and mitigation of behavioral symptoms of operator fatigue. An inherent difficulty at this level is that accumulating sleep debt is typically accompanied by a decline in an operator's ability to accurately self-assess his/her level of impairment. Consequently, there is considerable debate about the usefulness of self-rated fatigue measures as a Level 3 defense, despite their being cheap and easy to collect. As a counter-argument, how an operator feels may be relevant to the extent that it influences decisions about the use of personal countermeasure strategies (for example, drinking coffee or taking a nap). Checklists of personal fatigue risk factors (recent sleep history, time of day, time on task, and duration of continuous wakefulness) can help operators to assess their own risk of impairment, and that of their co-workers.

Vigilance monitoring devices are receiving increasing attention as a type of Level 3 defense. This approach is long-established in locomotive cabs, where there is typically an escalating series of warnings (a light on the control panel illuminates, then a warning hooter sounds, then the brakes are applied automatically) when a driver fails to press a button on an alertness device at required frequent intervals (for example every 60 seconds). A related concept is to have a series of escalating alarms when the operator fails to interact within a fixed time interval with the systems that he/she is controlling. This concept is applied by Boeing in its Crew Alertness Monitor installed on the flight decks of airplanes designed to fly long-haul routes.

Vigilance monitoring devices that monitor combinations of gaze direction, blink rate, and eyelid closure are receiving considerable attention in the trucking industry and for commercial aviation cockpits. Earlier versions were compromised because the monitoring system (video camera or infrared beam) could not track the eyes when the operator turned his/her head, but various solutions to this problem are being implemented. These devices aim to monitor declining alertness, but have the inherent weakness that it is possible to fall asleep and perceptually disengage from the environment without closing one's eyes.

Workplace performance monitoring offers another type of Level 3 defense. This has typically involved asking operators to undertake validated laboratory performance tests (such as the psychomotor vigilance task used in the experiments in Figures 17.1 and 17.2) at preset times across a work period. A disadvantage of this approach is that it takes the operator out of the active control loop. In addition, simple sub-tasks may have little relevance to operational performance, particularly where operators work in teams, such as in multi-crew aircraft cockpits.

An alternative approach is to embed monitoring of operator performance in the designed systems with which the operator interacts while working. In commercial aviation, consideration is being given to mining Flight Oriented Quality Assurance (FOQA) data for this use, although retrospectively rather than for real-time performance monitoring at present. The challenge is to link crew fatigue to identified excursions from established flight safety parameters measured by FOQA.

There is considerable potential for design level strategies to contribute to the improvement of Level 3 defenses. For example, self-rated fatigue measures can be incorporated into the operating interface so that rating scales are presented to operators at specified times (for example, just before top of descent in a flight operation), both as a reminder to the operator and as a routine means of collecting data to compare fatigue risk across work schedules. Validated workplace vigilance/ performance monitoring systems with real-time feedback to the operator would arguably represent a major breakthrough in Level 3 defenses. Such systems could also provide a source of routine data for fatigue risk monitoring. However, as with bio-mathematical models, there is an inherent risk that end users will see expensive Level 3 monitoring devices as a stand-alone technological solution for operator fatigue. This could be seen as relying on the ambulance at the bottom of the cliff.

Level 4 Defenses

Level 4 defenses require processes in a Fatigue Risk Management System for detecting and analyzing fatigue-related errors when they occur. Non-punitive reporting systems enable tracking of fatigue risk across operations and across time, and have been used successfully for over 10 years in a Fatigue Risk Management System developed by Air New Zealand (38). Key to maintaining the level of reporting is that the information is analyzed regularly, crews are provided with feedback about decisions taken, and where appropriate, duty schedules have been changed.

At this level, there is also great potential for designing systems that can mitigate the consequences of fatigue-related and other errors when they do occur (resilient systems). A new intravenous drug administration system for anesthesia is an example of the application of these concepts to medical practice (39). The system's design is based on broad understanding of the nature of human error (40) and specific understanding of drug administration errors, from detailed analysis of error reports. Spatial features of the system, and the use of color coding of classes of drugs, improve the selection and tracking of drugs and reduce the risk of administering the wrong class of drug, a type of error with high potential for patient harm. The use of color-coded pre-filled syringes wherever possible addresses the error-prone step of drawing drugs into syringes from ampoules, which are traditionally very similar looking for all classes of drugs. Syringes are passed under a barcode reader, which activates an announcement of the drug and its concentration, thus providing an additional cue enabling intervention before the anesthetist completes the highly rote sequence of actions and administers the drug to a patient. The barcode reading step also creates an automated record of all drugs administered and the timing of their administration.

Level 5 Defenses

In Figure 17.5, Level 5 defenses are processes for the investigation and analysis of fatigue-related incidents and accidents, and application of the lessons learned to reduce the likelihood of similar events recurring. Establishing the role of operator fatigue in an event requires: (a) evaluating the likelihood that the operator was experiencing fatigue-related impairment; and (b) evaluating whether actions or inactions of the operator contributed to the outcome, and whether these behaviors were consistent with fatigue-related impairment (41). Clearly, thorough accident investigations can provide valuable lessons learned upon which future safety improvements can be based. However, such lessons can come at a very high cost.

APPLYING SMS PRINCIPLES TO FATIGUE RISK MANAGEMENT

In organizations that have Safety Management Systems (SMS), fatigue-related operator impairment can be considered as one of the range of hazards that need to be managed. The following Table (17.1) outlines an example of how components of a Fatigue Risk Management System (FRMS) can be mapped to requirements from the International Civil Aviation Organization (ICAO) SMS Manual (42).

FRMS can thus be defined as:

a data-driven safety management system that provides a layered system of defenses to minimize, as far as is reasonably practicable, the adverse effects of fatigue on workforce alertness and performance, and the safety risk that this represents.

Such a system recognizes that operator fatigue risk cannot be eliminated in 24-hour operations because of the strong preference for sleep at night, driven by the circadian pacemaker. Thus fatigue must be managed proactively to minimize its impact on safety.

Table 17.1   Fatigue Risk Management System (FRMS) mapped to requirements from the International Civil Aviation Organization (ICAO) SMS Manual (42)

ICAO SMS Requirement	FRMS Example
Hazard Identification	
Reactive analysis based on reporting systems.	Voluntary system for reporting fatigue-related incidents and mandatory reporting of serious events.
Normal activity analysis using questionnaires or routine observations.	Questionnaires, sleep and fatigue monitoring, appropriate to the level of concern. Analysis of routinely collected performance measures, for example, FOQA data in commercial aviation, fatigue ratings prompted by the interface at key times.
Proactive analysis whenever a significant change is introduced.	Bio-mathematical modeling predicting fatigue levels across new duty schedules. Monitoring of sleep and fatigue during validation of new duty schedules.
Safety Management	
Suppression of risk.	Modifying duty schedules associated with high levels of operator fatigue.
Mitigation of risk.	Education of operators on personal fatigue management strategies to improve their sleep and manage their alertness. Provision of facilities where appropriate for napping/sleeping at work.
Strategies to maintain operational safety.	Error-resilient systems, task rotation, controlled napping, strategic use of caffeine.

THE EVOLVING REGULATORY ENVIRONMENT

As has been described throughout this chapter, operator fatigue is multifaceted and has multiple causes. Traditional hours-of-service regulations directly address only time-on-task fatigue, by limiting the duration of work. The need for sufficient time for sleep is addressed indirectly, by restrictions on minimum breaks away from work, but the protection offered is limited because most hours of service regulations do not differentiate between sleep opportunities at night, and sleep opportunities at less favorable times in the circadian pacemaker cycle. In the defenses-in-depth paradigm, hours of service regulations represent a single Level 1 defensive layer. In contrast, the FRMS approach does not rely on a priori decisions about the factors most likely to be causing fatigue. Rather, it is data driven, monitoring where fatigue risk actually occurs and where safety may be jeopardized, and having a layered system of defenses to mitigate and manage that risk.

A further limitation of hours of service regulations is that they are a one-size-fits-all approach that is applied across a broad range of operations in any given sector. This can result in a proliferation of variations or exemptions. For example in 1991, the UK Civil Aviation Authority introduced hours of service regulations for air traffic controllers. When the scheme was evaluated in 1997, over half the airfields covered by the regulations had approved modifications (43). It can be difficult to evaluate the likely safety consequences of a series of variations which are not part of a more comprehensive safety case. In contrast, FRMS are based on each organization developing a safety case based on their detailed understanding of their own operational risk. This safety case must be approved by the regulator and audited at regular intervals.

Legislation in a number of countries now permits transport operators to develop an FRMS as an alternative to complying with the prescriptive hours of service limits (44).

CONCLUSION

The performance capacity of human operators varies systematically across the daily cycle of the circadian pacemaker, and shows dose-dependent, cumulative degradation with insufficient sleep and extended time awake. These effects are grouped under the catch-all term of operator fatigue, and they affect human/machine interactions, particularly in non-routine situations. Innovative design-level strategies that account for these dynamics of operator behavior have exciting potential to improve fatigue risk management in complex operations. There are many opportunities for designers to contribute to improvements in this vital area of safety, in collaboration with the sleep/fatigue research community.

REFERENCES

1. National Transportation Safety Board. (1999). *Evaluation of US Department of Transportation Efforts in the 1990s to Address Operator Fatigue*. Safety Report NTSB/SR/99–01. Washington, DC.

2. Transportation Safety Board of Canada. (1997). *A Guide for Investigating for Fatigue*. Transportation Safety Board of Canada, Gatineau, Quebec.

3. Gander, P.H., Marshall, James I., Le Quesne, L. (2006). Investigating Driver Fatigue in Truck Crashes: Trial of a Systematic Methodology. *Transportation Research: Part F* 9:65–76.

4. National Transportation Safety Board. (2009). NTSB reiterates its commitment to ridding fatigue in transportation during sleep awareness week. NTSB News SB-09–10. Available at www.ntsb.gov/pressrel/2009/090306.html.

5. Amalberti, R. (2001). The paradoxes of almost totally safe transportation systems. *Safety Science*, 37, 109–126.

6. Connor, J., Norton, R., Ameratunga, S., Robinson, E., Civil, I., Dunn, R., Bailey, J., Jackson, R. (2002). Driver sleepiness and risk of serious injury to car occupants: population based case control study. *BMJ*, 324, 1125–1129.

7.   Dawson, D., Zee, P.H. (2005). Work hours and reducing fatigue-related risk: good research vs. good policy. *JAMA*, 294, 1104–1106.

8.   Gander, P.H., Purnell, H.M., Garden, A.L., Woodward, A. (2007). Work Patterns and Fatigue-Related Risk Among Junior Doctors. *Occupational and Environmental Medicine*, 64, 733–738.

9.   Gander, P.H., Merry, A., Millar, M.A., and Weller, J. (2000). Hours of work and fatigue-related error: a survey of New Zealand anaesthetists. *Anaesthesia and Intensive Care*, 28(2), 178–183.

10. Barger, L.K., Ayas, N.T., Cade, B.E., et al. (2006). Impact of extended-duration shifts on medical errors, adverse events, and attentional failures. *PLsS Medicine*, 3, 2440–2448.

11. Barger, L.K., Cade, B.E., Ayas, N.T., Cronin, J.W., Rosner, B., Speizer, F.E., and Czeisler, C.A. (2005). Extended work shifts and the risk of motor vehicle crashes among interns. *N Engl J Med*, 352(2), 125–134.

12. Ayas, N.T., Barger, L.K., Cade, B.E., et al. (2006). Extended work duration and the risk of self-reported percutaneous injuries in interns. *Journal of the American Medical Association*, 296, 1055–1062.

13. Lockley, S.W., Cronin, J.W., Evans, E.E., Cade, B.E., Lee, C.J., Landrigan, C.P., Rothschild, J.M., Katz, J.T., Lilly, C.M., Stone, P.H., Aeschbach, D., and Czeisler, C.A. (2004). Effect of reducing interns' weekly work hours on sleep and attentional failures. *N Engl J Med*, 351(18), 1829–1837.

14. Landrigan, C.P., Rothschild, J.M., Cronin, J.W., Kaushal, R., Burdick, E., Katz, J.T., Lilly, C.M., Stone, P.H., Lockley, S.W., Bates, D.W., and Czeisler, C.A. (2004). Effect of reducing interns' work hours on serious medical errors in intensive care units. *N Engl J Med*, 351(18), 1838–1848.

15. Flight Safety Foundation. (2005). Fatigue Risk Management System helps ensure crew alertness, performance. *Flight Safety Digest*, 26, 16–19.

16. Stewart, S. (2006). An integrated system for managing fatigue risk within a low cost carrier. In: Enhancing Safety Worldwide. *Proceedings of the Flight Safety Foundation International Aviation Safety Seminar*, Paris, October 23–26. Alexandria, VA, Flight Safety Foundation; 2007.

17. Reason, J. (1997). *Managing the risks of organizational accidents*. Aldershot, UK, Ashgate Publishing Limited.

18. Dawson, D., McCulloch, K. (2005). Managing fatigue: it's about sleep. *Sleep Med Rev*, 9(5), 365–380.

19. Wesensten, N.J., Belenky, G., Thorne, D.R., Kautz, M.A., Balkin, T.J. (2004). Modafinil vs. caffeine: effects on fatigue during sleep deprivation. *Aviat Space Environ Med*, 75(6), 520–5.

20. Saper, C.B., Scammell, T., and Lu, J. (2005). Hypothalamic regulation of sleep and circadian rhythms. *Nature*, 437, 1257–1263.

21. Gander, P.H., Gregory, K.B., Connell, L.J., Graeber, R.C., Miller, D.L., Rosekind, M.A. (1998). Flight crew fatigue IV: overnight cargo operations. *Aviat Space Environ Med*, 69, B26-B36.

22. Belenky, G., Wesensten, N.J., Thorne, D.R., Thomas, M.L., Sing, H.C., Redmond, D.P., Russ, M.B., Balkin, T.J. (2003). Patterns of performance degradation and restoration during sleep restriction and subsequent recovery: a sleep dose-response study. *J Sleep Res*, 12, 1–12.

23. Bonnet, M.H. (2005). Acute sleep deprivation. In: Kryger, M.K., Roth, T., Dement, W.C. (Eds.). *Principles and Practice of Sleep Medicine*. 4th edition. Philadelphia, Elsevier Saunders, 51–66.

24. Rupp, T.L., Wesensten, N.J., Bliese, P.D., Balkin, T.J. (2009). Banking sleep: realization of benefits during subsequent sleep restriction and recovery. *Sleep*, 32, 311–321.

25. Department of Transportation Federal Motor Carrier Administration. (2000). Hours of service of drivers: driver rest and sleep for safe operations. *Federal Register*, 65(85), 25540–25611. Washington DC. Available at https://www.fmcsa.dot.gov/spanish/english/pdfs/050200p.pdf

26. Harrison, Y., Horne, J.A. (2000). The impact of sleep deprivation on decision-making: a review. *J Exp Psychol Appl*, 6(3), 236–49.

27. Nilsson, J.P, Soderstrom, M., Karlsson, A.U., Lenader, M., Akerstedt, T., Lindroth, N.E., Axelsson, J. (2005). Less effective executive functioning after one night's sleep deprivation. *J Sleep Res*, 14(1), 1–6.

28. Thomas, M.L., Sing, H.C., Belenky, G., Holcomb, H.H., Mayberg, H.S., Dannals, R.F., Wagner Jr., H.N., Thorne, D.R., Popp, K.A., Rowland, L.M., Welsh, A.B., Balwinski, S.M., Redmond, D.P. (2000). Neural basis of alertness and cognitive performance impairments during sleepiness. I. Effects of 24 h of sleep deprivation on waking human regional brain activity. *J Sleep Res*, 9, 335–352.

29. Braun, A.R., Balkin, T.J., Wesenten, N.J, Carson, R.E, Varga, M., Baldwin, P., Selbie, S., Belenky, G., Herscovitch, P. (1997). Regional cerebral blood flow throughout the sleep-wake cycle. An H2(15)O PET study. *Brain*, 120 (Pt 7), 1173–97.

30. Braun, A.R., Balkin, T.J., Wesensten, N.J., Gwardry, F., Carson, R.E., Varga, M., Baldwin, P., Belenky, G., Herscovitch, P. (1998). Dissociated pattern of activity in visual cortices and their projections during human rapid eye movement sleep. *Science*, 279(5347), 91–5.

31. Balkin, T.J., Braun, A.R., Wesensten, N.J., Jeffries, K., Varga, M., Baldwin, P., Belenky, G., Herscovitch, P. (2002). The process of awakening: A PET study of regional brain activity patterns mediating the reestablishment of alertness and consciousness. *Brain*, 125, 2308–2319.

32. Dorian, J., Roach, G.D., Fletcher, A., Dawson, D. (2007). Simulated train driving: self-awareness and cognitive disengagement. *Applied Ergonomics*, 38, 155–166.

33. Dorian, J., Roach, G.D., Fletcher, A., Dawson, D. (2006). The effects of fatigue on train handling during speed restrictions. *Transportation Research Part F*, 9, 243–257.

34. Thomas, M.J.W., Petrilli, R.M., Lamond, N.A., Dawson, D., Roach, G.D. (2006). Australian Long Haul Fatigue Study. In: Enhancing Safety Worldwide. *Proceedings of the 59th Annual International Air Safety Seminar*. Alexandria, US, Flight Safety Foundation.

35. Robens, Lord. A. (1972). *Safety and Health at Work. Report of the Committee 1970–1972*. London, Her Majesty's Stationery Office.

36. Signal, T.L., Gale, J., Gander, P.H. (2005). Sleep measurement in flight crew: comparing actigraphic and subjective estimates of sleep with polysomnography. *Aviat Space Environ Med*, 76(11), 1058–1063.

37. Flight Safety Foundation. (2005). The Singapore experience: task force studies scientific data to assess flights. *Flight Safety Digest*, 26, 20–40.

38. Fallow, G. (2008). Fatigue Management, Assessment and Evaluation: An Operational Perspective. *Presentation to the FAA Fatigue Management Symposium: Partnerships for Solutions*, Vienna, VA, June 17–19. Available at www.faa.gov/about/office_org/headquarters_offices/avs/offices/afs/afs200/media/aviation_fatigue_symposium/FallowAppComplete.pdf.

39. Webster, C.S., Merry, A.F., Gander, P.H., Mann, N.K. (2004). A prospective randomised clinical evaluation of a new safety-oriented injectable drug administration system in comparison with conventional methods. *Anaesthesia*, 59, 80–87.

40. Reason, J. (2000). Human error: models and management. *British Medical Journal*, 320, 768–70.

41. Transportation Safety Board of Canada. (1997). *A Guide for Investigating for Fatigue*. Transportation Safety Board of Canada, Gatineau, Quebec.

42. International Civil Aviation Authority. (2000). *Safety Management Manual (SMM)*. Doc. 9859 AN 460. Montreal, International Civil Aviation Authority; 2006.

43. Spencer, M.B., Rogers, A.S., Stone, B.M. (1997). *A review of the current Scheme for the Regulation of Air Traffic Controllers Hours (SCRATCOH)*. Defence Evaluation and Research Agency PLSD/CHS5/CR/97/020, Farnborough, England.

44. Gander, P.H., Hartley, L., Powell, D., Cabon, P., Hitchcock, E., Mills, A., Popkin, S. (2009). Fatigue risk management I: Organizational factors at the regulatory and industry/company level. *Accident Analysis and Prevention* (in press).

18

Transversal Perspectives on Human–Machine Interaction: The Effect of Age in Human–Machine Systems

Anabela dos Santos Simões, Marta Pereira, and Maria Panou

The recent demographic projections, as well as the effects of the ageing process and the increased human variability among older people, are important issues to be considered when focusing the effect of age in human–machine systems. This chapter addresses older people's characteristics and design requests to accommodate their needs in order to ensure efficient, safe, and comfortable human–machine interactions. Different contexts of use and the related environment are referred to as important issues to be considered in the technology design. Finally, the issue of safe mobility for older people is addressed presenting technological solutions with the related advantages and inherent risks.

1. INTRODUCTION

In most OECD member countries, the elderly population represents the fastest growing segment of the overall population. As one grows older, many structural and functional changes occur, leading to declines in the ability to perform common daily tasks and a continuous need for medication. However, in a healthy ageing process, particularly during active life, age-related decrements don't have significant direct effects on task performance if previous experience can be used, as older people develop some strategies to compensate their declines. Experience in a particular task performance is the main resource of older people to keep good scores in performing the same task. For this, a stable and user-friendly technical environment is required so that it allows for a more constant, exact, and rapid behavior, being also less effortful and more automatic. In complex and dynamic tasks, this should result in an increased ability to anticipate potential dangerous situations at an early stage from a few slight cues and consequently to react in an adequate way in useful time.

New technologies (NT) can create increased difficulties to older people resulting from the lack of previous experience and poor usability regarding age-related characteristics. The effect of age in human–machine interactions (HMI) should lead designers and engineers to a greater concern on the technologies design. Although the recent technological improvements, older people still complain of several difficulties when interacting with NT. These difficulties regard the information content, as well as the quality and the duration of the displayed information, which do not comply with the age-related declines and consequent limitations in information processing. Furthermore, a generation effect appears as another constrain in HMI when the user is an older person. Actually, nowadays older people rarely are familiarized with NT, which leads them to avoid, in a general way, their use.

The recent demographic projections, together with the effects of the ageing process and the increased variability among older people, as well as different contexts of NT use, complete the approaches to be considered when analyzing the effect of age in human–machine systems.

2. DEMOGRAPHIC TRENDS

Older adults represent the most rapidly growing segment of the population in all developed countries. Demographic projections in most industrialized countries show a significant increase in the number of people 65 years old and older. The ageing of Europe, also known as the graying of Europe, refers to the increase in the percentage of elderly population compared to workforce. This is a social phenomenon resulting, on one hand, from the baby boom generation growing older, and, on the other hand, from a decrease in fertility and mortality rates, accompanied by a higher life expectancy. The global ageing of population is considered an unprecedented, new phenomenon, all-pervasive, profound, and an enduring change in nature (UN in Ilmarinen, 2005). According to an OECD publication (1998), in 1960 the older population (aged 65 and over) accounted for 15 percent of the active population. By 2030, this could jump to 35 percent, with particularly strong growth after 2010. In the next 25 years, the number of persons of pensionable age will rise by a further 70 million, while the active population will rise by only 5 million. Increasing every decade, life expectancy has changed substantially over the last century. In the European Union (27 countries), life expectancy at birth was 75 years for men and 81 years for women, which was slightly better than in the US and lower than in Japan, which is the country presenting the fastest ageing of the population (Ilmarinen, 2005). In the US, the number of people 65 years and older is projected to grow from about 35 million in 2000 to more than 86 million in 2050 (US Census Bureau in Eby, Molnar and Kartje, 2009). In 2003, life expectancy at birth was estimated to be 74.8 years for males and 80.1 for females (Travel and History). As an indicator of well-being, life expectancy is translated into an increase in the expected number of healthy and functionally unrestricted years. This means that older people will be able to carry out an independent life until later age if the current mortality and morbidity trends remain unchanged (Ilmarinen, 2005). However, even if general trends in public health tend to give good health conditions to elderly people, it will be probable that increasing age will continue to be correlated to the appearance of disability (Oxley, 1998).

Baby boomers are approaching later life having experienced an explosion in consumer culture. According to Macunovich (2000), they were the first generation of children and teenagers with significant spending power, and that, combined with their numbers, fuelled the growth of massive marketing campaigns and the introduction of new products. They may have a very different approach to ageing and expectations about where and how to live than current generations of older people. In general, baby boomers had a higher level of education than any generation before them. In the US, about 88.8 percent of boomers completed high school, and 28.5 percent hold a bachelor's degree or higher (Travel and History). In Europe, baby-boomers had to discover their own success strategies concerning both educational opportunities and educational outcome; that is to say, they have written the prelude for the expanding educational system (Kivinen, Hedman, and Kaipainen, 2004).

Together with the ageing of the general population, there is an increase in the percentage of older drivers on the road. At the same time, with the increasing trend toward suburbanization, people of all ages, and especially older people, are becoming more dependent on their cars. In the more developed nations, where the use of private cars is more widespread, an increase in the number of older people combined with a decreasing proportion of younger members of society is more marked. The present generation of older people got their driving license about 40 years ago; they own their cars and still drive regularly. Being more educated than former generations and so more prepared to interact with machines, the technological era represents a challenge they want to face and deal with. This is also a challenge to systems designers and managers, who have to accommodate older people's needs. Due to their increasing representation in the population and being an important potential market, there is no excuse for disregarding their needs. Furthermore, they want and have the right to stay mobile and autonomous.

3. AGEING AND FUNCTIONAL ABILITIES

Ageing is a highly complex, dynamic, and slow process, involving many internal and external influences, including genetic programming and physical and social environments (World Health Organization, 1998). With increasing age, individuals experience some level of functional declines, specially associated with changes in sensation, perception, cognition, and also psychomotor functioning. These declines are reflected in difficulties in discriminating the relevant information and in the need of more time to process it. Actually, the main feature of the ageing process is the progressive slowness of behavior. These changes may induce some limitations in one or more activities of daily living and with increasing age the declines become more evident and severe.

Despite the age-related declines, older people can perform daily tasks safely and efficiently, compensating for their failures by using their remaining abilities in a deeper way. It seems that, for the same task performance, the same types of compensations for functional losses can be found among older people, resulting in common patterns that are different from those of younger people (Eby, Shope, Molnar, Vivoda, and Fordyce, 2000). Therefore, older people compensate for their impaired perceptual-motor functioning by, (1) adapting their behavior according to the circumstances of the task performance, and (2) by using their still available compensatory potential. However, the ability to compensate for age-related declines is related to the individual experience in each particular task. Compensation based on the task knowledge and experience is the reason why some performance decrements in laboratory tests are not replicated in daily task performance. In the context of driving, for instance, compensatory behaviors reduce the stress and anxiety felt by older drivers in some situations, as well as the risk of driving in these situations (OECD, 2001). Therefore, a greater experience on the task should lead to optimizing performance, which becomes more constant, exact, and more rapidly executed, less effortful and more automatic. This should result in an increased ability to anticipate potential risky situations at an early stage from a few slight cues and consequently to react in an adequate way and in useful time when required. Such increased control may improve the possibility of rectifying errors, provided that enough time is available. Moreover, as a pre-condition for the use of experience, a more stable and user-friendly environment would be required.

Even healthy older users are affected by age-related declines, which cause them some difficulties in human–machine interactions. As an example, they often avoid the use of an ATM as a result of several previous aborted interactions, mainly due to the need of more time to perform the task. Due to a generational effect regarding the use of NT, as well as some experienced difficulties in previous attempts or a simple reaction to change, older people avoid the use of NT as they cannot mobilize any previous experience to better support compensation behaviors.

In the case of driving, as older drivers have 40 years or more of driving experience, their functional impairments can be to some extent compensated for by changing driving habits and travel patterns. Therefore, older drivers avoid driving conditions that impose higher demands, such as driving at night, with poor weather conditions or during rush hours. The ability to compensate functional losses is often the key to living the later life as a period of continued usefulness, recreation, and productivity. This self-regulation may be a consequence of the insight of their own limitations once it was already suggested that older drivers who fail in performing self-regulations may be at higher risk (Molnar and Eby, 2008). Driving until over 80 years old, and refusing to give up driving, can in some cases be caused by the lack of insight regarding the impact of ageing on driving skills and the inappropriate perception of risk (Holland and Rabbit, 1992; Eby, Molnar, and Kartje, 2009). The great amount of driving experience that elderly drivers possess is also an important factor. The traffic experience acquired may give them the ability to anticipate some problematic situations and avoid the related risk.

4. HUMAN VARIABILITY

Human variability is the range of possible values for any measurable characteristic, physical or mental, of human beings. Differences can be trivial or important, transient or permanent, voluntary or involuntary, congenital or acquired, genetic or environmental. This means that each person is different from other people due to biological inheritance, education, cultural and social environment, and so on (inter-individual variability). Furthermore, each human being is submitted to a within-subject variability resulting from transient factors (fatigue, health condition, psychological state, and so on), as well as ageing.

In modern society, organizations and the related technological development impose fast, efficient, and precise actions to human beings. In order to ensure the success of those actions, resulting from good cooperation between humans and technologies, the different factors leading to the variability of performance must be identified and understood. These factors, resulting from the diversity of human characteristics and functioning, as well as their short-term and life-span variability, contradict the assumption of the stability of human activity over time that presides to the design and management of numerous technological systems. Indeed, there is no average human being; human variability, resulting from diversity or the instability of human activity, is actually an uncomfortable reality that systems designers and managers have to face and work with accordingly.

Different from machines, humans evolve with time, learning, acquiring experience, ageing and being temporarily tired or sick. Ageing is a highly complex, dynamic, and slow process, involving many internal and external influences, including genetic programming and physical and social environments (World Health Organization, 1998). With these different influences, each individual ages differently from others and, for the same person, each biological function ages at a different rhythm. This results in great variability in terms of physical, psychological, and behavioral changes with age and differences between subjects. An important source of variability refers to generational changes, so that today's elderly people differ from those of 20 years ago and those 20 years hence. These differences regard economic status, education, home location, and experience as new technologies (NT) users. Actually, the elderly from 20 years ago never did get experience on NT use even during their professional life whilst most elderly nowadays have already used some NT professionally or in their daily life. However, it seems that a generational effect on NT experience and regular use will always characterize older people's attitudes and behaviors regarding NT. This is probably due to the increasingly fast technological development, which leads to a permanent gap between the newer systems and the related user's knowledge and skills. In addition, most older adults being retired from their professional life, the related cognitive under-stimulation will plead in favor of some difficulties regarding NT use and the consequent avoidance in learning and using NT.

This great variability among older people gives rise to specific users' needs and requirements for every system design, particularly those systems for generalized and voluntary use, such as an ATM or transport-related technologies. In these cases, the difficulty in accommodating the needs of such a diverse population increases the complexity of designing and managing technology-based systems. From the users' side, new developments create increasing complexity for older users, resulting from multiple human–machine and social interactions, sometimes within unstable and dynamic environments. Globally, a more user-friendly system and environment will be easier and safer for every user, which gives a good reason for the increasing effort of designers and managers in accommodating the special needs of older and mobility-impaired users.

Despite an increasing individual diversity with ageing, it seems that, for the same task performance, older people develop the same type of compensatory behaviors for functional declines. As it has been said above, in a healthy ageing process, age-related decrements don't have a significant impact on task performance if previous experience can be used. In the context of NT, older people can rarely base learning and use on previous experience; thus, without this important resource, it is natural that older people avoid the use of any NT.

5. AGEING IN THE TECHNOLOGY ERA

New technologies can be used to empower older adults in the performance of common daily tasks, compensating for age-related sensory, physical, psychomotor, and cognitive limitations. However, due to their lack of familiarization with NT and the related generalized attitudes avoiding their use, they rarely get the related expected benefits. NT can provide easy communication to older people, which is an important way to fight isolation related to later life. In-vehicle technologies can compensate some age-related declines and help the driver in the performance of the driving task, allowing for a safe mobility. Furthermore, infomobility systems can assist older people in many daily activities from at-home shopping to way-finding or public-transport information. However, experience in a particular task performance is the main resource of older people to keep good scores in performing the same task; but the use of experience requires some stability on the level of technical and environmental conditions for the task performance.

In order to disseminate the use of every new technology by older people, systems must be designed in order to accommodate their special needs. Although a large percentage of communication and computing technologies were originally designed by young engineers for business purposes and targeting young users, there is a significant potential to use these devices to better serve the information and communication needs of older people. However, the increasing processing capabilities of those systems must be tailored to the specific needs and abilities of older users.

In the context of technology-based communications, Ryan, Giles, Bartolucci, and Henwood (cited by Kemper and Lacal, 2003) identified two patterns in the systems design that contribute to older adults' communication problems: under-accommodations and over-accommodations. Under-accommodations occur when the speaker or writer fails to consider how ageing affects speaking and listening; this puts older adults at risk of social isolation and neglect because they lead to comprehension failure and hence to the possibility of misunderstanding, deception, and exploitation. Over-accommodations occur when the speaker or writer is over-reliant on negative stereotypes of ageing, which also put older adults at risk because they are often perceived by older adults as insulting and patronizing and so may disengage them from full participation in a conversational interaction. Furthermore, the authors suggest that over-accommodations to ageing may trigger negative self-assessments by older adults of their own communicative competence and thus contribute to a downward spiral of sociocognitive limitations. Both under- and over-accommodations represent barriers to older adults' communication as they lead to a rejection of a system in consequence of perceived difficulties or inappropriateness. Therefore, designing NT with older people in mind is a main request for an appealing and easy use of any system.

5.1. Working Life within Human–Machine Systems

Recent demographic trends focusing on the age of active populations are fostering new interest in older workers. In the US, it was expected that by 2010 the number of workers aged 55+ would be about 26 million, which reflects a 46 percent increase since 2000; and by 2025 this number will increase to approximately 33 million (Czaja and Moen, 2003). The labor force of both genders is expected to increase, although participation rates are projected to be slightly greater for older women than for older men. There will also be an increase in the number of workers over the age of 65 (US General Accounting Office in Czaja and Moen, 2003). In EU15, demographic projections estimated a decrease of the labor force 20–29 years old in 20 percent between 1995 and 2015 against an increase of workers 50–64 years old in 26 percent for the same period (Pestana, 2003). This could create labor shortages, especially in skilled and managerial occupations.

Since the 1980s, the explosion of new technologies in society and working life have led older workers to some kinds of exclusion: in a general way, they were excluded from training activities, and new tasks related to recent technological systems were allocated to younger workers, who were considered more competent. Actually, many companies considered that older workers were too close to retirement to justify an investment in training, which excluded them from opportunities for increasing their competencies. Therefore, they left earlier than expected from working life having a self-perception of inability to continue working in the technological era. This has implications for mental health as it has been stated on the recommendation N.R. (90) 22 (Council of Europe, 1990). Nowadays, employers have to turn their attention toward older workers due to the slowed growth in the number of younger workers. Some companies are turning to older workers to fill their positions and are providing flexible employment arrangements, such as part-time work, telecommuting, and financial benefits to retain or recruit older workers (Czaja and Moen, 2003).

In this context, there is a need to develop strategies to prepare for and accommodate an ageing work force. According to Czaja and Moen (2003), this requires understanding (1) the characteristics of older workers and the growing population of older adults who do not work; (2) the potential implications of ageing for work and work environments; (3) the technological and social characteristics of existing jobs and work environments; and (4) the triggers, dynamics, and processes moving people into and out of employment. When addressing these issues, the authors made a distinction between *older* workers and *retirees* in their 50s, 60s, and early 70s and those in their late 70s, 80s, and 90s. Understanding the differences among the various subgroups within the older adult population will become increasingly important, mainly due to the baby boomers moving into and through their 60s.

With the new demographic projections, it will be impossible to keep this attitude regarding older workers. Life span education and training policies will ensure their adaptability to technological changes. However, two important aspects must be taken into account: (1) the importance of basing learning and acquisition of new skills in previous experience, which is the prime request for the success of learning and will eliminate any feeling of anxiety or reaction to change; and (2) the importance of appropriate design in order to ensure systems user-friendliness, and so provide easy and efficient human–machine interactions. It should be highlighted that age-related declines are not much evident during active life as they are compensated for by experience. Furthermore, work-related demands represent a cognitive stimulation that can retain the ageing process. That's why cognitive declines, for instance, are much more evident after retirement due to the lack of daily cognitive stimulation.

5.2. Older Life Challenges

After retirement, the lack of a continuous cognitive stimulation resulting from work-related demands leads to more evident declines or even impairments. One of the impaired activities may be driving, since driving performance may decline with age. However, older people can drive safely, compensating for their failures by using their remaining abilities in a deeper way. From a road safety perspective, Davidse (2006) refers the following driving-related difficulties and weaknesses of older drivers as the most important needs for support:

a. difficulty in judging whether other road users are moving and at what speed they approach the intersection (motion perception);
b. overlooking other road users while merging and changing lanes (peripheral vision and flexibility of head and neck);
c. overlooking traffic signs and signals (selective attention);
d. reaction time increases as the complexity of the traffic situation increases (speed of processing information and decision-making, performance under pressure of time).

Based on these driving-related difficulties, some assistive devices can provide important support to the driver (Davidse, 2006):

e. drawing attention to approaching traffic;
f. indicating road users located in the driver's blind spot;
g. assisting the driver in directing his/her attention to relevant information;
h. and/or providing prior knowledge on the next traffic situation.

Despite their difficulties and higher fatal crash risk (Eby, Molnar and Kartje, 2009), older people are very reluctant to give up driving. The private car gives older people a feeling of independence and freedom, allowing them to stay involved in their community and participate in well-being-related activities. For this, the following issues must be considered: (1) the provision of new in-vehicle technologies with relevance to compensate for age-related limitations; (2) the provision of training as a cognitive stimulation to retain age-related declines and the systems-learning allowing for appropriate use; (3) the systems usability ensuring their user-friendliness and safety benefits.

6. TRANSPORT-RELATED HMI AND OLDER USERS

In the transportation field, both passengers and drivers have to perform different types of HMI along with the travel chain: from trip planning to the arrival and way out from the transport network. Interacting with a ticket machine, driving a car or using any transport-related information system involves specific HMI. Each interaction being centered on the subject's reaction to perceived stimuli, the interface quality remains a key point with its properties of user-friendliness, usability, transparency, and so on. These attributes have a great importance for a perfect coupling of human and machine, but they are not sufficient to ensure the success of the user's actions, particularly in complex and dynamic situations (Bellet et al., 2003). Actually, the stability of the environment in which those interactions occur makes the difference regarding the easiness of the system learning and use, as well as the related safety issues.

The use of public transport nowadays involves a set of HMI resulting from the integration of new technologies providing static information about the network, real-time dynamic information, ticketing, and so on. The provision of such information and services represents an incentive to the use of public transport as it makes the system easier despite the increasing complexity of the transport network. In the context of driving a car, the introduction of new technologies is supposed to improve mobility and safety. However, a major concern should guide the systems design and deployment so that the assistance provided by any device should not compromise safety, particularly to elderly users.

6.1. Intelligent Transport Systems

The deployment of novel technology in the transportation field has been occurring progressively and it's expected that the future will lead unconditionally to the presence of more and more systems. The primary focus of Intelligent Transport Systems (ITS) is to provide improvements in safety, efficiency, and environmental performance of all modes of transport including air, sea, road, and rail. Regarding road transportation, ITS users include road network operators, transport service providers, fleet owners, as well as the simple traveler (Panou and Bekiaris, 2004).

It is believed that ITS have the potential to change the driving experience, both in the near and far future, by promoting driving safety, trips efficiency and also increasing the drivers' comfort (Green, 2001). The concept of providing real-time information to increase safety and improve mobility is very appealing; however, the mainstream motor industry has largely ignored an important group of users during this technological evolution and also in the process of the systems design: the elderly (Harriots, 2005). As many transport technologies target drivers in private vehicles because cars are the dominant mode of transport and a high-value consumer good, much more attention should be paid to one of the drivers' groups that has been increasing considerably: elderly drivers. Nowadays, an increasing number of elderly people hope to spend their latter years participating in several activities and living in a dynamic and autonomous manner through the use of their own vehicles, maintaining their driving as long as possible.

In-vehicle technologies can have particular value for older drivers as they can assist them to increase their driving activity over time helping them to manage their driving-related difficulties. Systems may allow them to drive in conditions in which they might otherwise have refrained from driving, and this is done by lessening some of the effects caused by the age-related declines (Meyer, 2003). In fact, the ageing population introduces a special challenge in transport systems due to issues concerning the systems' functionality and safety, as well as the users' frailty. Freedom of movement provides innumerable opportunities related to different aspects of daily life, which can be easily reached with the use of NT (OECD, 2003). In order to be used in an efficient way, the development of new in-vehicle technology has to be based on the notion of *user-centered design*. This means that the needs of older users have to be considered in the entire design process, in order to adapt the product adequately to the users' characteristics. These usability considerations are extremely important since they will define users' acceptance and satisfaction, as well as safety and efficient use (Meyer, 2003).

7. SAFETY AND MOBILITY SOLUTIONS FOR OLDER PEOPLE

New technologies play an important role in compensating for age-related declines. The following systems can increase safe mobility and provide personal assistance to older drivers (Davidse, 2004; Meyer, 2003; OECD, 2003):

- *collision-avoiding systems* that can assist drivers at intersections;
- *automated lane-changing and merging systems* that can help in selecting gaps to cross and also take care of the changing or merging action;
- *blind-spot and obstacle-detection systems* providing support for the detection of close objects that are near a slow-moving vehicle, being also very useful while parking the car;
- *night-vision displays* that enhance vision at night by providing an intense image of the forward scene;
- *intelligent cruise-control* that can help maintain the same speed and also keep a determined safe distance from the vehicle ahead;
- *driver-information systems* providing information about the roads, traffic, and weather condition broadcasts, helping to plan the trip, providing information about vehicle maintenance and other important matters.

Even knowing that the use of NT can be an advantage to elderly drivers, it should be clear that the introduction of a new device into the car is not always easy and will not lead directly to an improvement in safety. It must be remembered that these systems may not be readily accepted due to a natural age-related aversion to NT. However, it is probable that in future generations this will be less of an issue because the elderly will be more familiar with intelligent technologies at an early age (Shaheen and Niemeier, 2001). Anyway, due to the fact that the elderly may be starting to use on-board devices, it is important to consider them when designing NT.

Collision-avoidance systems can be of great help for older drivers as they provide critical information in various forms of alerts and warnings, their main goal being the avoidance of any crashes and the reduction of the severity of imminent crashes (Linder, Kircher, Vadeby, and Nygardhs, 2007). Besides the advantages the in-vehicle systems can bring, their introduction into the car may lead drivers to alter the pattern of behavior usually activated in normal driving conditions (Meyer, 2003). However, the use of NT can increase the amount of information that drivers have to identify, perceive, process, and respond to, and may increase the complexity of the driving situation (Green, 2001). Increasing difficulty in the driving task can create serious problems for all drivers, but may have the most considerable effects on older drivers (Stamatiadis, 1993). The key rests primarily on the design of on-board systems.

Well-designed interfaces provide a means of helping all groups of drivers, especially the elderly, because adequately adapted devices can augment impaired sensory abilities and reduce cognitive processing requirements (Baldwin, 2002). The design of a system should also consider the prediction of the user's reactions to a new technological system as it is a way to prevent misuses and to improve the system itself.

7.1. Usability and Safety Concerns

The safety benefit from an in-vehicle intelligent system can be smaller than expected. Meyer (2003) points out four reasons for it:

1. Drivers may not use the system properly and fail to obtain the safety benefits. This improper use can be considered as misuse, meaning that the user did not use the system as it was intended by the designer. The improper operation or action over the device may have happened unintentionally as the user may believe that it was correct and appropriate to do a specific action. This may occur when the available information in the form of instructions or warnings is insufficient or inadequate.
2. Overconfidence is the reason for some bad outcome. Using a system can create a feeling of safety that may induce a driver to trust too much on it and take greater risks than he/she would without the device. Because drivers may feel more protected with the new device they can expose themselves to greater danger, thinking that the system will maintain a lower level of risk. Additionally, it must be remembered that systems can fail or give false alarms. These malfunctions can lead to accidents because the drivers' attention given to the aspect covered by the system may be reduced.
3. Drivers may develop other behavioral patterns as a consequence of the system introduction. Systems may alter the way people drive: for example, drivers might reduce the number of actions important for safety because they believe that the device will do the job for them.
4. Another important reason for the smaller safety benefits is the lack of adaptation of systems to older drivers' characteristics. Compared to other groups of drivers, older people possess distinct characteristics that are translated into different ways of behaving in specific situations. For example, these drivers may take longer to perceive and understand a system false alarm which can lead to inadequate behaviors and to a faster disregard on the systems safety benefits.

All the above factors leading to bad outcomes result from design pitfalls leading to a bad usability of the system. The increasing number of elderly drivers in consequence of demographic changes justifies highlighting design concerns regarding older users. Generally, there is not a need for specific systems addressing older drivers' needs, but a system designed with older people in mind is surely much more user-friendly and safer for all.

7.2. New Technology-Based Applications for a Safe Mobility of Older People

Aiming at promoting and supporting the mobility of older people, several ITS applications have been and are being designed and deployed. ASK-IT applications represent an example of technological developments addressing the mobility improvement of elderly and disabled people. ASK-IT was an EC co-funded project that lasted for four years and ended on December 2008. It involved 51 partners across Europe with the aim of developing an extended ambient intelligence space for the integration of functions and services for elderly and disabled people across various environments (car, bus, airplane, home, work, leisure, and sport). In its quest to support the user in a holistic manner, ASK-IT focused on geo-referenced and personalized transport and tourism services. Emphasis was on seamless service provision, independent of the media, user location (that is, indoors, outdoors, in a city, during a trip, and so on), user type and residual abilities. The developed system is based on an open reference ontology, to provide in a one-stop-shop over 80 existing and new services, ranging from transportation, tourism and leisure, to personal support services, work, business and education and, finally, social relations and community building services.

One of the main user groups of ASK-IT was the elderly, ranging from their early 50s and going up to the 85+. ASK-IT applications were designed for all types of devices, encompassing PCs, laptops, PDAs, mobile phones, infokiosks and domotic platforms and were specifically designed to be elderly-friendly. They were tested in eight sites in Europe (Athens/Thessaloniki, Bucharest, Genoa, Helsinki, Madrid,

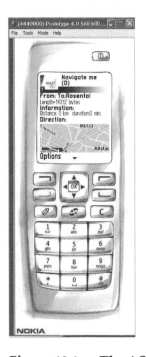

Figure 18.1   The ASK-IT UI in different types of mobile phones and PDAs and for different types of services

Newcastle, Nuremberg, and The Hague) with 149 elderly users (out of 672 users in total). The test results proved that ASK-IT is an ideal integrated service composition for the elderly, as it can provide them in a one-stop-shop mode all the information they require to perform a trip from origin to destination. They find it particularly beneficial that they could get, either before the trip or during it, information on multimodal transportation, tourist attractions, other points of interest, and emergency support services and other personal support services were always at hand. The major requirement of the elderly users in terms of content is related to the quality of service, which must be guaranteed for all connected services, as well as the need to get all relevant information in their own language. In terms of user interface (UI), ASK-IT applications were appreciated but the users require enhanced interaction possibilities (that is, larger text, more voice interactions), especially for the PDA and mobile phones. Most of these requirements are related to necessary improvements of the devices themselves. It is a remarkable paradox that they prefer the mobile phone to get the information (as the elderly are not expert users of PDAs and PCs) and yet the device limitations make mobile phones UI the most difficult to be used by them. Relevant recommendations on mobile phones' enhanced functionality have been taken up by AEGIS, another Integrated Project that is currently running.

Building on these results, OASIS Integrated Project, aiming at the quality of life enhancement of the elderly, develops and interconnects a number of services covering all the aspects of life where this specific user group needs support, that is, independent living, autonomous mobility and support at work. The services are to be provided through PDAs, mobile phones, PCs, and so on, following a common user interface style guide.

Among the services currently being designed and developed, elderly-friendly transport information services are included. Pedestrian navigation and route guidance are supported. For the pedestrian navigation, the planning of a special attribute trip is possible through the HMI, where the elderly user can plan a "scenic" or "safe" or "calm" route/trip, specific to the individual needs and preferences of each user (maximum walking distance accepted, maximum number of transport mode changes accepted, taxi preference, POIs on route preferences, existence of assistance services en route, avoidance of dense traffic and intersection crossings without traffic lights (such as pedestrian crossings), and so on). Thus, safety and comfort mobility needs of the elderly are supported and even to the individual level by the personalization of service. For the route guidance, elderly driver-friendly in-car (on-board and off-board) navigation is provided, avoiding heavy traffic and specific (difficult) traffic scenarios to enhance elderly drivers' safety and comfort. The system has its own definition for "safe" and "comfortable" for an elderly driver, based on literature and accident surveys (that is, through calm traffic, avoiding traffic jams, complex roundabouts, U-turns, negotiation of unsignalized T-junctions, and so on). The user can add/extract some of these features, thus personalizing the system (through tick-box selection). In all cases, the system monitors the user feedback and "learns" his/her behavior and preferences. It then employs Intelligent Agents technology to individualize the service, always allowing the user to be in control, view his/her preferences and even delete/alter them.

Thus, ASK-IT and OASIS initiatives spearhead the quest for elderly-friendly and inclusive application of modern technologies (in-vehicle, information, navigation, driver support, …) through properly adapted and even personalized content, HMI and holistic services.

8. CONCLUSIONS

Interacting with an NT is a big challenge to older people for several reasons: first, the generation effect leads them to avoid interacting with new devices; second, they seem to have difficulty in learning how to use a new device and so they need to be helped and taught; third, the interaction with a new technology as a secondary task creates great difficulties in managing the prime situation due to an important increase in mental workload and consequently the related risk. However, NT can be a factor of better quality of life for older people, particularly in the transport domain, but unless the systems interfaces and the forecast interactions will be ergonomically designed and the provision of some training will be considered, the interaction with the system will overload and confuse the older user. In the case of driving a car, since most in-vehicle systems require drivers to change their driving habits, this change may be difficult, and the need to adopt new habits may deprive the elderly of the extensive driving experience they have acquired over the years, which is their main resource. Another issue that should be considered and lead to further research is the long-term effects of using some in-vehicle technologies that cooperate with the driver in the driving task. In older age, a cognitive under-stimulation in terms of collecting and memorizing spatial information could lead to a great dependence on a route guidance system, making the person unable to drive without that information. The same may occur by the use of a collision-warning system, which could affect situation awareness. Therefore, the induced behaviors by the systems use should be studied in order to prevent potential decreases in fitness for driving. For each system, the side effects on driving behaviors and attitudes should be identified in order to develop adequate countermeasures.

REFERENCES

Baldwin, Carryl L. (2002). Designing in-vehicle technologies for older drivers: application of sensory-cognitive interaction theory. *Theoretical Issues in Ergonomics Science*, 3, 4, 307–329.

Bellet, T., Tattegrain-Veste, H., Chapon, A., Bruyas, M.-P., Pachiaudi, G., Deleurence, P., and Guilhon, V. (2003). Ingénierie cognitive dans le contexte de l'assistance à la conduite automobile. In G. Boy (Ed.), *Ingénierie Cognitive*. Paris: Lavoisier.

Council of Europe. (1990). Retrieved 2009, from https://wcd.coe.int/com.instranet.InstraServl et?command=com.instranet.CmdBlobGetandInstranetImage=570832andSecMode=1andD ocId=593426andUsage=2.

Czaja, S., and Moen, P. (2003). Technology and Employment. In R.W. Pew and S.B. Van Hemel (Eds.), *Technology for adaptive aging*. Washington DC: The National Academies Press.

Davidse, R. (2006). Older drivers and ADAS—Which Systems Improve Road Safety? *IATSS Research*, 30 (1).

Davidse, R.J. (2004). Older drivers and ITS: stronger together? *Proceedings of International Conference on Traffic and Transport Psychology*. Nottingham.

Davidse, R. (2006). Older drivers and ADAS. Which Systems Improve Road Safety? *IATSS Research*, 30, 1.

Eby, D., Shope, J.T., Molnar, L.J., Vivoda, J.M., Fordyce, T.A. (2000). *Improvement of Older Driver Safety Through Self evaluation: The Development of a Self-Evaluation Instrument*. UMTRI Technical Report 2000–04.

Eby, D., Molnar, L., Kartje, P. (2009). *Maintaining safe mobility in an aging society.* CRC Press, London: Taylor and Francis.

Green, P. (2001). Variations in task performance between young and older drivers: UMTRI research telematics. *Association for the Advance of Automotive Medicine. Conference on Aging and Driving.* Michigan.

Harriots, P. (2005). Identification of vehicle design requirments for older drivers. *Applied Ergonomics,* 36, 255–262.

Holland, C., and Rabbit, P. (1992). People's awareness of their age-related sensory and cognitive deficits and the implications for road safety. *Applied Cognitive Psychology,* 6, 217–231.

Ilmarinen, J. (2005). *Towards a Longer Worklife*: *Ageing and the Quality of Worklife in the European Union.* Finish Institute of Occupational Health. Helsinki.

Kemper and Lacal. (2003). Addressing the Communication Needs of an Aging Society. In R.W. Pew, and S.B. Van Hemel, *Technology for adaptive aging.* Washington DC: The National Academies Press.

Kivinen, O., Hedman, J. and Kaipainen, P.M. (2004). Educational Mechanisms of the Inheritance of Life-Chances: From Baby Boomers to Subsequent Generations. *Paper presented at the annual meeting of the American Sociological Association,* San Francisco.

Linder, A., Kircher, A., Vadeby, A., and Nygardhs, S. (2007). *Intelligent Transport Systems (ITS) in passenger cars and methods for assessment of traffic safety impact. A literature review.* VTI.

Macunovich, D.J. (2000). *The Baby Boomers.* Retrieved 2009, from http://newton.uor.edu/DepartmentsandPrograms/EconomicDept/macunovich/baby_boomers.pdf

Meyer, J. (2003). *Personal vehicle transportation.* In R.W. Pew and S.B. Van Hemel (Eds.), *Technology for adaptive aging.* Washington DC: The National Academies Press.

Molnar, Lisa J., and Eby, David W. (2008). The Relationship between Self-Regulation and Driving-Related Abilities in Older Drivers: An Exploratory Study. *Traffic Injury Prevention,* 9, 4, 314–319.

OECD. (1998). *Maintaining Prosperity in an Ageing Society.* Organisation for Economic Cooperation and Development. Paris.

OECD. (2001). *Ageing and transport. Mobility needs and safety issues.* Organisation for Economic Cooperation and Development, Paris.

OECD. (2003). New transport technology for older people. *Proceedings of the Organisation for Economic Cooperation and Development-MIT International Symposium.* Massachusetts.

Oxley, P.R. (1998). Transport et vieillissement de la population. ECMT Conference. Paris: Organisation for Economic Cooperation and Development.

Panou, M., and Bekiaris, E. (2004). ITS clustering and terminology: one concept with many meanings. *Research in Transportation Economics,* 8, 49–67.

Pestana, N.N. (2003), Trabalhadores Mais Velhos: Políticas Públicas e Práticas Empresariais, Cadernos de Emprego e relações de Trabalho, Direcção-Geral do Emprego e das Relações de Trabalho, Lisboa.

Shaheen, S., and Niemeier, D. (2001). Integrating vehicle design and human factors: minimizing elderly driving constraints. *Transportation Research Part C,* 9, 155–174.

Stamatiadis, N. (1993). Older drivers and IVHS technologies. *Proceedings of 26th International Symposium on Automotive Technology and Automation.* Aachen, Germany.

Travel and History. Retrieved 2009, from www.u-s-history.com/pages/h2061.html.

World Health Organization. (1998). *Growing Older. Staying Well: Ageing and physical activity in everyday life.* Geneva.

19
Error on the Flight Deck: Interfaces, Organizations, and Culture

Don Harris and Wen-Chin Li

Commercial aviation is without doubt one of the safest forms of passenger travel. For the majority of the past half-century there has been a steady decline in the commercial aircraft accident rate. However, over the last three decades it has been noticeable that the serious accident rate has remained relatively constant at approximately one per million departures (Boeing Commercial Airplanes, 2007). If this rate remains unchanged, with the current projected increase in the demand for air travel (assuming that the market eventually recovers after recent world events) this will mean that there will be one major hull loss almost every week by the year 2015.

Initial efforts to enhance aircraft safety were aimed at system reliability, structural integrity, and aircraft dynamics. The airworthiness regulations governing the design of commercial aircraft, for example the European Aviation Safety Agency (EASA) Certification Specification part 25 (CS 25) and Federal Aviation Regulation (FAR) part 25: Airworthiness Standards (US Department of Transportation, 1974), still reflect these earlier concerns. However, as reliability and structural integrity have improved over the last 50 years, the number of accidents resulting from such failures has reduced dramatically, and so has the overall number of accidents and accident rate. What this has meant, though, is that human error is now the principal threat to flight safety. In a worldwide survey of causal factors in commercial aviation accidents, in 88 percent of cases the crew was identified as a causal factor; in 76 percent of instances the crew was implicated as the *primary* causal factor (Civil Aviation Authority, 1998). However, many people refer specifically to "pilot error" as if it is something special (it isn't). The errors pilots make are no different in their causes and nature to those made by human beings in other walks of life. It is merely their context that is unique and unfortunately the consequences are potentially far more severe. While human (or pilot) error is without doubt the major contributory factor in aircraft accidents, a diagnosis of "error" in itself says very little. It is not an explanation; it is merely the very beginning of an explanation. Dekker (2001) proposed that errors are systematically connected to features of a pilot's tools and tasks and that error has its roots in the surrounding socio-technical system. The question of human error or system failure alone is an oversimplified belief in the roots of these failures.

WHAT IS PILOT ERROR?

Although "error" is a term used practically everyday it is not an easy term to define precisely once it is considered more closely. Hollnagel (1998) suggests three criteria must be fulfilled before any action can really be described as "erroneous".

- *Criterion problem:* There needs to be a specified performance criterion or standard against which performance can be compared.
- *Performance shortfall:* There must be an action that leads to a measurable performance shortfall.
- *Volition aspect:* There must be the opportunity for the person to act in such a way that would not be considered erroneous.

The criterion problem has two facets to it. An error may only be termed an "error" in one (or both) of two circumstances. If a pilot's actions fall short of what is required from an external verifiable viewpoint (that is, what is required by "the system") then it is an "error". If the action executed is not what the pilot intended to do, then there is a failure to perform compared against some internal (but less verifiable) criterion. However, what may be an "error" from an external perspective may not be an "error" from an internal perspective. Formal safety requirements tend to view error from an external (system-oriented) perspective, which many would say is ultimately what is required. However, simply viewing error in this manner can result in wrong conclusions about the etiology of the "error" being drawn and hence inappropriate remedial actions may be suggested as a result.

Errors are almost always associated with a negative outcome of some kind: a performance shortfall. Just occasionally though, people perform unintended actions (an "error" as judged against some internal criterion) that turn out to be for the better (in terms of the external, verifiable criterion for system performance). These serendipitous actions are rarely designated as "errors", although from a psychological/internal perspective (as opposed to a system perspective) they are clearly failures. Alexander Fleming's discovery and isolation of penicillin in 1928[1] is often described as accidental but rarely described as erroneous! Taken from a human/system reliability perspective, however, outcomes are more important than processes, hence such a fortuitous "error" this would not be regarded (from a system viewpoint) as actually being an error.

Finally, taking Hollnagel's third point, an "error" can only be considered an "error" if the person committing the "error" has the possibility of avoiding it. If an action was unavoidable it cannot be considered to be an "error" (although from a system perspective it may degrade the system—but this is taking an external viewpoint). Flying into a hurricane, either deliberately or through negligence, would

---

1   Penicillin was isolated from a mould growing in an uncleaned Petri dish left in the laboratory that was observed to inhibit bacterial growth.

be considered an error; flying into a microburst would not be considered erroneous if either the warning came too late or if it was not detected at all.

However, volition is not an "all or nothing" thing. This is where a socio-technical systems approach to the roots of human error enters the fray. To draw on Reason's (1990) terminology, in this approach the people at the "sharp end" (the pilots in this context) fall into traps left for them by the people at the "blunt end" (those removed from day-to-day operations: the managers, designers, regulators, and so on). The idea implicit in this approach to the description and causation of "error" is that the performance requirements of the task (an objective criterion which is either met or not met by the operator at the "sharp end") are either fulfilled or not fulfilled as a result of resources and constraints imposed by those elsewhere in the system who are several steps removed from operations. That is, despite what pilots may think, they often do not have complete volition. This theme is very much evident in the current major models of organizational safety/accident causation that will be considered later (for example, Reason, 1990; Reason, 1997).

To illustrate, consider the American Airlines flight 587 accident near New York. The principal cause of the accident to this Airbus A300 was attributed to "unnecessary and excessive rudder pedal inputs" on the part of the First Officer flying the aircraft (National Transportation Safety Board, 2004). As a result of these large rudder pedal inputs the aircraft's vertical stabilizer and rudder separated in flight. The engines then subsequently separated and the aircraft broke up killing all 260 people onboard. However, was this just simply pilot error or did the pilot simply fall into a trap that had been left for them by design and organizational flaws geographically and temporally remote from the accident? It was claimed that American Airlines' crews operating the A300 had never been trained concerning extreme rudder inputs (an organizational failure in the specification of the training provided) and that the subsequent rudder failure was caused by a flaw in the design of the aircraft (a design shortcoming in the aircraft). Such rudder inputs should not lead to a catastrophic rudder in a civil aircraft. It could even be argued that this was a failure in the aircraft certification process—a failure of regulation and governance of the industry. Pilot error is merely a starting point for an explanation of how this accident came about, not an end in itself. It can be seen that Dekker's (2001) assertion that errors are systematically connected to aspects of a pilot's tools, tasks, and the organizational context was certainly true in this case.

To round off this initial prologue a dissenting voice from Woods, Johannesen, Cook, and Sarter (1994) is worth considering providing a different perspective. They suggest that "error" is always a judgment made in hindsight:

> The diversity of approaches to the topic of human error is symptomatic that "human error" is not a well-defined category of human performance. Attributing error to the actions of some person, team or organisation is fundamentally a social and psychological process and not an objective, technical one. (Woods, Johannesen, Cook, and Sarter, 1994)

However, from a practical perspective it is undeniable that people in the aviation industry occasionally do things that they shouldn't do, or don't do things that they should do (whether they mean to or not). These actions and/or inactions degrade the system and can cause accidents. To be pragmatic, let's call these things "errors" (note that this considers these problems from a system perspective; an "error" is in some way a failure in the system). However, the terms "error" and "blame" should never be conflated. These terms are not synonymous.

The remainder of this chapter looks at the underlying factors that may help to contribute to errors being made on the flight deck as a function of the pilot's tools, tasks, and the organizational context. But as aviation is an international business the chapter concludes by examining cultural determinants and perspectives on human error.

THE PILOT'S TOOLS AND TASKS

During the last half century the skills required to fly a large commercial aircraft have changed considerably, mostly as a result of advances in control and display design and the technology of automation. The pilot of a modern commercial aircraft is no longer a "hands-on" stick and rudder flyer (they have not been for a long time): they are now a manager of flight crew and of complex, highly-automated aircraft systems. These highly automated systems started to be introduced in commercial aircraft during the "glass cockpit" revolution of the 1980s. While the systems on these aircraft offered a considerable advance in safety over their "clockwork cockpit" forbearers, new types of error began to occur in these flight decks. This was exemplified by accidents such as the Nagoya Airbus A300–600, the Cali Boeing 757 accident, and the Strasbourg A320 accident.

Many of us have attempted to pull a door with a handle on it even through the labels clearly says "push". The handle has an "affordance" (Norman, 1988): its design encourages you to pull it despite instructions to the contrary. This is a typical instance of a design induced error. Harris, Stanton, Marshall, Young, Demagalski, and Salmon (2005) provided a list of common design induced errors made on a day-to-day basis reported by pilots flying a particular type of modern highly automated airliner. These can be found in Table 19.1.

Although such errors would at first appear quite trivial (and most of these events are spotted almost immediately and rectified) on a flight deck their consequences can be dire. The crash of Air Inter flight 148 near Strasbourg was attributed to such a design induced error. The primary cause of the accident was that the crew left the autopilot in vertical speed mode when they should have selected flight path angle mode on the Flight Management and Guidance System console (see Figure 19.1). The crew entered "33" intending a 3.3° descent angle, however as the aircraft was in vertical speed mode this resulted in a rate of descent of 3,300 feet per minute (over three times the rate intended). The display of vertical speed or flight path angle was made on the same display element (at the right hand end of the panel) the only difference being the incorporation of a decimal place when in flight path angle mode. Mode selection was made using a switch in the center of the panel.

As a result of such accidents, the US Federal Aviation Administration (FAA) commissioned an exhaustive study of the interfaces in these modern flight decks. The ensuing report, *The Interfaces Between Flightcrews and Modern Flight Deck Systems* (Federal Aviation Administration, 1996), identified many major design deficiencies and shortcomings in the design process of modern commercial airliner flight decks. The report made criticisms of the flight deck interfaces, identifying problems in many systems. These included pilots' autoflight mode awareness/indication; energy awareness; position/terrain awareness; confusing and unclear display symbology and

Table 19.1   **Percentage of pilots reporting having made common design-induced errors during the approach and landing phase while performing an autoland in a modern "glass cockpit" airliner**

Error	%
Flaps	
Checked the flap position and misread it	4.3%
Moved the flap lever further or not as far as intended	17.4%
Landing gear	
Omitted to put the landing gear down until reminded	19.6%
Airspeed	
Initially, dialled in an incorrect airspeed on the Flight Control Unit by turning the knob in the wrong direction	39.1%
Having entered the desired airspeed, pushed or pulled the switch in the opposite way to the one that you wanted	26.1%
Adjusted the heading knob instead of the speed knob	78.3%
Altitude	
Entered the wrong altitude on the Flight Control Unit and activated it	15.2%
Entered an incorrect altitude because the 100/1,000 feet knob wasn't clicked over	26.1%
Believed you were descending in flight path angle and found that you were in fact in vertical speed mode or vice versa.	8.7%
Failed to check ALT (Altitude) mode was active	8.7%
Heading	
Entered a heading on the Flight Control Unit and failed to activate it at the inappropriate time	34.8%
Failed to check HDG (heading) mode was active	23.9%
Approach system	
Tried to engage APPR (approach) mode too late so that it failed to capture	28.3%
Pressed the wrong button when intending to engage APPR such as EXPED (expedite)	6.5%
Failed to check APPR was active	28.3%
Localizer	
Incorrectly adjusted heading knob to regain localizer and activated the change	4.3%
Glideslope	
Failed to monitor the glide slope and found that the aircraft had not intercepted it	39.1%
Other	
Had an incorrect barometric air pressure set	45.7%
Set an altitude "out of the way" and then out of habit pulled the altitude knob	15.2%

Source: Adapted from Harris, Stanton, Marshall, Young, Demagalski and Salmon, 2005.

Figure 19.1   Airbus A320 Flight Management and Guidance System glareshield panel

nomenclature; a lack of consistency in FMS (Flight Management System) interfaces and conventions, and poor compatibility between flight deck systems. The FAA Human Factors Team also made many criticisms of the flight deck design process. For example, the report identified a lack of human factors expertise on design teams, which also had a lack of authority over the design decisions made. There was too much emphasis on the physical ergonomics of the flight deck, and not enough on the cognitive ergonomics. Fifty-one specific recommendations came out of the report. The most far-reaching of these with regard to the reduction of error on the flight deck as a product of the pilots tools were that:

> The FAA should require the evaluation of flight deck designs for susceptibility to design-induced flightcrew errors and the consequences of those errors as part of the type certification process, and ... The FAA should establish regulatory and associated material to require the use of a flight deck certification review process that addresses human performance considerations.

As a direct result of the FAA report, in July 1999 the US Department of Transportation gave notice of a new task assigned to the Aviation Rulemaking Advisory Committee (ARAC). This was to provide advice and recommendations to the FAA administrator to *"review the existing material in FAR/JAR 25 and make recommendations about what regulatory standards and/or advisory material should be updated or developed to consistently address design-related flight crew performance vulnerabilities and prevention (detection, tolerance and recovery) of flight crew error"* (US Department of Transportation, 1999).

This regulation has now been developed and incorporated into the European airworthiness requirements by the European Aviation Safety Agency as Certification Specification 25.1302. These requirements apply to both the Type Certification and Supplemental Type Certification processes for large transport aircraft.

Perhaps the true significance of the establishment this regulation is that for the first time, there is a specific regulatory requirement for "good" human factors on the flight deck. It is an attempt to eradicate many aspects of pilot error at source. However, such rules relating to design can only address the fabric of the airframe and its systems so the new regulation can only minimize the likelihood of error as a result of poor interface design. It cannot consider errors resulting from such factors as poor training, inappropriate implementation of procedures, and so on. These aspects of aircraft operations are covered elsewhere in the airworthiness regulations. Although this segmentation of the regulations is logical from a regulatory perspective, from a human factors viewpoint, which assumes that the root causes of human error are often many and inter-related, this does pose some considerable challenges. For example, how can a system be evaluated for its error potential (in this case the flight deck) without explicit knowledge of the skills, knowledge, and abilities of the potential users of the system (that is, the pilots)?

However, the design of the flight deck interfaces cannot be separated from the aircraft's operating procedures. Complex interfaces, while potentially more flexible, are also more error-prone (there are far more opportunities for error). With regard to checklists and procedures various axioms have been developed over the years. Reason (1988) observed that:

- The larger the number of steps, the greater the probability that one of them will be omitted or repeated.
- The greater the information loading in a particular step, the more likely that it will not be completed to the standard required.
- Steps that do not follow on from each other (that is, are not functionally related) are more likely to be omitted.
- A step is more likely to be omitted if instructions are given verbally (for example in the "challenge and response" format).
- If steps are given in written form (as in a checklist) the items towards the end of the sequence are more likely to be omitted.
- Interruptions during a task which contains many steps (for example, the implementation of a pre-flight checklist) are likely to cause errors in the form of either a slip or a lapse.

Formal error identification techniques implicitly consider both the design of the flight deck interfaces and the procedures required to operate them simultaneously. Furthermore, they can be applied at the early design stages to help avoid design induced error. Most formal error identification methods operate in a similar way. They are usually based on a task analysis followed by the subsequent assessment of the user interfaces and task steps to assess their error potential. SHERPA (Systematic Human Error Reduction and Prediction Approach—Embrey, 1986) has been assessed as being one of the more sensitive and reliable generic error prediction methodologies suitable for use on the flight deck (Harris, Stanton, Marshall, Young, Demagalski, and Salmon, 2005) and is typical of this type of technique. The method operates by trained analysts making judgments about which error modes are credible for each task step based upon the analysis of the work activity involved. In the SHERPA technique error is regarded as a direct consequence of the design of the hardware and the operations employed. Although there is a strong behavioral element inherent in the methodology, the psychological root of the error is of little or no consequence. Secondly, error is defined strictly from a system perspective: any operations likely to degrade the system are categorized as errors. SHERPA also provides the facilities to incorporate the mitigation and management of errors into the analysis process (the error "troika"—prevent error, trap error, or mitigate its consequences). An Extract of a SHERPA analysis (the initial hierarchical task analysis—HTA— including an extract of plans) plus a section of the subsequent error identification phase is provided in Figure 19.2 and Table 19.2 (from Harris, Stanton, Marshall, Young, Demagalski, and Salmon, 2005).

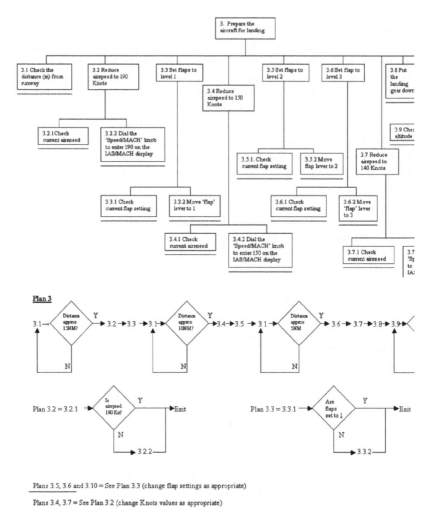

Figure 19.2   Extract of HTA for landing aircraft

Other error prediction methodologies employing a similar approach but developed specifically for the aviation domain have been developed (for example, the Human Error Template—Stanton, Harris, Salmon, Demagalski, Marshall, Young, Dekker, and Waldmann, 2006) which has demonstrated even greater degrees of sensitivity and reliability.

However, formal error prediction methodologies only really address Reasons' skill-based (and perhaps some rule-based) errors within a fairly well defined and proceduralized context. Hence they can only help in protecting against errors which relate either to the flight deck interfaces or their associated operating procedures. These error identification methods cannot cope with higher level decision-making errors, such as the rule-based errors that may occur when engaged in a non-diagnostic procedural management or creative problem-solving task (see Orasanu, 1993). They are quite limited in this respect. To understand the roots of these errors another approach is required.

Table 19.2   Extract of SHERPA analysis

Task step	Error mode	Description	Consequence	Recovery	P	C	Remedial measures
3.2.2	A3	Pilot turns the Speed/MACH selector knob the wrong way	The wrong airspeed is entered and the aircraft speeds up instead of slowing down	3.2.1	M	M	–Clearer control labeling –Auditory signal informing increase/ decrease
3.2.2	A6	The pilot dials in the desired airspeed using the wrong control knob, i.e., the heading knob	Before capture, the auto-pilot will attempt to switch course to the speed value entered causing the aircraft to leave the glideslope	Immediate	M	H	–Improved control labeling –Improved separation of controls

Notes: In this extract, error mode A3 is an operation in the wrong direction; error mode A6 is an operation in the correct direction but on the wrong object. Estimates (low, medium or high) of the probability of occurrence and criticality of the error are given in columns labelled P and C, respectively.
Source: Harris, Stanton, Marshall, Young, Demagalski and Salmon, 2005.

THE ORGANIZATION AS AN ERROR-PROMOTING CONDITION

Reason's (1990) model of human error posited that active failures (the errors proximal to the accident, associated with the performance of front-line operators—in this case the pilots) and latent failures (distal errors and system misspecifications, which lie dormant within the system for a long time) serve to combine together with other factors to breach a system's defenses. Reason (1997) observed that complex systems are designed, operated, maintained, and managed by human beings so it is unsurprising that human decisions and actions at the higher organizational level are implicated in many accidents (see the earlier example of the accident to American Airlines flight 587). The active failures of pilots (errors) have a direct impact on safety; however, latent failures are spawned in the upper levels of the organization and are related to its management and regulatory structures.

While Reason's model was extremely influential in providing a theoretical framework to describe the manner by which higher organizational levels contributed to error on the flight deck, it did not suggest remedial solutions. Based upon Reason's model, Wiegmann and Shappell (2003) developed HFACS (Human Factors Analysis and Classification System) to service such a need. HFACS was originally designed as a framework for investigating and analyzing human error accidents in US military aviation operations (Wiegmann and Shappell, 1997). However, its authors have also demonstrated its applicability to the analysis of accidents in US commercial aviation (Wiegmann and Shappell, 2001; Shappell, Detweiler, Holcomb, Hackworth, Boquet, and Wiegmann, 2007) and US general aviation (Shappell and Wiegmann, 2003). They claim that HFACS bridges the void between theory and practice by providing safety professionals with a theoretically based tool for identifying and classifying human errors in aviation mishaps. As it is based upon Reason's model the system focuses on both latent and active failures (and their inter-relationships) at various levels within the organization and by doing so it facilitates the identification of the underlying causes of pilot error.

HFACS examines human error at four levels. Each higher level is assumed to affect the next downward level in HFACS framework (see Figure 19.3).

- Level-1 "Unsafe acts of operators" (active failures proximal to the accident): This level is where the majority of causes in the investigation of accidents are focused. Such causes can be classified into the two basic categories of errors and violation. It is at this level that the error predictions made by techniques such as SHERPA apply.
- Level-2 "Preconditions for unsafe acts" (latent/active failures): This level addresses the latent failures within the causal sequence of events as well as more obvious active failures. It also describes the context of substandard conditions of operators and the substandard practices they adopt. It will be noted that the sub-categories of "Technological Environment" and "Physical Environment" encompass issues described in the previous section concerned with the design of the flight deck as an error-promoting factor.
- Level-3 "Unsafe supervision" (latent failures): This level traces the causal chain of events producing unsafe acts up to the front-line supervisors.
- Level-4 "Organizational influences" (latent failures and system misspecifications, distal to the accident): This level encompasses the most elusive of latent failures, fallible decisions of upper levels of management which directly affect supervisory practices and which indirectly affect the actions of front-line operators.

Focusing on the "unsafe acts of operator" (Level-1) is akin to treating a fever without understanding the underlying illness that is causing it. Wiegmann and Shappell (2003) classified "preconditions for unsafe acts" (Level-2) into seven sub-categories. These can be regarded as what Reason (1990) described as the psychological precursors to unsafe acts.

The role of supervisors is to provide their personnel with the facilities and capability to succeed and to ensure the job is done safely and efficiently. Level-3 in HFACS is primarily concerned with the supervisory influence both on the pilots and their operational environment. HFACS contains four categories of "unsafe supervision"; "inadequate supervision"; "planned inappropriate operation"; "failure to correct a known problem", and "supervisory violation".

The corporate decisions about resource management are based on two conflicting objectives: safety and on-time, cost-effective operations. The decisions of upper-level management can affect supervisory practices, as well as the conditions and actions of operators. However, these organizational errors often go unnoticed due to the lack of framework to investigate them. These elusive latent failures were identified by Wiegmann and Shappell (2003) as failures in "resource management"; "organizational climate" and "organizational process".

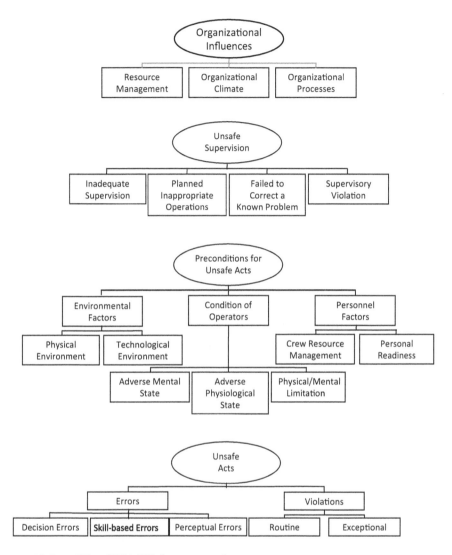

Figure 19.3   The HFACS framework

Note: Each upper level is proposed to affect items at the lower levels.
Source: Wiegmann and Shappell, 2003.

Although HFACS was based directly on an organizationally-based theory of failure (Reason, 1990; Reason, 1997) at the time it was derived there was little or no quantitative data to support the theoretical model upon which it was based. Recent work has, however, established strong statistical relationships describing empirically the cause/effect relationships between various components at the four different organizational levels in the framework, giving support to the underpinning theory behind the framework. Data have been analyzed both from military aviation (Li and Harris, 2006) and commercial aviation (Li, Harris and Yu, 2008) which have provided an understanding of how actions and decisions at higher managerial levels within organizations promulgate throughout them to result in operational errors and accidents.

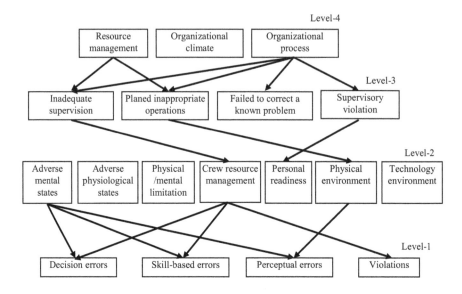

Figure 19.4   Significant associations between categories at the four levels in the HFACS framework for accidents involving commercial aircraft

Source: Li, Harris, and Yu, 2007.

The HFACS analysis of 41 commercial aircraft accidents by Li, Harris and Yu (2008) demonstrated that inadequacies at HFACS Level-4 ("organizational influences") had associations with further inadequacies at HFACS Level-3 ("unsafe supervision" — see Figure 19.4). The category of "organizational process" was particularly important; this was associated with inadequacies in all the categories at the next level and hence indirectly was at the root of operational errors resulting in accidents. "Resource management" issues (such as inadequate/inappropriate selection; staffing and training; excessive cost cutting and providing unsuitable equipment, and a failure to remedy design flaws) also showed strong relationships with the Level-3 categories of "inadequate supervision" and "planned inappropriate operations". Poor decision-making by upper-level management adversely influenced the personnel and practices at the supervisory level, which in turn affected the psychological pre-conditions for error (Level-2) and hence the subsequent actions of the pilots. The category of "CRM" was the key precursor to error here but it should be noted that inadequacies in CRM practices themselves were influenced by several higher level organizational issues (see Figure 19.4). Poor CRM was subsequently associated with "decision errors" (such as selecting an inappropriate strategy; improper in-flight planning) and "skill based errors" and "violations" in operating procedures. The category of "adverse mental states" encompasses such things as a loss of situational awareness; distraction, and mental fatigue due to stress. It is perhaps not too surprising that such mental states pre-disposed accident involved pilots to all the main categories of human error. This study provides some understanding of how actions and decisions at higher managerial levels in the operation of commercial aircraft subsequently results in errors on the flight deck and accidents. To reduce significantly the accident rate these "paths to failure" relating to such organizational and human factors must be addressed.

However, it should also be noted that this study was undertaken by the analysis of accidents of civil aircraft from Taiwan (Republic of China—RoC). This begs the obvious question: if organizational culture influences the prevalence of error on the flight deck, does national culture also play a part?

NATIONAL CULTURE AND PILOT ERROR

Aviation accident rates differ across regions. Asia and Africa have higher accident rates than either Europe or America (Civil Aviation Authority, 1998). Analysis of the underlying causal factors also shows differences between the regions. There has been a great deal of debate about the role of culture in aviation mishaps; however, culture is only cited on relatively few occasions as having a role to play in the causation of the accident (Helmreich, 1994; Soeters and Boer, 2000). Culture helps to fashion a complex framework of national, organizational and professional attitudes and values within which groups and individuals function. Cultures can be divided into different levels; for example, families, organizations, professions, regions, and countries. Culture is at the root of action; it underlies the manner by which people communicate and develop attitudes towards life. Kluckhohm (1951) proposed:

> Culture consists in patterned ways of thinking, feeling and reacting, acquired and transmitted mainly by symbols, constituting the distinctive achievements of human groups, including their embodiments in artifacts; the essential core of culture consist of traditional ideas and especially their attached values.

It is essential to consider the cultural determinants of behavior, including error. A culture is formed by its environment and evolves in response to changes in that environment, therefore, culture and context are really inseparable (Merritt and Maurino, 2004).

Using the HFACS taxonomy as a basis for a cross cultural comparison, Li, Harris and Chen (2007) observed that in a meta-analysis of previous studies seven categories exhibited significant differences between three different regions. These differences were not related to the nature of the final errors committed by the pilots on the flight deck but were mostly concerned with contributory factors at the higher organizational levels. The differences were related to organizational processes, organizational climate, resource management, inadequate supervision, physical/mental limitations, adverse mental states, and decision errors.

Li, Harris, and Chen's (2007) analysis showed that Taiwan and India, both countries which have a high power-distance culture (according to Hofstede, 2001), have a higher frequency of events in the "organizational influences" (HFACS Level-4) category compared to the US (a low power-distance culture). The corporate environments in Taiwan and India both prefer tall organizational pyramids with centralized decision structures and have a large proportion of supervisory personnel. In these cultures subordinates expect to be told what to do. On the other hand, the working environment of US exhibits low power-distance. It is also a culture high on individualism. Much flatter organizational structures are preferred with a relatively small proportion of supervisory personnel (Hofstede, 2001). US airlines also had fewer instances of factors at HFACS Level-3 "unsafe supervision" compared to the other two countries. It was suggested that the culture in the US of low power-distance and high individualism promoted greater efficacy in addressing safety-related issues by promoting open discussion by all personnel and that the organizational structures allowed greater autonomy of action than in the Taiwanese or Indian cultures, which were less reactive as a result of their preferred "tall" organizational structures which served to discourage autonomy of action, especially at the lower managerial levels. It was suggested that the nature of the proactive management style with few communication barriers between organizational levels in low power-distance cultures was the key to promoting aviation safety.

The only HFACS category that exhibited differences between the cultures examined in the error rates observed by the pilots on the flight deck was that of "decision-making" (HFACS Level-1). The Taiwanese preference for collective (rather than individual) decisions may explain the over-representation of poor decision-making being implicated in accidents. Individual decision-making skills may not be as well developed in this society. On the other hand, the US has a culture which prefers individual decision-making and responsibility for the self. Making decisions, implementing them, and taking responsibility for their consequences is a central part of life in a low power-distance culture (such as the US) and hence is well practiced.

However, culture has a much deeper, more insidious part to play in the causation and trapping of error on the flight deck (Harris and Li, 2008). CRM "failures" implicated in many accidents occurring to Asian carriers have been attributed to "culture" (specifically issues relating to communication between crew members in high power-distance cultures). This is a half-explanation (at best) and a vast over-simplification of the underlying problem. CRM principally works on two aspects of the error "troika". Good CRM should be aimed at preventing errors and/or trapping errors. The basic operating philosophy in the commercial flight deck centers on the concept of two pilots cross-monitoring each other's actions. Standard operating procedures are performed on a "challenge and response" basis. The system of "monitor and cross-monitor" and "challenge and response" is predicated upon the belief that the pilots, irrespective of rank, will alert each other to irregularities or errors. However, implicit in this is an assumption of low power-distance. This CRM philosophy is predicated upon a Western cultural assumption.

There are also fundamental differences in the mental models of people in different cultures. Westerners tend to adopt a function-oriented model connected to a task-oriented operating concept, resulting in a preference for a sequential approach to undertaking tasks (inherent in checklists and SOPs). The Asian preference is for an integrated, thematic approach; hence a task-oriented operating concept contradicts their preferred method of working (Rau, Choong, and Salvendy, 2004; Roese and Zuehlke, 1999). While a First Officer's reluctance to question errors made by the Captain may be attributable to the interaction of culture and CRM, a lower rate of compliance with procedures and/or the higher rate of procedural error observed on Chinese flight decks (Yu, Li, and Harris, 2007) could be a product of design and procedures that are not congruent with South East Asian mental models.

Research in cross-cultural ergonomics has tended to concentrate upon issues such as the user interface (Roese and Zuehlke, 1999) or attitudes towards the use of automation (Sherman, Helmreich, and Merritt, 1997). Such research also usually addresses only a single user interacting with the equipment. However, on the flight deck the pilot interface dictates how the crew as a team will undertake their tasks. The architecture of the modern flight deck is arranged to facilitate the cross-monitoring of pilots' actions and the execution of procedures (Kelly, 2004). While this is an effective approach to trapping or mitigating error in Western cultures, it is less effective in Asian cultures (Yu, Li and Harris, 2007). Furthermore, the aircraft manufacturers are not totally responsible for producing interfaces with an implicit Western bias. The airworthiness regulations and advisory material (for example, FAR 25—US Department of Transportation, 1974; Certification Specification 25—European Aviation Safety Agency, 2008; Advisory Circular AC 25–11A—US Department of Transportation, Federal Aviation Administration, 1987) contain these cultural biases. This has profound implications for new aircraft being developed in South East Asia; for example, the ACAC (AVIC Commercial Aircraft Company) ARJ21 Regional Jet.

CONCLUSIONS—AND MORE COMPLEXITY ...

Dekker (2001) asserted that errors were connected to the pilot's tools, tasks, and their organization. This is only partially the case. The pilot's tools, tasks, and organizational context are all culturally driven, with the tools and tasks primarily determined from a Western perspective. It is argued that the potential for error on the flight deck increases when the pilot's tools, tasks and the airline organization are not culturally congruent with the underlying design assumptions as expressed through the pilot interface and its associated standard operating procedures. At the root of all of this are the airworthiness and operations regulations, themselves written and implemented from a Western European/North American perspective.

Unfortunately, there is one more level of complexity in the determination of the root causes of pilot error on the flight deck. Independent analysis of the mid-air collision over Ueberlingen occurring on July 1, 2002 by groups of British and Taiwanese accident investigators using the HFACS methodology demonstrated that there were cultural differences in the causal attributions underlying the active errors on the flight deck and in the air traffic control center that led to the collision (Li, Young, Wang, and Harris, 2008). Woods, Johannesen, Cook, and Sarter (1994) opined that "error" is a judgment made in hindsight. However, it would seem to be a judgment made in hindsight from a particular cultural perspective; and in an international business like the aviation industry, this cannot be easily ignored.

REFERENCES

Boeing Commercial Airplanes. (2007). *Statistical Summary of Commercial Jet Airplane Accidents: Worldwide Operations 1959–2007*. Seattle WA: Boeing Commercial Airplanes.

Civil Aviation Authority. (1998). *CAP 681 Global Fatal Accident Review 1980–1996*. London, UK: Civil Aviation Authority.

Dekker, S.W.A. (2001). The re-invention of human error. *Human Factors and Aerospace Safety*, 1, 247–266.

Embrey, D.E. (1986). SHERPA: *A systematic human error reduction and prediction approach.* Paper presented at the International Meeting on Advances in Nuclear Power Systems, Knoxville, Tennessee.

European Aviation Safety Agency. (2008). *Certification Specification Part 25 (Amendment 5).* Cologne: European Aviation Safety Agency.

Federal Aviation Administration. (1996). *Report on the Interfaces between Flightcrews and Modern Flight Deck Systems.* Washington DC: Federal Aviation Administration.

Harris, D. and Li, W.-C. (2008). Cockpit Design and Cross-Cultural Issues Underlying Failures in Crew Resource Management. *Aviation Space and Environmental Medicine,* 79(5), 537–538.

Harris, D., Stanton, A., Marshall, A., Young, M.S., Demagalski, J.M., and Salmon, P. (2005). Using SHERPA to Predict Design-Induced Error on the Flight Deck. *Aerospace Science and Technology,* 9(6) 525–532.

Helmreich, R.L. (1994) The anatomy of a system accident: The crash of Avianca flight 052. *International Journal of Aviation Psychology,* 4, 265–284.

Hofstede, G. (2001). *Culture's Consequences: Comparing Values, Behaviors, Institutions, and Organizations Across Nations.* California: Sage Publications.

Hollnagel, E. (1998). *Cognitive Reliability and Error Analysis Method.* Oxford: Elsevier Science.

Kelly, B.D. (2004). Flight deck design and integration for commercial air transports. In D. Harris (Ed.), *Human Factors for Civil Flight Deck Design.* Aldershot: Ashgate, 3–32.

Kluckhohm, C. (1951). The Study of Culture. In D. Lerner and H.D. Lasswell (Eds.), *The Policy Sciences.* Stanford, CA: Stanford University Press, 86–101.

Li, W.-C. and Harris, D. (2006). Pilot error and its relationship with higher organizational levels: HFACS analysis of 523 accidents. *Aviation, Space and Environmental Medicine,* 77(10), 1056–1061.

Li, W.-C., Harris, D. and Chen, A. (2007). Eastern Minds in Western Cockpits: Meta-analysis of human factors in mishaps from three nations. *Aviation Space and Environmental Medicine,* 78 (4), 420–425.

Li, W.-C., Harris, D. and Yu, C.-S. (2008). Routes to failure: analysis of 41 civil aviation accidents from the Republic of China using the Human Factors Analysis and Classification System. *Accident Analysis and Prevention,* 40(2) 426–434.

Li, W.-C., Young, H.-T., Wang, T. and Harris, D. (2007). International Cooperation and Challenges: Understanding Cross-cultural Issues in the Processes of Accident Investigation. *International Society of Air Safety Investigators Forum,* 40(4), 16–21.

Merritt, A. and Maurino, D. (2004). Cross-cultural factors in aviation safety. In M. Kaplan (Ed.), *Advances in human performance and cognitive engineering research.* San Diego, CA: Elsevier Science, 147–181.

National Transportation Safety Board. (2004). *In-Flight Separation of Vertical Stabilizer, American Airlines Flight 587, Airbus Industrie A300–605R, N14053. Belle Harbor, New York, November 12 2001. Aircraft Accident Report NTSB/AAR-04/04.* Washington DC: National Transportation Safety Board.

Norman, D.A. (1988). *The Psychology of Everyday Things.* New York: Basic Books.

Orasanu, J.M. (1993). Decision-making in the cockpit. In E.L. Wiener, B.G. Kanki, and R.L. Helmreich (Eds.), *Cockpit resource management.* London: Academic Press Limited.

Rau, P-LP., Choong, Y.-Y., and Salvendy, G. (2004). A cross cultural study on knowledge representation and structure in human computer interfaces. *International Journal of Industrial Ergonomics,* 34, 117–129.

Reason, J.T. (1988). Stress and cognitive failure. In S. Fisher and J. Reason (Eds.), *Handbook of Life Stress, Cognition and Health*. New York: John Wiley.

Reason, J.T. (1990). *Human Error*. Cambridge: Cambridge University Press.

Reason, J.T. (1997). *Managing The Risks Of Organizational Accidents*. Aldershot: Ashgate.

Roese, K. and Zuehlke, D. (1999). Design of User Interfaces for Non-European Markets. In D. Harris (Ed.), *Engineering Psychology and Cognitive Ergonomics: Volume Four—Job Design, Product Design and Human–computer Interaction)*. Aldershot: Ashgate, 165–172.

Shappell, S., Detwiler, C., Holcomb, K., Hackworth, C., Boquet, A., and Wiegmann, D. (2007). Human Error and Commercial Aviation Accidents: An Analysis Using the Human Factors Analysis and Classification System. *Human Factors*, 49, 227–242.

Shappell, S.A. and Wiegmann, D.A. (2003). *A Human Error Analysis of General Aviation Controlled Flight Into Terrain Accidents Occurring Between 1990–1998 (Report no. DOT/FAA/AM-03/4)*. Washington, DC: Federal Aviation Administration.

Sherman, P.J., Helmreich, R.L., and Merritt, A.C. (1997). National Culture and Flight Deck Automation: Results of a Multination Survey. *International Journal of Aviation Psychology*, 7, 311–329.

Soeters, J.L. and Boer, P.C. (2000). Culture and flight safety in military aviation. *International Journal of Aviation Psychology*, 10, 111–133.

Stanton, N.A., Harris, D., Salmon, P., Demagalski, J.M., Marshall, A., Young, M.S., Dekker, S.W.A., and Waldmann, T. (2006). Predicting Design Induced Pilot Error using HET (Human Error Template)—A New Formal Human Error Identification Method for Flight Decks. *The Aeronautical Journal*, 110 (February), 107–115.

US Department of Transportation—Federal Aviation Administration. (1987). *Advisory Circular AC 25–11A—Transport Category Airplane Electronic Display Systems*. Washington DC: Author.

US Department of Transportation. (1974). *Federal Aviation Regulations (Part 25—Airworthiness Standards)*. Revised January 1, 2003. Washington, DC: US Department of Transportation.

US Department of Transportation (1999). Aviation Rulemaking Advisory Committee; Transport Airplane and Engine: Notice of new task assignment for the Aviation Rulemaking Advisory Committee (ARAC). *Federal Register*, 64, 140 (July 22, 1999).

Wiegmann, D.A. and Shappell, S.A. (1997). Human Factors Analysis of Postaccident Data: Applying Theoretical Taxonomies of Human Error. *International Journal of Aviation Psychology*, 7, 67–81.

Wiegmann, D.A. and Shappell, S.A. (2001). Human Error Analysis of Commercial Aviation Accidents: Application of the Human Factors Analysis and Classification System. *Aviation, Space and Environmental Medicine*, 72, 1006–1016.

Wiegmann, D.A. and Shappell, S.A. (2003), *A Human Error Approach to Aviation Accident Analysis: The Human Factors Analysis and Classification System*. Aldershot, England: Ashgate.

Woods, D.D., Johannesen, L.J., Cook, R.I. and Sarter, N.B. (1994). *Behind human error: Cognitive systems, computers and hindsight*. Columbus, OH: CSERIAC.

Yu, C.-S., Li, W.C., and Harris, D. (2007). To Be or Not to Be? Decision Errors or Violations in Aviation Accidents. *Proceedings of the Eighth International Conference on Naturalistic Decision-making*. June 3–6, 2007, San Francisco, CA.

20

The Diminishing Relevance of Human–Machine Interaction

Erik Hollnagel

No man is an island entire of itself; every man is a piece of the Continent, a part of the main.

John Donne (*c*.1572–1631)

The purpose of human–machine interaction design is to ensure that the tasks of the human–machine system can be accomplished as efficiently and reliably as possible. This type of design depicts the interaction as a well-defined activity, as evidenced by the commonly used formal methods. The three underlying assumptions are that system boundaries are well-defined, internal and external interactions are similar, and that humans and machines are reactive. While these assumptions may be reasonable for tractable systems which only are loosely coupled to their environment, they are not tenable for intractable systems with tight couplings to their environment. In these cases the boundaries are relative to the chosen level of description, and activities of necessity become open-loop. The design of such systems requires the adoption of a larger or more global perspective, and the goals change from maintaining local stability to persistence defined as the ability to absorb change and disturbance and still maintain an effective relationship with the environment.

INTRODUCTION

The topic of Human–Machine Interaction (HMI) has had a checkered history. By rights, HMI could have been a subject of study at least as soon as humans started to use machines that were not powered by the humans themselves, that is, machines which used an external power source and which therefore in some way had to be controlled. While a few such machines have existed for millennia, the widespread use of technology in work is usually dated to the start of the Industrial Revolution in the late eighteenth century, which marked the beginning of the uneasy relationship between humans and machines. Consider, for instance, the first modern locomotive, Stephenson's "Rocket," which on September 15, 1830 inaugurated the Liverpool and Manchester Railway. A locomotive is, by any means, a machine that has to be controlled by humans in order to carry out the intended function, namely to travel safely and efficiently along the railway. (Ironically, the opening of the Liverpool and Manchester Railway was also the occasion of the first railway accident.) In other words, the locomotive-engineer unit is a human–machine system and therefore an almost exemplary case of human–machine interaction. Yet the study of HMI was not born in 1830. HMI did not even exist as a recognizable scientific discipline one hundred years later, when the industrialized societies had come to depend heavily on human–machine systems of all kinds.

Human factors (or human factors engineering) saw the light of day around 1945. The purpose was literally to "engineer" the human factor into increasingly complex systems. This had become necessary because rapidly evolving technology had made it possible to build systems where the human, rather than the machine, was the limiting factor for overall performance. Although this might have been the start of the study of human–machine interaction, the recognition of HMI as a discipline lay still some years ahead. If we follow the principle of associating a discipline with the publication of a journal bearing the name, then HMI can be dated to the end of the 1960s. It was, however, at that time called man–machine interaction as in the title of the International Journal of Man–machine Studies (IJMMS) that was first published in 1969. Interestingly enough the name of the journal changed in 1994 to the International Journal of Human–computer Studies. In other words, man–machine interaction (which, by the way, soon was called human–machine interaction) transformed into human–computer interaction. This was, of course, a consequence of the proliferation of computers large and small in all types of human activity. Indeed, human–computer interaction (HCI) — which in the US mysteriously is called Computer–Human Interaction or CHI — almost totally dominated the field in the 1990s. Today there is perhaps a return to the study of HMI proper, by whatever name it may be called. Whereas a computer in the early 1980s was seen as a special kind of machine, we are now at a stage where most kinds of human–machine interaction takes place by means of computers, which have become so ubiquitous that they in most cases go unnoticed.

1. THE USE OF ARTIFACTS

HMI, and HCI/CHI, can be viewed more generally as a case of human interaction with technological artifacts, or as the use of artifacts in work. This is the position of Cognitive Systems Engineering (CSE, Hollnagel and Woods, 1983) — which incidentally was proposed at a time when HMI had not yet become HCI. In CSE every artifact, which in practice means everything that is designed, is by definition created with a specific purpose or objective in mind. The best known implication of that is that artifacts always are designed with a specific user, or group of users, in mind. In HMI, the issue of user modeling has consequently been an important concern for many years, as evidenced by a large number of journal papers, books, and even specialized conferences (for example, Norman and Draper, 1986; Noyes and Baber, 2001; Rich, 1979).

With the advent of information technology the use of artifacts largely became synonymous with the interaction between a user and an application represented by the artifact. (Needless to say, the application in itself is also an artifact although it may be less tangible.) Two systems — or two entities — can be said to interact if they can mutually have an effect upon one another. In HMI, one aspect of the interaction is the effect that the artifact has on the user; the other is the effect that the user tries to achieve by means of the (perceived) options provided by the artifact, for instance via direct manipulation interfaces, with all the problems that may involve (Hutchins, Hollan and Norman, 1985). Although HMI nominally refers to the interaction between the human and the machine/computer, the latter is in actual fact a mediator rather than the focus of the interaction as such (for example, Carroll and Campbell, 1988).

Most research in HMI took for granted that it was legitimate to consider the human–machine dyad as a system made up of two principal components—the user (human) and the machine or application (computer). Although this assumption is so common that it rarely is made explicit, it is nevertheless significant in its implications.

- One implication is that there is a clearly identifiable, and therefore also clearly describable, boundary between the human–machine system and its environment.
- A second implication is that the interaction between the system and the environment can be described in the same way as the interaction between the human and the machine, that is, in terms of input and output.
- A third, but not the least important, implication is that both human and machine are reactive, which means that the interaction can be described as taking place in a closed loop.

The obviousness of the conventional boundaries is evident from the very term used to label this scientific field, namely human–machine interaction. Yet it cannot be taken for granted that this way of decomposing the system is equally reasonable for all purposes. It may make sense if we are considering issues of ergonomics or display design. It may also make sense vis-à-vis the traditional definition of a system as "a set of objects together with relationships between the objects and between their attributes" (Hall and Fagen, 1969, p. 81). Yet the "objects" need not be physical objects but may just as well be functions. Thus if we consider a pilot in the cockpit of an aircraft or the way a skilled artisan uses her tools, the units of analysis may be entirely different.

2. THINKING SMALL

The predominant approach to design may—polemically, at least—be called "thinking small," as opposed to "thinking big." (Needless to say, this is not meant as a value judgment of any kind, hence with a derogatory connotation; it is simply a description.)

It is a consequence of the three implications listed above that the design and analysis of systems can use formal methods and be based on a decomposition, not only of the system but also of the activities into separate parts, such as in task analysis. One example of that is the Jackson System Development (JSD) approach (Sutcliffe, 1988), which forms the basis of a well-known usability engineering method, MUSE (a Method for Usability Engineering; cf. Lim and Long, 1994). The MUSE method comprises three phases called the information elicitation and analysis phase, the design synthesis phase, and the user interface specification phase. The essential MUSE representation is that of a network. In order to produce this it is necessary that all actions or tasks can be identified and that each can be characterized in detail. It is also necessary that tasks can be:

> decomposed to derive a system task model and a user task model respectively. Bearing in mind possible influences from the manual task described by the user task model, the functional design of the interactive system is pursued via the system task model. Thus, human–machine or mixed tasks in the system task model are decomposed further to define "human" and "machine" subtasks and actions. (Lim, 1996, p. 45)

In order to analyze the actions or tasks of the human–machine system as described here it is necessary that the system has a well-defined boundary. In the absence of that, it will be impossible to determine which activities take place within the system and which activities take place in the environment. The communication among the activities/tasks within the system is in terms of inputs and outputs, that is, the exchange of data or information. The standard representation is that of a flow chart or a network consisting of nodes with connecting lines, and the purpose of the design is to describe all possible connections.

Although design methods focus on the human–machine system and only pay scant attention to the environment, it seems reasonable to assume that the exchanges between the human–machine system and its environment take place in the same way, that is, in terms of specific inputs and outputs. That such exchanges are required is obvious from the fact that the human–machine system does not exist in splendid isolation (leaving aside issues such as how to provide the energy and other resources necessary for the system to do its work). The human–machine system has been designed to do something, usually described as a type of processing of information or materials. The human–machine system can therefore itself be described as a state machine with inputs and outputs.

This takes us to the third implication, namely that the system is reactive. Whenever some input has been received, some processing takes place to produce some output. This is the case for the human–machine system as a whole, as well as for each activity or node in the system. In the technological world, functions do not begin by themselves, but must be called from the outside. If the outcome is not satisfactory, a function may either be called again, or an alternative function may be called. In this way the system functions according to the principles of closed-loop control, that is, as a feedback-regulated system. In a human–machine system the same reasoning is applied to the humans. In other words, they are assumed to respond to the signals and information they receive (and perceive), but not to act independently. In particular, they are not assumed to do anything that has not been anticipated by the system design. If they did that, the "machine" would by definition be unable to respond, and the human–machine system would therefore be unable to function as it should.

This "thinking small" approach to design is well-supported by formal methods, such as hierarchical task analysis (Kirwan and Ainsworth, 1992) and task networks (Laughery, 1998; Zachary et al., 2001). There is no reason to question the efficiency of these approaches as they have been the basis of many successful applications. But as they all have been based on certain assumptions (to wit, the three implications mentioned above), their validity relies on these assumptions being correct. If for some reason that is no longer the case, the methods and techniques may well have to be changed.

3. JOINT SYSTEMS

When the interest for HMI design became commonplace in the early 1980s, it was quite reasonable to "think small" as described above. Work systems were more often independent than interconnected, and it was therefore sufficient to focus on the control of the local system. This independence was due to the state of the technology, both the limited speed and power of computers and the lack of interconnectivity. The environment in which the human–machine system found itself was characterized by loose couplings and linear interactions. Because the human–machine systems was only coupled to a few other systems, developments took place at a moderate pace with few surprises. It was therefore also reasonable to focus on what is now known as human–machine interaction at the "sharp end," cf. Figure 20.1.

Since the 1980s the technological systems that surround us have increased significantly in complexity, both because the technology in itself has become more powerful and because we have made ourselves dependent on the systems we created. Applications of computing technology were in the early 1980s large, explicit, and infrequent—and typically visible as such—while today they are small, implicit, and ubiquitous. Indeed, many of the artifacts that we use for work today are almost unnoticeable in practice, especially if they comprise information technology. It is therefore no longer sufficient to focus on HMI at the "sharp end." What happens at the "sharp end" is increasingly determined by what happens not only at the

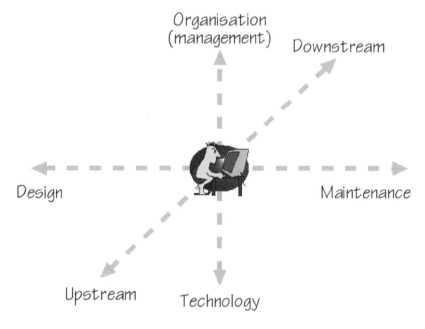

Figure 20.1   Narrow focus on HMI

"blunt end" but around the HMI, in a temporal as well as geographical sense. The focus of HMI must consequently be extended in several directions. A "vertical" extension is needed to cover the entire system, from technology to organization. One "horizontal" extension is needed to increase the scope to include both design and maintenance. A second "horizontal" extension is needed to include both upstream and downstream processes. Altogether, the situation today therefore looks more as shown in Figure 20.2.

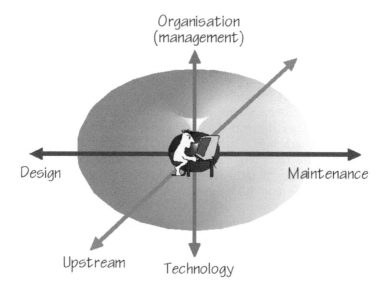

Figure 20.2   Wide focus on HMI

The increasing complexity not only affects each human–machine system in itself but also means that systems become more closely coupled, that is, that the interaction and dependency between them increases. This creates a kind of vicious circle where technological innovations create new possibilities and enable the construction of new and improved systems. We use these to make our lives "easier" and therefore quickly come to depend upon them. The increasing demands to efficient and reliable functioning in turn require further technological innovations, which—unintentionally—may create new possibilities, and so on. The effects of increasing complexity and closer coupling were characterized by Perrow (1984), who described them using the two concepts of tight coupling and complex interactions. Without going into details, the main effects can be summarized as shown in Table 20.1.

In 1984 Perrow referred to rather large, complex industrial systems. His warnings were therefore not noticed by the HMI research community. But as a consequence of the technological progress, many systems are today tightly coupled to others, sometimes by design but more often by coincidence (or lack of forethought). The tighter couplings not only mean that the systems become more complex to use in terms of actual operation, monitoring and control, but also that it becomes more difficult to maintain the notion of a well-defined system. The boundaries are no longer absolute but relative.

Table 20.1   Characteristics of complex, coupled systems

Tight coupling	Complex systems
Delays in processing not possible	Common-mode connections
Invariant sequences	Feedback loops
Little slack or substitution possible, in supplies/ equipment/personnel	Interconnected subsystems/Limited substitutions
Buffers and redundancies are designed in	Multiple and interacting controls
Only one method to achieve a goal	Limited understanding

Most human–machine systems today are so complex, and exist in environments so complex, that there are too many details to consider, that some modes of operation may be incompletely known, that functions are tightly coupled, and that they consequently may change faster than they can be described. The net result is that such systems are underspecified or intractable. Tractable systems can be completely described or specified, while intractable systems cannot. For systems that are underspecified or intractable it is clearly not possible to prescribe tasks and actions in detail, hence to design the HMI in detail. Instead, the HMI must be variable or flexible rather than rigid. In fact, the less completely the system is described, the more is performance variability needed. The differences between tractable and intractable systems are summarized in Table 20.2.

The primary concern in any system is to maintain control so that the intended functioning is not jeopardized. As long as the environment is relatively stable and predictable (both in terms of what might happen and in terms of what reactions are needed), it is reasonable to consider the systems by itself, to "think small," and to strive towards maintaining equilibrium conditions for the system's functioning. But when

Table 20.2   Tractable and intractable systems

	Tractable system	Intractable system
Number of details	Descriptions are simple with few details	Descriptions are elaborate with many details
Comprehensibility	Principles of functioning are known	Principles of functioning are partly unknown
Stability	System does not change while being described	System changes before description is completed
Relation to other systems	Independence	Interdependence

the environment becomes unstable and unpredictable and the HMI consequently becomes intractable, it is necessary to "think big," to try to comprehend the overall picture, and therefore to enlarge the scope of the system.

3.1 Joint Systems

Conventional design assumes that it is meaningful to speak about a system and its environment, that is, that a well-defined boundary exists. But defining or setting the boundary of a system is no trivial matter. The fact that we habitually accept one type of description, for instance the ubiquitous human–machine system, does not mean that this is the only way in which it can be done, or that it is inherently meaningful. It has been common practice in engineering and human factors to base the boundary on structural considerations, for example, referring to physically distinct entities. The human–machine system, for instance, distinguishes between humans and machines because of differences in physical rather than functional qualities.

The human–machine system may for example be air traffic controllers at their work station or pilots in their cockpit. Yet two pilots in a cockpit can also be seen together as a system—the flight crew—for which cockpit automation and flight management systems constitute the environment (cf. Figure 20.1). From another perspective, the airplane, that is, pilots plus flight control and automation is the system—the flight—for which the air traffic management (ATM) is the environment. It is also possible to consider the pilots and the ATM as one system—the traffic flow—in which case the environment is the airlines, the airports, and so on. Many analyses of the possible effects of new technology, such as the TCAS-II system (Mellone and Frank, 1993), tacitly assume that we are referring to a well-defined system (for example, the pilots in the cockpit), and that the boundaries of that system remain unaffected by the change. This assumption can unfortunately not be taken for granted.

The alternative to basing the definition of the boundaries on system structures is to base them on system functions. If we consider the system as a joint cognitive system (JCS), meaning a combination of one or more cognitive systems with one or more artifacts, then the boundaries can be derived using the guidelines shown in Table 20.2 (further details can be found in Hollnagel and Woods, 2005). The functional criterion is here whether the JCS is able to maintain control, that is, whether it is able to meet

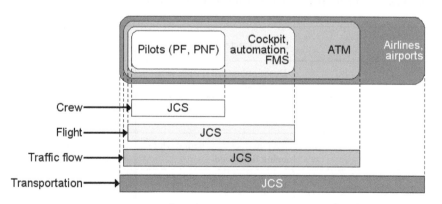

Figure 20.3   Joint cognitive systems for flying

its objectives. According to the principles summarized in Table 20.2, the JCS should as far as possible be designed to include all that is necessary to maintain control. In other words, the boundaries should be extended so that uncontrolled disturbances from the environment are excluded as far as possible (Hollnagel, 2001).

The first step of any design must therefore be to consider what the real objectives are, that is, what the reasons are for introducing a new function or feature. This will help to understand the different ways the boundaries of the system can be defined, and therefore the choice of a proper perspective to understand the nature of the interactions between systems and their environments.

Table 20.3   A pragmatic definition of the JCS boundaries

	Objects that can be effectively controlled by the JCS	Objects that cannot be effectively controlled by the JCS
Objects whose functions are important for the ability of the JCS to maintain control	Objects are included in the JCS	Objects are not included in the JCS
Objects whose functions are of no consequence for the ability of the JCS to maintain control	Objects may be included in the JCS	Objects are excluded from the description as a whole

4. THINKING BIG

Because we live in—and design for—a world that is far more complex than it was a quarter of a century ago, it is no longer meaningful to refer to the single, localized human–machine system. While "thinking small" still is necessary when it comes to the many details of human–machine interaction, "thinking small" must be complemented by "thinking big," that is, by considering the larger picture as well. "Thinking big" does not mean that the focus should shift from the local to the global systems, but rather that we should think of the local and the global systems at the same time. Design concepts and methods should consequently be developed to help us keep different perspectives in mind simultaneously.

One way of illustrating the consequences of "thinking big" is to take the three implications put forward in the introduction and consider their opposites. The three implications were (1) that there is a well-defined boundary between the human–machine system and its environment; (2) that the system-environment interaction can be described in the same way as the human–machine interaction; and (3) that human and machine both are reactive.

4.1 Boundaries are Relative rather than Absolute

If we look at the characteristics of tightly coupled systems (left-hand column of Table 20.1), then it is easy to see that such systems can be found in many different places and not just in complex, industrial processes. Because of the tight couplings, a system's ability to perform may depend on what happens outside the nominal system boundary. If the performance of a specific human–machine system becomes totally dependent on what happens around it, then it makes sense to adopt a different perspective and consider the human–machine system in a larger context. The boundaries are effectively extended so that the variability that dominated performance now is included as part of the system. Only in this way will it be possible effectively to design to achieve control.

The boundaries should ideally encompass everything a joint system does in order to be in control of the situation. Since this is not always feasible, the design may instead consider the ways in which a system can extend its control to include other joint systems. Control can, for instance, be improved by constraining the performance of other systems since this reduces the variability and unpredictability of the environment. The locus of control, however, remains within the joint system under consideration.

The current need of the information society is to extend control because we become increasingly dependent on the use of artifacts (social and technological). The challenge to researchers is to develop ways in which we can describe and understand how control is extended, specifically the tools and tricks that people invent or learn to use. The challenge is also to identify the control requirements on different levels and then facilitate these via design. This must clearly go beyond interface design, which is just the mediation of interaction, to co-agency (Hollnagel and Woods, 2005).

4.2 Internal and External Relations

When a system is conceived of and designed, regardless of the level of description and the definition of the boundaries, the primary goal is to ensure that it functions in an effective manner. This is usually tantamount to maintaining a state of functional equilibrium, where deviations in output are reduced or eliminated by feedback control. In the design of the local system it is therefore legitimate—and perhaps even necessary—to think of it as regulated by a closed loop.

For the design of the local system and of the human–machine interaction the primary concern is to make everything as predictable and regular as possible. If the machine responds in an unpredictable fashion, or if the options for information presentation and control are not stable, the user will have to cope with a design-induced but completely unnecessary complexity. In the interaction between the system and its environment it is impossible to achieve the same level of predictability because the presence of tight couplings leads to intractability and under-specification. The reason is not that the systems in the environment are complex as such, but rather that there are so many of them and that their connectivity is so massive. The variability of each system may be small, but in combination this may lead to unexpected effects as explained by the principle of functional resonance (Hollnagel, 2004).

In consequence of that, design cannot be predicated on the ability to make exhaustive analyses. Whereas the system under consideration may be considered as a finite state automaton, the environment cannot. This means that the interaction between the system and the environment cannot be described in the same way as the interaction between the human and the machine, that is, in terms of input and output. Instead the interaction has to comprise feedforward control, that is, to be open-loop. The environment is partly unpredictable not only in terms of what may happen but also in terms of when it may happen. The understanding is always approximate and the effects are never certain. Whereas the interaction between human and machine may be characterized by the gulfs of evaluation and of execution (Norman and Draper, 1986), the interaction between the system and the environment is characterized by temporal limits to understanding and intrinsically uncertain consequences of action (Merton, 1936).

4.3 Performance must be Proactive as well as Reactive

If we combine the two previous points, that boundaries are relative rather than absolute and that the interaction with the environment is of an open-loop nature, it is practically a consequence that the system's performance cannot exclusively be reactive. In order to be able to cope with the complexity of the environment, it is necessary to be proactive and to anticipate what is expected to happen.

One way of arguing for this is to note that all systems exist in a dynamic environment and that the speed of the internal processes often is insufficient to keep up with the rate of change of the environment. In other words, the time it takes the system to note and respond to an external event—whether it is a request, a command, or simply a noticeable change of one kind or another—may be so long that the response comes too late. The obvious solution is to increase the speed of the internal processes, but while that may work for technological systems it does not work well for humans. Another solution is to slow down the rate of change of the environment, for instance by dampening the variability or by changing the boundaries to bring part of the environment under control. This solution also has its obvious limitations. A third option is to base the response on a partial assessment or on expectations instead of waiting until a complete understanding has been achieved. It can indeed be argued that it is necessary to respond from an approximate understanding in order for the system to survive, at least if the dynamics of the environment outpace the speed of the system. Humans are easily able to do that and usually do it well. Unfortunately, they are also prone to doing it in situations where it is not strictly necessary. It seems to be an inherent feature of human action, and it is therefore wise to take it into account when the interaction is specified (cf. Hollnagel, 2009).

5. CONCLUSIONS

The design methods of human–machine interaction reflect the basic conditions of the 1980s, even though these conditions no longer are valid. Whereas it was defensible in the 1980s to focus on the local system and to "think small," the nature of the environment has changed beyond recognition. Rather than being something a bit remote, manageable by pairing inputs and outputs, it is now a "blooming, buzzing confusion" made up of countless, interconnected systems. This not only taxes the individual system's ability to persevere but also challenges the appropriateness of our design methods.

The design ideal has for many years been to maximize usability by making the interface and the interaction as simple and easy as possible. This has created an approach to interface design that can be called information structuring

(Hollnagel, 1997). Designing for simplicity based on information structuring can be a powerful technique if both the target functions and the interaction are well defined, that is, if the situation can be constrained to match the premises of the design. If this is not possible, the alternative is to design for complexity. The essence of coping with complexity is to be able to control — or manage — the internal and external variability. This is tantamount to being able to predict the future developments of the process and to act on these predictions. In other words, effective performance must be based on feedforward as well as feedback. Feedback is safe but consumes much time, while feedforward is risky but gains time.

Good system design requires the ability to think big while thinking small. It must at the same time ensure the stable functioning of the local system and the persistence and survival of the larger, global system. This requires not only a revision of many commonly held design ideals, but also the development of methods that do not have decomposition as their main principle. Human–machine interaction is less relevant today than it was 25 years ago. System design instead requires a perspective that emphasizes the intrinsic ability of joint systems and organizations to adjust their functioning prior to, during, or following changes and disturbances, so that they can sustain required operations under both expected and unexpected conditions.

REFERENCES

Carroll J.M. and Campbell, R.L. (1988). *Artifacts as psychological theories: The case of human–computer interaction*. IBM Research Report RC 13454, Watson Research Center, Yorktown Heights, NY.

Hall, A. D. and Fagen, R. E. (1968). Definition of system. In W. Buckley (Ed.), *Modern systems research for the behavioral scientist*. Chicago: Aldine Publishing Company.

Hollnagel, E. (1997). Designing for complexity. In G. Salvendy, M.J. Smith and R.J. Koubek (Eds.), *Seventh International Conference on Human–computer Interaction*, September 24–29, San Francisco.

Hollnagel, E. (2001). Extended cognition and the future of ergonomics. *Theoretical issues in Ergonomics Science, 2*(3), 309–315.

Hollnagel, E. (2004). *Barriers and accident prevention*. Aldershot, UK: Ashgate.

Hollnagel, E. (2009). *The ETTO principle: Why things that go right sometimes go wrong*. Aldershot, UK: Ashgate.

Hollnagel, E., and Woods, D.D. (1983). Cognitive systems engineering: New wine in new bottles. *International Journal of Man–machine Studies, 18*, 583–600.

Hollnagel, E., and Woods, D.D. (2005). *Joint cognitive systems: Foundations of cognitive systems engineering*. Boca Raton, FL: Taylor and Francis Books, Inc.

Hutchins, E.L., Hollan, J.D. and Norman, D.A. (1985). Direct manipulation interfaces. *Human–computer Interaction, 1*(4), 311–338.

Kirwan, B., and Ainsworth, L.K. (Eds.). (1992). *A guide to task analysis*. London: Taylor and Francis.

Laughery, K.R. (1998). Modeling human performance during system design. In E. Salas (Ed.), *Human-technology interaction in complex systems*. JAI Press.

Lim, K.Y. (1996). Structured task analysis: An instantiation of the MUSE method for usability engineering. *Interacting with Computers, 8*(1), 31–50.

Lim, K.Y. and Long, J.B. (1994). *The MUSE method of usability engineering.* Cambridge University Press.

Mellone, V.J. and Frank, S.M. (1993). Behavioral impact of TCAS II on the National Air Traffic Control System. In R. Jensen (Ed.), *Proceedings of the Seventh International Symposium on Aviation Psychology.* Columbus, OH: Ohio State University.

Merton, R.K. (1936). The unanticipated consequences of social action. *American Sociological Review, 1* (December), 894–904.

Norman, D.A. and Draper, W. (1986). *User-centered system design: New perspectives on human–computer interaction.* Hillsdale, NJ: LEA.

Noyes, J.M. and Baber, C. (2001). *User-centered design of systems.* London: Springer Verlag.

Perrow, C. (1984). *Normal accidents: Living with high risk technologies.* New York: Basic Books, Inc.

Rich, E. (1979). User modeling via stereotypes. *Cognitive Science, 3*(4), 329–354.

Sutcliffe, A. (1988). *Jackson system development method.* New York: Prentice Hall.

Zachary, W., Campbell, G.E., Laughery, K.R., Glenn, F., and Cannon-Bowers, J.A. (2001). The application of human modeling technology to the design, evaluation and operation of complex systems. *Advances in Human Performance and Cognitive Engineering Research, 1,* 199–247. Elsevier Science Ltd.

Conclusion and Perspectives

From Automation to Interaction Design

Guy A. Boy

Automation is certainly a very important topic in human–machine interaction. Why do we automate? Several chapters in this volume addressed this question. Typically, we automated because we want to improve safety, efficiency and/or comfort. In the same way commercial aircraft cockpits and offices have been highly automated during the eighties, cars and other safety-critical systems are now highly automated. Automation frequently created drastic changes in people's work practices. Instead of a smooth evolution, they had to adapt to a professional revolution. This is what happened with the arrival of glass cockpits and fly-by-wire technology. There is always a period of adaptation that may lead to incidents and accidents. Figure 21.1 shows the evolution of the number of hull losses with time for the traditional cockpits and the glass cockpits. It is clear that there was a period, between 1982 and 1984, where the glass cockpit curve was worse than the traditional cockpit curve; but eventually it became much better within the next few years. It should also be said that the curve continued to decrease from 1995 to 2005 despite the increase of departures (Flight Safety Foundation, July 2006). In fact, the shape of the second curve is almost identical as the first one; it is an exponential-shape curve that reaches a minimum horizontal asymptote.

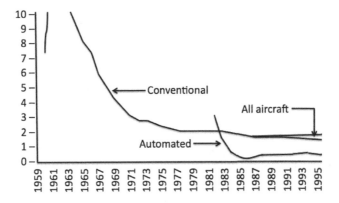

Figure 21.1   **Evolution of hull losses for conventional cockpits and glass cockpits (automated) per million of departures, presented by Airbus Industrie at the Flight Safety Conference in 1997**

As a general statement, we could claim that this kind of curve, related to safety, characterizes a specific automation revolution and its life cycle. Asymptote reaching characterizes the maturity evolution of a specific automation revolution. More generally, we could put any criterion or metrics related to safety, efficiency or comfort on the ordinate axis (Figure 21.2). Segment M represents the maturity period. Region A represents the acceptability area, as the sum of relevant parameter values, for example, number of casualties, bad performance or discomfort situations, over the maturity period M.

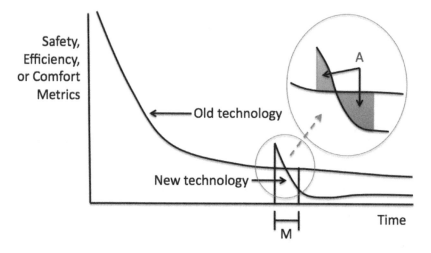

Figure 21.2   Generic maturity curve of a technology

The identification of appropriate M and A thresholds is crucial to assess if a technology will succeed or become obsolete according to contemporary acceptable practices and life styles. In addition, it is important to identify the best time t_D for final-product delivery and actual use. If this time t_D is within the maturity period M, we usually talk about surprises when unacceptable events occur. When t_D is after the maturity segment M, there are still residual unacceptable events but they are more due to routine practice and complacency than to unknown events or behaviors.

Therefore, the main issue in human-centered design is to take into account the maturity period M and the acceptability area A within a design and development process envelope. In particular, appropriate estimations of M and A should contribute to derive the delivery time of a product. This means that human-in-the-loop simulations (HITLS) have to be developed and carried out to enable enough as realistic as possible use experience that creates the conditions for the emergence of as many "surprises" as possible before delivery time. In aeronautics, the certification process is typically implemented to this end during that period. The main problem today comes form the fact that industry always wants to reduce the maturity period M and develop at the lowest possible costs. Maturity takes time and appropriate efforts! This is why visionary and competent leaders are required for maturity management. Processes like the Capacity Maturity Model (CMMi) are not effective when they are reduced to dry reporting, financial management, and little and/or inappropriate technical integration.

Today, industry is producing technology using a multitude of agents worldwide. Consequently, integration and coordination are two crucial processes that need to be better understood and managed. Not so long ago, products were designed and manufactured within integrated organizations where people knew each other. Products were much simpler than they are today though. Quality was insured by the technological glue that this integrated way of working was naturally providing. Today, work is performed in isolated places where the turnover of people is high. We are in a very dry interconnected set of networks with people who are not familiar with each other. Parts are described on paper or electronic media, but their description is not as deep as integration requires. This is why new types of integrators and coordinators are required. They often are not there. We even do not know what their profiles could be. This final chapter tries to investigate directions that we could take to improve our understanding of such integration and coordination processes and jobs.

For a long time, automation consisted in transferring a single cognitive function from a human to a machine. Autopilots were single mechanisms that controlled one parameter at a time, for example, speed or altitude. The first evolution consisted in multiplying the number of these automata. During the eighties, a first integration on flight decks was performed through the development of the flight management systems (FMS). A new type of automation was born. It led to the design and development of even more complex systems. However now, complexity comes from different causes, mainly software property issues. Today, software is everywhere, buried into various kinds of systems. It is interesting to note that we now talk about interactive cockpits, not because flight controls are interactive but because there is a pointing device and graphical displays! Pilots barely touch flight controls nowadays. They enter set points into systems that do the job for them. They have become managers of machine agents. Not only the nature of automation has changed; interactive technology through software is now an unavoidable reality. We have moved from automation design to interaction design.

Why interaction design has become so important? The primary reason is that software is embedded in many systems and tools. We do not use the tools in a physical manner anymore; we interact with them. Most mobile phones are computers that enable us to communicate via various resources including telephony, email, and the Internet. They enable us to store large quantity of data including text, music, photos and movies, which can be sent to other mobile phones or computers connected to a network. Human and machine agents interact between each other either directly or via other human and/or machine agents. A machine agent such as a modern mobile phone is a software-intensive system.

I had an interesting experience when I first designed a computer-supported meeting environment. The goal was to use computers to speed up a brainwriting process. Brainwriting is a very efficient technique that enables to gather viewpoints from a set of people in a limited period of time (Warfield, 1971; Boy, 1996). In addition, it enables the elicitation of agreement and disagreements between these people. This technique was commonly carried out using sheets that people could filled in and annotate other's viewpoints, expressing their agreements or disagreements. Transferring this technique in a computer-supported environment seemed to be easy. However, we had several surprises. First, we thought that we needed to limit each viewpoint elicitation to a fixed period of time. The main problem was that some of the participants had difficulty in using the software and lost their time understanding the way they had to interact. Consequently, they did not enter any viewpoint in the system. We understood that a human facilitator should manage this time limit, and we totally redesign the user interface. Second, there were people who were very efficient in writing down their ideas, and others who were slower. Therefore, there were people who were waiting for another participant to be finished. We understood that computers could be used to improve this inconvenience. All these surprises were not possible to elicit before the whole groupware was implemented and actually used. This is why we did many human-in-the-loop simulations before reaching an acceptable mature system.

In the previous example, we saw that interaction is not only between people and machines; it is also between people themselves through technology. Sometimes software magnifies the repercussions of these interaction issues. Some other times, it solves problems that could not be solved without software. More generally, we need to better understand when human and/or machine agents can solve problems and when they are problems enablers. Interaction design is about defining roles of these various agents. I would say roles of the cognitive functions that these agents use to perform what they have to do in a given context using the resources that they have. Interaction design is also about mastering both context and resource spaces where design-induced cognitive functions are really defined.

Interaction design moves us into the multi-agent world necessarily, because either systems are multi-agent themselves, or people have several cognitive functions to perform in a given context using several resources, or people and software-intensive machines are so interconnected that they behave like a society of agents. Software is an interesting matter. It is highly flexible. It can be easily modified locally. However, it becomes a tremendously complex matter globally, that is, in interconnected human and machine systems. Nowadays, complexity of interconnected software-intensive systems comes often more from the interconnections between the parts than from the complexity of the parts themselves. The use of email is a good example, for example, mailing list may provoke gigantic messes when they are not correctly used; writing and reading an email may not be interpreted in the same way according to context because email is both an oral and written support; it is very difficult to correctly express and interpret emotions in a quickly written short text.

The mix of human and machine agents now leads to a biological-like global system that is very difficult to study because it is difficult to isolate small-enough parts that can be studied in isolation. This is called separability. As an analogy, it is impossible to study the human heart isolated from the rest of the body. In addition, a machine agent does not have the same capabilities as a human agent, for example, emotions. In the same way it takes a long time to know how to write an expressive and effective text, it takes a long time to know how to use a software-intensive system safely, efficiently and comfortably. We are moving into a new world where not only technology has to be mastered, but also where people need to rapidly adapt to different types of interactions. People will always remain people with their basic functions and behaviors; it is the nature of interaction with other human and machine agents that is changing. It is also clear that interactions that will be the most natural will stay; the others will become obsolete in a relatively short period of time. This is where interaction maturity will have to be studied.

Interaction design is also about inventing new kinds of machines. Ubiquitous computing is certainly one of the emerging technologies that contributes to foster interaction design. Mark Weiser said: "The most profound technologies are those that disappear. They weave themselves into the fabric of everyday life until they are indistinguishable from it" (Weiser, 1991). The term "disappear" means that users of such technologies do not notice either their complexity or even their presence. Other authors have talked about seamless interfaces or tangible bits (Iishi and Ullmer, 1997), disappearing computer (Streitz, 2001; Streitz and Nixon, 2005) or invisible computer (Norman, 1998).

A good book is not only a well-written volume, it is a book that is used, cited, annotated, strikeout and that fosters the emergence of new things. It is the social context that this book creates that makes of it a "good book." Finally, syntax has to disappear to the benefit of semantics and pragmatics, the real meaning and projection. It is important to realize that, in our industry today, syntax in the form of reporting is predominant because financial management imposes it. Reporting without meaning cannot sustain any good product. For that matter, reporting should disappear, in the technological sense already described, to become a semantic glue between involved actors towards the success of the product being developed.

Human-centered design requires human requirements shaping the activity generated by the various tasks supported by the technology being designed. It is always impossible to anticipate all contexts in which this technology will be used. This is why appropriate scenarios must be developed to support the design process (Carroll, in this volume). Scenarios prefigure the use of the technology being developed. They should be developed by a team of knowledgeable users in the field where this technology will be used. Scenarios are good enablers for decision-making during the design and development process. However, they do not enable avoiding human-in-the-loop simulations, which may take a reasonable amount of time and number of knowledgeable users.

There are various levels of interaction in a multi-agent system. At the local level, each agent should be able to interact with his/her/its environment in the most natural way. Actions means should be as affordable as possible at the right time, and more generally in the right context. As Saadi Lahlou already said "People experience difficulties in interpreting new things for which there is no social representation." (Lahlou, in this volume). These social representations, which emerge in the maturity segment M, should be discovered as soon as possible, typically during the design process. The use of social representations in multi-agent communications is the most sophisticated model of interaction that I previously denoted "communication by mutual understanding" (Boy, 2002). However, we should not forget that there are two other possible models of interaction that are supervision and mediation. In the former, a knowledgeable agent supervises the interaction between the other agents. This happens when interacting agents do not know each other, that is, when they do not have appropriate social representations. In human–machine interaction, the supervisor could take the form of an instruction manual, a context sensitive help or an expert person. In the latter mode, agents may not have social representations of the other agents, but they can communicate through a meditative space. Mediation could be done via other agents usually called facilitators, diplomats, or lobbyist. User-friendly interfaces, and the desktop metaphor in particular, that were developed during the eighties, are typical examples of such meditative spaces. A continuum between these three models of interaction (Figure 21.3) was presented in a recent paper (Boy, 2009).

Back in 1986, I was working on the orbital refueling system (ORS) of the space shuttle trying to better understand how an astronaut could safely and effectively monitor and control the ORS. At that time, I proposed a model of the evolution of the performance of a human–machine system (HMS) with respect to various levels of autonomy and available knowledge during the life cycle of the technology being deployed (Figure 21.4). HMS performance increases up to an optimum P_O when automation increases and the autonomy of the machine increases. This optimum of performance corresponds to currently available knowledge in anticipating surprises. Passed this optimum, HMS performance decreases down to an end point related to technological limitations. This part of the curve from P_O to P_{TL} correspond to what Ear Wiener called clumsy automation (Wiener, 1989). The more human–machine interaction knowledge increases together with technological possibilities, the more this optimum moves up to the right. When full automation is possible, the optimum corresponds to point P_{FA}.

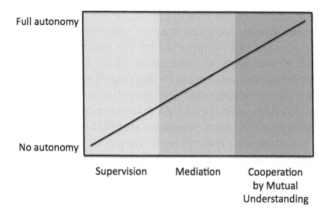

Figure 21.3   **Interaction models from no-autonomy to full-autonomy of agents**

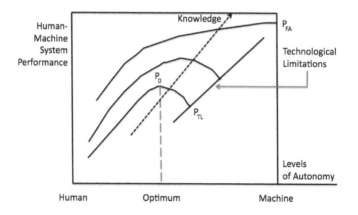

Figure 21.4   HMS performance versus levels of autonomy

Source: Boy, 1986.

At a more global level, that is, between large groups of agents, interaction can be categorized with respect to the three interaction models also. I will follow the claim that an agent can be represented as a society of agents (Minsky, 1985); therefore, what has been said for two interacting agents will hold for two interacting societies of agents. As a matter of fact, if we come back to the cognitive function representation, we can say that an agent has several cognitive functions that are usually interconnected. From this representational point of view, we can draw cognitive functions maps that model relevant interactions between agents. This is typically what I called cognitive function analysis (Boy, 1998).

As Figure 21.3 shows, cooperation by mutual understanding promotes agent's autonomy. However, the more agents are autonomous, the more they need to be coordinated, not necessarily because they do not have a good model of the other agents, but because they may have personal reactions to events and personal intentions that other agents should be aware of. Coordination is usually supported by rules, procedures, contracts between agents and a community culture. These kinds of coordination support create constraints that agents need to deal with. When these constraints are too rigid, agents need to find alternative solutions to contextual problems. In other words, the definition of these constraints should allow for flexibility when creativity is required, that is, in unforeseen or abnormal situations where human agents have to urgently make decisions and act. This explains why human agents always need to keep a high degree of competence and experience, for example, aircraft pilots today.

In some specific cases, human agents may not need to have such competence and experience. These are the cases where mature and reliable technology allows for human errors and machine failures with no dangerous repercussions. These are the cases where the AUTOS pyramid has been fully understood and effectively used (see my introduction in this volume). We also could interpret this as knowing all possible contexts of interaction and having all possible resources to keep an acceptable stability of a multi-agent system. Unfortunately, we need to remember that we live in an open world, that is, anything can happen and we do not have infinity of resources to solve all problems. This does not means that we have to stop defining scenarios and running simulations. This means that we will always have surprises, and discover as many as we can before they could happen in the real world. The main question is to measure the repercussions of such possible surprises. Answers to this question are mainly related to the type of criteria, ethics and philosophy that we adopt.

In this handbook, we introduced several concepts such as organizational automation (Boy and Grote, in this volume) and thinking small and thinking big (Hollnagel, in this volume). Earlier, Etienne Tarnowski (2006) introduced the concept of four loops of automation (Figure 21.5). He described the first loop as flying around the center of gravity of the aircraft, which is the role of the aircrew. The reaction time is around 500 milliseconds, and this level is very much mature for a long time following the introduction of autopilots circa 1930s. The second loop concerns the guidance on a basic trajectory, that is, a simple flight segment on a 15 seconds horizon. The third loop was introduced around the mid 1980s with the implementation of the flight management system (FMS) that is able to follow an entire flight plan. FMS deserves a monitoring scan of about one minute to keep perfect situation awareness. Today, the fourth loop is incrementally appearing with the emergence of air traffic management (ATM) where the average time constant is about 10 minutes.

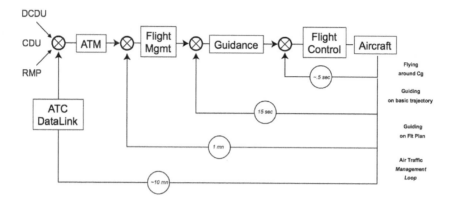

Figure 21.5   Tarnowski's four looks of flight automation

There are a variety of systems that support ATM such as the Controller-Pilot Data Link Communications (CPDLC), with various interfaces in the cockpit such as the Datalink Control and Display Unit (DCDU), the Control and Display Unit (CDU) and the Radio Management Panel (RMP). All these terms show that there is more software, and the nature of interaction between the various agents changes. Of course, this representation is a simplification of what really happens in the cockpit. In addition, the growth of such embedded loops is not finished and we anticipate more loops coming in the near future.

We do not need to forget that one of the main users of this air system is nevertheless the passenger, and more generally people who are involved in or benefit/suffer from the aviation system. For that matter, we could say that there is another loop coming that will take into account people from various points of view such as decreasing pollution, solving flight delays, managing airport and so on. More software will be developed and used. The nature of interaction between agents will keep changing again. We then keep in mind the three types of interactions already described to better understand interaction problems in the future.

Interaction design is not only a question of style; it is also a question of time management, especially in life-critical systems. No need to say that this issue becomes even more important when human errors or systems failures occur. Mastering time in human–machine interaction takes time! Maturity again. It took about two decades to be able to use the mouse and hypertext-based tools invented by Douglas Engelbart in the mid-sixties at Stanford Research Institute. It took three decades to put together the appropriate technologies to use Internet, as we know it nowadays. Today, we have faster computing machines, but software is more complex for various kinds of reasons such as security and reliability. Maturity today is mostly a matter of mastering complexity. This complexity is not only in the systems themselves, but also in the interconnections between these systems. The difficulty is that these interconnections are context-sensitive. Consequently, it is practically impossible to figure out correctly the appropriate design without iterative tests using human-in-the-loop simulations.

The context issue is not new. In my 1998 book on cognitive function analysis, I alread gave an account on context in human-centered design, based on Mantovani's work (1996). Mantovani proposed three levels of context interpretation (Figure 21.6).

These three mutually-inclusive levels can be represented as follows: Level 1 is context construction, that is, social context; Level 2 is situation interpretation, that is, everyday situations; Level 3 is local interaction with the environment, that is, artifact use. Level 1 is more general than Level 2 which is more general than Level 3. At level 1, the social context is determined by *values* that are very general goals determined by the *culture* (Thomas and Alaphilippe, 1993). At Level 2, the psychological level, *motivations* are more precise but less persistent than attitudes, and are influenced by values and needs. At Level 3, the biological level, *needs* are biological strengths such as eating, drinking or sleeping. Mantovani describes Level 3 using the user-task-artifact triangle (see my Introduction of this handbook). He proposes equivalent triangles at Level 2, that is, interests-goals-opportunities, and Level 1, that is, action-history-structure. Mantovani's three level model can be interpreted as follows (Figure 21.6): a user may have situated interests for action in a given context; the task that a user performs is based on situated goals coming from a social history; and the tool (artifact) is built from opportunities that arise from a cultural structure.

In interaction design, we sometime break the smooth traditional evolution induced by these mutually inclusive triangles. We often talk about technological revolutions (back to Figure 21.1 in this chapter). When we designed the first fly-by-wire aircraft, for example, we created a brand new artifact because technology enabled to do it; this was an opportunity that made a break with the conventional aircraft controls. Since the beginning of aviation (social history), flying an aircraft is an art in the sense of developing flying skills that pilots are using. These emboddied skills are mainly sensorimotoric. The introduction of fly-by-wire technology provoked the emergence of a new type of skills that are more cognitive, removing the previous sensorimotoric skills. The goal is no longer to fly the aircraft, but to manage the systems that are actually flying the aircraft. Consequently, the task became higher-level flight management. A new type of job was born. Since then, we put more software between pilots and the mechanical parts of the aircraft in order to improve safety, efficency and comfort. As a result, flying has become safer and safer to the point that new problems arise from situation awareness in cases of unanticipated events and complacency in routine situations.

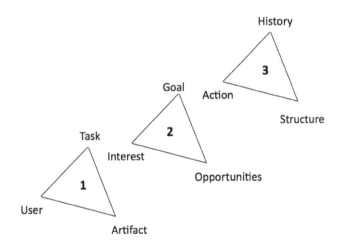

Figure 21.6 **Three levels of context interpretation**

In this handbook, there are several descriptions and references to situation awareness. It is interesting to notice that the human visual channel is always over utilized, and other modalities often left totally unused. For example, the tactile modality is a more precise cue than visual and auditory modalities. There are many life-critical situations where tactile and olfactory channels could be very useful and even unique cues for appropriate situation awareness. Adaptive multimodal user interfaces are also likely to improve situation awareness. In our everyday life, multimodal redundancy is necessary in most situations; why technology do not provide affordances for such multimodal redundancy? Since this last chapter is devoted to perspectives, it would be good to identify multimodality requirements specific to the most relevant life-critical tasks and situations for improving safety, efficiency and comfort. We need to improve currently available multimodality user interfaces to address specific usability needs of users through software (for example, context-sensitive adaptive multimodal user interfaces), hardware (for example, interface elements integration or not) and redundancy of modalities.

A substantial amount of work has been performed on multimodal interfaces (Oviatt and Cohen, 2000; Oviatt, 2002; Reeves et al., 2004). According to Sarter's guidelines for the design of multimodal interfaces, modalities should be chosen first, then they should be mapped to tasks and types of information, they should be combined, synchronized and integrated, and finally multimodal information presentation should be adapted to accommodate changing task contexts and circumstances (Sarter, 2006). Guidelines are good but they do not sufficiently take into account people experience to be used systematically. There is a need for a theory useful and usable in the real-world that encapsulates human intentions and responses together with several modalities. In particular, crossmodal switching time and attention shift (Spence et al., 2000), especially after interruptions, should be reduced. For example, multimodality is typically implemented to reduce cognitive load in human–machine interaction. For certain applications, there is evidence that cognitive load is decreased with multimodal redundancy (Ruiz et al., 2006). Even if a theory of organized multimodal integration patterns during human–computer interaction has already been proposed (Oviatt et al., 2003), we need to develop an approach that takes into account cognitive stability to better analyze, design and evaluate multimodal human–machine systems (HMS). In addition, more specific knowledge of the actual technology being developed should be considered because this technology will create a specific human–machine context that will influence the way modalities should and will be implemented and used.

Many methods were developed and used to perform cognitive task analysis (CTA) and cognitive function analysis (CFA) in order to identify cognitive demands that affect resources such as memory, attention and decision-making (Klein, 1993; Schraagen, Chipman and Shalin, 2000; Boy, 1998). These methods should be adapted to study usability and usefulness of multimodal HMS. They should be able to tell us what kind of modality is appropriate for a given task or function in a given context. Should it be adaptable or adaptive? Should it be associated with another modality to make signal more salient to human operators? We anticipate that these methods will focus on the definition of context. This is why storyboard prototypes first and human-in-the-loop simulations are mandatory to support evaluations of multimodal HMS. Context awareness plays also an important role in priority management for example (Funk, 1996; Funk and Braune, 1999) on the flight deck especially after an alarm (Boucek, Veitengruber and Smith, 1977) or an interruption (McFarlane and Latorella, 2002). Multimodal interfaces should be able to provide appropriate context awareness. Smith and Mosier (1986) provided user interface design guidelines to support the flexibility of interruption handling, but there is more to do on context sensitivity using multimodal interfaces. More recently, Loukopoulos, Dismukes and Barshi (2009) analyzed the underlying multitasking myth and complexity handling in real-world operations. As a matter of fact, flight deck multimodal interfaces should be intimately associated with checklists and operational procedures (Boy and De Brito, 2000). Paper support could also be considered as an interesting modality.

Whenever a new artifact is designed, manufactured and delivered, it has to be used within a well-understood socially-shared regulatory framework. An important issue remains open; how can we correctly allocate human issues between design and actual operations support and regulations? Human operator fatigue risk, for example, "has traditionally been addressed at the regulatory level through prescriptive limits on hours of work and rest" (Gander, Graeber and Belenky, this volume), but "fatigue risk reduction strategies should be incorporated into the design of human–machine systems where operator fatigue can be expected to have an impact on safety." Again, maturity is reached when all elements of the AUTOS pyramid (Introduction of this volume) are sufficiently well understood and articulated.

Even if the topical choices that we made in this handbook were made to cover some important human-centered designer's needs, they may not be all relevant to your specific design enterprise or task. Indeed, interaction design is a complex domain where expertize and experience needs to be gained over time from trial-and-error, and of course successes. Most importantly, designers and engineers should always keep in mind the crucial need for integration of Technology, Organizations and People (iTOP), without forgetting that technology always follows a maturity curve that needs to be constantly assessed ... there is always something to improve! Design will be really human-centered when as many actors as possible, who deal with the technology being developed and used, will be effectively involved or taken into account, by highly competent technical leaders, in the various phases of its creation, construction, use, refinement, maintenance and obsolescence.

REFERENCES

Boucek, G.P., Veitengruber, J.E. and Smith, W.D. (1977). *Aircraft alerting systems criteria study. Volume ii: Human Factors Guidelines and Aircraft Alerting Systems*. FAA Report FAA-RD-76–222, II. Washington, D.C.: Federal Aviation Administration.

Boy, G.A. (1986). An Expert System for Fault Diagnosis in Orbital Refueling Operations. *AIAA 24th Aerospace Sciences Meeting*, Reno, Nevada, US.

Boy, G.A. (1996). The Group Elicitation Method for Participatory Design and Usability Testing. *Proceedings of CHI'96, the ACM Conference on Human Factors in Computing Systems*, Held in Vancouver, Canada. Also in the *Interactions Magazine*, March 1997 issue, published by ACM Press, New York.

Boy, G.A. (1998). *Cognitive function analysis*. Ablex/Greenwood, Westport, CT, US ISBN: 1–567–50376–4.

Boy, G.A. (2002), Theories of Human Cognition: To Better Understand the Co-Adaptation of People and Technology, in Knowledge Management, Organizational Intelligence and Learning, and Complexity. In L. Douglas Kiel (Ed.), *Encyclopedia of Life Support Systems (EOLSS)*, Developed under the Auspices of the UNESCO, Eolss Publishers, Oxford,UK, www.eolss.net.

Boy, G.A. (2007). Perceived Complexity and Cognitive Stability in Human-Centered Design. *Proceedings of the HCI International 2007 Conference*, Beijing, China.

Boy, G.A. (2009). The Orchestra: A Conceptual Model for Function Allocation and Scenario-based Engineering in Multi-Agent Safety-Critical Systems. *Proceedings of the European Conference on Cognitive Ergonomics*, Otaniemi, Helsinki area, Finland; September 30–October 2.

Boy, G.A. and de Brito, G. (2000). Towards a categorization of factors related to procedure following and situation awareness. *Proceedings of HCI-Aero 2000*, Cepadues, Toulouse, France.

Burn, J. (2006). *2005: The year review. Return of the Killers*. Aviation Safety World, Flight Safety Foundation, July. www.flightsafety.orghttp://www.flightsafety.org.

Funk, K. (1996). A functional model of flight deck agenda management. *Proceedings of the Human Factros and Ergonomics Society 40th Annual Meeting*. Santa-Monica, Ca, pp. 254–259.

Funk, K. and Braune, R. (1999). The AgendaManager: A knowledge-based system to facilitate the management of flight deck activities. *World Aviation Congress*, San Francisco, CA. SAE and AIAA.

Iishi, H. and Ullmer, B. (1997). Tangible Bits: Towards Seamless Interfaces between People, Bits and Atoms. *Proceedings of CHI'97*. Atlanta, GA, US, pp. 234–241.

Klein, G.A. (1993). *Naturalistic decision-making: Implications for design*. Wright Patterson AFB, OH: Crew Systems Ergonomics Information Analysis Center.

Loukopoulos, L.D., Dismukes, R.K. and Barshi, I. (2009). *The multitasking myth: Handling complexity in real-world operations*. Ashgate, UK.

Mantovani, G. (1996). Social context in HCI: A new framework for mental models, cooperation, and communication. *Cognitive Science*, 20, pp. 237–269.

McFarlane, D.C. and Latorella, K.A. (2002). The scope and importance of human–computer interaction design. *Human–computer Interaction*, Volume 17, pp. 1–61.

Minsky, M. (1985). *The Society of Mind*. Simon and Schuster, Boston.

Norman, D.A. (1998). *The invisible computer: Why good products can fail, the personal computer is so complex, and information appliances are the solution*. Cambridge, MA: MIT Press, ISBN 0–262–14065–9.

Oviatt, S. and Cohen, P. (2000). Multimodal interfaces that process what comes naturally. *Communications of the ACM*, March, Volume 43, No. 3.

Oviatt, S. (2002). Multimodal interfaces. In J. Jacko and A. Sears (Eds.), *Handbook of Human–computer Interaction*. LEA, Hillsdale, NJ.

Oviatt, S., Coulston, R., Tomko, S., Xiao, B., Lunsford, R., Wesson, M. and Carmichael, L. (2003). Toward a theory of organized multimodal integration patterns during human–computer interaction. *ICMI'03 Proceedings*, November 5–7, Vancouver, BC, Canada.

Reeves, L.M., Lai, J., Larson, J.A., Oviatt, S., Balaji, T.S., Buisine, S., Collings, P., Cohen, P., Kraal, B., Martin, J.C., McTear, M., Raman, T.V., Stanney, K.M., Su, H. and Wang, Q. (2004). Guidelines for multimodal user interface design. *Communications of the ACM*, January, Volume 47, No. 1.

Ruiz, N., Taib, R. and Chen, F. (2006). Examining the Redundancy of multimodal input. *OZCHI'06 Proceedings*, November 20–24, Sydney, Australia.

Sarter, N. (2006). Multimodal information presentation: Design guidance and research challenges. *International Journal of Industrial Ergonomics*, 36, pp. 439–445.

Schraagen, J.M., Chipman, S.F., and Shalin, V.L. (2000). *Cognitive task analysis*. Mahweh, NJ: Lawrence Erlbaum Associates, Inc.

Smith, S.L. and Mosier, J.N. (1986). *Guidelines for design user interface software*. Report ESD-TR-86–278. MITRE, Bedford, MA.

Spence, C., Pavani, F. and Driver, J. (2000). Crossmodal links between vision and touch in covert endogenous spatial attention. *Journal of Experimental Psychology: Human Perception and Performance*. 26, pp. 1298–1319.

Streitz, N. (2001). Augmented Reality and the Disappearing Computer. In: Smith, M., Salvendy, G., Harris, D., Koubek, R. (Eds.), *Cognitive engineering, intelligent agents and virtual reality*. Lawrence Erlbaum, pp. 738–742.

Streitz, N. and Nixon, P. (2005). The Disappearing Computer. *Communications of the ACM*, 48 (3), March, pp. 33–35.

Tarnowski, E. (2006). *The four loops of automation in the latest commercial airplanes, and what about the future?* Keynote speech. HCI-Aero'06, Seattle, WA, US.

Thomas, R. and Alaphilippe, D. (1993). *Les Attitudes*. Que sais-je? Paris: Presses Universitaires de France.

Warfield, J.N. (1971). *Societal systems: Planning, policy and complexity*. John Wiley and Sons, New York.

Wiener, E. (1989). *Human factors of advanced technology ("Glass Cockpit") transport aircraft*. NASA Contractor Rep. 177528. See also Richard I. Cooketal et al., *The Natural History of Introducing New Information Technology into a Dynamic High-Risk Environment*, 1990 Proceedings of the Human Factors Society, 429.

Weiser, M. (1991). The Computer of the twenty-first century. *Scientific American*, 265(3), pp. 94–104.

Index

Page numbers in *italics* refer to figures and tables. A footnote reference is referred to with *f*.